Garden Plants &
Gardening Techniques

Garden Plants &
Gardening Techniques

The definitive guide to 2,500 garden plants, and step-by-step
instructions on how to plant and care for them

ANDREW MIKOLAJSKI & JONATHAN EDWARDS

LORENZ BOOKS

This edition is published by Lorenz Books,
an imprint of Anness Publishing Ltd
Hermes House, 88–89 Blackfriars Road, London SE1 8HA
tel. 020 7401 2077; fax 020 7633 9499
www.lorenzbooks.com; info@anness.com

© Anness Publishing Ltd 2001, 2008

UK agent: The Manning Partnership Ltd; tel. 01225 478444; fax 01225 478440;
sales@manning-partnership.co.uk

UK distributor: Grantham Book Services Ltd; tel. 01476 541080; fax 01476 541061;
orders@gbs.tbs-ltd.co.uk

North American agent/distributor: National Book Network; tel. 301 459 3366; fax 301 429 5746;
www.nbnbooks.com

Australian agent/distributor: Pan Macmillan Australia; tel. 1300 135 113; fax 1300 135 103;
customer.service@macmillan.com.au

New Zealand agent/distributor: David Bateman Ltd; tel. (09) 415 7664; fax (09) 415 8892

Publisher: Joanna Lorenz
Managing Editor: Judith Simons
Editor: Mariano F.X.P. Kälfors
Designer: Michael Morey
Indexer: Helen Snaith
Editorial Reader: Jonathan Marshall
Production Controller: Ben Worley

ETHICAL TRADING POLICY
Because of our ongoing ecological investment programme, you, as our customer, can have the pleasure and
reassurance of knowing that a tree is being cultivated on your behalf to naturally replace the materials used to
make the book you are holding. For further information about this scheme, go to
www.annesspublishing.com/trees

Previously published as *An Encyclopedia of Garden Plants and Techniques*

PUBLISHER'S NOTE
Although the advice and information in this book are believed to be accurate and true at the time of going to
press, neither the authors nor the publisher can accept any legal responsibility or liability for any errors or
omissions that may be made.

Contents

Introduction 6

INTRODUCTION

Nowadays we are bombarded with images of beautiful gardens, in magazines, books and on TV. A whole host of makeover programmes has made a garden even more desirable, but the effect of these is negative as well as positive. While good design and unusual plants are now available to everyone, and at an affordable price, the confidence to set to and turn a vision into a reality is sometimes lacking. While it is entertaining to watch an unpromising plot transformed into an idyllic garden in the space of a weekend, most people are aware that real gardens take a little longer, especially if you have to do all the work yourself - as most of us have to. Plus the experts will not be there to advise on layout, the best plants for your needs, or how to look after the garden once it is made. The perception of many a novice gardener is that there is a lot to learn. In a sense that is true, and you can guarantee that most experts would tell you they know only a fraction of what there is to know and that they are learning all the time. It is equally true that the art of gardening can be boiled down to a few basic principles, and anyone who is prepared to get their hands dirty will soon find that there is little more to it than common sense.

This book is aimed primarily at beginners. Even if you do not know the difference between an annual and perennial, a fern and a cactus, this book will help you. But it is also intended as a source for more experienced gardeners, to dip into if you are tackling a new project, making a vegetable garden or adding

ABOVE: This primarily herb garden with a charmingly informal design, based on fluid shapes and an irregular layout, gives plenty of scope for growing a variety of plants.

a water feature, for instance, as well as unravelling the mysteries of compost making. Even gardeners of long standing are sometimes perplexed by such matters as pruning, and, again, you will find straightforward advice here.

The approach is essentially practical: not only do you need to know how you should tackle any particular aspect of gardening, but why you might want to do it in the first place, as well as the best timing and the pitfalls you might meet on the way. A strong element of the book is aftercare: what you need to do once a certain element has been created in the garden— a lawn, for instance — to help it carry on looking its best. Gardens are like people: neglected, they become dejected, but quickly perk up with the appropriate attention.

The plant directory is divided into sections that are designed to make plant selection easier, and includes tips on growing the plants, ideas for their use in the garden and plant associations.

Ultimately, the best way to learn about gardening is to set to and make a garden. This book should help you along the way and will hopefully become the tool you reach for alongside your trowel, spade, fork and gardening gloves.

ABOVE: Bulbs like these alternating red and white tulips, underplanted with *Anemone blanda*, are ideal for formal spring borders.

LEFT: Dwarf box hedging keeps this functional kitchen garden neat and tidy, with sunflowers adding the perfect decorative touch.

GARDENING
TECHNIQUES

FUNDAMENTAL GARDENING SKILLS

Most people find a garden a relaxing place, but for the gardener the pleasure is immeasurably increased. Firstly, there is the fun of deciding on a design, then the satisfaction of preparing the ground and planting, followed by the sense of achievement from the careful maintenance that keeps plants looking their best.

The appeal of gardening

In recent years, interest in gardening has mushroomed, and there has been an increasing demand for advice and information. Garden designs are becoming more imaginative, although one of the most appealing things about gardening is that you don't need any special skills or experience to start you off. Basic gardening is not only fulfilling and great fun, but is so easy to achieve that nobody is excluded. Perhaps even more important is that everyone can garden to their own level and in their own way, investing as much time and money as their own particular circumstances will allow.

This sunny border has been planted with a range of hot-coloured perennials, creating a bright, cheerful atmosphere.

Getting it right

To be an efficient gardener you need to master a few basic but very important skills, so that you avoid mistakes and get the most from the plants in your care. Many techniques are common sense, such as choosing the right plant for a particular position and knowing when to water, but other skills such as sowing, planting and pruning require knowledge and a bit of practice to get right. In this section, we guide you step-by-step through all the essential garden tasks you will need, whether creating a garden from scratch or caring for an existing one.

How to use this section

The key to successful gardening is careful planning so that it meets both your needs and aspirations. The first part of this section helps you to design and plan a garden, whether you have a new, empty plot or are converting an existing design. Each step is explained, from assessing what you have and its potential to making new plans and turning them into reality.

Any garden is only as good as the soil that sustains it. For this reason, this section includes a dedicated chapter that explains exactly how to assess the soil in your garden, the various steps you can take to improve it, and how to prepare the ground ready for planting.

A stone urn planted with white and soft purples creates a lovely calm effect. Containers require a lot of watering but they do add an extra dimension to the garden.

Magnolia x *soulangeana* 'Amabilis' is a magnificent sight in mid-spring.

Columbines can be grown in the open border, but are frequently found in open woodland in the wild. Follow nature and grow them in shady borders or under a tree.

You will find plenty of practical growing techniques, arranged according to the types of plants: trees and shrubs; climbers; and flowers. In addition, this section looks in depth at particular areas of the garden that have techniques specific to them, including lawns; patios and containers; water and rock gardens; and greenhouse gardening.

There is an extensive section on the kitchen garden, explaining how to grow the most popular vegetables, herbs and fruit, whether in a dedicated plot or integrated into the rest of the garden.

The chapter on propagation runs through all the main methods of sowing, taking cuttings and layering to make increasing your stock of plants straightforward.

Many fundamental techniques apply to most if not all the areas of the garden. They are brought together in one section covering all the basics, from choosing an essential tool kit to weeding, mulching, feeding, watering as well as pest and disease control.

Finally, there is a seasonal checklist, to remind you to carry out the essential tasks in all areas of the garden at the right time.

This section contains over 150 step-by-step sequences to guide you through many of the more complicated gardening techniques. Throughout, there is information to help you choose the right plants for a specific situation or purpose, and green tip boxes that give simple suggestions on how to incorporate environmentally friendly techniques into your gardening. Both beginners and experienced gardeners will find this section the ideal reference guide to achieve the garden they want.

Busy herbaceous borders full of strongly growing plants help to keep the weeds down, and so require less maintenance. A planting scheme like this is unbeatable in midsummer.

Planning your garden

Gardening is much more than just growing plants. To make a garden appealing, it is just as important that the setting in which the plants are placed is right. You can have your garden designed and constructed by professionals, but it will cost a great deal and the chances are that it won't give you as much satisfaction as creating a garden by your own efforts.

Only you can decide what is best for your garden. Tastes in gardens vary enormously, and the best test of a new design is whether it pleases you. Use the planning techniques suggested to experiment on paper — you will soon develop the skills that will enable you to design your garden with confidence. A well-thought-out design will ensure you make the best use of your space, and planning it is an enjoyable challenge in itself.

A well-planned garden will have points of interest all year round. Here, a border of brightly coloured tulips is a welcome sight in spring.

Assessing your garden

Whether you have the blank canvas of a new garden or are trying to make improvements to an existing design, the first step is to decide exactly what you want as well as what changes you will have to make to achieve your ideal garden.

What do you want?

This may seem a simple question, but in practice it can prove problematic, especially if there are two gardeners in the house. The easiest way to decide what you really want is to make several lists. Write down all the things in the existing garden that cannot be changed, such as the position of an established tree or a pond, as well as other features you want to keep. Then make a list of everything you really

A greenhouse takes up a lot of space in a small garden, so consider whether the use you make of it would make it worthwhile.

Garden priorities

Wish list	Essential	Desirable
Structural features		
1. Paving/decking	[ ]	[ ]
2. Gravel area	[ ]	[ ]
3. Lawn	[ ]	[ ]
4. Pond/water course	[ ]	[ ]
5. Summerhouse	[ ]	[ ]
6. Tool shed	[ ]	[ ]
7. Greenhouse	[ ]	[ ]
8. Vegetable garden	[ ]	[ ]
Utility features		
1. Washing line	[ ]	[ ]
2. Compost heap	[ ]	[ ]
3. Cold frame	[ ]	[ ]
4. Dustbin (trash) area	[ ]	[ ]
5. Built-in barbecue	[ ]	[ ]
6. Sandpit	[ ]	[ ]
7. Garden store	[ ]	[ ]
Decorative features		
1. Raised bed	[ ]	[ ]
2. Shrubbery	[ ]	[ ]
3. Herbaceous border	[ ]	[ ]
4. Wildlife area	[ ]	[ ]
5. Arch/pergola	[ ]	[ ]
6. Rock garden	[ ]	[ ]
7. Small water feature	[ ]	[ ]

want in the new design. Invariably, you will have to prioritize this "wish list" to establish which items are most important. Remember to include utility items, such as a rotary washing line or compost heap. If you find prioritizing difficult, then score each feature as either essential or desirable. In this way you can be sure to include all the essential features as well as some of the desirable ones if there is the space.

HOW TO MEASURE

Use a 3m (10ft) retractable tape measure and pegs to measure a small area. For larger areas, it would be easier to hire or buy a 30m (100ft) surveyors' tape.

Measure the plot

The next step in planning a new garden or making alterations to an existing design is to assess what the current garden has to offer and to consider its limitations. The best way to do this is to draw a rough plan of the existing plot, by eye at first, on a piece of paper and record its overall dimensions.

Small rectangular gardens are very easy to measure, and sometimes the boundary can be calculated simply by counting fence panels and multiplying by the length of a fence panel and a post. In most cases, however, you will need to measure the plot with a tape measure. A long surveyors' tape measure is extremely useful. Having someone else to hold the other end of the tape will make measuring a lot easier. Note down any changes in level from side to side or down the length of the plot. Hammer in pegs at 1m (3ft) intervals, and then work out the direction and extent of the gradient, using a piece of straight timber and a spirit (carpenter's) level.

Triangulation

Sometimes it may be difficult to measure the position of a feature, such as a tree or a pond, using right angles. Triangulation is a way of fixing the position of an object in relation to the things around it.

Find two points already fixed on your plan: the corners of the house are often used. Measure the distance from each of the two points to the object. Transfer these measurements into the scale you are using on your plan. Set a pair of compasses (a compass) to each of the scale distances in turn and scribe an arc in the approximate position. When the second arc intersects the first one your point is established.

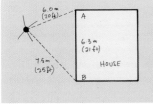

It is important to plan out a formal garden quite accurately before you start any practical work in order to get the proportions right.

HOW TO MAKE A SKETCH

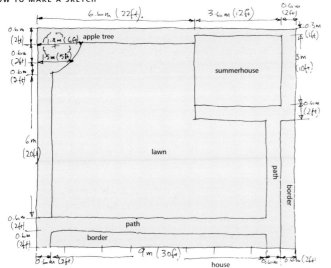

Make a rough visual sketch by eye, keeping permanent features roughly in proportion. Only include features you know you want to keep. Leave plenty of space to add measurements.

Plot the position of fixed features

Next turn your attention to the positions of permanent features, such as trees as well as other structural elements that you wish to keep in the new design. Most objects can be measured in right angles from a base line, such as the wall of the house, on your plan. If an object does not fall in a straight line from this point you will need to use triangulation (see box above left) in order to fix its position, so that it can be placed accurately on your rough sketch.

If your garden is small, sketch the whole plot in one go. If it is too big to do this, sketch it in sections that you can join together later when you draw up a scale plan.

Making plans

Drawing up an accurate plan is the best way to avoid making expensive mistakes later on. Once you have a basic plan that is drawn to scale, you can try out new ideas and see how the different elements fit together.

Draw a scale plan

Using the measurements noted down on your rough sketch of the garden, draw up a scale plan of the area being designed on graph paper, indicating the position of all the permanent features. A scale of 1:50 is suitable for most gardens (that's 2cm in the plan for every 1m in the garden, or ¼in to 1ft). However, if you are planning a large area, a scale of 1:100 (1cm per 1m or ⅛in to 1ft) may be more practical. Drawing your plan to scale will also make it easier to estimate quantities of materials, such as paving. Once you are sure they are accurate, ink the main lines in so that they show up clearly. Then, on an overlay

of acetate or tracing paper, use cross-hatching in a variety of colours to indicate areas of sun and shade at different times of the day. This information will be invaluable when you come to thinking about planting plans.

Try out new ideas

Cut out shapes from another piece of graph paper to represent the different features you want in your new garden design. You can then move the features around or alter the sizes of different elements without having to redraw the plan each time. When you are satisfied with the arrangement, draw them in position on an overlay.

Practical planning

Before ordering materials and beginning work, mark out as much of the design as possible in your existing garden. Mock up the overall shape of larger features to help you

HOW TO USE YOUR PLAN

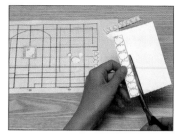

It's helpful to draw and cut out scale features that you want to include in your finished design, such as a raised pond, summerhouse or raised beds. These can be moved around until they look right, but use them as aids only. If you try to design around them, your garden will almost certainly lack coherence.

visualize the impact they will have on the rest of the garden. You could use bamboo canes as an arch or trellis, a piece of garden hose for the edge of a lawn or planks of wood to indicate the edge of a patio or path. Tall canes indicating the position of important features or key plants will

HOW TO DESIGN YOUR GARDEN

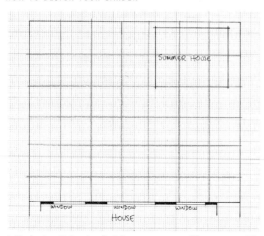

1 The basic grid Transfer all of the measurements of features you wish to retain from your first sketch on to graph paper. Superimpose on to this grid the type of design you have in mind: based on circles, diagonals or rectangles. Most gardens work best with the grid lines about 2m (7ft) apart. Using overlays or photocopies, try out features that you would like to include in their approximate positions. Moving around scale features, cut out of paper, is helpful.

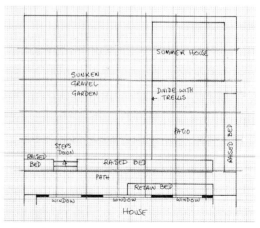

2 The rough Using an overlay or photocopies, sketch in your plan. If you can visualize an overall design, sketch this in first, then move around the cut-out features to fit. If you have not reached this stage, sketch in the features you have provisionally positioned but adjust them as the big design evolves. Make many attempts – the best plan will emerge once you have tried out lots of options. Don't worry about planning details at this stage apart from the important focal points in the design.

Getting inspired

If you are short of inspiration or cannot find a solution to a particular problem in your garden, don't be shy of being inspired by others and adapting their ideas to fit your circumstances. After all, it's what the professionals do all the time. Look at magazines and books to help decide which style appeals to you most. Also collect pictures of features that you like when you are reading magazines, and take pictures of your own when you visit other people's gardens and gardening shows. Note down any plant combinations that catch your eye; they may well come in useful later on.

DECIDING ON A PATTERN

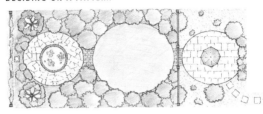

CIRCLES
A circular pattern is good at disguising the sometimes predictable shape of a rectangular garden. The circles can be overlapped, if necessary.

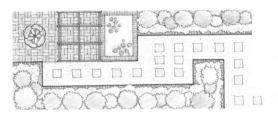

RECTANGLES
A rectangular theme is a popular choice and is effective if you want to create a formal look, or divide up a long narrow garden into smaller sections.

show how much screening they are likely to offer. By observing the shadow at different times of day you'll also know whether shade is likely to be a problem for other plants or in a sitting-out area.

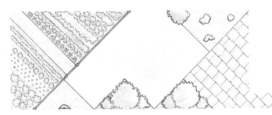

DIAGONALS
A diagonal grid pattern will create a sense of space by taking the eye along and across the garden. It is best to use a grid that is at 45° to the house.

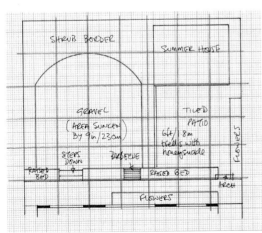

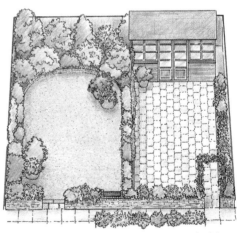

3 The detailed drawing Details such as the type of paving should be decided now – not only because it will help you see the final effect, but also because you need to work to a plan that uses multiples of full blocks, slabs or bricks if necessary. It will also help you to budget for your plan. Draw in key plants, especially large trees and shrubs, but omit detailed planting plans at this stage.

4 Visualize the finished result Before starting construction it is worth being absolutely sure what the end result will look like. If you can draw, sketch out how you plan your garden to look. You may wish to make a 3-D model of your garden, using coloured card, wooden matches and other household items, such as straw, cotton wool (cotton balls) and lentils or rice, to represent the texture of different materials. Think about the garden as it will appear at different times of the year.

Lawns and alternatives

Grass lawns have been the main feature of most domestic gardens for many years, but recent trends in garden design have provided a range of other options to consider for covering the ground.

Why choose a lawn?

A lawn is quick and easy to lay, requires little skill to maintain and looks good when it is well cared for. It is perhaps the best all-round surface and is one of the cheapest methods of covering large areas of ground. When regularly mown and trimmed, a lawn provides an attractive open space that sets off all the surrounding features and provides cohesion to the overall design. There are two main grades of domestic lawn. High quality putting- or bowling-green lawn is the most ornamental, but it requires a lot of attention and fairly frequent mowing to keep it in tip-top condition. For most people, though, a standard lawn, also called a family or utility lawn, is perfectly adequate. It is harder wearing and requires cutting less often, so it takes a lot less time to maintain. Although there are special lawn grass mixes for difficult situations, such as shade, a lawn requires more maintenance if the growing conditions are not ideal.

A lawn is one of the most important elements in a garden for many people, creating a sense of open space that lets the garden "breathe".

Lawn alternatives

In some situations such as deep shade a ground covering of shade-loving plants may be a better option. Also consider alternative coverings where mowing would be difficult or dangerous, such as on a steep slope. If you don't want a grass lawn but still require an open space in the middle of the garden, there are a number of other options you can use to cover the ground.

Herb lawns In a sunny, well-drained site a few herbs, such as camomile, thyme and comfrey, are sufficiently low growing to create a lush lawn effect. Although they are tough enough to be walked on occasionally, these plants are not hard-wearing so are not suitable for children's play areas or high-traffic walkways. Try *Thymus serpyllum* or choose the non-flowering camomile variety *Chamaemelum nobile* 'Treneague'.

HOW TO PLANT GROUND COVER PLANTS

1 Dig over the area and clear the ground of weeds at least a month before planting. Hoe off any seedlings that appear in the meantime. Rake the ground level before planting.

2 Water the plants in their pots, then set them out about 15–20cm (6–8in) apart, in staggered rows to work out the positions and to check you have sufficient plants.

3 Tease out the roots and plant to the original depth. Firm in the soil around the roots. Water thoroughly and keep well watered for the first season.

HOW TO LAY GRAVEL

1 Excavate the area to the required depth – about 5cm (2in) of gravel is sufficient in most cases. Don't disturb the soil to a greater depth than you need to.

2 Level the ground. Lay punctured, heavy-duty black polythene or a semi-permeable membrane over the area to suppress weed growth. Overlap strips by about 5cm (2in).

3 Tip the gravel on top of the base sheet and spread it evenly over the surface, making sure it is about 5cm (2in) thick. Use a rake to get the gravel level.

Ground cover plants Choose easy-care plants – low-growing conifers and heathers as well as the rose of Sharon (*Hypericum calycinum*), for example – to cover difficult or dangerous areas, such as steep slopes where you do not intend to walk. They will quickly smother the ground with a knee-high, weed-suppressing thicket of foliage. Apart from a once-a-year tidy up, they don't need any maintenance.

Flowering carpet Under trees and shrubs a flowering carpet of bulbs can be particularly effective. If you plant early varieties they will bloom before the overhead foliage emerges and then be hidden from view at other times. Choose shade-tolerant species that are suited to the impoverished conditions and mulch the soil well to conserve moisture and prevent weeds.

Gravel A popular option with many designers, gravel, pebbles and other aggregates are versatile and easy to lay. There are now many attractive grades and mixes to choose from including coloured glass chippings. If laid over a semi-permeable landscape fabric these surfaces are practically maintenance free. They are also easy to combine with plants to create a natural-looking effect.

Paving and decking These permanent ground coverings are maintenance-free, and there is a wide range of materials available to suit any garden design. Paving requires a lot of work before laying, particularly on a sloping site, and is an expensive option, requiring some skill. Decking is more versatile as it can be cut to fit any space and can be raised so that the ground does not have to be levelled beforehand. Decking requires basic do-it-yourself skills and costs about the same as paving.

PLANTING THROUGH GRAVEL

Draw back the gravel and make a cross-shaped slit in the base sheet. Plant normally, then firm in the plant, water well, and replace the flaps of the base sheet before re-covering with gravel.

Lawns are not the best option for every garden. In a small courtyard other coverings, such as gravel, might be a more sympathetic or appropriate material.

Patios

Paving requires careful thought and planning because, once laid, it is difficult and expensive to alter. First, consider what you want your paved area for and then identify the ideal position for a patio or paved area.

The purpose of the patio

A patio provides a smooth, level, hard surface on which to sit and relax and entertain. For these reasons patios are usually best sited in a spot that is not overlooked by neighbours and that is in a convenient position near to the house. If you want to use your patio for sunbathing it will need to catch the sun for much of the day, and if you want it for entertaining a site close to the kitchen would be most convenient.

In a north-facing garden, the best place to site a patio may be at the bottom of the garden to catch the maximum amount of sun. It may be more convenient to have two smaller areas of paving: one for sunbathing and one near to the house for entertaining. Wherever you decide to site your patio, make sure that the outlook is pleasing and that it is well screened; the privacy will create a relaxing atmosphere.

Deciding on a size

The size of the patio should also be determined by what you want to use it for. To accommodate a standard patio set of table and four chairs, you would need a paved area at least 3 x 3m (10 x 10ft) but preferably larger, about 4 x 4m (13 x 13ft), so that there is room to walk around the furniture comfortably while it is in use. However, in a small garden, the patio can dominate the garden and create an unbalanced effect in the overall design. In this situation you may be better off paving the whole garden and using planting

HOW TO LAY PAVING

1 Excavate the area to a depth that will allow for about 5cm (2in) of compacted hardcore topped with about 3–5cm (1–2in) of ballast, plus the thickness of the paving and mortar.

2 On top of the layers of hardcore and ballast, put five blobs of mortar where the slab is to be placed – one at each corner, and the other in the middle.

3 Position the slab carefully, bedding it down on the mortar. Over a large area of paving, create a slight slope to allow rainwater to run off freely.

4 Use a spirit (carpenter's) level placed over more than one slab to ensure that the slab is as close to horizontal as you want. Use a small wedge of wood under one end of the level to create a slight slope over the whole area if necessary. Tap the slab down further, or raise it by lifting and packing in more mortar.

5 Use spacers of an even thickness to ensure regular spacing between the paving slabs. Remove these later, before the joints are filled with mortar.

6 A day or two after laying the paving, go over it again to fill in the joints. Use a small pointing trowel and a dryish mortar mix. Finish off with a smooth stroke that leaves the mortar slightly recessed. This produces an attractive, crisp look. Brush any surplus mortar off the slabs before it dries.

pockets, raised beds and plenty of containers to provide visual interest in the garden.

Even in a large garden, expanses of paving can appear austere. You can break up this appearance by combining styles of paving as well as planting up the patio itself. Don't be tempted to overdo it because the effect will look too fussy and undermine the calm atmosphere.

Soften the boundary between the patio and lawn, perhaps with a low wall, designed with a planting cavity.

Check the depth of the foundation before you lay the paving. If it adjoins the house, make sure that the paving will end up at least 15cm (6in) below the damp-proof course.

Choosing materials

There is an incredibly wide range of materials suitable for garden paving. Which you choose is largely a matter of personal preference, although each type does have its own advantages and disadvantages. Try to choose a paving material that is sympathetic to the overall design and to the style of your house. Using materials that are already used elsewhere in the garden will help create a co-ordinated effect. Regularly shaped paving works well in a formal setting, whereas paving that consists of smaller units or a range of paving sizes is often a better choice if you are trying to create a more relaxed feel. If you are combining different materials, make sure they are the same thickness to make laying easier.

RIGHT
The top row shows (from left to right) natural stone sett, clay paver, brick, artificial sett.

The centre row shows a range of the different shapes of concrete paving blocks available.

The bottom row shows some of the colours and sizes of concrete paving slabs available.

Grouping containers together presents an attractive display to brighten up the patio. Here, *Clematis* 'Prince Charles' is planted in a chimney pot next to some potted chives.

Decking

Garden decking is a popular choice these days and in many situations is often the best option. It can be cheaper and easier to construct than paving, especially on a sloping site, and provides a hard, flat surface that is functional and looks good too.

Designing with decking

Decking can be tailor-made to suit any garden design. Its essentially natural appearance makes it ideal for informal gardens where you can make the most of the warm tones of the timber. Decking also looks good in a bold, contemporary garden design. Indeed, it can be made the main focal point by choosing an eye-catching design and colouring it with woodstain. In a formal setting, emphasize the clean lines of a deck by using stepped edges.

Different designs can be achieved by fixing planks in different ways (see opposite), but on the whole, it is best to keep any pattern fairly simple. In some countries there are building codes that may have to be met. If in doubt, seek professional help with the design, even if you intend to construct it yourself.

Timber decking provides a durable, practical and easy-to-care-for floor surface. It makes a refreshing change from a patio made of paving slabs or bricks. Adding containers will help to make the deck a pleasant place to sit in summer.

HOW TO MAKE A DECK

1 Level the area, then use bricks or building blocks to support your decking. Calculate the position of each row. Each timber bearer should be supported in the middle as well as the ends. Excavate the soil and position the brick.

2 Position each block so that about half of it sits in the soil – it is important that air circulates beneath the bearers. Tap down each block to ensure it is level, adding or removing soil if necessary.

3 Use a spirit (carpenter's) level to ensure that the blocks are level. If the ground is unstable, set the bricks or blocks on pads of concrete. Make sure that they are level, or the final decking will not be stable.

Which timber?

Decking can be made from hardwood, pressure-treated softwood or plain softwood. Hardwood decks made from white oak or western red cedar are durable and practically maintenance free, but they cost a lot more to construct. Decking made from pressure-treated (tanalized) softwood is less expensive and reasonably easy to maintain, but requires seasonal maintenance, while plain softwood decking needs regular maintenance and is prone to rotting, so it is not very durable. Clad the deck with non-slip grooved planks spaced about 6mm (¼in) apart to allow for expansion and to allow water to drain away freely. Attach them with galvanized nails or screws. All decks should also be laid on a sheet of semi-permeable material such as landscaping fabric.

Choosing a deck

The easiest way to create a deck is to use ready-made decking tiles that can be laid straight on to a firm, flat surface, such an old patio, roof terrace or firmed hardcore. For a better result, lay the tiles on top of a

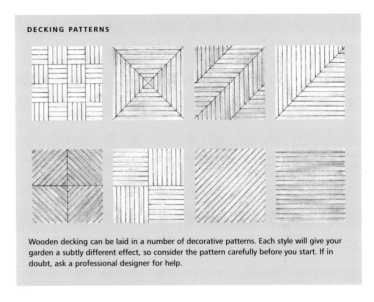

DECKING PATTERNS

Wooden decking can be laid in a number of decorative patterns. Each style will give your garden a subtly different effect, so consider the pattern carefully before you start. If in doubt, ask a professional designer for help.

framework of pressure-treated timber and treat any cut ends or joints with wood preservative. You can also get decks in kit form, and these are very easy to put together and a good choice where the deck isn't fitted into a particular space, such as an island deck part-way down the garden.

Custom-made decking, supplied and fitted by a professional supplier, is the most convenient but most expensive option. Specialist suppliers will take on the whole process, from planning, checking local planning regulations and getting the permissions necessary to constructing the deck. With custom-made decking you can be more ambitious with split levels, walkways and even raised decks to give the perfect view of the garden.

4 Use wood preservative on the bearers if necessary. Space out the bearers on the block supports. Add extra bearers near the ends and sides of the decking, where planks (boards) will need extra support.

5 Your bearers may not be long enough to stretch the whole length of the deck, in which case make sure joints are made above a block. Use a damp-proofing strip between each block and bearer to prevent water seeping up.

6 Add a plastic sheet to suppress weeds, then saw the decking planks to size and treat with a preservative. Nail in position with galvanized nails leaving gaps of about 6mm (¼in) between planks to allow for expansion.

Beds and borders

The position, size and shape of beds and borders should be considered at the outset of a new garden design, as they have an enormous influence on the way the garden is viewed.

Changing the perspective

Most gardeners consider beds and borders essential, both to grow specific plants and to add interest to the shape of the garden. It is quite easy to change the shape of a border, so consider whether the existing design is making the most effective use of perspective. For example, narrow borders that simply follow the boundary lines will make a narrow garden seem narrower and a short garden shorter.

Create the illusion of space in a small garden by disguising the boundary. Wider borders provide the opportunity to combine a range of plants that together will either hide the boundary from view or break up its outline, effectively camouflaging it. Dividing the garden horizontally will also make the garden more intriguing because at least part of the design is hidden from view, encouraging the casual visitor to explore. In a short garden, use a long, curving border cutting across the garden to make it seem longer, emphasizing the longest dimension, the diagonal.

Breaking up a lawn

A large area of grass can make a garden look plain, and you may want to add a feature such as an island bed or a border alongside a path.

HOW TO CREATE A CIRCULAR BED

1 Insert a post in the centre of the proposed bed. Attach one end of a piece of string to the post and the other end to a bottle filled with sand or soil.

2 Walk slowly around the post, keeping the string taut and the bottle tilted, so that the sand or soil trickles out and marks the outline of the circle.

HOW TO CREATE AN OVAL BED

Place two posts in the ground and loosely tie a piece of string around them. Experiment with the distance between the posts and the length of the piece of string to get the size and shape of bed you require. Place a bottle filled with sand or soil inside the loop of string and walk around the posts, keeping the string taut. The sand or soil will trickle out, creating the outline of a perfect oval.

HOW TO CREATE AN IRREGULAR BED

Use a flexible garden hose to work out the size and shape of an irregular bed. Once you are happy with the shape of the bed, remove a line of turf around the inside edge of the hose to mark it out.

3 Once the circle is complete, the turf can be cut from within the marked area in order to produce a perfectly circular bed.

This will break up the garden visually, and also give you the chance to grow more flowers and shrubs. It can sometimes be more effective to cut a bed towards one end of the lawn rather than in a central position. This can make the most of your lawn by taking the eye across it to the flower bed.

It is important to keep an island bed looking neat as it is a key focal point. However, by choosing low-maintenance plants such as alpines, and mulching with an attractive layer of gravel, an island bed doesn't need to be time-consuming.

Choosing plants

It is essential to choose the right combination of plants for each part of the site. First, consider what you want the plants to do. If you want year-round cover you will need a high proportion of evergreens to provide the screen. But a garden made from evergreens alone becomes very static and lacking in interest. In this situation, make the key plants that block the sight lines evergreen, but fill in and around them with a range of deciduous plants, bulbs and herbaceous plants to add seasonal variety and excitement.

Beds of lavender flank a narrow path. It's a good choice of plant: brushing past the lavender will release its delicious scent.

HOW TO PREPARE THE GROUND

1 Since flowerbeds and borders are likely to be undisturbed for many years it is important to clear the area of weeds first. There are three ways of doing this: spray with weedkiller, skim off the surface with a hoe, or cover with polythene for several months.

2 Dig the first trench to one spade's depth across the plot, and transfer the soil you have removed to the other end of the plot using a barrow where it will be used to fill in the final trench.

3 Fork a layer of well-rotted compost or manure into the bottom of the trench to improve the soil structure and to provide nutrients for the plants.

4 Dig the next trench across the plot, turning the soil on to the compost in the first trench. Add compost to the new trench and then dig the next.

5 Continue down the border until the whole of the surface has been turned. Add some compost to the final trench and then fill with the soil taken from the first.

6 If possible, dig in the autumn and allow the winter weather to break down the soil. In spring, take out any new weeds and rake over the bed.

Raised beds

Although they are time consuming and expensive to build, raised beds can solve a range of gardening problems, such as poor soil or bad drainage, but they are also useful for adding interest to flat plots or for providing level ground in sloping gardens.

Designing with raised beds

Raised beds offer so many advantages that it is surprising they do not feature in more gardens. They are ideal for adding height and interest to otherwise boringly flat gardens, but equally they are a practical solution to providing level areas on sloping ground. In small gardens they can be combined with paving to produce an intimate courtyard garden. Raised beds can be a functional square or rectangle, or designed to fit a corner in the garden.

Choosing the right soil

Raised beds hold a lot more soil than containers, so they are much easier to look after and you can grow much bigger plants. They also offer the opportunity to grow plants in your garden that otherwise would fail to thrive. For example, if your soil is poor or badly drained, raised beds can be filled with good quality imported loam. Indeed, if you fancy growing plants that like a specific

HOW TO MAKE A RAISED BED USING BRICKS

1 Mark out the shape of the bed using short pointed stakes and string. Use a builders' set square (triangle) to ensure the correct angles. Define the lines with a thin stream of fine sand or use line-marker paint.

2 Dig out along the markings to a depth of 30cm (12in) and width of 15cm (6in). Fill with concrete to within 5cm (2in) of the top. Firm down, level and leave for 24 hours to set. For concrete, use 1 part cement to 4 parts ballast.

3 Build up four or five courses of bricks and set each into mortar, checking with a spirit (carpenter's) level at every stage.

4 Clean up the mortar while it is still wet with a pointing trowel. Leave it to harden.

5 Before filling with soil, coat the inside of the wall with a waterproof paint.

6 Put in a layer of rubble topped with gravel for drainage. Fill with topsoil and stir in a layer of a good potting medium.

7 Plant up the raised bed in the usual manner and water in well.

8 The completed bed planted with a selection of culinary herbs and wild strawberries.

type of soil, such as acid-loving rhododendrons, raised beds filled with ericaceous compost (soil mix) will provide that opportunity even if your garden soil is not suitable.

The soil in raised beds warms up more quickly than garden soil so you can start off new plants earlier in spring, which is useful if you grow early vegetables or flowers. For anyone who finds bending difficult, raised beds are particularly welcome.

Which material?

Traditional permanent raised beds made from bricks or blocks are built in much the same way as solid brick retaining walls, the only differences being that the walls in a raised bed are built vertical rather than slightly sloping. They can be made from bricks or blocks mortared together, with "weep-holes" (vertical joints free of mortar) every metre (yard) or so along the base of each wall to allow water to drain out. Check the bricks are frostproof; ordinary housebricks may not be suitable. In a cottage-style garden, dry-stone walls also make good raised beds, with crevices used to grow plants.

Raised beds can also be constructed from wood. Old railway sleepers (railroad ties) were traditionally recommended, but designer mini-sleepers are more readily available from garden centres, either as individual logs that can be nailed together tailored to suit any position, or as part of a raised bed kit, which is easily slotted together. Pressure-treated softwood gravel boards, which will withstand damp, are an economical material for making simple raised beds for the vegetable garden. Alternatively, once the boards have been stained they will make an attractive feature container on the patio.

Growing a mix of fragrant herbs in a raised bed will bring the scents, colours and textures closer to you, making a feature of this attractive part of the garden.

HOW TO MAKE A RAISED BED USING WOOD

1 Set the log edging in position and tap it into place. Check with a spirit (carpenter's) level. If you are using flexible edging, drive in stakes to which you nail the edging.

2 On geometric shapes, as shown here, nail the corners together with rust-proof nails.

3 Fill with soil, ensuring that you create the correct conditions for the types of plant you are intending to grow. Heathers will need an acid soil to grow well.

4 Plant up the raised bed and water the plants in well. Mulch the ground with shredded bark or gravel to retain moisture.

Paths

Paths exert a strong influence on the design and sense of movement in a garden, so consider the effect during the planning process. It is also essential to match the construction to the type of use a path will receive.

Designing with paths

A path's design should reflect the overall theme of the garden. In a formal setting straight paths with clean lines will reinforce the formality of the design, whereas in an informal garden gently meandering paths will be more appropriate. Try to avoid straight paths that lead the eye directly to the bottom of the garden, because they will be less inviting and make the plot seem smaller. Calm the feeling of movement by adding changes in direction along the path and create a sense of mystery by allowing the path to disappear from view – behind a garden structure or border, for example.

Which path?

There are three main types of path: functional paths that are constantly used come rain or come shine; occasional paths that are largely ornamental and are used infrequently or not at all; and temporary paths that are rolled out for specific jobs. All paths should have a slight slope or camber to prevent puddles forming in wet weather.

Regularly used paths

A well-used path needs to be at least 60cm (2ft) wide and have an all-weather surface. If laid against the side of the house the path needs to be at least 15cm (6in) below the

HOW TO LAY A GRAVEL PATH

1 Excavate the area to a depth of about 15cm (6in), and ram the base firm.

2 Provide a stout edge to retain the gravel. For a straight path, securing battens by pegs about 1m (3ft) apart is an easy and inexpensive method.

3 Place a layer of compacted hardcore. Add a mixture of sand and coarse gravel (you can use sand and gravel mixture sold as ballast). Rake level and tamp or roll until firm.

4 Top up to within 2.5cm (1in) of the edge or battens with the final grade of gravel. In small gardens the size often known as pea gravel looks good and is easy to walk on. Rake the gravel level.

A winding gravel path, bordered with carefully chosen cottage garden plants, is an inviting way to the front door.

damp-proof course and slope gently away from the house to shed water.

The amount and type of traffic a path will carry is one of the main considerations when you decide the type of path to opt for. Paved paths, using concrete slabs set on blobs of mortar on a solid base of rammed hardcore, are the best choice for an all-weather path that's used for regular foot and light wheeled traffic (bikes, wheelbarrows etc). This type of path is expensive, a lot of work to construct and not very adaptable.

Paved paths made from small unit paving blocks bedded into a layer of sharp sand on top of well-firmed soil are less expensive and are easier to construct. They can be adapted to any design, but you do need to have solid edges to the path to keep the paving in place. These can be wooden, concrete or simply a row of blocks set in a foundation of concrete.

Gravel paths are simple to construct on firmed soil with an underlay of membrane. They can be made any shape, including complicated curves. Little maintenance is required apart from removing the odd weed and the occasional rake to keep it looking neat. Unfortunately, the gravel tends to be kicked into nearby borders and may get walked into the house.

Occasionally used paths

Paths constructed for largely ornamental reasons can be made from a wider range of materials. In general, choose a material that is in keeping with its surroundings and will provide a solid footing. Stepping stones made from the paving used elsewhere in the garden can look good set into the lawn to provide access to the washing line. Under trees or through a shrubbery, log stepping stones or a path of chipped bark can be more appropriate.

Neat edging

For a period garden, Victorian-style rope edging looks appropriate. You can use it either to retain a gravel path or as an edging to a paved path.

Wavy edgings such as this are also reminiscent of some of the older styles of garden, but they can also be used in a modern setting to create a formal effect.

HOW TO LAY BRICKS AND BLOCKS

1 Excavate the area and prepare a sub-base of about 5cm (2in) of compacted hardcore or sand-and-gravel mix. Set an edging along one end and side first. Check that it is level, then lay the pavers on a bed of mortar.

2 Once the edging is set, lay a 5cm (2in) bed of sharp sand over the area. Use a straight-edged piece of wood to level the surface. Position the pavers, butting them tightly to the edging and to each other.

3 Brush loose sand into the joints of the pavers with a broom. Hire a flat-plate vibrator to consolidate the sand or tamp the pavers down with a club hammer used over a piece of wood.

4 Brush in more sand and repeat the vibrating process once more for a firm, neat finish. To avoid damage do not go too close to an unsupported edge with the vibrator. The path should be ready to use straight away.

Walls

Although walls are mainly thought of as a structure to provide security and privacy along the boundary, they are also useful within a garden for building terracing on a sloping plot as well as a range of other features, including raised beds, barbecues, garden screens, seats and plinths for containers and ornaments.

Most builders' merchants have a wide range of bricks suitable for garden walls. Bricks come in many colours and finishes and these are just a small selection of the many available.

Designing with walls

Walls can be made from a wide range of materials so can be constructed to suit any style. Substantial or prominent walls, such as those used along the boundary, will fit in more easily with the rest of the garden if they are constructed of the same material used for the house. Smaller walls within the garden can be designed to reflect the overall design of the garden. They can also be combined with other materials, such as wooden trellis, to help soften the overall effect.

Which wall?

There are basically four types of wall: free-standing walls for boundaries and screens; solid retaining walls for terracing; loose dry-stone walls also for terracing; and retaining walls for raised beds. All walls require some skill to construct, so if you are in doubt seek professional advice.

Plants for wall crevices

Aubrieta deltoidea
Campanula portenschlagiana
Dianthus deltoides
Erinus alpinus
Erodium reichardii
Geranium sanguineum var. *striatum*
Mentha requienii
Pratia pedunculata
Saxifraga paniculata
Scabiosa graminifolia
Sedum spathulifolium

Foundations

All walls need a concrete foundation along their entire length. The higher the wall, the wider and deeper the foundations have to be. For walls up to 75cm (30in) high the foundations should be 10cm (4in) deep and about twice as wide as the wall being constructed. For walls over 75cm (30in) high, foundations should be 15cm (6in) deep and about three times as wide as the wall.

Boundary walls

The way a boundary wall is constructed will also depend on how high you want to build it. A small wall at the front of the house could be made from single bricks, 10cm (4in) thick, if it is up to 45cm (18in). Any higher, and you will either have to use a double brick wall, 23cm (9in) thick, or build supporting piers every couple of metres (yards) along a single brick wall. Walls over 1.2m (4ft) need a double-brick construction and supporting piers. Add coping stones on top of the wall to help shed water and to protect the bricks.

BRICK BONDING

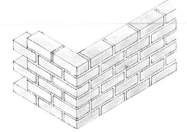

Running bond or stretcher bond The simplest form of bonding used for walls a single brick wide.

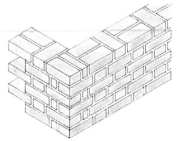

Flemish bond Creates a strong bond in a wall two bricks wide. Bricks are laid lengthways and across the wall in the same course.

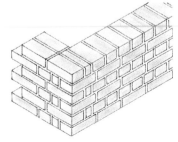

English bond Used for a thick wall where strength is needed. Alternate courses are laid lengthways then across the wall.

Retaining walls

Solid retaining walls are made from bricks or blocks mortared together. The wall will have to be strong enough to hold back the weight of the soil behind it. For this reason, always use the double-brick construction method but this time lay the foundations and build the wall so that it slopes back slightly. Leave weep-holes (vertical joints free of mortar) every metre (yard) or so along the base of the wall to allow water to drain out from the soil. Pack in rubble behind the weep-holes and cover with coarse gravel to prevent soil washing out and to stop the weep-holes from becoming blocked with soil.

Dry-stone walls also make good retaining walls up to 1m (3ft) high. Again the wall needs to be built so that it leans back slightly. The blocks should be selected so that they interlock as much as possible, leaving few gaps. Pack rubble behind the wall as you go to help secure each layer in place. Any large crevices can be planted with suitable plants.

Retaining walls provide an excellent opportunity to experiment with climbers and wall shrubs.

A wall is cloaked in the scented creamy white flowers of *Rosa* 'Climbing Iceberg'.

HOW TO BUILD A WALL

1 All walls require a footing. For a low wall this is one brick wide; for larger and thicker walls the dimensions are increased. Excavate a trench about 30cm (12in) deep and put 13cm (5in) of consolidated hardcore in the bottom. Drive pegs in so that the tops are at the final height of the foundation. Use a spirit (carpenter's) level to check that they are level.

2 To form the foundations, fill the trench with a concrete mix of 2 parts cement, 5 parts sharp sand and 7 parts 2cm (¾in) aggregate, and level it off with the top of the pegs. Use a straight-edged board to tamp the concrete down and remove any air pockets.

3 When the concrete foundation has hardened for a few days, lay the bricks on a bed of mortar, adding a wedge of mortar at one end of each brick as you lay them. For a single brick wall with supporting piers, the piers should be positioned at each end and at 1.8–2.4m (6–8ft) intervals, and can be made by laying two bricks crossways.

4 For subsequent courses, lay a ribbon of mortar on top of the previous row, then "butter" one end of the brick to be laid.

5 Tap level, checking constantly with a spirit (carpenter's) level to make sure that the wall is level and vertical.

6 The top of the wall is best finished off with a coping of suitable bricks or with special coping stones sold for the purpose.

Fences

One of the most popular choices for marking a boundary, fences offer instant privacy and security. They are less expensive to construct than a wall and need less maintenance than a hedge.

Designing with fences

There is a huge selection of fencing styles in a range of different materials, including various woods, metals and plastic, so you should have no problem finding a style that will enhance your garden. In the front garden fences with a more open structure are often used. Examples include picket or post-and-rail fences, ranch-style fences and post-and-chain fences. They do not provide privacy or much security, but they are an attractive way of marking the boundary.

In most back gardens, a boundary fence should recede from view, so choose something robust enough to support climbers and wall shrubs that will help disguise it. However, in certain circumstances you might want to make a feature of a fence. Painting with a woodstain used

A fence has been erected to screen the practical corner of the garden from view. It is strong enough to support a climber.

elsewhere in the garden or to co-ordinate with a nearby planting scheme will emphasize its presence.

Which fence?

The most popular type of fence is the ready-made panel, which comes in various forms, including horizontal lap, vertical lap and interwoven. They are also available in several heights including 1.2m (4ft), 1.5m (5ft) and 1.8m (6ft). Fencing panels are very cheap and easy to put up between regularly spaced, well-anchored posts. Most fencing panels are rather flimsy and have a lifespan of less

HOW TO ERECT A RANCH-STYLE FENCE

1 The posts of a ranch-style fence must be well secured in the ground. Use 10cm (4in) square posts, set at 2m (6½ft) intervals. For additional strength add 8cm (3in) square intermediate posts. Make sure the posts go at least 45cm (18in) into the ground. Concrete the posts into position, then fill in with soil.

2 Screw or nail the planks (boards) in place, making sure that the fixings are galvanized. Use a spirit (carpenter's) level to check that the planks are horizontal. Butt-join the planks in the centre of a post but try to stagger the joints on each row so that there is not a weak point in the fence.

3 Fit a post cap to improve the appearance and also protect the posts. Paint with a good quality paint recommended for outdoor use. Choose the colour of the paint carefully; you will need to keep white paint clean in order for the fence to look good.

than ten years, even when regularly maintained. For a better quality and longer-lasting wooden fence, opt for the close-board fencing. Here, a structure of posts with two or three cross-members, called arris rails, is constructed before cladding with wooden strips. These are sometimes thinner along one edge than the other and are overlapped when nailed to the arris rails. Alternatively the fence can be regular, where the pales are nailed on to the arris rails butted together with no spaces between them and without overlapping.

Posts

With all types of fence, the posts should be durable. For preference choose a naturally rot-resistant hardwood, but pressure-treated softwood is more commonly available. With panel fencing they are set 1.8m (6ft) apart to accommodate the panel, but with close-board fencing they are usually spaced more widely – 2.4–3m (8–10ft). Either buy posts that are long enough for the bottom section to be buried into the ground and held firm with concrete, or buy posts the same height as the fence and secure them with special fencing spikes.

Planning permission

Check with your local planning authority before erecting a new wall or fence to make sure there are no restrictions. In certain circumstances, particularly in front gardens near to a highway or in designated conservation areas, there may be restrictions on the type and height of boundary you are allowed to erect. Normally, you require planning consent for any wall more than 1.8m (6ft) high and for a wall more than 1m (3ft) high that abuts a highway.

HOW TO ERECT A PANEL FENCE

1 Post spikes are an easier option than excavating holes and concreting the post in position. Use a special tool to protect the spike top, then drive it in with a sledge-hammer. Check with a spirit (carpenter's) level to ensure it is absolutely vertical.

2 Insert the post in the spike, checking the vertical again, then lay the panel in position on the ground and mark the position of the next post. Drive in the next spike, testing for the vertical again.

3 There are various ways to fix the panels to the posts, but panel brackets are easy to use. Simply nail the brackets to the posts.

4 Lift the panel and nail in position, through the brackets. Insert the post at the other end and nail the panel in position at that end.

5 Check the horizontal level both before and after nailing, and make any necessary adjustments before moving on to the next panel.

6 Finish off by nailing a post cap to the top of each post. This will keep water out of the end grain of the timber and extend its life.

Other garden structures

Pergolas, trellises and arches are not only quick and easy to construct but, if correctly positioned, can also effectively transform the appearance of a garden. Flatpack kits are now available in a variety of materials and styles to suit both traditional and contemporary gardens.

Designing with arches, trellises and pergolas

Arches can perform several functions in the garden. They look lovely when positioned over a path and festooned with colourful climbing plants. Ideally, the structure should frame a distant object, such as an ornament, or focus the eye on the path as it leads tantalizingly out of sight into the next area of the garden. Arches can also be used to link borders either side of the garden to give the overall design coherence.

Trellises can be used to divide the garden into separate "rooms" and add a strong vertical dimension to an otherwise flat garden scheme. If you are looking for a more subtle application, a trellis can provide a secluded corner for a garden seat, creating a peaceful sitting area or arbour.

A pergola is simply an open structure, often placed over a patio adjacent to the house to create an intimate area for outdoor entertaining. It can be covered in shading materials, such as netting or bamboo screens, or a more natural covering of climbers. Pergolas also can be used away from the house, forming a covered walkway along the sunny side of the garden or a point of focus in the middle of the garden. Being a larger structure means that a pergola lends itself to supporting quite vigorous climbers, such as wisteria, which would swamp an arch or trellis.

Adding a fence or trellis will not only give your garden a strong sense of design, but it also provides a wonderful opportunity to grow climbers.

Choosing materials

In an informal or country-style garden, structures made from rustic poles blend naturally into their surroundings. These can be bought as ready-made structures from fencing suppliers or made from fresh-cut wood. Rustic poles are usually roughly jointed and nailed together with galvanized nails. Rustic structures are not usually as strong as other types and often require more cross-members to improve their rigidity and strength.

If you are using sawn timber for arches and pergolas, choose timber that has been pressure-treated with preservative to prevent it rotting.

HOW TO ASSEMBLE AN ARCH

1 The simplest way to make an arch is to use a kit, which only needs assembling. First, establish the post positions, allowing a gap between the edge of the path and post, so that plants do not obstruct the path.

2 Dig four 60cm (2ft) deep holes to hold the posts. Alternatively, choose a kit with shorter posts for use with fence spikes. Drive the spikes in with a special tool, using a spirit (carpenter's) level to ensure they are vertical.

There are two main styles of wooden pergola: traditional and oriental. The traditional style has fewer, larger roofing timbers with square-cut ends, while oriental-style pergolas have bevelled ends.

You can also get plastic-coated tubular metal arches, arbours and pergolas. These are lightweight and so easier to put up than wooden versions. Their stylish appearance makes them suitable for use in contemporary garden designs.

HOW TO JOIN RUSTIC POLES

If you need to attach a horizontal pole to a vertical one, saw a notch of a suitable size in the top of the vertical one so that the horizontal piece will fit snugly on top.

To join two horizontal pieces of wood, saw two opposing and matching notches so that one sits over the other. Secure the two pieces with galvanized nails or screws.

To fix cross-pieces to horizontals or uprights, remove a V-shaped notch, using a chisel if necessary to achieve a snug fit, then nail into place with galvanized nails.

Use halving joints where two poles cross. Make two saw cuts halfway through the pole, then remove the waste timber with a chisel. Secure the two pieces with galvanized nails or screws.

Bird's mouth joints are useful for connecting horizontal or diagonal pieces to uprights. Cut out a V-shaped notch about 3cm (1in) deep and saw the other piece of timber to match the shape. You may need to use a chisel to achieve a good fit.

Try out the assembly on the ground, then insert the uprights in prepared holes and make sure these are secure before adding any further pieces. Most pieces can be nailed together, but screw any sections subject to stress. Use rust-free screws and nails.

3 Position the legs of the arch in the holes. Backfill with the excavated earth and compact with your heel. Check that the legs are vertical using a spirit level. If using spikes, insert the legs and then tighten any securing bolts.

4 The next stage is to construct the overhead beams of the arch. Lay both halves on a large flat surface and carefully screw the joint together at the correct angle. Use galvanized screws to protect the arch from corrosion.

5 Fit the overhead beams to the posts. In this example they slot into the tops of the posts and are nailed in place.

Preparing the soil

Cultivation is the basis of all good soil husbandry and is the starting point of most gardening activity. Even a garden run on a no-dig system requires thorough cultivation to get it off to a good start.

Digging is the best way of removing weeds and other unwanted debris from the soil, breaking up compacted layers and incorporating organic matter. It also brings pests to the surface so that they can be eaten by birds and introduces air into the soil. However, once planted and mulched with a thick layer of organic matter there may be no need to dig it again provided the soil is not walked on, which will compact it.

Well-rotted garden compost is one of the best soil conditioners. Every garden should have a compost heap, where grass clippings, leaves and other vegetable matter can be left to rot down. Not only is this material absolutely free, but it is an environmentally sound practice.

Look after your soil and it will look after you – requiring less effort and providing reliable bumper harvests.

Know your soil

It is essential that you understand what type of soil you have in your garden and its level of fertility before you can take steps to improve it. Several simple soil-testing kits are available to help you.

Understanding your soil

All soils are made up of the same basic ingredients: clay, silt and sand. It is the proportions of these that determines the type of soil you have.

Clay soil This heavy soil is generally fertile, but is sticky and difficult to work. The tiny clay particles pack together tightly with few air spaces between them, so the soil cannot drain freely and remains wet for longer. This causes problems in spring, because the soil is too wet to be cultivated and remains colder for longer. Soils with a high clay content have a poor structure and compact easily when walked on, further impeding drainage. When clay soils dry out in summer they crack badly and form solid lumps.

Sandy soil The particles in sandy soil are mainly larger and irregularly shaped, which means that water

It is essential that you choose plants that like the prevailing soil conditions in your garden. The rock rose (*Helianthemum*), for example, will thrive in neutral to alkaline soil in a dry, sunny spot.

drains freely and there are plenty of air spaces between the particles. The downside of free-draining, sandy soils is that nutrients are very easily leached (washed) out, which leaves the soil impoverished. Free-draining soils are also more prone to drought during dry spells. However, they are quicker to warm up after winter and easy to work, so are ideal for sowing early crops in spring.

Silt soil In terms of particle size, silt falls roughly between clay and sand. The soil is usually fertile. Silty soils are reasonably free-draining, but like clay soils they are easily compacted.

Loamy soil This type of soil contains both clay and sand particles as well as silt, and in many ways they offer the best of all worlds, being highly fertile and reasonably well drained, but still fairly moisture-

HOW TO TEST THE SOIL FOR NUTRIENTS

1 Collect a soil sample from 10cm (4in) below the surface. Take a number of samples, and mix together for a representative test.

2 Follow the instructions on the kit. Mix one part of soil with five parts of water. Shake well in a jar, then allow the water to settle.

3 Draw off some of the settled liquid from the top few centimetres (about an inch) for your test.

retentive. Loamy soils also warm up quickly in spring so are suitable for growing early crops.

The other essential factor about your soil that will affect the plants you can grow is its acidity or alkalinity. This is measured on a pH scale, of which the mid-point, 7, is neutral. Anything higher than that is increasingly alkaline, anything lower is increasingly acidic. Most plants prefer a neutral to slightly acidic soil (down to pH 5.5), although they will tolerate slightly alkaline conditions (up to pH 7.5). A few plants, such as azaleas, need acidic conditions to thrive; others, such as lilacs, prefer slightly alkaline soils.

Assessing your soil

If you have a new garden or are planting a new area, it is worth finding out what your soil is like so that you can improve it before planting. The first step is to check the drainage by digging holes about 30cm (12in) deep randomly across the area. Fill each with water and see how quickly it drains. If it all disappears within 24 hours all is

Reducing soil acidity

The acidity of your soil can be reduced by adding lime some weeks before planting and working it in thoroughly with a rake. First, check the soil with a soil-testing kit to see how much lime is required.

well. If the hole is still partly full after that time, you may have a drainage problem. In most cases this can be overcome by digging deeply and incorporating plenty of well-rotted organic matter and grit into the soil. Otherwise, you will have to get land drains installed or build raised beds.

Testing your soil

Cheap and reliable soil-testing kits are available from garden retailers that will indicate the nutrient balance in your soil and its pH level. For this to be of value you must test a representative sample of soil. The most reliable way of doing this is to lay four canes on the soil surface in a large W shape, then use a trowel to

Soil-testing kits of various degrees of sophistication are widely available, such as this electronic meter to test the pH level.

dig a small hole, about 15cm (6in) deep, at each point of the W, making a total of five holes. Scoop out some soil from each hole and place it in a garden sieve over a bucket. This will remove any debris and large pieces of organic matter. Mix the soil from the different holes thoroughly before testing. Make sure you do not test contaminated areas, such as where a compost heap has been, otherwise the results will not be representative of the garden as a whole.

4 Use a pipette to transfer the solution to the test chamber in the plastic container supplied with the kit.

5 Select a colour-coded capsule (one for each nutrient). Put the powder in the chamber, replace the cap and shake well.

6 After a few minutes, compare the colour of the liquid with the shade panel shown on the container.

Improving your soil

With the knowledge of what your soil is like, you can take positive steps to improve it through the incorporation of well-rotted manure and compost and thorough digging.

HOW TO CARRY OUT DOUBLE DIGGING

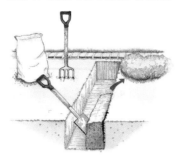

Soil conditioning

Organic matter, such as well-rotted farmyard manure, garden compost or mushroom compost, will improve all but peaty soils, which are already rich in the material. It improves the structure of heavy soils by allowing water and air in, and helps sandy soils by acting as a sponge, holding on to moisture. It also provides food for beneficial soil-borne creatures, such as earthworms, which further aerate the soil.

When well-rotted, organic matter is practically odourless it is ready to add to the soil. Do not use fresh or partly rotted organic material because the micro-organisms will use nitrogen to complete the process and this will be extracted from your soil.

Heavy soils are best dug in late autumn, to allow the large clods to be broken down by frost action. Loamy soils can be dug at any time in winter, as long as the soil conditions allow. Light, sandy soils are best cultivated in spring to avoid loss of nutrients through leaching in winter.

Forking

Light, recently cultivated soils can be simply forked over to the full depth of a garden fork, incorporating organic matter as you work. The soil is roughly turned and placed back in the same position. Remove any weeds and other debris by hand.

Digging

There are three main methods used to dig the garden, simple, single and double digging, although there are variations of each.

1 Dig a wide trench, placing the topsoil on a plastic sheet to one side to be used later when filling in the final trench.

2 Break up the subsoil at the bottom of the trench, adding well-rotted manure to the soil as you proceed.

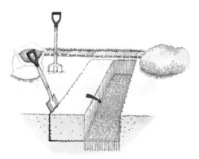

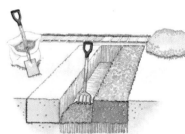

3 Dig the next trench, turning the topsoil over on top of the broken subsoil that is in the first trench.

4 Continue down the plot, taking care that subsoil from the lower trench is not mixed with topsoil from the upper.

Simple digging As its name suggests this is the least complicated to do. It is useful for cultivating lighter soils and for removing weeds. The spade is forced vertically into the soil to the full depth of the blade and the handle is eased back to lever the earth up. The spade is turned and the soil deposited in the same place but inverted, burying annual weeds at the bottom of the excavation. Perennial weeds and other debris are removed by hand, and clods of soil are broken up with sharp jabs of the spade. Repeat the technique across the plot. When the other side is reached, step back about 15cm (6in) and repeat the procedure across the plot.

Preparing for planting

You should prepare the soil for planting in the spring, when the surface of the soil is dry. Simply rake level using a soil rake, removing any stones that have made their way to the surface as well as any weed seedlings. Any remaining clods should break down readily to form a breadcrumb-like structure (known as a fine tilth), which is ideal for sowing and planting. If necessary, suitable fertilizers can be added at this point.

Avoid walking on the soil at any time because your weight will cause compaction. Instead, always lay short planks on the surface to spread your weight and work from these.

Single digging Used on heavier soils, this is a very good technique for incorporating organic matter into the upper layer of soil. It follows the same process as simple digging, except a trench about 30cm (12in) wide is excavated across the plot and the soil deposited on one side. A layer of well-rotted garden compost or manure is placed in the bottom of the trench. Moving 15cm (6in) back, the next row is dug, but the excavated soil is thrown forward to fill the first trench. After two passes across the plot the first trench will have been filled and a second trench created. This process is repeated until the entire plot has been dug. The excavated soil from the first trench is moved to the other end of the plot to fill the last trench.

Double digging This goes one step further and is used to break up compacted subsoil or for preparing deep beds for hungry crops. After excavating each trench, use a garden fork to loosen the subsoil at the bottom of the trench and mix in well-rotted organic matter or grit to improve the drainage if required. Then follow the procedure for single digging. It is important not to mix the soils from each layer.

This border was prepared thoroughly before planting. The soil was dug over to remove weeds and stones and to improve the soil structure. Plenty of organic compost was added to improve drainage. The end result is a border full of strong, healthy plants that requires little maintenance.

Using a cultivator

It is worth considering mechanical digging if you have a large plot to cultivate. However, you will need to clear the perennial weeds beforehand, and cultivators are hard work and noisy to operate. If a mechanical digger is used repeatedly on the same plot, the soil structure will suffer and a compacted layer can form just below the maximum depth of penetration of the blades.

HOW TO PREPARE FOR PLANTING

1 Break down the soil into a fine crumbly structure, and level with a rake before sowing.

2 Any large clods that still exist should be broken down with a spade or fork or the back of a rake. Try to avoid walking on the soil as this will cause compaction.

3 Once the soil is reasonably fine, rake it level. At the same time remove any large stones and other debris.

Making compost and leafmould

Composting is good for your garden and good for the environment. It is a convenient way of getting rid of garden waste and will also save you money, so it is well worth making the effort to do it.

Garden compost

Making your own compost is sound sense. It returns organic matter and nutrients to the soil that would otherwise be lost. It is also a very convenient way of getting rid of waste. There are environmental benefits, too, as composting recycles material that would otherwise find its way to landfill sites. Producing your own compost will save you money, because it means you need to buy less organic matter to improve your garden soil.

To compost successfully and efficiently you need the right equipment and an understanding of the principles of the decomposition process. Although you can compost organic waste perfectly well in a loose heap, it looks untidy and tends to decompose unevenly unless carefully managed. In most gardens a compost bin is a far better option.

WHAT TO COMPOST

A wide range of organic material from both the garden and household can be composted including (clockwise, from top left) most kitchen waste, weeds, shredded prunings and grass clippings.

Ideally, a bin should contain at least 1 cubic metre (about 30 cubic feet) of waste to allow it to heat up adequately and compost material quickly. The bin can be a simple structure made from old pallets nailed together to form a box or a neater home-made version fashioned from second-hand, tanalized fencing timber. Do not use untreated timber because it will rot along with the

A bonus crop

After the compost has been turned in the compost bin you can use it to grow a bonus crop of vegetables. Simply cover the top of the compost with about 15cm (6in) of garden soil and plant hungry vegetables, such as marrows (large zucchini), pumpkins or cucumbers. They will benefit from the heat generated by the decomposing compost and the extra nutrients made available.

contents. Alternatively, you can buy a ready-made compost bin, but make sure you choose one that will hold sufficient organic waste. The compost should be easily accessible when it is ready to use.

What can you compost?

Almost all organic waste material from the garden and household can be recycled, but to decompose quickly and form a crumbly, sweet-smelling, fibrous material, the right ingredients must be combined. Ideally, add dry material, such as prunings, old newspapers and straw, with equal quantities of green, wet

HOW TO MAKE COMPOST

1 A simple compost bin, which should be about 1m (3ft) square, can be made using cheap, pressure-treated fencing timber, or by nailing four flat pallets together.

2 Pile the waste into the bin, taking care that there are no thick layers of the same material. Grass clippings, for example, will not rot down if the layer is too thick because the air cannot penetrate.

3 It is important to keep the compost bin covered with an old mat or a sheet of polythene (sheet vinyl or plastic). This will help to keep in the heat generated by the rotting process and will also prevent the compost from getting too wet in bad weather.

organic waste, such as grass clippings. Before adding to the compost heap, make sure that dry and woody material is chopped finely with secateurs (pruners) or a garden shredder. Do not add meat, fish, fat or other cooked foods to the compost bin because they will attract vermin. Also throw away perennial weed roots and annual weeds that are setting seed because these may survive the composting process.

Mix up the material before adding it to the compost bin or add the material in layers no more than 15cm (6in) deep.

Speeding up composting

There are several actions you can take to minimize the time it takes for the composting process to be completed. Give the decomposition process a kick-start by adding a proprietary compost activator or a spadeful of well-rotted compost from a previous bin to each layer of material added. This will provide extra nitrogen and introduce the necessary micro-organisms needed for decomposition. Fill the bin as quickly as you can so that there is sufficient organic material to heat up and decompose quickly. Make sure that the material is moist enough when it is added. Check after a few weeks to see if it has dried out and water if necessary.

So the material does not get too wet, cover it with a lid, piece of old carpet or sheet of plastic. If the compost does get too wet, turn out the bin and mix in more dry material before refilling the bin. Insulate the bin in winter with bubble polythene or old carpet so that the core of the heap does not cool down. Turn the decomposing organic matter after about a month so that the material on the outside is placed in the centre of the bin. This will introduce air and produce a more uniform compost at the end of the process. After about two months in summer and up to six months in winter the compost should be ready to use.

Making leafmould

Autumn leaves are another source of useful organic matter. If you have a small garden, fill black plastic bags with leaves, add a little water if the leaves are dry and seal by knotting

Chicken wire attached to four wooden posts makes an ideal container for autumn leaves. The leafmould can be used on the garden after about a year.

the top. Puncture a few holes in the sides with a garden fork to allow air in before putting the bags in an out-of-the-way place, such as behind the shed. The leaves take about a year to break down into a rich, crumbly texture, which can then be used on the garden. Speed the process by adding a few handfuls of grass clippings to each bag before sealing.

In a large garden make a special enclosure with chicken wire and corner posts. Cover with carpet to prevent the leaves from blowing away.

4 After about a month, turn the contents of the compost bin with a fork to let in air and to move the outside material, which is slow to rot, into the centre to speed up the rotting process. If you have several bins, it is easier to turn the compost from one bin into another.

5 When the bin is full, you may want to cover the surface with a layer of soil and use it to grow marrows (large zucchini), pumpkins or cucumbers. If you want to use the contents as soon as possible, omit the soil and keep the compost covered with plastic.

Compost

Good garden compost is dark brown, fibrous and crumbly. It has a sweet earthy smell, not a rotting one. Compost can be used straight away or left covered until required.

Choosing and using fertilizers

Plants need a range of essential nutrients to grow well. The amount of fertilizer you use and how often you need to apply it will depend on your soil and the types of crops you are trying to grow.

Essential nutrients

In nature a nutritional cycle occurs whereby plants take nutrients from the soil as they grow, then eventually die and rot, allowing the nutrients to return to the soil. In the garden you can mimic this process to some extent by recycling all your organic waste in a compost bin and using the compost to return nutrients to the soil. A proportion of the organic matter is not returned, however, so the soil needs replenishment from other sources. Fertilizers are a convenient method of providing the nutrients that are needed for healthy growth. Your choice will depend on the nutrients already available from your soil and the type of growth you want to encourage.

There are three macro- or primary nutrients, nitrogen (N), phosphorus (P) and potassium (K), the proportions of which are expressed as a ratio of N:P:K on the labels of fertilizer packs. Each macro-nutrient promotes a different type of growth.

If they are to flower reliably year after year, perennials and shrubs, such as this camellia, should be given the nutrients they need. Fertilizer rich in potassium encourages good flower production.

Nitrogen This nutrient encourages leafy growth, so it is useful for adding to leafy crops such as spinach and cabbages.

Phosphorus An essential nutrient for healthy roots, phosphorus also promotes the ripening of fruit.

Potassium Available in the form of potash, this promotes flowering and good fruit production.

Three other nutrients, calcium, magnesium and sulphur, are needed in smaller quantities and are known as secondary nutrients, and seven more, boron, chlorine, copper, iron, manganese, molybdenum and zinc, are also essential but in very small amounts. These are known as micro-nutrients or trace elements.

Types of fertilizer

Fertilizers are grouped according to their mode of manufacture or origin. Organic fertilizers are derived from naturally occurring organic materials, such as animals and plants. Some of the most widely used are bonemeal (high in phosphorus), fishmeal, fish,

HOW TO ADD ORGANIC MATERIAL

1 Organic material such as well rotted garden compost or farmyard manure is high in nutrients. Fork in when the soil is dug. For heavy soils this is best done in the autumn.

2 If the soil has already been dug, the organic material can be lightly forked in or left on the surface. The worms will complete the task of working it into the soil.

3 In autumn, and again in spring, top-dress established plants with a layer of well-rotted organic material.

INORGANIC FERTILIZERS

ORGANIC FERTILIZERS

balanced general fertilizer

sulphate of ammonia

blood

bonemeal

potash

superphosphate

seaweed

fish, blood and bone

blood and bone, hoof and horn (high in nitrogen) and seaweed meal (also high in nitrogen). They are slow acting because they have to be broken down by micro-organisms in the soil before the nutrients they contain become available to plants. The rate of breakdown of the fertilizer varies according to the prevailing conditions: if it is warm and moist breakdown speeds up; when it is cold or dry it slows down. Nutrients are thus released when plants need them most and are growing strongly. For these reasons organic fertilizers are acceptable to most organic growers.

Inorganic fertilizers are man-made. Most are manufactured, but a few, such as rock potash, are naturally occurring minerals that are mined. They are concentrated and usually quick acting because they are soluble in water so are immediately available to the plants. Although effects can be immediate, such fertilizers are easily leached from the soil by heavy rains, especially in winter and on well-drained soil.

These fertilizers can be further grouped according to the amount of N, P and K they contain. As the name suggests, balanced fertilizers (also known as complete fertilizers) contain an equal proportion of each macro-nutrient, an N:P:K of 7:7:7 being typical. Specific fertilizers, on the other hand, have different ratios of N:P:K. They are usually sold labelled as beneficial for particular plants, such as lawns or roses. Straight or simple fertilizers are the final group and these supply just one of the macro-nutrients, such as superphosphate (phosphorus), or potassium sulphate (potassium).

To make selection even more complicated, some fertilizers are supplied in combination with other chemicals, such as a fungicide, insecticide or herbicide. They are a convenient but usually an expensive way of buying fertilizer. Slow-release fertilizers are inorganic fertilizers that have been coated in a special resin so that the nutrients are released slowly over time. They

mimic organic fertilizers in that they release more nutrients when the soil is warm and moist, just when the plants need it.

You can buy slow-release fertilizers that will last from a few weeks to the whole season. Because they cannot be washed away they are particularly suited for use in containers that are regularly watered throughout the growing season.

Fertilizers are also available in liquid formulations. Liquid growmore or liquid seaweed extract will promote general plant growth, but a high-potash feed, such as rose or tomato fertilizer, will encourage flowers and the formation of fruit.

Foliar feeds

Dilute fertilizer solutions can be applied to, and absorbed through, the plants' foliage. They are quick acting and useful for giving plants a boost part-way through the growing season or for correcting a deficiency.

Lawns

A lawn has a dramatic effect on the atmosphere of a garden. When it is kept neat and tidy it will greatly enhance the overall appearance as well as act as a calming visual counter-balance to busy and colourful beds and borders. If you have just moved into a new house the best way to get the garden started is to lay a new lawn. You do not have to worry about the size or shape at this stage because it can be easily changed later on when you have formulated your overall garden design.

When you design a new lawn it is important to keep the shape simple to reduce the time you will have to spend mowing and edging. Tight curves and corners might look dramatic, but they are awkward to cut. If the lawn runs right up to the base of a wall or fence consider installing a mowing edge so that you do not have to stop and trim wayward grass stems. An edging strip is also a good idea along borders, reducing maintenance time still further.

A long lawn draws the eye to the end of the garden. Rhododendrons spilling out on to the grass help soften the edges of the lawn.

Creating a new lawn

The decision to create a new lawn is not one to be taken lightly, but it does give you the opportunity to give your garden a top quality surface. A new lawn is best laid in spring or early autumn.

Seed or turf?

The main consideration once you have decided to have a new lawn is whether to grow it from seed or lay turf. Seed is cheaper, costing less than a quarter of the price of turf, and is easier to do. It is also more flexible because you can wait until the weather and soil conditions are just right. Turf, on the other hand, has to be put down almost as soon as it is delivered and is hard work to lay.

Preparing the ground

First dig over the area, clearing the ground of weeds, including the roots of perennials. If sowing seeds, leave for a week or two to allow any weed seeds to germinate. These will need to be killed using a weedkiller spray (choose a type that leaves the area safe for replanting within a few days) or by hoeing.

Creating a level surface

A few days after killing the surface weeds, rake the ground level using a soil rake and remove any stones or other debris that have come to the surface. Then tread the whole area using tiny shuffling steps with the weight on your heels. Repeat this process until an even, level and firm surface has been produced. It is worth investing the time and effort to create a perfectly level bed whether you are sowing seed or laying turf, as this will improve the appearance of your lawn later.

HOW TO SOW A NEW LAWN

1 Dig the ground thoroughly, removing deep-rooted perennial weeds. Rake the soil level. Use pegs marked with lines drawn 5cm (2in) down from the top as a guide, having checked with a spirit (carpenter's) level on a straightedge that the pegs are level.

2 Allow the soil to settle for a week, then consolidate it further by treading it evenly to remove large air pockets. The best way to do this is to shuffle your feet over the area, first in one direction then at right angles.

3 Rake the consolidated soil to produce a fine, crumbly structure suitable for sowing seeds. If you can, leave the area for a couple of weeks to allow weed seeds to germinate. Hoe them off or use a weedkiller that leaves the ground safe for replanting within days.

4 Use string to divide the area into strips a metre (yard) wide and divide the strips into squares with bamboo canes or stakes. Move the canes along the strips as you sow.

5 Use a small container that holds enough seed for a square metre (yard). Make a mark on it if the amount only partly fills the container. Scatter the seeds as evenly as possible with a sweeping motion of the hand.

6 Hire or buy a calibrated granular fertilizer spreader to sow large areas quickly. Check the delivery rate over sheets of paper first and adjust the spreader until the correct amount is being applied per square metre (yard).

HOW TO LAY A LAWN WITH TURFS

1 Dig and consolidate the soil as described for seed, but there is no need to leave it for a few weeks to allow weed seeds to germinate: the turf will prevent them from sprouting. Start by laying the turf along a straight edge.

2 Stand on a plank while you lay the next row, as this will distribute your weight. Stagger the joints between rows to create a bond like brickwork. Turf in a long roll will have fewer joints but again these should not align.

3 Tamp down each row of turf to eliminate air pockets with the head of a rake, then roll the plank forwards to lay the next row. Brush sandy soil, or a mixture of peat and sand, into the joints to help bind the turfs together.

Planting the lawn

A couple of days before laying turf or sowing seed, scatter a general fertilizer at the recommended rate over the area and rake lightly into the surface of the soil. If sowing seed, choose a windless day, preferably when rain is forecast and lightly rake the grass seed into the surface. It is a good idea to protect the area with fine mesh netting to keep off birds and cats.

For both seed and turf, keep the area well watered, if it does not rain heavily, until the grass is well established. For turf this should be about two weeks, for seed it will be considerably longer.

A good-quality lawn invites you into the garden, leading the eye smoothly to beds and borders. If your lawn is in very bad condition it is worth considering starting from scratch and sowing seed or laying turf to get the effect you want.

Looking after your lawn

A lawn needs regular mowing throughout the growing season. Other maintenance tasks such as removing moss and weeds, seasonal feeding and watering and other lawn treatments may also be necessary to keep it in tip-top condition.

Mowing and trimming

From the time the grass starts to grow in early spring it will need to be cut and trimmed regularly until the end of the growing season. The first spring cut should be made when the lawn is dry after the grass reaches about 8cm (3in) long. Brush off any wormcasts before you mow. Make sure the blades of the mower are set high so that they trim off just a couple of centimetres (less than 1in). Gradually lower the cutting height over the next few mows until it is cutting the grass back to 4cm (1½in). Collect lawn clippings from the early cuts. Thereafter, mow the lawn every time the grass has grown about 2cm (¾in). You do not need a grass box to collect the clippings if you mow this often because they can be left on the lawn as a mulch, returning nutrients to the soil.

Controlling moss

A lawn that contains a lot of moss should be treated by applying a specially formulated moss killer to the grass in the autumn or spring. Use a treatment recommended for the season. The mixture known as lawn sand, sometimes used to kill moss, is fine in spring, but it contains too much nitrogen for autumn use. Moss is fairly easy to eliminate using a lawn treatment, but to achieve long-term control you need to tackle the underlying causes that encourage moss. A lawn becomes colonized by moss because the grass is not growing vigorously enough. This could be due to poor drainage, too much shade or soil that is too acidic – if you are unsure, check it using a simple pH kit. Where shade is the problem, thin out any overhanging branches of trees or cut back shrubs.

Killing weeds

Isolated weeds can be removed with an old kitchen knife or treated using a spot weedkiller. You may need to treat areas of established perennial weeds several times to kill them completely. Where the problem is more widespread use an overall lawn treatment. On a small lawn apply a granular weedkiller using a hand shaker pack or apply a liquid weedkiller using a watering can fitted with a weedkiller dribble bar. Large lawns are quicker and easier to treat by applying a granular weedkiller using a calibrated fertilizer spreader. Coarse grass weeds can also spoil the appearance of a lawn and are not affected by lawn weedkillers. You can either dig out the coarse grasses by hand and reseed the bare patch, or weaken the weed grass over time by slashing through the patches with a sharp knife each time you mow.

HOW TO REMOVE WEEDS

1 Use a special weeding tool or a knife to prise up single weeds. Push the tool in next to the root and lift the plant out with a lever action as you pull with the other hand. Even deep-rooted plants can be removed like this.

2 Widespread weeds are best controlled by a selective weedkiller, ideally in spring. They are usually applied as a liquid, using a dribble bar attached to a watering can. Always mix and apply as recommended by the manufacturer.

3 If there are just a few troublesome weeds, spot treatment may be a more economical and quicker method. Brush or dab on a selective weedkiller. Be careful not to kill the grass as well as the weeds.

4 Make any necessary lawn repairs. If you have had to lift a lot of weeds growing close together, leaving a bare patch in your lawn, sprinkle grass seeds over the area.

FEEDING YOUR LAWN

If your lawn is in poor condition and
needs reviving, apply a lawn feed.
Choose one formulated for the season:
spring and summer feeds have much
more nitrogen than autumn feeds.

If you want your lawn to remain green all summer, you will have to water it regularly during dry
spells. A water sprinkler takes much of the hard work out of this tedious task.

Feeding and watering

A vigorously growing lawn is less
likely to be colonized by weeds and
mosses. Keep the grass growing
strongly by ensuring it receives
plenty of water in long, dry spells.
Apply a high-nitrogen lawn feed once
a year in spring and use a slow-
release formulation feed throughout
the growing season. If you also have
a problem with moss or weeds use a
combined lawn weed and feed, or
lawn weed, feed and moss killer.

Clearing the lawn

Where there is no obvious sign of
moss but the lawn still feels spongy
when you walk on it, the problem is
likely to be the build-up of dead
grass stems at the base of the lawn,
known as thatch. When the thatch
gets more than 1cm (½in) thick it
starts to suffocate the lawn and
must be removed, a technique known
as scarifying. Use a spring-tine or

wire lawn rake and vigorously rake
out the thatch. This is hard work, so
if you have a large area to deal with
it is worth considering buying or
hiring a powered lawn rake to do the
job. Scarify your lawn thoroughly
once a year in autumn.

Falling leaves also cause a problem
and must be removed, otherwise the
grass beneath will turn yellow from
lack of light and be prone to disease.

HOW TO REMOVE THATCH

Grass clippings, leaves and other debris form
a thatch at the base of grasses in your lawn
which can stifle them. Remove it with a spring-
tine rake. Raking also removes moss.

HOW TO COLLECT LEAVES

1 Don't let autumn leaves lie on your lawn
for long or the grass underneath will suffer.
Clear the leaves up with a lawn rake.

2 Rake the leaves into piles and scoop them
up with a pair of short planks (boards).
Choose a still day when the leaves are dry to
make the job pleasant.

Repairing your lawn

Many lawns receive a lot of wear, especially during the summer months. Fortunately, the autumn is an ideal time to make repairs. Use the following techniques to tackle humps and hollows, badly draining soil, bare patches, broken edges and areas that are simply worn out.

Bumps and hollows

When an uneven lawn is cut the high points will show up as light green because the grass is being cut too short and the low points as dark green patches. If the problem is widespread, you would be better off topdressing the whole lawn, but if you have just a few isolated bumps or hollows you can cure them using the following technique. Use a sharp spade or half-moon edging tool to make a H-shaped cut in the lawn centred over the bump or hollow. Carefully undercut the turf either side working from the central cut and peel back the turf to expose the soil beneath. Then either remove sufficient soil to level the bump when the turf is relaid, or top up with fine soil if you are levelling a hollow. Fill any gaps with an equal-parts mixture of sieved garden soil and sharp sand.

Repairing any broken edges will give your beds and borders a neat finish, essential when the impact of your garden design relies on straight lines.

Bare patches

Repair any bare patches in the lawn by using a garden fork to scratch the surface and gently loosen the soil. Then incorporate a general fertilizer such as growmore at the rate of 50g (2oz) per square metre (yard), before firming with the back of a soil rake. Sow grass seed over the top at the rate of about 35g (1½oz) per square metre (yard) for really bare patches and about 20g (1oz) per square metre (yard) if over-sowing sparse areas. Cover the seed

---

Aeration

Surface drainage can be impeded if the grass has become compacted because of excessive wear. You can overcome this by a technique known as aeration. Small areas are best treated with a garden fork. Simply spike it into the grass, pushing the tines into the ground to a depth of about 15cm (6in), spacing the holes about 5cm (2in) apart. For larger areas of lawn consider hiring a powered spiker or slitter instead. Fill the holes with sharp sand or a mixture of soil and sand for poorly drained soils, or use peat or very fine, well-rotted compost if the ground is sandy. Autumn is the best time to aerate your lawn.

1 If the grass growth is poor this could be because the soil is poorly drained. Aerate the lawn by pushing the prongs of a fork into the ground.

2 Gently brush a soil improver, such as sharp sand or a mixture of soil and sand, into the holes made by the fork.

with a light scattering of sieved garden soil and then water with a fine-rosed watering can. Protect the area from birds and cats by covering with a piece of garden fleece, held down with stones. Water again during dry spells until the new grass is well established.

Heavy wear

Areas that receive constant wear, such as under children's play equipment or at the bottom of steps on to a lawn, need to be reinforced if they are going to cope. If the lawn is used as a shortcut to another part of the garden consider incorporating stepping stones to take the impact. Where children's play equipment cannot be moved to spread the wear and tear around, reinforce the grass with heavy-duty plastic mesh. Cut the grass short, then peg the mesh down over the area so that it is held completely flat. Allow the grass to grow up through the mesh over the winter. When you come to mow next spring, the mesh will be hidden from sight, well below mower blade height so that you can mow straight over the top.

HOW TO RECUT AN EDGE

Insert a half-moon edging tool about 8cm (3in) into the soil. Lever the soil forwards to form a gulley with one vertical side against the lawn and one curved side against the border. Remove any grass to prevent it rooting.

HOW TO REPAIR A BROKEN EDGE

1 Use a half-moon edging tool or a spade to cut a rectangle around the affected area.

2 Push a spade under the rectangle, starting from the broken edge. Keep the thickness of the slice of grass as even as possible.

3 Reverse the turf so that the undamaged part of the turf is against the edge of the bed and the broken edge is within the lawn. Fill the hole caused by the damage with sifted soil and firm it down well.

4 Brush soil into the joints to help the grass knit together quickly and water well. Sow grass seed in the patched area, matching the type of grass if possible. Cover until the seed has germinated.

Broken edges

Isolated broken edges on lawns, perhaps caused by a careless heel or spade, are easy to repair. Use a sharp spade or half-moon edging tool to cut out a square at the edge of the lawn that encloses the damaged area. Undercut the turf and then turn it around 180 degrees so that the broken area is within the lawn and the straight part aligns with the edge of the lawn. Top up the damaged area with sieved garden soil if necessary, then level and firm with the back of a soil rake. Reseed as described for bare patches (above).

If the lawn is broken and uneven all along the edge of a border it is worth re-cutting to improve the appearance of your garden. Mark out where you will re-cut, using a board as a guide for straight edges or a length of garden hose for curved ones. Insert a sharp spade or half-moon edging tool into the soil. Lever back the handle and push the soil forwards to form a gulley with one vertical side against the lawn and one curved side against the border. Remove any unwanted grass to prevent it rooting into the border and becoming a weed problem.

Reducing maintenance time

The shape of a lawn – whether square, rectangular or irregular – will have a great influence on the amount of time it takes to keep it neat as well as the style of garden you are trying to create.

Lawn size

Obviously the larger a lawn the more time it will take to mow. This can, however, be offset somewhat by choosing a mower with a cutting width to match the size of your lawn. For a large lawn – more than 250 square metres (300 sq yards) – look for a mower with a cutting width of at least 35cm (14in). If you have a small lawn – less than 50 square metres (60 sq yards) – a mower with a cutting width of 25cm (10in) would be sufficient. A mower with a 30cm (12in) wide cut would be the best option for lawns in between these two extremes.

Wider mowers are usually more expensive, so consider whether the extra cost is worth it. The extra manoeuvrability of a smaller mower might be better in a smaller garden, with fewer straight runs.

Naturalizing bulbs in the lawn gives you a good excuse to leave the grass uncut.

The shape of the lawn

You can reduce the time and effort involved when mowing by keeping the shape of your lawn simple. Simple shapes often look more appealing than complicated fussy ones in any case. If your existing design has obstacles, such as island beds and specimen trees, you could reduce the amount of stopping and starting as well as the length of edge to be trimmed by joining the beds together or extending borders from the sides to incorporate them.

HOW TO CREATE A MOWING EDGE

1 A mowing edge of bricks or paving slab will prevent overhanging flowers smothering the edge of the lawn. Mark out the area of grass to be lifted using the paving as a guide. To keep the new edge straight, use a half-moon edger against the paving. Then lift the grass to be removed by slicing it off with a spade.

2 Remove enough soil to allow for the depth of the slab or brick and make a firm base by compacting gravel or a mixture of sand and gravel where the paving is to be laid. Use a plank of wood to make sure it is level. Allow for the thickness of the paving and a few blobs of mortar.

3 It is best to bed the edging on mortar for stability, but because it will not be taking a heavy weight, just press the slabs on to blobs of mortar and tap level with a mallet. The slabs should be laid evenly and flush with, or very slightly below, the lawn. Use a spirit (carpenter's) level to double-check.

If you have more than one lawn in your garden, consider joining them into one. Small lawns in the front garden often take more time to look after than the main one at the back. You may be better off getting rid of the small lawn altogether and replacing it with an area of gravel.

Mowing edges

It is a good idea to create a mowing edge if your garden is bounded by a border. It will mean the grass always has a neat edge and you won't damage overhanging border plants when you mow. On a large lawn the edging can be wide, especially if you have large, trailing plants that are likely to flop over the edge of the bed. If the lawn is small, however, use narrow edging so that it will look in proportion with the rest of the garden.

Cutting to different heights

If you have a large lawn consider leaving part of it to grow longer between cuts so that your workload is reduced. Keep broad "pathways" cut regularly, cut other areas with the blade set higher, and mow only every second or third time. Some areas can remain uncut except for a couple of times a season, which will allow wildflowers to thrive. Do bear in mind that very long grass cannot be cut with a standard mower and you will have to use a nylon-line trimmer or hire a powered sythe.

HOW TO FIT AN EDGING STRIP

1 Make a slit trench along the lawn edge with a spade, then lay the strip alongside the trench and cut to length. Place the edging strip loosely into the trench.

2 Backfill with soil for a firm fit. Press the strip in gently as you proceed. Finish off by tapping it level with a hammer over a straight-edged piece of wood.

HOW TO FIT WOODEN EDGING

Cut the roll to length using strong pliers to cut the wires and insert the edging in a narrow trench. Join the pieces by wiring them together. Backfill with soil for a firm fit. Use a hammer over a piece of wood to tap it down. Use a spirit (carpenter's) level to check the edging is level.

A mowing edge will lessen your work on a lawn, as the mower can get right up to the edge of the bed. You may have to trim any spreading grass stems, but this will only be necessary occasionally.

Planting in and around the lawn

Adding plants to your lawn can transform the appearance of your garden. Bulbs and wildflowers will provide seasonal interest, while trees and shrubs will add height and structure. Bear in mind that the more obstacles you place in the lawn the longer it will take to mow and trim, and you will break up the sweep of an uncluttered lawn.

Naturalized bulbs

In the wild, bulbs naturally form dramatic flowering drifts of colour under trees. This effect can be reproduced in the garden by planting bulbs in a natural-looking style. Early spring bulbs are a particularly good choice because they not only give a spectacular show but will be

out of the way before mowing starts in earnest. You need to wait six weeks after flowering before mowing the naturalized area. If you want to grow later-flowering bulbs this way, you would be better off creating a wildflower meadow, which does not need cutting until late summer.

To get a natural distribution of bulbs, toss them gently on to the lawn and plant them where they land. Clumps of bulbs are best planted by removing a whole turf with a sharp spade, planting at the correct depth, firming the soil and then replacing the turf. If you use this method, make sure you maintain the informal arrangement of the bulbs. Individual bulbs can be planted using a cylindrical bulb planter. If you are

Bulbs to naturalize in grass

Camassia	Galanthus
Chionodoxa	Leucojum
Colchicum	Muscari
Crocus	Narcissus
Erythronium	Ornithogalum
Fritillaria	Scilla

planting many bulbs, choose a model with a long handle and foot bar, which can be used like a spade. Push the planter vertically into the soil and remove a core that is deep enough for the bulb being planted. After positioning the bulb replace the core and carefully tread level. Bulbs susceptible to rot should be planted on gravel to improve drainage.

HOW TO NATURALIZE BULBS IN A LAWN

1 If you have a lot of small bulbs to plant in a limited area, try lifting an area of turf. Use a spade or half-moon edging tool to make a H-shaped cut.

2 Slice beneath the grass with a spade until you can fold back the turf for planting. Try to keep the spade level so the soil removed is an even thickness.

3 Loosen the ground, as it will be very compacted. If you want to apply a slow-acting fertilizer, such as bonemeal, work it into the soil at the same time.

4 Avoid planting in rows or regimented patterns. You want the bulbs to look natural and informal, so scatter them and plant where they fall.

5 Use a trowel or a bulb planter for large bulbs, making sure the bulb will be covered with twice its own depth of soil when the grass is returned.

6 Firm the soil then return the grass. Firm again if necessary to make sure it is flat, and water well. Water the grass again in dry weather.

7 Special bulb planters can be used for large bulbs. The planters remove a cylindrical core of soil.

8 Place the bulb at the bottom of the hole on a bed of gravel to improve drainage, if necessary, and replace the plug of earth.

Wildflower meadow

The easiest way to create a wild-flower meadow is to sow it like a lawn using a special wildflower and grass mix. You can convert an existing lawn by clearing patches and sowing a wildflower seeds mixture, or by planting pot-grown species directly into the grass.

Feed meadows or lawns containing wildflowers in spring, but use an autumn formulation lawn feed which contains less nitrogen than spring formulations, reducing grass growth.

The meadow will need cutting just twice a year: once in early spring and the second time in mid- to late-summer after the flowers have seeded. Small areas can be cut using a nylon-line trimmer, but larger areas are more easily cut with a powered scythe, which can be bought or hired.

HOW TO PLANT A LAWN TREE

1 Mark a circle 60–120cm (2–4ft) in diameter, using a trail of sand. Lift the grass, removing about 15cm (6in) of soil at the same time.

2 Insert a stake on the side of the prevailing wind. Place off-centre in the hole to allow the rootball to occupy the central position.

3 Check that the hole is deep enough for the rootball by placing the potted tree in the hole. After planting, the soil should be level with the original soil-mark on the trunk.

4 Replace the soil in layers, firming carefully with the heel of your boot as you go. Secure the tree to the stake, and then water well. Mulch the bed to suppress weeds.

Trees and shrubs

The grass underneath a tree or shrub in a lawn is often of poor quality. Its leaves block the light while they are on the tree and suffocate the grass when they fall in the autumn. Specimen trees and shrubs are best grown in a bed cut into the grass.

HOW TO SOW AND PLANT WILDFLOWERS

1 The most satisfactory way to create a wildflower meadow is to sow a special mixture of wildflower seeds. Remember to completely clear the ground of all perennial weeds before you start.

2 To bury the seeds, simply rake in one direction and then in the other. It does not matter if some seeds remain on the surface. Keep the area well watered until the seeds germinate. Protect from birds if necessary.

3 For a very small area, wildflower plants may be more convenient. You can raise your own from seed or buy them. Plant into bare ground or in an existing lawn. Keep the plants well watered until established.

Trees and shrubs

An essential element in most gardens, trees and shrubs provide structure and height as well as acting as foils for other plants. Attractive specimens are eye-catching focal points, while others can be used for specific purposes, such as creating a living boundary or smothering the ground with a carpet of foliage. It is essential to choose the right plant for the function and position you have in mind.

Trees and shrubs should be regarded as permanent additions to the garden and so soil preparation and planting are critical to success. If you get these right, most good garden varieties will establish quickly and thereafter largely look after themselves. In a mature garden, you will need to master techniques to help you keep your plants within bounds or even to move an overcrowded specimen to a new position where it has the space to grow and fulfil its potential.

Trees and shrubs form a vital part of the garden, with a surprising variety of colours and shapes giving structure and, in the case of evergreens, interest throughout the year.

Buying trees and shrubs

Trees and shrubs are permanent additions to the garden and so need to be chosen with care. Many grow into large specimens, taking up a lot of garden space, so make sure you choose varieties that offer more than one season of interest to ensure they offer real value for money.

Buying plants

Trees and shrubs can be bought as container grown, containerized (grown in the field; potted for sale), rootballed or root wrapped (grown in the field; lifted with soil around the roots) or bare root (grown in the field; lifted without soil around the roots) depending on the type of plant and the supplier. Generally, container-grown plants will establish more quickly but are more expensive. Rootballed and bare-root plants are usually available in the autumn or early spring, while container-grown plants are available all year round.

Choosing trees

Most gardens can accommodate just one or two fully grown trees, which will take up a large proportion of the available planting space. It is vital, therefore, to make the correct choice. There is quite a wide range of trees available from garden centres and an even wider choice from specialist nurseries and by mail-order or on the Internet.

To make choosing easier, the first thing you should do is disregard those types of trees that are simply not suitable. Unless you have a very large garden, most can be rejected on the basis of their ultimate size. But other criteria, such as the preferred position (sun or shade) and the soil type in your garden, can also be used to narrow down the choice available. Plant labels, plant catalogues and websites will give this information, or you can check your selections in the plant directory section.

With a much-reduced list of possible candidates, the next step is to consider what features you want the tree to have. Should it be evergreen? When should it bear flowers or fruits? Is scent important? Would your garden benefit from autumn colour or winter interest such as attractive stems or bark? Again, use the information at the point of sale to help you decide.

Once you have made a choice, the next decision is the size of tree you buy (see right). Large trees make an instant impact and might be the best option if your garden is newly laid out and would benefit from the added height and structure a large tree would offer. However, younger specimens – three to five years old, say – generally establish more quickly than older trees. After a few years young trees will often catch up with and even overtake larger ones. Smaller trees are also much cheaper.

MAIL-ORDER PLANTS

Many trees and shrubs are available from mail-order companies. The young plants are mailed in special packages that minimize damage during transit.

ROOTBALLED PLANTS

A rootballed *Taxus* (yew). The ball of soil around the roots of the plant is held together by a net and strong elastic bands. It protects the roots and prevents desiccation.

BARE-ROOT PLANTS

During the dormant season, bare-root plants are often sold with a wrap to protect their roots. If it is too frosty or wet to plant them, leave in the wrappings until conditions improve.

Specialist nurseries carry a wide range of trees and shrubs. Many have a mail-order service, which can be invaluable if the nursery is not easy for you to reach.

What size tree?

Trees are generally sold as two sizes: standards and half-standards, although you may find variations from some suppliers. Standards have a clear trunk to 1.8m (6ft) or so and are ideal for large trees that will form a specimen in a lawn or at the back of a border. Half-standards have a clear single stem, to at least 1.2m (4ft), and are useful planted in a mixed border or to provide a focal point nearer the edge. You can also buy trees as single-stemmed young plants (known as whips) or with new side branches (known as feathered maidens), which you can train yourself into a half-standard or standard by removing the lower branches as the tree grows.

Choosing shrubs

A garden or area of a garden can accommodate more shrubs than trees, so you can choose plants that offer spectacular displays for a relatively short period. However, it is important to create collections of shrubs that flower at different times to extend the period of interest. If you are planting a large area, plant shrubs in groups of threes or fives to achieve a more natural-looking overall display. Also include a proportion of evergreens to provide structure and colour to the borders in winter – as a rule, aim for about two-thirds evergreen to one-third deciduous plants.

What to look for

When buying trees and shrubs, whether container grown, rootballed or bare root, the signs to look out for are the same. Choose a plant with a well-balanced shape and healthy looking foliage with no signs of pest or disease damage. Grafted plants should have a strong, well-healed union. Look for plants that are well established in their pots but avoid those that have roots coming through the bottom of the pot or where roots are circling inside the pot because these have been left too long in their container. Also avoid plants with unnaturally yellowing leaves or weeds in the container because they have been neglected. Faded labels are also a sign the plant has been hanging around too long.

Look for healthy plants of bushy habit (centre) without any signs of leaf yellowing (right), stunted, straggly growth (left), or premature leaf fall, which may be caused by irregular watering.

Planting trees and shrubs

Trees and shrubs need to get off to the best possible start if they are to establish quickly. The secrets of success are preparing the ground well, preventing competition from other plants and keeping the new specimen well watered.

When to plant

Generally, the larger the specimen, the more work it will be to plant successfully. Container-grown deciduous plants can be planted at any time of the year, but they will establish more quickly and be easier to look after if they are planted in spring or autumn when the soil is moist and warm, which encourages rapid root growth and so establishment. Bare-root specimens, however, have to be planted during the dormant season, which is between autumn and spring. Evergreens, particularly conifers, are best planted in late spring so that they have time to establish before the onset of winter.

How to plant

If planting in a lawn, remove a 1m (3ft) wide circle of turf. Dig a hole large enough to accommodate the full spread of the roots (for bare-root plants) or twice as wide as the rootball for all other types. The hole should be the same depth as the rootball. Fork over the soil in the bottom of the hole. Place all excavated soil on a sheet near to the planting hole. Traditionally, the soil would be augmented with well-rotted manure and a handful of bonemeal, but recent research has shown that it is more beneficial to mulch after planting to prevent competition from weeds and to help retain soil moisture around the roots.

Water the rootball thoroughly before planting and allow it to drain. If staking, drive in a stake at this

Trees often look best planted in isolation on the lawn. Here, the pale pebbles at the tree's base draw the eye to the feature, and enhance the decorative red leaves.

HOW TO PLANT A CONTAINER-GROWN SHRUB

1 Before you start, check that the plant has been watered. If not, give it a thorough soaking, preferably at least an hour before planting. This ensures that the rootball is moist and has the ability to absorb water after it has been planted.

2 If the soil in the bed has not been recently prepared, fork it over, removing any stones, weeds and other debris. Add a slow-release fertilizer and fork it into the soil well. If you use bonemeal, apply the fertilizer wearing rubber or vinyl gloves.

point. Position the tree or shrub at the same depth as it was in the pot or the nursery bed – there is usually a tell-tale dark soil mark on the stem about 5cm (2in) above the highest root. With container-grown specimens, tease out the roots from around the rootball before planting to encourage them to spread into the surrounding soil. Check the planting depth by laying a cane across the planting hole, then add or remove soil as necessary.

Backfill the first few centimetres (inch) of the hole with the excavated soil, and give bare-root trees or shrubs a gentle shake to settle the soil. Firm the first layer around the roots with your heel before adding a second layer and repeating the process until the hole is filled. This will prevent any air pockets. Also check that the specimen is upright from time to time as you work. With trees that you are staking, fit the tie. Water well, then cover the soil around the new tree or shrub with an 8cm (3in) deep layer of well-rotted, loose organic mulch. In exposed gardens, protect the tree or shrub after planting by erecting a windbreak and add rabbit guards if these are a pest in your garden.

How to stake a tree

If you are planting a tree over 1.5m (5ft) tall, hammer in a stake on the windward side of the tree to leave just 60cm (2ft) above ground level. Normally this can be done before positioning the tree.

If planting a large specimen you may need to put in the stake after planting, angling it to avoid the rootball. When planting bareroot specimens, spread the roots around the stake.

1 Place a strong stake of rot-resistant wood or one treated with preservative in the hole, knocking it in so that it cannot move.

2 Place the tree in the hole, pushing the rootball up against the stake, so that the stem and stake are 8–10cm (3–4in) apart.

3 Firm down the soil around the plant with the heel of your boot.

4 Although it is possible to use string, proper rose or tree ties provide the best support. Fix the lower one 15cm (6in) above the soil.

5 Fix the second tie near the top of the stake, slightly below the head of the plant.

6 Water the ground around the plant thoroughly and mulch with chipped bark or a similar material.

3 Dig a hole twice as wide as the rootball. Place the plant, still in its pot, in the hole and check that the hole is deep enough by placing a stick or cane across the hole: the top of the pot should align with the top of the soil. Adjust the depth of the hole accordingly.

4 Remove the plant from its pot, being careful not to disturb the rootball. If it is in a plastic bag, cut the bag away rather than trying to pull it off. Place the shrub in the hole and pull the earth back around it. Firm the soil down around the plant and water well.

5 Finally, mulch round the shrub, covering the soil with 5–8cm (2–3in) of chipped bark or similar material. This will not only help to preserve the moisture in the soil but will also help to prevent weed seeds from germinating.

Moving trees and shrubs

It is of course best to plant a tree or shrub in its final position, but even in the best planned garden this isn't always practical. Moving established plants, even small ones, is hard work and needs careful forethought. However, with a few helpers and good preparation, many plants can be moved successfully.

When to move trees and shrubs

The best time for transplanting most established trees or shrubs is during the dormant season (late autumn to early spring). However, the soil should not be waterlogged or frozen as this will damage the soil structure and make it more difficult for the plant to re-establish itself. Spring planting gives a full season's growth before the winter; an autumn move allows the plant to develop a good root system before spring. Evergreens, including conifers, are best moved in mid-spring when the soil is moist and warm enough to encourage rapid root growth.

What size rootball?

The rootball diameter and depth should depend on the size of the plant you are trying to move. The diameter should be about the same as the spread of the branches of shrubs and about one-third the height of a tree. The depth of the rootball depends on the type of soil in your garden. The lighter the soil the more penetrating the roots and so the deeper the rootball will have to be. For example, a 30cm (12in) deep rootball on clay soil may need to be twice that depth on a light, sandy soil. Bear in mind that rootballs with soil attached can literally weigh a ton if you are moving a small tree or large shrub. Make sure you have sufficient help before you start.

HOW TO MOVE A SMALL SHRUB

1 Before moving a shrub, make sure that the planting site has been prepared and the hole excavated. Water the plant well the day before moving it.

2 Dig a trench around the plant, leaving a large rootball (the size depends on the size of the plant). Carefully sever any roots that you encounter to release the rootball.

3 Dig under the shrub, cutting through any vertical taproots that hold it in place.

4 Rock the plant to one side and insert sacking or strong plastic sheeting as far under the plant as you can. Push several folds of material under the rootball.

5 Rock the shrub in the opposite direction and pull the sacking or plastic sheeting through, so that it is completely under the plant.

6 Pull the sacking round the rootball and tie it firmly at the neck of the plant. The shrub is now ready to move. If it is a fairly small plant, one person may be able to lift it out of the hole and transfer it to its new site.

7 If the plant plus the soil is heavy, it is best moved by two people. Tie a length of wood or metal to the sacking. With one person on each end, lift the shrub out of the hole.

8 Lower the transplanted shrub into the prepared planting hole. Unwrap and remove the sheeting from the rootball. Make sure that the plant is in the right position, refill the hole, and water well.

Root pruning

The chances of successfully moving very large shrubs and trees can be improved by pruning the roots in advance of the move, a technique known as root pruning. It should be done up to a year before the move.

To root prune, simply dig the vertical trench at the correct distance from the tree or shrub and sever any roots you find, then refill the trench with soil. The plant will produce more fibrous roots in the soil nearer to the trunk, and these will form part of the rootball, increasing the plant's chances of survival after the move.

A shrub may need to be moved because it is too vigorous and is crowding out other plants, or because the re-design of its bed makes a move desirable. Prune the shrub after planting if required to create a balanced shape. Water the shrub well throughout the first growing season.

Making moves

Before you start, decide on the new position of the plant and prepare the planting hole, which should be about twice as wide and as deep as the rootball. Fork over the bottom of the hole, incorporating a bucketful of grit on heavy soils to improve drainage.

Use a spade to cut a slit-trench around the tree or shrub being moved to mark out the size of the rootball and to sever any roots near to the surface. Then cut a second slit-trench about 30cm (12in) further out and dig out the soil in between to form a trench around the specimen. Make this trench as deep as the rootball.

Undercut the rootball from the trench by inserting the spade at an angle of about 45 degrees all the way round. Small rootballs should then be completely undercut and can be wrapped. Larger rootballs may need further excavation to expose any vertical roots under the middle of the rootball.

After the rootball has been freed, carefully rock it back and slip a sheet of folded heavy-duty polythene or hessian (burlap) under one side then rock it over the other way and then pull the folded polythene through. Tie the corners of the sheeting over the top of the rootball around the main stem to form a neat package, so that the soil is held firmly. Use rope or strong string to reinforce the rootball on all sides.

Move the tree or shrub by pulling on the polythene sheeting, not the trunk. Use a short plank (board) or pair of planks as a ramp out of the hole and then drag it to its new position or get a gang of helpers to lift it. It may be easiest to fix a pole to help carry the tree or shrub.

Replant immediately and water and mulch well. Stake if necessary. Spray the foliage of evergreens after planting and every few days for the first month to help prevent scorching. It is also worth putting up a windbreak around conifers. Keep all transplants well watered throughout the first growing season.

Even very small conifers such as this *Chamaecyparis lawsoniana* 'Bleu Nantais' are hard work to move. Always check the final height and spread of a plant before choosing where to plant it.

Aftercare of trees and shrubs

Once they are established, most trees and shrubs will look after themselves. However, it can take more than a growing season to reach this point of independence. There are also some ornamental types that produce much better displays if they are given a little extra pampering.

Watering techniques

The main reason new trees and shrubs fail in their first season is because they cannot take up sufficient water. Since they have not had time to root into the soil, new specimens should be treated like container-grown plants elsewhere in the garden. Water them thoroughly once a week in dry weather or if your soil is well drained, rather than giving them a light sprinkling every day. Aim to give new shrubs at least a full watering can of water and new trees twice this amount each time you water.

It is essential that the water soaks the soil around the plant and doesn't run off elsewhere. There are a number of techniques you can employ to make sure this happens. Insert a plastic pipe at an angle into the soil

This evergreen *Pieris japonica* had sufficient water in its first year after planting, and now produces an everchanging display of foliage with very little maintenance required.

so that the bottom is at the root zone and the top just proud of the soil surface. Fill the pipe with gravel so that other rubbish cannot accumulate in it and pour water into the pipe each time you water. Alternatively, ridge up the soil about 30cm (12in) away from the main stem to create a

moat each time the plant is watered. The water will then have time to soak into the soil exactly where it is needed. A more sophisticated method is to use circles of seep hose or leaky pipe with a snap-lock connector around individual plants and clip these to a hosepipe (garden hose) each time you water. The water will be released slowly without running off. If you are planting a whole garden, consider installing an automatic watering system.

Mulching

There are many benefits to mulching the newly planted tree or shrub with organic matter. It smothers the ground, preventing weed seeds from germinating and getting established. It also prevents water evaporation from the soil, helping to conserve soil moisture. As it is incorporated into the ground by soil-living creatures, such as earthworms, it helps improve the soil structure and

HOW TO LOOK AFTER TREES AND SHRUBS AFTER PLANTING

A newly planted tree or shrub needs to be watered well in order to become established.

Mulch with straw or garden compost to conserve the moisture in the soil.

releases valuable plant nutrients as it decomposes. A mulch also helps to insulate the soil from excessive heat in summer and cold in winter.

A wide range of materials can be used for mulching. Apply a 5–8cm (2–3in) deep layer around new plants and top up to this layer each spring thereafter. Around established shrubs and trees you can use grass clippings as a free organic mulch. Although some nitrogen is removed from the soil by micro-organisms as the clippings are broken down, only the very surface layer is affected.

Weed control

Limiting weed growth is important in the first few years but is less so as the canopy fills out. Keep all weeds under control during the early years. Use a hoe shallowly around each plant to avoid damaging the roots and hand weed near shallow-rooted plants, such as azaleas, as well as trees and shrubs, such as lilac, that are prone to suckering (throwing up shoots from below ground level) if they suffer root damage. If a weed gets established, use a chemical spot weedkiller to deal with it.

WEEDING AROUND TREES AND SHRUBS

Using a hoe to remove weeds from around young trees or shrubs is the surest way of catching them all. It is best carried out in hot weather so that any weeds hoed up die quickly.

As its name suggests, *Hippophaë rhamnoides* (sea buckthorn) is tolerant of strong, salt-laden winds and can be planted as a windbreak to protect frailer plants. Its long, silvery green leaves, yellow flowers and orange berries are all decorative in their own right.

Windbreaks

A severe winter storm can cause considerable damage to trees and shrubs, sometimes breaking whole branches. If your garden is exposed you should consider erecting some sort of windbreak. In the short term this can be a special plastic windbreaker, but in the longer term it is probably better to create a more permanent solution by planting a living windbreak. A number of trees and shrubs can be used for this, and it should be fairly easy to find one that fits seamlessly into your garden design.

Leyland cypress grow very fast, and, for this reason, they are often used as windbreaks, but are best avoided for more suitable alternatives. They are thirsty, hungry plants that take a lot of nutrients from the soil for some distance around the roots. They also continue to grow rapidly past their required height.

It is best to get the windbreaks established before the shrubs or ornamental trees are planted, but if time is of the essence, plant them at the same time, perhaps temporarily shielding both from the winds with windbreak netting.

Good windbreak plants

Acer pseudoplatanus (sycamore)
Berberis darwinii
Buxus sempervirens (box)
Cotoneaster simonsii
Fraxinus excelsior (ash)
Griselinia littoralis
Hippophaë rhamnoides
  (sea buckthorn)
Ilex (holly)
Ligustrum ovalifolium (privet)
Lonicera nitida (box-leaf honeysuckle)
Pyracantha (firethorn)
Rosmarinus officinalis (rosemary)
Sorbus aucuparia (rowan)
Taxus baccata (yew)

Conifers

After years in the wilderness, slow-growing dwarf conifers are now coming back into fashion. They are easy to grow, require practically no maintenance and offer year-round interest.

Grouping conifers

Conifers can be grown as single specimens or in groups, in a mixed border with other shrubs, perennials and bulbs or in a special conifer area, where a variety of forms can be combined to good effect. Although an evergreen conifer display is very low maintenance and looks good all year, it can seem static, because it remains exactly the same from one season to the next.

Choosing a position

Most conifers prefer a position in full sun, but many will tolerate partial shade or being in deeper shade for just part of the day. They will not grow well in dense shade or waterlogged soil, however. If your soil is heavy, you could try draining it, improving the structure, by adding plenty of well-rotted organic matter and grit before planting, or creating a special conifer raised bed. Many slow-growing dwarf conifers also do well in containers.

Conifers develop a range of habits, including upright, conical and spreading. Planted together in the garden they can make a striking group.

HOW TO PLANT A CONIFER

1 Place the conifer in the prepared hole and check the planting depth. The soil mark should be at the same level as the surrounding soil.

2 When the plant is in position, untie the wrapper and slide it out of the hole. Avoid disturbing the ball of soil around the roots.

3 Replace the soil around the plant and firm down to eliminate large pockets of air. Apply fertilizer, if necessary, and water well.

Planting

The best time to plant conifers is mid-spring, when the soil is moist and starting to warm up. This allows the plants to establish before the onset of winter. However, container-grown conifers can also be planted at other times of year (particularly early autumn), provided they are kept well watered in summer and protected from cold winds in winter. If the weather or soil conditions are not suitable for planting when the conifers arrive, plant them roughly in a trench in a sheltered spot (known as heeling in) until conditions improve. Do not take container-grown plants out of their pots until you are ready to plant them properly.

Plant conifers in the same way as other trees and shrubs but after planting protect the plants from cold and drying winds by erecting plastic windbreak netting held up on well-anchored posts as a windbreak. Once the conifer is well established this protection can be removed. Tall trees may also need staking to prevent damage from storms.

Do not feed conifers unless they are showing signs of starvation (unnatural yellowing foliage). If they are given too much food, conifers

4 It is worth mulching the ground after planting. It will conserve moisture, and some mulches, such as chipped bark, look attractive.

HOW TO REMOVE A COMPETING LEADER

Where two or more leaders have formed a fork in the conifer tree, leave the strongest unpruned. Cut away the other stem or stems at the point of origin.

will grow more quickly, producing lush, often uncharacteristic, growth that does not look attractive and is prone to damage caused by drying and cold winds.

Pruning

Conifers do not need extensive pruning and most are best left to assume their natural shape, with the occasional pruning of an overly long shoot. Occasionally, however, you may need to undertake more substantial pruning if the conifer starts to get too big for its position.

Plants can be clipped annually with shears to keep them small and neat. Do not prune back to leafless brown stems because these will not re-sprout. Cut back whole stems to restrict the size of ground-hugging conifers, making the cut under a newer, shorter shoot that will hide it. Conifers that have become too overgrown should be removed.

Another problem that should be pruned out as soon as it occurs is reversion: all-green growth on variegated forms. Use secateurs (pruners) to remove these vigorous shoots, otherwise they may dominate the more decorative foliage.

If the remaining leader is not growing strongly upright, tie a cane to the conifer's main stem. Tie the new leader to the cane to encourage vertical growth.

Most conifers produce resinous sap that bleeds freely from the stems if they are cut while the tree is in active growth. Pruning is therefore best carried out from autumn to mid-winter while the tree is dormant. Use sharp, clean pruning tools as blunt blades will snag the wood and may provide an entry point for disease. Wear gloves and goggles and, if you are using power machinery, the protective clothing recommended.

Aftercare

Once established, conifers will largely look after themselves. Mites and aphids can be problems on pines and spruces respectively, causing the needles to drop and producing unsightly bare stems. Aphids are easy to control with insecticidal sprays, but mites are more persistent (you may wish to get in a professional to treat an affected specimen). Mites are particularly active during warm, dry years when conifers are under stress. You can help prevent outbreaks by watering conifers during a drought and spraying the foliage occasionally to increase air humidity. Do this in the evening to avoid scorching the foliage on a sunny day.

Hedges

A living screen makes an excellent marker for a garden boundary and an attractive garden divider. Hedges will be around for a long time, so careful preparation before planting and regular maintenance are essential to keep them looking good.

Choosing a hedge

Many shrubs and some trees make excellent hedging plants, and the species will be largely a matter of personal preference. However, there are a few key points to bear in mind when you are making your selection.

First, decide whether you want a deciduous or evergreen hedge. An evergreen hedge will provide cover throughout the year but a deciduous one is often hardier and so is better in cold or very exposed positions. A few deciduous plants, such as hornbeam and beech, offer the best of both worlds because they keep their dead leaves on the plant until spring. You will also have to decide whether you want to grow it informally (unclipped) or formally (clipped).

Perhaps the most important consideration is the desired height of the hedge, and you must match the vigour and ultimate height of the hedging plant to this. If you choose a fast-growing variety for a small hedge, for example, the results will be quick, but you will need to trim it many times each growing season and the overall appearance of the hedge may deteriorate with time. Remember that the taller the desired height of the hedge, the more work it will be to maintain – anything over 1.5m (5ft) will be difficult to clip from ground level.

How much time and effort you are prepared to devote to your hedge is also something to consider. Although the thought of having a hedge that needs clipping just once a season can be appealing, the growth that it puts on means the trimming task is a lot of work. You may prefer to spread the work by choosing a hedge that responds to pruning several times each growing season. Alternatively, if you want a low-maintenance option choose a compact, slow-growing variety or consider having a no-prune informal hedge instead.

Planting a hedge

Hedges are planted in the same way as other trees and shrubs. Instead of making a planting hole for each plant, however, you simply prepare the planting trench for the whole hedge in one go. Bear in mind that this will be hard work, especially on heavy soils.

In the autumn, when weather and soil conditions allow, dig over a strip 60–90cm (2–3ft) wide, double digging down its entire

HOW TO PLANT A HEDGE

1 Prepare the ground thoroughly. Excavate a trench at least 60cm (2ft) wide and fork in plenty of manure or garden compost.

2 Add fertilizer at the rate recommended by the manufacturer. Use a controlled-release fertilizer if planting in the autumn.

3 Use a garden line, stretched along the centre of the trench, as a positioning guide. If the area is windy or you need a particularly dense hedge, plant a double row.

4 Use a piece of wood cut to the appropriate length as a guide for even spacing. Make sure the roots of bare-root plants are well spread out. If planting container-grown plants, tease out some of the roots before planting.

5 Firm the plants in and water well. Water the hedge regularly in dry weather for the first season. Mulch to keep down weeds until the hedge is filling out, after which it should suppress weeds naturally.

length. For shorter, less vigorous hedges you can get away with single digging. Remove any weeds and other debris as you proceed and incorporate plenty of well-rotted manure or garden compost into the soil and a handful of bonemeal for every 1m (3ft) of hedge. Allow the soil to settle for a fortnight before planting or delay planting until spring.

Aftercare

The general care after planting a hedge is exactly the same as for any other tree or shrub. However, as a general rule, vigorous deciduous hedging plants, such as privet, should be cut back to 15cm (6in) and evergreens and flowering shrubs cut back by about one-third after planting to encourage thick growth from the base of each plant. Pruning is not required after planting for slower growing deciduous plants, such as beech, and all types of conifers until they have reached the desired height of the hedge.

Annual pruning of an established hedge will vary according to the variety. As a general rule, prune flowering hedges, such as quince or firethorn, after the flowering is over and use secateurs (pruners) rather than shears or hedge trimmers for hedges of large-leaved plants such as cherry laurel.

SHAPING A CONIFER HEDGE

Conifer hedges are best shaped with an inward slope, called a batter, to prevent damage by heavy snowfalls and allow light to reach lower parts of the hedge.

HOW TO PRUNE A HEDGE

1 Take the hard work out of clearing up trimmings by laying down a cloth or plastic sheet under the area you are clipping and move it along as you go.

2 When you use shears, try to keep the blades flat against the plane of the hedge as this will give an even cut. If you jab the shears forward with a stabbing motion, the result is likely to be uneven.

3 When trimming the top of a formal hedge, use canes and string as a guide to help you get it completely flat.

4 Keep the blades flat when you cut the top of a hedge. If it is a tall hedge, you will need to use steps rather than trying to reach up at an angle. Stand back from the hedge periodically to check that the trim is even.

5 Power trimmers are much faster than hand shears and, in consequence, things can go wrong more quickly. Concentrate on what you are doing and have a rest if your arms feel tired. Wear adequate protective gear and take the appropriate precautions if you are using an electrically operated tool.

6 Some conifers are relatively slow growing and produce only a few stray stems, which can be cut off with secateurs (pruners) to neaten them. Secateurs should also be used for large-leaved shrubs, such as *Prunus laurocerasus*. This avoids the leaves being cut in half by mechanical or hand shears, which always looks a bit of a mess and can encourage die-back.

Routine care

Some trees and shrubs need regular maintenance to produce their best displays. Pruning is the main task, but there are a few other important techniques worth carrying out.

Feeding

Trees and shrubs are often fed with bonemeal at planting time but, once established, feeding should not be necessary except in a few special circumstances. If your soil is very poor or free-draining give an annual application of a general fertilizer around each plant in spring. Some free-flowering shrubs, such as roses and lilacs, will produce a better display if given a high-potash fertilizer such as tomato fertilizer or rose feed, in spring and early summer.

Foliar feed can also be applied as an emergency measure when soil nutrients are in short supply or unavailable because of drought, for example. The feed is very dilute and can be easily applied, even to quite large plants and large areas, using a hose-end feeder fitted to the end of a garden hose. The nutrients are readily absorbed through the leaves.

Get better, long-lasting displays from flowering shrubs by applying a high-potash feed in spring.

Deadheading

The removal of fading, dying or dead flowerheads after flowering (known as deadheading) not only improves displays directly by tidying up the plant, but also prolongs and improves flowering over time by encouraging the plant to put its energy into growth and flower production rather than producing seeds. With nearly all trees and most shrubs deadheading is not practicable, but it is particularly worth the effort for repeat-flowering shrubs, such as large-flowered (hybrid tea) and cluster-flowered (floribunda) roses, as well as free-flowering plants such as lilacs. Pinch off the old blooms between finger and thumb or

HOW TO DEADHEAD RHODODENDRONS

1 Deadheading stops the plant putting energy into seed production that could be used for new flowers or foliage. New growth emerges below the flower truss.

2 Pinch out the dead flowerheads, using your finger and thumb to minimize potential damage to the emerging new leaves.

3 After the flowerhead is removed, the point at which soft and tender new leaves will emerge can clearly be seen.

HOW TO DEADHEAD HEATHERS

Trim heathers with shears after flowering. Cut just below faded flowers but avoid cutting into the old wood because it will not resprout.

use a pair of garden snips or secateurs (pruners) for tougher stems. Shrubs that produce a lot of small flowers, such as heathers, are usually easier to deadhead using a pair of shears.

A few shrubs, such as magnolias and rhododendrons, produce next year's blooms just behind those produced this year, so you need to be careful not to break these off too. Hydrangeas are the exception to the deadheading rule because the old blooms should be left on the plant to protect next year's buds in winter. Only in early spring should the faded flowerheads be removed.

Winter protection

If you have any shrubs that are of borderline hardiness for your area, it is worth protecting them over the winter. Even normally hardy shrubs may need protection during a severe

or unseasonably cold spell. Cold and wind or a combination of the two are the main problems. Evergreens in particular can be scorched by cold winds in winter, especially if the soil is frozen, because the plant is unable to replace the water it loses through its leaves. The easiest way to protect individual plants is to erect a windbreak supported on wooden stakes. Groups of small shrubs can be protected by covering them with netting firmly anchored on all sides and held off the plants on canes topped with upturned pots. A more long-term solution is to choose hardy trees or shrubs as windbreaks.

Some shrubs, such as hardy fuchsias and eucalyptus, will die down to ground level in cold winters and sprout again in the spring. In severe spells of cold weather, however, the roots can be killed, so they are worth protecting with an insulating layer of leaves or straw. Make an enclosure over the root area using plastic mesh and fill it with dry leaves in autumn, or cover the roots with a 15cm (6in) layer of bark chippings. This can be removed in spring and used as a border mulch.

HEAVY SNOW FALLS

Some evergreens, particularly conifers, are susceptible to damage caused by the weight of accumulated snow. The plant can be either pulled out of shape or have limbs broken. Prevent damage by tying up susceptible plants before winter or routinely knock heavy falls of snow from exposed plants before damage is caused.

A few shrubs, such as bay, cordylines and myrtle, are worth wrapping up in winter. Make an insulating duvet out of two layers of fine-mesh netting stuffed with insulating material. Wrap the plants in late autumn or early winter and uncover them in early spring.

HOW TO PROVIDE WINTER PROTECTION

1 To protect a tender shrub using a shield, insert three stout stakes firmly into the ground around the plant, then wrap a plastic sheet or several layers of horticultural fleece around the outside of the stakes. Tie securely and peg down the bottom to secure.

2 If you don't want to erect a shield, perhaps on aesthetic grounds, cover the plant with a large plastic bag or horticultural fleece sleeve, pegged to the ground, when very severe weather is forecast. Remove it afterwards.

Shrubs worth deadheading

Azalea	Paeonia
Camellia	Pieris
Choisya	Rhododendron
Erica	Rosa
Hypericum	Syringa
Kalmia	

Pruning basics

Most trees and shrubs will need an occasional prune to maintain health, control their size and improve the display of flowers or foliage. It is a straightforward process provided you use the correct pruning technique and get the timing right.

Pruning tools

Despite having acquired a reputation for being difficult, all pruning follows a few basic rules, which are easy to understand and to put into practice. The first rule is to have good quality tools with sharp, clean blades. Sharp well-maintained blades will make clean cuts without damaging the surrounding tissues left on the plant. By keeping the blades clean you will also minimize the chance of spreading disease when you prune. If you are removing diseased material it is a good idea to use a garden disinfectant to wipe the blades between cuts.

It is also important to use the right pruning tools for the thickness of the stem. For cutting stems up to 1cm (⅜in) thick use a pair of secateurs (pruners), for stems 1–3cm (½-1¼in) thick a pair of long-handled loppers would be best. For stems more than 3cm (1¼in) thick you will need a pruning saw.

Pruning cuts should also be made in the right way. As a rule, cut just above an outward-facing, healthy looking bud (or pair of buds) so that new growth does not increase the congestion in the centre of the plant. Make the cut angled away from the bud so that it sheds water. With shrubs such as potentilla and spiraea, which have a lot of thin, wiry stems, pruning in this way is not practicable. You will get just as good a result if you use shears to cut back the plant. Indeed, recent research has shown that even thick-stemmed bush roses can be "rough pruned" without a noticeable decline in their health or flowering potential.

Simple pruning

Most shrubs and trees do not require regular pruning, but some will produce bigger and better displays of flowers

GOOD AND BAD PRUNING CUTS

1 A good pruning cut is made about 3mm (⅛in) above a strong bud. It should be a slanting cut, with the higher end above the bud. The bud should generally be facing outward from the plant rather than inward; the latter will throw its shoot into the plant, crossing and rubbing against others, which should be avoided. This is an easy technique and you can practise it on any stem.

2 If the stem has buds or leaves opposite each other, make the cut horizontal, about 3mm (⅛in) above the buds.

3 Always use a sharp pair of secateurs (pruners). Blunt ones will produce a ragged or bruised cut, which is likely to provide easy access to disease spores.

4 Do not cut too far above a bud. The piece of stem above the bud is likely to die back and the stem may well die back even further, causing the loss of the whole stem.

5 Do not cut too close to the bud, otherwise the bud might be damaged by the secateurs (pruners) or disease might enter. Too close a cut is likely to cause the stem to die back to the next bud.

6 It is bad practice to slope the pruning cut towards the bud because this makes the stem above the bud too long, which is likely to cause die-back. It also funnels rain on to the bud, and moisture can collect in the join which may cause rot or other problems.

HOW TO PRUNE

1 Cut any diseased or damaged wood back to sound wood, just above a strong bud. It may be necessary to cut right back to the main stem. The wood is quite easy to spot. It may not be dead, but still in the process of turning brown or black. Damaged wood will not grow and may harbour diseases.

2 Crossing stems should be removed while they are still young, otherwise friction may damage them and let in disease spores. They also make the bush look congested if not removed, and make it harder to prune. Use secateurs (pruners) to cut the stem at its base where it joins the main branch.

3 Tips of stems often die back, especially those that have carried clusters of flowers. Another cause of die-back is when the young growth at the tip of shoots is killed by frost. If the die-back is not cut out, it can eventually kill off the whole shoot. Cut the shoot back into good wood, just above a strong bud.

if they are pruned in the right way and at the right time. If left to their own devices, however, even those types that don't normally need pruning will become congested with unproductive wood. For this reason the most basic form of pruning can be applied to all woody plants and is often known as the three Ds: the removal of dead, diseased and damaged stems. This can be done at any time of the year.

If you want to go a step further the pruning method you use and the time you prune will depend on what you are trying to achieve. For example, if you are pruning to

improve flowering you will need to know whether the shrub you are about to prune blooms on wood produced during the previous season or on new wood produced during the current season. However, if you do not know anything about the shrub

you could use the fail-safe one-in-three method. Prune one-third of the shrub back to the ground every year, choosing the oldest stems, so no stem is more than three years old. The one-in-three technique is also a good way of rejuvenating old shrubs.

This *Olearia x haastii* puts forward a glorious display of white flowers in summer. After flowering, prune back the oldest one-third of the shoots following the one-in-three method.

No-prune shrubs

Aucuba japonica
Berberis thunbergii
Choisya ternata
Cordyline australis
Cotoneaster microphyllus
Euonymus fortunei
Fatsia japonica
Genista lydia
Magnolia stellata
Prunus laurocerasus
Skimmia japonica

Pruning popular shrubs

Most of the popular shrubs can be grouped according to their pruning requirements. Prune little and often, ideally once a year, rather than waiting many years until the plant is overgrown and unmanageable.

Better flowering

Shrubs such as *Buddleja davidii*, large-leaved hebes, *Hydrangea paniculata*, lavatera and *Potentilla fruticosa*, which flower on the current year's growth and bloom from midsummer, need pruning in early spring, just before new growth starts. Prune out as much of last year's growth as you want – the harder you prune the more new growth will be produced.

Early-flowering shrubs, such as escallonia, forsythia, *Kerria japonica* and philadephus, which bloom before midsummer, generally produce their blooms on wood produced during the previous season. In this case, prune as soon as flowering has finished by cutting back one in three of the old shoots to a new shoot

Salix integra 'Hakuno-nishiki' should be pruned annually in early spring to ensure its colourful foliage gives the best display.

lower down or a plump outward-facing bud. The new growth put on during the summer months will flower the following year.

Better foliage and stems

Many shrubs, such as *Cornus* (dogwood), *Rubus cockburnianus*, *Salix alba*, *Sambucus nigra* and *Spiraea japonica* 'Goldflame', are principally grown for their foliage displays or brightly coloured stems. These shrubs should be pruned in early spring by removing all the previous year's growth to near ground level or to a low framework of woody stems. This pruning will encourage larger, more brightly coloured foliage in spring and summer and more colourful stems in winter.

Evergreen foliage

Most shrubs grown for their evergreen foliage are pruned only when they need restricting or when diseased or damaged wood is found. Some shrubs, however, such as *Elaeagnus pungens*, *Griselinia littoralis*, *Lonicera nitida*, *Photinia × fraseri*, *Prunus laurocerasus*, *Prunus lusitanica* and *Viburnum tinus*, may need pruning to keep them in shape. Cut back overly

---

HOW TO PRUNE BACK HARD FOR COLOURED FOLIAGE AND STEMS

1 Plants such as this *Rubus cockburnianus* are cut back to the ground annually in spring to prevent growth becoming congested. The colour on young stems is more pronounced so the plant is more attractive if all the canes have been produced in the current year.

2 Cut the old canes to just above the ground using secateurs (pruners). The height you cut to is not critical as new shoots will grow from the base. Although pruning does not come much simpler than this, it is not without its hazards. Protect your hands from thorny stems by wearing thick gloves.

3 You may find it easier to use long-handled pruners (loppers) to prune thick canes. Do not worry about trying to cut back to a bud as new growth will come from the base.

4 Little will be visible, but if you prune in spring new shoots will appear in a few weeks. By the end of the growing season the new shoots will be as long as those removed in the pruning, forming a bushy and compact plant.

HOW TO PRUNE GREY-LEAVED SHRUBS

1 Grey-leaved foliage plants like this brachyglottis look their best with lots of new growth on compact plants. Prune annually from a young age to keep them looking good.

2 Small plants such as cotton lavender, *Santolina chamaecyparissus,* can be pruned hard in early spring provided they are not too old and woody. If new growth is visible near the base of the plant, cut the stems back to within about 5–10cm (2–4in) of the ground.

3 Cut back to just above a young shoot or a developing bud. Do not cut into wood that is very old and thick. Confine the severe pruning to shoots that grew last summer. The plant will look bare when you have finished, but will soon regrow.

long stems and thin out congested stems in late spring. Small-leaved evergreens can be clipped with hand (hedge) shears, but for large-leaved kinds use secateurs (pruners). Formally shaped shrubs may need to be pruned more often if they begin to look untidy. Avoid cutting back to older wood if you can.

Grey-leaved shrubs

Prune shrubs with grey leaves, such as lavender, *Santolina chamaecyparissus, Artemisia abrotanum, Helichrysum italicum*

subsp. *serotinum* and *Senecio,* to keep plants compact and the foliage dense. Trim lightly in spring once plants are well established and repeat each spring by cutting back new growth to just above a pair of leaves, about 5–10cm (2–4in) from the old wood. Do not cut back into old wood because this is unlikely to re-sprout.

Pruning large shrubs

When pruning old thick stems on shrubs and limbs from trees it is best to use a pruning saw. The main

problem with cutting large branches is that their weight tends to rip the branch free before the pruning cut has been completed, producing a ragged finish and tearing the branch and bark from well below the cut. This can provide an entry point for disease. To prevent this, make the first cut beneath the branch and upwards until about half-way through. Then cut downwards, about 2.5cm (1in) further out than the first cut. The branch will break off and the cut can then be straightened.

HOW TO PRUNE THICK STEMS

1 Choose a point about 5cm (2in) or more from the position of the final cut and make a saw cut from beneath the branch. Continue sawing until you are about halfway through or until the weight of the branch begins to bind on the saw.

2 Next, make a downward cut from the top of the branch about 2.5cm (1in) or so on the outside of the first cut. When the saw has cut to level with the first cut, the weight of the branch is likely to make the branch split or tear along to the first cut.

3 Sawing from above, cut through the branch at the desired point. Now you have removed most of the weight of the branch, it should be possible to cut cleanly through the branch and thus finish the pruning.

Pruning bush and standard roses

For years rose pruning has been presented as a complicated affair of well-defined rules and precise, well-timed cuts. Then, a few years ago, new research showed it might all be a waste of time. So how should you prune your roses?

Why do roses need to be pruned?

Rose pruning is important for two main reasons. The first is that, left unpruned, the plant will get big and straggly, with an ugly bare base; the second is that the stems will bear flowers for only a few years before becoming exhausted. Pruning tackles both problems in one go, keeping the plant small and the shoots young and vigorous.

Pruning roses correctly

The same basic rules apply when rose pruning as for any other shrub, so use sharp, clean blades and a pair of thornproof gloves.

Bush roses The traditional method of pruning bush roses is probably still the most reliable. Cut back all the stems of large-flowered (hybrid tea) roses by about half their length. Cut back old stems of cluster-flowered (floribunda) roses to the base. The remaining younger stems of cluster-flowered roses should be pruned back to about 45cm (18in).

All cuts should be made just above a healthy, outward-facing bud using a cut that slopes slightly away from the bud so that the lower edge of the cut is still above the top of the bud. You should also remove all dead, damaged or weak wood and thin out the centre of the plant. Pruning should be carried out annually in early spring.

It is now known that, although the results won't be quite as good, all bush roses can be pruned roughly, cutting all stems back to 15–20cm

LARGE-FLOWERED BUSH

Cut out any badly positioned, diseased or dead wood (shown here coloured orange-brown) close to the base. This will leave fewer stems about which pruning decisions have to be made, and the extra space makes the job easier. Shorten the remaining stems by about half, cutting to an outward-facing bud.

STANDARDS

Prune an ordinary standard rose (left) by shortening the summer's growth by about half. Prune a weeping standard (right) by cutting back each long shoot to a point where there is a new one to replace it. If no suitable replacement shoots can be found, do not prune the main stems; instead, shorten the sideshoots on the flowered stems to two buds.

(6–8in) once every few years without worrying about cutting to just above a bud. You can even use a hedge trimmer if you have a lot of roses and time is short.

CLUSTER-FLOWERED BUSH

First cut out any badly placed or very old shoots that are dying or diseased (shown here coloured orange-brown), then shorten the remaining main shoots to about 45cm (18in), or about one third of their length. Cut back to an outward-facing bud where possible.

SHRUB

Pruning should always be modified to suit the growth characteristics of the plant but, as a guide, shorten the main stems by between a quarter and a half, and any sideshoots that remain by about two-thirds. Cut out any badly positioned growth and remove weak, diseased or dying stems completely.

Standard roses Prune lightly as cutting back severely will encourage over-vigorous shoots that may spoil the shape. Shorten the main stems in the head and any sideshoots.

Newly planted roses

It is worth pruning new roses in early spring to encourage new shoots from the base. Reducing the amount of top growth will also give the roots a chance to get established. The stems of bush roses and new growth on standard roses should be cut back by about half their length while those of shrub roses and miniatures should be cut by about a quarter.

Prune standards in late winter or early spring, but prune weeping standards after flowering, in summer.
Shrub roses Prune lightly, either annually or once every other year. Remove between a quarter and a half of the new growth and cut out any dead, diseased or congested growth.
Miniature roses These require little or no pruning other than to keep growth thick and compact. Use shears to trim back vertical new growth in spring. Again cut out any dead, diseased or weak growth.

This floribunda rose has been well pruned and now displays plenty of new, vigorous growth and an abundance of flowers.

HOW TO PRUNE ROSES

1 Moderate pruning is the most appropriate for established large-flowered roses. Cut back all the main stems by about half, or to within 20–25cm (8–10in) of the ground. Cut to an outward-facing bud to keep the centre of the bush open, with no congestion.

2 You can treat cluster-flowered roses in the same way, but if you prune some shoots severely and others lightly, flowering may be spread over a longer period. Prune the oldest shoots back close to the base, but those that grew last year by about one third only.

3 Whichever type of rose you are pruning, cut back any dead or diseased shoots to healthy wood. Also remove any very thin, spindly shoots, cutting either to their point of origin or to two or three buds from the base of the shoot.

Problem solving

Although trees and shrubs are usually trouble free, there are some problems that can occur from time to time, especially if the plant is not growing well or if there is a prolonged spell of dry weather.

Pests and diseases

Generally speaking, a good garden plant that is vigorous and growing well will simply shrug off most pests and diseases. If the plant is suffering from stress, such as water shortage in a drought, it might succumb. However, if the source of the stress is removed (by watering in this example) most established trees and shrubs will recover by themselves. This is fortunate, because using chemical controls on large plants is expensive and often quite impracticable. Many pests will attack the foliage of trees and shrubs, eating holes or defoliating whole twigs. This will almost always be localized and have little impact on the tree as a whole, however. Similarly, diseases tend to disfigure the plant if weather conditions allow, but the effect is usually temporary, and most plants will soon recover. There are a few more serious

BOTRYTIS

Botrytis is a fluffy grey-white/brown fungal mass formed on seedlings or on growth damaged by other causes such as frost. Use a fungicide on seedlings. Remove the affected parts of a mature plant, cutting back into live wood, then spray with fungicide.

exceptions, such as fireblight, honey fungus, canker and silver leaf. If you think your plant has one of these diseases, check the symptoms in a good plant pest and disease encyclopedia before taking action.

Plant fails to establish

Failure to establish can be the result of a number of problems, but the most common is that the soil conditions are inappropriate for the plant in question. Check the pH of your soil and test for the presence of nutrients such as nitrogen, potassium and phosphorus. Look up

LEAF-CUTTING BEE

Neatly notched leaves indicate the presence of leaf-cutting bees. Damage is largely cosmetic and will not affect the health of established plants. Bees are beneficial pollinators and the small amount of damage caused does not justify the use of chemicals.

the conditions the plant prefers in a good plant encyclopedia. If the soil conditions were correct for the plant, the problem might have occurred if the shrub was planted incorrectly. Another reason for plants failing to establish is a shortage of water after planting. It is important to always water well until established.

Foliage problems

Variegated plants often spontaneously produce an all-green shoot that is more vigorous than its more ornamental counterparts. This is known as reversion. It is important

Suckers

Some trees and shrubs are prone to producing shoots from the roots below ground (known as suckers). If the plant is grown on a rootstock, as with many roses, the sucker shoot will bear flowers of the rootstock variety rather than of the ornamental plant. The rootstock is usually much more vigorous, and could eventually take over the ornamental plant, and so the sucker should be removed. Do not prune off the shoot at ground level because this will encourage even more suckers. Instead use the following technique.

1 Remove suckers at their point of origin – you will have to excavate the soil to expose the bottom of the sucker.

2 If possible, pull the sucker off; otherwise, try to cut it off flush with the main stem using a sharp knife.

CUTTING OUT REVERSION IN SHRUBS

Green-leaved shoots have appeared in this *Spiraea japonica* 'Goldflame'. If left, they may take over the whole plant. The remedy is simple. Remove the offending shoots back to that part of the stem or shoot where the reversion begins.

to cut out all reverted shoots as soon as you can because if they are left they will outgrow the ornamental shoots, eventually dominating the whole plant. Variegated plants that are planted in deep shade also lose their variegation. In this case, you will need to move the plant to a more suitable position.

Discoloured leaves can also be a problem on all plants. Yellow leaves, for example, can be caused by a range of problems. Lack of water and starvation are common causes, but lack of iron can be the cause when lime-hating plants are grown on chalky soil. You can either give the plant a fillip with a dressing of chelated iron or you will have to move it to a container filled with ericaceous compost (acid soil mix.)

Leaves with scorched edges are usually a sign of drought, but they can result from hot winds in summer and, on evergreens, cold winds in winter. Severe late frosts can burn the edges of new growth in spring too. Established plants will recover and disfigured stems can be pruned out. If the problem recurs year after year, you will either have to provide shelter or move the plant to a more sheltered position. During hot,

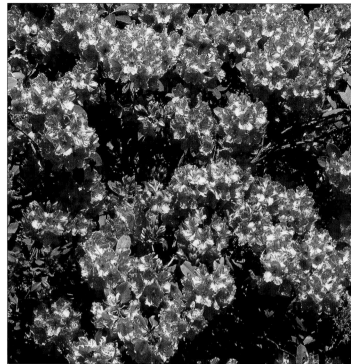

Azaleas are a form of rhododendron. In a good year, if protected from unseasonally late frosts, they produce masses of flowers, making a spectacular spring display.

sunny weather in summer shrubs that like lightly shaded conditions can also suffer from scorched leaves. Plants with golden foliage are particularly vulnerable.

Flower problems

Many flowering shrubs don't flower well for a few years while they are getting established, so be patient. If your plant's flowering has declined it might need feeding with a high-potash fertilizer. If the shrub has been pruned recently you may have used the wrong method or pruned at the wrong time of the year.

Early flowering shrubs can lose their blooms to late frosts, while those that flower later in the year can drop buds in response to drought.

A few large-flowered shrubs, notably roses, are also susceptible in prolonged periods of wet weather to a physiological problem (known as balling) that causes the blooms to rot on the plant.

DEADHEADING CAMELLIAS

Some cultivars of *Camellia japonica* do not shed their flowers as they fade, and will need deadheading regularly.

Gardening with climbers

Climbing plants have much to offer the modern gardener. They are fairly easy to grow and usually take up little growing space.

Climbers have many uses and are an important element in most gardens. They are often trained up supports to cover walls and fences or tied into free-standing structures. Many are suitable for scrambling through mature trees and shrubs or for use as weed-suppressing ground cover.

There is a wide range of climbers, varying in both vigour and preferred position, so it is important to choose carefully. Match the climber to the size of the support as well as the prevailing conditions in your garden. There are climbers to suit almost any situation, including most soils in sun or shade. When you are buying climbing plants follow the same rules as for shrubs.

Walls offer perfect support and protection for climbers such as this *Clematis montana* 'Elizabeth', which produces a mass of flowers in early spring.

Planting climbers

Most climbers should be planted in the same way and at the same time as trees and shrubs, although the technique varies slightly depending on the type of support they are being trained against.

Preparing the soil

The soil next to vertical surfaces, such as walls and fences, is usually drier than the soil in the rest of the garden because the ground is in the rain shadow of the wall or fence. Walls also draw water from the soil, further reducing the moisture content. It is essential, therefore, to improve the water-holding capacity of the soil before planting and to set the climber a little way away from the wall so that the roots have a chance to spread out. This is also the best method when planting next to free-standing supports. Before you plant a new climber it is a good idea to put up the support. Prepare the soil by digging it over thoroughly and removing any debris, which can include builders' rubble if the border has not been properly dug before. Incorporate plenty of organic matter as you go.

Planting

Once the soil has settled, dig a hole 30–45cm (12–18in) away from the wall or fence, large enough to accommodate the full spread of the roots (for bare-root plants) and about twice as wide as the rootball for container-grown types. The planting hole should be the same depth as the rootball.

As you dig, place all excavated soil on to a sheet next to the planting hole. Fork over the soil in the bottom of the hole. Add well-rotted manure or organic matter, such as garden compost to the soil as well as a handful of bonemeal and gently fork it in (use latex gloves for protection when handling bonemeal). Remove container-grown specimens

Match the vigour of the climber to the climbing space available. This *Rosa* x *alba* 'Alba Semiplena' grows to 2m (6ft) high.

from their pots and tease the roots out from around the rootball before planting to encourage them to spread into the surrounding soil.

With the exception of clematis, position the climber at the same depth as it was in the pot or the nursery bed – look for a soil mark on the stem – angling it back at 45 degrees towards the bottom of the support. Check the planting depth by laying a cane across the hole, then add or remove soil as necessary.

Backfill the first few centimetres (inches) of the hole with the excavated soil and give bare-root climbers a gentle shake to settle the soil. Firm the first layer around the roots with your hands before adding a second layer and repeating the process until the hole is filled. Water in well and cover the soil around the new specimen with an 8cm (3in) deep layer of well-rotted, organic mulch but take care not to pile it up against the stems.

HOW TO CHOOSE A CLIMBER

1 Many climbers are sold in containers. Look for strong-growing plants with plenty of shoots arising from the base of the plant.

2 Small plants with fewer stems are sometimes available. They are usually cheap but will probably need good aftercare if they are to establish themselves properly.

3 Check the root system by sliding the plant from its container. Reject the plant if the roots are congested or tightly coiled around the pot. The root system of this plant is in good condition.

HOW TO PLANT CLIMBERS

1 Dig over the proposed site, loosening the soil and removing any weeds. If the ground has not recently been prepared, work some well-rotted organic material into the soil to improve soil texture and fertility.

2 Add a general or specialist shrub fertilizer to the soil at the dosage recommended on the packet. Work into the soil around the planting area with a fork. A slow-release organic fertilizer is best.

3 Water the plant in the pot. Dig a hole that is much wider than the rootball. The hole should be next to a free-standing support or at least 30cm (12in) from a wall or fence, and angled back towards the support.

4 Stand the plant in its hole and place a cane across the hole to check that it is at the same level. Take the plant from the pot or cut the bag away. Holding the plant steady, fill in the soil. Firm as you go with your hands.

5 Train the stems of the climber up individual canes to their main support. Tie the stems in with string or plastic ties. Even twining plants or plants with tendrils will need this initial help. Spread them out, so that they ultimately cover the whole of their support.

6 Water the climber thoroughly. Put a layer of mulch around the plant, to help preserve the moisture and prevent weed growth. Do not pile mulch up against the stems of the climber, however.

Planting near established plants

The soil next to established trees and shrubs is often dry and full of roots and it may be difficult for a climber to become established.

The best position for a new plant is at the edge of the tree or shrub canopy, where water will run off when it rains – the "drip zone". When digging the planting hole try as far as possible to do this without disturbing the surrounding soil or any major roots. Cut off any minor roots that become exposed in the planting hole. Improve the soil with well-rotted garden compost and bonemeal, and then line the sides of the planting hole with pieces of old timber. This will give the climber a chance to establish without suffering from too much competition from surrounding plants. The timber will eventually rot away without you having to remove it.

Planting clematis

It is good practice to plant clematis about 8cm (3in) deeper than other types of climber so that the bottom of the stems are below ground level. Then, if the clematis suffers from wilt, which kills all top growth, it will be able to produce new shoots the following year from unaffected buds at the base of the stems underground.

Providing wall support

When choosing a support for a climbing plant it is important to take into consideration the method by which it climbs. Some climbers such as ivy can be grown on a bare brick wall, but most will need a trellis to support them as they grow.

Types of climbers

Climbers hold on to their supports in a number of ways. Some are self-clinging and can cover a vertical surface without the need for any support at all. Ivies and climbing hydrangeas, for example, produce modified roots on their stems that attach themselves to rough surfaces, while other climbers, such as Virginia creeper, produce tiny suckers that will stick to any surface, including glass. Many self-clinging climbers need a support or another plant to climb up but will hold on by themselves. Clematis, for example, have twining leaf stalks, and passion flowers and sweet peas produce tendrils. A few plants, such as akebia, honeysuckle and wisteria, have twining stems that coil snake-like

SELF-CLINGING CLIMBERS

Hydrangea anomala subsp. *petiolaris* clings to wall surfaces by putting out modified roots.

around their supports. There are also climbers, including climbing and rambler roses, that are not self-clinging and need to be tied in to their supports.

Supports for vertical surfaces

There are several types of support to choose from, but it is important to provide one that matches the size and vigour of the climber it is to

TWINING CLIMBERS

Clematis have twining leaf stalks that grow round a supporting structure.

support. Against a wall or fence you have the choice of fixing trellis panels, expanding trellis or plastic mesh to the surface or attaching a series of sturdy parallel wires.

Trellis panels Wooden or plastic panels are very strong and look attractive. They are also easy and quick to erect, but they are fairly costly. Trellis panels are available only in a small range of specific

HOW TO TRAIN A CLIMBER OR WALL SHRUB ON WIRES

1 Without supporting wires or a trellis, a wall shrub will grow out in all directions.

2 Drill pilot holes into the wall and insert vine eyes to support the wires. If you use vine eyes with a screw fixing, insert a plastic or wooden plug in the wall first. Vine eyes are available in several lengths, the long ones being necessary for vigorous climbers, such as wisteria, that need wires further from the wall.

3 The simplest vine eyes are wedge shaped. Hammer them directly into the masonry and then feed the wire through a hole. Although wedge-shaped eyes are suitable for brick and stone walls, the screw type are better for wooden fences and posts.

HOW TO FIX A TRELLIS TO A WALL

1 The trellis should be sturdy and in good condition. Ensure it has been treated with wood preservative. Take the trellis panel to the wall and mark its position. The bottom of the trellis should be about 30cm (12in) from the ground. Drill holes for fixing the spacers and insert plastic or wooden plugs.

2 Drill the equivalent holes in the wooden batten and secure it to the wall, checking with a spirit (carpenter's) level that it is horizontal. Use a piece of wood that holds the trellis at least 2.5cm (1in) from the wall. Fix another batten at the base, and one halfway up for trellis more than 1.2m (4ft) high.

3 Drill and screw the trellis to the battens, first fixing the top and then working downwards. Check that the trellis is straight using a spirit level. The finished trellis should be secure, so that the weight of the climber and any wind that blows on it will not pull it away from its fixings.

sizes, so are suitable for only some climbers and walls.

Expanding trellis This is sold in a compact form, is easier to transport than panels, but is not as strong. It comes in specific sizes, but expansion can be adjusted to fit an area.

Plastic mesh This is cheap but less robust than trellis panels. It is also less pleasing to the eye until it is covered with growth.

Wires and netting Fixing vine eyes into a wall to support galvanized wire is time-consuming, but once up, wires are a good support for climbers. Even when not covered with plants they are barely visible, and are very versatile, covering any shape or size of surface. If you are growing annual climbers, such as morning glory and sweet peas, less robust netting or even string can make a suitable support.

Access for maintenance

To make maintenance of the wall easier in the future, consider attaching the bottom of the trellis panel to the bottom spacer batten with galvanized hinges so that when the screws fixing the panel to the other battens are removed the panel can be swung away from the wall or fence, providing easy access for repointing or painting.

4 Thread galvanized wire through the hole in the vine eye and wrap it around itself to form a firm fixing. Thread the other end through the intermediate eyes (set at no more than 2m/6ft intervals and preferably closer) and fasten the wire around the end eye, keeping it as taut as possible.

5 Spread out the main stems and attach them to the wires, using either plastic ties or string. Tie at several points, if necessary, so that the stems lie flat against the wall and do not flap about in the wind.

6 When all of the stems are tied in to the wires they should form a regular fan shape. Tying the stems in like this, rather than allowing the climber to grow up the wall naturally, covers the wall better and encourages the plant to produce flowering buds all along the top edge of the stems.

Providing free-standing support

It is not always convenient to grow a climber against a wall, and a free-standing support gives flexibility in planning which climbers to grow and where to place them. Climbers can be used to shield an unsightly part of the garden from view as well as adding variety to already attractive areas.

Growing into established plants

If you wish to grow a climber through a tree or a shrub, you must make sure that you have compatible candidates. Neither plant should compete unduly for moisture or nutrients or both will suffer. The established plant must also be strong enough to bear the weight of a full-grown climber, which can be

considerable. Hedges and apple trees are good candidates for large climbers. The tree should be neither too young nor too old: a young tree may be smothered by the vigorous climber, while the additional burden may be too much for an older, weaker tree during winter storms.

Position the climber on the side of the prevailing wind so that it will blow the stems into the support as it grows. After planting the climber, hammer in a short stake next to it and attach one end of a piece of rope to the stake. Tie the other end of the rope up into the canopy of the supporting plant. Untie the climber from its supporting cane that was supplied when you bought it and unravel the stems. The climber can

then be tied into the rope and the longer stems up into the canopy of the tree or shrub. Do not, as is sometimes recommended, secure the bottom of the rope by looping it under the rootball because the climber is likely to be pulled out of the ground by the first strong gust of wind that catches the branch holding the other end of the rope.

Arches and pergolas

Garden structures, such as arches and pergolas, are available in a wide range of styles. The style you choose should fit in with the rest of the garden design and be strong and large enough to support the chosen climbers. There are many ready-made kits on sale in a variety of materials.

PLANTING A CLIMBER NEXT TO AN ESTABLISHED SHRUB

1 Choose a healthy shrub, such as this *Salix helvetica*, and preferably one that flowers at a different time from the climber.

2 Dig a hole at the edge of the supporting shrub so that the climber will receive rain. Improve the soil if necessary.

3 Using a cane, train the climber, such as this *Clematis alpina*, into the shrub. Spread out the shoots so it grows evenly through the shrub.

4 Water the new plant thoroughly and mulch if necessary. Continue to water, especially in dry weather, until the climber is established.

The white flowers of the scented rambling rose 'Seagull' look spectacular against the dark green of the conifer it is climbing through.

Single posts, tripods and hoops

Many climbers are suitable for training up single posts, often called pillars, although it is probably best to avoid very vigorous climbers. If space permits, a series of pillars can be erected along a path, linked garland-fashion by chunky rope along which climbers can grow. Climbers also look effective trained up tripods or, alternatively, you can make your own supports from canes.

Training a climber over a hoop allows you to direct the growth so that it covers the available space with an abundance of flowers. Bending the new growth into curving arches encourages flowering buds to be formed along the whole stem rather than just at the tip. A hoop will also keep the climber in proportion to the border in which it is growing, and is a useful method of growing vigorous plants in a limited space.

Whichever free-standing support you choose, it is essential that it is anchored securely into the ground.

The rich purple flowers of *Clematis* 'Jackmanii' can be seen clearly as it climbs up a tripod, bringing interest to an otherwise neglected corner of the garden. Once it is fully grown, the clematis will cover the support completely, so that the tripod cannot be seen.

HOW TO ERECT A PILLAR FOR A CLIMBER

1 Dig a hole at least 60cm (2ft) deep. Put in the post and check that it is upright. Backfill with earth, ramming it firmly down as you work. In exposed gardens a more solid pillar can be created by filling the hole with concrete.

2 Plants can be tied directly to the post but a more natural support can be created by securing wire netting to the post. Self-clinging climbers such as clematis will then be able to climb by themselves with little attention from you other than tying in wayward stems.

3 Plant the climber a little way from the pole. Lead the stems to the wire netting and tie them in. Self-clingers will take over, but plants such as roses will need to be tied in as they grow. Twining plants, such as hops, can be grown up the pole without wire.

Aftercare of climbers

Most climbers are easy to look after and, apart from pruning, require the minimum of care. Do keep an eye out for potential problems, however, as early action is most effective. A little general maintenance will keep your plants in tip-top condition.

Watering and mulching

Most climbers are planted in dry soil at the base of walls and fences, which is why they are more likely to suffer from drought during prolonged dry spells. Always keep climbers well watered until they are established. Thereafter, soak the soil thoroughly once a fortnight during a period of drought or if the climber is showing signs of stress.

Each spring top up the loose organic mulch so that it is about 8cm (3in) thick but is not piled against the stems of the climber. The mulch will not only help to retain moisture in the soil but will also prevent any competition from weeds.

Feeding

With new plants, apply a general-purpose fertilizer on the surface of the soil in spring. Thereafter, if your soil is very poor or free-draining apply an annual dressing of a general fertilizer around each plant in spring. Some free-flowering climbers, such as roses, will produce even better displays if given a high-potash fertilizer, such as rose feed, in spring and early summer. Foliar feed can also be applied using a hose-end feeder fitted to the end of a garden hose. The nutrients are readily absorbed through the leaves.

Keeping plants tidy

Tie in new growth while it is still flexible enough to be bent into position against the support. Prune out any dead, diseased or dying growth as well as any unwanted, crossing stems. Also remove any all-green shoots produced on variegated climbers (known as reversion) to

Using grass clippings

For a free organic mulch use grass clippings (not treated with weedkiller) in an unobtrusive area, such as at the back of a border or the bottom of the garden, to mulch established climbers each spring. Top it up throughout the mowing season. This is not only a cheap and effective mulch but is also a convenient way of getting rid of lawn clippings.

prevent these more vigorous green shoots from overwhelming the rest of the climber. Check old ties to make sure they are secure and are not constricting the stems.

The removal of fading flowers (known as deadheading) on climbers is desirable although not always practicable if the climber is large or not very accessible. Deadheading not only makes the climber look neater, but also encourages better and longer-lasting flowering displays by stopping the climber wasting energy in producing unwanted fruits and seeds. Where the fruits or seedheads are of ornamental value, simply deadhead parts of the climber that are hidden from view so that you get the best of both worlds.

Winter protection

Although walls and fences give some protection in winter, climbers that are of only borderline hardiness may need extra protection during cold years or in colder areas. Draping a sheet of hessian (burlap) over the climber is the traditional method, but a double layer of horticultural fleece will also do the trick. For real protection, create an insulating duvet by stuffing straw or other insulating material under the sheeting. Remove all winter protection when milder weather returns in spring.

HOW TO TIE IN NEW SHOOTS

Once you have pruned out the old stems of ramblers and climbers, tie in vigorous new shoots to replace them.

HOW TO DEADHEAD CLIMBERS

As the flowers die, remove the flowerheads. This not only makes the climber tidier but also promotes further flowering. With tall climbers, however, this may not always be practicable.

CLEMATIS WILT

Some forms of clematis, mainly large flowered hybrids and *montana*, are susceptible to wilt. This disease is caused by the fungus *Ascochyta clematidina*. The top-growth dies back and, left unchecked, the disease may affect the whole plant. If your clematis shows signs of wilt prune it hard. If it has been planted deeply enough it will usually recover. Drenching with fungicide at monthly intervals in the growing season may help, but if wilt is a persistent problem, replace your clematis with one less susceptible to the disease.

HOW TO PROTECT AGAINST FROST

For light protection against unseasonal frosts a temporary cover such as shade netting or hessian (burlap) can be used to protect new shoots and early flowers. If the climber is grown against a wall, hang the cover from the gutter or from some similar support. Fasten the netting securely so that it remains attached, even in windy weather.

This *Solanum* has been well cared for and is in good condition. The plant has been securely tied to its support, and trained so that it is not growing over the windows or into the guttering. Regular mulching and feeding with a high-potash fertilizer will help improve flowering.

Pruning clematis and wisteria

Most climbers can be kept in good shape and flowering well by simply removing unwanted growth and pruning out any dead, dying or diseased stems. A few popular types, however, including clematis, wisteria and roses, require special pruning for best results.

Pruning clematis

Clematis has gained a reputation for being difficult to prune, mainly because not all clematis are pruned in the same way. However, as long as you know when your clematis flowers and can tell whether it produces blooms on old stems or new growth produced during the current year, you won't go far wrong.

Clematis can be divided into three groups: those that produce all their flowers on old wood (known as pruning group 1); those that produce blooms on both old wood and new growth produced during the current season (known as pruning group 2); and those clematis that flower only on new growth (known as pruning group 3).

Clematis 'Pagoda' is a group 3 clematis, so the flowers are borne on new stems. Hard pruning in winter will lead to a good display of flowers the following summer.

CLEMATIS PRUNING GROUPS

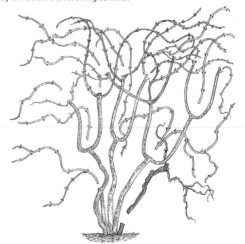

Group 1 These clematis need pruning only when they outgrow their space. Cut out sufficient branches to reduce congestion and take those that encroach beyond their space back to their point of origin.

Group 2 After cutting out all the dead, damaged or weak growth, remove any wood that is making the clematis congested, cutting back to a pair of buds.

HOW TO PRUNE WISTERIA

1 In late summer shorten the long shoots produced this year. Unless required for further spread, cut back to about four or six leaves.

2 In midwinter shorten the summer's growth further, cutting back to just two or three buds, so the shoots are 8–10cm (3–4in) long.

WISTERIA TWO-STAGE PRUNING

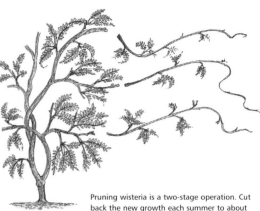

Pruning wisteria is a two-stage operation. Cut back the new growth each summer to about four leaves and reduce this even further with a winter pruning.

Group 1 The spring-flowering clematis belong to this group. Some are vigorous, such as *C. montana*, while others are more restrained. Cut back vigorous species as necessary to keep them in check, but others in this group need little pruning other than the removal of dead, damaged or diseased stems. Prune back unwanted stems to their point of origin or to a pair of plump buds.

Group 2 This group includes late spring and early summer varieties that flower mainly on old wood early in the season and later produce a smaller flush on this year's growth.

They need little pruning other than the removal of dead, damaged or diseased stems. Congested growth can be thinned out by pruning back stems to their point of origin or a pair of plump buds. Alternatively, cut half the stems back to a pair of buds before growth starts to increase the number of blooms produced later in the year.

Group 3 The clematis in this group flower in late summer. Cut back all stems during the winter or early spring to the lowest pair of buds.

Pruning wisteria

Wisteria has an undeserved reputation for being difficult to prune, but in this case it is because it is pruned in two stages, in late summer and then in winter. The pruning itself is straightforward: simply cut back all the whippy new growth to four or six leaves in late summer and then, when the leaves have fallen and it is easier to see what you are doing, cut the same stumps to just two or three buds from the main stem.

Group 3 These clematis should have all the growth cut back in winter or early spring to the first pair of sound buds above the ground.

Clematis pruning groups

Group 1	Group 3
C. alpina	'Abundance'
C. armandii	'Bill MacKenzie'
C. cirrhosa	'Comtesse de
C. macropetala	Bouchaud'
C. montana	'Duchess of
	Albany'
Group 2	'Etiole Violette'
'Barbara	*C. flammula*
Jackman'	'Gravetye
'Daniel Deronda'	Beauty'
'Ernest	'Hagley Hybrid'
Markham'	'Jackmanii'
'Lasurstern'	'Perle d'Azur'
'Marie Boisselot'	*C. rehderiana*
'Nelly Moser'	*C. tangutica*
'The President'	'Ville de Lyon'
'Vyvyan Pennell'	'Victoria'

Pruning climbing roses and honeysuckle

Climbers that are grown for their flowers, such as roses and honeysuckles, require only light pruning from time to time to achieve a profusely flowering plant.

Climbing roses

When trained up walls or along fences climbing roses may not need pruning annually, other than to remove dead or dying growth, but regular pruning will keep the plant vigorous and flowering well, with the blooms low down, where they can be appreciated. Roses trained over free-standing supports need annual pruning to keep them within bounds.

Climbing roses can be divided into two main groups: those that produce blooms in one flush on short sideshoots from an established framework of stems, and those that are repeat-flowering, bearing blooms in a series of flushes throughout summer. Once-flowering climbers should be pruned after flowering by removing up to one-third of the stems, starting with the oldest. Cut

back near to the base or to a new sideshoot produced low down. If there isn't much new growth, cut back older branches to about 30cm (12in) to encourage more next year. Trim sideshoots on other stems to two or three leaves.

Repeat-flowering climbers or those that produce attractive hips should be pruned in winter to remove the weakest and oldest stems. Trim any sideshoots on the remaining stems to within two or three buds.

Rambler roses

These roses have a single flush of blooms in summer, which are produced on growth that was formed the previous year. They produce long shoots from the base. For each vigorous new young shoot prune out an unproductive old one back to ground level after flowering. Do not prune out an old shoot unless there is a new one to replace it, but remove completely any very old, dead or diseased wood.

PRUNING A CLIMBING ROSE

On a well-established, once-flowering climber, cut out one or two of the oldest stems to a point just above a new shoot near the base.

PRUNING A RAMBLER ROSE

Ramblers are straightforward to prune. Cut out old canes that have flowered, taking them back to a point where there is a new replacement shoot.

HOW TO PRUNE A ONCE-FLOWERING CLIMBING ROSE

1 These climbing roses have a stable framework of woody shoots and are always pruned in summer after flowering, so they can seem intimidating to prune. Fortunately, these roses usually flower even with minimal pruning, provided you keep the plant free of any very old stems and any dead and diseased wood.

2 Cut out one or two of the oldest stems each year to encourage new growth. Cut old stems off just above young replacement shoots near the base. If there are no low-growing shoots, choose one that starts 30–60cm (1–2ft) up the stem, and cut back to just above this level.

3 If there are strong young replacement shoots, prune back a proportion of stems that have flowered to just above the newer growth. Tie them in if necessary. If possible, always prune to an outward-facing bud or shoot.

4 Go along the remaining stems and shorten the sideshoots, pruning back to leave two or three buds. Do not remove more than a third of the stems, otherwise flowering will suffer next year.

HOW TO PRUNE A RAMBLER ROSE

1 Prune the rambler rose after flowering – late summer is a good time. Older, congested plants can be more off-putting than younger ones, but all rambler roses are fairly straightforward to prune if you work on them methodically.

2 Once you have a well-established rambler, try to balance the shoots that you remove with those available to replace them. First, cut out any dead or damaged shoots or those that are very weak and spindly. Do not remove very vigorous, young shoots.

3 Cut out old stems that have flowered, but only where there are new shoots to replace them. This will vary from plant to plant and year to year. Shorten the sideshoots on old stems that have been retained (those that have flowered) to leave two or three leaves.

4 Tie in the flexible new shoots to the support. Wherever possible, tie loosely to horizontal wires or a trellis. After pruning, rambler roses will produce new stems from the base, rather than growing taller on existing stems, which gives them a lower, more spreading habit.

Honeysuckle

These climbers can be divided into two groups: those that flower on the current year's growth and those that bear blooms on stems produced last year. Those that flower on new wood do not need regular pruning unless they outgrow their allotted space. In this case, cut back all stems in winter to allow for the new growth the following season. If the climber gets overcrowded remove about one-third of the oldest stems, cutting back to near ground level. Honeysuckles that flower on the previous year's growth should have old growth that has flowered cut back to a newer shoot produced lower down on the stem.

HOW TO PRUNE HONEYSUCKLE

1 Prune honeysuckle only if it has become sparse at the base and the flowers are too high, or if the tangled mass of stems is too thick. This sometimes happens if the plant is grown on a trellis of limited height: when the stems reach the top, they cascade downwards and begin to grow upwards, using the already tangled stems for support.

2 If you prune back hard you will lose flowers for a season or two. Avoid this by shearing off only dead or badly placed shoots, especially those beneath healthy growth. You could use secateurs (pruners), but the job will be very tedious among the mass of tangled stems.

3 If it is done carefully, the plant will not look very different yet much of the redundant growth will have been removed. As you will almost certainly have severed stems that remain entangled, you may notice dead stems, which will need to be pulled out; sever the stems in several places if this helps to disentangle them.

Tackling overgrown climbers

Overgrown and unproductive climbers can be given a new lease of life by hard pruning. The method you use will depend on the type of climbers you are tackling.

Renovation pruning

If your climbers have got out of control or produce all their flowers out of sight at the top of the plants, you may need to take decisive action. The best time to carry out drastic pruning of climbers is during the dormant season, between autumn and spring. When there are no leaves it is easier to see what you are doing and make the cuts in the right place. Choose a mild day to make the task as pleasant as possible and arm yourself with a good pair of secateurs (pruners) and long-handled loppers. For stems over 3cm (1¼in) thick you will also need a special pruning saw.

Overgrown clematis

Clematis are often left unpruned for years so that the climber ends up as a mass of bare, non-flowering stems at the base with the few blooms produced way up on top. All clematis respond well to pruning back hard: cut back stems to within 1m (3ft) of the ground. Those that flower on new wood can be cut back even harder, to 30cm (12in). If your clematis flowers on old wood, you will not get any blooms for a year or two, but thereafter the climber will flower with renewed vigour.

Climbing and rambler roses

If they are neglected climbing roses slowly get bigger and bigger, forming large gnarled bare stems at the base with the flowers produced on growth higher up on the plant. Tackle an overgrown monster by removing one stem in three back to a newer shoot lower down or cut right back to the base if there is not one. Repeat over a three-year period to reinvigorate the plant completely.

Rambler roses by contrast throw up new shoots from the base, and these form impenetrable thickets of thorny growth if left to their own devices. In this case, thin out the tangle of stems by removing all but the newest shoots.

Honeysuckles

These often form a top-heavy mass of spindly shoots, and when they are grown on free-standing supports and fences they tend to catch the wind and rock the support. The best way to tackle an overgrown honeysuckle is to trim back all the thin growth on the top to reveal the main stems. These can then be pruned with secateurs (pruners). Reduce their number by removing awkwardly placed stems and the oldest ones

HOW TO PRUNE A SELF-CLINGING CLIMBER

1 Vigorous self-clinging climbers can reach great heights if planted against a tall wall. They may need pruning to keep shoots clear of windows and doors, or areas where they can cause damage such as blocking gutters or loosening roof tiles.

2 The actual pruning, best done in early spring, is very simple but you may need ladders to reach the offending stems. If necessary pull the shoots clear of the wall (this may require some force) so that you can use the secateurs (pruners) freely.

3 On this wall, a hard edge after the plant has been cut back is acceptable, but around windows you may prefer to cut the shoots by different amounts to avoid a clipped or straight-line appearance.

Evergreen plants such as this ivy 'Green Ripple' can be particularly difficult to prune as it is hard to see the stems under the leaves. When pruning is necessary, carry out the task methodically, working your way along the wall.

HOW TO RENOVATE A NEGLECTED CLIMBER

1 This neglected climbing rose has lost vigour and is flowering very poorly, and so needs renovative pruning.

2 Use loppers to cut back old growth that is too thick for secateurs (pruners).

3 Thick stems may need a pruning saw. Support the branch to prevent it tearing off bark from the main stem.

4 Use a sharp knife to pare off the rough edges of any large pruning wounds.

first. If all else fails, honeysuckles respond well to hard pruning, so if yours gets out of hand try cutting it back in winter to within 30cm (12in) of the base. It should regrow, although it may be a couple of years before it is flowering well again.

RENOVATING HONEYSUCKLE

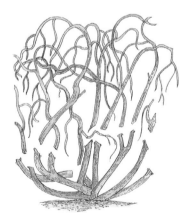

If you prune honeysuckle hard you will lose flowers for a season or two, but in the long term you will have fresh growth that you can retrain. This drastic treatment means that the support will look bare for a while, but new shoots should grow fairly rapidly in the first summer. Tie the new shoots in or train them to the support to give even and relatively untangled growth.

Hard pruning can sometimes restore all of the former glory of a rose, such as this 'Frühlingsgold', which is now showing a healthy crop of primrose-yellow flowers.

Gardening with flowers

Flowers provide the eye-catching highlights of each season. In spring, early bulbs produce a succession of colour until early summer, when exotic bulbs make their brief but triumphant entrance. Glorious annuals then make their mark, along with early-flowering perennials — shooting stars that transform the shape, colour and feel of the border.

As the summer marches on, the banks of summer bedding are dwarfed by the long-flowering, daisy-faced perennials, which, in turn, link up with the late summer and autumn perennial fireworks. Even after the early frosts a few flowers soldier on, supplemented by colourful autumn-flowering bulbs. Evergreen perennials combine with winter bedding and the subtle charm of dainty winter bulbs to complete the cycle.

Irises and primulas produce a stunning combination of fresh, bright colours to liven up an informal border in spring.

Buying bulbs

The plants grown from bulbs are superb for adding much-needed colour to spring borders, but there are other types, flowering at other times of the year, that are equally rewarding. It is important to choose bulbs suited to the conditions your garden has to offer.

Selecting bulbs

Bulbs can be bought from garden centres, from gardening websites on the Internet or by mail order from specialists. Most are sold as dry bulbs during the dormant season, either loose or in prepacks. A few select varieties are available as container-grown plants in spring.

Dry bulbs can deteriorate quickly in the warmth of a garden centre and so are best bought as soon as they arrive – check with your local branch to find out in advance when they are due to take delivery. In general, bulbs sold loose are more variable in quality than those sold in prepacks, but you have the opportunity to select the best and leave poorer

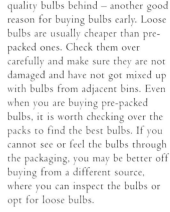

Bulbs is an umbrella term, referring to tubers and corms as well as true bulbs. A bulb's internal structure and external shape give vital clues to identifying them. True bulbs (such as the galtonia, shown top) have onion-like leaves within them, while corms (such as the gladiolus, bottom) have solid flesh and, usually, a regular outline like a bulb. Tubers (such as the anemone, centre) also have solid flesh within, but their outline and shape is often more lumpy and irregular.

quality bulbs behind – another good reason for buying bulbs early. Loose bulbs are usually cheaper than pre-packed ones. Check them over carefully and make sure they are not damaged and have not got mixed up with bulbs from adjacent bins. Even when you are buying pre-packed bulbs, it is worth checking over the packs to find the best bulbs. If you cannot see or feel the bulbs through the packaging, you may be better off buying from a different source, where you can inspect the bulbs or opt for loose bulbs.

What to look for

Bulbs should be firm to the touch, with the outer skin (called the tunic) as complete as possible. The skins should not be loose, cracked or showing signs of mould. Avoid bulbs that are soft, which indicates rot, or hard and mummified. Also reject bulbs that are covered in soil or shooting at the growing point or producing roots from the base. Before you make your final selection, press the base of each bulb to make sure it is firm – if it is soft it could indicate basal rot.

When buying daffodils, pick bulbs with only one or two "noses" (growing points), avoiding those with multiple noses because they are less likely to flower well in the first season.

Bulbs from the wild

Selling garden bulbs is big business, and each year unscrupulous dealers trade in bulbs that are taken from the wild – either stolen from native woodland or uprooted from countries around the world. Do not buy bulbs in bulk unless you are sure of the source.

A massed display of *Tulipa praestans* 'Fusilier' is very effective as each stem has up to six flowers.

Choosing the right bulb

Naturalizing in woodland	Normal borders
Allium	*Allium*
Anemone (some)	*Anemone* (some)
Chionodoxa	*Chionodoxa*
Crocus	*Colchicum*
Cyclamen	*Convallaria*
Eranthis	*Crocus*
Erythronium	*Cyclamen*
Fritillaria (some)	*Eranthis*
Galanthus	*Erythronium*
Leucojum	*Fritillaria*
Muscari	*Galanthus*
Narcissus	*Hyacinthus*
Scilla	*Iris*
Tulipa	*Leucojum*
	Muscari
	Narcissus
Dry borders	*Ornithogalum*
Amaryllis	*Oxalis*
Iris (bulbous)	*Puschkinia*
Cyclamen	*Scilla*
Gladiolus	*Trillium*
Nerine	*Tulipa*
Tigridia	

Muscari armeniacum (grape hyacinth) thrives in most places and multiplies freely. It is ideal for planting in bold drifts amongst shrubs or in woodland.

Which type?

Make sure you have a good idea of what you are looking for before you buy your bulbs and do not buy on impulse. Different species of bulbs like different conditions, and it is important to choose a suitable type for the position you have in mind. Also consider the colour, size and flowering time of the bulbs so that they fit in with your existing planting schemes. If you are combining several species of bulb, either choose types that flower at the same time for a dramatic splash of colour or combine forms that flower at slightly different times to provide a succession of colour throughout the season.

In the green

Some bulbs, notably snowdrops (*Galanthus*) and snowflakes (*Leucojum*), do not transplant very well as dormant bulbs and often do not survive drying out. Instead, buy them shortly after flowering has finished when they are still in leaf (known as "in the green"). Ask at your local garden centre if they supply these bulbs in the green and make sure you buy them as soon as they are available. Otherwise, you will have to go to a specialist supplier.

BULBS FROM SEED

A drift of bluebells makes a soft haze under the canopy of the trees. The display looks better massed, with many plants, so these bluebells have been allowed to self-seed freely. This is an economic way of raising a large number of plants.

Growing bulbs

Bulbs are among the easiest plants to grow and so are an ideal starting point for newcomers to gardening. They need little more than planting and watering to get going and require very little maintenance thereafter.

Planting

As a rule, bulbs should be planted as soon as they are bought. Autumn- and spring-flowering types produce new roots in autumn and should be planted in late summer or early autumn. The main exceptions are tulips, which are best planted in late autumn. Plant bulbs in well-prepared, weed-free soil. If it is poor incorporate a sprinkling of slow-release fertilizer, such as bonemeal.

The depth of planting and spacing depends on the size of bulb. As a rule, all bulbs should be planted in a hole that is three times as deep as the bulb. For example a 5cm (2in) deep daffodil bulb will need a 15cm (6in) deep hole so that the bulb is covered by 10cm (4in) of soil. Similarly, a 1cm (½in) deep crocus corm will need to be planted 3cm (1½in) deep. Small bulbs should be about 2.5–5cm (1–2in) apart and larger bulbs 8–10cm (3–4in) apart.

Creating a natural effect

To get an instant effect you will need to plant bulbs quite thickly – say 70–140 per square metre (7–14 per square foot), depending on the size of bulb. Some bulbs, such as daffodils, spread mainly by offshoots from the bulb so that they form larger and larger clumps. Others, such as crocuses and chionodoxa, will seed themselves, so that after four or five years the original display will be transformed with the new plants.

If you want to create a natural-looking planting scheme it is important to plant in irregular clumps.

HOW TO PLANT BULBS

1 Fork over the ground before planting and, if the plants are to be left undisturbed for some years, try to incorporate plenty of organic material, such as rotted garden compost or manure. Many bulbs like well-drained soil but nevertheless benefit from plenty of organic material, which will hold moisture and nutrients.

2 Avoid adding quick-acting fertilizers in the autumn. Controlled-release fertilizers that provide nutrients according to the soil temperature can be used, but they are best employed in spring. Instead, rake a slow-acting fertilizer, such as bonemeal, which contains mainly phosphate, into the surface, or apply it to the planting holes.

3 Where there is space and the plants will benefit from planting in an informal group or cluster, dig out a hole about three times the depth of the bulbs and wide enough to take the well-spaced bulbs.

4 Space the bulbs so that they look like a natural clump, using the spacing recommended on the packet as a guide. Wide spacing will allow for growth and multiplication, but if you intend to lift the bulbs after flowering, closer spacing will create a bold display.

5 Draw the soil back over the bulbs, being careful not to dislodge them in the process. Firm the soil with the back of the rake rather than treading it down, which may damage the bulbs and compact the soil.

6 So that you do not disturb the bulbs when you are weeding, mark their position with canes. Don't forget to include a label.

If you are planting several varieties together, do not mix them up, but keep them in roughly separate clumps for the best effect. The easiest way to get a natural distribution of bulbs is to toss them gently on to the ground and plant them where they land. Individual bulbs can be planted using a cylindrical bulb planter. Push the planter vertically into the ground and remove a core of soil that is deep enough for the bulb being planted. After positioning the bulb replace the core and firm down. Clumps of bulbs are best planted by digging a trench or hole with a spade and planting in this.

Planting bulbs the correct way up

Most bulbs have an obvious top and bottom and present no problem. Others, especially tubers, can lack an obvious growing point. If in doubt, plant them on their side – the shoot will grow upwards and the roots down.

Some bulbs that do have an obvious top are planted on their side because the base tends to rot in wet soil, though these are rare exceptions. *Fritillaria imperialis* is sometimes planted in this way. It is always worth planting vulnerable bulbs on a bed of grit or sand to encourage good drainage around the base and prevent them from rotting.

Bulb planner

Type of bulb	planting time	depth	spacing	flowering time
Allium	early autumn	5–8cm (2–3in)	15–30cm (6–12in)	late spring to early summer
Anemone	early autumn	5cm (2in)	10cm (4in)	late winter to mid-spring
Arum	midsummer	15cm (6in)	10cm (4in)	mid- to late spring
Begonia	spring	2.5cm (1in)	23–30cm (9–12in)	summer
Chionodoxa	early autumn	2.5–5cm (1–2in)	8cm (3in)	late winter to mid-spring
Colchicum	late spring	8cm (3in)	10–15cm (4–6in)	autumn
Crocus, spring	late summer	5–8cm (2–3in)	10cm (4in)	spring
Crocus, autumn	midsummer	5–8cm (2–3in)	10cm (4in)	autumn
Cyclamen	late summer	2.5cm (1in)	15cm (6in)	autumn to spring
Eranthis	late summer	2.5–5cm (1–2in)	10cm (4in)	late winter to mid-spring
Erythronium	late summer	5–8cm (2–3in)	10cm (4in)	mid- to late spring
Fritillaria	early autumn	5–8cm (2–3in)	15–45cm (6–18in)	spring
Galanthus	late summer	8–10cm (3–4in)	10cm (4in)	late winter to mid-spring
Gladiolus	mid-spring	8–10cm (3–4in)	10–15cm (4–6in)	midsummer
Hyacinthus	early autumn	10cm (4in)	20cm (8in)	spring
Iris reticulata	autumn	8–10cm (3–4in)	10cm (4in)	midwinter to early spring
Leucojum	late summer	8–10cm (3–4in)	10–20cm (4–8in)	mid- to late spring
Lilium	mid-autumn	10–15cm (4–6in)	15–45cm (6–18in)	late spring to late summer
Muscari	late summer	5–8cm (2–3in)	10cm (4in)	spring
Narcissus	late summer	5–12cm (2–5in)	10–20cm (4–8in)	spring
Nerine	spring	2.5cm (1in)	15cm (6in)	late summer to early autumn
Ornithogalum	mid-autumn	5–8cm (2–3in)	10–15cm (4–6in)	spring
Puschkinia	early autumn	5–8cm (2–3in)	8cm (3in)	spring
Scilla	late summer	5–8cm (2–3in)	5–10cm (2–4in)	spring
Sternbergia	midsummer	8cm (3in)	12cm (5in)	autumn
Tigridia	late spring	5–8cm (2–3in)	15cm (6in)	late summer
Tulipa	late autumn	8–15cm (3–6in)	10–20cm (4–8in)	spring

Aftercare of bulbs

Bulbs need very little routine aftercare, although deadheading, weeding and keeping the bulbs well fed and watered will help to make sure that they give good displays for years to come.

Deadheading

Most bulb displays benefit from regular deadheading to remove dead and dying flowers. Not only does this keep the display tidy, but it also stops the bulbs using up vital energy in producing unwanted seed. This is draining on their food reserves and can adversely affect their flowering performance the following season. Some bulbs, including alliums and bluebells, should be deadheaded to prevent them from self-seeding prolifically and becoming invasive.

Do not remove the foliage from bulbs until at least six weeks after flowering. This will allow the bulb to build up plenty of reserves for the following year's flowering display. Ideally, leave bulb foliage until it has turned brown.

Narcissus 'Tête-à-Tête' is a welcome sight in spring. Once flowering has finished, the leaves should not be cut back for at least six weeks to allow the bulbs a chance to build up reserves of nutrients ready for flowering the next year.

After removing the foliage from daffodil bulbs, use a hoe to break up the soil and fill any holes that would provide easy access for narcissus bulb flies.

Weed control

Growing bulbs and dormant, shallowly planted small bulbs are best weeded by hand. It is safe to weed around deeply planted bulbs with a hoe while they are dormant as long as you keep the blade near the surface.

Individual deep-rooted perennial weeds can be controlled with a wipe-on weedkiller containing glyphosate, which is applied directly to the leaves of the weed. If the border is heavily infested with perennial weeds, you would be better off lifting the bulbs when they are dormant and thoroughly digging over the border to remove all traces of the perennial weed roots before replanting.

Once you have achieved weed-free soil, many bulbs, including daffodils, tulips and lilies, benefit from a thick mulch of loose organic matter, such

HOW TO LIFT DAHLIA TUBERS

1 Dahlias are not hardy and should be lifted and overwintered in a frost-free place. Lift the tubers once frost has blackened the foliage. First, cut off the stems to about 15cm (6in) above the ground and remove stakes.

2 Use a garden fork to lift the clump of tubers, inserting it far enough away to avoid the risk of spearing the tubers. If possible, do this when the soil is fairly dry.

3 Carefully remove as much soil as possible before taking the tubers into a shed or greenhouse to dry off. This will be easier if the soil is not too wet.

as well-rotted manure or garden compost. This not only prevents further weeds from germinating, but it also helps retain soil moisture. The mulch will improve the nutritional value and structure of the soil as it is broken down by soil-borne creatures.

Feeding

Unless you are growing bulbs for a single season and then discarding them, all bulbs, apart from those naturalized in grass, will benefit from feeding. If you feed bulbs growing in a lawn you will encourage the grass to grow more vigorously, which may obscure the flowering display. On poor soils give bulbs a top-dressing of sulphate of potash two or three times during the growing season, otherwise a single application of a balanced, slow-release fertilizer, such as growmore is usually sufficient. Do not use high-nitrogen fertilizers because they encourage leafy growth at the expense of the flowering display.

Lilies reward care and attention with a sumptuous display. Deadhead the flowers to keep the bed looking its best and weed regularly to prevent unwanted plants from gaining toe-hold.

Winter care

Some bulbs, such as tuberous begonias, are frost tender and will perish if left outside in winter. Others, such as dahlias or gladioli, are well protected below the ground and will probably survive a mild winter provided the soil does not become too wet. Except where winters are mild and frosts do not penetrate more than a few centimetres (inches) into the soil, it is best to lift vulnerable bulbs and overwinter them in a cool, frost-proof place.

HOW TO STORE TUBERS

1 Stand the tubers upside down so that moisture drains easily from the hollow stems. Using a mesh support is a convenient way to allow them to dry off. Keep them in a dry, frost-free place.

2 After a few days the tubers should be dry enough to store. Remove surplus soil, trim off loose bits of old roots and shorten the stem to leave a short stump. Label each plant.

3 Pack the tubers in a well-insulated box with peat, vermiculite, wood shavings or crumpled newspaper placed between them. Store in a frost-free location. Check from time to time, and discard any that feel soft, which could be a sign of rot.

Buying annuals

The usual definition of an annual is a plant that grows and dies or is discarded in a year. Annuals can be raised from seed or bought as plants in a range of stages of development. The way you decide to buy them will depend on how many you need, the amount of time you have and how much you are prepared to spend.

Annuals in the garden

Widely available and cheap to buy, annuals offer a quick, easy and, above all, cheap way of adding instant colour to your garden. Annuals come in a wide range of colours from very bright to soft and subtle shades. They can be used almost anywhere in the garden from beds and borders to patio containers, hanging baskets and window boxes – they can even be used to decorate the vegetable plot.

Raising plants from seed

This is a cheap and easy way to raise a lot of plants. Hardy annuals can be sown directly in autumn but half-hardy annuals should not be planted outside until the threat of frost has passed. You may need propagating facilities and somewhere to grow the plants on. A few types of annual have to be sown in early spring to be in flower by early summer, but most can be sown in mid-spring. Seeds generally germinate at a temperature of 15–18°C (59–65°F), but some may need temperatures as high as 21°C (70°F) to germinate reliably. Quick-maturing annuals, such as alyssum and French marigold, can be sown as late as late spring and still produce a good display.

Choosing annuals

Traditionally, the best way to get annuals was to raise the plants yourself from seed. Although

HOW TO CHOOSE ANNUALS

1 Young plants are sometimes grown in small cells, known as plugs. These are cheaper than those in larger packs, but can become potbound. Plants left too long in the cells can be starved if the tangled mass of roots cannot find enough food. The plants should be potted on and allowed to grow for a while before being planted out.

2 When they are grown individually in larger cells, young plants have plenty of room to develop good root systems. Plants can stay in these larger packs longer and with less danger of becoming overcrowded.

3 Some of the best plants come in individual pots, but they are more expensive to buy because more work was required to raise them. The plants have more compost (soil mix) in which to grow and can be left in the pots longer than when in packs or plugs.

4 When choosing plants always check the root system. It should be evenly spread and not overcrowded (right). If the roots have wound themselves around the inside of the pot and are obviously overcrowded (left), you should reject the plant.

bedding plants were available in garden centres, the choice was very limited and the quality variable. In recent years, however, there has been a revolution in bedding plants, with many types being offered as seedlings, individual tiny plants and flowering plants in cellular packs or individual containers. The range being offered increases every year, and many are the most recent and

best varieties available. This is an ideal way of buying bedding without having to go to the trouble or risk of raising your own from seed, and if you want a range of different species it can be cost effective too. Some bedding plants, notably pelargoniums, are expensive to buy as seed, and it is quite tricky to raise plants early in the season, so buying a few ready-grown plants can make

Sowing times for annuals

Type	sowing time	minimum sowing temperature
Ageratum	mid-spring*	18°C (65°F)
Alyssum	late spring	15°C (59°F)
Antirrhinum	early spring*	10°C (50°F)
Begonia	early spring*	21°C (70°F)
Dianthus	mid-spring	18°C (65°F)
Gazania	early spring	15°C (59°F)
Impatiens	mid-spring*	21°C (70°F)
Lobelia	early spring*	15°C (59°F)
Nemesia	mid-spring	18°C (65°F)
Nicotiana	mid-spring*	18°C (65°F)
Pelargonium	early spring	21°C (70°F)
Petunia	mid-spring*	18°C (65°F)
Salvia	early spring	18°C (65°F)
Tagetes (African)	mid-spring	15°C (59°F)
Tagetes (French)	late spring	15°C (59°F)
Verbena	mid-spring	21°C (70°F)
Viola x wittrockiana	mid-spring	15°C (59°F)
Zinnia	late spring	18°C (65°F)

Key: * = sow on surface of compost (soil mix) because seeds need light to germinate.

Popular bedding plants, such as these marigolds, can be bought as seed, seedlings, plugs and flowering plants.

good economic sense. Buying ready-grown bedding plants is, however, an expensive way of buying a lot of the same type of bedding for something like a massed bedding scheme.

Tender summer bedding often appears in the garden centres before the last frost has occurred, so make sure that you have somewhere cool but frost-free to keep your plants until they can be safely planted out. Otherwise, wait before buying and let the garden centre take the risk.

Which way to buy annuals?

Whether you decide to grow annuals from seed or buy them as plants will probably depend on the amount of money and time you have, how big an area you intend to cover and the time of year you start.

Seed Good for unusual varieties and is a cheap way of growing lots of the same variety of plant.

Seedlings Overcomes the need to buy propagation equipment and is a cheap way of growing a few dozen of the same variety.

Plugs A cheap way to grow a few plants of the same variety. Easier than seedlings or raising from seed.

Cellular packs Plants are growing in their own cell, so good for plants such as *Impatiens* that resent root disturbance when planting.

Small pots Individual plants that are slightly larger and more expensive than those sold in plugs or cellular packs, but good for planting a single container or hanging basket.

Individual pots Mature plants, often in flower. They are expensive, but ideal for creating instant displays.

What to look for

Plants should be compact and, unless naturally coloured, should have healthy green leaves. Avoid any plants with unnaturally yellowing foliage – a sign of starvation – or a blue tinge to the outer leaves, which is a tell-tale sign that the plant has been allowed to get too cold. Don't buy seedlings (or plants) that are tall and straggly because they have been packed together too tightly for too long, and check the compost (soil mix) to make sure that it is moist but not waterlogged. Avoid plants that have any signs of pest and disease attack, such as aphids in the growing tips and under the leaves. Always make sure that plants you buy have been hardened off properly by the garden centre: ask if you are not sure.

The annuals should not be in flower unless they are sold in summer, in cellular packs or individual pots. Pinch off flowers and buds when you plant so that the new specimen establishes quickly.

Sowing annuals

Hardy, half-hardy and tender annuals are a cheap and easy way of adding colour to your garden. They are perfect for filling gaps and for making a cheerful display in a new garden before you have had a chance to draw up longer-term plans or before perennials and shrubs have filled their allotted space.

Types of annual

Hardy annuals can be sown directly into the soil in autumn and they will survive the winter unprotected ready to produce flowers in the late spring or early summer. Half-hardy annuals cannot tolerate frost, so they should either be grown in a greenhouse, hardened off and planted in late spring, or sown directly into the soil once there is no danger of frost.

Tender annuals must be raised in a greenhouse in order for them to flower early in the year.

Sowing direct

Some people are put off growing annuals because they have sown them *in situ* outside and the seeds have failed to come up or the results have been sparse and patchy. The secret to success is good soil preparation and careful sowing.

The soil does not need to be very fertile, because many annuals can tolerate fairly impoverished conditions. A week or two before sowing, cultivate the soil and remove any weeds, stones and other debris. Rake the soil level and remove any lumps. Cover with clear plastic to warm the soil and encourage weed

seeds to germinate. Hoe lightly just before sowing to kill off the new flush of weed seedlings.

The easiest way to sow directly is to scatter the seed in rows. For a more natural effect, combining several varieties, mark out the seed-bed into irregular blocks. A series of arcs drawn with sand is usually recommended, but any shape will do.

Press a cane into the soil to create drills at the correct spacing (see the seed packet for details), varying the direction of the drills in each block. Sow the seed thinly, at the recommended spacing, and lightly cover with soil or compost (soil mix). Weed as necessary, and when the seedlings are large enough to handle, remove the weakest to leave the plants at the correct spacing.

SOWING HARDY ANNUALS

1 It pays to prepare the ground thoroughly by clearing it of weeds and raking the surface to a fine, crumbly tilth.

2 If you are growing just for cutting, sow in rows in a spare piece of ground, but if you want to make a bright border of hardy annuals, "draw" your design on the ground with sand or grit.

3 Use the corner of a hoe or rake to draw shallow drills, but change the direction of the drills from one block to the next to avoid a regimented appearance. Check the packet for spacing between rows.

4 Scatter the seeds as evenly as possible in each marked out area. If the weather is dry, run water into the bottom of each drill first and allow it to soak in.

5 Write and insert a label, then cover the seeds by raking the soil back over the drills. Try not to disturb the seeds unnecessarily.

6 Water the area thoroughly, particularly if the soil is dry and rain is not forecast. Continue to water in dry weather until the seedlings have emerged.

If time is short or if you have a large area to cover, you can broadcast sow. In this case measure out sufficient seed for each sector and place it in the palm of your hand. Then carefully scatter it over the area as evenly as possible by tapping your hand gently. Use a soil rake to mix the seed into the surface soil. Weed and thin out overcrowded plants as before.

Weeding around annuals that were broadcast sown can be a nightmare because it is so difficult to tell the weed seedlings from the flowers. Sowing in rows does overcome this problem to some extent, especially if you use sterilized potting compost to cover the drills after sowing. The lines of flower seedlings stand out clearly, making identifying weeds less of a problem.

Using a greenhouse

Heavy soils, wet weather and prolonged cold spells can take their toll, even with hardy annuals. You can still win the day if you have a greenhouse or cold frame, by raising hardy annuals from seed in trays (flats) – just as you would tender annuals and vegetables.

Sowing in trays is far less wasteful of seed than sowing directly outside, and the results are more predictable. Sowing in trays also means that you can place the plants exactly where they are needed, producing better displays. If space under glass is at a premium, you can still have the best of both worlds by sowing most of the seeds directly into the bed and, say, 10 per cent in trays to use for filling gaps and in places where direct sowing is impracticable.

It is important that any annual raised in the greenhouse is hardened off thoroughly before planting outside in its final position.

HOW TO SOW OR PLANT A MIXED BORDER

1 Remove any old plants and weeds from the area. Dig over the soil, taking care that you do not disturb the roots of nearby plants, and add well-rotted organic material if the soil has not been rejuvenated recently.

2 Work well-rotted compost into the soil and break the soil down to a fine tilth. If the soil is impoverished, add a base dressing of slow-release general fertilizer and rake into the surface before sowing or planting.

3 If sowing, carefully level the soil with a rake before scattering the seed evenly over the ground. Rake in and water using a watering can fitted with a fine rose. When the seedlings appear, thin them to the desired distance apart.

4 Bedding plants can be used instead of seeds. Arrange the plants in their positions before you start to plant as changes are easy to make at this stage. Try to visualize the final height and spread, and do not be tempted to plant them too close together.

The intricate flowers of *Nigella damascena* (love-in-a-mist) make it a popular choice for the border. This is a hardy annual, so sow seeds directly in the autumn.

Growing annuals

Vigorous but delicate young bedding plants need to be planted carefully at exactly the right time, otherwise they will receive a check in growth and may never recover.

Planting

Prepare the ground by digging over the soil and removing weeds and other debris. Incorporate well-rotted organic matter, such as manure or garden compost, if the soil is poor. Make sure all the plants have been hardened off well beforehand and keep tender bedding in a frost-free place until it is safe to plant outside.

The stems of young bedding plants are delicate and easily damaged, so it's advisable to handle them by their rootball or leaves rather than holding them by the stems. For this reason the best way to remove the plant from its container is by turning it upside down in the pot with the plant between two fingers and tapping the pot or pushing on its base to dislodge the

HOW TO PLANT EDGING

1 Prepare the soil, removing any weeds and adding some well-rotted compost if the soil is impoverished. Break the soil down to a fairly fine consistency. Set up a garden line at an even distance from the actual edge of the border. Alternatively, for a curved border, use a standard measure, such as a length of stick, between the edge and each plant.

2 Plant the edging plants along the line at the correct spacing (depending on the variety), checking the distance between each one with a measuring stick. Firm in each plant and water. For an informal planting, you can use a mixture of plants in uneven rows so that the edging merges into the other plants in the border.

rootball. Plant at the same depth as the plant was in the pot and firm the soil lightly around the rootball. Water well after planting.

Late frosts

Protect new bedding from damaging late frosts by covering plants with a double layer of horticultural fleece or sheets of newspaper when late frosts are forecast. If unprotected tender plants are touched by frost, minimize the damage by covering them in the morning, before the temperature rises, to slow down the thaw. It is the rapid thaw that causes most damage to plant tissues.

Hardening off bedding plants

About two weeks before you want to set out your bedding plants, they will need to be weaned off the cosy temperatures inside the greenhouse to the harsher environment outdoors. This is known as hardening off. It simply means that you get plants slowly accustomed to conditions outside over a period of time. Normally, this is done with a cold frame. Start off by opening the top slightly on mild days and closing it at night, then increase this ventilation each day until the top is removed altogether. If you don't have a cold frame you can use shelves near vents in the roof of a greenhouse to harden plants off or construct a makeshift cold frame out of a large cardboard box cloche or layers of horticultural fleece in a sheltered part of the garden.

Puddling in

If your soil is dry or you are planting during a warm spell in summer, use a special technique called puddling in. Water the plants well in their pots as usual. Prepare the planting hole and fill it right up with water. When the water has had a chance to soak away, position the plant and replace the soil around the roots. Water thoroughly after planting and keep well watered until established.

An informal edging of *Chrysanthemum tenuiloba* 'Golden Fleck' sprawls out over a path.

Bedding planner

Bedding type	planting distance
Ageratum	20cm (8in)
Alyssum	15cm (6in)
Antirrhinum	23cm (9in)
Begonia	15cm (6in)
Dianthus	20cm (8in)
Gazania	20cm (8in)
Impatiens	20cm (8in)
Lobelia	15cm (6in)
Nemesia	20cm (8in)
Nicotiana	30cm (12in)
Pelargonium	30cm (12in)
Petunia	25cm (10in)
Salvia	20cm (8in)
Tagetes (African)	20cm (8in)
Tagetes (French)	20cm (8in)
Verbena	25cm (10in)
Viola x wittrockiana	20cm (8in)
Zinnia	25cm (10in)

HOW TO PLANT ANNUAL CELLULAR PLANTS

1 Several hours before planting out, or the evening before, water the tray of plants and leave them to stand so excess water drains away. The plants are less likely to be stressed by the move if they are growing well.

2 Remove a plant from the pack by pressing on the bottom. In strips, where the plants are not segregated, remove the lot from the pack and carefully remove one, trying not to tear off too many of its neighbour's roots.

3 Using a small trowel, dig a planting hole that is wider and slightly deeper than the plant's rootball.

4 Adjust the depth of the planting hole so that the top of the rootball is level with the surrounding soil.

5 Fill in the hole around the plant with soil and gently firm down with your hands.

6 Water the plant with a watering can fitted with a fine rose. Keep well watered thereafter until the plant is well established.

Aftercare of annuals

Once they are established and growing well most annuals will look after themselves, but to get better and longer-lasting displays you need to pamper them a little.

Watering and feeding

Keep an eye on annuals because they will be among the first plants to indicate if they are running short of water or nutrients. Even before planting out they may show signs of starvation: poor growth and yellowing lower leaves. While still in their containers water them with a balanced liquid feed.

Once established in the ground, most bedding won't need regular feeding, but to get the best flowering displays apply a high-potash feed every month while they are actively growing. It is important not to let annual bedding suffer from drought. If they are allowed to wilt some, such as lobelia, are reluctant to recover, while others, including verbena, will be more susceptible to diseases such as powdery mildew.

For sheer architectural grandeur there is little to beat the giant spires of *Verbascum* (mullein), which tower 2.1m (7ft) or more above the border.

PINCHING OUT

If left to their own devices, many annuals will grow up as a single stem. In a bedding scheme this would result in a forest of tall spindly spikes rather than a desirable carpet of foliage and flowers. To avoid this effect, pinch out the growing tip of each main spike. The stem will produce sideshoots and the plant will become completely bushy and much more attractive. Cut through the stem with a sharp knife just above a leaf joint.

FEEDING

An application of high-potash fertilizer during the growing season will help promote better flowering. If using granular feed, take care not to get any on the leaves. Apply the fertilizer at the manufacturer's recommended dosage, as given on the package.

SUPPORTING

In exposed gardens taller annuals may need supporting. Use sticks pushed into the ground around the clump. Bend the sticks over and weave or tie their tops together to create a network through which the stems will grow. Alternatively, use special plant supports.

General care

Some annuals, such as antirrhinums, tend to produce a single main stem that will get taller through the summer. You can encourage bushier growth by pinching out the growing tip after planting. If necessary, repeat the process a couple of weeks later by pinching out the tips of the sideshoots that are produced.

Taller annuals may also benefit from staking, especially in exposed gardens or borders. Traditionally, twiggy sticks have been used, pushed into the ground around young plants with the tops woven together to form a firm support. Alternatively, use any of the plant supports that you would for perennials.

Pests and diseases

Slugs and snails have a particular liking for some bedding plants. Put down beer traps or patrol the garden after dark with a torch (flashlight) when these pests are most active and collect and dispose of any you see. Protect new plants with slug-proof barriers, such as cut-down large

TIDYING UP

Some edging plants spread out over the grass, possibly killing it or creating bald patches, as this *Limnanthes douglasii* (poached-egg plant) has done. If the plant has finished flowering, it can be removed completely. Otherwise, just cut back the part that is encroaching on the grass. If cascading over a path, there may be no problem, although it could still cause people to stumble.

plastic drinks bottles, or surround plants with a layer of grit or broken eggshells, which slugs and snails find uncomfortable to cross. If all else fails, scatter slug pellets sparingly around susceptible plants.

Mammals and birds can also be a problem in some areas: use suitable barriers and netting to protect plants if these are pests in your garden.

Deadheading bedding plants

A few plants need to be deadheaded regularly to keep flowering well. If left, the plants will produce seeds at the expense of new flowers, and some, such as sweet peas (*Lathyrus odoratus*), will stop flowering altogether. Large-flowered bedding plants, such as pelargoniums, are also worth deadheading as a matter of routine. Many types of bedding have too many tiny flowers to make deadheading worthwhile, but a few, such as pansies, will flower better if you cut back leggy stems with scissors. Ageratum, calendula, dianthus, erigerons, marigolds, mesembryanthemums, mimulus, osteospermum, phlox and poppies are also worth deadheading.

If you have masses of soft-stemmed bedding, such as begonias and impatiens, you could try speeding up the process by deadheading with a nylon-line trimmer, but this is a tricky procedure to get right without damaging or destroying the plants. After deadheading clear up the discarded material and compost.

WEEDING

Where plants are close together, the best way to remove weeds is either to pull them out by hand or to dig them out using a hand fork. Perennial weeds must be dug out whole and not simply chopped off or they will soon resprout. Where there is more room, hoes can be used in a border, but take care to avoid the delicate plants. In hot weather hoed-up weeds can be left to shrivel, but it looks neater if they are removed to the compost heap.

MULCHING

It is a good idea to apply or renew a mulch after weeding. As well as helping to prevent weeds from reappearing, this will also preserve moisture. Composted bark, chipped bark or gravel will set the plants off well. You could also consider using garden compost or leaf mould as a mulch. Other mulches such as black polythene, grass clippings and straw work well but look unattractive.

DEADHEADING

Regular deadheading helps to ensure a continuing supply of new flowers. If any of the flowers are allowed to run to seed, vital energy that would otherwise be channelled into producing new blooms is used up. Removing dead flowers and any developing seedheads helps to conserve this energy.

Buying perennials

Spring is the best time to buy perennial plants. Garden centres, specialist nurseries and gardening websites offer the greatest range of varieties at this time of year, and the plants will also be coming into growth and be ready to plant.

Evergreen perennials

Ajuga	Helleborus
Artemisia	Heuchera
Bergenia	Kniphofia
Carex	Lamium
Epimedium	Pulmonaria
Euphorbia	Sempervivum
Festuca	Stachys

Winter-flowering perennials

Anemone nemorosa (wood anemone)
Eranthis hyemalis (winter aconite)
Euphorbia rigida
Helleborus niger (Christmas rose);
    H. orientalis (Lenten rose);
    H. purpurascens
Iris unguicularis (Algerian iris)
Primula vulgaris (primrose)
Pulmonaria rubra (lungwort)
Viola odorata (sweet violet)

Choosing perennials

Perennials are a large and varied group and there are types to suit every garden situation, regardless of soil type or whether the garden is in sun or shade. Most perennials are herbaceous, which means they die back to ground level during the winter months and then produce new growth each spring from dormant underground roots.

A few perennials are evergreen, however, keeping their leaves throughout the winter. Some even flower in the winter, so it may be worth considering planting a winter garden to enjoy in the colder months of the year. Some shade-tolerant perennials can be grown beneath a deciduous tree or shrub, so that they are in full view when at their best, but hidden from sight the rest of the year.

The wide choice of perennials can be bewildering for the beginner so it is a good idea to consider exactly what you want from each plant from the start. That way you can drastically reduce the number of options available to make the selection a more manageable task.

Another tip is to start by visiting your local garden centre, which will stock only a limited range of plants, all of which should be suitable for growing in your area.

Spring in the cottage garden heralds the appearance of ever-popular perennials such as primulas and columbines.

Buying pot plants

It is a good idea to choose perennials sold in 9cm (3½in) pots because they will establish more quickly than larger plants and cost you a lot less. The exception to this rule is if you want a large number of the same variety, for ground cover, for example. In this case, a bigger plant that is well established in its pot is worth buying because it can be divided into many smaller sections before planting.

It is also worth buying a few perennials, such as peonies and Japanese anemones, in large pots because they tend to sulk if they get potbound in tiny containers. Perennials in larger pots are also worth opting for if you are buying later in the season, because plants in smaller containers will have suffered more from irregular watering.

What to look for

Choosing the healthiest plants you can will ensure your garden display looks its best. The points to consider change throughout the year.
Early spring If you buy plants early in the season, before new growth

Planting perennials in the right combination can make for a truly spectacular summer display. Here, *Tanacetum parthenium* has been planted with *Galega* x *hartlandii* 'Alba' to create a bright white border, softened with the yellow centres of the tanacetum flowers and green foliage.

starts, make sure the perennials have recently been delivered from the nursery and are not left-over stock from the previous season. Weeds, faded labels and scruffy pots are all tell-tale signs of older plants.

Late spring Once new growth starts, choose plants that have fresh, healthy-looking, new shoots and foliage with no signs of pests or diseases. Make sure the plants are well established in their pots and avoid those with loose compost (soil mix) because they probably have been only recently potted up and are not ready to be planted out. Avoid plants with lots of bright green leaves because they will have been forced into growth and need hardening off before planting.
Summer and autumn Later in the season, choose plants with strong, even growth that look as if they have been well cared for. Avoid those plants with weeds, straggly foliage and lots of roots growing out of the base of the pot. The foliage of most perennials naturally turns yellow in autumn, so don't let this put you off at this time of year.

BUYING POT PLANTS

Most perennials are now bought in pots. You should find a reasonable range in your local garden centre suitable for growing in your area. Before you buy, always check that the plant is healthy and free from pests or disease, and make sure that the surface of the soil is free of liverwort.

HARDENING OFF

Make sure that perennials have been hardened off properly before you plant. If not, place them in a cold frame for a week or two. Close the top in the evening and on cold days, otherwise ventilate freely. Be aware of the weather, and if frost threatens, cover the frame with insulation material.

Growing perennials

Perennials should be considered permanent residents of the garden and so soil improvement should be carried out before planting. If you are planting a new bed, dig the area thoroughly and remove all weeds and other debris, including the roots of perennial weeds. Improve the soil by incorporating plenty of well-rotted organic matter, such as farmyard manure or garden compost. Also add a base dressing of a slow-release fertilizer, such as bonemeal.

Planting

Nearly all perennials are now sold as container-grown specimens, which means that they can be planted out at any time of the year as long as the ground is not frozen or waterlogged. However, they will establish a lot more quickly if they are planted either in spring or autumn. Summer planting can be hard work, because new additions will need regular watering during dry spells.

Before removing the plants from their pots place them on the bed and adjust the arrangement until you are satisfied with the result. Larger specimens can be used individually, but smaller perennials and ground cover plants are best grouped in odd numbers of threes or fives if you want to achieve a natural-looking scheme. Also bear in mind that herbaceous perennials die back in winter, so you might want to include a proportion of evergreen plants or evergreen trees and shrubs to provide structure and interest throughout the coldest months.

Water the perennials thoroughly while they are still in their containers and leave to drain. When you have decided on the positions of the plants, dig planting holes. Starting with the central perennials, plant them at the same depth as they are

HOW TO PLANT PERENNIALS

1 Always prepare the soil first. Dig it deeply, remove weeds, and incorporate a fertilizer and well-rotted garden compost if the soil is impoverished. Most perennials are sold in pots, so space them out according to your plan. Change positions if the associations don't look right.

2 Water thoroughly about half an hour before knocking the plant from its pot, then dig a planting hole with a trowel. If the roots are wound tightly around the rootball, carefully tease out a few of them first. Work methodically from the back of the border or from one end.

3 Carefully firm the soil around the roots to remove any large pockets of air.

4 Always water thoroughly after planting and keep plants well watered in dry weather for the first few months.

in their pots. Firm the soil around them, not too heavily, and water well. Finally, apply a mulch, 5–8cm (2–3in) deep, of loose organic material, taking care not to pile it up against the plant stems.

Raising perennials from seed

Many perennials are also easy to grow from seed. This is much cheaper than buying container-grown plants and many perennials grown this way will flower in their first year, while nearly all will be in bloom by their second summer. It is particularly well worth raising plants from seed if you want a lot of one variety such as ground cover plants, or are planting a new garden from scratch.

Seed can be sown in several ways: outside in a well-prepared seedbed; in a cold frame between early spring

Good perennials to raise from seed

Achillea	*Helenium*
Aquilegia	*Lobelia*
Coreopsis	*Lupinus*
Gaillardia	*Polemonium*
Geum	*Viola*

and midsummer; or in pots of fresh compost (soil mix) as you would sow bedding plants and vegetables. When the seedlings are large enough to handle, prick them out into 8cm (3in) pots. As soon as the young plants are well established they can be planted out into their final flowering positions.

Lupins make a good border plant, and their attractive flowers also have a distinctive, peppery scent. If you want a massed planting of lupins it may be worth raising them from seed.

HOW TO SOW SEED IN OPEN GROUND

1 Prepare the soil in the bed thoroughly, carefully removing all weeds and the roots of perennial weeds and breaking the soil down into a fine tilth with a rake.

2 Draw out a shallow drill with a corner of a hoe. It should be about 1cm (½in) deep. Keep the drill straight by using a garden line as a guide.

3 If the soil is dry, water the drill with a watering can and wait until the water has soaked in before sowing.

4 It is essential to mark the ends of the row, to help you identify the seedling flowers when weeding and hoeing later on.

5 Sow the seed thinly along the drill. Larger seed can be "station sown" at intervals.

6 Gently rake the soil back into the drill, covering over the seed. In dry weather water regularly and do not allow the soil to dry out.

Aftercare of perennials

Maintaining beds and borders is part of the enjoyment of gardening, and gives you a chance to examine the perennials thoroughly, to check on their general health and well-being and to admire their beauty at close quarters.

Feeding

Once they are established, perennials don't require regular feeding unless they are growing on poor soil or are becoming congested. Apply an annual feed of balanced fertilizer in the spring. Scatter 70g per square metre (2oz per square yard) around the plants, taking care not to get any fertilizer on their foliage. Over-crowded perennials are best lifted and divided in either spring or autumn to reinvigorate them.

Staking

It is worth staking taller-growing perennials or types with large blooms that are prone to flopping in windy conditions or heavy rain. Perennials grown in exposed gardens or plants that are crammed together may also benefit from some form of support.

Perennials that produce just one or two tall stems are best staked individually with a bamboo cane and string. Clump-forming perennials are easier to support with special interlocking structures, which are available from most garden retail outlets. If you are on a tight budget you can make your own support from short pieces of old bamboo cane linked together with string. Alternatively, use twiggy sticks pruned from beech or another well-branched deciduous woody plant during the dormant season.

Pests and diseases

If you choose good varieties, most plants do not suffer from pests and diseases unless they are under stress – during a drought, for example. A few types, however, including hostas and delphiniums, are prone to slug damage when they are first planted and each year as the new shoots emerge. Try to prevent damage by reducing pest numbers, and use barriers of sharp grit and roughly crushed eggshells that these pests don't like to cross. If your plants are

still suffering from damage, scatter slug pellets around susceptible plants early in the season before any new shoots emerge or get some slug-destroying nematodes from a biological control supplier.

Deadheading

Many repeat-flowering perennials can be persuaded to produce bigger and longer-lasting displays by regular deadheading. For most perennials, simply nip the fading flowers off just above the first leaf down the stem to encourage a second flush of blooms. For perennials such as delphiniums and hollyhocks, which throw up flower spikes, cut back to the first sideshoot lower down on

HOW TO STAKE PERENNIALS

Proprietary hoops with adjustable legs can be placed over a clump-forming perennial. The new shoots grow through the grid, gaining support from the frame and eventually hiding it.

Tall flowering stems can be staked individually by tying them to a cane that is shorter than the eventual height of the plant and hidden from sight behind the stem.

Wire netting can be used vertically, creating cylinders, held firmly in place with posts. The plant grows up through the centre, with the leaves coming through and covering the sides.

Perennials that are worth deadheading

Aconitum	Erigeron
Alcea	Gaillardia
Anchusa	Geranium
Centaurea	Leucanthemum
Chrysanthemum	Lupinus
Delphinium	Penstemon
Digitalis	Scabiosa

CLEARING AWAY SUMMER BEDDING

Old bedding plants are ideal for the compost heap. Being non-woody, they rot down easily, making excellent compost.

TOP-DRESSING PERENNIALS

In autumn apply a mulch of garden compost around the crowns of your perennials. This will help to conserve moisture.

the stem when the last bloom on the original flower spike starts to fade. These sideshoots will develop to flower during late summer. Some early-flowering perennials, notably hardy geraniums, look untidy by midsummer and so are worth cutting back to ground level with shears. If watered and given a feed, they will produce an attractive mound of new leaves and perhaps even a further flush of flowers later in the season.

Cutting back

At the end of the season, most perennials start to look tatty as the foliage begins to die back. In early autumn cut back the foliage to near ground level with shears or secateurs (pruners) for thicker stems and consign them to the compost heap. Shred or chop up woody stems before adding to the compost heap to speed the decomposition process.

The crowns of borderline hardy species should be covered with an insulating layer of leaves held in place with fine netting or a 15cm (6in) thick layer of bark chippings.

The insulating layer should be removed in spring after the worst of the cold weather is past and before new growth starts.

A few perennials, including agapanthus, chrysanthemums, red-hot pokers, schizostylis and sedums, are worth leaving intact over the winter months because they have attractive seedheads. These can be particularly eye-catching on a sunny morning after a hoarfrost.

Hostas are sometimes subject to viruses, usually apparent as a yellowing in blotches on the leaf surface. Dig up and burn any affected plant to prevent the spread of the virus.

Patios and containers

Tubs, baskets and other containers can be filled with annuals and short-lived perennials to brighten up your patio. Planted with perennials, climbers, shrubs and even trees they provide a long-term structure in an otherwise empty part of the garden.

Anything that can hold soil and has drainage holes can be used for planting. Pots are the most popular option, but hanging baskets, troughs, window boxes, wall-mangers and urns can look equally attractive, and provide a splash of colour at eye-level.

Containers are made in a range of materials. Terracotta has a natural tone and fits with almost any garden design or planting scheme. Plastic pots are cheap and lightweight but may not be sufficiently stable for tall plants. Wood and stone have a natural appeal and are suitable for almost any setting, but metal or fibreglass containers may be better options for contemporary designs.

This garden makes the most of a small space with the clever use of containers. They make the patio an inviting area to step into.

Planting window boxes and baskets

Window boxes, troughs and hanging baskets filled with annual bedding plants are an ideal way of adding colour and interest to all parts of the garden in summer. They can also be used to brighten up the dull, dark days of winter by planting them with evergreens and winter-flowering perennials.

Choosing a hanging basket

When you are choosing a basket, opt for the biggest you can find – ideally 40cm (16in) – because this holds twice as much compost (soil mix) as the most popular size – 30cm

(12in). It will also weigh twice as much, so make sure you buy suitable brackets and have a system of watering that doesn't involve lifting the hanging basket down each time.

There are basically two types of hanging basket: open-mesh wire baskets and solid-sided plastic baskets. The open-mesh style, which includes wrought iron types, is the most common but in many ways the most difficult to master. The wire mesh is plastic coated to prevent corrosion, and the large holes make planting the sides easy. However, they will dry out more quickly than solid-sided baskets,

HOW TO PLANT A HANGING BASKET WITH ANNUALS

1 Stand the basket on a large pot or bucket to make it easier to work. Carefully place the liner in position so that it fills the basket.

2 Half fill the liner with compost (soil mix), then mix in some water-retaining granules to help prevent the basket drying out. Add some slow-release fertilizer; this will overcome the need to feed throughout the summer.

3 Cut holes 4cm (1½in) across in the side of the liner. Shake some earth off the rootball of one of the plants and wrap it in a strip of plastic. Poke it through the hole, remove the plastic and spread out the roots. Add more compost containing water-retaining granules and slow-release fertilizer.

4 Plant up the rest of the basket, packing the plants much more tightly together than you would in the open ground. Smooth out the surface of the compost, removing any excess or adding a little more as necessary. Water, then keep the basket indoors until all danger of frost has passed.

although this can be overcome by using a waterproof liner. Solid-sided plastic baskets cannot be planted at the sides, so the display is less appealing, but they need watering less often, especially if there is a built-in water reservoir.

Types of liners

Open-mesh baskets need to be lined before they can be planted to stop the compost (soil mix) falling out. Traditionally, a 5cm (2in) thick layer of sphagnum moss was used, but this is expensive, and many gardeners have turned to alternatives on environmental grounds. This has led to the appearance of manufactured liners in a variety of materials, including recycled wool and cotton, coconut fibre and foam.

Window boxes

The type of window box you choose should fit comfortably with the style of your house. There is a wide range of materials and styles to choose from: stone and terracotta look attractive as they age but they are fairly heavy. Plastic, wood and galvanized tin window boxes are all lighter options.

HOW TO PLANT A WINDOW BOX WITH ANNUALS

1 Assemble all the items you will need. If the window box is light, assemble it on the ground. If it is heavy, make it up in position, especially if it is to be fixed high up.

2 Place irregularly shaped stones over the drainage holes to prevent the compost (soil mix) falling through.

3 Partially fill the window box with compost containing water-retaining granules. These granules will help retain moisture so that the planted window box will not require watering so frequently.

4 Plant the flowers to the same depths as they were in their pots or trays. For instant impact, postion plants closer together that you would in open ground.

5 Regular feeding is important: the nutrients in the compost will quickly get used up. Add a liquid feed to the water every week or push special slow-release fertilizer tablets into the compost at planting time.

6 Water thoroughly. The plants will soon spread out to fill the window box. If the box has been planted away from its final position, it can be left for a while until the plants are all in full flower before being put on display.

Trouble-free plants for hanging baskets

Flowers	Foliage
Begonia	Cineraria
Bidens	Glechoma
Brachycome	Hedera
Felicia	Helichrysum
French marigold	petiolare
Gazania	Lysimachia
Heliotrope	Plectranthus
Impatiens	
Osteospermum	**Trailers**
Pelargonium	Anagallis
Petunia	Convolvulus
Portulaca	sabiatus
Scaevola	Diascia
Verbena	Fuchsia
Viola	Lotus
	Nasturtium
	Pelargonium
	Sanvitalia
	Sutera

Pale orange pansies make this an eye-catching summer hanging basket.

Planting tubs

The beauty of tubs and other large containers is that with the minimum of effort they will transform a patio, bringing the bright colours of the garden closer to the home. They can be filled with annuals or bulbs for a seasonal display, or planted with small ornamental trees or shrubs.

Which compost?

It is important to choose a good-quality compost (soil mix) if you want reliable results in your container. There are three main types: traditional loam-based composts and peat-based mediums or those based on a peat-substitute.

Loam-based composts These are made to a special formula and contain a mixture of soil, peat and sand. They are heavy and variable in quality, but maintain their structure and nutrients well over a long period of time. Loam-based composts are ideal for long-term schemes and permanent plants in containers.

Peat-based composts Lighter and easier to use than loam-based composts, these composts are a good choice for planting bedding.

Peat-substitute composts These new composts are based on composted bark, coir or other organic waste material. Use in the same way as peat-based composts.

Planting containers

Although the traditional technique of adding broken pots to the bottom of the tub is not necessary, if you are planting top-heavy trees or shrubs, a heavy layer of stones will improve stability. If you are planting shallow-rooted bedding plants in a deep container you can save compost and reduce the weight of the container by filling the bottom third with polystyrene (styrofoam) chips. In small containers, which are more prone to drying out, consider using a special hanging basket compost, which contains a wetting agent to help the water soak in. Some plants, such as camellias and azaleas require acid conditions and so are best planted using a specially formulated ericaceous compost (acid soil mix).

HOW TO PLANT IN A CONTAINER

1 Filled tubs and pots can be heavy to move, so plant them where they are to be displayed. Cover the drainage holes with a layer of broken pots, gravel or chipped bark.

2 Use a loam-based compost (soil mix) for permanent plants such as trees and shrubs. A peat-based or peat-substitute compost is a better bet for annuals.

3 Choose a tall or bold plant for the centre, such as *Cordyline australis* or a fuchsia, or one with large flowers such as the osteospermum that has been used here.

4 Fill in with bushier plants and trailing types around the edge. Choose bright flowers if the centrepiece is a foliage plant, but place the emphasis on foliage effect if the focal point is a flowering plant.

5 Water thoroughly. If much of the surface of the compost is visible, you can add a decorative mulch such as chipped bark, which will help conserve moisture; with a dense planting, there is no need.

HOW TO PLANT A PERMANENT CONTAINER FOR WINTER AND SPRING INTEREST

1 When creating a winter interest display, choose attractive evergreen plants with contrasting habit and form. Here, a dwarf conifer and small-leaved variegated ivies have been used with spring flowering bulbs to provide a colour boost in the spring.

2 Position the bulbs on the surface first so that they are evenly spaced around the container. Small bulbs that multiply freely, such as *Muscari armeniacum*, scillas, chionodoxas and *Anemone blanda*, can usually be depended upon to improve year by year.

3 When you are happy with the position of the bulbs, plant them with a trowel, being careful to disturb the roots of the conifer and ivies as little as possible. Water the container thoroughly and mulch if necessary.

Planting large specimens

A useful technique that will save a lot of effort when planting a semi-mature specimen in a large pot is to partly fill the container with compost. Remove the pot from the specimen plant and position the pot where you want the plant to go, making sure it is at the right level. Then pack compost around the empty pot and use it as a mould for the plant's rootball. Remove the empty pot, and simply slip the plant into position. Lightly firm the soil to remove air pockets. Top up the container with compost if necessary and water thoroughly. After watering cover the surface with large pebbles for an attractive ornamental effect. The extra weight will also help keep the specimen in position.

Flowers for containers

Ageratum (floss flower)
Antirrhinum (snapdragon)
Begonia
Bidens
Brachyscome
Cerinthe
Chrysanthemum
Dianthus (carnations, pinks)
Echium
Felicia
Laurentia (syn. *Isotoma*)
Lobelia
Myosotis (forget-me-not)
Nicotiana (tobacco plant)
Schizanthus (butterfly flower; poor
    man's orchid)
Senecio
Tagetes (marigold)
Tropaeolum (nasturtium)
Viola x *wittrockiana* (pansy)

Lathyrus odoratus (sweet pea), one of the best-loved of all fragrant annuals, can be used as trailing plants, instead of growing them to climb up an obelisk or frame.

Planting perennials in containers

Some hardy perennials make ideal container plants. Although they do not flower for as long or as prolifically as bedding plants, they are generally easier to look after and can cope with a wider range of different conditions.

Perennials for containers

When you choose perennials for containers, select plants that have decorative foliage so that they look attractive throughout the growing season. Evergreen plants will also offer winter interest. Several perennials, including hostas and agapanthus, make excellent specimen plants. If the flowers are their main feature, as in the case of agapanthus, they can be given a prominent position while in bloom and then tucked out of the way at other times of the year. Where foliage is the main attraction, as in the case of hostas, the plant can be given a prominent position for most of the summer. Some smaller perennials, such as lamium and *Festuca glauca* (blue fescue), can be combined with

Corners in the shade

This permanent window box contains three different sorts of fern, and is ideal for a dark, damp, shady spot. These conditions are disliked by many plants, but ferns will thrive here. Provided the plants are not allowed to dry out, they will grow happily for many years.

other plants to create a permanent container display or used as a long-term filler between bulbs and seasonal bedding. This will save you time and money in the long run because you won't have to buy so many bedding plants to fill your pots.

Many perennials are also more tolerant of shady conditions than annual bedding plants and so are useful for brightening the gloom in these areas. Ideal candidates include hostas, hardy ferns and variegated ivy. Other perennials, such as diascias and sempervivums, are drought-tolerant and can go for long periods between waterings, so are ideal for hot sunny spots, or for window boxes or baskets that aren't easily accessible for watering.

HOW TO PLANT AN URN

1 Assemble the items you will need: a terracotta pot, your choice of plant (in this case, a cordyline), some stones to cover the drainage holes, compost (soil mix), slow-release fertilizer (either loose or in pellets) and water-retaining granules.

2 Cover the bottom of the container with small stones or some pieces of broken tile or pottery, to prevent the compost washing out of the drainage holes.

3 Partly fill the pot with a good-quality potting compost – loam-based compost is best for permanent displays. If you wish, mix some slow-release fertilizer and water-retaining granules into the compost before you fill the pot.

Perennials for containers

Acanthus	Incarvillea
Achillea	Lamium
Agapanthus	Pulmonaria
Anthemis	Sedum
Artemisia	
Aquilegia	**Invasive**
Astrantia	**perennials**
Diascia	Aegopodium
Doronicum	Convallaria
Euphorbia	Gunnera
Festuca	Houttuynia
Geranium	Persicaria
Helleborus	Phalaris
Hosta	Physalis

LEFT
The foliage and flowers of the perennials *Stachys byzantina* and *Nepeta* x *faassenii* blend perfectly in a container.

Unusual containers

Containers also give you the opportunity to grow plants that would otherwise struggle in your soil conditions as well as invasive perennials that would swamp your borders or even your whole garden. The giant ornamental rhubarb, for example, *Gunnera manicata*, can reach 2 x 2m (6 x 6ft) in a moist spot, but in a large container, such as a half-barrel, it can be kept to a more manageable size.

Alpines grow well in containers, too, thriving on the good drainage and airy conditions. The container also brings their dainty form and intricate markings closer to the eye where they are more easily appreciated. When they are grown in a trough, they can be combined with other dwarf plants and rocks to create an attractive miniature landscape or alpine bed.

4 Scoop a hole in the compost and insert the plant, positioning it so that the top of the rootball is level with the surface of the compost.

5 Place any extra plants that you wish to include around the edge of the main plant. Add more compost to fill any gaps and firm down. Insert a fertilizer pellet at this stage if fertilizer granules were not added to the compost mixture.

6 Water thoroughly. The plants will soon grow and fill out the container.

Patio trees and shrubs

Tough, drought-tolerant trees and shrubs make superb container plants, and they can be used to create a focal point or to provide shelter and shade on the patio.

Planting for a patio

Trees and shrubs add structure to permanent containers just as they do to other planting schemes around the garden. Although almost any species can be grown in a pot, it's a good idea to choose trees and shrubs that are not too vigorous to avoid having to carry out regular pruning and repotting. Trees and shrubs can be used as effective focal points around the garden, and when they are grown in a container you can alter the way a garden is viewed by moving the plants around. They also provide shelter and privacy on the patio during the summer months as well as adding colour and interest throughout the rest of the year.

By planting trees and shrubs in containers you can grow types that would not thrive in your garden soil. For example, if your soil is alkaline

A small tree in a container can be moved around the garden at will. A change in position will draw attention to both the tree and its surroundings.

you will not be able to grow acid-loving plants such as heathers, rhododendrons, camellias and azaleas in the border, but you could grow them in containers filled with ericaceous compost (acid soil mix). You can also grow exotic plants that

are not hardy in your area provided you have somewhere frost free, such as a conservatory or greenhouse, to keep them safe over winter.

Which container?

Choose any large, wide-bottomed container with drainage holes that will be stable once it is planted up. Wooden tubs, half-barrels and even empty water tanks can be used. Ideally, the container should be on outdoor castors to make moving it around easier. However, if this is not possible, position the container carefully before planting because it will be difficult to adjust its position afterwards. For a small collection of plants a tub of at least 45cm (18in) diameter will be required, filled with a loam-based compost (soil mix).

Choosing trees and shrubs

If you are looking for a focal point, choose neat plants with dense foliage, such as box or bay, but if you want to add a little colour too, choose a variegated shrub, such as *Aucuba japonica*. Seasonal displays from

HOW TO PLANT A TREE OR SHRUB IN A TUB

1 Choose a large tub or pot with an inside diameter of at least 45cm (18in), unless you are planting very small shrubs. Make sure it is heavy (clay or stone, for instance, not plastic) and place pieces of broken clay pots or chipped bark over the drainage hole.

2 Part-fill the tub or pot with a loam-based compost (soil mix). Do not use lightweight alternatives because the weight is required for stability.

3 Knock the plant from its pot, and if the roots are tightly wound round the rootball carefully tease out some of the roots so that they will grow into the surrounding soil more readily.

HOW TO PLANT A CLIMBER IN A HALF-BARREL

1 Fill a half-barrel with a loam-based compost (soil mix). You need a large, deep container and heavy potting mixture, which will secure the canes as well as the plants.

2 Plant the climbers, using the right number of plants. For instance, in a barrel of this size, you will need three to four clematis. Angle the root-ball of the plant so that it points slightly inwards.

3 Tie the canes together with string or use a proprietary plastic cane holder. If the growth reaches the top of the canes, it will tumble down again and make the planting look even denser.

shrubs, such as rhododendrons and camellias, can also be very effective. By growing them in containers you have the added advantage that once the flowers fade, the tub can be moved to a less prominent position for the summer. The type of shrub you choose can also influence the general ambience of the garden – for example, by combining a yucca or cordyline with the lush leafy growth of *Fatsia japonica* (false castor oil plant) to create a steamy, tropical atmosphere around the patio.

Two types of trees make excellent container plants: slow-growing specimens with attractive foliage, which can be left largely to their own devices, and fast-growing trees, which respond to annual heavy pruning to keep them in check. Vigorous trees, such as eucalyptus, *Betula pendula* (silver birch) and *Salix* (willow), are ideal for adding instant maturity to a new garden and can have all their new growth cut back in early spring to create eye-catching multi-stemmed or lollipop shapes. Containers are also an ideal way of growing trees that sucker and would otherwise be a nuisance in the garden. As with other plants, trees vary in their ability to cope with a lack of moisture, so if you find regular watering a problem, choose a drought-tolerant tree such as *Caragana arborescens* (pea tree).

4 Test the plant for size and position. Add or remove soil as necessary, so that the top of the rootball and soil level will be 2.5 – 5cm (1–2in) below the rim of the pot to allow for watering.

5 Backfill the soil around the roots firmly, because trees and shrubs offer a great deal of wind resistance. Water thoroughly after planting, thereafter water as necessary including during the winter months.

Shrubs for containers

Arundinaria	Hydrangea
Aucuba	Juniperus
Berberis	Picea (dwarf
Buxus	forms)
Caragana	Rhododendron
Chamaecyparis	Rosmarinus
Choisya	Skimmia
Cordyline	Viburnum
Euonymus	Yucca
Fatsia	

Permanent container aftercare

Growing plants in permanent containers requires a fair amount of maintenance. They require regular feeding and watering: perhaps more watering than other containers because the plants are bigger. Many will also need annual repotting, pruning or tidying up to keep in good shape. But don't be put off as there are all sorts of advantages to growing plants in this way.

Perennials

These plants fall into three broad groups when it comes to their aftercare: short-lived perennials that need replacing every few years; long-term perennials that need dividing every other year to maintain a neat habit and good flowering; and a few long-term perennials, such as agapanthus, that flower better if they are a little pot-bound. Instead of dividing these perennials, simply replace the top few centimetres (inch) of compost (soil mix) with fresh each spring and push a few slow-release fertilizer pellets into the compost.

All perennials will need tidying up at the end of the season. Remove all yellowing stems and leaves. Pests, such as slugs and snails, which can be a menace in the border are often less of a problem in pots. However, powdery mildew, which can ruin aquilegias and pulmonarias among others, is more serious because container-grown plants are more likely to suffer from stress caused by uneven watering. If the attack occurs early in the season spray with a systemic fungicide, but later attacks are best ignored.

Lily-of-the-valley (*Convallaria majalis*) grows very well in containers and will thrive in the shade, where its delicately scented white flowers stand out from the greenery.

HOW TO PROTECT FROM COLD

1 If you are using plastic bubble wrap or horticultural fleece, wrap it around the plant in its container, allowing a generous overlap, and cut it to the correct size using sharp scissors. For particularly vulnerable plants, cut enough for a double layer.

2 Place four or five tall canes in the container and wrap the protective sheeting around the plant. If you are using a sleeve, it can be simply slipped over the canes.

3 If you are using plastic bubble wrap, leave the top open for ventilation and a gap at the bottom to permit watering if necessary. If you are using horticultural fleece, tie the top closed to help to conserve warmth.

Trees and shrubs

Most trees and shrubs require little regular maintenance, apart from an annual tidy up with secateurs (pruners) to remove any unwanted growth or to tidy the overall shape of the plant. Some clipped specimens, such as bay, will require trimming more often through the growing season to keep their neat form. Flowering shrubs, such as rhododendrons and camellias, are worth deadheading once the flowers start to fade to tidy the display.

Every couple of years in spring, permanent specimen plants will need repotting. Where practicable move them to a larger pot or repot into the same container. To do this you will first need to remove the plant from its pot – this is easier said than done with a large specimen, but pulling the pot on to its side will help. Use your fingers to remove any loose compost from around the rootball and trim any roots that are winding around the base of the pot. After cleaning the container, place a

PROVIDING SUPPORT

Check the potential size of any climber you plant and place canes in the container to support it. With regular feeding and watering, a small climber will send up strong stems that can be trained into a permanent structure around cane supports. It may be necessary to tie in the climber as it grows.

Topiary

Choose compact slow-growing trees and shrubs for topiary: yew and box are the best, but holly, privet and box-leaf honeysuckle are also good. Topiary can either be created from an existing shrub or the shrub can be trained into shape using a special wire frame.

Prune the topiary by hand, using secateurs (pruners) to snip out one stem at a time. Once the shape has been formed, trim it over with a pair of small clippers.

Even small topiaries may take several years to achieve the desired shape, but the effort is definitely worth it, so be patient.

little fresh compost in the base and position the specimen so that it is at the same level as before. Trickle fresh compost down the sides of the rootball, carefully pushing it down with a short stick to get rid of any air pockets. Top up with compost and add slow-release fertilizer pellets before watering thoroughly.

GENERAL CARE FOR PLANTED CONTAINERS

1 Most composts (soil mixes) contain fertilizer, but it will run out after about six weeks. Either feed plants with a liquid fertilizer every time you water or add a slow-release fertilizer to the compost each spring that will last for the whole growing season.

2 Leave the top of the compost as it is, or cover it with a decorative mulch, such as large pebbles or gravel. These not only give the container an attractive finish but also help keep the compost cool and prevent water from evaporating.

3 Water the container thoroughly and continue to do so at regular intervals. During hot weather, this is likely to be at least daily. Occasional watering will also be necessary during dry spells in the winter months.

Planting up a patio

Don't restrict yourself to planting in containers to bring life to your patio because there are many attractive plants that are well-adapted to growing in cracks, crevices and planting pockets in and around the patio.

Creating large planting pockets

Planting pockets large enough for a small shrub or climber can be created by lifting one or two adjacent slabs from part of the patio. Choose an area that is not used very often and away from points of access. Prise up the slab with a garden spade or use a cold chisel and club hammer if it is cemented into position. Use a garden fork to break up the rubble or hardcore base before removing it. Dig down about 30cm (12in), removing any additional hardcore and subsoil, then use a garden fork to loosen the soil in the bottom of the hole. The soil is likely to be fairly poor quality, so incorporate plenty of organic matter, such as well-rotted garden compost, and top up with fresh topsoil from elsewhere in the garden or use a loam-based compost (soil mix).

PLANTING IN PAVING

Chisel out a space in your paving to a depth of at least 5cm (2in). Add loam-based compost (soil mix) and plant your seedling. Trickle more compost around the roots and firm in. Water regularly, using a fine mist sprayer to avoid washing the compost away.

Plant the pocket as you would a bed, putting the larger plants in first and then filling the gaps with the smaller plants. All plants should be drought-tolerant. Take care not to create an obstruction or hazard when using larger plants. After planting, water thoroughly and cover the surface of the compost with a decorative mulch of pebbles to prevent weeds germinating and help retain water. Continue to water until the plants are established.

Planting cracks in paving

Cracks between paving stones and at the edge of the patio, which often get colonized by weeds, can be used to grow a range of ground-hugging, drought-tolerant plants that are tough enough to be walked on occasionally. They will also prevent the weeds from returning.

To prepare the crack, first remove any weeds. Perennial weeds are best killed with a translocated weedkiller that will kill the whole plant, including the roots. Use a screwdriver to dig out the loose material between the paving slabs, reaching down as far as possible. Fill the crack with a loam-based compost (soil mix), poking it into the hole with the screwdriver to eliminate any air pockets. Level the compost and firm gently.

If you are planting seeds directly into the crack, sow them thinly and evenly. Use a garden sieve to dust compost over the seed, then water with a fine mist sprayer or a watering can fitted with a fine rose to prevent the seed and compost from being washed away. Thin seedlings when they are large enough to handle, leaving the strongest.

HOW TO CREATE A LARGE PLANTING POCKET

1 Lift one or two paving slabs, depending on their size. If they have been mortared into position, loosen the slabs with a cold chisel and club hammer, then lever them up with the chisel or a crowbar.

2 If the paving slab has been bedded on concrete, break this up with a cold chisel and club hammer. Fork over the soil, adding well-rotted garden compost or manure and a slow-release fertilizer.

3 Plant the shrub or climber, firming it in well and watering thoroughly. Arrange decorative pebbles or gravel to make the feature more attractive and reduce the chance of soil splashing on to the paving.

PLANTING IN A DRY-STONE WALL

Press moist loam-based compost into the crevice using a small dibber or your fingers. Firm in to avoid air pockets. Insert the plant into the crevice and add more soil. Keep the compost moist until the plants become established by spraying with a fine mist.

If you are using small plants in the crack, press the rootball between your palms to form a wedge shape. Carefully ease the rootball between the paving stones and water well.

Continue to water the crack as needed, until the plants or the seeds are established, especially during prolonged dry spells.

Planting crevices in walls

Garden walls or walls around raised beds can be planted using a similar technique to that described for cracks. The crevice in the wall will have to be made large enough to accommodate the rootball of the plant and deep enough for the plant to become established. Only drought-tolerant plants can be used.

Place a small, flat stone at the base of the crack to prevent the compost from falling out before you position the plant and pack in more compost around its roots. Water carefully until the plant is well established. You can sow seed directly into the crevice by mixing the seed with some compost in your hand, moistening it and pressing it into the crevice.

Good specimens for planting in the patio

Plants for cracks	Plants for crevices	Plants for pockets
Aubrieta deltoidea	*Globularia cordifolia*	*Armeria maritima*
Dianthus deltoides	*Lewisia tweedyi*	*Campanula*
Erinus alpinus	*Saxifraga callosa*	*portenschlagiana*
Scabiosa graminifolia	*Sedum spathulifolium*	*Cerastium tomentosum*
Thymus	*Sempervivum*	*Sedum telephium*
	Thymus	*Veronica prostrata*

Erinus alpinus   *Thymus serpyllum*   *Veronica prostrata*

The formality of regular shaped paving edged in brick has been softened with an exuberant planting of low-growing herbs. The herbs spill out of their planting pockets and from cracks between paving slabs in this charmingly informal patio.

Watering container plants

Keeping plants moist is of critical importance throughout the growing season and watering should be continued, although less frequently, during the winter months. It can be time-consuming, but there are many techniques and products that can be employed to make the job easier.

Hanging baskets

A large basket that holds plenty of compost (soil mix) will retain water better than a smaller basket. Line wire-mesh baskets with polythene before planting. Use a special hanging basket compost that contains a wetting agent to make watering easier. Incorporate water-retaining granules that hold on to water longer and choose drought-tolerant plants that can go for longer periods without water and recover well if they do suffer a shortage.

Patio containers

Choose the largest container you can and line porous containers, such as those made from terracotta, with a sheet of polythene, taking care not to cover the drainage holes. Mix water-retaining granules into the compost before planting, or trickle water-retaining granules into holes made with a bamboo cane into the compost in existing permanent containers. Cover the surface of all containers with a mulch of stone chippings or pebbles to prevent moisture evaporating.

Watering problems

When a container plant goes short of water, the compost can dry out and be difficult to rewet. If the water sits on the surface without soaking in, add a drop of washing-up liquid (dishwashing detergent) to the watering can before watering. This will act as a wetting agent, making it

Hanging baskets are vulnerable to drying winds and should always be kept well watered.

HOW TO USE WATER-RETAINING GRANULES

1 Pour the recommended amount of water into a bowl. Scatter the granules over the surface, stirring occasionally until it has absorbed the water.

2 Add the hydrated granules to compost (soil mix) at the recommended rate. Mix the hydrated granules thoroughly before using the compost mixture for planting.

Watering acid-lovers

Acid-loving plants growing in ericaceous compost (soil mix) will suffer if they are watered with hard water, direct from the tap. If you live in a hard-water area, either collect rainwater (which is slightly acidic) in a water butt or add an old teabag to a full watering can and let it stand for 24 hours before watering.

easier for the water to be absorbed. Alternatively, place a few ice-blocks on the surface of the compost. These will slowly soak into the surface as they melt, and you will then be able to water as normal.

In severe cases of drought, the rootball may shrink away from the sides of the container so any water simply runs between the rootball and the inside of the pot and out of the drainage holes. Prevent this from happening by adding compost to the top of the rootball and pushing it in to fill any gaps. Then water.

During hot periods it is best to water in the early morning or late evening to minimize evaporation.

Water acid-loving plants, such as this variegated pieris, with rainwater collected in a water butt if you live in a hard water area.

HOW TO WATER CONTAINERS

1 One of the easiest ways of watering is with a watering can. This allows you to deliver just the right amount of water to each plant. However, it is very time-consuming, so only really suitable for a small number of containers. Always make certain that the soil is well soaked and that you have not just dampened the surface.

3 For large collections of containers, a hose-end trigger spray is a more efficient method of watering. If you have several hanging baskets to water, consider buying a spray lance (wand) instead.

Watering equipment

A wide range of aids to make watering easier are available. Choose one that can cope with the types of containers you have and that fits in with your watering regime. Watering cans and garden hoses fitted with a hose lance (wand) make watering containers a lot easier. You can either direct the hose at individual plants or mount the hose so that a group of plants is watered by the spray.

Self-watering containers, which have a reservoir of water, are widely

2 You can apply water more quickly to established containers using a watering can without a rose fitted, but it is still hard work and quite time-consuming.

4 If you have not used a slow-release fertilizer, you can feed your plants at the same time as watering them by adding a liquid fertilizer to the watering can. Feed containers once a week when plants are growing rapidly or flowering a lot.

available, and are especially useful in hot, sunny poistions. However, if you have a number of containers you can make your life even easier by installing an automatic watering system. This is basically a network of small-bore tubes attached to a water source. It delivers water to each container by way of an adjustable drip nozzle pegged into the compost. The system can be made completely automatic by adding a water timer or watering computer to the outside tap (faucet).

Water and rock gardening

Water features add a new dimension to your garden, providing colour, movement and gentle sound, which can be used to create a relaxing atmosphere. If well planned and given the right setting, water features are easy to look after and a joy to behold.

The most important consideration when creating a water feature is to site it correctly. It needs a sunny, open position well away from overhanging trees and dense shade. Choose a type of pond that complements the style of your garden and position it where it will be most appreciated.

When creating a pond, consider adding other complementary features to your garden at the same time. A bog garden blurs the divide between pond and garden and allows you to grow some wonderful plants, while a rock garden can be as natural or as dramatic as you like.

The purple flowers of *Iris sibirica* make a striking edging to a charming and informal garden pond.

Small water features

No contemporary garden would be complete without introducing water somewhere in the design. With modern equipment, small water features are easy to install.

Choosing a feature

Creating a water feature used to require considerable planning and some serious excavation, but the development of easy-to-install kits and reliable low-voltage submersible pumps means that even a novice can build an attractive, working feature in less than a day. Of course, careful planning is advisable to avoid errors, but once you have decided on a suitable position, the time required to install a water feature is short.

There is a huge range of features to choose from, but they can be grouped according to their function: a watercourse, which creates a stream effect; spouts, where a jet of water spills from a wall mask; gurgle ponds, where a water spout splashes over a feature such as a heap of pebbles; and still-water pools.

Bear in mind that the temperature of a small pond, situated in a suntrap, may fluctuate too much for fish to thrive.

Moving water features

All small features with moving water have the same basic equipment: a submersible pump and a reservoir to hold the water. The reservoir can be bought for the purpose or made from anything that holds water, from an inexpensive central-heating header tank to a hole lined with flexible pond liner. The reservoir needs only to be deep enough to completely cover the pump with water, but larger reservoirs are much easier to maintain because they require topping up less frequently, especially in summer.

HOW TO MAKE A PEBBLE FOUNTAIN

1 Mark out the diameter of the reservoir and dig a hole slightly wider and deeper than its dimensions. Place a shallow layer of sand at the bottom. Ensure the reservoir rim is slightly below the level of the surrounding soil.

2 Backfill the gap between the reservoir and the sides of the hole with soil. Firm in. Create a catchment area by sloping the surrounding soil slightly towards the rim of the reservoir. Place two bricks at the bottom to act as a plinth for the pump. Then position the pump.

3 Ensure the pipe used for the fountain spout will be 5–7cm (2–3in) higher than the sides of the reservoir. Line the catchment area with a plastic sheet and either cut it so the plastic drapes into the reservoir, or cut a hole in the centre for the fountain pipe. Fill with water.

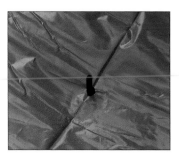

4 Position the plastic sheet over the reservoir, with the fountain pipe protruding through the hole and fit the fountain spout.

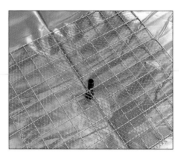

5 Place a piece of galvanized mesh (large enough to rest on the rim of the reservoir) on top to support the weight of large wet cobbles. If you are using small stones, place a smaller mesh on top of the larger one to prevent them falling through.

6 Cover the area around the pump with a layer of cobbles. Check the height of the spout is satisfactory. When you are happy with the fountain, finish arranging the cobbles.

The finished gurgle fountain gives interest to what would otherwise have been a neglected corner of the garden.

Plants for miniature ponds

Acorus gramineus 'Variegatus'
Azolla filiculoides
Dwarf water lilies
Eichhornia crassipes
Juncus effusus f. *spiralis*
Marsilea quadrifolia
Trapa natans

What size pump?

The size of pump you require will depend on the amount of water needed to produce the effect you want. A small water feature will require a pump with a flow rate of about 450 litres (about 120 gallons) per hour, while a large fountain will need one that can supply 650 litres (about 170 gallons). If you want to combine features or have a watercourse you will need a much larger pump (see product packaging for details).

The easiest way to create a small water feature with moving water is to sink a reservoir into the ground so that it is about 5cm (2in) below the surrounding soil. Then create a catchment area for the feature by sloping the soil around the hole towards the reservoir, so that when it is lined with heavy-duty polythene or a flexible pond liner, water will drain back into the reservoir. Position the pump in the reservoir and cover with heavy-duty steel mesh and smaller mesh to prevent smaller pebbles from falling through. Arrange cobbles and pebbles on the mesh to hide the reservoir and the catchment area to create a pebble fountain.

You can change the display by adding a millstone or another focal point, or by adding different types of fountain jet on the outlet pipe of the pump to create all manner of display fountains.

Alternatively, use a piece of pipe to connect the outlet pipe to a wall mask or a free-standing waterspout.

Still patio pools

You can create a small attractive pool from a half-barrel or large bucket. Sink it into the ground or stand it on the patio as a raised pool. If the container is not properly sealed, line it with flexible pond liner, stapling the top edge just out of sight below the rim. Trim carefully to neaten the edges and cover the bottom with a layer of gravel. Fill with water and allow to stand for a few days before planting with dwarf pond plants such as dwarf water lilies, corkscrew rush and the variegated form of the Japanese rush.

Larger raised pools are available in kit form from garden retailers or they can be made from fibreglass liners supported with brick walls.

HOW TO PLANT A MINIATURE POND

Choose an attractive watertight container such as a sturdy bucket and fill it with water. Plant with dwarf or miniature varieties of *Nymphaea* (water lily) and *Eichhornia crassipes* (water hyacinth).

Making a pond

After deciding on the best position for a pond in your garden, you need to consider its style and dimensions as well as the construction materials.

Planning a pond

A self-sustaining pond that does not require constant maintenance should be as big as possible. Whatever the shape, it should have at least 5 square metres (over 50 square feet) of surface area, and so that it doesn't heat up too quickly in summer or get too cold in winter it also needs to be at least 60cm (24in) deep over much of that area. A marginal shelf 23cm (9in) wide and about 15cm (6in) below the surface of the water around the edge is needed to accommodate plants that like their roots in water but their shoots and leaves in the air. Before excavating, check that there are no underground obstructions, such as pipes and cables.

Lining a pond

A pond can be made with a rigid, pre-formed liner or with a special flexible liner. Rigid liners are usually made from plastic or fibreglass and

A brick or paved edge creates a fairly formal effect, but the pond has been made more interesting by using the excavated soil to build up a raised bed behind it.

they come in a range of shapes and sizes to suit most styles of garden. Rigid liners tend to be on the small side, with little space for marginal plants, and are more work to install. A flexible liner, made from PVC, butyl rubber or heavy-duty polythene, gives you a lot more control over the design of your

pond. It can be pleated at the corners to fit a rectangular or square-shaped pond, and it is particularly suitable for an informal pond because it can be folded to fit any shape you want. It does, however, require some skill to create a convincing shaped pond, and the liner can be easily damaged, especially on stony soil.

HOW TO INSTALL A FLEXIBLE LINER

1 Mark out the shape of the pond with garden hose or rope for curves and pegs and string for straight edges, then remove any turf and start to excavate the pond. Redistribute the topsoil to other parts of the garden.

2 Dig the whole area to about 23cm (9in) deep, then mark the positions of the marginal shelves. Each should be about 23cm (9in) wide. Dig the deeper areas to 50–60cm (20–24in) deep. Angle all the vertical sides so they slope slightly inwards.

3 Check the level as you work. Correct discrepancies using sieved garden soil. Make sure there are no sharp stones on the base and sides that might damage the liner, then line the hole with builders' sand.

What size flexible liner?

Flexible liners are available in a range of sizes. To calculate the size you will need for your pond, use the following formula:

Length = 2 x maximum depth + maximum length of the pond

Width = 2 x maximum depth + maximum width of the pond

For example, a pond that is 3 x 2m (10 x 6ft) with a maximum depth of 50cm (20in) will require a flexible liner that is 4 x 3m (13⅓ x 9⅓ft).

Edging the pond

The style of edging and the material used should reflect the formality of the pond and the materials used elsewhere in the garden. A formal pond looks best with a neat, straight edge of paving, while an informal one can be paved with irregularly shaped stones or small unit paving, which can follow the gentle curves of the pond. Around the edge of a wildlife pond, a sloping pebble beach would be appropriate so that visiting wildlife can enjoy a bathe and a drink.

HOW TO INSTALL A PRE-FORMED RIGID LINER

1 Transfer the shape to the ground by inserting canes around the edge of the unit. Use a garden hose, rope or sand to mark the outline on the ground.

2 Remove the unit and canes and excavate the hole to approximately the required depth, following the profile of the shelves as accurately as possible.

3 Use a spirit (carpenter's) level and straight-edged board, laid across the rim, to check it is level. Measure down to check that it is the required depth.

  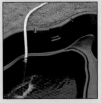

4 Remove any large stones. Put the pond in the hole, then add or remove soil to ensure a snug and level fit. Check with a spirit level that the pond is level.

5 Remove the pond and line the hole with damp sand if the soil is stony. With the pond in position and levels checked again, backfill with sand or fine soil, being careful not to push the pond out of level.

6 Fill with fresh water and backfill further if necessary as the water level rises, checking the level frequently to make sure the liner has not moved. Allow to stand for a few days before stocking with plants.

4 On stony soil, you may need to line the hole further with loft insulation or special pond liner underlay. Trim the liner underlay so that it fits neatly into the hole.

5 Ease the liner into position without stretching it unduly. Choose a warm day because this will make it more flexible. Weigh down the edges with stones, then fill the pond slowly. Ease the liner into position so that it follows the contours as the pond fills.

6 Once the pond is full, trim back the excess liner to leave an overlap of at least 15cm (6in) around the edge. Cover the overlapping liner with paving or other edging. To disguise the liner, overlap the water's edge by 2.5cm (1in).

Stocking a pond

It is essential to choose the right blend of aquatic plants to create a natural balance in your pond. Select plants that suit the size of the pond so they don't need regular chopping back to keep them in check.

Types of water plant

Pond plants can be grouped according to the depth of water they require.

Deep-water plants These plants, which include *Nymphaea* (water lily), are essential to the overall health of the pond because the leaves cover the surface and provide shade, which discourages the growth of algae and offers a cool retreat for fish.

Marginal plants The roots of marginal plants are in water but the stems and leaves grow above the surface. Most flower for only a short time between late spring and late summer, so try to combine varieties with different flowering times to prolong the period of interest. In addition, include plants with attractive foliage, such as the variegated irises *I. pseudacorus*

An informal pool, where nature is allowed to have its way, will soon become a haven for wildlife.

'Variegata' or *I. laevigata* 'Variegata', or *Schoenoplectus lacustris* subsp. *tabernaemontani*, which lasts for months.

Submerged aquatic plants Although not as ornamental as other plants, submerged aquatics are important for keeping the pond healthy. They use up excess nutrients that would otherwise encourage blanketweed and other algae. They also oxygenate the

water, improving the environment for fish and other pond creatures. Add around ten bunches per square metre (yard) of pond surface area.

Free-floating plants These plants, together with those that live in deep water, provide shade for fish and discourage the growth of algae. Aim to cover about one-third of the surface area with floating foliage.

HOW TO PLANT AQUATICS

1 Fill a basket sold for water plants with special aquatic compost. The hessian (burlap) liner will help prevent the soil from falling through the mesh sides of the basket.

2 Remove the plant from its container and plant it in the basket at its original depth, using a trowel to add or remove aquatic compost as necessary. Firm it in well.

3 Cover the aquatic compost with gravel to help keep it in place when you put the container in the pond and to minimize disturbance by fish. Soak the plant in a bucket of water to remove air bubbles.

Planting

The easiest way to introduce an aquatic plant is to use a special planting basket. If you use one of the traditional mesh-sided baskets, line it with hessian (burlap) before planting so the compost does not wash out. The extra lining will not be necessary if you are using a modern micromesh aquatic basket. Use specially formulated aquatic compost because standard potting compost (soil mix) will allow nutrients to leach out, encouraging excessive algae growth. Good quality topsoil can also be used if you find it difficult to get aquatic compost.

Although you can put more than one plant in a large basket, you are better off planting singly so that individual plants can later be removed and divided or replaced more easily. Top the basket with a 2cm (½in) deep layer of pea gravel to stop fish disturbing the compost and muddying the water. Soak the basket in a bucket of water before positioning it in the pond.

HOW TO PLANT AN OXYGENATOR

Submerged aquatic plants are called oxygenators and are essential for the health of the pond. To plant an oxygenator such as *Lagarosiphon major* (curly water thyme), tie it to a stone, then drop it in the water. The plant will root in the sediment at the bottom of the pool.

INTRODUCING FISH

Never place fish directly in the pond. First acclimatize them by floating the plastic bag that you transported them in on the surface of the water for an hour. This will allow the water temperatures to equalize gradually, after which the fish can be allowed to swim out of the bag.

STOCKING A WILDLIFE POND

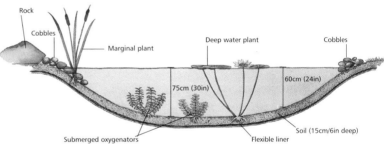

This pool has a sloping edge to allow birds and animals to reach the water easily. Surround it with lush plantings and long grass to provide cover for visiting wildlife.

4 Once thoroughly soaked, carefully place the plant on the shelf at the edge of the pool so that the container is covered by 3–5cm (1–2in) of water.

Trouble-free pond plants

Deep-water plants
Nymphaea 'Attraction'
   N. 'Aurora'
   N. 'Ellisiana'
   N. 'Froebelii'
   N. 'Pygmaea Helvola'
Nymphoides peltata (water fringe)
Orontium aquaticum (golden club)

Marginal plants
Acorus calamus 'Variegatus'
Butomus umbellatus (flowering rush)
Caltha palustris 'Flore Pleno'
   (marsh marigold)
Iris laevigata 'Variegata'

Myosotis scorpioides
Pontederia cordata (pickerel weed)
Schoenoplectus lacustris
Typha minima

Submerged and floating plants
Azolla filiculoides (fairy moss)
Eichihornia crassipes (water hyacinth)
Eleocharis acicularis (hair grass)
Fontinalis antipyretica
Hydrocharis morsus-ranae
Ranunculus aquatilis
Stratiotes aloides (water soldier)
Trapa natans
Utricularia vulgaris

Pond care

Once established, a well-planned and constructed pond will largely look after itself. There are, however, a number of seasonal tasks worth carrying out that will help maintain the equilibrium.

Spring

Once the coldest weather is over, you can remove the netting keeping out wind-blown leaves and exchange the pond heater for a pump. The pond will come to life in mid-spring, when marginal plants put on new growth, the first lily pads appear and on a mild day fish can be seen at the surface. This is the time to start feeding the fish and to carry out a pond spring clean. Scoop any dead or rotting leaves from the pond to prevent them from fouling the water.

Mid- to late spring is an ideal time to add new plants to your pond. It is worth adding special fertilizer tablets to the compost of established plants. Make sure they are pushed well into the compost so that nutrients do not leach out into the water and encourage the growth of algae. If the pond tends to go green with algae at this time of year, place a barley straw pad (available from garden retailers) in the pond.

A mature specimen of the water lily *Nymphaea* 'Attraction' in early summer.

Summer

Choose a warm, fine day in late spring or early summer to remove and divide overgrown plants.

Fish will need feeding on a regular basis throughout summer. Try to feed in the morning and clear away any uneaten food left floating on the surface of the water after about 10 minutes using a fine-mesh fishing net. This will prevent it from sinking to the bottom and rotting.

Pond problems often occur in summer. Use a jet of water from a hose to knock off sap-sucking pests

from water lily pads. Spreading filaments of blanketweed should be scooped out with a bamboo cane or wire rake. Before placing it on the compost heap, leave the weed on the side of the pond for a couple of hours to allow any pond creatures to make their way back into the pond. Use a fine-mesh net to scoop out floating duckweed, which can quickly spread over the surface of a pond. Top up the water level as necessary and clean the filter of the pump if there appears to be a blockage. In heavy, thundery weather you may

HOW TO DIVIDE A WATER LILY

1 Lift the water lily in spring, put it in a bowl of water and wash it free of compost. Trim back any over-long roots with secateurs (pruners) and remove any damaged leaves.

2 Using a sharp knife, cut the rhizome into pieces, making sure that each section has roots and leaves or leaf buds.

3 Pot the sections up into pots of aquatic compost. Add a layer of gravel to prevent the compost being disturbed. Put the pot in a bowl of water and keep it in a shaded place. New leaves will appear within a few months.

HOW TO OVERWINTER TENDER AQUATICS

1 Net a few plants in good condition. They may already be deteriorating in the cooler weather, so don't save any that appear to be rotting or badly damaged.

2 Put a handful of the plants in a plastic container of pond water. Don't overcrowd them – use extra containers rather than allow them to touch. Some gardeners put a little soil in the bottom to provide nutrients.

3 Keep the plants in a light, frost-free place, such as a greenhouse. You might be able to keep them on a cool windowsill. Top up or change the water occasionally so that it does not become stagnant.

see fish gasping for air at the surface. Increase oxygen levels in the water by turning on the pump or by playing a jet of water from a hose on to the surface.

Autumn

The main tasks of autumn are to clear away the dying foliage of marginal plants and to prevent leaves from nearby deciduous trees from falling into the pond. Cut down marginals so that the tops of their stems are above the water surface when the pond is full. Remove any other organic material. Place tender aquatics in a bucket of pond water

somewhere cool but frost free, such as a greenhouse, until spring. In early autumn use a high-protein fish food to help fish build up sufficient reserves to survive the winter, then when the weather cools stop feeding altogether. Remove the pond pump, store carefully and replace with a pool heater, which will help keep at least part of the water's surface ice free in freezing weather.

Winter

If you completed all the pond-care tasks on time in autumn, little needs to be done other than to keep the pond clear of fallen leaves that are

still blowing about the garden and to make sure that at least part of the pond's surface remains free of ice during prolonged cold weather.

The easiest way to clear an area of ice is to stand a pan of hot water on the surface to melt a hole. Never hit the ice with a hammer to try to break it up because this will send shock waves through the pond that can harm fish. If a substantial ice-sheet has formed on the pond, you could siphon off a couple of inches of water from underneath the ice. The layer of air will help to insulate the water and prevent any more water from freezing.

SUMMER MAINTENANCE

Submerged oxygenators, such as *Lagarosiphon major*, and rampant growers, such as *Myriophyllum aquaticum*, will clog the pond unless you clear them out periodically. Remove the excess with a net or rake.

HOW TO PREPARE A POND FOR WINTER

1 A small pond can be protected from the worst of the leaf fall with a fine-mesh net. Anchor it just above the surface of the pond. Remove the leaves regularly and eventually take the netting off.

2 If you cannot cover your pond with a net, use a fish net or rake to remove leaves regularly – not only from the surface but also from below the surface. Decomposing leaves in the pond will pollute the water.

Bog gardens

Marshy bog gardens associate
particularly well with water features,
helping to create a natural setting,
but they are also worth considering as
features in their own right because
they allow you to grow a wider
range of plants in your garden.

Deciding on a site

Bog gardens are areas of permanently
wet soil that are suitable for growing
marginal and wetland plants. They
look particularly effective alongside
water features, where the lush foliage
and colourful flowers help to
integrate pools into the rest of the
garden. A bog garden can be either
planted in a permanently waterlogged area in your garden or created
in a dry spot using a pond liner.

The soil in a bog garden must be
kept moist, which may mean regular
watering during the summer months.
Before planting a bog garden
consider installing a seep hose under
the soil for automatic watering.

Creating a bog garden

A bog garden is very easy to create.
If you are building a pond at the
same time you can simply extend the
excavation and use a single piece of
flexible liner to line both the pond

CREATING A BOGGY MARGIN TO A POND

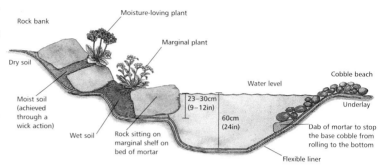

Adding a boggy margin to a pond will make it more attractive and help integrate it into the
surrounding garden. It is the perfect spot to experiment with unusual moisture-loving plants.

and the bog area. However, you can
also create a bog garden near to an
existing water feature or make it a
feature in its own right. Simply
scoop out an area about 45cm
(18in) deep with sloping sides and a
flat base to the hole. Don't make it
too small, otherwise the soil will be
prone to drying out, but try to keep
the widest part no more than 2m
(6ft) across so that it will be easy to
reach and maintain the plants in the
centre. Line the hole with sand as
you would a pond and then cover
with a flexible liner.

If you are building the bog garden
at the same time as the pond, make

a ridge of stones along the border
between the two and lay some fine-
mesh netting on the bog garden
side along the inside of the stones.
This will stop soil washing through
the stones and muddying the pond.
To allow excess water to drain away,

Good bog garden plants

Aruncus	Hosta
Astilbe	Iris
Caltha	Ligularia
Cardamine	Lysichiton
Filipendula	Lobelia (some)
Hardy ferns	Primula (some)
Hemerocallis	Zantedeschia

HOW TO PLANT A BOG PLANT

1 Adjust the position of the bog plants while
they are still in their pots until you are
satisfied with the arrangement. Water each
container well and allow to drain before
planting the centre of the bog garden first.

2 Make a planting hole slightly larger than
the container and plant at the same depth.
Firm the soil carefully around each plant.

3 Level the soil over the bog garden after
planting is complete and cover the surface
with a layer of loose organic mulch to help
prevent moisture loss. Take care not to pile
the mulch against the stems of the plants.

HOW TO PROPAGATE BOG PLANTS BY SEED

1 Fill the base of a seed tray with stones for drainage, then fill with aquatic compost to within 1cm (½in) of the top.

2 Firm down the aquatic compost with a tray of the same size, but do not compact it. Moisten the compost by standing the tray in shallow water for a couple of hours until the surface of the compost darkens with moisture.

3 Scatter the seeds thinly and cover with compost. Spray regularly to keep the compost moist. When they are big enough to handle, pot up the seedlings and grow them on.

make a few well-spaced holes in the bog garden liner and cover with a 5cm (2in) layer of grit. Trim the flexible liner to leave a 15cm (6in) overlap on all sides before filling the bog garden with a mixture of three parts topsoil to one part well-rotted organic matter. Allow the soil to settle for a couple of weeks and then mix in a slow-release fertilizer. Water well before planting up with your chosen bog plants. Start in the centre and work your way outwards. As a finishing touch, cover the liner flap with decorative pebbles or other stones. Alternatively, if it is next to a border, cover it with a thin layer of soil or mulch.

Careful planting of the bog garden will help to make a subtle transition to the wider garden.

Rock gardens

Like ponds or watercourses, rock gardens benefit from an open site. If planned well, they can each enhance the other. In a level garden the soil excavated during pond installation can be used to form the base.

Building a rock garden

When you build a rock garden, aim as far as possible to create as natural-looking outcrop, otherwise it will take on the appearance of a rock-encrusted heap of soil. The most important ingredient is the rocks, which are more likely to "gel" as a rocky outcrop if they are of the same natural stone. Choose a type of rock that has clear strata lines running through it and an attractive texture and colour. Limestone and sandstone are perhaps the best rock types, but it is possible to create an attractive feature from other types of rock.

You will need a range of sizes of rock – anything from 15kg (33lb) to 100kg (well over 200lb) – so make sure you have help to manoeuvre the larger stones. If you live near a quarry, use this as your source, otherwise suppliers can be found in local directories, and a limited selection of rocks is offered at some garden centres.

Rock gardens are perfect for growing a selection of alpine plants.

HOW TO BUILD A ROCK GARDEN

1 The base of the rock garden is a good place to dispose of rubble and subsoil excavated if you have dug out a pond.

2 Use a special soil mixture for the top 15–23cm (6–9in), especially if soil excavated from a pond is used. Mix equal parts of soil, coarse grit and peat (or peat substitute) and spread evenly over the mound.

3 Lay the first rocks at the base, making sure that the strata run in the same direction, and add more soil mixture around them.

Designing a rock garden

The design should suit the situation. On sloping ground you can build a natural-looking outcrop or a series of terraces or a combination of the two for a very large rockery. On a level site a more acute outcrop, with strata lines at a 45 degree angle, can work well, or choose a series of flattish stones to create a pavement effect with horizontal strata lines.

Careful planning is essential. Mark out the site using string and improve drainage if necessary – if you have heavy soil this may mean digging a hole 30cm (12in) deep, half-filling it with rubble and covering it with a layer of sharp sand before topping with good-quality, free-draining topsoil mixture.

Building a rockery on a slope

If practicable start at the bottom of the slope and build in layers. Choose the best-looking stone to start building your rockery and position it in the middle so that the strata lines angle gently back into the ground. About one-third of the stone will be underground, so you will have to scoop out a hole to accommodate it. Then add stones either side so that the strata lines

HOW TO PLANT A ROCK GARDEN

1 Position the plants while still in their pots so that you can see how they look and adjust if necessary. Alpines are a good choice of plant for a rock garden.

2 Use a trowel to take out a hole a little larger than the rootball. You can buy narrow trowels that are particularly useful for planting in the crevices between rocks.

3 Make sure that the plant is at the correct depth, then trickle gritty soil around the roots and firm it well.

4 Finish off by covering the exposed surface with more grit to improve drainage and protect leaves from splashing mud.

fall away at exactly the same angle. Make sure that each stone is set firm before positioning the next by ramming soil around the rock. Repeat the process for each layer of the rockery, then fill any gaps with a free-draining mixture consisting of equal parts of good quality topsoil, peat (or peat substitute) and coarse grit. Then plant and mulch the surface with stone chippings to match the rocks used in the rockery.

4 Lever the next row of rocks into position. Using rollers and levers is the best way to move heavy rocks around.

5 As each layer is built up, add more of the soil mixture and consolidate it around each of the rocks in turn.

6 Make sure that the sides slope inwards and make the top reasonably flat rather than building it into a pinnacle. Position the plants, then cover the exposed soil with a layer of stone chippings.

Vegetable gardening

Growing your own vegetables is one of the most satisfying aspects of gardening. On a large plot you can even become self-sufficient if you plan carefully and are able to put in the necessary time and effort. Even in a small garden you can grow a wide range of vegetables, which will reduce your grocery bills and provide tasty meals throughout the year.

There are a number of factors to consider before you embark on redesigning your plot to grow vegetables. First, look at the garden itself, its location, aspect, soil type and size. Second, assess the labour force: how good are you at gardening and how much time will you be able to devote to tending your crops? Don't forget holidays, because these tend to fall at the most inconvenient times. Then, consider whether you intend to grow vegetables to eat fresh or to produce sufficient for winter storage. Finally, draw up a list of the vegetables you like to eat.

Wigwams or tepees of long bamboo canes support runner beans.

Planning a kitchen garden

The initial planning is the most important part of growing a range of vegetables for the kitchen. It is essential to plan for a continuous supply and to avoid gluts and shortages.

Choosing a style

Careful planning will help you to achieve a continuity of supply of vegetables for the kitchen table. Timing is critical, and the best way to get this right is to work out when you want particular crops to reach maturity and then to work backwards to decide on the best possible sowing dates.

There are three main systems for growing vegetables: in rows in a designated plot; in permanent vegetable beds; and randomly mixed throughout the garden. The last is perhaps the most aesthetically pleasing in a small suburban garden, but vegetable crops have to compete with neighbouring plants for light, moisture and nutrients, which

reduces growth and subsequent yields. For this reason most gardeners prefer the traditional method of growing vegetables in a dedicated area that can be kept clear of other plants and prepared specifically with the needs of the vegetables in mind.

Recently, a system of permanent beds, called no-dig beds, has become fashionable. The vegetables are grown in beds surrounded by permanent paths, which means that they can be grown more closely together, and yields are higher because the soil is not compacted by trampling. This system also requires less effort to prepare the soil – often no digging is needed once the system is set up – and because rows are much shorter, access to all parts of the vegetable area is easier. Furthermore, because the plants are grown close together the opportunities for weeds to become established are minimized. This system can also be

Sowing crops in rows in a designated vegetable plot makes weeding much easier.

used effectively in a small garden, especially if you choose a decorative material for the paths.

Creating no-dig beds

Plan the design of the beds carefully. A series of straight beds may be the most suitable design on an allotment, but in a small garden a system of interlocking beds could be more attractive. However, do not choose too intricate a scheme because this will reduce the amount of growing space and undermine the advantages of growing vegetables in this way.

The beds should be about 1.2m (4ft) wide, so that the centre can be reached from either side, and the paths should be about 30cm (12in) wide. If you want wheelbarrow access you will need to increase the path width accordingly. Use tanalized gravel boards 15cm (6in) wide to make the sides. Support them with stakes 45cm (18in) long and 5cm (2in) square, at the corners and at 1m (3ft) intervals along the sides. Dig the beds over thoroughly, then

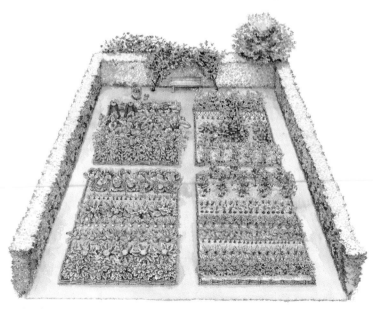

When there is room in the garden, a dedicated plot is the most productive way of growing vegetables. Dividing the vegetable garden into beds makes crop rotation much simpler.

scoop the topsoil from the paths into the beds and top up with a mixture of equal parts of well-rotted organic matter and topsoil. Cover the paths with a weed-suppressing membrane and cover this with chipped bark or another all-weather material.

Crop rotation

If you grow the same family of vegetables on the same ground year after year, soil-borne pests and diseases will build up, reducing yields. The easiest way to avoid this on permanent vegetable plots and beds is to use a crop rotation system over three or four years. This method of gardening also has the advantage of using your time in the garden efficiently. For example, a plot can be heavily manured when it is dug in the autumn, providing ideal conditions for cabbages. The following year the plot can simply be dug over, ready for planting root crops, which do not like the soil to be too rich.

Crops are grouped by their family. Grow each group in a different area, then rotate the crops around the areas with each year. There are four main groups.

Brassicas This family includes broccoli, Brussels sprouts, cabbage, calabrese, cauliflowers, kale, kohl rabi and radishes.

Legumes The vegetables in this group include peas, French (green) beans, runner beans and broad (fava) beans.

Onion family This group includes shallots, garlic, leeks and spring onions (scallions) as well as onions.

Root crops Potatoes, parsnips, swedes (rutabaga), beetroot (beets), carrots and turnips are all defined as root crop vegetables.

If you are using a four-year rotation system, each of these crops can be grown in a different bed, but if you are working on a three-year system, combine the legume and onion crops in one bed. It may also be worth creating a permanent bed

Vegetable beds filled with colourful, strongly growing crops can be as attractive as more conventional ornamental plants.

to grow crops such as asparagus, rhubarb, artichokes and sea kale. Whether you adopt a three- or four-year rotation, make sure that brassicas, in particular, are moved every year.

HOW TO PLAN A THREE-YEAR CROP ROTATION

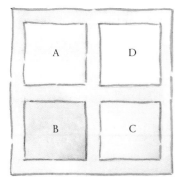

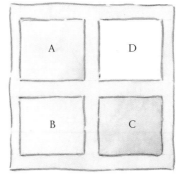

Year 1
There are four beds in the vegetable garden. Crops are grown in a four-year or three-year rotation system.

Bed A	Onions and legumes
Bed B	Root crops
Bed C	Brassicas and lettuces
Bed D	Permanent

Year 2
With the exception of certain vegetables, which need a permanent site, the crops are planted in a different bed each year.

Bed A	Brassicas and lettuces
Bed B	Onions and legumes
Bed C	Root crops
Bed D	Permanent

Year 3
Moving the crops in this way helps to prevent pests and diseases lingering from one year to the next and allows efficient soil management.

Bed A	Root crops
Bed B	Brassicas and lettuces
Bed C	Onions and legumes
Bed D	Permanent

Sowing vegetables

Most vegetables are raised from seed, but the techniques you use will depend on the time and facilities you have available and on the crops you want to grow.

Buying vegetable seed

There is an extensive range of crops available by mail order from seed companies, from gardening websites and from garden centres. If you are buying by post, order seeds during the winter months when you are planning your next year's planting so that you are ready to sow in early spring. There are three main ways of sowing, and the method you use will depend on the crops you grow.

Sowing indoors

Indoor sowing in pots or modular seed trays (flats) is an ideal way of getting vegetables off to an early start. This approach gives the most reliable results, but it is expensive because you need to invest in equipment, such as a propagator, and provide somewhere heated to grow them on. The main advantage is that you can sow exactly when you want to, regardless of the weather and soil

SOWING INDOORS

After sowing seeds in blocks or trays, they should be thoroughly watered and then placed in a warm position for germination.

conditions. It is a good system for crops such as tomatoes, which are expensive to buy as seed, and tender crops, such as courgettes (zucchini), which need to be kept under cover until the threat of frost has passed.

Sowing in seedbeds

Some crops, notably brassicas, are best sown in a specially prepared area and then transplanted when they reach a suitable size. The main advantage of this system is that you can use your best piece of ground to raise the crops from seed and give them extra attention during this

SOWING IN A SEEDBED

Crops planted in a seedbed can be protected from bad weather with cloches. They are transferred to their final position in late spring.

critical growing period. Raising plants in a seedbed also makes it practical to protect the seedlings from the worst of the weather using cloches. This system is of particular value for widely spaced crops that would otherwise occupy a lot of growing area while still young. It is not suitable for crops that resent root disturbance, however.

Sowing direct in rows

Many crops are best sown direct in the rows where they are to grow on to maturity. This is a good system for crops, such as broad (fava) beans

HOW TO SOW SEEDS IN DRILLS

1 Most vegetables grown in rows, such as carrots, are sown in drills. Use a garden line to make sure the drills – and therefore the rows – are straight.

2 Open up a shallow drill with the corner of a hoe or rake. Refer to the seed packet for the recommended depth.

3 Flood the drills with water before sowing if the weather is dry. Do it before sowing rather than after so that the seeds are not washed away or into clumps.

TECHNIQUES FOR SOWING SEED AND PLANTING BULBS

1 Parsnip, carrot, onion and parsley seeds are sometimes germinated then mixed with wallpaper paste, placed in a bag and squeezed over the soil. This is called fluid sowing.

2 Carrots must be sown thinly. Mix the seed with a little silver sand, which makes it easier to sow both thinly and evenly.

3 Large seeds, such as peas, can be sown individually, at the correct spacing in a wide drill. Make sure the trench is the right depth.

4 Shallots are spaced about 15cm (6in) apart. Push the bulbs into the drill so that the tips are just protruding. Pull the soil back around them with a hoe or rake.

and peas, that can be set out at the correct spacing and for crops, such as carrots and radishes, that do not like to be moved once they have germinated. The main drawback is that you waste seed in having to thin plants to the correct spacing, and through variable germination and losses from pests and diseases.

Fluid sowing

In dry soil or during the summer months germination from direct sowing can be erratic. One way to overcome this is to use a technique called fluid sowing. Pre-germinate the seed on sheets of moist kitchen paper. When the roots are just showing, before the leaves open, mix the seeds with a half-strength, fungicide-free wallpaper paste or a special sowing gel. Put the mix into a plastic bag and make a small hole by cutting off one corner. Twist the top of the bag to prevent the paste oozing out, then squeeze out the mixture into the prepared seed drill as if you were icing a cake.

4 Sprinkle the seeds evenly along the drill. Do this carefully now and you will save time later when you have to thin the seedlings.

5 Cover the row of seeds with compost (soil mix) if your soil is stony.

6 Use a rake to return the excavated soil to the drills. Rake in the direction of the row, not across it, otherwise you might spread the seeds and produce an uneven row.

Planting vegetables

A limited number of vegetables are now available to buy, either as seedlings or as plants in pots. They can be good value if you want just a few plants or for those vegetables that are tricky to raise from seed. Plant out these vegetables as soon as you can. You will also need to plant out the crops sown under glass, and those grown in seedbeds.

Buying plants

If you are buying plants from your local garden centre, ask when the next delivery is due and visit as soon as possible afterwards so that the plants are not left in inappropriate conditions. Choose stocky plants with dark green leaves and no signs of discoloration. Yellow leaves are a sign of starvation, and a blue tinge could indicate that the plants have been allowed to get too cold. Also avoid plants with signs of pests and diseases, such as speckled leaves, and check growing tips for pests, such as aphids, which not only weaken plants but also transmit diseases, such as leaf viruses.

PLANTING BOUGHT SEEDLINGS

This courgette (zucchini) has been grown in a fibre pot so that the roots are disturbed as little as possible when it is planted out. Buying seedlings of frost-tender plants is a good option if you are not able to provide the conditions that are needed to germinate the seeds yourself.

Planting vegetables in rows makes it much easier when weeding as you will be able to identify more easily what are weeds and what are wanted plants.

Vegetable planner

Vegetable	germination temperature	sowing depth	planting distance in rows	distance between rows
Bean, broad (fava)	5°C (40°F)	5cm (2in)	15cm (6in)	50cm (20in)
Bean, French (green)	10°C (50°F)	5cm (2in)	8cm (3in)	45cm (18in)
Bean, runner	10°C (50°F)	5cm (2in)	15cm (6in)	60cm (24in)
Beetroot (beet)	7°C (45°F)	2.5cm (1in)	5cm (2in)	15cm (6in)
Broccoli	5°C (40°F)	5cm (2in)	60cm (24in)	60cm (24in)
Brussels sprouts	5°C (40°F)	5cm (2in)	60cm (24in)	1m (3ft)
Cabbage	5°C (40°F)	5cm (2in)	30cm (12in)	30cm (12in)
Calabrese	5°C (40°F)	5cm (2in)	25cm (10in)	30cm (12in)
Carrot	7°C (45°F)	2.5cm (1in)	8cm (3in)	15cm (6in)
Cauliflower	5°C (40°F)	2.5cm (1in)	45cm (18in)	60cm (24in)
Courgette (zucchini)	15°C (60°F)	2.5cm (1in)	1m (3ft)	1m (3ft)
Leek	7°C (45°F)	2.5cm (1in)	23cm (9in)	23cm (9in)
Lettuce	5°C (40°F)	1cm (½in)	30cm (12in)	30cm (12in)
Marrow (large zucchini)	15°C (60°F)	2.5cm (1in)	1m (3ft)	1m (3ft)
Onion	7°C (45°F)	1cm (½in)	4cm (1½in)	23cm (9in)
Parsnip	7°C (45°F)	1cm (½in)	15cm (6in)	30cm (12in)
Pea	5°C (40°F)	2.5cm (1in)	5cm (2in)	45cm (18in)
Radish	5°C (40°F)	1cm (½in)	1cm (½in)	15cm (6in)
Spinach	10°C (50°F)	1cm (½in)	15cm (6in)	30cm (12in)
Swede (rutabaga)	5°C (40°F)	2.5cm (1in)	15cm (6in)	30cm (12in)
Sweetcorn (corn)	10°C (50°F)	2.5cm (1in)	35cm (14in)	35cm (14in)
Tomato	15°C (60°F)	2.5cm (1in)	40cm (16in)	45cm (18in)
Turnip	15°C (60°F)	2.5cm (1in)	13cm (5in)	23cm (9in)

PLANTING MODULE SEEDLINGS

Cabbages and cauliflowers are often raised in modules so that the seedlings receive less of a shock when they are transplanted. Many modules are designed so that you can remove the plant by gently squeezing the base while gently supporting the plant at the top.

HOW TO MINIMIZE ROOT DISTURBANCE WHEN PLANTING PEAS

1 Start off the seeds in a length of old gutter. Block the ends and fill with soil. Sow the seeds about 5–8cm (2–3in) apart and cover with soil. Place the gutter in a greenhouse or cold frame, and water regularly to keep the soil moist.

2 When the seedlings are ready to plant out in their final position in the garden, make a shallow drill with a draw hoe. Carefully slide the peas out of the gutter and into the row. The seedlings will need to be thinned out as they grow.

Planting out vegetables

Hardy vegetables, such as cabbages, Brussels sprouts and other brassicas, that have been kept outside should be ready for planting out in the garden as soon as soil conditions allow. However, plants displayed under cover at the garden centre will need hardening off before being planted out. You will also need to harden off plants you have grown from seed in a greenhouse or a cold frame. It is important not to buy tender varieties too early in the season, otherwise you will have to keep them in a sheltered position until the risk of frosts has passed.

When planting out vegetables, try to minimize the root disturbance so that the plants don't suffer a check in growth. Water the seedlings before planting and set them out at the same depth as they were in the container. Use a garden line and cane marked with the correct spacing to make planting easier. Most vegetables are planted in straight rows, but sweetcorn (corn) should be planted in blocks of short rows because they are wind pollinated and need other plants growing on all sides to ensure a good set. Plant seedlings and container-grown plants at the correct distances apart.

If the weather is bad or the soil conditions prevent immediate planting, keep container plants well watered. If the delay is over two weeks, repot into the next size pot.

HOW TO TRANSPLANT SEEDLINGS GROWN IN A SEEDBED

1 Loosen the soil with a fork or trowel. It is best to lift each plantlet individually with a trowel, but if they have not been thinned sufficiently this may be difficult.

2 Plant with a trowel and firm the soil well. A convenient way to firm soil around the roots is to insert the blade of the trowel about 5cm (2in) away from the plant and press it firmly towards the roots.

3 Brassicas need to be planted firmly. Test this by tugging a leaf after planting. Always water in thoroughly after transplanting.

Growing legumes and onions

Beans, peas, onions and leeks are essential ingredients in the kitchen and can be very rewarding to grow in the garden.

Legumes

Treat most beans as half-hardy annuals and either sow them indoors in early spring, ready for planting out after the last frost, or sow direct outside into prepared soil in late spring. However, broad beans and peas can be sown direct outside in late winter or early spring.

Broad (fava) beans Sow 5cm (2in) deep and 15cm (6in) apart in a no-dig bed or 10cm (4in) apart in double rows spaced 50cm (20in) apart elsewhere. Sow an early crop in mid-winter under the protection of cloches, or in late winter, and a main crop in early spring. Pinch out 8cm (3in) of the growing tip as the first beans start to form to discourage aphids. Water well from this stage and provide support in exposed gardens using stout bamboo canes and string either side of the row.

Runner beans Sow indoors in deep pots in early spring and plant out after hardening off when the threat

HOW TO PLANT RUNNER BEANS

Runner beans should be planted against a wigwam of canes to provide support as they grow.

of frost has passed. Alternatively, sow direct outside against a supporting tent or wigwam of 1.8m (6ft) canes, spaced 15cm (6in) apart with 60cm (24in) between rows about a fortnight before the expected last frost. Sow spares to replace early losses. A second sowing in late spring will ensure a continuous crop until autumn. Mulch between rows and protect young plants from slugs. Do not allow pods to mature on the plant, otherwise cropping will be

Few things taste better than garden-fresh beans. Surpluses can be easily frozen for later in the year.

reduced. Grow over arches between no-dig beds for a decorative and productive feature.

Dwarf French beans (green beans) These tender plants need to be sown or planted out after the last frost. Sow beans 5cm (2in) deep in pots and then plant out in rows in mid-spring under the protection of cloches. Alternatively, the beans can

PINCHING OUT BEANS

Pinching out the tops of broad (fava) beans is good practice because it discourages aphids. The tops can then be boiled and eaten.

STAKING BEANS

Taller varieties of broad beans will need supporting with string tied to canes, which should be set at intervals along the rows.

SUPPORTING PEAS

Wire netting can be used to support shorter varieties of peas.

be planted 15cm (6in) apart in a no-dig bed or 8cm (3in) apart in rows. The rows should be spaced 45cm (12in) apart. A second crop of beans can be sown direct outside in mid-spring. Mulch between rows and protect young plants from slugs. Water well while pods are forming and provide support in exposed gardens with pea sticks or netting.

Peas Autumn sowings overwintered outside are often recommended for early crops of peas but are invariably disappointing. A more reliable method is to sow in lengths of guttering in early spring and plant out under cloches when about 8cm (3in) tall after hardening off. Later crops can be sown direct outside in a 15cm (6in) wide trench about 5cm (2in) deep, with staggered rows set 5cm (2in) apart. Make several sowings in succession every fortnight until early summer. Protect the peas from birds and mice. Mulch between rows to conserve soil moisture and water well while pods are forming. Taller varieties will need pea sticks or netting support.

The onion family

Bulbous vegetables including onions, leeks, garlic and shallots are very easy to grow and store, making them one of the most straightforward types of vegetables to provide a year-round supply for the kitchen. They can be raised from seed or grown from mini-bulbs (sets).

Onions Sow in early spring for a late summer harvest, or midsummer for a spring crop of Japanese varieties. Keep plants weed-free. There is no need to water unless the summer is particularly dry. Spring onions (scallions) should be sown in succession from mid-spring until early summer for a continuous supply throughout the summer

PLANTING OUT LEEK SEEDLINGS

Use a dibber to make a hole in the ground. The plant can then be dropped into the hole, and the earth firmed in around it.

months. In no-dig beds sow onions 5cm (2in) apart, or, elsewhere, sow in drills, that are about 1cm (½in) deep and 23cm (9in) apart. Thin out the plants to 4cm (1½in) apart once the seedling has straightened and later to 10cm (4in). Rows of spring onions need be only 10cm (4in) apart.

Onions raised in containers in the greenhouse should be planted out 10cm (4in) apart. Alternatively, plant onion sets in mid-spring about 10cm (4in) apart in rows that are spaced 23cm (9in) apart. Protect newly planted sets from birds. Hoe the soil carefully to keep the rows of onions free of weeds.

Leeks Sow in a well-prepared seedbed in drills about 1cm (½in) deep and 23cm (9in) apart, thinning the plants to 23cm (9in) apart. Pull up soil around the stems to blanch them. Make sure that you do not get soil between the leaves. Plant out greenhouse-raised plants and transplant seedlings raised in a seedbed when 20cm (8in) high. Plant into 15cm (6in) deep holes spaced 15cm (6in) apart in rows 30cm (12in) apart.

EARTHING UP LEEKS

As the leeks grow earth (hill) them up by pulling the soil up around the stems to blanch them. This will give the leeks a better flavour.

Shallots Sow as for onions, planting sets in early spring 15cm (6in) apart in rows 23cm (9in) apart during early spring. Keep the crop free from weeds, and water if necessary. Apply a mulch between the rows to conserve moisture.

Garlic Plant cloves during late winter or early spring about 2.5cm (1in) deep in rows spaced 15cm (6in) apart. Treat as described for shallots.

PLANTING OUT SHALLOTS

Once the shoots of container-grown shallots are about 10cm (4in) high, plant out in the garden, spacing them about 15cm (6in) apart, in rows that are 23cm (9in) apart.

Growing root crops

Root vegetables, which include crops such as carrots, parsnips and turnips, are reasonably easy to grow provided your soil is deep and not too stony. Root crops are biennials, which means that during their first year they build up reserves in a storage root to enable them to flower well the following year.

Cultivation

Most root crops prefer an open, sunny site. The soil should be light, and should not have been recently manured. Root crops prefer a moist soil, so you may have to water them in dry weather. They are usually hardy, and the vegetables can be left in the ground over winter, to be harvested as needed.

In very stony ground, root crops such as parsnips and carrots may fork and produce rather stunted growth. To avoid this, use a crowbar to make deep holes at the correct planting distance and fill them with potting compost (soil mix) so that the seeds can be sown in this.

A flourishing row of carrots coming to maturity.

HOW TO PLANT IN STONY SOIL

1 If the soil is very stony or of poor quality it is worth making improvements before planting. Use a crowbar to make a conical hole at the required planting distances.

2 Fill the hole with potting compost (soil mix). Sow the seed in the middle and then cover with more earth.

Beetroot (beets) Sow bolt-resistant varieties under cloches in early spring for an early summer crop, followed by a late spring sowing for a summer harvest. An early summer sowing will provide a crop in autumn and winter. Sow seed in a well-prepared seedbed in drills about 2.5cm (1in) deep and 15cm (6in) apart, spacing seeds 5cm (2in) apart. The seeds are in fact usually made up of a cluster of seeds and so produce several seedlings close together. Thin to leave the strongest plant at each station. When roots reach 2.5cm (1in) across, thin again by removing every other plant.

Carrots Sow carrot seeds under cloches in early spring for a crop by early summer. Sow maincrop varieties in succession every few

THINNING CARROTS

Thin carrots only if necessary as they resent disturbance. Choose a still, muggy evening to prevent the smell of carrots travelling and betraying their presence to carrotflies.

weeks from mid-spring for a midsummer crop to early summer for an autumn crop. A late sowing can also be made in late summer under cloches for a tender winter crop. Sow in a well-prepared seedbed in drills about 1cm (½in) deep and 15cm (6in) apart, thinning plants to 8cm (3in) apart when they are large enough to handle. Hand weed to keep the rows clear. Put up a 75cm (30in) high barrier of insect-proof

Beetroot growing in a raised bed. The bulk of the vegetable's swollen root sits on top of the ground so that you can watch its progress and determine when it is ready to harvest.

WATERING

Fennel plants, like root vegetables, need plenty of moisture. In dry periods you may have to water them to keep the crop healthy, but a good mulch should help.

mesh around the crop to prevent carrotfly. If necessary, cover the tops of developing carrots with soil to prevent them going green.

Parsnips Sow in mid-spring for a late summer harvest in a well-prepared seedbed in drills about 1cm (½in) deep and 30cm (12in) apart. Sow a few seeds together at 15cm (6in) intervals along the row, thinning seedlings to leave the strongest plant at each station.

Swede (rutabaga) Sow in late spring for an early autumn harvest in a well-prepared seedbed in drills about 1cm (½in) deep and 15cm (6in) apart. When large enough to handle, thin plants in stages until 30cm (12in) apart. Watch out for flea beetle.

Turnips Sow early varieties under cloches in early spring followed by crops sown in succession from mid-spring to early summer. A late sowing can also be made in late summer under cloches for spring greens. Sow in a well-prepared seedbed in drills about 1cm (½in) deep and 23cm (9in) apart, thinning to 13cm (5in) apart when they are large enough to handle.

Fennel Sow the seeds in early to midsummer in drills 1cm (½in) deep and 45cm (18in) apart. Thin the seedlings to 23cm (9in). When the bulbs begin to swell, draw up the soil around them to blanch, which will improve the taste.

Potatoes Although potatoes are relatively easy to grow, they take up a great deal of space and rewards are relatively low. However, they are worth growing if you particularly like an unusual variety or if you are fond of new potatoes, which are fairly expensive in the shops.

Place seed potatoes in the light to sprout (known as chitting) at a temperature of about 10°C (50°F). For an early crop, plant under cloches in late winter through a black polythene mulch, setting seed potatoes about 15cm (6in) deep and 30cm (12in) apart with 60cm (24in) between rows. Cover with a double layer of garden fleece to help insulate the crop.

Space later crops slightly wider and protect emerging shoots from frost by earthing up – pulling soil from between the rows to form a mound over the row. This will also eliminate weeds. You can also grow an early crop for a midwinter harvest in a large container, such as an empty plastic dustbin.

PLANTING POTATOES

Seed potatoes should be planted out after being placed in the light to sprout.

Growing leafy vegetables

Leafy vegetables such as cabbage, cauliflower and Brussels sprouts are all members of the brassica family and so can be treated in a similar way. They all suffer from the same range of pests and diseases, but these can largely be avoided if you use the right techniques.

Cultivation

Most brassicas do best in an open, sunny site in a soil that is fertile but free-draining. They do not like a soil that is too acid and it may be worth adding lime to bring the soil down to a pH of 6.5–7. You may have to protect Brussels sprouts, which grow fairly tall, from the wind. Some brassicas, such as savoy cabbages and Brussels sprouts, taste better after they have experienced a winter frost.

Brussels sprouts Sow under cloches in early spring for a late summer crop, wait until mid-spring for an autumn and winter harvest. Treat as for cabbages, except that the transplants should be 60cm (24in) apart in rows 90cm (36in) apart.

Stake tall varieties in winter and remove yellowing leaves. Firm soil around plants in winter if they are loosened by frost. There is a large amount of space between plants, so it may be worth intercropping with lettuces or radishes.

Cabbages By choosing the right combination of varieties you can have cabbages all the year round. Spring cabbages are sown in midsummer for cropping from early spring the following year, summer cabbages are sown under cloches in early spring for harvesting from midsummer onwards, while winter cabbages are sown in mid- to late spring for a crop from autumn until the middle of spring the following year. Sow in a well-prepared seedbed in drills about 1cm (½in) deep and 15cm (6in) apart, thinning plants to 8cm (3in) apart. When five leaves have developed on the seedlings they are ready for transplanting to their growing position. Space seedlings 30–45cm (12–18in) apart in the row and between rows depending on

Cauliflowers are sometimes scorched by the hot sun. Protect from discoloration by covering them with the inner leaves.

the variety. Make 15cm (6in) deep holes, firming well after planting. Place a 15cm (6in) square collar of carpet underlay, slit to the centre, around each seedling to protect against adult cabbage rootfly. Also cover with garden fleece or insect-proof mesh after planting to prevent butterflies from laying their eggs on your plants, and protect against birds. Keep weeds under control.

Cabbage plants can be started in a cold frame before moving to their final growing position.

This block of healthy Brussels sprouts has been inter-planted with red cabbages to create a highly decorative effect in the kitchen garden.

Cauliflowers More difficult to grow than other members of the cabbage family, cauliflowers are grouped into winter, summer and autumn varieties. All are sown from mid- to late spring to mature from early spring, early summer and early autumn respectively. Treat as for cabbages, but space the transplants 60cm (24in) apart both ways. It is important that the cauliflowers' growth is not checked because this causes irregular and undersized heads. Ensure the plants always have plenty of water.

Kale and broccoli Treat as for cabbages but space the transplants 45cm (18in) apart both ways. Stake tall varieties in winter and remove yellowing leaves. Firm soil around plants if they are loosened by frost. Kale should be kept steadily growing because it is slow to recover from any checks. Water during any dry spells.

Salad crops

These vegetables are the best crops for new gardeners to start with because they can be fitted in around other plants, even grown in flower beds and mixed borders. They grow

Lettuces grow relatively quickly and can be ready for harvesting from 5 to 12 weeks after sowing, depending on the variety. Start early sowings under glass; otherwise, sow directly into the bed.

HOW TO WEED

Weeding with a hand fork is often the best option when delicate plants are spaced very closely together.

and mature quicky and tend to suffer from fewer problems than many other vegetables.

Lettuces You can achieve a year-round harvest by selecting the right combination of varieties and sowing in succession. Sow undercover or under cloches in early spring for a crop in late spring and then follow this at intervals with further sowings made when the previous sowing has produced sturdy seedlings. Sow in a well-prepared seedbed in drills about 1cm (½in) deep and 30cm (12in) apart, thinning plants to 30cm (12in) apart when they are large enough to handle. Cover with insect-proof mesh to protect from insect pests (especially aphids) and birds. Slugs can also be a problem, so protect plants from these.

Radishes Site radishes between other slower-growing crops to make efficient use of space. Sow under cloches from early spring followed by crops sown in succession from mid-spring to early summer. A late sowing of winter radish can also be

made in late summer under cloches for a late autumn harvest. Sow in a well-prepared seedbed in drills about 1cm (½in) deep and 15cm (6in) apart in summer, or 23cm (9in) apart in winter. Thin seedlings if necessary to 2.5cm (1in) apart. Protect against birds and slugs and keep weeds under control.

HOW TO INTERCROP LETTUCES

Lettuces can be planted between slower growing plants. Here, they will be harvested before the cabbages overshadow them.

Protecting vegetables

The vegetable garden, with its rows of closely growing crops, is an ideal breeding ground for many pests and diseases. Always take preventative action before any problem gets out of hand.

Good garden hygiene

Most insect pests are fairly easy to control with chemicals, but in the vegetable garden it is always worth considering techniques that will help to prevent the pest from becoming a problem in the first place, making spraying unnecessary.

Plant debris and weeds will provide vital overwintering sites for pests and diseases and so must be cleared away to prevent problems persisting from one season to the next. Burn or throw away the material rather than composting to reduce the risk of the problem returning.

Most pests and diseases will not get a foothold if your plants are growing well at all times. Choose disease-resistant varieties whenever

A mixed garden that contains plenty of flowers will attract a host of welcome natural predators such as ladybirds (ladybugs) and hoverflies. They will attack any pests that arrive in the garden.

possible (see opposite) and, if you buy container-grown vegetables, choose healthy stock. It is essential that crops do not suffer a check in

growth due to lack of moisture or nutrients as this will weaken their ability to fight off an attack. Inspect vegetables regularly to spot pest and disease outbreaks early and take remedial action as promptly as possible. Caught early enough, most plants will recover from the pest or disease attacks.

USING NETS

Birds and butterflies can be kept at bay with fine-meshed nets.

USING WIRE NETTING

Wire-mesh nets can be used to guard your crops against rabbits and rodents.

PROTECTING BRASSICAS

Protect young brassicas from cabbage rootfly by placing a collar around the base of each plant. The collar can be made of plastic, felt or even a square of old carpet; the important factor is making a barrier.

Timing

Most pests have an annual life cycle, so if you understand when the pest is most likely to be a problem you can avoid it. For example, peas sown before early spring and after late spring will not be in flower when the pea moth is on the wing so cannot be attacked. Similarly, carrots sown by late spring will be harvested before midsummer to avoid carrotfly, and later sowings of brassicas can avoid the worst of the flea beetle attacks.

Barriers

Many pests can be out-smarted by using barriers. For example, after planting cabbage plants, place a 15cm (6in) square collar of plastic or carpet underlay, slit to the centre, around each seedling. This will prove to be an effective barrier to the cabbage rootfly adults as they try to lay their eggs. Similarly, seedlings that are susceptible to slugs and snails should be protected with individual cloches made from cut-down plastic drinks bottles.

Other pests, such as carrotfly and cabbage caterpillars, can be combated using physical barriers surrounding the crop. By putting up a 75cm (30in) high fence of insect-proof mesh around your carrots you can successfully prevent the low-flying carrotfly from reaching your plants. To deter cabbage caterpillars, cover susceptible crops with horticultural fleece or insect-proof mesh after planting to stop the adult butterflies from laying their eggs on your plants. Lay the crop cover loosely over the plants so that there is plenty of room for growth, burying the edges around the crop to prevent pests gaining access. These covers are also effective against other flying pests, including aphids.

Disease-resistant varieties

Brussels sprouts	powdery mildew	'Adonis', 'Cascade', 'Citadel', 'Cor', 'Icarus', 'Odette', 'Tavernos', 'Topline', 'Troika'
Cabbages	downy mildew	'Derby Day', 'Stonehead'
Calabrese	clubroot	'Trixie'
Courgettes (zucchini)	mosaic virus	'Defender', 'Supremo'
Leeks	rust	'Bandit', 'Conora', 'Poribleu', 'Poristo'
Lettuces	downy mildew	'Avondefiance', 'Challenge', 'Dolly', 'Musette', 'Soraya'
Marrows (large zucchini)	mosaic virus	'Tiger Cross'
Parsnips	canker	'Arrow', 'Avonresister', 'Gladiator', 'Javelin', 'Lancer', 'White Gem'
Potatoes	blackleg	'Kestrel', 'Maxine', 'Pentland Crown', 'Saxon'
	blight	'Cara', 'Maris Piper', 'Pentland Dell', 'Romano', 'Stirling', 'Valor';
	virus	'Pentland Crown', 'Sante', 'Wilja'
	nematode	'Accent', 'Cara', 'Concorde', 'Maris Piper', 'Nadine', 'Pentland Javelin', 'Sante'
	scab	'Accent', 'Carlingford', 'Nadine', 'Pentland Crown', 'Swift', 'Wilja'
	spraing	'Accent', 'Premiere', 'Romano'
Swedes (rutabaga)	mildew	'Marian'
Tomatoes	leafmould and wilt	'Blizzard', 'Counter', 'Dombito', 'Estrella', 'Shirley'

Pest-resistant varieties

Carrots	carrotfly	'Nandor', 'Nantucket', 'Flyaway', 'Sytan'
Lettuces	root aphid	'Avondefiance', 'Beatrice', 'Malika', 'Musette', 'Sabine'
Potatoes	eelworm	'Cara', 'Maris Piper', 'Pentland Javelin'
	slugs	'Pentland Dell', 'Romano'

USING HORTICULTURAL FLEECE

Physical barriers can be used to protect crops against pests. Here, fleece is used to cover brassicas to prevent butterflies from laying their eggs on the plants.

Harvesting vegetables

A well-planned kitchen garden will have a succession of crops that are ready to pick over a long period. The best time to harvest vegetables varies, of course, but the following guide will help you pick your vegetables in their prime.

Peas and beans

Pick peas when the pods swell and they have reached their full length. Harvest mangetout (snow) peas as soon as the blossom drops and pods are about 8cm (3in) long. Pick sugarsnap peas as the peas are just starting to form, but before the pods swell.

Pick over all pea plants regularly to ensure a continuous supply. After harvest is complete, put the plants on the compost heap.

Pick runner beans when they reach a usable size – say 15cm (6in). Pick French (green) beans when they have reached their full length, which is usually about 10cm (4in), but before the seed starts to swell. Both runner and French beans need to be picked regularly, before they get stringy, to ensure a continuous supply. Wait to harvest broad (fava) beans until the seeds have formed but before the stalk goes woody.

Root crops

Harvest beetroots (beets) when the roots are large enough to use but still tender, which is usually when the root starts to produce a square shoulder. Twist off the foliage but leave the stalks 5cm (2in) long to prevent bleeding.

Radishes and early carrots should be pulled as soon as they are large enough to use for the sweetest, most tender roots. Maincrop carrots should be lifted for storing at the end of the growing season. Cut off the leaves to prevent the root from going rubbery.

Turnips, parsnips and swedes (rutabaga) can be pulled as soon as they are large enough to use, or they can be left in the soil until needed and gently lifted with a fork. Twist off the leaves before storage.

Potatoes

Harvest early potatoes when the flowers open. The tubers should be the size of a large hen's egg and the skin should rub off easily. You do not have to dig up the whole plant, simply delve into the soil with your hands and remove tubers that have reached the right size, leaving undersized ones to develop further.

Maincrop potatoes should be harvested when the topgrowth (known as haulm) turns yellow and dies down and the skin on the tubers does not rub off. Remove the haulm and add it to the compost heap, then wait a week before lifting the potatoes. Remove all the tubers you find, even if they are too small to use, so they do not become a weed problem the next year.

Leafy vegetables

Spinach is harvested when the leaves are still young and tender; remove the fully developed outer leaves so that the younger inner ones can grow on. Repeat this process as the plant

HOW TO HARVEST VEGETABLES

Runner beans should be harvested regularly. Pick them over carefully to remove all maturing beans to ensure a continuous crop.

Harvest root vegetables such as carrots and parsnips by digging a fork well under the root and levering them out.

Lift maincrop potato tubers with a fork once the foliage has died down. You can leave them in the ground for longer if penetrating frosts are not likely to be a problem, but lift promptly if pests such as slugs appear.

grows to get a continuous supply. Harvest cabbages when the heads are firm and fleshy, and cauliflowers when the curds are firm and pure white but before they start to separate.

Vegetable fruits

Tomatoes should be harvested with a stalk when ripe and just starting to soften. At the end of the season you can pick unripe tomatoes to ripen off the plant. Place in a drawer with a banana skin to help the process.

Courgettes (zucchini) should be picked when young and firm and about 10cm (4in) long. Harvest regularly to ensure a continuous supply. Harvest marrows (large zucchini), squashes and pumpkins when they are large enough. At the end of the season remove all mature fruit before the first frost.

Pick sweetcorn (corn) when the tassels on the end of the cob turn brown and milky sap oozes from kernels when they are punctured with a fingernail. If the sap is watery the cob is not ready to be harvested.

HOW TO RIPEN ONIONS

1 Ripening can be hastened once onions near their maximum size by bending over their tops so the bulbs are exposed to as much sun as possible. As soon as the foliage has turned a straw colour and is brittle, lift the onions with a fork and leave them on the surface with their roots facing the sun for a week or two to dry off.

2 In wet seasons, finish off the hardening and ripening process by laying the onion bulbs on netting or wire mesh that is supported above the ground so that air can circulate freely. If the weather is very damp, cover the bulbs with cloches until you can store them.

The onion family

Harvest spring onions (scallions) as soon as they are large enough, before the bulb has started to form.

Maincrop onions should be harvested when mature. Loosen the soil under the bulbs when the tops topple over to speed the process. Lift completely about two weeks later. In wet years or on wet soils it may be necessary to lift the bulbs and dry them on mesh sheets or netting somewhere dry for a few weeks before storing.

Leeks can be harvested small or as mature vegetables. They can be left in the soil until needed, when they should be gently lifted with a fork.

Some vegetables are harvested by cutting through the stems as and when they are required. Swiss chard is a good example of this method of harvesting. The stem is cut close to the base. Some gardeners prefer to twist or snap the stems off at the base rather than cutting them.

Harvest cauliflowers by cutting the stem with a sharp knife just below the first ring of leaves.

Pick tomatoes as they become ripe, which will usually be when they turn red all over. Leave the stalk on.

Storing vegetables

If you have a glut of vegetables at the end of the season or want to have a continuity of supply throughout the winter, there are a number of techniques you can use to store them successfully.

Short-term storage

Although many vegetables can be stored in the freezer, it is best to save this method for crops that freeze particularly well and those that cannot be stored in any other way, because freezer space is usually limited. Some vegetables can be stored for short periods in the crisper drawer at the bottom of the refrigerator, where leafy crops such as lettuce can be kept for a fortnight or more – again, space will be limited. For longer term storage of most vegetables try the following methods. Store only perfect vegetables and make sure they are clean and dry before storage.

HOW TO STORE ROOT CROPS

1 Carrots, like most root crops, can be stored in trays of just-moist sand or peat (peat moss or peat substitute). Place a shallow layer of peat in the bottom of a deep tray and then lay rows of carrots on top.

2 Sprinkle peat over the carrots. Place another layer of carrots on top and cover these with more peat. Repeat with more layers until the tray is full, topping off with a final layer of peat.

Packing in boxes

Many root crops, including carrots, parsnips, swedes (rutabaga), turnips and beetroot (beets), can be stored in boxes of sand in a cool, dark place, such as a garage or shed. Twist

off the foliage and pack the roots into sturdy boxes filled with moist sand, peat or peat substitute. Place the boxes in a frost-free area. This is a good method of storing root crops if you have particularly heavy soil that is difficult to work in winter or pest problems that might attack the roots if left outside in the ground.

Storing in sacks

Potatoes are best stored in purpose-made, double-thickness paper sacks (available from garden centres) because they keep out light and yet allow the movement of air that reduces the chances of rotting. Potatoes must be kept dark in a place where the temperature does not dip below 4°C (40°F); an insulated shed or garage is ideal.

Using nets

A few crops, including onions, shallots, garlic, marrows (large zucchini), pumpkins and cabbages, can be successfully stored in open-mesh nets. Hang up the nets in a well-ventilated, frost-free, dry place such as a garage.

It is essential that onions and shallots are completely dry before they are stored. Place them in trays or nets in a cool but frost-free place such as a cellar, shed or garage. Check the onions regularly, throwing away any that show signs of rot.

LEAVING CROPS IN THE GARDEN

Many root crops can be left in the ground insulated with straw.

Some hardy crops, including leeks, Brussels sprouts, cabbages and these red-topped turnips, can be left outdoors and harvested only when needed.

Storing dry

Onions, shallots and garlic also can be stored dry. Place them on trays, or twist string around the neck ends and hang up them up. Choose a dry and well-ventilated place such as a garage or shed to prevent rot. Peas and beans can also be stored dry. Lay the pods out to dry and remove the seeds when the pods are brittle. Put them in air-tight containers stored in a frost-free place.

Leaving in situ

Some root vegetables, such as carrots, swedes and turnips, as well as leeks and Brussels sprouts, can be left in the ground until needed. Root vegetables will go dormant in winter, but Brussels sprouts will continue to develop in milder spells. Cover root crops with an insulating mulch of straw or other insulating material to keep out the worst of the frost and use labels to indicate the ends of rows to help you find the roots when the topgrowth has disappeared. Lift extra supplies in advance of severe frosty weather because it is impossible to dig up root crops if the ground is frozen.

HOW TO STORE VEGETABLES

Place the largest potatoes in sacks and store them in a cool but frost-proof place. Paper sacks are best, but if you can't obtain them, use plastic sacks and cut some slits with a knife to provide some ventilation.

Many vegetables, such as marrows (large zucchini), can be stored in trays. Make sure that they do not touch each other.

A simple way of stringing garlic is to thread a stiff wire through the dry necks of the bulbs. The bulbs can also be tied on string and hung in a dry, airy place.

Herb gardening

The word "herb" is defined as a plant, some part of which – roots, stem, leaves, flowers or fruit – is used for flavouring food, or for medicine or scent. There is enormous variety in the types of plants understood to be herbs, and most gardeners find room for at least one or two. Beauty of foliage and flower, countless scents and tastes, cures for various ailments: herbs offer all these things and more.

You can grow herbs in special parts of the garden, creating separate beds for individual varieties for easy picking, or combining them with cottage-garden flowers to create a wonderful relaxed atmosphere. The beauty of herbs is that they blend perfectly with all kinds of design, from the strictly formal with neatly clipped box hedging to the cheerful informality of the cottage garden. This chapter will explain how to cultivate and harvest these rewarding and varied plants.

Alternating clumps of purple and green-leaved sage, *Salvia officinalis*, line a gravel path, giving a very decorative effect.

Buying herbs and designing a herb garden

Herbs are among the most popular garden plants, and room is usually found for them in any garden. Many gardeners prefer to grow herbs in a dedicated bed, while others like the convenience of a container of herbs by the kitchen door.

Selecting herbs

You can grow many herbs from seed or buy them as plants. Seed is the cheaper option, especially if you require a large number of plants, and it is the best way to grow specimens of basil and borage, which resent root disturbance. Some herbs, such as golden and variegated forms of marjoram, mint, sage and thyme, do not come true from seed.

Garden centres and other retail outlets offer a wide range of herbs in pots, and this is a good way of buying shrubby herbs, such as rosemary and bay, of which you will require just one or two specimens. Although it is a convenient way of buying herbs, it could prove costly for herbs that are used in larger quantities, such as chives and basil. Herbs can also be bought in pots from supermarkets. These have been

forced under cover and need to be hardened off carefully if you intend to plant them outside.

Grow the herbs that you like to eat and use most often in the kitchen. The most popular herbs are basil, bay, chervil, chives, dill, marjoram, mint, parsley, rosemary, sage, tarragon and thyme, but you might prefer to grow sorrel, fennel and savory if you like fish, or lemon grass, ginger, coriander (cilantro) and garlic chives for Asian dishes.

What to look for

Choose stocky, healthy-looking plants with plenty of leaves and a balanced shape. If you buy plants in early spring, make sure they have been hardened off properly before planting them out. Inspect plants carefully for signs of pests and diseases. Some problems are specific to different types of herbs. For example, check the undersides of mint leaves for tiny orange spots, which are the tell-tale sign of mint rust disease; inspect parsley plants for pale lines in the leaves, which are a sign of celery fly damage; while the stems of bay trees should be

checked for scale insect. Always look at the growing tips of all herbs for signs of aphids. As with other plants, buy specimens that are not showing signs of stress from over- or under-watering and avoid plants that are showing signs of neglect, such as weeds in the pot or roots growing through the pot's drainage holes.

Creating a herb feature

The best place to grow herbs is outside the kitchen door, where they will be close to hand when they are needed. Many herbs are drought-tolerant, so are ideal for growing in containers, but if you use a lot of herbs, a designated herb garden would be appropriate and useful.

Designing a herb garden

A dedicated herb garden can form a decorative focal point to a garden design. Formal gardens often look best in a traditional shape such as a wheel marked out using small unit paving or a knot garden surrounded by a low hedge of clipped dwarf box. Attractive contemporary designs include a chequer-board effect made using paving slabs.

BUYING HERBS

Two plants of verbena (vervain), one strong-growing and healthy, the other past its best and struggling.

This *Mentha* (mint) is becoming pot-bound with roots conforming to the shape of the pot and trying to escape out of the bottom.

For large orders of a single herb, buying rooted cuttings can be cost-effective. Here, purple sage and golden thyme have been propagated in plug trays.

HOW TO MAKE A RAISED HERB BRICK WHEEL

1 Use string and canes to mark a circle, then measure off equal points on the circumference for the spokes. Sink a length of earthenware (clay) sewage pipe in the centre.

2 Trace over the whole design with fine sand or line-marker paint.

3 Excavate a trench for the bricks and fill it with dry concrete mix to form a firm footing.

4 Build the outer circle and spokes with one or two courses of bricks, set in mortar. A herb wheel does not have to be very high; two or three courses of bricks should be sufficient.

5 Fill in the sections of the wheel and the earthenware pipe with rubble and gravel to provide drainage. Then add topsoil.

6 Plant up the herb wheel with a selection of culinary herbs, such as sage, thyme, rosemary and lemon verbena. Water in well and add an organic mulch. Continue to water until the herbs are established.

Herbs in containers

Many herbs used in the kitchen come from Mediterranean countries and like well-drained soil conditions. They are pretty drought-tolerant, making them ideal for container plants. Some herbs are even suitable for growing in hanging baskets. A few herbs require large containers if you choose to grow them this way, the main examples being deep-rooted herbs, such as fennel, which produce vertical taproots, and larger shrubby herbs, such as rosemary and bay. Moisture-loving herbs such as sweet cicely are suitable for growing bags.

Choose a reasonably deep container, at least 15cm (6in), to give them plenty of root run. You can either grow individual herbs in different pots or group herbs with similar cultural requirements in a larger pot. This will make looking after the herbs more straightforward. Short-lived herbs or those that are used up quickly, such as basil and chives, are worth growing in their own pot, which can be sunk rim-deep into the larger container holding the herb collection. The smaller container can be slipped out easily and replaced when necessary without disturbing the other herbs.

Interlocking containers are now available, and these allow you to grow the herbs separately, but they can be assembled so that they look like a single container.

Many of the most useful culinary herbs grow well in hanging baskets. Position the basket outside the kitchen door for convenience.

Growing herbs

The versatility of herbs is one of their great advantages in the garden. If you provide the right conditions, herbs are generally easy to grow, rewarding you with their colourful, fragrant flowers and foliage as well as their usefulness to flavour dishes in the kitchen.

Positioning herbs

Most herbs grow best in full sun with some protection from cold winter winds. The soil should usually be light and free-draining with plenty of organic matter forked in. Lavender, in particular, will not grow well in a very heavy clay soil. There are some herbs, however, that can cope with heavier soils and light shade. These include angelica, borage, chives, fennel, lemon balm, lovage and mint. It always makes sense to go with the conditions and not against them, so a hot, dry site will suit Mediterranean herbs, while

Restricting invasive herbs

A few herbs, such as mint, are very vigorous and will quickly spread and overwhelm neighbouring plants if given free rein in the border. The easiest way to restrict their ambitions is to confine the roots by planting them in a large pot or bottomless bucket sunk into the border. As long as the rim of the pot is proud of the surface, the roots will be kept within bounds. However, it is still worth checking the plant from time to time to make sure that flopping stems have not rooted outside the pot.

Companion planting

Many herbs have a reputation for repelling insect pests and are used as companion plants by organic gardeners for protecting vulnerable plants such as roses, fruit and vegetables from insect attack. Rue, cotton lavender, curry plant, tansy and southernwood are all strongly aromatic and are said to discourage many types of pest.

Camomile has a reputation for improving the health and vigour of surrounding plants.

Pennyroyal, planted in paving, is thought to keep ants away.

Summer savory, planted in rows next to broad beans (fava beans), provides them with some protection from aphids.

Chives and garlic are often planted to discourage the aphids that can damage roses.

a heavy moist soil suits plants that like streams and meadows. Looking at how a plant thrives in its natural habitat will tell you how best to grow it in the garden.

It is not essential to grow herbs in a specially designated herb bed. Individual herbs are delightful additions to flower borders and beds. Chives and parsley, for example, are useful edging plants, while stately bronze fennel will be an eye-catching addition to a mixed border. Low-growing herbs such as camomile and

thyme can be planted in cracks in paving in paths and on patios. Choose a variety that grows well in these conditions.

Growing herbs from seed

Raising your own plants from seed is not only very rewarding, it is also the best way to stock your herb garden economically. Sow seed thinly in seed compost (soil mix), using plug trays. The advantage of using these trays is that when the plants are transferred to a pot, there is little

HOW TO PLANT A HERB GARDEN

1 Newly planted box trees line this wooden-edged herb bed and provide a framework inside which the herbs will be laid out. First prepare the site by thoroughly weeding and forking over to break up the soil, then rake the ground level.

2 Work out the eventual spread of the herbs and decide how much room to give each plant. A helpful method is to "draw" on the soil with sand trickled out of a pot. If you make a mistake, it can be easily erased and the design begun again.

Choosing herbs

Hanging baskets	Borders
Basil	Angelica
Marjoram	Artemisia
Sage	Bay
Thyme	Catmint
Winter savory	Chervil
	Chives
Containers	Curry plant
Basil	Fennel
Bay	Hyssop
Camomile	Lavender
Marjoram	Marjoram
Parsley	Mint
Rosemary	Parsley
Sage	Rocket (arugula)
Summer savory	Rosemary
Thyme	Sage
Winter savory	Thyme

Planting herbs in the garden

Prepare the site by eliminating all weeds, especially perennials. Dig the soil well and rake it over. If you are creating a dedicated herb garden, with each plant allocated to a certain space, plan out the design before you start. Transferring a design to the soil can be made simple by using sand poured from the hole in the bottom of a container. If you make a mistake it is easy to rake the soil over and start again.

Thoroughly water all pot-grown plants several hours prior to planting, then knock them out of their pots by giving a sharp rap on the bottom of the container. Plant the herb at the same depth it was in the pot, firming the soil well around the roots afterwards. Water generously and label unless you are quite sure of the names of the different herbs.

A herb garden from container-grown plants can be created at any time of year, provided it is kept well-watered, but early spring is probably the best time as it will give the plants a full season to establish before the trials of winter.

root disturbance, so the growth of the herb is not checked. This method of sowing suits borage, dill and chervil in particular.

Alternatively, you can sow seed into a well-prepared seed bed in spring. Parsley must only be sown when the soil has warmed up in spring, and trying too early can result in poor germination.

Bay prefers a sheltered, sunny position. They are evergreen, frost hardy plants, so are ideal for growing in a container close to the house for year-round interest. Protect from severe weather, however. This specimen has been grown by plaiting (braiding) three stems.

3 Remove the herbs from their pots and plant them carefully, at the same level as they were in the container. If you want to keep the pots for reuse, then scrub them well with soap and water.

4 Water each plant thoroughly and keep them watered in dry weather until they are established. Avoid planting on a hot day; just before rain is ideal.

5 The newly planted herb garden looks rather bare, but it won't be long before the plants grow to fit their allocated space. It can be tempting to plant too close together for a more immediate effect, but this will lead to overcrowding later.

Aftercare of herbs

Most herbs are easy to grow, requiring little maintenance and generally remaining free from pests and diseases. There are, however, a few seasonal tasks that will ensure you get the most from your plants.

Watering

Herbs in pots need regular watering in summer and even in well-drained beds and borders annual herbs may need the occasional watering during prolonged drought. Make watering pots easier by leaving the compost (soil mix) 2.5cm (1in) below the rim of the pot and cover the surface with gravel to help reduce water loss through evaporation.

Do not use a high-nitrogen inorganic fertilizer on herbs because this encourages soft sappy growth, prone to aphid infestation and unable to stand the stress of droughts. The herb will also lack fragrance and aroma.

Mint is an extremely vigorous plant once established, but keep an eye on young plants during hot spells and water if necessary.

HOW TO PRUNE COTTON LAVENDER

1 Keep cotton lavender (*Santolina rosmarinifolia*) neat and compact by regular pruning. Use a pair of shears to clip the bush into shape. Do not prune back as far as the older, woody stems; there should be plenty of greenery below the cut stems.

Weeding

In the border it is essential to keep on top of weeding throughout the growing season. Weeds not only compete with the herbs for light, moisture and nutrients, but they also harbour pests and diseases. Hand weed or hoe annual weeds and use a hand fork to dig out perennial weeds complete with their roots to stop them re-sprouting. If it is impossible to remove the weeds completely because they are growing among the herbs, cut the leaves of the perennial

Mulching helps to keep beds and borders weed-free. Gravel is a good choice for herbs that like free-draining soil.

2 When the plant has been pruned into a dome shape it will quickly put on new growth. Clipping about twice a year will keep the bush compact and neat.

weeds back to ground level and repeat the process each time they sprout. This weakens the weeds and may even kill them.

Mulching

In spring each year top up the loose mulch to prevent weed seeds from germinating and to help reduce moisture loss from the soil surface. Use an organic mulch, such as bark chippings, around herbs, such as lovage and sweet cicely, and those that like a moist root run, and a gravel mulch around herbs, such as thyme and marjoram, which prefer well-drained conditions.

Pruning

Remove any all-green shoots from naturally variegated plants because these will be more vigorous and will outgrow the variegated foliage. Some herbs are also worth pruning annually to keep them looking neat and to prevent them from self-seeding and becoming a weed problem. Use shears to trim small flowering plants, such as thyme and chives, and secateurs (pruners) on woody shrubby herbs, such as rosemary and bay, to keep them in shape. Some herbs, such as fennel, become coarse in stem and leaf if left unpruned. Cut back early to make plenty of young growth for cooking. Use secateurs (pruners) to cut the stems almost to ground level.

You don't have to let pruning go to waste; healthy leaves can be used in the kitchen or frozen for later use.

Overwintering herbs

Summer is the usual time for harvesting herbs, but the normal growing season can be extended by covering selected plants with cloches in early autumn to keep them growing for a few more weeks. To get year-round supplies of herbs, you can lift and pot up a few plants of perennial herbs, such as mint and marjoram, in autumn and move them indoors where they will sprout new leaves.

You can also maintain a supply of annual herbs, such as basil and parsley, by sowing in late summer in pots and keeping plants on a sunny windowsill or in a heated greenhouse or conservatory.

HOW TO PROTECT HERBS IN AUTUMN

Protect late-sown herbs, such as parsley, with cloches to ensure a supply of fresh leaves.

HOW TO POT UP HERBS FOR WINTER USE

1 Mint is an easy plant to force indoors, or in a cold frame or greenhouse. Lift an established clump to provide a supply of roots to pot up.

2 Select only pieces with healthy leaves (diseased leaves are common by the end of the season). You can pull pieces off by hand or cut through them with a knife.

3 Plant the roots in a pot if you want to try and keep the plant growing indoors for a month or two. Three-quarters fill a 20cm (8in) pot with compost (soil mix), then spread out the roots and cover with more compost.

4 If you want a supply of tender fresh leaves early next spring, cut off the tops of the mint plants and put the roots in seed trays (flats) or deeper boxes. Cover with soil. Keep in a cold frame or the greenhouse for an early harvest in spring.

5 Chives also respond favourably to lifting for an extended season. Lift a small clump to pot up. If it's too large you should be able to pull it apart into smaller pieces.

6 Place the clump in a pot of soil, firm well and water thoroughly. The pot of chives, if kept indoors, should continue to provide leaves after those outdoors have died back, and will produce new ones earlier next year.

Harvesting and storing herbs

Herbs need to be picked regularly to maintain a continuous supply of fresh, young leaves. If you want to store herbs for winter use, however, you should make sure that you harvest them at their best.

When to harvest herbs

The best time to harvest herbs for later use varies depending on the part of the plant you are harvesting. Large leaves should be picked individually, but smaller-leaved herbs can be picked in sprigs and stripped before processing.

Most herbs are best harvested in early summer, just before they come into flower, although leafy herbs, such as mint, are best cut back to near ground level to encourage a second flush of young, aromatic leaves later in the season. If you are storing flowers, pick them at their peak as soon as they have opened. Again, smaller flowers can be picked on sprigs, ready

WHEN TO HARVEST HERBS

Harvest herbs when they are at their peak, usually before they flower. Cut them on a dry day, avoiding times when they are wilting in the heat. Harvest the best leaves, not the older leaves lower down the plant.

for processing in the kitchen. If you are collecting seeds, cover seedheads with a paper bag as they are becoming ripe, then cut off the seedheads and

keep them somewhere warm and dry until the seeds are released. Root herbs, such as horseradish, should be harvested in autumn.

Harvesting herbs for storage

Choose a fine, dry day when the sun is out but before the foliage starts to wilt to capture the essential oils that give herbs their distinctive flavour and aroma. The foliage must be dry when it is harvested, so wait until any dew has evaporated before you start. This will help to prevent the herbs from going mouldy while they are drying. Choose only the best material for storing, avoiding leaves that show signs of age or pest and disease attack. Cut the herbs with sharp garden snips or secateurs (pruners) so that the plant tissue is not crushed. Pick little and often because herbs that are processed quickly will retain their flavour. Handle the herbs as little as possible.

HOW TO HARVEST MARJORAM FOR DRYING

1 Small-leaved herbs, such as marjoram, are easily air-dried. Cut bunches of healthy material at mid-morning on a dry, warm day.

2 Strip off the lower leaves, which would otherwise become crushed and damaged when the stems are bunched.

3 Twist a rubber band around a few stems to hold them tightly together. Gather as many bunches as you need.

1 Pick seedheads just as they are ripening. At this stage the seeds should readily come away from the stalks. Place on a tray and leave the seeds for a few days in a warm, dry place until they have completely dried.

2 Once the seeds are thoroughly dried, tip them into a glass jar with an airtight lid. Store in a cool, dry, dark place.

The best method of storing soft-leaved herbs, such as parsley and mint, is to freeze them. Chop up the herb and place in ice-cube trays. Top up with water and freeze. This has the advantage of keeping the herb's colour.

Storing herbs

Some herbs, such as thyme, can be dried with no loss of flavour, but others are best stored in infusions to retain their distinctive taste. Soft-leaved herbs can be frozen.

Drying Hang up sprigs of individual herbs in bunches in a well-ventilated, warm, dry, dark place, such as an airing cupboard (linen closet). Root herbs should be cleaned and cut into small pieces and dried in the oven at a low temperature on a baking tray. Store dry herbs in airtight containers. Herbs should be kept in the dark, so store in a cupboard (closet) or, if herbs will be kept on open shelves, place them in opaque containers.

Freezing Whole leaves can be placed in clearly labelled plastic bags and then kept in the freezer. Alternatively, the leaves can be finely chopped and frozen with water in an ice-cube tray. Individual frozen cubes can be added to dishes as required.

Infusions A popular method with some cooks is to create infusions using good-quality olive oil or wine vinegar. The infusion can be of a single herb, such as basil, or two or three different herbs, and used to add flavour to dishes, such as pizzas and salads.

DRYING HERBS

Bunches of herbs can be dried by hanging them in a dry place where they are out of direct sunlight.

Herb mixtures

Different herbs can be combined in a number of distinctive mixtures. Bouquet garni, for example, is a combination of several herbs, such as bay, parsley, marjoram and thyme. Sprigs of the herbs are tied together or placed in a muslin (cheesecloth) bag, which is cooked with the dish and removed before serving.

Greenhouse gardening

A greenhouse offers many gardening opportunities and challenges. It can transform your gardening activities, extending the season and increasing the range of crops you can grow. The enclosed environment means you can give plants exactly the conditions they need to grow fast and well, but unfortunately it is also the ideal environment for pests and diseases.

The health of the plants in the greenhouse will depend on your management skills, and a productive greenhouse requires almost constant attention. Fortunately, there are many products to help you, including thermostatically controlled heaters to keep the greenhouse warm in winter and automatic vent openers to keep it cool in summer. There is also a range of special equipment for automating the time-consuming task of watering. Careful planning of the layout of the greenhouse and of the cropping programme will help make efficient use of your time and space.

A greenhouse enables you to grow a far wider range of plants than would otherwise be possible.

Controlling the greenhouse environment

The temperature inside a greenhouse can quickly rocket out of control on sunny days in spring and summer, sometimes soaring to over 50°C (120°F). Equally, in winter it can drop low enough to cause damage to frost-tender plants. Use the following strategies to keep the temperature in the greenhouse under control.

Providing ventilation

There are three basic methods you can use to prevent overheating in the greenhouse: ventilation, shading and damping down.

Providing ventilation is the best way to control temperatures during the early days of spring. Opening a roof vent and a vent in the side of the greenhouse will allow the hot, humid air that has risen to the top of the greenhouse to escape, while at the same time drawing cooler, dryer air through the side vents. This is known as the chimney effect, and it is an extremely effective cooling technique until the temperatures outside start to rise in late spring. You can take the hard work out of opening the vents by installing automatic vent-openers throughout

CHECKING THE TEMPERATURE

A maximum/minimum thermometer is ideal for keeping track of the temperature inside a greenhouse, warning you to adjust the conditions before the plants start to suffer.

the greenhouse. This mechanism opens the greenhouse windows as soon as a specific pre-set temperature is reached.

You can increase the flow of air through the greenhouse by opening more and more vents – and even the door – but eventually, in the hottest weather, this method alone will not be sufficient to cool your greenhouse to the correct temperature.

Splashing or spraying water over the greenhouse floor helps to create a humid atmosphere. This traditional technique is known as damping down. It is especially beneficial for crops, such as aubergines (eggplant), and cucumbers, but most plants appreciate a moist atmosphere on hot days. Carry out damping down frequently on very hot days as the humidity helps to reduce the temperature.

Providing shade

The second strategy to avoid overheating is to prevent the sun's rays, which heat up the greenhouse, from entering. The easiest way to do this is to put up greenhouse shading. There are three main types: indoor shading fabric, which is fixed to the inside frame of the greenhouse; roller blinds, which are attached to the outside of the greenhouse; and a special whitewash paint, which is applied to the glass in spring and removed in autumn when light levels decline.

Roller blinds are best because they prevent the sun's energy from entering the greenhouse, but they are most expensive and awkward to adjust. Shading fabric is cheap and easy to adjust, but it absorbs some

VENTILATING

It is vital not to let greenhouses overheat. Opening the windows at the right time is not always possible if you are not at home during the hottest part of the day, but automatic vent-openers will do the job for you.

SHADING

It is important to keep the sun out of the greenhouse during the hottest part of the year. Shading, in the form of temporary netting, helps to keep the temperature down and also protects the plants from the scorching effects of the sun.

of the sun's energy and so is less effective. Shading wash is both cheap and effective, but once applied it is on for the whole season regardless of the weather. However, there is a type, called Varishade, which turns opaque when it gets wet, so allowing more light into the greenhouse when it rains. In a greenhouse used to grow a variety of plants, use sun-loving plants, such as tomatoes, to shade other plants by growing them on the sunny side of the greenhouse.

Damping down

During the long, hot days of summer, especially if there is little air movement outside, the greenhouse temperature can still rise too high. You can help cool things down using the traditional technique of damping down. This is where all surfaces, including the floor and staging, are sprayed with water in the morning. As the temperature increases, energy will be absorbed by the water as it evaporates and is carried out of the greenhouse in the form of water vapour.

Protecting from cold

During the winter it is important not to let your greenhouse get too cold, as this could damage any tender plants or seedlings. One of the best ways to heat a greenhouse is to install an electric heater. A thermostat will ensure that no heat (or money) is wasted, because the appliance only comes on when the temperature drops below a certain point. Heating bills can be reduced with insulation. A cheaper alternative to double glazing is to line the greenhouse with sheets of clear polythene (plastic) containing air bubbles. If you have just a few plants, a heated propagator may be sufficient for your needs.

An unusually shaped greenhouse with a steeply pitched roof not only looks different from conventional greenhouses but has the advantage that the steep sides absorb the low winter sun more easily, making heating the greenhouse more economical.

HEATING

Electric fan heaters are very efficient. When equipped with thermostats, they come on only when extra heat is required. They can also be used to circulate the air on still, damp days, reducing the risk of fungal disease caused by stagnant air.

INSULATING

Insulating the greenhouse is important during the cold winter months, helping to keep heating costs down as well as preventing any violent fluctuations in temperature. Polythene (plastic) bubble insulation is cheap and efficient and easy to install.

Watering and feeding

In the greenhouse plants are especially vulnerable to a shortage of moisture and nutrients. Establishing a routine of providing both water and fertilizer will ensure that your plants remain healthy.

When to water

Watering is probably the most difficult technique to get right in the greenhouse because it depends on such variable factors as the time of year, the plants chosen and their stage of growth, light levels, where the plants are growing and the temperature in the greenhouse.

Do not wait until a plant starts to wilt before you water it since this means it is already under stress, leading to reduced growth and yields. It is essential to check plants regularly to make sure they do not run short of water, and this may mean more than once a day in summer. The best way to judge the moisture is to

Plants in growing bags, whether they are grown outside or in a greenhouse, quickly use up the moisture and nutrients available in the compost (soil mix). They will require regular watering and feeding throughout the growing season.

push your finger into the compost (soil mix) of each pot. If the compost about 2cm (¾in) below the surface is dry, it needs watering; if it is moist, leave it for another day.

Making watering easier

If you have a greenhouse full of plants checking individual pots is clearly impracticable. Fortunately, there are a number of ways you can

HOW TO WATER GREENHOUSE PLANTS

Plants should be watered before they show obvious signs of distress, such as wilting. With bushy plants it is not possible to judge by the appearance of the potting compost (soil mix), and you really need to feel below the surface, but this is time-consuming if you have many plants.

Moisture indicators for individual pots can be helpful for gardeners who find it difficult to judge the soil or if there are just a few plants, but they are not practicable if you have a whole greenhouse full of plants.

Capillary matting is an ideal way to water most pot plants in summer. You can use a proprietary system fed by mains water or improvise with a system like this one, which uses a length of gutter for the water supply. You can keep it topped up by hand, with special water bags or from a cistern.

take much of the hard work out of watering. First, by planning the layout and positioning of plants carefully you can make watering a lot easier, for example, by grouping together containers with similar requirements. Second, it is worth investing in simple watering devices.

Capillary watering If you have a lot of small containers a sandbench is worth considering. It is fairly simple to make out of a strong wooden box about 15cm (6in) deep. Line it with heavy-duty polythene (plastic) and place a 2.5cm (1in) layer of pea gravel on the bottom. Add a further 10cm (4in) of horticultural sand on top of this and stand the pots and trays on the sand. When the sand is wet the plants in the containers will draw up as much moisture as they require via capillary action.

A similar system involves using capillary matting. Cover a flat surface with heavy-duty plastic and

If you are watering by hand, use the can without a rose unless you are watering seedlings. This will enable you to direct water more easily to the roots rather than sprinkling the leaves. Use a finger over the end of the spout to control the flow, or stick a rag in the end to break the force.

HOW TO FEED GREENHOUSE PLANTS

A liquid fertilizer is applied at the same time that you water, but you must remember to do it regularly. There are both soluble powders and liquids, which can be diluted to the appropriate strength.

then lay the matting on top. Drape one end of the plastic sheet and matting into a reservoir, such as a trough or a short piece of guttering fitted to the end of the bench. When the reservoir is filled with water it will soak the matting so that the containers placed on it can draw up all the moisture they require. Remember to keep the reservoir topped up with water.

Drip watering Another option is to install a drip irrigation system. You can buy bladder bags that supply a single drip nozzle (similar to a medical drip) or a micro-bore drip irrigation system, or make your own out of a large plastic drinks bottle. Cut the bottom off the bottle and make a small hole in the bottle top. Fix a galvanized screw into the hole and insert the upended bottle into the compost. When the bottle is filled, water will slowly leak out, past the screw, keeping the compost moist between waterings. Keep an eye on the reservoir and top up as necessary. This method is ideal for watering larger pots and growing bags.

Fertilizer sticks and tablets that you push into the container are a convenient way to administer fertilizer if you don't want to apply liquid feeds regularly. Most release their nutrients over a period of several months.

Automatic watering Both capillary and drip systems can be made completely automatic by plumbing them into the mains. You can either use a water timer or computer to regulate the watering periods or install a header tank with a ballcock valve to act as a reservoir.

Feeding

The amount of food a plant requires depends on how fast it is growing. Fast-growing crop plants grown in containers will need feeding once a week from about six weeks after potting up. Use a high-potash liquid feed, such as tomato fertilizer, for all flowering and fruit-bearing crops and a high-nitrogen feed for leafy vegetables. Follow the manufacturer's instructions for application rates. Vegetables in the greenhouse are gross feeders that quickly deplete the nutrients in the compost (soil mix). To save time, mix slow-release fertilizer granules into the compost for ornamental and foliage plants. This will provide sufficient food for several months.

Troubleshooting

The greenhouse offers the perfect breeding ground for many pests and diseases. Many can be prevented by growing the crops so that they are vigorous enough to withstand most problems, but some insects and diseases will need to be controlled.

Avoiding problems

There are many things you can do to prevent pests and diseases taking over. Keep the growing environment as clean and uncluttered as possible, clearing away rubbish and washing and sterilizing used pots.

In the winter, clear out the greenhouse and give it a thorough clean. Wash down the insides with a garden disinfectant and scrub all the surfaces, including the path, benches and frame. Clear any algae that is trapped between glass overlaps and clean out the awkward mouldings of an aluminium frame. As you bring plants back inside, inspect them for signs of pest and disease attack. Always use sterilized pots and

If you have had an infestation of pests or diseases, fumigation is a good way to rid the greenhouse of the problem. You may be able to keep the plants in while you carry out the process, or you may have to fumigate in an empty greenhouse. Check the label.

compost (soil mix) when sowing and planting. If you buy plants make sure they are free from pests and diseases so that they do not introduce problems into your greenhouse.

Make sure that you provide the right environment for your plants so that they are growing strongly and do not suffer a check in growth. Use your time while watering to inspect plants closely, especially the growing tips and undersides of leaves, for any early signs of pest or disease activity and take action promptly when necessary. If you are vigilant you should be able to avoid having to use chemical controls.

Some infestations can be prevented by covering vents with insect-proof mesh. If there are insects in the greenhouse, use sticky traps, which consist of sheets of yellow plastic covered with a non-drying glue. This form of non-chemical control is becoming popular for a wide range of flying pests, and works particularly well in a greenhouse.

If a pest or disease attack is severe make sure you select the right chemical for the problem and follow the manufacturer's instructions given on the label.

HOW TO CONTROL PESTS IN THE GREENHOUSE

If vine weevil grubs destroy your plants by eating the roots, try controlling them with a parasitic nematode. A suspension of the nematodes is simply watered over the compost (soil mix) in each pot.

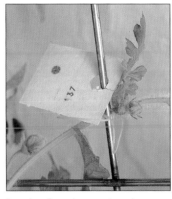

A number of greenhouse pests can be successfully controlled with other insects. The beneficial insects are released, here from a sachet, on to the susceptible plant in order to attack the pests. There are predatory wasps and mites that will attack whitefly larvae, spider mite, soft scale insects and thrips.

Biological controls

Most plants in the greenhouse are grown to eat, so avoid spraying them with insecticide as far as possible. Fortunately, there are a number of biological measures to control pests.

Several common garden pests can be controlled by other insects, which either eat or parasitize the pest. For example, the small wasp, *Encarsia formosa*, will control whitefly, while a predatory mite, called *Phytoseiulus*, can be used against spider mite attacks, and nematodes can be used to attack vine weevils.

Introduce the biological control as soon as the first signs of attack are noticed, remove yellow sticky traps and do not use chemicals that might kill the biological controls. Be patient, and accept there will be some damage before the biological agent takes effect.

Common pests and diseases

Identifying the problem is the first step to eradicating it.

Spider mite This pest can attack a wide range of greenhouse crops throughout the summer. Leaves become speckled, eventually turning yellow, and later webbing can be seen. The tiny insects are visible. Prevent problems by thoroughly cleaning your greenhouse in winter and increase the humidity in the greenhouse by damping down and misting the plants because this pest likes a dry atmosphere.

Whitefly This pest attacks a wide range of plants, especially tomatoes, peppers and aubergines (eggplant). Small white flies congregate on the undersides of leaves and fly up in a cloud when disturbed. Use a car vacuum to suck up flying pests or hang up yellow sticky traps.

Damping off This disease affects all types of seedlings, causing them to

French marigolds have been planted with a row of tomatoes in this greenhouse. They are thought to ward off whitefly from the tomatoes, a technique known as companion planting.

keel over like felled trees. It is a particular problem in the spring. Apply a suitable fungicidal drench before sowing, use sterile pots and compost, and space seedlings to improve air flow. Water from below.

Grey mould Velvety patches appear on leaves, fruit and stems of most crops, especially tomatoes, cucumbers and lettuces. Prevent outbreaks by keeping the greenhouse well ventilated and clear away yellowing foliage and other debris.

Powdery mildew A white powdery coating forms on leaves of many crops, including cucumbers, especially during the summer months. Keep the compost (soil mix) moist but keep the atmosphere dry by careful ventilation, and avoid wetting the leaves. Try growing mildew-resistant varieties if the problem recurs.

Growing tomatoes

There is nothing quite like the flavour of a freshly picked, home-grown tomato. To get the best crops, choose a good variety and don't neglect it at any stage.

Growing methods

Tomatoes are easy to raise from seed but need to be sown early in the year and require a high temperature to germinate. This means you will need a propagator set to 18°C (65°F) to get them started and somewhere heated to 21°C (70°F) to grow them on. On the other hand, you could buy plants that are ready for planting out much later in the year saving you time, trouble and money. Make sure that you choose a healthy-looking, stocky plant, showing no signs of yellowing leaves or pest or disease attack. Plant tomatoes out when they are showing colour (the flowers are beginning to open) in their first truss.

Greenhouse tomatoes can be grown in two main ways: in the greenhouse border and in containers, such as pots or growing bags. A third method, called ring culture, is also used by some growers but it has never gained popular appeal, despite the lower maintenance it requires.

HOW TO RAISE TOMATOES

1 With ring culture, the water-absorbing roots grow into a moist aggregate and the feeding roots into special bottomless pots filled with a potting compost (soil mix). Take out a trench about 15–23cm (6–9in) deep in the greenhouse border and line it with a waterproof plastic to minimize contamination by soil-borne diseases.

2 Fill the trench with fine gravel or coarse grit, then place the special bottomless pots ("rings") on the aggregate base. Fill them with potting compost and plant the tomatoes into the rings. Water into the rings at first. Once the plant is established and some roots have penetrated the aggregate, water only the aggregate and feed through the pot.

3 Planting directly into the greenhouse border gives the plants' roots a chance to spread out, making it less likely that the plants will suffer from a lack of water or nutrients. You will need a cane or string to support the plant as it grows.

4 Growing bags are less trouble than ring culture to set up, but you will have to feed plants regularly and watering can be more difficult to control unless you use an automatic system. Insert a cane through the bag or use a string support.

5 String makes a simple and economical support. Fix one length of wire as high as practicable from one end of the greenhouse to the other, aligning it above the border. Fix another wire just above the ground, attaching it to a stout stake at each end of the row. Tie lengths of string between the top and bottom wires, in line with each plant.

6 There is no need to tie the plant to its support. Loop the string around the growing tip so that it forms a spiral.

Tomatoes in the border This is the best method of growing tomatoes for the beginner or anyone else who finds routine watering a chore. The plants will have a lot more space for their roots to roam, so they will be less dependent on you for food and water. You will need to improve the soil with well-rotted organic matter before planting and to incorporate a general fertilizer at the rate recommended by the manufacturer. You will still need to water the plants thoroughly every couple of days during the height of summer.

The main drawback of border planting is that soil-borne problems build up after a few years, so once every few years it is a good idea to dig out the soil and replace it with fresh from the garden.

Tomatoes in growing bags This convenient method is now probably the most popular way of growing tomatoes. Clean, fresh compost (soil mix) is used each year, which means there is no carry-over of soil-borne pests and diseases. Using growing bags also means the greenhouse can be cleaned out properly in winter to eliminate any overwintering pests. However, bags cost money, and plants will need regular feeding and watering at least once a day during the hottest weather.

The other option is to pour the contents of the growing bag into a large pot or bucket with drainage holes drilled in the base. This means that the compost (soil mix) is much deeper, with more volume per plant, so that the plants can last longer between waterings.

Training tomatoes

Cordon tomatoes are trained with a single main stem. They will need to be supported by canes or pieces of string tied to strong overhead wires. Strings are either tied to the bottom of the plant or looped under the rootball when planting. If plants are in growing bags, consider buying one of the special metal supports now available from garden retailers. Tie the plant loosely to the support straight after planting, then tie in any extension growth each week as the plant grows.

Remove any sideshoots that grow from the leaf joint with a sharp knife or simply break them off using your finger and thumb. If you accidentally break the main leader of the tomato plant while you are training it, leave the top sideshoot to train up in its place. When the tomato plant reaches the top of the support or has produced seven trusses, pinch out the growing tip so that the plant

puts all its energy into producing fruit. Remove leaves from the base of the plant as they start to yellow. Pick the tomatoes when they are fully coloured.

TRAINING CORDON PLANTS

Use a sharp clean knife to remove large sideshoots. Small ones can be pinched between thumb and finger.

RIPENING TOMATOES

At the end of the growing season, tomatoes grown outdoors can be ripened in the greenhouse. Strip off the lower leaves and hang the plants upside down.

Growing cucumbers and peppers

In most years in temperate climates, cucumbers and (bell) peppers can be grown successfully only under the protection of a greenhouse. Plant in mid-spring for an early crop that will last all summer long. Both will be a welcome sight in summer salads.

Cucumbers

Choose seeds of an all-female variety, as the cucumbers are less likely to be bitter. Sow two seeds on their sides in pots or modules in early spring in a heated greenhouse or in mid-spring in an unheated one. Provide a temperature of around 25°C (80°F) for speedy germination.

When the seeds germinate discard the weaker seedling. After about a month, the cucumber seedlings should be planted out, with as little root disturbance as possible. It is important to maintain a temperature of 16°C (60°F) thereafter.

Cucumbers are best grown as cordons, with a single stem tied to a vertical supporting cane or piece of string tied to an overhead wire. Tie in the plant as it grows using plant ties. Pinch out any sideshoots, flower buds and tendrils that appear until the seventh leaf. Thereafter, leave the flowers and tendrils and pinch out the sideshoots.

When the plant reaches the top of the support, pinch out the growing tip and leave the top two sideshoots to grow. These can be trained along the top wire and then down towards the floor.

Water the cucumbers regularly, keeping the soil moist at all times and throwing water on the floor of the greenhouse to keep the atmosphere humid.

Once the fruit starts to develop, feed the plants with a high-potash liquid feed once every two weeks.

Many modern cucumbers produce only female flowers, but some greenhouse varieties produce both male and female blooms (the female flowers have a small embryo fruit behind the petals). Pinch out male flowers before they have a chance to pollinate the female ones, because the resulting cucumbers will taste bitter.

Maintain a temperature of about 21°C (70°F). Harvest the cucmbers when they are large enough, which is usually when their sides are parallel. Cut the fruit with a short length of stalk. Pick cucumbers frequently to encourage the development of more fruit.

The most popular sort of cucumber is long with a smooth skin, and can only be grown under glass. It is a climbing variety.

There has been a recent rise in the popularity of both growing and eating (bell) peppers. Green peppers are the unripe fruit, yellow peppers are the first stage in the ripening process, and the final stage is red peppers. All peppers can be eaten raw, or cooked.

Chillies

Related to (bell) peppers, the fiery flavour of chillies is indispensable in many cuisines including Indian, Thai and Mexican. Chillies are sometimes grown as house plants, but they will do better if grown in a greenhouse, following the same growing technique as used for peppers. Remember to water the chillies often and feed with a liquid fertilizer about once a fortnight.

Peppers

Sow seeds for (bell) pepper in spring at 21°C (70°F) in seed trays or modules. Keep at a temperature of 18°C (65°F) after germination. Prick out seedlings into individual pots when they are large enough to handle. Once established, lower the temperature to 16°C (60°F) to grow on. As soon as they are big enough, transfer the young plants to the greenhouse border, growing bags or large pots. If you use growing bags, plant two or three peppers to a bag.

Pinch out the tops of young plants when they get to 15–20cm (6–8in) to make them bush out. If the plants get above 45–50cm (18–20in) they may need to be supported with canes or string. Tie plants in loosely.

Water the peppers as necessary and feed every fortnight once the fruit starts to swell using a tomato fertilizer. Peppers can be harvested from midsummer onwards. The fruit

Some plants, such as (bell) peppers, are usually grown in a greenhouse although they can be grown outside in the open air. The plants will do much better in a greenhouse as they are assured of a constant temperature and humidity. You will find the plants have an increased yield of fruit and will continue producing fruit over a longer period.

is ready when the skin turns glossy, usually when it is about the size of a tennis ball. Pick the first fruit when green to encourage more to develop. Subsequent fruits can be picked at the green or coloured stages.

Peppers enjoy the same kind of growing conditions as tomatoes, so they make ideal companions. If you do decide to grow both, make sure you grow the peppers on the sunny side of the greenhouse so they are not shaded by the faster growing and much taller tomato plants.

Good cucumber and (bell) pepper varieties

Cucumbers	Peppers
'Brigit'	'Ace'
'Carmen'	'Ariane'
'Fenumex'	'Bell Boy'
'Femspot'	'Canape'
'Flamingo'	'Golden Bell'
'Pepinex 69'	'Gypsy'
'Petita'	'Luteus'
'Telegraph'	'Rainbow'
'Telegraph Improved'	'Redskin'
	'Yellow Lantern'

Growing other greenhouse crops

Many other crops, including aubergines, melons, salad vegetables and herbs, can be grown in a greenhouse. Combine crops that need a similar growing environment for the best results.

Melons can be grown very successfully in a greenhouse; the plants are supported on a wire frame and the ripening fruit is held in a net. Harvest the fruit when the flower end gives slightly when pressed gently.

Lettuces

Sow seed in trays from late winter to early spring at 13°C (55°F). Prick out when the seedlings are large enough to handle into individual pots. Plant out in the border or growing bags (old ones used for a previous crop of tomatoes are ideal), spacing them 15cm (6in) apart in the border and planting 12 to a standard growing bag. Lettuces grow relatively quickly and will be ready from 5 to 12 weeks after sowing, depending on the variety. Make a succession of sowings every fortnight or so through the spring and early summer for a continuity of supply throughout the summer.

Melons

Sow seed singly on edge and place in a heated propagator set to 18°C (65°F). Once germinated, grow them on at 16°C (60°F). When each seedling has four true leaves plant them out two plants to a growing

Greenhouse flowers

A wide range of flowers can be raised in the greenhouse, both to populate beds and containers outdoors and to provide colourful pot plants for the house. *Abutilon*, *Browallia*, *Calceolaria*, *Celosia*, *Cuphea*, *Gerbera*, *Gloxinia*, *Hibiscus*, various primulas, *Schizanthus* and *Streptocarpus* are all good choices. They can be raised from seed in a propagator and grown on at around 13°C (55°F), or bought as small plants from a garden retailer and grown on.

bag or singly in large pots filled with growing bag compost (soil mix).

Plant the seedlings shallowly, with 2.5cm (1in) of the rootball proud of the surface to prevent stem rot. The plant will need support as it grows. Use plastic netting, or erect a series of sturdy horizontal wires, spaced 30cm (12in) apart, and tie the melon loosely to a vertical cane secured to the wires. Continue to tie in the plant as it grows and remove any sideshoots until it reaches the first wire. Allow two sideshoots to develop and tie these to the horizontal wire either side of the main stem. Repeat this process as the plant grows until there are shoots trained along all the wires.

Pinch out the growing point of the main stem when it reaches the top wire. Also pinch out the growing

point of each of the sideshoots when they have produced five leaves. New shoots will be produced from the leaf joints of the sideshoots, and these should be pinched out after the second leaf has formed.

When there are female flowers (those with a slight swelling behind the flower) on all the sideshoots, use a male flower to pollinate them by dabbing pollen from the male flower into the female ones.

Keep plants well fed and watered and the atmosphere humid thereafter. Remove any further flowers and sideshoots as they develop. Support the fruit in an individual net as it grows. Harvest melons when the fruit is ripe. A good indication is when the melon smells sweet and it gives slightly when pressed at the flower end of the fruit.

Aubergines

This plant is sometimes called eggplant due to the white, egg-shaped fruit produced by some varieties. The aubergine is an extremely versatile vegetable and is widely used in Mediterranean cooking.

Aubergines are related to tomatoes, and are just as easy to grow. However, they do need a long growing season to get reliable crops. This means sowing in late winter in a propagator set to 21°C (70°F). Soak the aubergine seeds overnight before sowing. Prick out seedlings individually as soon as they are large enough to handle, then grow them on at a temperature of 16°C (60°F). Plant out the seedlings three in a growing bag or singly in large pots filled with growing bag compost (soil mix). Use canes or string to support the plants once they get to about 45–60cm (18–24in) high. Tie the stems in loosely.

Keep the plants well fed and watered and keep the atmosphere in the greenhouse moist. Pinch out the tips of the plants when they reach about 38cm (15in) high to encourage the formation of fruit. Pick when shiny and about 15cm (6in) long, which should be from midsummer onwards.

Herbs

It is worth ensuring you have a good supply of herbs to use throughout the winter. Pots of herbs can be kept growing throughout the autumn by moving them into the greenhouse before the first frost. Keep them well watered but do not wet the foliage.

Herbs, such as clumps of chives and mint, which have been growing in a border, can be potted up and moved into the greenhouse in late autumn so that they are ready to harvest in spring.

Both parsely and basil require a high germination temperature of 18°C (65°F) and benefit from starting off in a greenhouse in mid-spring, before being potted up into a large container and moved outside for the summer.

This swelling fruit shows the glorious purple colour of the most common aubergines (eggplant). Only harvest when the fruit is fully ripe and shiny, otherwise the aubergine will taste bitter and not be worth eating.

GROWING AUBERGINES OUTDOORS

Aubergines (eggplant) can be grown in pots indoors and moved to large containers in a sheltered position outside when the weather is warmer. Plants that are not grown under glass take longer to mature, and the fruit will not be ready for harvesting until the autumn.

PINCHING OUT AUBERGINES

You will have bushier plants if the growing tip is pinched out when the aubergine plant is about 30cm (12in) high. Allow only one fruit to develop on each shoot. Pinch out the growing tips of these shoots three leaves beyond the developing fruit.

Reliable greenhouse varieties

Lettuces	Aubergines
'Cynthia'	'Black Beauty'
'Kellys'	'Black Bell'
'Kwiek'	'Black Enorma'
'Marmer'	'Black Prince'
'Novita'	'Bonica'
	'Dusky'
Melons	'Easter Egg'
'Amber Nectar'	'Long Purple'
'Charentais'	'Moneymaker'
'Classic'	'Short Tom'
'Honeydew'	'Slice Rite'
'Galia'	
'Ogen'	
'Superlative'	
'Sweetheart'	
'Venus'	

Fruit gardening

You do not need a large garden to grow a few fruit trees and bushes. It is possible to train trees in many styles against walls and fences or use them as garden dividers. There are even dwarf forms of popular fruits that are small enough to grow at the edge of a border or in containers.

Once established, fruit trees and bushes are able to compete with other plants for soil moisture and nutrients and so can be accommodated all around the garden. Make sure that they are planted in a sunny spot and that there is sufficient access to carry out essential maintenance tasks such as pruning, spraying and harvesting.

If you want to grow a lot of fruit, you would be better off allocating a separate area of the garden where the fruit trees, bushes, canes and vines are easier to manage and protect. Before planting any fruit it is essential to prepare the ground thoroughly because most plants will occupy the same spot for many years.

This pear tree has been beautifully trained into a fan, which is supported on wires, but it could also be grown against a wall.

Planting a fruit garden

When choosing which fruit to grow in your garden, consider the position you are intending to plant them in. Select good specimens of reliable and trouble-free varieties that you like to eat.

Buying fruit trees

It is important to choose healthy and vigorous specimens when you are buying fruit. Whether you buy bare-root or container-grown plants is a matter of personal preference: most varieties are available as both. Garden centres usually offer a limited range, but for the best choice and for unusual varieties or for trained forms you will probably find that you need to visit a specialist nursery.

When choosing a fruit tree, look for one with a sturdy, straight main trunk and several well-spaced branches that are not too vertical. This is important because the angle between the branch and the trunk will determine how strong the branch will be in later years and, therefore, how much fruit the tree can bear.

An apple tree that has been well cared for when young will fruit for many years, needing little maintenance once it is established.

Fruit tree varieties are all grafted on to a rootstock, and it is essential that you choose a type to suit your particular needs (see box below). It is also important to check that the union between the fruiting variety and rootstock is well healed and strong – look for a bulge about 15cm (6in) above the ground. When you buy plum or cherry trees you should also check the branches for rough areas of bark and oozing sap (a sign of canker disease) as well as foliage with a silvery sheen (a sign of silver leaf disease). Avoid buying suspect plants.

Buying bush and cane fruits

Look for varieties that have been "certified", which means they have been inspected and approved as being of a certain quality.

Currants All types should have three or four equally strong, well-spaced branches of about pencil thickness so the plant forms a well-balanced bush. Many redcurrants and white currants are sold on a short, clear stem, about 10cm (4in) long, but all blackcurrants shoot from the ground.

Choosing a rootstock

Fruit tree varieties are grafted (joined) on to a range of different rootstocks, which vary in their vigour. If you choose a dwarfing rootstock you will get a slower growing, smaller tree, but if you choose a vigorous rootstock you will get a much faster growing, larger fruit tree.

Dwarf rootstocks are good for planting in restricted spaces and produce trees that are easy to manage. Vigorous rootstocks are worth considering if you want a larger tree, if your soil is very poor, or if the tree will get a lot of competition from surrounding plants.

The rootstocks of apples and pears have been given codes; those of cherries and plums have names.

Rootstock	vigour	eventual size
Apples		
M27	very dwarf	1.8m (6ft)
M9	dwarf	2.4m (8ft)
M26	semi-dwarf	3m (10ft)
MM106	semi-vigorous	4.5m (15ft)
MM111	vigorous	5.5m (18ft)
Cherries		
Colt	semi-dwarf	4.5m (15ft)
Pears		
Quince C	semi-dwarf	3m (10ft)
Quince A	semi-vigorous	3.5m (12ft)
Plums		
Pixy	semi-dwarf	3m (10ft)
St Julien A	vigorous	5.5m (18ft)

PLANTING A FRUIT TREE OR BUSH

When you are planting a fruit tree or bush, always make sure that it is planted at the same depth as it was in its container or in its nursery bed.

TYING IN A NEWLY PLANTED TREE

Make sure that a newly planted fruit tree is anchored to a stake. Attach the tie firmly, but not too tightly, approximately 30cm (12in) above the ground.

PROTECTING TRAINED FRUIT

Fruit trees and bushes that are trained against a wall can be protected against birds with netting over a home-made frame. A similar frame can be covered with plastic sheeting to protect the blossom from frosts.

PROTECTING BARK

Damage to trees from rabbits and deer can be prevented by using wire guards.

Gooseberries These plants are also sold on a short stem about 10cm (4in) long. Choose one with a balanced head of three or four well-spaced and equally strong branches.
Raspberries When choosing, look for single, strong canes, each of about pencil thickness.
Blackberries and other hybrid berries Choose plants with at least two shoots of pencil thickness. Do not buy plants that have split stems or uneven colouring to the stems because this is a sign of neglect and possibly disease.

Planting fruit trees and bushes
Prepare the ground thoroughly before planting fruit trees and bushes, ensuring that you remove all perennial weeds. Dig in plenty of organic material.

As long as the weather is neither too wet nor too cold the best time to plant is between late autumn and mid-spring. If bare-rooted plants are delivered when you cannot plant them, heel them in (plant in a shallow trench, with their stems leaning at an angle close to the ground) temporarily until they can be planted in their permanent position. Container-grown plants can be planted at other times of the year, but they need more attention to make sure that they survive.

Fruit trees and bushes should be planted to the same depth as they were in their pots or nursery bed when you purchased them. If a tree needs staking, place the stake in the ground before planting. Water the plants in thoroughly and keep them watered in dry weather until they are well established. Apply a mulch around the base of the plant in order to help preserve moisture as well as to keep the weeds down. Remove any weeds that do appear. You may also find it necessary to use wire guards around the trunks or netting over the branches to protect fruit trees and bushes from pests such as rabbits, deer or birds.

Growing trained fruit trees

Although free-standing fruit trees look lovely, the best way to grow fruit trees in a small garden is as trained forms against boundaries and as garden dividers. Not only do they take up less room, but there are practical advantages to the method.

Siting trained fruit trees

A sunny wall or fence offers several advantages for training fruit. The trees are well supported and branches well spaced. Walls and fences help to protect the blossom from cold winds and frosts in early spring, and encourage rapid ripening of fruit in late summer. Another advantage is that all parts of the tree are within reach, making maintenance straightforward. It will be easier to protect against birds in summer, frost in spring and cold in winter, as well as diseases, such as the dreaded peach leaf curl disease.

The best option for training fruit trees is to buy a ready-trained tree in a container from a fruit specialist, but you can do it yourself using a single-stemmed (maiden) tree.

PRUNING A CORDON

In summer, cut back any new sideshoots to three leaves and new growth on existing sideshoots to the first leaf.

In winter, thin out any of the older spurs if they have become congested, then cut back the main stem's new growth to 15cm (6in).

Supporting fruit trees

If you do not have a sturdy wall or fence to grow the tree against, make a free-standing support from fence posts high enough for the form you are training. Space the posts 1.8m (6ft) apart and set them in concrete, with the end posts braced with an angled strut (also set in concrete). String heavy-duty fencing wire horizontally between the posts, using screw-in, galvanized vine-eyes and tensioning bolts at either end. The first wire should be 30cm (12in) above the soil, with subsequent wires 45cm (18in) apart. When growing a tree against a wall, have the first wire 30cm (12in) above the soil and subsequent wires 15cm (6in) apart.

Training and pruning cordons

Cordons have a single stem trained at an angle of 45 degrees. After planting at the correct angle, tie a bamboo cane behind the main stem and to the top wire. Prune sideshoots to just above the third bud. In the first summer, tie extension growth to the cane and prune back any new shoots from the main stem to above the third bud. New shoots produced from the stubs of sideshoots produced last year should be pruned to their first leaf. Each winter, thereafter, cut back the main stem's new growth to within 15cm (6in). Once the tree reaches the top of its support, cut any extension growth to the first bud. Each summer all new shoots produced from the stubs cut back the previous year should be pruned to the first leaf.

HOW TO FIX SUPPORTING WIRES TO A WALL

1 To support trees against walls, use wires held by vine eyes. Depending on the type of vine eye, either knock them into the wall or drill and plug before screwing them in.

2 Pass heavy-duty galvanized wire through the holes in the eyes and fasten to the end ones, keeping the wire as tight as possible.

PRUNING A FAN-TRAINED TREE

The main aim when pruning a fan tree is to maintain the fan shape. In spring, cut out any new sideshoots that are pointing towards or away from the wall. If necessary, reduce the number of new shoots to about one every 15cm (6in).

In summer cut back all new shoots to about six leaves, leaving any that are needed to fill in gaps in the main framework. In autumn, after cropping, further cut back the shoots to three leaves.

Training and pruning fans

Fan-trained trees have up to ten equally spaced ribs radiating from the main stem. It is a good way of training fruit trees because the fan produces a large number of fruit-bearing stems.

After planting, cut back the main stem to just above the first bud which should be about 5cm (2in) above the bottom wire. Tie in two bamboo canes to the supporting wires either side of the tree at angles of 45 degrees. The following summer select two sideshoots and tie them into the canes as they grow. Remove all others. During the dormant season cut back sideshoots to about 45cm (18in). The following summer, untie the first pair of canes and lower the canes, with branches attached, to the lowest horizontal wire each side of the tree. Tie in another pair of canes at 45 degrees and tie two new suitably placed shoots to them. Remove any unwanted shoots to their first leaf.

Repeat the process each year to create a symmetrical, fan-shaped tree. Once established, it will still need regular pruning to remove unwanted or badly positioned new shoots and to keep it fruiting well, because the fruit is borne on one-year-old wood. Always prune in summer to avoid silver leaf disease.

Training and pruning espaliers

Espalier trees have three or four horizontal tiers of branches trained along the supporting wires. Follow the method described for pruning fans, except the main stem is retained and trained vertically. Each winter the main stem should be pruned back to just above the horizontal wire, and the sideshoots are trained along canes held at 45 degrees in their first year, then lowered to the horizontal wire in their second. Each summer all unwanted new shoots should be pruned to the first leaf and suitably placed new shoots tied into the next pair of canes. Once the tree covers the support, cut back the extension growth of the main stem to one bud above the top wire and treat each branch as described for a cordon.

Growing a fan-trained peach tree against a wall creates an ideal environment for the tree and looks attractive. All parts of the tree are within reach and so maintenance is easier.

Growing apples and pears

Apples and pears can be grown in a variety of ways, ranging from free-standing specimens for the middle of a lawn or border to neatly trained types for growing against a fence or a wall or other type of supporting framework.

Planting

If you are growing more than one tree, in an orchard for example, you will need to space the trees according to their eventual size, which is dependent on the rootstock. Trees on dwarfing rootstocks can be planted 1.5m (5ft) apart, while trees on vigorous rootstocks should be up to 7m (25ft) apart.

Container-grown fruit trees can be planted at any time of the year, but they will establish more quickly and be easier to look after if they are planted in spring or autumn when the soil is moist and warm, which encourages rapid root growth and so establishment.

Bare-root specimens, however, have to be planted during the dormant season, which is between autumn and spring. The planting technique for fruit trees is the same as that described for ornamental trees and shrubs.

Good apple and pear varieties

Eating apples	'Grenadier'
'Discovery'	'Howgate
'Fiesta'	Wonder'
'Greensleeves'	
'James Grieve'	**Pears**
'Jonagold'	'Beth'
'Katy'	'Concorde'
'Sunset'	'Conference'
	'Doyenné du
Cooking apples	Comice'
'Bramley's	'Williams' Bon
Seedling'	Chrétien'

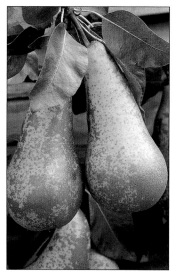

Conference pears have a distinctive elongated shape. These healthy specimens are ripe for picking and enjoying.

Malus 'John Downie' is one of the best varieties for making crab apple jelly.

Pruning free-standing trees

Despite a popular belief that apple and pear trees are difficult and time-consuming to keep in shape, if you buy trees that have been well trained, they will require the minimum of care. Pruning is best carried out in mid- to late winter. First, cut out dead or diseased stems and any new shoots that are crossing or touching. Also cut out any very upright-growing shoots. Then shorten about half of the remaining new growth to maintain a well-balanced overall shape. Every few years you may have to remove one or two larger branches so as to maintain the balanced shape and keep the tree from becoming congested in the centre.

General care

Three or four years after planting, start feeding all fruiting trees as a matter of course each spring. Apply a general fertilizer at a rate recommended by the manufacturer,

on the ground under the canopy of the tree. Then top up the loose organic mulch so that it is about 8cm (3in) thick over the same area. Established trees do not need watering, although a thorough soaking every couple of weeks during a prolonged drought will ensure that crop yields are not affected. Spraying garden trees against pest and disease attacks is not normally worthwhile.

Harvesting and storing

Fruits are ripe when they separate from the tree with their stalk intact. Gently twist the fruit in the palm of your hand: if it comes away it's ready to pick. In general, the fruit on the sunny side of the tree will ripen first.

Not all varieties of apples and pears store well. Early varieties of eating apples should not be stored. Choose only perfect fruit of average size. Small fruit tend to shrivel and large fruit tend to rot. Separate

PRUNING A FREE-STANDING TREE

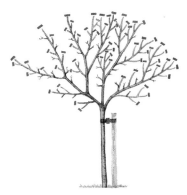

After planting cut back the leader to about 75cm (30in) above the ground. Leave any sideshoots that appear just below this cut and remove any others lower down. The following year reduce all new growth by about half. This will form the basic framework. Subsequent pruning is restricted to reducing the length of new growth by about a third and removing overcrowded growth.

different varieties because they store for different durations. Keep the fruit in moulded paper trays in ventilated cardboard boxes, both of which are often available free from supermarkets. Place boxes in a cool, dark, frost-free place and check at least once a week to remove deteriorating fruits.

Apples are not only delicious when they are picked straight from the tree, many varieties also retain their qualities when stored. This crop of ripening apples will make for a successful harvest.

HOW TO HARVEST APPLES AND PEARS

Apples and pears are removed from the tree with a twist of the wrist. The stalks should remain attached to the fruit.

HOW TO STORE APPLES AND PEARS

Apples, pears and quinces can be stored in trays in a cool, dry place. It is best if they are laid in individual screws of paper or moulded paper trays so that the individual fruits do not touch. The length of storage time depends on the variety.

Growing other tree fruit

Plum and cherry trees can be grown in a number of ways, ranging from full-sized standards to pyramid bushes. They can also be trained as fans against walls and fences.

Choosing a site

Fruit trees grow best in a moisture-retentive but free-draining soil, so it is worth digging in plenty of well-rotted organic matter before planting. Cherries, in particular, do not do well on dry or shallow soil. All need full sun to thrive, although acid cherries are more tolerant of shady conditions.

General care

Apply a general fertilizer at the rate recommended by the manufacturer, under the canopy of each peach and nectarine tree. Plums and cherries respond to a slightly higher rate of feed, so apply a general fertilizer at approximately double the rate that you would use for other trees. Fruit trees should be mulched each spring with loose organic material, such as well-rotted garden compost, so that it is about 8cm (3in) thick. Water in prolonged dry spells. Wall-trained trees should also be watered regularly while fruit is swelling.

Reducing vigour

You can keep young plum trees small and fruiting well using a technique called festooning. During the summer pull down the main stems into a horizontal position by tying strings to their tips and tying the other ends to the trunk. This reduces sap flow. During the following summer prune back the main shoots and tie down in the same way the new shoots that were produced. In time, you end up with a smaller, slightly weeping tree that fruits well.

Eat damsons fresh when they are fully ripe. Surplus fruit can be frozen whole or used to make jams and jellies. Damsons are suitable for cooking once they have coloured.

PRUNING A SOUR CHERRY FAN

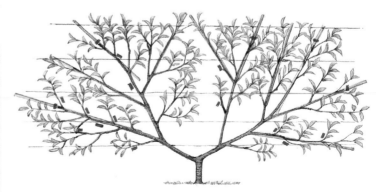

Once established, there are two purposes to pruning a cherry fan: to keep the fan shape and to ensure that there is a constant supply of new wood. When you are pruning to keep the shape, remove any shoots that are pointing in the wrong direction. For renewal pruning, cut back in summer one-third of the shoots that have fruited, preferably as far back as the next new shoot. Tie these new shoots to the cane and wire framework.

Peaches and nectarines blossom early in the year, when only a few pollinating insects are about, so it is worthwhile hand-pollinating the blossom with a soft paintbrush to ensure a good set of fruit.

During cold spells in early spring, it is worth covering fruit trees with insulating hessian (burlap) or a double layer of horticultural fleece to protect the blossom from frost. Later in the year, use netting to protect ripening fruit from the birds.

Peach leaf curl disease distorts leaves and can eventually weaken the tree. You can prevent new leaves from becoming infected by clearing away infected leaves once they fall and by covering the tree from early winter until late spring so that rain cannot wet the foliage. The fungal disease is spread by rain splash.

Pruning and training

Plums should be pruned in summer to avoid silver leaf disease. Once the basic shape of the tree has been established, cherries and plums need little pruning apart from the removal of dead, diseased or congested growth. Sour cherries are produced on one-year-old wood and should be pruned after the fruit has been harvested. Cut back about one-third of the fruiting stems to the first new shoot lower down the stem.

Plum and sweet cherry trees, on the other hand, produce most of their fruit at the base of one-year-old and older shoots. This means that they are not suitable for training as cordons or espaliers but can be trained as fans. After formative pruning of a fan-trained tree has established the framework, you need to make sure there is a constant supply of new growth that will bear the fruit. In summer cut back all shoots that have fruited to a

PRUNING A FRUIT TREE

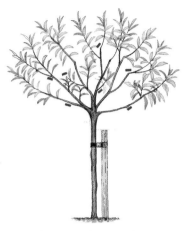

For a free-standing fruit tree such as this peach, not a great deal of pruning is required. In spring cut back some of the older barren wood as far as a new replacement shoot. Remove any awkwardly placed branches and keep the bush open and airy. Avoid making large cuts, because this is likely to allow canker to infect the tree.

new shoot lower down. Then tie in this new shoot to the supporting cane as a replacement for the one you have removed. Also prune out any unwanted growth to maintain the overall shape of the fan.

Peaches and nectarines can be grown as free-standing trees, but they are most successful when grown as a fan against a south-facing wall or fence. Not only does the support provide protection during early spring when the blossom is susceptible to frost damage, but it also captures more of the sun's energy during the summer, improving the chances that the fruit will ripen successfully.

Harvesting and storing

Pick fruit as soon as it is ripe. You can also pick plums slightly under-ripe for storage in the salad drawer of your refrigerator for a couple of

weeks. Sweet cherries, nectarines and peaches do not continue to mature after picking, so do not harvest until they are ready. Ripe fruit is best eaten straight away, although it will last a few days if kept somewhere cool. Gluts of fruit can be made into jam and preserves, or plums and sweet cherries halved and stoned (pitted) and then frozen whole.

Good fruit tree varieties

Plums	
'Cambridge Gage'	'Garden Anny'
	'Garden Lady'
'Czar'	'Garden Silver'
'Marjorie's Seedling'	'Garden Gold'
	'Peregrine'
'Merryweather'	'Rochester'
'Oullins Gage'	'Terrace Amber'
'Victoria'	'Terrace Diamond'

Cherries	Nectarines
'Morello' (acid)	'Early Rivers'
'Stella'	'Garden Beauty'
'Sunburst'	'Golden Glow'
	'Lord Napier'
Peaches	'Nectarella'
'Bonanza'	'Terrace Ruby'
'Duke of York'	

Patio peaches and nectarines

Dwarf peaches, such as 'Bonanza', and those in the Garden and Terrace series, as well as dwarf nectarines, such as 'Nectarella' and 'Golden Glow', are suitable for growing in pots on the patio. Use a large container filled with soil-based compost (soil mix). Hand-pollinate with a soft brush and keep frost free (in a conservatory or heated green-house) until late spring when the plant can be moved outside. Feed with a high-potash liquid feed, such as tomato fertilizer, every fortnight throughout the growing season. Net ripening fruit against birds.

Growing bush fruit

Gooseberries and currants are more tolerant than many other fruit and can be grown in partial shade, although better crops and earlier harvests will be achieved in full sun. Red- and white currants need a well-drained site, but blackcurrants can tolerate poorly drained soil.

Planting

For best results plant bush fruits in a moisture-retentive but free-draining soil that does not get waterlogged in winter. They can be grown as free-standing bushes, novelty hedges or as trained forms against a fence or other support. On an exposed site, a wall or fence will provide protection, especially in spring when late frosts can reduce yields considerably.

Gooseberry bushes should be spaced 1–1.5m (3–5ft) apart, depending on the vigour of the variety. Blackcurrant bushes should be spaced 1.5m (5ft) apart. Red- and white currants, grown as bushes, should be spaced 1.2m (4ft) apart or, as cordons, should be spaced 45cm (18in) apart.

HOW TO PRUNE A GOOSEBERRY BUSH

On an established gooseberry bush, cut back the new growth on the leaders in winter by about half and reduce all other new growth to two buds. In summer, remove any damaged wood, crossing branches, suckers and basal growth to keep the centre of the bush airy and prevent it becoming congested.

Pruning and training

Gooseberries and currants can be grown as airy, open-centred bushes or as cordons against a supporting framework. Gooseberries and blackcurrants are produced on shoots that are one or more years old, so bushes will produce a crop even if you do not prune them. However, the stems will soon become very congested and picking will be difficult.

Gooseberry bushes After planting, prune back three or four well-spaced sideshoots by about half to an upward-facing bud. Remove all other shoots. In the following winter cut back two new shoots on each sideshoot by about half to form the main framework of the bush and at the same time remove any shoots congesting the centre. Cut back any other new growth to two buds so that they form fruiting spurs. Thereafter, prune in summer to keep the centre of the bush open and healthy. In winter, cut back any growth from the framework branches by about half and all other new growth to two buds.

Gooseberry cordons After planting, cut back the main shoot by about half and tie it in to an upright bamboo cane fixed to the support. Prune off any sideshoots to leave two buds. Thereafter, prune in late summer, cutting back new sideshoots to 10cm (4in) from the main trunk. In winter cut back the leading shoot by a third. Once the cordon has reached the top of its support, cut it back to one bud instead.

Blackcurrant bushes This fruit can only be grown on bushes. Prune established blackcurrants in winter, removing one-third of the stems starting with the oldest, cutting back to 2.5cm (1in) above the ground. Alternatively, they can be pruned when harvesting.

Red- and white currant bushes After planting, select three or four well-spaced sideshoots and cut them back by about half to an upward-facing bud. All other shoots should be removed. The following winter cut back two new shoots on each sideshoot by about half to form the main framework of the bush and remove any shoots congesting the centre. Cut back any other new growth to two buds so that they

Gooseberries can be grown as single cordons. This is achieved by tying them into canes, which are supported by horizontal wires.

Blackcurrants and redcurrants are delicious when ripe, picked fresh from the garden.

form fruiting spurs. In subsequent years, prune in summer to keep the centre of the currant bush open and healthy. In winter, cut back extension growth from the framework branches by about half and other new growth to two buds.

Red- and white currant cordons

After planting a cordon, cut back the main shoot by about half its length and tie it in to an upright bamboo cane fixed to the support. Prune back any sideshoots to leave two buds. Thereafter, prune in late summer but cut back new sideshoots to leave about five leaves. In winter cut back the leading shoot by a third. Once the cordon has reached the top of its support, cut it back to one bud instead.

Good bush fruit varieties

Gooseberries	Blackcurrants
'Careless'	'Baldwin'
'Greenfinch'	'Ben Lomond'
'Invicta'	'Ben Nevis'
'Lancashire Lad'	'Ben Sarek'
'Leveller'	'Black Reward'
'Whinham's Industry'	'Boskoop Giant'
	White currants
Redcurrants	'White Dutch'
'Laxton's No. 1'	'White Grape'
'Red Lake'	'White Versailles'

General care

Apply a general fertilizer at the rate recommended by the manufacturer around each fruit bush annually in spring. Mulch each spring with loose organic material, such as well-rotted garden compost.

Bush fruits are largely trouble-free, although American gooseberry mildew disease can be devastating if it is allowed to take hold. If your bushes show symptoms (powdery patches on young leaves), prune back affected branches by about a third before spraying the rest of the bush with a suitable fungicide. The variety 'Invicta' is resistant to mildew.

Sawfly caterpillars can strip leaves from gooseberries in late spring; pick off any caterpillars by hand and kill them. You may also need to protect bushes with netting from bud-stripping bullfinches in winter and the ripening fruit from other birds in summer.

Harvesting and storing

Gooseberry bushes that are developing a lot of fruit can be thinned in late spring and the unripe fruit used for cooking, allowing the

HOW TO PRUNE BLACKCURRANTS

After planting, cut blackcurrants back to a single bud above the ground. The following winter, remove any weak or misplaced growth. Subsequent pruning can take place either in winter or when harvesting. Remove dead and diseased stems and cut out up to a third of two-year-old or older wood.

The simplest method of preserving bush fruits is to freeze them.

rest to swell and ripen to be eaten fresh. Gooseberries will not all ripen at once, so you will have to pick over the bushes several times. The fruit can be kept for a few weeks in a cool place or made into preserves.

Blackcurrants can be picked and pruned at the same time. Simply cut back all fruiting stems to 2.5cm (1in) from the ground above a plump bud and then take the laden stems to the kitchen for stripping. Pick or prune off sprigs of red- and white currants while the fruit is well coloured but still shiny. All currants can be kept for a couple of weeks in a cool place, or frozen or made into preserves.

HOW TO PRUNE OTHER CURRANTS

After planting a red- or white currant bush cut back each main shoot by about half. During subsequent pruning, in summer, aim to form an open bush. In winter, cut back all new growth on the main shoots and reduce the new growth on all sideshoots to two buds. Remove any dead and diseased stems.

Growing cane fruit

Raspberries, blackberries and hybrid berries such as loganberries are easy to grow. Blackberries will even produce a decent crop if they are grown against a north-facing wall.

Raspberries

This crop needs a sunny, sheltered spot and a well-drained but moisture-retentive soil to do well. Raspberries dislike winter wet, so grow them on a ridge of topsoil if your soil is heavy. Space plants 38–45cm (15–18in) apart in the row. After

planting, cut back the stems to about 30cm (12in), cutting just above a bud. The following spring cut back the old stem to ground level as new shoots emerge.

Raspberries can be grown against a free-standing support or alongside a fence. The easiest form of support consists of stout posts at 3m (10ft) intervals along the row with horizontal fencing wire strung between the posts and held taut with tensioning bolts. Only two wires are needed, one running about

60cm (24in) from the ground and the second at a height of about 1.2m (4ft).

There are two types of raspberry: summer fruiting and autumn fruiting. By far the most common are the summer-fruiting varieties, which bear fruit on canes produced the previous year. Autumn-fruiting raspberries, on the other hand, produce their fruit at the tips of the canes produced during the current season. Prune summer-fruiting raspberries in early autumn by removing all shoots that have fruited back to ground level and tying in new shoots to the support. If there are too many shoots to space about 8cm (3in) apart on the support, cut out the weakest. Autumn-fruiting raspberry canes should be cut back to ground level after harvesting. New shoots produced from below ground in spring will bear fruit in the following autumn.

Blackberries and hybrid berries

Although blackberries prefer a sunny spot, they are much more tolerant than other types of fruit and can be grown in shade and on any type of soil. Space plants 1.8–3m (6–10ft) apart depending on the vigour of the variety. Do not plant blackberries too deeply; the soil should only just cover the roots. Blackberries and most hybrid berries need a support. This can be constructed as described for raspberries, but the horizontal wires should be spaced just 30cm (12in) apart, with the lowest wire 1m (3ft) from the ground and the highest wire at about 1.8m (6ft).

The easiest way to train blackberries and hybrid berries is to use a fan method. Select one new cane to be trained along each wire on one side of the plant, then tie in the canes as they grow. The following

HOW TO ERECT POSTS AND WIRES

1 Knock a stout post well into the ground at the end of the row of cane fruit. It may be easier to dig a hole and insert the post before backfilling and ramming down the earth.

2 Knock another post at an angle of 45 degrees to the vertical to act as a support to the upright post. Nail firmly using galvanized nails so that the upright post is rigid and will support the tension of tight wires.

3 Fasten the wires around one end post and pull tight along the row, stapling it to each vertical post. Keep the wire as taut as possible. If necessary, use eye bolts on the end posts to tension the wire.

4 Fasten the canes – in this case raspberry canes – to the wire with string or plant ties. Space the canes out evenly along the wire so that the maximum amount of light can reach the leaves.

year do the same on the other side of the plant. Once canes have fruited in autumn, cut them back to ground level and tie in new ones to replace those that have been cut out.

General care

Hand-weed around the plants rather than using a hoe so that you do not damage their shallow roots. Every spring, apply a general fertilizer, at the rate recommended by the manufacturer, on either side of the row. Mulch each spring with loose organic material, such as garden compost, and remove any suckers that appear away from the row.

HOW TO PICK CANE FRUIT

Small cane fruit, such as raspberries and blackberries, should be carefully picked between thumb and finger. The fruit should be placed in small containers so that they are not squashed or bruised.

Good cane fruit varieties

Autumn raspberries	**Blackberries**
'Autumn Bliss'	'Ashton Cross'
'Fallgold'	'Bedford Giant'
	'Fantasia'
Summer raspberries	'Loch Ness'
'Delight'	'Oregon Thornless'
'Glen Clova'	
'Glen Moy'	**Hybrid berries**
'Glen Prosen'	'Loganberry LY59'
'Julia'	'Loganberry L654'
'Leo'	'Sunberry'
'Malling Admiral'	'Tayberry'
'Malling Jewel'	'Vietchberry'

TRAINING BLACKBERRIES: ALTERNATE BAY

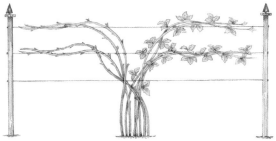

There are several methods of training blackberries. One method is to tie all the new growth to one side of the wirework. After fruiting, remove the previous year's growth from the other side and then tie next year's new growth on that side. Repeat each year.

TRAINING BLACKBERRIES: ROPE

A second way to train blackberries is temporarily to tie in all new growth vertically to the wirework and along the top wire. The current fruiting canes are tied in groups horizontally. These are removed after harvesting and the new growth is tied into their place.

TRAINING BLACKBERRIES: FANS

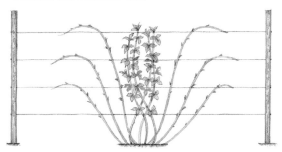

The new blackberry canes are temporarily tied vertically and along the top wire, while the fruiting canes are tied in singly along the horizontal wires. Any excess canes are removed. After fruiting, these canes are taken out and the new growth is tied into their place.

TRAINING RASPBERRIES: POSTS AND WIRES

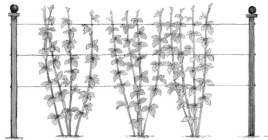

Raspberry plants are set at intervals of 38–45cm (15–18in). Each year, new raspberry canes are thrown up. When fruiting has finished on the old canes, these are cut out and the new canes are tied to the wires in their place. This sequence is followed every year.

Growing strawberries

To get a reliable crop of strawberries it is important to choose a good variety and grow them well. There are several excellent varieties, which can give a succession of fruit over a long period.

Planting strawberries

Strawberries should be planted into soil that has not been used for growing them for at least the last five years. Choose a sunny, sheltered site with well-drained soil and add plenty of well-rotted manure before planting. Plant bare-root strawberries on a slight ridge at the same depth as they were in the field. Container-grown strawberries should be planted slightly deeper so that the rootball is just covered with soil. Space plants 45cm (18in) apart, with 75cm (30in) between rows.

Plant through a mulch of black polythene (plastic) to prevent weeds. Lay over the prepared bed where the soil has been ridged slightly in the centre and plant through cross-shaped slits. Bury the edges of the polythene to keep it in place.

On this plant a succession of stages can be seen, from flowers to ripe fruit. Strawberries eaten immediately after picking taste best.

Succession of strawberries

Because different varieties of strawberry are ready to harvest at different times, if you choose the right combination you can achieve a succession of fruit through the early summer. Very early varieties, such as 'Pantagruella', can be brought on even earlier under cloches to give you a garden crop in late spring – or even earlier if grown in pots or a growing bag in an unheated greenhouse. Follow this with an early variety, such as 'Idil', and a mid-season variety, such as 'Tenira', and finally a late variety, such as 'Bogota', for a continuous harvest until late summer. You can extend the season

MULCHING WITH STRAW

Place a layer of straw under the leaves of the strawberry plants in order to prevent the developing fruit from getting muddy or covered with dirt.

MULCHING WITH MEMBRANE

Strawberries can be grown through a polythene (plastic) mulch. This not only protects the fruit from mud splashes but also reduces the need for weeding and watering.

Good strawberry varieties

Summer-fruiting strawberries	Perpetual-fruiting strawberries / Alpines
Summer-fruiting strawberries	'Royal Sovereign'
'Bogota'	'Tamella'
'Cambridge Favourite'	'Tenira'
'Cambridge Vigour'	**Perpetual-fruiting strawberries**
'Cambridge Rival'	'Aromel'
'Domanil'	'Gento'
'Hapil'	'Ostara'
'Honeoye'	'Red Rich'
'Idil'	'St Claude'
'Jamil'	
'Korona'	**Alpines**
'Pantagruella'	'Alexandria'
'Redgauntlet'	'Delicious'
	'Yellow Wonder'

Replacement crops

Strawberries produce their best crops in the second or third year after planting, then yields tend to fall and the health of the plants deteriorates as pests and diseases take a hold. Therefore, it is a good idea to replace the whole strawberry bed every few years with new, vigorous plants set in fresh soil. The cheapest way to do this is to raise your own plants by rooting runners from healthy, heavy-cropping plants.

PROTECTION AGAINST FROST

Strawberries can be protected against frost with cloches.

PROTECTION AGAINST BIRDS

A tunnel of wire netting can be used to protect the fruit from birds. The netting can be in short sections for easy removal and storage.

further by planting a perpetual strawberry variety, such as 'Aromel', which will continue to produce fruit into the autumn provided it is given the protection of cloches if cold weather threatens. Even winter and early spring crops can be achieved in a heated greenhouse.

General care
Keep strawberry beds free of weeds at all times. Hand-weeding is best, so as not to disturb the roots. Keep plants watered until they are established. Water strawberry plants as necessary when the fruits are swelling and in the autumn when the following year's flower buds are formed. Apply a general fertilizer, at the rate recommended by the manufacturer, either side of the row in midsummer.

Strawberries are vulnerable to a number of pests and diseases. If you do not wish to use chemical controls you will need to remain vigilant at all times and clear fading foliage and rotting fruit as soon as they are noticed. Aphids and slugs are the main pests, but watch out for botrytis if the season is moist. Protect ripening fruit from birds by covering the rows with nets held off the crop on wire hoops.

Harvesting and storing
Check ripening strawberries every day and pick when the fruits are red all over. Eat fresh straight away or keep somewhere cool for a few days. Surpluses can be frozen for purée or made into jam.

CARE AFTER FRUITING

After summer-fruiting strawberries have produced their fruit, cut off all the leaves and burn or compost them, along with the straw mulch, to help prevent the spread of diseases.

PROPAGATING FROM RUNNERS

1 After fruiting, the strawberry plant sends out a series of runners that root along their length to produce new plants. This method of propagation is called layering.

2 The layered plants can be dug up once they have rooted and used to start a new bed.

Propagation

The thrill of seeing your first seeds germinate or your first cutting take root is often when the gardening bug really gets a grip on a beginner. There are many ways you can increase your stock of plants, and the method you choose will depend on the type of plant you are growing, although some plants can be propagated using a variety of techniques.

All annual flowers and vegetables are raised from seed, and this is a useful way of growing some perennials and shrubs that you want a lot of – for ground cover or for a hedge, for example. But perennials, shrubs, climbers and trees can also be reproduced vegetatively by taking cuttings or by layering, and this might be more appropriate if you want just a few plants of a particular variety.

You do not need elaborate equipment, but your success rate will increase if you can provide the right environment. So, if you want to raise a lot of new plants, you should consider investing in a thermostatically controlled propagator.

The white, fragrant flowers of *Lilium regale* make it a popular plant. It can be propagated by seed in early autumn.

Sowing seed

Raising plants from seed has got to be one of the most satisfying aspects of gardening and is probably the easiest way of growing a lot of the same plant within a tight budget.

Collecting seed

If you want a lot of one particular plant or are propagating plants for sale at a plant fair, for example, many flowers can be raised successfully from seed collected from your own garden. Bear in mind, however, that seed from a named variety may not grow into a plant that is exactly the same as its parent.

To save your own seed, simply cut the seedhead just before it is fully ripe and place it in a paper bag in a dry, airy room where it will finish ripening. For plants that eject their seed, you will need to cover the seedhead with the paper bag before you remove it from the plant.

Sowing techniques

To raise plants successfully early in the season you will need to keep the sown seeds somewhere warm, such as in an airing cupboard (linen closet) or a thermostatically controlled propagator, and have somewhere frost-free, such as a windowsill or heated greenhouse, to grow them on.

Seed is available in various forms, and the method of sowing varies according to the type you are growing. Always check the seed packet for details such as whether the seed needs light to germinate, its sowing depth, germination and growing-on temperatures, and use this information as a guide before you start.

Many seeds are now available pre-treated for more reliable germination (known as primed, chitted or pre-germinated seed). Such seeds are more expensive, but they are worth considering for expensive and difficult-to-germinate subjects. Some seed suppliers also offer coated or pelleted seed, which is larger and easier to space when sowing. This eliminates the need for pricking out, and will reduce the wastage from discarding seedlings.

Planning ahead

It makes sense to plan ahead if you intend to sow a lot of plants from seed. This will not only make the most efficient use of your time, equipment and available space, but it will also help even out the workload.

The best way to organize a programme is to decide when you want the plants and to work backwards to decide on a sowing date. Make sure that you have the time and growing space at each stage of development. It's a good idea to make a seed organizer out of an old

COLLECTING SEED

1 Most self-sowing flowers will drop their seed without need for assistance but to make sure that seed does fall on the soil, tap ripe seedheads to dislodge and scatter the seed before discarding the dead flowers.

2 Seed can also be collected by tapping the seedhead over a sheet of paper. Remove any bits of seed case and pour the seed into a paper bag, labelled with the plant's name, until it is required. Store in a cool, dry place.

Germinating seed

A few types of seed will not germinate reliably unless given a special treatment before sowing – check the seed packet for details. The seeds of sweet peas, for example, have a particularly hard coat that needs to be softened by soaking in water for 24 hours before sowing or breached by nicking the seedcoat with a sharp knife or rubbing it with sandpaper.

Other types of seed need a period of cold (known as stratification) before they will germinate. In nature this is the winter period, and the easiest way to provide this is to sow the seed in autumn and overwinter it in a cold frame. However, you can mimic the process at other times of the year by mixing seed with moist sand and placing it in a refrigerator for one to three months, depending on the type of seed.

shoebox with weekly dividers to help you keep track. If you need to sow several batches of the same seed over a period of time (such as with many salad crops) move the seed packet after sowing to the next date in the organizer. In general, sow twice as much seed as you need mature plants to allow for erratic germination and losses along the way.

The best way to sow most seed is in a seed tray (flat) using a sowing compost (soil mix) because you can control the conditions accurately and so achieve more reliable germination. However, it is worth sowing some types of seed, such as hardy annuals and many vegetables, in their final position, direct into a specially prepared seedbed.

HOW TO SOW IN THE GARDEN

1 Sow the seed along the drill, taking care not to sow too thickly, to reduce the amount of thinning that will be necessary.

2 Rake the soil into the drill over the seed. Gently tamp down the soil along the row with the flat of the rake and lightly rake over.

Sowing small seed

Some plants, such as lobelias and impatiens, have dust-like seed that is very difficult to sow thinly and evenly. You can make the job a lot easier by mixing the seed with a little dry silver sand before sowing. The sand will effectively "dilute" the seed, making it easier to sow, and, because it is light in colour, you will be able to see which areas of compost have been sown.

SOWING IN CELLULAR BLOCKS

Fill the blocks with compost (soil mix) and tap on the table to settle down. Sow one or two seeds in each cell. Cover lightly with compost. Remove the weaker seedling after germination.

HOW TO SOW IN TRAYS

1 Fill the seed tray (flat) with seed compost and tamp down the compost lightly to produce a level surface. Sow the seed thinly across the compost.

2 Cover with a thin layer of compost (unless the seed needs light to germinate), lightly firm down and label the tray. Labelling is very important as many seedlings look the same.

SOWING IN POTS

Fill the pot with a good sowing compost (soil mix), tap it lightly on the bench and sow from one to three seeds in each pot. Once germinated, the weaker seedlings can be removed, leaving one to grow on.

HOW TO USE A PROPAGATOR

1 Place the seeds in a propagator. Adjust the temperature of heated propagators as required – seed packets should indicate the best temperature, but you may need to compromise if different seeds need different temperatures.

2 This propagator is unheated and should be kept in a warm position in a greenhouse or within the house. Start opening the vents once the seeds have germinated to begin the hardening-off process.

Pricking out and aftercare

Once the seeds have germinated, they need to be given the perfect growing conditions to produce independent, healthy and vigorous plants suitable for planting in their permanent position.

Pricking out

Poor seedling care is the most usual reason for failure when raising new plants from seed. The aim is to provide a suitable growing environment where the plants can establish and develop without receiving a check in growth. This means that the seedlings indoors

need to be spaced (pricked) out either into seed trays (flats) or other containers, and those raised outside need to be transplanted or thinned out to the correct spacing.

As soon as they are large enough to handle safely, space seedlings into prepared seed trays (flats) or modules or into individual pots filled with fresh compost (soil mix). Gently lift each seedling individually, holding it by a leaf (never the stem), and support the root system with a dibber, plant label or pencil. Position the seedling at the correct spacing at the same depth as it was before,

spreading its delicate roots carefully. Water the tray of seedlings from below by standing it in a bowl of water until the surface of the compost darkens. Place the seedlings somewhere bright but shaded from direct sunlight and mist occasionally if they threaten to flag. Maintain the correct growing-on temperature (depending on the type of plants you are growing) until they are ready to plant out.

If conditions outside are not suitable, you may have to keep the plants growing in limited amounts of compost for several weeks. If they

HOW TO PRICK OUT SEEDLINGS INTO MODULES

1 Choose a module that suits the size of plant. A small seedling, such as ageratum, will not need such a large cell as, say, a dahlia. Fill the cells loosely with a suitable potting mixture (soil mix). Strike the compost off level with a straightedge but do not compress it. It will settle in the cells once the seedlings have been inserted and watered.

2 Loosen the seedlings in the tray or pot you are pricking out from and if possible lift them one at a time by their seed leaves. Never hold seedlings by their stems as this can damage them. The seed leaves are the first ones to open, and they are usually smaller and a different shape from the true leaves.

3 Use a tool designed for the purpose, or improvise with a pencil or plant label, to make a hole large enough to take the roots with as little bending or disturbance as possible. Gently firm the compost around the roots, being careful not to press too hard. Water thoroughly, then keep the plants in a well-lit spot but out of direct sunlight.

HOW TO PRICK OUT SEEDLINGS INTO POTS

1 Fill small pots with potting mixture (soil mix) and firm it lightly, using the base of another pot. Loosen the compost around the seedling to be transplanted with a small dibber or transplanting tool. Hold the seedling by its leaves, not the stem.

2 Make a hole in the centre of the pot, deep enough to take the roots. While still holding the seedling by a leaf, gently firm the potting mixture around the roots, using a small dibber or a finger. Do not press too hard, as watering will settle the mixture around the roots.

3 Water carefully so that the soil settles without washing the plant out. Keep in a warm, humid place out of direct sunlight. Labelling individual pots is tedious, so you may prefer to group individual varieties into trays, and use just one label.

begin to show signs of starvation (yellowing lower leaves) water them with a dilute liquid feed. Also space plants as necessary so that the leaves do not touch.

About two weeks before you want to plant out, they will need to be weaned off the cosy temperatures found inside the greenhouse to the harsher environment outdoors. This is known as hardening off.

Transplanting

A few flowers, such as wallflowers, and vegetables, such as cabbages and Brussels sprouts, are best sown in specially prepared nursery seedbeds and then transplanted to their final growing position when they are large enough to move. This allows you to grow the plants in an out of the way spot until they are large enough. Water the seedbed well before you intend to transplant the seedlings and lift them carefully, holding the plant by the leaf rather than the stem. Replant them as quickly as you can, firm well and water thoroughly once more.

Thinning

Seedlings sown directly outside should be thinned in two stages. When the majority of the seedlings have emerged and are large enough to handle, thin the rows to half their final spacing. Then allow the partially thinned seedlings to grow on before thinning again to their correct spacing. In this way you are more likely to get the final spacing right. Choose a fine day when the soil is moist to thin the plants. Re-firm any seedlings loosened while thinning and water the row well afterwards. With some plants you can use thinnings to fill any gaps in the rows, while some vegetable thinnings can be used in the kitchen.

HOW TO TRANSPLANT SEEDLINGS

1 Water the row of seedlings, the previous night if possible, but at least a few hours before transplanting. This will soften the earth and make transplanting easier. It will also reduce the stress the seedlings are under.

2 Using a hand fork, dig up, rather than pull out, the plants to be moved. Only dig up the plants as you need them. Do not dig them up all at once and leave them lying around or they will dry out.

3 Using a garden line to keep the row straight and a measuring stick to make sure that the distances are equal, replant the seedlings using a trowel.

4 Gently firm in each plant and rake the soil around them in order to tidy it up and to remove footprints and uneven soil. Water the seedlings carefully.

There is really nothing to surpass the delicate paper-tissue flowers of the *Papaver somniferum* (opium poppy), which are followed by large, grey-green seedheads. It is fairly easy to collect the seeds for propagation and grow them up, ready to plant outside in the spring.

Spring cuttings

Many plants, including shrubs and herbaceous plants, can be propagated easily from cuttings. Spring is a good time to take cuttings as the young plants will grow quickly. It is always worth experimenting if there is a plant that you want to propagate but are not sure if a softwood or basal cutting is suitable. The chances are that some will root.

Different types of cuttings

There are several types of cuttings that make use of plant material in its different stages of development at various times of the year. Softwood and basal cuttings are taken in spring from the new, soft growth. In summer, semi-ripe and heel cuttings can be taken from material that is starting to ripen and go woody at the base. Hardwood cuttings are fully ripe shoots, and these cuttings are taken in winter.

Softwood cuttings

Although softwood cuttings are usually taken in spring, while the plant is putting on new growth that is soft and green, material can also

Pelargoniums such as this 'Little Gem' propagate well from softwood cuttings. A cutting taken early in spring will be sufficiently mature to flower by the summer.

be taken from tender perennials in late summer. These cuttings are then overwintered as rooted cuttings as an insurance against winter losses. Choose healthy, non-flowering shoots that are typical of the plant and cut off material just above a leaf joint using a sharp knife or pair of

secateurs (pruners). Collect the cuttings early in the day while they are turgid (firm, not wilted) and keep in a plastic bag to prevent them wilting. Prepare the cuttings by trimming the stem just below a leaf joint to make a cutting 2.5–8cm (1–3in) long depending on the type

HOW TO TAKE SOFTWOOD CUTTINGS

1 Take cuttings from non-flowering shoots. A good guide to length is to cut the shoot off just above the third joint below the growing tip. Here a softwood cutting is taken from a pelargonium.

2 Remove the lowest pair of leaves with a small sharp knife. Trim straight across the base of each cutting, just below the lowest leaf joint. You can dip the ends in a rooting hormone, but the cuttings usually root quite readily without.

3 Insert about five cuttings around the edge of a 13cm (5in) pot containing a cuttings mixture (soil mix) and firm gently. Keep in a light, warm position but out of direct sun. Be careful not to overwater, otherwise the cuttings will rot. Pot up individually when rooted.

of growth that the plant produces. Remove the lowest pair of leaves and the growing tip from longer cuttings and insert them around the edge of a pot filled with moist, fresh cuttings compost (soil mix). The success rate for some types of plant can be increased by using a rooting hormone. Some types of rooting hormone also contain fungicide, which may be worth buying if the plant you are propagating is particularly vulnerable to disease.

It is important that the softwood cuttings are not allowed to wilt, so either place them in a covered propagator or cover the pot with a clear plastic bag held off the cuttings by short canes and secured by a rubber band. Place in a well-lit spot shaded from direct sunlight. Puncture the bag or ventilate the propagator when the cuttings start to root. Pot up into containers when they have sufficient roots.

Basal cuttings

Some plants, such as asters, chrysanthemums and dahlias, produce almost no woody growth, and can be propagated from new shoots produced at the base of older stems in spring and early summer. These are called basal cuttings.

When the new shoot reaches about 5–10cm (2–4in) long, with the first leaves starting to unfurl, use a sharp knife to cut it off cleanly from the crown. Insert it in a pot filled with cuttings compost. Several more cuttings can be placed around the edge of the pot.

Cover the pot with a plastic bag, held in position with a rubber band, and place the pot on a shady windowsill. Alternatively, use a heated propagator for quick results. After a few weeks, rooted cuttings can be potted up individually.

HOW TO TAKE BASAL CUTTINGS

1 Take short cuttings from the new growth at the base of the plant. Place the cuttings in a plastic bag until they are required so that they don't wilt.

2 Trim the base of the cuttings. Cut through the stem just below a leaf joint and then remove all the leaves, except for a few right at the top.

3 Place the cuttings in a pot of well-drained compost mix (soil mix) with added grit, perlite or vermiculite. You can root several in the same pot.

4 Label the pot, including the date on which you took the cuttings. Water the pot and place it in a propagator. You can use a plastic bag, but ensure that no leaves touch the bag. Seal with a rubber band.

Rooting hormones

You can increase your chances of success with most stem cuttings, particularly those that are reluctant to root, by using a rooting hormone. When applied to the cut surface at the base of the cutting, the hormone encourages root formation and increases the speed of rooting. Rooting hormones are usually formulated as powders, but you may also come across liquids and gels.

To avoid contaminating the hormone, tip a small amount into a saucer. Dip the cutting's cut end into the hormone, shaking off excess if you use powder, and insert into the compost (soil mix). After treating the batch of cuttings, discard any powder that is left over in the saucer. Rooting hormone deteriorates rapidly, so buy fresh stock every year to make sure of its effectiveness.

Apply a rooting hormone to plants such as this fuchsia to help increase the chance of successful propagation.

Summer cuttings

During the summer months you can increase your stock of many shrubs, climbers and perennials using semi-ripe and heel cuttings. This is one of the easiest ways to propagate plants and is usually successful.

Timing

When plant growth begins to slow down in summer, new shoots start to ripen and turn woody at the base, and are suitable for semi-ripe cuttings.

To test that the plant is at the correct stage of development, hold the main stem steady and bend the shoot over. If the shoot breaks it is either too soft and sappy or too hard and woody, but if it is springy and returns to its original position when you let go, it is at just the right stage of development.

Semi-ripe cuttings

During late summer, select non-flowering, healthy shoots that are typical of the plant and cut off material just above a leaf joint using a sharp knife or a pair of secateurs (pruners). Prepare the cuttings by trimming the stem just below a leaf joint to make a cutting 2.5–10cm (1–4in) long, depending on the type of growth the plant produces. Then treat as for softwood cuttings.

Heel cuttings

The cuttings of some plants, notably conifers, root better if taken with a small sliver of wood pulled from the main stem, known as a heel cutting. This is because the plant produces more hormones at this point and so the propagation is often more

successful. Select material of a suitable length, depending on the growth of the plant, and carefully pull it backwards up the stem so that it rips a small piece of older wood with it (known as a heel). Use a sharp knife to trim the heel to neaten up any rough edges so that it is 1–2cm (½–1in) long. Then dip the cut end of the prepared cuttings in rooting hormone before inserting the cuttings around the edge of a pot of cuttings compost (soil mix) or evenly spaced in a seed tray, then water well.

Making a border propagator

Summer cuttings are easy to root and need no special equipment. You can root most types in a simple border propagator in the garden.

HOW TO TAKE SEMI-RIPE CUTTINGS

1 Cut a length of the current season's growth. Trim each cutting just below the second or third leaf beneath the terminal leaves at the stem tip. Cut off the lowest one or two leaves from the base of each cutting.

2 Remove a sliver of bark about 1–2.5cm (½–1in) long from the base of each cutting, opposite the lowest leaf bud.

3 Dip the base of each cutting into hormone rooting powder and then tap it gently on the side of the tub to remove any excess.

4 Insert the cuttings into pots of well-drained compost mix (soil mix) with added grit, perlite or vermiculite.

5 Water well and mist the leaves with water to prevent the cuttings from wilting.

6 Label the cuttings and tent them in a clear plastic bag supported on canes.

Wounding cuttings

If you have had problems rooting cuttings from a particular plant, try increasing your chances of success by removing a sliver of stem from the base of the cutting while you are preparing it. Apply rooting hormone to the wound before inserting into the compost (soil mix).

Choose a position in a sheltered spot in light shade for most of the day. Dig a trench 5cm (2in) deep about 25cm (10in) wide and fill it with sharp sand. Make hoops 50–62cm (20–25in) out of stiff wire (old coat hangers work well). Insert the prepared cuttings into the sand and water well. Push wire hoops every 15cm (6in) along the trench and cover with a piece of opaque or white plastic, such as a plastic bag, which should be buried in the soil on one side and held down with bricks at the ends and along the other side. Check periodically to see if the cuttings need watering and to remove any that are starting to rot. When most of the cuttings have rooted carefully slash the cover for ventilation, then after a couple of weeks remove it and plant out or pot up the rooted cuttings.

Like other camellias, *C. transnokoensis* can be propagated by semi-ripe cuttings taken in late summer. Take the cutting from a healthy looking stem to increase the chances of success.

HOW TO TAKE HEEL CUTTINGS

1 Select a strongly growing, non-flowering sideshoot from the parent plant and grasp it near its point of origin. Pull it sharply away from the main stem, tearing off a tail (heel) of bark from the main stem.

2 Trim the heel of the cutting with a small sharp knife, if necessary, cutting at an angle. Carefully strip off the foliage from the bottom half of the cutting with your finger and thumb.

3 Immerse the cutting in a fungicide solution to prevent disease problems. Dip the base of the cutting in hormone rooting powder and tap off the excess.

4 Insert the cuttings in a pot of cuttings compost (soil mix) to half its length using a fine dibber or skewer. Water well to seal the surface of the compost and leave to drain.

5 Blow up a plastic bag large enough to hold the tray and seal the tray inside. Place in a cool, shady spot outdoors. The bag should fog over. Water again if it dries out, then reseal until the cuttings have rooted.

Autumn and winter cuttings

When plants go dormant in winter some can still be propagated from hardwood cuttings and a few from root cuttings. This is the easiest way of propagating some deciduous trees and shrubs.

Root cuttings

There are a few popular plants that are difficult to propagate by other methods. Some of these can be raised successfully from root cuttings, which are taken during the dormant season. You can either lift a whole plant or leave it in the ground and dig around the edges to find suitable cuttings material. Select vigorous, healthy roots of about pencil thickness if possible and cut from the parent plant. Prepare the cuttings so they are about 5–10cm (2–4in) long, making a straight cut nearest the crown and an angled cut furthest away (so that you can tell which way up the cutting is). Dip the cutting in a fungicide powder before inserting vertically around the edge of a pot filled with a well-drained mixture of equal parts of grit and compost (soil mix), so that the straight cut is just proud of the surface. Top up with a thin layer of grit so that you can still see the top of each cutting and water well. Place in a cool, sheltered spot such as a cold frame or under a cloche in the garden.

If the roots are thinner than pencil thickness, lay them horizontally on the surface of the compost, before covering with grit.

Hardwood cuttings

These cuttings are taken from current year's shoots of deciduous woody plants that are fully ripe. When the plant has lost its leaves, select vigorous and healthy stems of around pencil thickness. Trim them off the

HOW TO TAKE ROOT CUTTINGS

1 Lift a young but well-established plant for the cuttings. If you don't want to use the whole plant for cuttings, and prefer to leave the parent plant largely undisturbed, remove soil from one side so that you can get to the roots. If the plant has large, fleshy roots, cut some off close to the main stem or crown.

2 You should be able to make several cuttings from each root by cutting it into lengths about 5–10cm (2–4in) long. To help you remember which way up they are, cut them horizontally at the top and diagonally at the bottom.

3 Fill a pot with a gritty potting mixture (soil mix) and insert the cuttings using a dibber or pencil to make the hole. The top of the cutting should be just above the top of the potting mixture.

4 Sprinkle a thin layer of grit over the surface, leaving the cuttings just visible. Label the pot so that you don't forget what it contains. Place in a cold frame or greenhouse and keep the potting mixture just moist.

5 Some plants, such as border phlox, and rock plants, such as *Primula denticulata*, have thin roots. These can be laid horizontally, so don't make sloping cuts to indicate the bottom. Just cut into 2.5–5cm (1–2in) lengths.

6 Fill a seed tray with a gritty compost and firm it level. Space the cuttings out evenly over the surface, then cover them with a layer of the gritty potting mix. Keep moist but not too wet in a cold frame or greenhouse.

Suitable plants for autumn and winter cuttings

Root cuttings	Hardwood cuttings
Acanthus	Aucuba
Bergenia	Berberis
Campanula	Buddleja
Dicentra	Buxus
Echinops	Cornus
Eryngium	Cotoneaster
Gaillardia	Escallonia
Geranium (hardy	Forsythia
varieties)	Hebe
Gypsophila	Kerria
Monarda	Leycesteria
Papaver orientale	Ligustrum
Phlox	Lonicera nitida
Primula	Philadelphus
denticulata	Ribes
Pulsatilla vulgaris	Rosa
Romneya coulteri	Salix
Stokesia laevis	Sambucus
Symphytum	Spiraea
Trollius	Weigela
Verbascum	

HOW TO TAKE HARDWOOD CUTTINGS

1 Choose stems of pencil thickness that are firm and hard but not too old. With shrubs such as *Cornus* you should be able to make several cuttings from one shoot. Make the first cut straight across the stem, just below a node, and a second, angled cut about 25cm (10in) above the first.

2 A rooting hormone is not essential, but it should increase the success rate. Moisten the bases of the cuttings in water then dip them into a rooting powder. You can use liquid or gel rooting hormones, in which case there is no need to dip the end in water first. Treat only the base end of each cutting.

3 Make a slit trench by pushing a spade into the ground and levering it backwards and forwards. The trench should be a little shallower than the length of the cuttings. Choose an unobtrusive spot in the garden to leave the cuttings undisturbed for a year.

4 Sprinkle some grit or coarse sand in the base of the slit trench if the ground is poorly drained. This will help to prevent water-logging around the cuttings.

5 Insert the cuttings 8–10cm (3–4in) apart, making sure that they are upright against the back of the slit and leaving about 5–10cm (2–4in) above the ground.

6 Firm the soil around the cuttings, to eliminate the pockets of air that would cause the cuttings to dry out. Water and label. Remember to water in dry weather.

plant using secateurs (pruners) just above a bud or pair of buds. Prepare the cutting so that it is about 25–30cm (10–12in) long, making a horizontal cut at the bottom and an angled cut at the top. Wound difficult-to-root subjects and dip the cut ends in hormone rooting powder.

Hardwood cuttings are usually rooted outside in a sheltered spot. After preparing the soil by digging and weeding, make a 15–20cm (6–8in) deep, V-shaped slit trench, with one side vertical, using a spade. Fill the bottom 5cm (2in) of the trench with sharp sand and then insert the cuttings about 8–10cm (3–4in) apart along the trench. Refill the rest of the trench with soil, firm lightly and water well. Leave the cuttings *in situ* for the whole of the following season, watering and weeding as necessary. Then plant out rooted cuttings the following autumn, one year after taking the cuttings.

Layering

This easy method of propagation is a useful way of increasing some shrubs and climbers that cannot readily be propagated from cuttings.

Simple layering

Layering is a method of getting a growing shoot to produce roots while it is still attached to the "parent" plant. There are several variations on the technique, and the one you use will depend on the plant and the type of growth it produces.

To make a simple layer choose a strong, actively growing shoot that is representative of the plant and showing no signs of pest or disease attack. It should also be low down on the plant and flexible enough to bend down to the ground without snapping. If there are no suitable stems, prune the parent plant back during the dormant season to encourage the production of suitable material next year.

Carefully dig over the area of ground next to the plant where the layer is to be rooted, removing weed roots and improving the soil with grit and well-rotted organic matter. Trim any sideshoots from the stem to be layered, leaving the growing point intact. Then bend down the stem to the soil and mark where it touches the ground about 30cm (12in) behind the growing tip. Use a trowel to dig a shallow trench along the line of the stem at this point. Carefully bend the stem to form a right angle about 20cm (8in) behind the growing tip and secure it into the bottom of the hole using a piece of stiff wire. Tie the growing tip vertically to a short bamboo cane.

More difficult-to-root plants will benefit from a slit cut on the underside of the stem. Dust the wound with rooting hormone and peg into position. Replace the soil around the layer, firm lightly and water well. Leave for 6–18 months until the layer has rooted well, then cut it from the parent and plant it elsewhere in the garden.

Serpentine (compound) layering

Some plants, especially climbers such as clematis, wisteria and honeysuckle, produce long, flexible shoots that can be layered several times along their length. The stem is buried at several points along its length, with the growing tip out of the ground, as for simple layering (see above). Make sure that each loop of the stem exposed above the soil has at least one bud. Separate and plant out the layers once rooted.

French layering

Some multi-stemmed shrubs, such as *Cornus* (dogwood) and acers, can be layered by burying the entire stem just below the surface of the soil. First, peg down the stem on to the soil surface in early winter so that all the buds break at the same time in spring. Once new sideshoots are about 5cm (2in) long, lower the stem into a shallow trench and cover with soil, taking care not to damage

HOW TO LAYER

1 Find a low-growing shoot that can easily be pegged down to the ground. Trim off the leaves just from the area that will be in contact with the soil.

2 Bend down the stem until it touches the ground. Make a hole about 10cm (4in) deep, sloping toward the parent plant but with the other side vertical.

3 Twist or slit the stem slightly to injure it. Peg it into the hole with a piece of bent wire or a peg, using the vertical back of the excavation to force the shoot upright.

4 Return the soil and firm it well. If you keep the ground moist, roots should form, and within 6–18 months you may be able to sever the new plant from its parent.

HOW TO AIR-LAYER

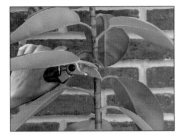

1 Air-layering is a useful technique to propagate plants whose stems cannot easily be lowered to ground level. Begin by using secateurs (pruners) to remove a few leaves from the point on the stem where you want to make the layer.

2 Using a sharp knife, carefully make an upward slit about 2.5cm (1in) long, below an old leaf joint. Do not cut more than halfway through the stem, otherwise it may break.

3 Cut a piece of plastic that is large enough to wrap around the stem of the plant, making a wide sleeve with space to add a thick layer of moss. Fix the bottom of the sleeve a short distance below the cut with a twist-tie or adhesive tape.

the shoots and leaving the tops exposed. As they grow, carefully earth up the sideshoots – leaving at least 5cm (2in) of shoot exposed – until a ridge of soil about 15cm (6in) high has been created. Separate and plant out layers once rooted.

Tip layering

A few plants, notably blackberries and hybrid berries, can be easily propagated by tip layering. This is a process whereby the tip of a suitably placed shoot is pegged into prepared soil and left until it roots.

4 Brush a small amount of rooting hormone compound (powder or gel) into the wound to speed rooting. Then pack a little sphagnum moss into the wound to keep it open.

5 Pack plenty of damp sphagnum moss around the stem to enclose the wound, then cover with the sheet of plastic and secure at the top with another twist-tie or tape. Make sure that the moss is kept moist, and carefully check for roots after a month or so. When well rooted, sever from the parent to pot up.

Mound layering

Some small bushy shrubs, such as heathers, can be propagated by mound layering (also known as stooling or burying). This is where the whole plant is covered with soil – a useful technique for replacing old woody specimens that have gone bare at the base.

First, thin out the shoots so that soil can be pushed between those that remain. Carefully pile a free-draining soil mixture on in layers, making sure there are no air pockets, until just 5–10cm (2–4in) of each shoot is above the mound of soil. Keep well watered throughout the summer. Separate and plant out layers once they are rooted.

1 Prepare a sandy, friable mixture of garden soil, sand and compost (soil mix). Mound this carefully around the stems of the plant, spreading the stems apart with your fingers if necessary. Cover the stems to within 5–10cm (2–4in) of their tips.

2 Keep the mound well watered during dry spells in the summer. You may need to replenish the mound if heavy rainfall washes away some of the soil. The shoots should have rooted by late summer, when they can be separated from the parent plant and potted up or planted out.

Division

Many fibrous-rooted plants, including a few shrubs and most perennials and aquatic plants, can be propagated by division. It is also the best way to keep them growing strongly and flowering well.

Timing

Division is best carried out straight after the plant has flowered so that you do not miss the display the following year. However, most experts recommend dividing plants in spring or autumn, depending on how much time you have to spare in each season. Dividing in spring is probably better for plants of borderline hardiness, so that they have time to settle in before they have to face their first winter, while autumn is best for hardier types, because the soil is still warm and moist – ideal for quick establishment.

Some perennials, such as astilbe, liriope and solidago, respond to regular division. Others, such as agapanthus, alstroemeria, eryngium and helleborus, do not like being disturbed and can take several years to recover from the process.

Techniques

The precise technique used to divide a fibrous-rooted plant will depend on the type of root system it produces and how long it has been since the plant was last divided, but the principle is the same. For most perennials you should be able to ease the crown apart using two border forks pushed and pulled while back to back. This method avoids damaging the roots. For old, neglected plants that have produced a solid mass of roots you will need to use a sharp spade to slice the crown into sections. Some plants, such as asters and campanulas, produce a loose mass of roots that

Propagate *Caltha palustris* (kingcup or marsh marigold) by division in spring or autumn.

HOW TO PROPAGATE PLANTS BY DIVISION

1 Water the congested plant to be divided during the previous day. Dig up a clump of the plant, in this case the Michaelmas daisy, *Aster novi-belgii*.

2 Insert two forks back-to-back into the plant and lever apart by pushing the handles together and apart. Keep on dividing until the pieces are of the required size.

3 A few of the most vigorous pieces of the plant can be replaced in the bed, but dig over the soil first, removing any weeds and adding some well-rotted organic material.

4 Alternatively, small pieces of the plant can be potted up individually. After watering, place these in a closed cold frame for a few days, before hardening off.

HOW TO DIVIDE PLANTS WITH TANGLED ROOTS

1 Many plants, such as these kniphofias, have very tangled roots or grow in heavy soils that will not easily fall away.

2 Shake the plants in a bucket of water so that the soil is washed from the roots. Wash with a hose if the soil is very difficult to remove.

3 Once the soil is washed away, most plants break up surprisingly easily into individual sections, each with a growing point.

can be teased apart by hand. Others, such as hostas and red-hot poker, are so compact you will have to use an old kitchen knife or pair of secateurs (pruners) to divide them up.

Dividing perennials

Choose a dry day when the soil is still moist but workable. Lay out a plastic sheet in a clear space, such as on the lawn or nearby patio, to work on. Then clear as much old foliage from the plant to be divided as possible so that you can clearly see what you are doing. Use a garden fork to loosen the soil around the plant, then carefully move it on to the plastic sheet. Choose your tool – spade, border forks, old kitchen knife or secateurs (pruners) – and split the old crown into smaller chunks – each will need a proportion of the shoots and roots. Replant the young and vigorous outer sections into well-prepared soil and discard the exhausted woody core. Firm all divisions after replanting and water well until established.

Plants with horizontal rhizomes, such as bergenias and irises, can be cut into sections with a sharp knife or secateurs. Cut back leaves of tall plants by half to prevent wind-rock and then replant the rhizome at the same depth as it was before.

4 Some plants do not come apart very easily. If this is the case, separate the sections with a sharp knife, making certain that each section has a bud.

5 Once the plants have been cleaned and divided, they can be potted up individually and then kept in a shaded cold frame until they have recovered.

HOW TO DIVIDE RHIZOMES

1 Divide plants grown from rhizomes, such as this flag iris, when they get congested. Lift the clump and cut away the oldest parts. Replant only the newest growth.

2 Trim the leaves by about half to prevent wind-rock. Replant the pieces of rhizome on a slight ridge of soil, covering the roots but leaving the tops exposed.

Propagating bulbs

Bulbs look best planted *en masse* in borders or naturalized in grass, where they will increase naturally if left undisturbed. Some types, however, may become congested and need dividing or you may wish to propagate them to grow elsewhere.

Dividing bulbs

Bulbs increase naturally once they are planted in the garden and will form clumps. The easiest method of propagation is, therefore, simply to lift an established clump and divide it up before replanting. Daffodils, for example, can be lifted about six weeks after flowering when the foliage has started to die down. Clear soil from the bulbs and pull off any offsets to be replanted along with the healthy parent bulbs. The offsets of bulbs such as *lachenalia* are best removed when growth is just beginning. Lilies produce offsets, but these are joined firmly to the parent and should be severed with a sharp knife. The new corms of crocuses and colchicum are produced on top of the old ones, which are dead and should be separated and thrown away. A few bulbous plants, including anemones, form knobbly tubers with several growing points. These can be lifted and cut up with at least one growing point on each division, before being dusted in fungicide and replanted.

Stem bulbils, bulblets and pips

A few types of lily bulb, including the tiger lily, produce small bulbs called bulbils or bulblets at the leaf axils up the stem. These should be removed about a fortnight after the plant has flowered and planted out or potted up. The largest will reach flowering size within a year.

Bulbs can be encouraged to produce bulbils by burying about half the ripened stem at a 45-degree

HOW TO DIVIDE BULBS

1 Lift the clump when flowering has finished, but before the leaves have died back completely, using a fork to reduce the risk of damage. Try to avoid spearing the bulbs. Loosen the soil all round, then insert the tines of the fork beneath the bulbs to lift them.

2 Unless you require a large number of individual new bulbs, prise apart the clump into three or four pieces and then replant the pieces immediately. They will produce good-size clumps that will look well established next season.

3 Replant the bulbs straightaway, before they can dry out. Plants that produce small bulbs can be replanted with a trowel; a spade may be better for larger ones.

4 Firm the soil after planting, making sure that there are no large air pockets where the roots may dry out. Water well if the weather is dry. Carefully fork in a general fertilizer around the plants.

angle in a bed of leafmould after flowering. Bulbils will form on the underground portion. Stem-rooting lilies produce bulbils underground if they are mulched with a thick layer of loose organic material. The bulbils can be separated when the lily stem dies down in autumn.

On some types of ornamental onion and leek, pips are formed at the top of the flowering stem as the flowers go over. To propagate, simply remove these from the plant and pot up the healthiest looking pips. The largest should reach flowering size within two years.

It is easy to propagate lilies, such as *Lilium martagon*, to create a spectacular summer display of flowers.

Scaling and chipping

Each scale of a lily bulb can be separated from an established plant and encouraged to produce one or more bulblets. This is a relatively simple technique that is best carried out in late summer or early autumn, before the roots have begun to grow. Similarly, some bulbs, including daffodils, hyacinths and snowdrops, can be propagated by chipping – a technique whereby the bulb is sliced into sections, each of which has a proportion of the basal plate. The cut surfaces are then dusted in fungicide and allowed to dry before planting. Each separate piece should produce a new plant.

HOW TO PROPAGATE LILIES FROM SCALES

1 Take a clean, dormant bulb and snap off some outer scales, as close to the base as possible. Be careful not to damage the scales as you remove them from the bulb.

2 Put the scales in a bag of fungicide, and gently shake to coat them. Prepare a mixture of equal parts peat (or an alternative) and perlite or vermiculite in a plastic bag.

3 Dampen the mix. Shake the scales free of excess fungicide and place them in the bag. Store in a warm, dark place for 6–8 weeks and plant up when bulblets appear on the scales.

Basic techniques

There are a range of basic gardening techniques, such as weeding, watering and feeding, that are common to most if not all parts of the garden. They are all easy to understand and take little skill to master, so it is worth spending some time getting these techniques right because they can have a considerable impact on the rest of your gardening.

Carrying out simple tasks correctly can often save you hours of time later. Weeding, for example, is best carried out before you plant up a bed. Once the flowers and shrubs have been planted and a thick layer of mulch added, the bed will need very little weeding.

Once the basic tasks have been mastered, you will have the time to carry out more elaborate and challenging techniques. Do remember to take sensible safety precautions to prevent injury and ensure gardening remains a pleasure.

As well as being the ideal place to store your tools, equipment and other gardening materials, a shed can be an attractive retreat in its own dusty way.

Essential tool kit

You don't need a shed full of tools to be able to garden successfully, but you will find some items indispensable and can build up your kit as you go.

Choosing tools

If tools are going to be used they need to be effective, convenient and comfortable to use, and it is always worth trying out new tools before making your selection. Always buy the best you can afford, because well-made and well-maintained garden tools will last a lifetime.

Tools for digging You will need some form of digging tool, such as a spade or fork. A spade is perhaps the more versatile but a fork is better on stony ground or if you find digging particularly hard work. Smaller, easy-to-use border forks are also available. Whatever digging tool you select, choose a make that is strong, with a comfortable handle that is long enough to prevent you stooping when you dig; long-handled versions are available to suit taller gardeners. Make sure

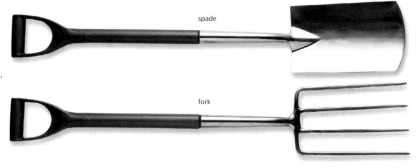

spade

fork

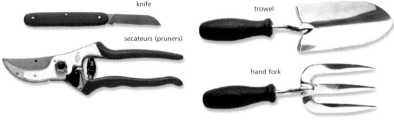

knife

secateurs (pruners)

trowel

hand fork

pruning saw

gloves

dibber

Rosa 'Zéphirine Drouhin', *Clematis* 'Lady Betty Balfour' and *Vitis coignetiae* need regular pruning to keep them in good shape. Use secateurs (pruners) or long-handled loppers to cut them back.

Lawn care equipment

If you have a lawn you will need a range of specialist equipment, including a mower with a cutting width to suit the size of your lawn, a pair of shears or a nylon-line trimmer to keep the edges in trim and a spring-tined (wire or lawn) rake with springy, wire-like tines set at an angle for combing through grass to remove dead leaves, moss and thatch.

the grip of a D-shaped handle is wide enough to be comfortable when you are wearing gloves. Stainless steel tools are more expensive but might be worth the investment if your soil is particularly heavy. If you intend to do a lot of digging choose tools with a tread (a flat area on top of the blade to put your foot on) because this will be more comfortable and be less damaging to your footwear.

Tools for weeding Most gardeners will find a hoe of some kind invaluable. The style you choose is a personal matter, but Dutch and draw hoes have stood the test of time. Again, choose one with a handle that is long enough for your height and make sure the head is securely fastened to the shaft. The Dutch hoe is the easier to master and more versatile, using a simple push and pull action to chop off weeds just below the soil surface. The shape of a draw hoe makes it easier to draw up soil around plants and to use among plants in existing borders.

Tools for levelling soil There are several types of rake, each designed for very specific purposes, but for most gardeners a soil rake is most frequently used. It usually has about a dozen, equally spaced, solid metal, vertical teeth and is used for levelling soil and removing stones before planting or sowing.

Tools for cutting These are also an essential element in the basic gardening tool kit. A well-made, straight-bladed, all-purpose knife is top of the list because it has a multitude of uses around the garden. A sturdy pair of secateurs (pruners) for deadheading and most types of pruning is also essential, but if serious pruning is contemplated, a pair of long-handled loppers or a pruning saw will be needed, too.

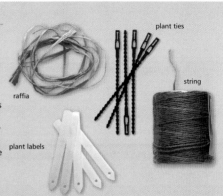

Labelling and tying

When you are working in the garden, it is useful to have a tray of odds and ends, such as string, raffia, plant ties and labels. You never know when you might need them. For example, wayward shoots of climbers may need fixing to their supports, or you may be sowing seeds or planting seedlings that you need to be able to identify.

raffia

plant ties

string

plant labels

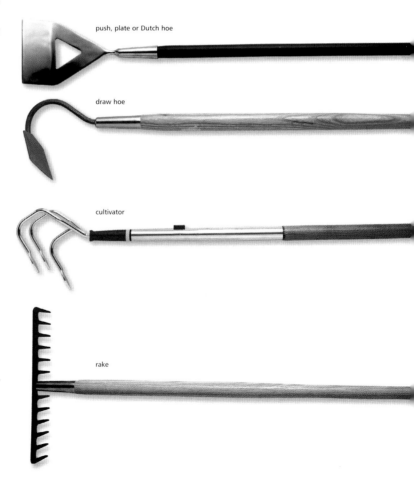

push, plate or Dutch hoe

draw hoe

cultivator

rake

Weeding

Weeds are nothing more than plants growing where they are not wanted. There are several techniques you can adopt to reduce the number of weeds in the garden and, therefore, the time spent weeding.

Controlling weeds

There are two types of weeds: annual weeds, such as groundsel and chickweed, which grow from seed, flower and set seed again in one season; and perennial weeds, such as dock, bindweed, couch grass and thistle, which survive for more than two growing seasons and often many years. It is important to remove all weeds before they flower and set seed, otherwise you will be weeding for many seasons to come – after all, a single weed can scatter many thousands of viable seeds near and far.

Weeds will be able to grow only if there is bare soil waiting for them to colonize, so you can go a long way to preventing weeds by covering all the bare soil in your garden: by planting up your borders and filling any gaps with ground cover plants or mulches. Alternatively, you can use a special chemical between established woody plants, such as trees and shrubs, to inhibit the germination of weed seeds. Such products will also damage the new growth of desirable plants, so they are not suitable for mixed borders containing herbaceous perennials or bulbs.

The best way to tackle weeds depends both on the type of weeds you have and where they are growing. In general, annual weeds are easy to control by using a hoe in open spaces between plants and by hand to remove weeds among ornamental plants. Perennial weeds are more difficult to eliminate because you have to remove the entire root as well as the topgrowth, otherwise the weed is likely to re-sprout. This can be hard work with some weeds, such

HOW TO WEED

Deep-rooted perennial weeds that have long, penetrating roots are best forked up. Loosen the roots with a fork, and hold the stem close to its base as you pull up the whole plant. If you don't get all the root out, the plant may re-grow.

Hoeing is one of the best forms of annual weed control, but it needs to be done fairly regularly. Slice the weeds off just beneath the soil, preferably when the soil is dry. Keep beds and borders as well as the vegetable garden hoed throughout the growing season.

Contact chemical weedkillers are useful if you need to clear an area of ground quickly and easily. Some types, which normally kill only the top growth so are better for annuals than problem perennial weeds, leave the area safe to replant after a day.

Systematic weedkillers kill the whole plant. Large areas can be sprayed, but some formulations can be painted on the leaves so will not harm other plants. Some types break down immediately in the soil.

Mulches are an effective method of controlling weeds. In the vegetable and fruit garden various forms of matting and plastic sheeting are a cost-effective method.

Where appearance matters, use a mulch of an organic material, such as chipped bark or garden compost. If the ground is cleared first a mulch at least 5cm (2in) – ideally 8cm (3in) – thick will suppress most weeds.

USING CHEMICAL WEEDKILLERS

A chemical weedkiller is best used to kill persistent weeds when first preparing a bed. Avoid using chemicals near fruit, vegetables or herbs. Always follow the manufacturer's instructions on the packet.

as dandelions and thistles, which produce a carrot-like taproot, and for brittle-rooted weeds, such as couch grass and bindweed, which send out roots in all directions, it can be close to impossible. Indeed, if these weeds have become established in your garden, you may have to dig up the entire border and painstakingly remove every weed root you can find before replanting the ornamental plants. If this is not a practical option you could try exhausting the weeds into submission by removing all the topgrowth and repeating the process every time it re-sprouts.

Your final option is to use a chemical weedkiller, which should be applied according to the instructions on the pack. There are two main types: contact weedkillers, which kill the parts of the weed they touch; and systemic formulations, which are transported around the plant, killing all parts. Which you choose will depend on personal preference and where the weeds are growing.

Beds and borders

Hand-weed mixed borders and use a hoe to clear annual weeds from bare soil between plants. Perennial weeds can be removed by hand where practicable or killed with a spot treatment weedkiller. Large weeds are easier to treat with a glyphosate-based, ready-to-use spray, but cover all nearby ornamental plants with a plastic sheet before spraying and leave the sheet in position until the spray is dry.

Lawns

Remove isolated weeds by hand using an old knife or a special weeding tool. Alternatively, kill them using a spot weedkiller. If the weed problem is more widespread, it is more efficient to use a specially formulated lawn weedkiller.

Where moss is also a problem it is a good idea to use a combined moss and weedkiller treatment in spring.

Patios and paths

Remove individual weeds by hand using an old knife or a special weeding tool. Alternatively, kill them with a spot weedkiller. Where the problem is widespread use a path weedkiller, which will kill existing weeds and prevent further weed problems for the rest of the year.

Neglected areas

If there are no ornamental plants, dig over the entire area, hand-weeding as you go. If this is not practicable, remove all the topgrowth and cover the area with black plastic or old carpet for a few years. A glyphosate-based weedkiller is another option. Stubborn weeds, such as bramble, may need several applications, or you could use the more potent chemical, sodium chlorate, although you will not be able to plant the treated area for at least six weeks afterwards.

The close planting of vigorous perennials, such as *Dictamnus albus* (dittany), prevents weed seedlings from germinating and surviving.

Ground cover

Weeding is a time-consuming task, and it is best to prevent weeds from germinating in the first place if you can. Carpeting the ground with a mass of attractive foliage, which also makes an effective foil for other plants and may produce flowers itself, makes good gardening sense.

What is a ground cover plant?

To make a suitable ground covering, a plant needs to establish quickly and cover the ground with a dense layer of leaves, without any gaps where weeds could germinate. The principle is that the plant is so dense that little light can reach the ground and any weed seedlings that do manage to germinate are starved of light, become sickly, and soon die.

The ground cover plant should also be low growing, so as not to detract from the ornamental plants,

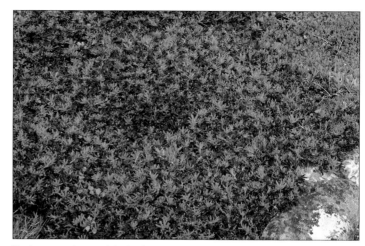

The dense ground cover subshrub *Lithodora diffusa* makes a vivid carpet of blue in spring.

and not so invasive that it swamps the whole bed. Although a wide variety of plants are labelled and described as suitable, relatively few make ideal ground cover.

Choosing the right ground cover

Low-growing ground cover plants are an ideal way of covering the soil between shrubs and trees in the border. Choose plants that are ground-hugging and can cope with the occasional trampling; you will need to tread on them to carry out maintenance to other plants.

Try to select plants with foliage that will contrast with the other plants, so that they set one another off. An underplanting of bulbs will provide seasonal variation and interest: tulips, spring-flowering dwarf narcissi and autumn-flowering colchicums are suitable. Some plants, such as heather or *Hypericum calycinum*, also have flowers to enhance their appearance.

Ground cover is also useful for areas where grass is not practical. For example, *Hypericum calycinum* is useful on slopes that are difficult to mow,

while *Vinca minor* is good for awkward areas at the bottom of a fence or alongside a driveway. Ground cover plants also make a low-maintenance option in the front garden.

A few ground cover plants, such as cotoneaster and prostrate junipers, produce stiff spreading foliage, which lends itself to covering eyesores such as manhole covers or ugly tree stumps.

Planting and aftercare

Although ground cover will prevent weeds from establishing, they do need to be planted into weed-free ground to start with. The best time to plant is autumn.

Prepare the ground by digging thoroughly and removing weeds, including the roots of perennial weeds. Incorporate well-rotted manure and a handful of bonemeal per square metre (yard). Take care not to damage the roots of existing plants if you are planting between or under them. When planting ground cover, do so either through a mulch matting or mulch after planting with an 8cm (3in) thick layer of loose

DIVIDING GROUND COVER

If you buy large ground cover plants in containers, they can be divided before planting for maximum cover. Gently knock the plant, such as this *Pachysandra terminalis*, out of its pot without damaging the roots. If the crown is too tough to pull or prise apart, try cutting through it with a knife. Replant larger pieces with several shoots and plenty of roots immediately. Smaller pieces can be potted up and grown on for a year before planting out into the garden. Keep new plants well watered until they are established.

HOW TO PLANT GROUND COVER

1 Clear the ground of weeds first, and be especially careful to remove any deep-rooted or persistent perennial weeds.

2 Add plenty of garden compost or rotted manure, then rake in a slow-release fertilizer or bonemeal. This will help the plants establish successfully.

3 Cover the area with a weed-suppressing mulching sheet. The special semi-permeable membrane allows water and air to penetrate to the soil.

4 Make crossed slits through the mulching sheet where you want to plant. Avoid making the slits too large.

5 Excavate holes and plant the ground cover, firming in well. If necessary, tease a few of the roots apart first.

6 Water thoroughly, and keep well watered. In prominent positions you could disguise the mulching sheet with a thin layer of soil.

organic mulch to prevent weeds from germinating before the ground cover can do the job. The distance between each of the ground cover plants will depend on the vigour of the plant you have chosen and how long you are prepared to wait for complete cover. Obviously, the closer the spacing the more plants you will need and the costlier it will be.

Good ground cover plants should remain pest and disease free and require little maintenance, other than an annual tidy up. This is best done in late autumn when deciduous leaves that have become trapped in the stems can be collected.

Good ground cover plants

Shrubs
Berberis thunbergii 'Atropurpurea Nana'
Calluna vulgaris cultivars
Ceanothus thyrsiflorus var. repens
Cotoneaster dammeri
Cotoneaster x suecicus 'Coral Beauty'
Erica carnea cultivars
Euonymus fortunei 'Emerald Gaiety'
Gaultheria procumbens
Genista lydia
Hebe pinguifolia 'Pagei'
Hypericum calycinum
Juniperus horizontalis Glauca Group
Juniperus squamata 'Blue Carpet'
Mahonia aquifolium
Vinca minor

Perennials
Ajuga reptans
Alchemilla mollis (lady's mantle)
Bergenia (elephant's ears)
Convallaria majalis (lily-of-the-valley)
Epimedium perralderianum
Geranium
Heuchera
Hosta sieboldiana
Houttuynia cordata
Lamium maculatum
Lysimachia nummularia (creeping Jenny)
Nepeta 'Six Hills Giant'
Pulmonaria (lungwort)
Rodgersia
Symphytum (comfrey)

Mulching

A mulch is a layer of material laid on the soil surface to discourage weeds from germinating and to prevent moisture loss. Organic mulches also improve soil fertility.

Types of mulch

The most natural mulch is loose organic material laid over the surface of the soil in a layer 8cm (3in) deep. In nature autumn leaves provide a blanket of organic matter, but in the garden we can use anything from chipped bark or cocoa shells to garden compost, leafmould or grass clippings. Non-organic mulches are used too, such as stone chippings and pebbles, or manufactured sheet mulches, as well as old carpet and black polythene.

A mulch helps to retain moisture in the soil by preventing water evaporating from the surface layer. Dark coloured mulches can also help warm the soil early in the season and promote rapid root growth in spring.

Organic mulches

These are popular because they are easy to use, adaptable and help to improve soil fertility as they slowly decompose and are incorporated into the soil by earthworms and other soil-dwelling creatures. Some, such as bark chippings, composted bark and cocoa shells, are attractive to look at and provide a useful foil for low-growing border plants and bulbs. Bear in mind that loose organic mulches, such as grass clippings, that have not been composted will deplete the levels of nitrogen in the soil surface as they decompose. They are suitable for use only between established plants or alongside a hedge.

Inorganic mulches

Loose inorganic mulches are particularly useful in certain areas of the garden. Pea gravel, for example, is ideal around alpines, which like well-drained conditions and would rot if surrounded with a loose

organic mulch. Similarly, stone chippings are often the best choice for covering the soil in planting pockets and between paving slabs in and around the patio. Pebbles, on the other hand, are ideal for mulching around plants, such as clematis, which like to have a cool root run, or as an attractive finishing touch to containers.

If you are planting a new bed or a specimen tree or shrub, specially made sheet mulches are an option worth considering. This material, also called mulch matting, is permeable and weed-proof. Lay the sheet over the prepared soil before

DIFFERENT TYPES OF MULCH

A border without any kind of mulch on the soil is prone to weed infestation and to loss of moisture.

Grass cuttings are readily available in most gardens. They are not attractive but can be used effectively between established plants at the back of borders, where they are not highly visible. Do not heap them on thicker than 5cm (2in) or they may heat up too much as they decompose, harming the plant.

Composted bark is an ideal material for mulching, being both effective and attractive. Do not use bark that is fresh, however, or the resin may harm the plants. Hedge and shrub prunings can be shredded and used after they have been composted for a couple of months.

This bright border has been well tended, resulting in the vigorous growth of healthy plants. An organic mulch of well-rotted garden compost was applied early in spring to return nutrients to the soil and to prevent weed seeds from germinating.

planting up a bed and simply cut cross-shaped slits in the sheet at each planting position. For larger plants, place a sheet over the soil around the specimen after planting, covering an area of at least 1sq m (1sq yard) around each plant. Sheet mulches are more effective weed barriers than loose organic mulches and do not need to be reapplied every spring. They do not, however, improve soil fertility and are unattractive. They are best disguised with a thin layer of soil or a mulch if used in prominent positions.

Semi-permeable mulching membrane, which has small holes in it to allow water and air to pass through to the soil, is available from many garden retailers. Measure out how much you will need, then cut the membrane to shape and lay it on the surface of the soil.

Mulching membrane is fairly unattractive so, in prominent positions, it is worth disguising it with a layer of gravel to improve the appearance of the border. Make sure that the membrane is flat and completely covered with stones.

Material mulches are not suitable to cover areas planted with bulbs or dormant herbaceous plants. In such positions, a loose organic or inorganic mulch such as gravel would be a better option.

Watering and feeding

Watering and feeding are among the most time-consuming tasks in the garden, especially if you have a lot of containers or own a greenhouse. Use the following techniques to help you work efficiently.

Watering

The ground must be thoroughly soaked after watering: a sprinkling will do little other than lay the dust. Effective watering should supply the equivalent of 2.5cm (1in) of rain.

Every gardener should have a watering can fitted with a fine rose, and this may be all that you need if your garden is small or if you do not grow many plants in containers. Most gardeners, however, will benefit from installing an outside tap (faucet) fitted with a hose on a reel. This will make transporting water around the garden straightforward, and the reel will keep your hose neat and tidy.

Ideally, the hose should be long enough to reach all parts of the garden, but if this is not possible it should certainly reach the areas that require the most frequent watering, such as the patio, greenhouse and kitchen garden. An adjustable nozzle at the end of the hose is a good idea as this will eliminate the need to keep returning to the tap to regulate the supply. If you have a lot of hanging baskets, window boxes or other out-of-the-way containers a hose lance (hose wand) that directs the water is a good investment.

A hose-end sprinkler is worth considering for large areas. Choose an oscillating or rotary type for the most even coverage. However, most garden plants do not need regular watering, even during a drought, and because the water is applied indiscriminately over the entire area a great deal is wasted. It is, moreover, tempting to leave the tap running for longer than is really necessary.

If you cannot afford the time to water all your plants on a regular basis, you can buy systems that will do the job for you. For most gardeners, the best option is a system of micro-bore tubes that carry water to individual plants. These networks usually have an adjustable nozzle fitted to regulate the correct amount of water. Such systems can be used for watering all types of container, including hanging baskets, and can also be linked to lengths of leaky pipe (sometimes called a seep hose or drip hose) for watering plants in

WATERING SYSTEMS

Most automatic watering systems have a control system to reduce the water pressure, and some act as a filter to prevent nozzles becoming clogged.

Drip-feed systems can be used for beds, borders and containers. T-joints allow tubes to be attached for individual drip heads.

The delivery nozzle of this drip-feed system is held in position with a pipe peg, so that the head can deliver water to an individual plant.

A seep or drip hose can be laid along a row of plants and will water only the immediate area. The water slowly seeps out of the pipe and soaks into the soil.

A timing device will turn water on and off automatically. You can preset the timing, so this is an ideal way of watering your plants while you are away on holiday.

HOW TO APPLY FERTILIZER

If it is necessary to pep up a flagging border towards the end of a long season, add a liquid feed to a watering can. Follow the instructions given by the manufacturer.

If you want to apply a foliar feed to a large number of plants, use a special applicator fitted to the end of a garden hose so that a measured amount is applied.

Dry fertilizer can simply be scattered on the soil around individual plants that need feeding, so there is no waste.

rows, such as in fruit and vegetable gardens. Plumbing the system to an outside tap (faucet) and including a water timer or watering computer will give a completely automatic watering system.

Feeding

The other regular task facing the gardener during the summer is feeding. Plants in containers will quickly deplete the fertilizer present in the potting compost (soil mix)

unless a slow-release fertilizer was added at the planting time. You will need to feed weekly from about six weeks after planting.

Some fertilizers are formulated for specific plants – tomatoes, roses and lawn grass are the best known – but most gardeners will also find a general fertilizer of some kind useful. These fertilizers are supplied in powder or liquid form and may need to be diluted or made up according to the manufacturer's recommendations. Alternatively, you can add a slow-release fertilizer to the compost in the form of pellets or granules. These will usually provide sufficient nutrients for a growing season.

When planting permanent borders of trees and shrubs, add a slow-release fertilizer, such as bonemeal, and improve the soil with well-rotted organic matter.

In a very small garden or in the greenhouse, a watering can is probably the most efficient way to deliver the appropriate amount of your chosen feed to individual plants. In a large garden a special attachment for a garden hose can be used to deliver fertilizer over a large area.

Collecting your own water

Place a water butt beneath the gutter of a greenhouse, shed or garage to catch the water as it runs off the roof. Rain water is slightly acidic so ideal for watering acid-loving plants, especially if you live in a hard-water area. It will also save water and money spent on metered water.

You can easily collect sufficient water in a water butt to keep a collection of acid-loving plants happy all summer long. If you are more ambitious you can now get kits to link water butts together to create a serious garden water storage system.

The butt should be easy to use, so make sure there is room to get a watering can under the tap. Keep the butt covered at all times so that the water remains sweet and clean.

You can also recycle water that has been used for washing or bathing in the house. Known as "grey-water", it is suitable for applying to established plants in borders and on lawns, but is best used immediately not stored.

Pests and diseases

The best way to control pests and diseases is to maintain a healthy garden environment and grow plants well so that they are able to shrug off or recover quickly from most attacks. It is also worth seeking out problem-free varieties that are naturally resistant to attack.

Deterring pests and diseases

Good garden hygiene is the most important factor in the battle against pests and diseases. Clear all debris from around the garden and put suitable material on the compost heap. Consign the rest to the dustbin or bonfire as soon as you can. Clean containers once you finish using them. Stay vigilant for the first signs of attack and take necessary remedial action as soon as possible. Keep weeds under control, including during the winter, because they can provide a convenient overwintering site for some problems.

Nectar-rich plants

Shrubs and trees	Iberis
Buddleia	Limnanthes
Crataegus	Lunaria
Viburnum	Matthiola
	Sedum
Flowers	Solidago
Arabis	
Aubrieta	
Erysimum	

Encouraging natural predators

A well-managed garden will be a dangerous place for pests because it is full of natural predators including birds, small mammals, amphibians, spiders and insects. You can increase the numbers of these natural predators by providing them with food, shelter and suitable places to breed. Frogs and toads, for example, are voracious eaters of slugs and will happily take up residence if you provide suitable places for them to

Natural predators

Introducing or encouraging beneficial insects can have a dramatic impact on the number of pests in your garden. Check which pests your plants are vulnerable to, and encourage their natural predators into your garden.

Ladybirds (ladybugs) and larvae – eat aphids, scale insects, mealy bugs and caterpillars

Hoverflies and larvae – eat up to 50 aphids a day

Lacewings – eat aphids, woolly aphids, spider mites, scale insects and caterpillars

Ground beetles – eat slugs, flat worms, cabbage and carrot rootfly (eggs and larvae), vine weevils and spider mites

Anthocorid bugs – eat vine weevil larvae, caterpillars, midge larvae and spider mites

Centipedes – eat slugs and snails

PREVENTING DISEASE

Thoroughly wash and clean pots, trays and equipment after use to get rid of loose soil that may harbour pests and diseases.

There are many beautiful garden plants that have the added advantage of attracting the natural predators of pests into the garden. This wallflower (*Erysimum*) is nectar-rich and will attract bees and butterflies, as well as hoverflies and lacewings.

WEEDING

Continue to weed vegetable and flower beds during the winter. Weeds can harbour pests and diseases that will attack plants later.

HOW TO TREAT MILDEW

1 Mildew is common in humid conditions, so apply a mulch to keep the roots moist but do not water the leaves.

2 Remove leaves affected by mildew. Severely damaged plants can be sprayed with a suitable fungicide.

hide and a pond where they can breed. Similarly, useful insects, such as hoverflies, can be lured into your garden by nectar-rich plants and a supply of insect pests. You can even provide a "hotel", made from bundles of bamboo, where they can safely hibernate.

Controlling pests and diseases

Stay one step ahead of the pests by sowing and planting at appropriate times and putting up traps and barriers. Protecting plants with suitable netting is probably the only solution to prevent damage caused by mammals such as rabbits. Isolated

attacks of snails and caterpillars can be picked off by hand and destroyed, while small colonies of aphids can be rubbed out between finger and thumb. Similarly, isolated disease symptoms can be pruned out and the affected material put in the dustbin or burned. Do not put any material that looks as if it has been attacked by disease in the compost bin, as this may spread the disease to other plants in the garden.

It is worth having a few chemicals to hand for the most intransigent pests and diseases. Slug pellets, for example, can be used sparingly around vulnerable plants, notably

hostas, when they are planted out, and each spring thereafter, before the new leaves emerge.

If you have problems with aphids, choose a selective treatment based on piricarb, which is specific to aphids. A systemic insecticide is also useful for all other insect pests. Choose one based on permethrin or dimethoate or a spray based on pyrethrum if you garden organically.

Combined chemical treatments can be very quick and effective. Many rose growers, for example, like to use a combined treatment to combat the three main rose diseases of blackspot, mildew and rust.

HOW TO DEAL WITH CATERPILLARS AND SLUGS

The best way to get rid of caterpillars, such as these on *Polygonatum odoratum*, is to pick them off by hand.

When slugs and snails eat holes in hosta leaves, the holes remain visible throughout the growing season. If you do not mind using slug pellets, scatter them around the plants.

Dishes and jars half-filled with beer or sweetened water and sunk into the ground will attract slugs and snails, which can be collected up and disposed of.

Safety in the garden

The garden can be a dangerous place if you are careless. Every year thousands of people are injured by garden equipment, particularly power tools. Fortunately, most of the injuries are avoidable if you take the necessary precautions when using the equipment.

Think ahead

Always take sensible steps to protect yourself when gardening. Wear thick gloves when handling rough materials and protect your eyes with goggles when pruning or working with twiggy stems.

Pruning

Move around a plant to prune it rather than stretching to your furthest reach. Use a steady ladder if you are cutting a hedge or climber over shoulder height.

Most accidents that involve a hedgetrimmer occur when the machine is in use, with lacerations, falls and electrocutions (with electric

Thorny plants, such as this rose 'Ispahan', should be pruned back from a path or a doorway to prevent the stems catching on passers-by.

models) coming top of the list. Make sure your machine has the basic safety features such as a short blade-stopping time, two-handed switches and special blade extensions that stick out beyond the reciprocating blades and prevent you cutting something accidentally.

Always use the appropriate clothing and a thick pair of gloves. Use a hedgetrimmer with care and don't try to rush the job. Keep both hands on the machine while it is in operation.

Lawnmowers

Most lawnmower accidents, on the other hand, occur when the machine is not being used. Be particularly careful while it is being cleaned, maintained or simply moved around. Check that the blade has stopped moving before removing the box, and disengage the machine from the power supply before touching the blade. Turn off the power supply to electric models and turn off the engine and disconnect the spark plug lead with petrol-driven machines. If the blades become clogged, use a stick to clear them.

Of the accidents that occur while a mower is being used, most are because the machine is being asked to do too much – either the grass is overgrown, wet or both – or is on a steep incline. If you have a steeply sloping lawn always mow across the slope rather than up and down it.

HOW TO PRUNE SAFELY

1 It is sensible to use a hedgetrimmer on a large or fast-growing hedge, but power tools such as this can be dangerous. Accidents often occur when you are in a hurry, so take your time and don't start pruning unless you know you can finish the job comfortably.

2 Pruning very tall climbers is a job that requires some care. Check that the feet of the ladder are steady on the ground. Do not attempt to reach too far above your head or stretch to the left or right. It is better to move the ladder than risk overbalancing.

Shredders

Most accidents occur either when the blades are being unblocked, or when the equipment is being used without the correct safety guards in place. Always wear eye protection and strong gloves. If you are using a shredder for a long period of time, wear ear defenders too. Never put your hand in inlets or outlets and only try to shred materials recommended by the manufacturer.

Using chemicals

If you are dealing with chemicals make sure you follow all of the manufacturer's instructions, including using protective equipment or clothing, such as waterproof gloves when handling concentrates, and washing your hands and the equipment thoroughly after spraying. Do not apply at rates not given on the packet or make chemical cocktails unless it is specifically advised in the instructions. Only apply chemicals when the prevailing weather conditions are suitable and make sure spray does not drift on to other areas of the garden. Always dispose of chemicals as directed.

ADDING BONEMEAL

It is advisable to wear protective gloves when you are adding bonemeal to the soil as there is a small risk of it harbouring disease.

USING POWER TOOLS

Always read the safety instructions supplied by the manufacturer carefully before using power tools, and follow them to the letter.

Essential tool maintenance

Having invested in a set of good quality gardening tools it makes sense to keep them in good condition. Not only will they last longer, but they will be easier and more efficient to use. Always keep bladed tools sharp so that they cut efficiently, causing as little damage to the plant tissue as possible – particularly important when pruning and propagating. It also makes sense to keep the blades of spades and hoes sharp. When storing tools make sure that all bare metal parts are clean, and have an oily rag to hand so that they can be lightly oiled before being put away. Larger tools such as border forks and spades that don't have a really sharp edge can be stood in an old bucket of oily sand when they are not needed.

Most garden cutting equipment does not require routine maintenance, other than cleaning and replacing worn blades. If you do intend to use a service centre, to service a petrol machine for example, do it at the end of the season rather than waiting until the centres are busy in the spring, when frustrating delays inevitably occur.

Power tool safety checklist

Bear in mind that most serious gardening accidents involve powered equipment, so always take extra care during its use.
• Do not attempt to use a power tool unless you are completely sure you can do so safely. Some tools, such as chainsaws, require a skilled operator.
• Read the manufacturer's instructions before you start.
• Never start a job unless you are sure you have time to finish: trying to complete work in a hurry may lead to an accident.
• Always check the equipment is in good working order.
• Ensure children and pets keep well away from the working area.
• Always use the recommended protective clothing and equipment.
• Always check that the equipment is turned off before moving it around.

Electrical equipment
• Never use in the wet.
• Always use an RCD (residual current device) or similar to help prevent electric shocks.
• Only use suitable extension cables and connectors for outside operation and for the equipment being used.
• Make sure your extension cables and connectors are in good condition and brightly coloured so they are easily seen.
• Never use a damaged cable or connector and always unplug electrical equipment before leaving it unattended.

Petrol-driven tools
• Always start petrol equipment outside or in a well-ventilated outdoor building.
• Never refuel while the machine is running.
• Store fuel in a safe and secure place, well away from heat sources.

Seasonal checklist

Many of the basic maintenance tasks required in the garden are seasonal: they depend either on a particular stage of growth or on environmental conditions to be effective. For example, it is important to choose the right time of year to prune roses otherwise you risk loosing a year's worth of flowers. It is, therefore, important to know the optimum time for each technique.

The following pages summarize the main tasks you are most likely to need throughout the year. These tasks are divided into the gardening seasons of spring; early summer; late summer; and autumn and winter, rather than the seasons of the year. The techniques are listed according to the areas of the garden they apply to. Use them as a quick guide to your gardening activities but remember that nothing in gardening is prescriptive, and the timing will depend on your garden, the weather and the time you have available.

Many gardeners enjoy the routine maintenance tasks needed throughout the year. Early preparation can pay dividends later.

Spring techniques

For many gardeners, spring is the most exciting time of the year. This is when plants begin to show signs of new life and the garden is full of promise. It isn't long before the first spring flowers make their spectacular appearance.

Beds and borders

Prune shrubs Prune early-flowering shrubs, such as forsythia, as soon as flowering is over. Prune grey-leaved shrubs, such as lavenders, to keep them compact and bushy.

Apply fertilizer After pruning shrubs apply a slow-release fertilizer on the ground during mid-spring to give them a boost.

Slugs and snails Protect emerging shoots of vulnerable plants, such as hostas, from the attention of slugs and snails.

Deadhead bulbs Remove fading blooms from bulbs but leave the foliage intact for at least a further six weeks.

Start weeding Remove weeds before they are able to flower and set seed.

Compost heap As soon as the weather warms up, turn the compost heap to ensure even composting.

Bluebells will naturalize in shady areas, providing a sweetly scented carpet in late spring.

Check equipment Make sure all garden tools and machinery are in good working order before you will be using them in earnest. Check that cutting tools are sharp and electrical equipment is safe, including cables and connectors.

New plants Mid-spring is an ideal time to plant all types of hardy plants, including deciduous and evergreen trees, shrubs and climbers and hardy herbaceous plants. Wait until late spring to plant conifers.

Lawns

First cut When the grass is dry, give the lawn its first cut. Set the cutting height of the mower to 2.5cm (1in). After a few weeks, reduce the cutting height to 2cm (¾in) for most lawns, or to 1.5cm (½in) for a fine finish.

New lawns Mid- to late spring is an ideal time to create a new lawn. Prepare the ground thoroughly as soon as weather conditions allow and either sow seed or lay turf.

Control moss Apply a moss killer in mid-spring when the grass is dry if your lawn has been colonized by moss over winter. Use a wire rake to

remove the moss at least a fortnight after applying the chemical control. If you need to give your lawn a boost too, use a combined moss killer and lawn fertilizer treatment.

Make repairs Remove any large weeds using an old kitchen knife and control coarse grasses by either digging them out or weakening them by slashing them with a knife each time you mow. Any bare patches can be reseeded in mid-spring.

APPLY FERTILIZER

Apply a slow-release fertilizer around shrubs to give them an added boost.

PLANT OUT

As soon as the ground begins to warm up, plant out crops brought on in the greenhouse.

Ponds

Position pump Remove the pool heater and replace the pond pump in mid-spring.

Feed fish Start feeding fish in the pond in mid-spring, as soon as they become active.

Plant up On a warm day in late spring or early summer plant up your pond or add new plants to an existing feature. Replace tender plants that have been overwintered in a frost-free place.

Greenhouse

Start sowing Make the first sowings of summer bedding plants and vegetables. Seedlings should be pricked out as soon as they are large enough to handle.

Tender perennials Overwintered tender plants, such as fuchsias and pelargoniums, should be given more water in mid-spring to start them into growth.

Harden off plants New plants that were raised in a cosy environment indoors need to be hardened off before being planted out to face the harsher conditions outside. This should start about two weeks before you plan to plant them out.

Pest watch Stay vigilant for the first signs of pests and disease. Take appropriate action as soon as you can.

Keep cool Make sure the greenhouse does not overheat by ensuring there is adequate ventilation and shading.

Kitchen garden

Feed fruit In mid-spring apply a general fertilizer to all fruit trees, bushes and canes.

Protect blossom Protect vulnerable early blossom from late frosts by covering with a double layer of horticultural fleece, taking it off during the day to allow pollinating insects to get access.

USE CLOCHES

Particularly tender plants should be protected with glass or plastic cloches until all threat of frost has passed.

Prepare seedbed Carefully prepare the area to be used as a seedbed as soon as the weather is suitable. Cover with a sheet of clear plastic to help warm the soil and encourage weed seed to germinate. Take off the sheet and lightly hoe off the weeds before sowing.

Clear ground Once the harvesting of overwintered vegetables is complete, clear the ground of debris and weeds, and cultivate the soil ready for the next crop.

PREPARE FOR PLANTING

In the vegetable garden, break the soil down to a fine tilth and rake in some general fertilizer before planting out seedlings.

Hardy vegetables Hardy seedlings can be planted out from mid-spring as soon as they are large enough and weather conditions allow. Harden them off in a cold frame first. Plant out onion sets and shallots.

Sprout potatoes In early spring place early potato tubers in a tray or an eggbox, eyes uppermost to encourage them to sprout (chit). Wait until mid-spring for maincrop potatoes. Plant earlies in mid-spring and maincrop in late spring.

Pale yellow primroses, tiny forget-me-nots and the delicate flowers of dicentras make a lovely fresh combination for a spring border.

Early summer techniques

This is the busiest time of the gardener's year, with plenty to do in every part of the garden. Seedlings and established plants will need constant attention.

Beds and borders

Position supports Place supports around tall herbaceous plants during late spring or early summer to prevent them flopping over when in full bloom. Stake single-stemmed plants, such as delphiniums and gladioli, with canes.

Plant containers Plant up hanging baskets and summer containers with bedding plants and place outside after the threat of frost has passed.

Feed container plants About a month after planting up containers (including growing bags) start to feed with liquid feed unless you added a slow-release fertilizer at planting time. Use a balanced feed on beds and borders and a high-potash fertilizer, such as tomato feed, for flowering and fruiting plants.

Deadhead flowers Remove faded blooms from repeat-flowering plants

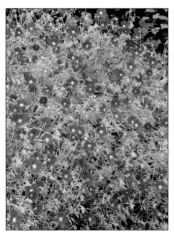
The hardy geraniums are one of the mainstays of the summer border. There is a wide range from which to choose.

Early flowering clematis (Group 1) should be pruned after blooming.

such as roses. Annual bedding should also be deadheaded where practical to encourage further flushes of blooms. Deadhead self-seeders, such as forget-me-nots and campanulas, to prevent them becoming a weed problem. Once flowering has finished, deadhead rhododendrons, taking care not to damage or remove the buds for next year that lie just below this year's blooms.

Pest watch Stay vigilant for the first signs of pests and disease attacks, especially aphids, which can attack plants all around the garden; take appropriate action promptly. Spray susceptible roses against blackspot, mildew and rust. Hand-pick any caterpillars and sawfly grubs.

Slugs and snails Continue to protect emerging shoots of vulnerable plants such as hostas against attacks from slugs and snails.

Water new plants Make sure new plants do not run short of water during their first growing season. Mulch after watering to help retain soil moisture and minimize competition from weeds. Also water container plants as necessary.

Prune shrubs Prune early summer-flowering shrubs, such as choisya, deutzia, kerria, lilac, philadelphus, spiraea and tamarix, as soon as the flowering is over.

Tie in climbers New growth produced by climbers should be tied into the support to keep the plant looking tidy and to avoid damage to the shoots. The stems will still be flexible and easy to manoeuvre in early summer.

Keep weeding Continue to remove weeds as they appear.

Lawns

Keep mowing Mow the lawn regularly as necessary, generally at least once a week but twice a week if the grass is growing strongly. During dry spells, growth will slow and the need for mowing will be reduced; also raise the cutting height of your mower.

Watering lawns Water new lawns throughout the summer. Established lawns rarely require watering. Even if they turn brown in summer they will soon recover following the first rains in autumn.

Lawn treatments Lawn weedkillers, moss killers and fertilizers can be applied any time the grass is growing strongly up until midsummer. If you intend to use more than one treatment, use a combined product.

Ponds

Plant up On a warm day in late spring or early summer plant up your pond or add new plants to an existing feature.

Tidy ponds This is an ideal time to refurbish overgrown or neglected ponds. Clear excessive growth of blanketweed using a rake or bamboo cane and leave it on the side for a day or two to allow any trapped pond creatures to escape back into

PLANT UP THE POND

Introduce new plants to the pond carefully. Flood the container with water and gently lower it to the appropriate depth.

This cottage garden, shown in early summer, is full of freshness and vitality as the borders begin to fill out with lush vegetation and flowers.

the water. Use a small net to remove duckweed. Divide and replant any overgrown plants.

Top up water During hot and windy spells keep the water levels topped up in ponds and in the reservoirs of all water features.

Greenhouse

Harden off plants Tender bedding plants and vegetables raised under glass need to be hardened off before planting in the harsher conditions outside. This should start about two weeks before you plan to plant out.

Keep cool Make sure the greenhouse does not overheat by providing adequate ventilation and shading. Damping down may be necessary in hot, sunny weather.

Train crops Tie in new growth on tomatoes and cucumbers and pinch out sideshoots.

Keep watering and feeding Plants that are in containers will need watering several times a day in warm weather in the greenhouse. Make your life easier by installing an automatic watering system. Feed all actively growing plants with a suitable liquid feed.

Pest watch Stay vigilant for the first signs of pests such as aphids, spider mites and whitefly and diseases such as botrytis and take appropriate action promptly.

Kitchen garden

Continue sowing Make successional sowings of salad crops to maintain a continuous supply. Thin or transplant previous sowings.

Plant tender vegetables By early summer it is safe to plant out the last of the tender vegetables, such as French (green) and runner beans. Be prepared to protect them with a double layer of horticultural fleece in colder areas if a late frost is forecast.

Protect strawberries Place a mulch layer of straw under strawberry rows to prevent the fruit touching the soil

and rotting. This will also prevent mud splash in heavy rain. Cover the plants with bird-proof netting before the fruits start to ripen.

Earth up potatoes Continue to earth up around emerging shoots and cover with a double layer of fleece on cold nights to protect them from frosts. By midsummer early potatoes will be ready for harvesting.

Propagate strawberries Peg down runners from healthy plants to form new plants. Grow directly into the bed or into pots filled with moist compost sunk rim-deep into the soil.

THIN SEEDLINGS

Remove the weakest seedlings to ensure the others have enough space to grow. Check the ideal space between each plant.

EARTH UP POTATOES

When the potato shoots reach 25cm (10in) high, draw in the soil along the rows to cover the stems.

Late summer techniques

Now is the time to enjoy the garden. Beds and borders will be filled with colourful blooms, and the vegetable garden will be producing a regular supply of crops.

Beds and borders

Feed container plants Continue feeding container plants unless you added a slow-release fertilizer at planting time. Use a balanced feed for general use and a high-potash fertilizer, such as tomato feed, for flowering and fruiting plants.

Watering Water containers daily throughout the summer months. In borders, concentrate on new plants, which should not go short of water during their first growing season.

Deadhead flowers Remove faded blooms from repeat-flowering plants, such as roses. Deadhead early-flowering perennials and annual bedding where practical to encourage further flushes of blooms. Trim straggly pansies. Deadhead self-seeders such as forget-me-nots and campanulas to prevent them becoming a weed problem.

Pest watch Stay vigilant for the first signs of pest and disease attacks, especially aphids, which can attack plants all around the garden; take

PROPAGATE TENDER PERENNIALS

Cut off a sideshoot just below a leaf joint, about 2.5–10cm (1–4in) long. Trim off the lower leaves and insert the cutting in a pot.

appropriate action promptly. Spray susceptible roses against blackspot, mildew and rust. Hand-pick any caterpillars and sawfly grubs.

Save seed Collect seed from plants you want to propagate. Cover the flower heads with paper bags and cut off when ripe.

Cut back shrubs Prune summer-flowering shrubs and hedges as soon as the display is over. Cut back fast-growing hedges and climbers, such as climbing and rambler roses. Pick lavender for drying.

Plant bulbs Plant autumn-flowering bulbs, such as sternbergia, in midsummer and spring-flowering bulbs in late summer. Also plant up winter containers.

CLEAR EDGING

Some edging plants, such as this poached egg plant, can spill out on to the lawn, causing bald patches. Remove completely or trim back.

Sow hardy annuals During late summer sow hardy annuals, such as calendula, candytuft and nigella, in prepared soil in the garden. During cold spells over winter, protect these with cloches or a double layer of garden fleece in cold areas.

Lawns

Keep mowing Mow when necessary, and during dry spells raise the cutting height of your mower.

Watering lawns Water new lawns throughout the summer. Established lawns should not require watering. Even if they turn brown in summer they will soon recover following the first rains in autumn.

Lawn treatments Lawn weedkillers, moss killers and fertilizers can be applied if the grass is growing strongly, up to midsummer. Use a combined product if necessary.

Ponds

Top up water During hot and windy spells keep the water levels topped up in ponds and in the reservoirs of water features.

Oxygenate the water If fish are gulping at the surface of the pond in close, thundery weather, turn on the fountain or direct a jet of water from the hose into the water to churn the surface and help oxygenate the water.

Prune rambling roses such as *Rosa* 'Bobbie James' as soon as flowering has finished in late summer. This allows plenty of time for shoots to grow, ready for next season's crop of flowers.

Deadhead aquatics Remove faded blooms from repeat-flowering marginal plants and from bog garden plants.
Thin plants Overcrowded water lily pads can be thinned out, as can overgrown submerged plants.

Greenhouse

Take cuttings Propagate tender perennials, such as pelargoniums, fuchsias and marguerites, by taking cuttings during late summer; overwinter the cuttings somewhere frost-free.
Keep cool Provide adequate shading and ventilation to prevent overheating. Damping down may be necessary on hot, sunny days.
Train crops Continue to tie in new growth on tomatoes and cucumbers and pinch out sideshoots.
Keep watering and feeding Plants in containers will need watering several times a day in hot weather; you may wish to install an automatic watering system. Feed actively growing plants.
Pest watch Continue to watch for signs of pests, such as aphids, spider mites and whitefly, and diseases such as botrytis and take appropriate action promptly.
Sow winter crops If you want to have a productive greenhouse in winter sow winter lettuce, as well as carrots and radishes for early spring.

This garden, a riot of colour, shapes and textures, looks its best at the height of summer.

TIE IN PLANTS

Keep an eye on plants that need support, such as tomatoes, and tie them in when necessary.

Kitchen garden

Keep watering Water all fruit and vegetable plants in containers as necessary. Plants with developing crops will also need watering during dry spells to prevent reduced yields. Also water potatoes and leafy vegetables, such as lettuce, during dry spells throughout the summer. Consider installing automatic watering to make the job easier.
Strawberries Prepare the ground for new fruit in autumn strawberry beds. Remove netting and mulch from fruited plants and cut back their foliage. Sever rooted strawberry runners pegged down in early summer from their parent plants.
Fruit bushes Prune blackcurrants after harvesting by removing the oldest stems.
Cane fruit Cut back canes that have fruited from summer-fruiting raspberries and tie in new canes to their support.
Harvest crops Pick fruit and vegetables as they reach the right stage of development. Some types of vegetable, including runner beans and courgettes (zucchini), need picking regularly, otherwise cropping will be reduced.

Autumn and winter techniques

This is the time to prepare the garden for bad weather. Make sure that all garden structures are sound and secure against wind and rain.

Beds and borders

Pot up tender perennials Tender perennials, such as pelargoniums, fuchsias and marguerites, should be lifted and potted up before the first frost to be overwintered in the greenhouse. If space is short, take cuttings instead.

Lift tender bulbs In colder areas, especially if the soil is heavy, tender bulbs such as gladioli should be lifted before the first frost and dried and stored somewhere frost-free. Check for rot every few weeks.

Plant bulbs There is still time to plant spring-flowering bulbs and winter containers.

Protect some shrubs Some shrubs are of borderline hardiness, depending on where you live. Protect vulnerable shrubs as well as hardy shrubs in exposed positions with a layer of windbreak netting lined with garden fleece, held taut between sturdy posts.

Tie in wall shrubs Check wall shrubs and tie in new growth as necessary. Protect not-so-hardy types such as ceanothus with a double layer of garden fleece. Tender shrubs and

Asters are one of the mainstays of the autumn garden. *Aster* x *frikartii* 'Mönch' flowers over a long period from summer to late autumn.

climbers will need an insulating layer of leaves or straw, held in place with fine-mesh netting.

Pruning Long whippy growth on roses in exposed sites should be cut back by about one-third to prevent wind-rock loosening the roots. Winter prune wisteria. Cut back all stems of any Group 3 clematis.

New plants The dormant season is an ideal time to plant bare-rooted trees, shrubs and hedging plants.

Protect containers Leave only frost-proof containers outside in winter. Other containers, and the tender plants growing in them, may need protecting in colder areas. Wrap pots with bubble polythene to prevent the compost (soil mix) freezing solid. Protect the plant in a double layer of garden fleece. Leave a space for evergreen plants to be watered.

Wrap conifers Protect conifer specimens from being splayed open by heavy falls of snow by wrapping fine-mesh netting or a piece of thick soft string around them. Conifer hedges should have accumulations of snow knocked off before they cause damage to the branches.

Check stakes and ties Most climbers and many trees will have ties holding them on to a support or stake. Check these in winter to ensure they are secure but not too constricting.

Protect rock plants Excessive winter wet can damage plants with woolly foliage, such as those found in the rock garden. Protect by covering them with an open-ended cloche or a sheet of glass held up on bricks.

Clear summer bedding Remove annual plants from the border and dig over the ground ready for planting in the spring.

Lawns

Lawn repairs Early autumn is the perfect time to carry out maintenance tasks such as spiking and scarifying as well as essential lawn repairs.

Final cut Make the final cut once the grass has stopped growing. Then clean and service the lawn equipment before storage.

Fallen leaves Clear fallen leaves from the lawn through autumn and early winter so they do not smother the grass. Do not walk on the lawn if it is very wet or frosted.

TIDY BORDERS

Clear summer bedding away and dig over the soil, removing large weeds. Rake the ground level so it looks neat and tidy.

PROTECT CONTAINERS

Protect vulnerable container-grown plants with a layer of insulation. Plastic bubble wrap is a good choice.

Ponds

Fallen leaves Keep fallen leaves out of ponds by covering the feature with a lightweight fine-mesh netting. Clear any leaves collected in the netting regularly to prevent them rotting and fouling the water.

Autumn tidy up Cut back marginal plants, but take care not to cut those with hollow stems too short – the cut stems should remain proud of the water surface all winter.

Prevent freezing Remove the pond pump and replace it with a pond heater in autumn. If you do not have a pond heater, keep at least one area of a pond that contains fish ice-free by melting a hole with a pan of hot water.

Greenhouse

Move tender plants Citrus trees and other tender shrubs growing in containers should be moved from their summer position on the patio to the protection of a heated greenhouse or conservatory.

Remove shading Clean shading wash from the glass or take down shading material or blinds to maximize the amount of light getting into the greenhouse in winter.

Put up insulation Fit polythene bubble insulation to the roof and walls of all the greenhouse to keep down heating costs and to help maintain an even temperature. Check that the heater is in good working condition. Unheated greenhouses also need additional insulation.

Clear crops Remove summer crops from the greenhouse and take down plant supports. Clean pots and other equipment so that they are ready for use in the spring.

Clean greenhouse On a mild day in autumn remove everything from the greenhouse and clean the structure, staging and floor with a garden disinfectant to help prevent pests and diseases overwintering successfully. Wipe pots of permanent plants and clear up all debris, such as fading flowers and yellowing leaves, to help reduce the problems of botrytis disease over winter.

Kitchen garden

Prevent problems Clear fallen fruit and leaves from under fruit crops to prevent pests and diseases from over-wintering ready to attack the crops next year. Tie grease bands around the trunks of fruit trees to trap the wingless female codling moths, which climb the trees and lay eggs.

Harvest vegetables Pick the last crops of beans and salad crops as well as squashes and tomatoes. Place cloches over tomato plants to help ripen the fruit or pick the green tomatoes and ripen in a fruit drawer containing a banana skin.

Harvest apples Late apples should be harvested when ready. Perfect fruit can be stored.

Encourage tomatoes to ripen by placing a cloche over them. If a severe frost is forecast, however, harvest the remaining fruit.

Winter digging Clear summer crops and dig over vacant heavy soil so that frost can break down large clods ready for planting next year.

Plant vegetables Plant garlic cloves, spring cabbages and broccoli in well-prepared ground.

Herbs Pot up herbs for winter use.

Pruning Complete all winter pruning of tree, bush and cane fruits.

New plants The dormant season is an ideal time to plant bare-rooted fruit trees, bushes and canes.

Prunus x subhirtella 'Stellata' has star-like pale pink flowers. It is an eye-catching feature in winter, flowering from late autumn to early spring, a time when the rest of the garden can appear dead.

DIRECTORY OF
GARDEN
PLANTS

PLANTS FOR YOUR GARDEN

The directory section is intended to be of practical value to gardeners. Plants are grouped according to type (trees, shrubs, perennials, etc.) and the descriptions are designed not only to allow for identification but to suggest how the plants can be used in the garden.

The number of plants available is constantly expanding, and it is obviously impossible to keep pace with every new introduction. One of the aims of this directory is to bring together tried and tested plants, which have already proved their value in gardens and can be expected to perform reliably for many years to come alongside newer introductions that are likely to appear on the market. A few unusual plants are included (for instance *Berberis temolaica*, *Lonicera × tellmanniana* and *Phillyrea angustifolia*), plants which need no special cosseting but simply deserve to be better known. It is often only the difficulties of producing stocks in large quantities that have kept them out of gardens.

This border has been designed in a "hot" colour scheme with a combination of red-flowered and purple-leaved plants, both hardy and tender.

The summer-flowering *Itea ilicifolia*, though hardy, benefits from the shelter of a warm wall.

Hardiness

All the plants in this book have been assessed for their hardiness, and for the US, the range of zones where they can be grown outdoors is given (see page 494). Most (apart from cacti and succulents and orchids) can be grown outdoors in most temperate areas, and are able to withstand lows of -15°C (5°F). Plants described as "borderline hardy" will need some form of protection from the coldest weather, either by growing them in a warm, sheltered spot (for instance in the lee of a sunny wall) or by covering them in winter with a dry mulch of straw or other similar material. However, severe lows in themselves are less detrimental to plants than cold, drying winds.

Hardiness in any case is relative, and the ability of many plants at least to survive cold is largely dependent on how hot the weather is the previous summer. Deciduous trees and shrubs, herbaceous bulbs that disappear below ground in winter have an in-built mechanism

for surviving unfavourable weather. During hot, dry periods, plant growth stops altogether. As the soil dries out, roots delve deeper in search of moisture, while bark thickens in the heat. The result is a tough, sturdy plant with an extensive root system that is better able to withstand severe cold than one that has grown sappy through excess moisture during the growing season. These plants are able to survive colder winters than usual, simply because the preceding summer was a hot one. Winter temperatures in certain regions with a Mediterranean climate for instance can drop as low as they do in temperate areas, but plants such as olives are able to survive simply because of the long hot summers that ripen the wood. Hence the necessity of growing plants of borderline hardiness in a microclimate where they can ripen sufficiently. The same applies to many bulbs, which are adapted to long dry summers and indeed need a good summer roasting in order to flower successfully.

How to use the directory

The directory section is divided into fourteen plant categories: Trees; Conifers; Shrubs; Perennials; Annuals and Biennials; Climbers; Roses; Bulbs (including corms and tubers); Alpines; Water Plants; Cacti and Succulents; Orchids; Ferns; and Grasses and Bamboos.

Each category features genus introductions in alphabetical order, accompanied by concise information on cultivation. These are followed by a selection of plant entries also organized alphabetically according to their most common and internationally accepted names.

A plant entry might be a species, hybrid or group of hybrids, a variant, or a cultivar. As well as a brief description, information is given on height and spread; best time of interest for flowers, foliage and fruits/berries/hips; and hardiness/zones.

Caption
A full botanical name is given with each photograph

Genus name
This gives the botanical name for a group of related species

Common name or names
These apply to the whole genus, if given

Genus introduction
This is a general description of the genus and may give the number of species or state that the genus is monotypic (there is only one species in the whole genus). There is also some information on preferred conditions and natural habitat, country or countries of origin, and occasional advice on how the plants can be used in the garden.

Cultivation
This section gives the level of sun or shade that the plants described in the selection either require or tolerate as well as advice on the type of soil in which they should be grown.

Hybrids
Occasionally, there is one entry for a group of hybrids.

Varieties and cultivars
The descriptions of cultivars, forms, subspecies, and varieties appears within the main plant entry. Heights and spreads are only included if they differ from those of the main plant entry.

Erigeron 'Quakeress'

ERIGERON
Fleabane
Useful daisy plants, suitable for a sunny border, these suit cottage garden-style plantings. There are a large number of hybrids; only the species described is well-represented in gardens.
Cultivation Best in fertile, moist but well-drained soil in sun. Taller varieties may benefit from light staking.

E. karvinskianus
(syn. *E. muconatus*)
Wall daisy
This spreading species has dainty white flowers from late spring to autumn. H to 30cm (1ft), S 1m (3ft). Hardy/Z 8–9.

E. hybrids
The following hybrids flower throughout summer but can also flower intermittently at other times. They are all hardy/Z 2–7. 'Dignity' has violet-blue flowers. H and S 45cm (18in). 'Dunkelste Aller' (syn. 'Darkest of All') has deep purple flowers with yellow eyes. H 60cm (24in), S 45cm (18in). 'Gaiety' has mid-pink flowers. H 60cm (24in), S 45cm (18in). The deservedly popular 'Quakeress' has white flowers flushed with pale lilac-pink. H 60cm (24in), S 45cm (18in). 'Schneewittchen' (syn. 'Snow White') has pure white flowers, which turn pink as they age. H 60cm (24in), S 45cm (18in).

Main plant entry
This gives the current botanical name of the plant in bold and can refer to a species, hybrid or hybrids, a variant, or a cultivar.

Synonym or synonyms
If given, this provides the synonym or synonyms for the main plant entry. A synonym is an alternative name for the same plant.

Common name or names
If given, this provides the common name or names for the main plant entry.

Hardiness ratings/Zones
This gives the plant's temperature tolerance as either tender, down to 5°C (41°F); half-hardy, down to 0°C (32°F); or hardy, down to -15°C. Plants described as "Borderline hardy" will need some form of protection from the coldest weather. A slightly different system is used in the US and Canada. Zones are based on the average annual minimum temperature for each zone. The smaller number indicates the northernmost zone it can survive in and the higher number the southernmost zone the plant will tolerate. In some cases only one zone is given for a plant entry. See page 494 for details of zones and a zone map.

Height and spread
This gives the average expected height and spread, though growth rates may vary, depending on location and conditions. If the height and spread are the same, then only one measurement is given. Metric measurements always precede standard measurements.

How plants are named

All living things are classified according to the binomial system, devised by the Swedish taxonomist Carl Linnaeus (1707–78) in his *Species Plantarum* (1753). Under the rules of this system, plants have Latin names consisting of the genus name (e.g. *Viburnum*) followed by the species epithet (e.g. *davidii*). Some genera comprise only one species, while others are vast. *Euphorbia*, for instance, is made up of some 2000 plants, annuals, perennials, shrubs and trees as well as some cactus-like plants, and is widely distributed. (Such genera are sometimes rather grandly described as "cosmopolitan".)

All members of a genus are assumed to have some relationship to each other (though this may not necessarily be immediately apparent to the naked eye) and different species can often be crossed with each other. At the higher level, some genera seem to be related to each other (roses, pyracanthas and rowans, for instance, which all have cup-shaped flowers in their wild state), suggesting some common ancestry, though much remains conjectural or relies on the evidence of fossilized remains.

Naming plants

Nomenclature is not an exact science, and although there are certain internationally agreed rules, how they are put into use is often a matter of individual prejudice. Botanists and taxonomists frequently disagree over which name certain plants should bear, and in many cases there can be no "right" answer, since much depends on individual opinion. Hence the advisability of retaining synonyms, which can be as valid as the name officially sanctioned. The well-known mile-a-minute plant (here *Fallopia baldschuanica*) has

Plant names can be a complex and confusing matter, and few gardening subjects have aroused such controversy in recent years as the naming of chrysanthemums.

migrated several times between *Polygonum* and *Fallopia*, with ports of call at *Bilderdykia*. The most radical and controversial changes in recent years involved those to *Chrysanthemum*, which properly is made up exclusively of annual species from the Mediterranean. The perennials (which include the many garden forms that are such a feature of the autumn garden, the so-called florists' chrysanthemums) have been assigned to *Dendranthema*. However, so deeply entrenched is the name *Chrysanthemum* that it has been widely retained both within the nursery trade and in a number of plant dictionaries, this one included.

It occasionally happens that two plants thought to be distinct, with two separate names, are discovered to be, in fact, one and the same, and here a decision has to be taken as to which name has precedence.

Cultivars

Many plant species have the genetic potential to assume different characteristics to adapt to changes in the environment. In the wild, the habitat will favour seedlings best suited to the prevailing conditions, while the rest will not survive. Hence any population of a particular species in the wild will look more or less the same.

In the more controlled conditions of a garden, the genetic potential becomes manifest, since gardeners are able to germinate and grow on a larger proportion of the seed. All manner of variations can arise: double flowers, albino forms, plants with variegated leaves, etc. Such forms, if they have garden potential and are sufficiently distinct from the species, are given names and known as cultivars (a contraction of "cultivated varieties") or selections of the species, and the name is put in single quotes as, for instance, *Viburnum tinus* 'Eve Price'.

Hybrids

Certain species can be crossed with each other to produce hybrids. This can occur in nature, but is more usually deliberately practised by plant breeders. Hybridization generally results in robust plants with bigger flowers. For instance, at Bodnant in Wales, *Viburnum farreri* was crossed with *V. grandiflorum* to produce *V. × bodnantense* (the cross indicating that the plant is a hybrid). Outstanding seedlings were given names, including 'Dawn' and 'Deben'.

Hybrids can be back-crossed with one of the parents, to consolidate a particular feature, or can be crossed with other species or hybrids. Some garden forms have such complex parentage that it becomes meaningless to try to ascribe them to one or other species or hybrid group. Indeed, if precise records were not kept, the ancestry of a plant can only be guess-work. Such plants are styled with the genus name followed by the cultivar name, e.g. *Campanula* 'Burghaltii'. Many roses and rhododendrons come into this category.

In general, garden forms can only be propagated vegetatively (cloning). Seedlings will revert back to the parent species (or one of them). Over time, the quality tends to deteriorate: repeated vegetative propagation is like photocopying a photocopy of a photocopy. Hence only the most vigorous of the older cultivars will stand the test of time, and there is good reason for replacing them with newly created hybrids. Many gardeners regret this, but while there is every reason to wish to preserve species that may be under threat in the wild to maintain the biodiversity of the planet, the disappearance of certain garden forms from cultivation does not represent a comparable loss.

Garden forms usually do not survive in the wild, but some species have been known to "escape", as with *Rhododendron ponticum*, from the Mediterranean, which has colonized areas of the UK and Ireland, to the extent that it has become a weed.

Name changes

As previously mentioned, nomenclature is never precise and can lead to disputes amongst botanists. For instance, the genera *Berberis* and *Mahonia* were formerly united in a single genus, and members of the two will in fact hybridize, suggesting that there is some close relationship between them. Many botanists would like to see them reunited. Recent research into cacti and bamboos has resulted in reclassification, and some species formerly considered to belong to separate genera are now thought to be related, and some species have been switched from one genus to another.

Name changes result in synonyms. A new name is not necessarily more valid than the old, and merely represents the opinion of whoever has come up with the new name. Although many gardeners despair at what seem like constant changes, there is usually a good reason for a change (even though agreement may not be universal). Sometimes it is best to be practical. *Chrysanthemum* is a case in point.

Names of cultivars that have been bred abroad and given foreign names are often given translated names (or even new names) once imported. There are arguments for and against this: on the plus side, it results in names that are easier to remember and spell; on the down side, it leads to potential confusion. Modern rules require translated names to be set in a different font and without quotes.

Hybrids with the same parentage are sometimes given group names. This usually happens when all the seedlings share similar characteristics and, while varying, make good garden plants. A case in point is *Lilium* African Queen Group, plants of which all have orange flowers, but with differing intensity of colour. Conversely, the same name is sometimes ascribed to two different plants, as is the case with the clematis 'Princess of Wales', a name that applies to two cultivars, one honouring Alexandra, wife of Edward VII, the other Princess Diana.

The breeding of orchids has been scrupulously recorded. This hybrid **Cymbidium** **Summer Pearl** **'Sonya'** has complex parentage.

Trees

A tree completes a garden. Whether it is grown for its flowers, fruits, foliage or overall appearance, a tree adds dignity and style to any garden. From mighty oaks to the more manageable Japanese maples, there is a tree for every type of garden, whether you have rolling acres or a suburban plot. Even if you have only a courtyard, balcony or roof garden, there are trees suitable for containers. Careful selection is necessary, however. Remember: a tree often outlives the gardener.

A flowering tree makes a splendid eye-catcher at the peak of its glory, dominating the garden.

Trees for your garden

Trees comprise a large and diverse group of plants that defies precise botanical classification. What distinguishes a tree from other forms of plant life is in fact no more than its overall appearance. Most people understand a tree as having a single woody trunk and a branching crown, while shrubs produce a number of stems from ground level. However, many trees can develop as multi-trunked plants, while certain shrubs become tree-like on maturity. Climatic factors also play a part: certain plants are unequivocally trees when growing at the foot of a mountain, for instance, but behave as shrubs at the mountain top, where strong winds will have a dwarfing effect, resulting in a thick trunk and gnarled branches. In isolation on open ground, trees will branch from ground level (or very near it) and be clothed in leaves; in forests, where the planting is denser and they are competing for light, they tend to develop tall, slim trunks, branching only near the top to form the characteristic leaf canopy. Generally, trees are assumed to have a height greater than 3m (10ft) and shrubs to be below that. But some weeping trees have a much shorter trunk than that and can in no way be mistaken for shrubs.

Trees occur in a range of plant families and have adapted to most environments except deserts and tundra. Most belong to the largest group, the angiosperms (all flowering plants). Gymnosperms include conifers and cycads, while even the most primitive plant group, the ferns and mosses (pteridophytes), includes the tree ferns (but treated as a fern in this book). Most trees are deciduous, shedding their leaves in autumn and experiencing a period of dormancy

The weeping willow is particularly alluring in spring, when its delicate, pale green emerging leaves cast dappled shade.

over winter, though some are evergreens that in favourable climates will be more or less permanently in growth. Evergreen trees tend to be less hardy than deciduous trees.

Essential to the planet's ecology, trees store carbon dioxide and produce oxygen, and the material they shed – leaves and twigs – breaks down in the soil to release nitrogen, carbon and oxygen to feed the next generation of plants. Their roots help prevent soil erosion, which is why they are often planted in railway cuttings and to retain the banks at the sides of motorways, and the vast amount of water stored in a mature tree helps prevent local flooding. Trees also provide food and shelter for a wide range of mammals, birds and invertebrates.

Most trees grown in gardens today are either species or very closely related to naturally occurring forms. A few have been extensively hybridized, however, most notably the Japanese maples (forms of *Acer palmatum* and *A. japonicum*) and flowering cherries (*Prunus*), resulting in a vast number of highly desirable garden plants.

Trees in the garden

Even the smallest of gardens should include at least one tree. Trees give an air of maturity and permanence to any plot, quite apart from whatever ornamental qualities they may possess, and have the additional benefit – inestimable to environmentalists – of attracting wildlife into the garden. Birds will perch and sometimes nest in the branches, as well as feed off any autumn fruits or berries. Trees also attract pollinating insects when in flower, and harbour a wide range of invertebrates in their bark. Before making a choice, however, you need to consider the impact the tree will make on the rest of the planting. Deciduous trees that cast dappled shade in summer but are bare in winter can be underplanted with dwarf spring bulbs for early interest, followed by shade-loving perennials later on, but the shade cast by evergreens will be too dense to allow much other plant life to thrive. In a very small garden, a narrow, columnar tree, such as *Prunus* 'Amanogawa', is often the best choice.

Trees have a range of ornamental qualities, but whether you are planning an avenue of mighty oaks or have room for only a small tree, think long and hard over which species to plant. Most trees will outlive you. If it is flowers that you want, you could scarcely do better than look to the magnolias, with sumptuous, waxy, chalice-like flowers in spring; for more delicacy, a flowering cherry (*Prunus*) could fit the bill. In favoured areas, a catalpa or paulownia would provide spring flowers, while *Acacia dealbata* (perhaps trained against a warm wall) will flower in late winter. Rather less exotic, but equally attractive in their way, as well as being tough and hardy, are the rowans (*Sorbus*) and hawthorns (*Crataegus*).

Many trees have a second period of interest in autumn when the fruits ripen. Crab apples (*Malus*) are among the best, and their red, yellow or orange fruits, as well as looking good and attracting birds, can be cooked or made into a preserve. Rowans also have spectacular trusses of berries, which often change colour or turn translucent as the temperature drops in winter.

That elusive moment when the leaves of deciduous trees change colour in autumn just before they are shed is one of the most keenly anticipated events in the gardening calendar. The display will vary from year to year, depending on the conditions of the season. One reliable performer is the katsura tree (*Cercidiphyllum japonicum* var. *magnificum*), whose leaves turn brilliant orange and then give off the scent of burnt toffee as they fall to the ground. Many of the acers produce glorious autumn colour, particularly the Japanese maples, as do amelanchiers, rowans and beeches (*Fagus*).

Trees that have attractive bark are interesting in every season of the year. The birches are especially noted for this feature.

Many trees are surprisingly effective in winter, and not only the evergreens such as hollies (*Ilex*) or *Quercus ilex*. *Prunus serrula*, for instance, has shiny mahogany red bark, while that of *Betula utilis* var. *jacquemontii* (to name only one birch from a genus outstanding for this very feature) is a gleaming white. Site them where they will be dramatically lit up by the winter sun.

If space is restricted, a surprising number of trees will do well in containers. Not the large forest trees, obviously, but any of the evergreens that take kindly to pruning, such as bay (*Laurus*) or holly, as well as more modest trees, such as Japanese maples (stylish in glazed Eastern-style pots). Citrus and acacias make a good choice for a conservatory or porch.

Fruit trees have two-fold attractions: breathtaking when in flower in spring, they earn their keep by providing edible crops in autumn.

The trees described below are deciduous unless otherwise indicated.

ACACIA
Wattle
The main drawback of this delightful genus is that few wattles are hardy enough to grow as freestanding specimens in any but favoured climates. In the right spot, however, they make airy, elegant trees, laden with scented flowers. They are sometimes used as pavement trees, to spectacular effect. In cold areas they can be grown in conservatories (porches), but need cutting back to restrict their size. The genus also includes some shrubs.
Cultivation Moderately fertile, lime-free soil in full sun, with shelter from strong winds.

A. dealbata
Mimosa, silver wattle
This evergreen Australian and Tasmanian species has silver-grey, fern-like leaves and masses of fragrant, fluffy yellow flowers in late winter to early spring. It is suitable for training against a warm wall. H 15m (50ft), S 10m (33ft). Borderline hardy/Z 9–10.

ACER
Maple
This is a huge and important genus, and there is a maple for every garden, large or small. *A. pseudoplatanus* (sycamore) is almost a weed in some gardens, but that should not blind you to the

Acacia dealbata

beauties of the other species. Maples suit a woodland planting or lightly shaded area.
Cultivation Acers tolerate most soil types, although *A. rubrum* does best in lime-free soil. Japanese maples like a leafy, fertile but well-drained soil. Smaller species are best in light shade. *A. palmatum* cultivars are particularly susceptible to frost, which can damage the young growth, and they do best in a sheltered spot.

A. capillipes
The young stems of this erect, deciduous Japanese species are reddish. The leaves open red, mature to mid-green and turn crimson and orange in autumn. The grey-green bark is striped white. H and S 10m (33ft). Hardy/Z 6–9.

A. × conspicuum 'Phoenix'
This is grown mainly for the beauty of its green bark, which turns vivid pink with silver stripes in winter. The autumn display is also good, with the leaves turning a bright golden-yellow. H 5m (16ft), S 3m (10ft). Hardy/Z 6–9.

A. davidii
Snake-bark maple, Père David's maple
Native to China, the species has (usually) spreading branches. The leaves are tinged bronze as they emerge and turn red and purple in autumn. The grey bark is striped white. It does best in semi-shade. H 6m (20ft), S 3m (10ft). Hardy/Z 6–8.

Acer × conspicuum 'Phoenix'

'George Forrest' has larger, red-stalked, dark green leaves, but the autumn colour is not as good. H 4m (13ft), S 2m (6ft).

A. griseum
Paperbark maple
Also native to China, this slow-growing species is one of the most outstanding members of a fine genus. The leaves turn a brilliant red before they fall in autumn, but the principal interest is the cinnamon-red bark, which peels to reveal a richer colour beneath. H and S 10m (33ft). Hardy/Z 6–8.

A. japonicum
Japanese maple, full-moon maple
The Japanese maples, which also include selections of *A. palmatum* (see below), are among the most attractive of all small trees, staying fairly compact and ending up as broad or broader than they are tall. They all have spectacular autumn leaf colour. The species is a spreading, rather shrubby tree. H and S 10m (33ft). Hardy/Z 6–8. **'Aconitifolium'** (syn. 'Filicifolium') is a slow-growing tree or large shrub, generally broader than it is tall. The soft green, deeply cut leaves turn vivid orange-red in autumn. H 5m (16ft), S 6m (20ft).

A. palmatum
Japanese maple
The species, which is native to Korea and China as well as to Japan, is a rounded tree or shrub

Acer griseum

Acer japonicum 'Aconitifolium'

displaying glorious autumn colour. H 8m (25ft), S 10m (33ft). Hardy/Z 5–8.
A. palmatum f. *atropurpureum* (syn. 'Atropurpureum') is notable for the vibrant purple of its leaves, in spring and autumn. H 8m (25ft), S 10m (33ft).
A. palmatum var. *dissectum* makes a dome-shaped tree with elegant ferny foliage, which turns red or yellow in autumn. It has a number of cultivars with coloured or variegated leaves. H and S to 4m (13ft) but usually less. Acers in the **Dissectum Atropurpureum Group** have similar colouring to *A. palmatum* f. *atropurpurem* but with very finely dissected leaves, giving the plant a more filigree appearance. Slow-growing, they eventually make attractive, dome-shaped, spreading trees. H and S 4m (13ft). **'Dissectum Nigrum'** (syn. 'Ever Red') has finely dissected, blackish-purple leaves and forms a low, rounded bush. H 3m (10ft), S 4m (13ft). **'Fireglow'** (syn. 'Effegi') carries rich burgundy-red leaves, which turn orange-red in autumn. This requires some sun to enhance the leaf colour. H and S to 3m (10ft). **'Kagiri-Nishiki'** (syn. 'Roseomarginatum') has pale green leaves margined with pink, later turning cream. H and S 3m (10ft). **'Katsura'** has the typical palm-shaped leaves of the species. Pale orange-yellow when young, they mature to a rich bronze, then redden in autumn. H 1.2m (4ft), S 2.5m (8ft). **'Ôsakazuki'** carries mid-green leaves, which turn brilliant orange, crimson and scarlet in autumn. H 5m (16ft), S 2.5m (8ft). The red-tinted leaves of **'Rubrum'** turn bright red in autumn. H 5m (16ft), S 2.5m (8ft). **'Sekimori'** has very finely divided, filigree foliage,

Acer palmatum f. atropurpureum

which is bright green, turning red or yellow in autumn. H and S to 3m (10ft).

A. platanoides
Norway maple
This fast-growing acer offers startling autumn colour, which is usually yellow but sometimes red. H 25m (80ft), S 15m (50ft). Hardy/Z 4–7. **'Crimson King'** has rich red-purple foliage. H 15m (50ft), S 5m (16ft). **'Drummondii'** is less vigorous with mid-green leaves that are variegated with creamy-white. H 12m (40ft), S 5m (16ft).

A. rubrum
Red maple, scarlet maple, swamp maple
This species has leaves that turn rich red-orange in early autumn. H 20m (65ft), S 10m (33ft). Hardy/Z 4–9. **'Scanlon'** is a slow-growing, densely upright form with good autumn colour. H 15m (50ft), S 5m (15ft).

A. shirasawanum 'Aureum'
Moonglow maple
A round-headed, slow-growing tree, with distinctive butter-yellow

Acer palmatum 'Rubrum'

leaves, which turn red in autumn. It needs some sun to colour the foliage but can scorch in full sun. H and S to 6m (20ft). Hardy/Z 6–8.

AESCULUS
Horse chestnut, buckeye
A spectacular show of late-spring flowers is just one of the attributes of these majestic trees. Most are for big gardens only, although A. pavia is well worth considering for a smaller plot. *Cultivation* Grow in moist, fertile, well-drained soil in full sun.

A. hippocastanum
Common horse chestnut
This giant of a tree, which is native to south-eastern Europe, has mid-green leaves. The white, candle-like flowers are spectacular in late spring. H 25m (80ft), S 20m (65ft). Hardy/Z 4–7.

A. × neglecta 'Erythroblastos'
Sunrise horse chestnut
This slender, slow-growing, conical hybrid has red leaf stalks and leaves that emerge cream and pink, then turn yellow before maturing green by midsummer. H 10m (33ft), S 8m (25ft). Hardy/Z 7–8.

A. pavia
(syn. A. splendens)
Red buckeye
A shrubby, North American species, this has mid-green leaves and upright panicles of bright red flowers in late spring to early summer. H 3m (10ft), S 2.5m (8ft). Hardy/Zone 6–9.

ALNUS
Alder
One of the few genera adapted to boggy conditions, alders are often planted near to water. *Cultivation* Alders will grow in any fertile soil in full sun.

A. glutinosa
Common alder
This species has purplish catkins (pussy willows) in late winter. Dark green leaves emerge from sticky buds in spring. H 25m (80ft), S 10m (33ft). Hardy/Z 4–7.

AMELANCHIER
June berry, snowy mespilus, serviceberry
These are charming trees for the spring garden, the dainty flowers appearing around the same time as tulips. They also provide good autumn colour and fruits that will attract birds. They make good specimen trees but are small enough for a mixed planting. *Cultivation* Grow in a lime-free soil in sun or light shade.

A. × grandiflora 'Ballerina'
A profusion of starry white flowers appears on this spreading, shrubby hybrid in spring. The leaves turn red and purple in autumn. H 6m (20ft), S 8m (25ft). Hardy/Z 4.

A. lamarckii
This beautiful small tree bears copper-red young leaves, which turn orange and red in autumn.

Aralia elata

The white spring flowers are followed by black berries. H 10m (33ft), S 8m (25ft). Hardy/Z 4–8.

ARALIA
Angelica tree
The genus includes some of the most elegant and architectural trees for the small garden. The species described makes a good specimen, but it can also be used in mixed plantings when young. *Cultivation* Fertile soil in partial shade, but they will tolerate full sun if the soil is reliably damp.

A. elata
(syn. A. chinensis of gardens)
Japanese angelica tree
This has spiny stems and coarsely toothed leaves, which turn yellow, orange or purple in autumn. White flowers appear in late summer to autumn. H and S 10m (33ft). Hardy/Z 4–9.

Aesculus hippocastanum

Betula albosinensis var. septentrionalis

ARBUTUS
Strawberry tree, madroña, manzanita

A genus with many attractions, not the least of which are the charming, strawberry-like fruits that give the trees their common name. (The fruits are edible, if on the insipid side.) The lily-of-the-valley-like flowers, which appear at the same time as the ripening fruits, are also beautiful. Add peeling bark to the list of attractions, and the surprise is that they are not more widely planted. There are two main reasons for this: not all are reliably hardy, and some will grow well only in acid soil.
Cultivation Most strawberry trees need lime-free soil in a sheltered position; *A. unedo* tolerates lime.

A. × andrachnoides
This evergreen hybrid has peeling, reddish-brown bark and clusters of small ivory-white flowers, which are borne between autumn and spring. Fruits appear only occasionally. H and S 8m (25ft). Hardy/Z 8–9.

Arbutus unedo 'Rubra'

A. unedo
This evergreen species has a spreading, sometimes rather shrubby habit. It is native to south-eastern Europe and the Middle East. The white flowers appear in autumn, at the same time as the strawberry-like fruits from the previous year ripen. The red-brown bark, which peels in shreds, is also an attractive feature. H and S 6m (20ft). Borderline hardy/Z 8–9. The form **'Rubra'** reaches the same size as the species, but has deep pink flowers.

BETULA
Birch

The genus includes some of the best garden trees. They are hardy and easy to grow in addition to being graceful and quick growing. Most have attractive, usually white, bark and good autumn leaf colour. They are among the most reliable trees for alkaline soils.
Cultivation Birches will grow in any fertile soil in sun or light shade; they also tolerate poor soil.

B. albosinensis var. septentrionalis
In a genus renowned for the beauty of its bark, this form of *B. albosinensis* (Chinese red birch) is outstanding for that feature. Creamy white when young, on mature specimens (those 15 or more years old) it develops a pinkish bloom and peels to reveal a mahogany red underlayer. The oval leaves are deep green, turning yellow in autumn and persisting on the tree until early winter. In favourable conditions trees can exceed the dimensions indicated, but only after 20 years or so. H 10m (33ft), S 6m (20ft). Hardy/Z 6–8.

B. ermannii
Erman's birch, gold birch, Russian rock birch
The species is native to Russia (the Kamchatka peninsula), Japan and Korea, and is valued by gardeners because of its beautiful peeling white bark, which is sometimes tinged pink or cream. This feature is particularly apparent on multi-stemmed trees. H 7m (23ft) or more, S 4m (13ft) or more. Hardy/Z 5–8.

Betula utilis var. jacquemontii

The vigorous **'Grayswood Hill'**, which has an attractive conical habit of growth, has pure white bark. H 7m (23ft) or more, S 4m (12ft) or more.

B. pendula
(syn. B. alba, B. verrucosa)
Silver birch
This familiar tree, which is native to Europe and northern Asia, has slightly drooping branches and greyish-white bark, which cracks attractively on mature specimens. It may not always be long-lived in gardens. H 25m (80ft), S 10m (33ft). Hardy/Z 3–8. Notable selections include **'Youngii'** (Young's weeping birch), which is less vigorous and has more pendulous branches. H 8m (25ft), S 5m (15ft). Hardy/Z 3–8.

B. utilis var. jacquemontii
(syn. B. jacquemontii)
This naturally occurring variety of the Himalayan birch has white bark, which makes it an outstanding plant for the winter garden. The oval leaves turn yellow in autumn. Many of the plants sold in the trade under this name are raised from seed collected in the Himalayas, so habits and growth rates can vary, but most will not exceed the dimensions indicated in 20 years. H 12m (40ft), S 5m (16ft). Hardy/Z 6–8. Selected seedlings include **'Grayswood Ghost'**, which has glossy leaves, the fast-growing **'Jermyns'**, which has rounded leaves and large catkins (pussy willows), and **'Silver Shadow'**, which has large,

drooping, dark green leaves; all three forms have particularly brilliant bark. H 12m (40ft), S 5m (16ft).

CATALPA
Indian bean tree

Catalpas are among the most impressive flowering trees, bearing orchid-like flowers in mid- to late summer. The large, soft leaves are also appealing, particularly in the coloured-leaf forms. Suitable trees for sheltered, sunny gardens, they are hardier than is commonly supposed, although flowers are not always freely borne in cold areas. They can also be grown as foliage plants in mixed borders and cut back hard annually in spring, which produces luxuriant foliage, albeit at the expense of the flowers. The common name refers to the seedcases, which dangle from the branches from late summer onwards.
Cultivation Grow in any fertile soil in sun. Provide protection from strong winds.

C. bignonioides
Southern catalpa, smoking bean
Native to the south-eastern United States, this has long seed pods hanging from the branches in autumn. Its most striking feature, however, are the panicles of orchid-like flowers, which are white marked with yellow and purple-brown. A mature catalpa in full flower is an impressive sight in midsummer. The large, soft green leaves are also handsome, making this a highly valued shade tree in hot climates. Flowering is

Catalpa bignonioides 'Aurea'

Cercidiphyllum japonicum var.
magnificum

reliable only during hot summers.
H and S 15m (50ft). Hardy/Z
5–9. **'Aurea'** is less vigorous. The
soft yellow-green leaves, tinged
bronze as they unfurl in spring,
benefit from some shade from
direct sun. Given that this tree is
more reluctant to flower than its
parent, plus the fact that it is
slightly tender, in cool climates it
is best treated as a pollard or
coppice and enjoyed for its leaves
alone. H and S 10m (33ft)
unpollarded.

CERCIDIPHYLLUM

The genus contains a single
species, which is native to western
China and Japan. It is a choice
tree for the garden grown for its
spectacular autumn foliage.
Cultivation These trees do best in
woodland conditions – in fertile
soil in light dappled shade – and
although they are tolerant of lime,
the best autumn colour occurs on
acid soil.

× *Citrofortunella microcarpa*

C. japonicum var. *magnificum*
(syn. *C. magnificum*)
Katsura tree
This rare Japanese upright species
has rounded leaves that turn
yellow, orange and red in autumn
and smell of toffee when they fall
to the ground. H 10m (33ft),
S 8m (25ft). Hardy/Z 5–9.

CERCIS

All six species in the genus are
small trees, with rounded leaves
and pea-like flowers in spring.
Cultivation The trees need fertile
soil in a sunny, sheltered spot
where the late-spring flowers will
not be damaged by frosts.

C. siliquastrum
Judas tree
The connotations of the common
name (this is supposedly the tree
from which Judas hanged himself)
do not militate against its garden-
worthiness. The species, which is
native to south-eastern Europe
and south-western Asia, is quick-
growing and produces dark pink
flowers on the bare wood in
spring. The kidney-shaped, blue-
green leaves turn yellow in
autumn. The tree can be trained
against a wall. H and S 10m
(33ft). Hardy/Z 8–9. The
shrubby form *C. siliquastrum* f.
albida has white flowers and pale
green leaves.

× CITROFORTUNELLA

The trees in this hybrid genus
(a cross between *Citrus* and
Fortunella) are easy to grow, being
hardier than most *Citrus*.
Cultivation Grow in neutral to
acid soil in full sun. Container-
grown plants can be clipped to
keep them within bounds.

× *C. microcarpa*
(syn. × *C. mitis*)
Calamondin
This evergreen tree bears fragrant
white flowers at the same time as
the fruits from the previous
season are ripening. H 3m (10ft),
S 2m (6ft). Half-hardy/Z 9.

CORNUS
Dogwood
The dogwoods are among the best
trees for a small garden. Some are
grown for their overall appearance

Cornus alternifolia 'Argentea'

and hence make good specimens,
while others have striking spring
flowers and good autumn leaf
colour. The genus also includes
many shrubs and a few perennials.
Cultivation They need fertile soil,
preferably lime-free, in sun or
light shade. The species described
need neutral to acid soil.

C. alternifolia
(syn. *Swida alternifolia*)
Pagoda dogwood, green osier
This species from eastern North
America is usually grown in the
variegated form **'Argentea'** (syn.
'Variegata'), one of the most
beautiful of small trees. It has a
distinctive tiered habit, but it is
slow-growing and takes several
years to develop its characteristic

'wedding-cake' appearance.
Careful staking is necessary
initially to establish an upright
leader. H 3m (10ft), S 2m (6ft).
Hardy/Z 4–8.

C. 'Eddie's White Wonder'
This conical tree or large shrub
has white flowers in late spring
and leaves that reliably turn
orange, red and purple in autumn.
H 6m (20ft), S 5m (16ft).
Hardy/Z 6–9.

C. kousa
White flowers in summer are
followed by red fruits on this
elegant species, native to Japan
and Korea. The wavy-edged leaves
redden in autumn. H 7m (23ft),
S 5m (16ft). Hardy/Z 5–8.

Cercis siliquastrum

Crataegus laevigata 'Crimson Cloud'

CRATAEGUS
Hawthorn

Despite their ubiquity as roadside plants, hawthorns make excellent garden trees, particularly in exposed situations and on poor, limy soils. They are tough and hardy and make excellent hedges, particularly in country gardens.
Cultivation Grow hawthorns in any fertile soil, preferably in full sun. They can be grown in exposed positions.

C. laevigata
(syn. *C. oxyacantha*)
Common hawthorn, may
Widely seen as a hedgerow plant in northern Europe, this bears white flowers in spring. These are followed in autumn by red haws, a valuable food source for birds. H and S to 8m (25ft). Hardy/Z 5–8. **'Crimson Cloud'** is a distinctive selection, producing brilliant red flowers with white centres, which are a strong contrast to the glossy,

dark green leaves. H and S 5m (16ft). **'Paul's Scarlet'** is one of the most popular of the hawthorns, but its double, deep pink flowers, produced in vast quantities, are usually sterile and haws are seldom produced. H and S 5m (16ft). Hardy/Z 5–8.

C. × lavallei 'Carrierei'
This spreading, densely branched hawthorn has glossy green leaves that turn red in late autumn and winter. Clusters of white spring flowers are followed by orange-red fruits. H 7m (23ft), S 10m (33ft). Hardy/Z 5–7.

C. persimilis 'Prunifolia'
(syn. *C. prunifolia*)
A compact, spreading hawthorn of garden origin, this bears clusters of white flowers in spring, which are followed by bright red fruit. The glossy, deep green leaves are tinted orange and scarlet in autumn. H 8m (25ft), S 10m (33ft). Hardy/Z 6–7.

EUCALYPTUS
Gum tree, ironbark
A familiar sight in many urban areas, eucalyptus are widely planted as pollution-tolerant street trees. Although potentially very large, they respond well to pruning. The foliage of most species changes shape as the tree matures, the juvenile leaves being generally considered the more attractive. Cutting back stems regularly ensures that trees retain their youthful appearance.
Cultivation Grow in any well-drained soil in full sun. (Some sources specify acid soil, but many species tolerate chalk.)

Crataegus laevigata 'Paul's Scarlet'

E. gunnii
Cider gum
This evergreen from Tasmania is one of the most versatile of garden trees. Not only can it be allowed to develop freely as a single- or multi-stemmed tree, but it can also be kept within bounds by hard pruning so that it can be grown as a shrub in a mixed border. Pruning also encourages the ready production of juvenile foliage, which is coin-shaped and a gleaming pewter grey. Unless cut back, mature trees can become unstable. H 20m (65ft), S 6m (20ft). Borderline hardy/Z 8–10.

E. pauciflora subsp. niphophila
(syn. *E. niphophila*)
Snow gum, alpine snow gum
This slow-growing evergreen tree is grown for its brilliant, peeling, cream and grey bark, which is shown to best advantage when the plant is grown as a multi-stemmed tree. The bluish-grey juvenile leaves are oval; adult leaves are sickle shaped. To retain the juvenile foliage, treat as a pollard. H and S to 6m (20ft). Hardy/Z 9–10.

E. perriniana
Spinning gum
An evergreen species from Australia, this has flaking, white,

Eucalyptus gunnii

Eucryphia glutinosa

green or grey bark and bluish-green, rounded juvenile leaves, while adult leaves are lance-shaped. It is best treated as a pollard. H 5.5m (18ft), S 2m (6ft). Borderline hardy/Z 9–10.

EUCRYPHIA

These trees deserve to be better known. Not only are the myrtle-like flowers beautiful, but they also appear late in the season, when few other woody plants are flowering. A mature eucryphia in full flower is an impressive sight. Choose among the species carefully because some are particular as to soil type.
Cultivation Plant in neutral to acid soil in sun or light shade in a sheltered spot. *E. × nymansensis* 'Nymansay' tolerates chalk.

E. glutinosa
Nirrhe
This slow-growing small tree or shrub from Chile is an excellent flowering tree for an acid site. The large white flowers cover the plant in mid- to late summer. In mild areas the tree is evergreen; in cold areas the leaves turn rich orange-red before falling in autumn. H 10m (33ft), S 6m (20ft). Hardy/Z 8–10.

E. × nymansensis 'Nymansay'
This columnar, evergreen hybrid is better known than *E. glutinosa*, probably because it tolerates alkaline conditions and has fragrant flowers. H 5m (16ft), S 2m (6ft), ultimately probably larger. Borderline hardy/Z 8–9.

Fagus sylvatica 'Purpurea Pendula'

FAGUS
Beech

The 10 species in this genus have a number of uses. While most – magnificent though they are – grow too large for the average garden, some are more modest and make fine specimens. Beech also makes a splendid hedge. While not evergreen, the faded leaves hang on the branches over winter in a most appealing way. The autumn colour of all beeches can be spectacular.

Cultivation Grow in any soil except wet, sticky clays. Forms with coloured leaves do best in full sun, but other forms prefer light shade.

F. sylvatica
Common beech

This large European species is widely planted in parks and large public gardens. It can be unstable as a large specimen and its branches are brittle, especially in strong winds. It is, however, the parent of a number of handsome

Fortunella japonica

selections. Those listed are both hardy/zone 4–7. The excellent **'Dawyck Gold'** is a narrow, conical, slow-growing tree with leaves that are bright yellow as they unfurl in spring, becoming paler by summer. The dead leaves are held on the tree over winter. For the best leaf colour, plant in a sunny position. H 6m (20ft), S 2m (6ft). **'Purpurea Pendula'**, the weeping copper beech, is popular as a specimen in gardens both for its elegant habit and its rich purple leaves, which turn red in autumn. H up to 5m (16ft) (but often less), S to 2.2m (7ft).

FORTUNELLA
Kumquat

The four or five species in the genus are popular for their orange-yellow fruits, which, unlike other types of *Citrus* (to which *Fortunella* is related), can be eaten whole. Kumquats are native to southern China, and they make good conservatory (porch) plants.

Cultivation In frost-free climates they will grow in any well-drained soil in full sun or light shade, but elsewhere they need protection from frost.

F. japonica
(syn. Citrus japonica, C. macrophylla)
Marumi kumquat, round kumquat

This small evergreen tree or shrub carries fragrant white flowers from spring to summer. These are followed by edible, oval, golden-yellow fruits, each up to 4cm (1½in) long. When grown in a container under glass the dimensions will be smaller than indicated here. H 3m (10ft), S 1.5m (5ft). Tender/Z 9.

GLEDITSIA

Few trees have the charm of gleditsias, which look graceful all year round. In areas where there are hot summers the stems turn almost black, creating a sensational contrast with the lime green leaves. They are excellent as specimens or underplanted with prostrate ceanothus.

Cultivation Grow in any well-drained soil in sun or light shade. They are tolerant of pollution.

Gleditsia triacanthos 'Sunburst'

G. triacanthos
Honey locust

This popular species, from North America, is usually represented in gardens by **'Sunburst'**. The leaves of this cultivar are bright yellow on emergence, changing to pale green by the end of summer. This does best in a sunny position, where it can be sheltered from strong winds, and it is definitely a better choice for a small garden than the more vigorous *Robinia pseudoacacia* 'Frisia', which it superficially resembles. H 12m (40ft), S 10m (33ft). Hardy/Z 5–9.

HIPPOPHÄE
Buckthorn

These attractive small trees and shrubs make good windbreaks or barrier plantings, but they also combine well with other plants in mixed borders, providing a good

Hippophäe rhamnoides

foil to flowering shrubs and herbaceous perennials.

Cultivation Buckthorns will grow in any well-drained soil, including sandy soil, in sun or partial shade. They are well adapted to coastal conditions and will withstand strong, salt-laden winds.

H. rhamnoides
Sea buckthorn

The spiny shoots of this native of Europe and temperate Asia are clothed in long, silver-green leaves. Small yellow flowers in spring (almost lost among the branches) are followed by showier orange berries in autumn. Male and female flowers are borne on separate plants, so for reliable berrying, plant members of both sexes. H and S 6m (20ft). Hardy/Z 3–8. **'Freisendorf Orange'**, **'Hergo'** and **'Leikora'** are female; **'Pollmix'** is male.

IDESIA

The genus, from China and Japan, contains only one species, an elegant, understated plant, which is probably at its best as a specimen in a minimalist-style garden or in light woodland.

Cultivation Idesias need neutral to acid soil in sun or light shade.

I. polycarpa

This is an unusual, spreading tree, with heart-shaped leaves, usually tinged bronze as they open in spring. Male and female flowers are carried on separate plants, so for the bright red berries that are a feature on female plants in autumn, trees of both sexes must be grown. H and S up to 12m (40ft). Hardy/ Z 7–9.

Idesia polycarpa

Ilex aquifolium 'J.C. van Tol'

ILEX
Holly

Indispensable plants in any garden for their healthy, glossy leaves, the hollies are either trees or shrubs depending on age and how they have been pruned (if at all). If you inherit a garden with a large holly, think twice before ousting it – it will undoubtedly be of venerable age. Holly also makes an excellent hedge. Berries will be produced only on females, which will need a pollinating male nearby, so choose carefully among the cultivars. (*I. aquifolium* 'J.C. van Tol' is self-pollinating.) Those listed here are evergreen.
Cultivation Grow in any fertile soil, in sun or light shade. Variegated forms produce their best leaf colour in full sun. They are tolerant of atmospheric pollution and wind.

I. aquifolium
Common holly, English holly
Seedlings of the species, which is native to northern Africa and western Asia as well as to Europe, often appear in gardens, but the many cultivars generally make more attractive plants. The following selections are all hardy/Z 7–9. 'Aurea Marginata Pendula' is a slow-growing, rounded, weeping tree with purple stems and spiny, glossy, bright green leaves that are margined with creamy yellow. It is a female form, producing red berries in autumn. It is an outstanding plant for year-round interest. H and S up to 3m (10ft). The male 'Ferox Argentea' carries very prickly dark green leaves margined with cream. H 6m (20ft), S 4m (13ft). 'J.C. van Tol' is self-fertile, with bright red berries among the plain leaves. H 6m (20ft), S 4m ((13ft). 'Silver Milkmaid', a female cultivar, has an open habit and leaves with white margins. The berries are scarlet. H 6m (20ft), S 4m (13ft). 'Silver Queen' (syn. 'Silver King'), which is a slow-growing male form, also has white-edged leaves. It has a dense, upright habit of growth. H 10m (33ft), S 4m (13ft).

KALOPANAX

The genus, which is native to China, Korea, Japan and parts of Russia, contains a single species, which, while not exactly beautiful, nevertheless makes a striking statement in the growing season with its maple-like leaves and, in winter, its barbed branches.
Cultivation Grow in any fertile, well-drained soil either in sun or light shade.

K. septemlobus
(syn. *Eleutherococcus pictus, E. septemlobus, Kalopanax pictus, K. ricinifolius*)
Castor aralia, tree aralia
This spreading tree has lobed, dark green leaves and large heads of small white flowers, which appear in autumn and are followed by small black berries. H and S 10m (33ft). Hardy/Z 5–9. The leaves of *K. septemlobus* var. *maximowiczii* are more deeply lobed. H and S 10m (33ft).

× LABURNOCYTISUS

This curiosity would be a talking point in any garden, although it is not an entirely beautiful tree. It is a hybrid of *Chamaecytisus purpureus* and *Laburnum anagyroides*, grafted on to laburnum seedlings. It retains some of the characteristics of both its parents.
Cultivation Grow in any well-drained, moderately fertile soil in full sun.

× *L.* 'Adamii'
This tree is grown for its laburnum-like flowers in late spring or early summer. Some are yellow (like laburnum), others purple (like *Chamaecytisus*), while a third group are purplish-pink, flushed yellow, all colours appearing simultaneously. H 8m (25ft), S 6m (20ft). Hardy/Z 6–8.

LABURNUM
Golden rain

These decorative trees with their long pendulous flowers have one drawback, which is a serious one for many gardeners: all parts of the plant are poisonous. Effective as they are as specimens, laburnums are at their most attractive when planted in avenues and trained as a tunnel. In a small garden, they can be very effective when planted as a pair and trained to make an archway.
Cultivation Plant in any well-drained soil in sun or light shade.

Kalopanax septemlobus var. *maximowiczii*

L. × watereri 'Vossii'
This laburnum, a naturally occurring hybrid of *L. alpinum* and *L. anagyroides*, is one of the best-loved trees, with its racemes of golden-yellow flowers, which are followed by pea-like seed pods. Initially upright, it becomes more rounded on maturity. H and S 8m (25ft). Hardy/Z 6–8.

LAURUS
Bay laurel, sweet bay

The small genus, which contains two species, is a typical plant of the Mediterranean littoral. In colder areas bays are usually grown as shrubs, principally for their leaves, which, while not edible in themselves, can be used to flavour a variety of dishes. Bay looks effective in containers and incomparably stylish when arranged in pairs to frame a doorway. It is also a good choice for a seaside planting.
Cultivation Plant in any well-drained soil in sun or light shade.

Ilex aquifolium 'Aurea Marginata Pendula'

Laburnum × watereri 'Vossii'

Laurus nobilis

Choose a sheltered spot in all but the warmest gardens because cold, drying winds can kill it.

L. nobilis
Bay laurel
This handsome evergreen foliage plant has glossy mid- to dark green leaves. The flowers, produced in spring, are inconspicuous. Although it can be grown as a standard, it is often pruned to a shape, such as a cone or ball. H 12m (40ft), S 10m (33ft). Borderline hardy/Z 8–10.

LIGUSTRUM
Privet
Most of the privets are shrubs, planted mainly as hedging, although they are widely considered inferior to many other evergreen hedging plants. The genus includes a number of fine trees, which are tough, tolerant plants.
Cultivation Grow in any garden soil in sun or shade.

L. lucidum
Chinese privet
The evergreen species, which originates in China, Korea and Japan, has oval, glossy, dark green leaves and white flowers in late summer. It can be kept smaller than the dimensions shown by regular clipping. H and S 10m (33ft). Hardy/Z 7–10.

MAGNOLIA
Sumptuous and stately, magnolias are among the most handsome of garden trees, as well as being among the hardiest. Drawbacks of

some of the species are their enormous size, slowness of growth and reluctance to flower until some 20 or more years after planting. Fortunately, most of the modern selections are free from these vices. All magnolias make incomparable specimens and are best appreciated when grown in isolation. A few are shrubs.
Cultivation Grow in well-drained, humus-rich soil in sun or light shade. Not all magnolias will tolerate chalky (alkaline) soil.

M. campbellii
The species is found in a range from the Himalayas to China. The large, cup-and-saucer-shaped flowers, to 30cm (12in) across and either white or pink, emerge in late winter to early spring before the glossy green leaves. H to 15m (50ft), S to 10m (33ft). Hardy/Z 7–9. The vigorous **'Charles Raffill'** is a well-known selection, with claret-stained, white flowers, opening from rose pink buds. H 10m (33ft), S 5.5m/18ft.

M. 'Elizabeth'
A conical tree, this bears fragrant, goblet-shaped, pale yellow flowers, to 15cm (6in) across, in mid- to late spring. The leaves are attractively tinged with bronze when they emerge. This needs acid soil. H 10m (33ft), S 6m (20ft). Hardy/Z 5.

M. grandiflora
Bull bay, laurel magnolia
One of the few evergreen magnolias, the species is native to the south-eastern United States. Sadly, it is less hardy than some other species. In an open situation, it makes a magnificent, broadly conical tree, with long, glossy, dark green leaves and citrus-scented, waxy-textured, creamy white, cup-shaped flowers, which are borne in late summer. It is tolerant of lime, and it may be grown against a wall in cold areas. H 18m (60ft), S 15m (50ft), less when wall-trained. Borderline hardy/Z 7–9. The selection **'Victoria'** is hardier than the species but has smaller flowers. The leaves are brownish-red beneath. Hardy/Z 6.

Magnolia campbellii

M. 'Heaven Scent'
This lovely spreading tree hybrid bears a profusion of fragrant, goblet-shaped, white flowers, heavily flushed with deep pink outside, from mid-spring to early summer. The leaves are glossy dark green, lighter green beneath. This needs to be planted in acid soil. H 10m (33ft), S 6m (20ft). Hardy/Z 5.

M. 'Pickard's Schmetterling' (syn. M. 'Schmetterling')
A spreading tree, this bears goblet-shaped, rich pinkish-purple flowers in mid-spring. The flowers open as the leaves emerge. H 10m (33ft), S 6m (20ft). Hardy/Z 5.

M. × soulangeana
The hybrid of *M. denudata* and *M. liliiflora* has given rise to a large range of garden-worthy plants, all with goblet-shaped

Magnolia 'Pickard's Schmetterling'

flowers from mid-spring and a candelabra-like habit as they mature. The plants are moderately tolerant of lime. The following are all hardy/Z 5–9. The slow-growing **'Amabilis'** has pure white flowers. H and S to 6m (20ft). The flowers of the conical **'Brozzonii'** are heavily flushed with purple on the outside and white within. They are produced over a long period from mid-spring to early summer. H and S to 8m (25ft). The large flowers of **'Rustica Rubra'** (syn. 'Rubra') are a dramatic deep purple. H and S to 6m (20ft).

M. sprengeri
This slow-growing species, which is native to China, carries large, cup-shaped, white or pink-tinged flowers in early spring before the leaves appear. It has a compact habit. H 20m (65ft), S 10m (33ft). Hardy/Z 7–9.

Magnolia × *soulangeana* 'Amabilis'

Magnolia sprengeri

Malus 'Evereste'

Mespilus germanica 'Nottingham'

MALUS
Crab apple

As well as a plethora of fruit-bearing trees (forms of *Malus domestica*), this genus includes a number of trees of purely ornamental value, although even with these it is worth bearing in mind that the fruits, small and hard though they are, can be cooked or made into jellies. These ornamental trees are smaller than the flowering cherries, to which they are, therefore, a useful alternative, and, having a more 'rustic' appearance, they suit cottage-style gardens.
Cultivation Grow in any ordinary, fertile garden soil which is not too wet, in sun or light shade.

M. coronaria
Wild sweet crab apple

The species, native to North America, is usually represented in gardens by the form '**Charlottae**', an attractive small tree. Fragrant, semi-double, pink flowers are borne in late spring, and these are followed by yellowish-green fruits. The leaves take on good autumn colour. H and S 9m (30ft). Hardy/Z 5–8.

M. 'Evereste'

In spring this conical small hybrid bears a profusion of large white flowers, opening from reddish-pink buds. The fruits, which develop in autumn as the leaves turn yellow, are bright orange to red. H 7m (23ft), S 6m (20ft). Hardy/Z 4.

M. floribunda
Japanese crab apple

A spreading species from Japan, this bears pale pink flowers in late spring and small yellow fruits in autumn. H and S 10m (33ft). Hardy/Z 5–8.

M. 'John Downie'

This is one of the finest crab apples, and the best for making jelly. The cup-shaped, white flowers, borne in late spring, are followed by quantities of egg-shaped, orange and red fruits. H and S 6m (20ft). Hardy/Z 5–8.

M. × robusta 'Red Sentinel'

This hybrid produces a wonderful display of deep glossy fruits, which stay on the tree for most of the winter. H and S up to 7m (23ft). Hardy/Z 4–8.

M. tschonoskii

A notable introduction from Japan, this strong-growing, erect species bears pink-flushed, white flowers in spring. Fruits ripen to glossy yellow (with a red flush) in autumn as the leaves turn orange, red and purple. H 12m (40ft), S 7m (23ft). Hardy/Z 5–8.

M. × zumi 'Golden Hornet' (syn. M. 'Golden Hornet')

A small, rounded tree with deep pink buds that open to white flowers in late spring. They are followed by a good crop of bright yellow fruits. H 10m (33ft), S 8m (25ft). Hardy/Z 5–8.

MESPILUS
Medlar

Although medlars have been known since the Middle Ages, they are not grown commercially, so most people are unaware of the unique delights of the fruits, which are edible only once they have been frosted (or 'bletted') on the plant. The flowers, in late spring, are also attractive. The one species in the genus makes a charming specimen.
Cultivation Grow in well-drained soil in sun or light shade.

M. germanica

This medlar is found growing wild in forests and woodlands in south-eastern Europe and south-western Asia. The white flowers, borne in late summer, are followed by rounded brown fruits. As an added bonus, the leaves turn yellow-brown in autumn. H 6m (20ft), S 8m (25ft). Hardy/Z 6–9. The most widely grown selected form is '**Nottingham**', which is less thorny than the species and has larger leaves.

MORUS
Mulberry

These handsome trees are sometimes found in old cottage gardens: they can live for several hundred years. Although the raspberry-like fruits are edible, mulberries are grown more for their stately overall appearance.
Cultivation Mulberries need fertile, humus-rich soil in full sun. For the best fruiting, provide some shelter from strong winds.

M. alba
White mulberry

The shiny, heart-shaped leaves of this mulberry turn yellow in autumn as the fruits ripen from white through red to black. The species is native to China. H and S 10m (33ft). Hardy/Z 5–9. '**Pendula**' is a weeping form, ideal for a smaller garden. Unfortunately, it does not fruit freely. H 3m (10ft), S 5m (16ft). Hardy/Z 5–9.

Morus alba 'Pendula'

PAULOWNIA

Only one species of this fairly small genus of deciduous trees is at all common, and the climate of your garden will determine how you grow it. Where summers are long and hot, it can make an excellent specimen, but in colder areas, where it is less likely to flower, it is best treated as a pollard, when the huge leaves make it an exotic-looking foliage plant for a mixed border.
Cultivation This needs well-drained fertile soil in full sun with shelter from wind.

P. tomentosa
Foxglove tree, empress tree, princess tree

The most usual common name of the species, which is native to central and western China, derives from the upright spires of foxglove-like, mauve flowers. Unfortunately, the overwintering flower buds are generally killed by frosts in cold climates. In areas with hard winters, therefore, it is usually best enjoyed for the hairy young shoots and leaves and cut

Paulownia tomentosa

Populus alba

back hard annually in early spring. The leaves on coppiced plants will be up to 60cm (2ft) across. H to 12m (40ft), S 10m (33ft) (uncoppiced). Hardy/Z 6–9.

POPULUS
Poplar, aspen, cottonwood
Lombardy poplars are a familiar roadside tree in Europe, but the genus contains many other handsome species, although the majority are suitable only for larger gardens. Poplars are fast growing and are useful for providing a barrier in a relatively short time. All have invasive roots, however, so take care not to plant them near buildings whose foundations they could damage.
Cultivation Most poplars will grow in any garden soil, including wet, sticky clay (as long as it is not waterlogged), in an open position.

P. alba
White poplar, abele
The species, from central and southern Europe, central Asia and northern Africa, is recognizable from the white, woolly undersides of the leaves (turning yellow in summer), which create a charming effect as they flutter in the breeze. H to 40m (130ft), S 15m (50ft). Hardy/Z 4–9. 'Richardii' is a more compact form, with leaves that are golden-yellow above and white beneath. H 15m (50ft), S 12m (40ft).

P. × candicans 'Aurora'
This decorative, slow-growing hybrid forms a pillar-like tree with oval leaves that are splashed with white, cream and pink. Some shelter is desirable if the leaves are not to scorch. Pollarded, it makes a pretty specimen in a small garden. H 15m (50ft), S 6m (20ft). Hardy/Z 5–9.

P. nigra
Black poplar
Although handsome, the species is eclipsed in popularity by the selected form **'Italica'** (Lombardy poplar), an elegant, narrowly columnar tree. It tends to be short-lived in cultivation and seldom reaches the dimensions indicated. H 30m (100ft), S 5m (16ft). Hardy/Z 3–9.

Prunus 'Pandora'

PRUNUS
Ornamental cherry
This large genus contains evergreens and deciduous plants, shrubs as well as trees. Apart from the fruiting varieties (cherries, plums, apricots, peaches and almonds), there are a huge number of ornamental ones, many being hybrids of Japanese origin. A cherry orchard is a spectacular sight when in flower in spring, and an ornamental cherry should be among the first choices for a flowering specimen.
Cultivation Grow ornamental cherries in any well-drained, moderately fertile soil in full sun. A little lime seems to suit them.

P. 'Amanogawa'
(syn. P. serrulata 'Erecta')
This is an upright ornamental cherry with, usually, semi-double, shell-pink flowers in late spring. The leaves, which are tinged with bronze when young, redden in autumn. It is an ideal specimen for a small garden, but is also effective when planted in pairs or

Prunus 'Hillieri'

Prunus 'Shirofugen'

avenues. H 8m (25ft), S 4m (13ft). Hardy/Z 6–8.

P. 'Hillieri'
A spreading tree, this hybrid bears clusters of soft pink flowers in mid-spring. H and S to 10m (33ft). Hardy/Z 6.

P. 'Okame'
This cherry is laden with clusters of carmine-pink flowers in spring. The leaves turn orange and red in autumn. H 10m (33ft), S 8m (25ft). Hardy/Z 5–8.

P. 'Pandora'
This makes a spreading tree, with deep pink buds in early spring opening to paler pink flowers. Good autumn leaf colour adds to its attractions. H 10m (33ft), S 8m (25ft). Hardy/Z 6–8.

P. sargentii
Sargent cherry
A spreading species from Japan, Korea and Russia whose pale lilac-pink flowers are followed by cherry-like fruits that ripen to a glossy crimson. The leaves are a magnificent crimson and orange in autumn. It may grow too large for most gardens. H 25m (80ft), S 20m (66ft). Hardy/Z 5–9.

P. serrula
(syn. P. tibetica)
Tibetan cherry
This species from western China is usually planted for its gleaming mahogany red bark which peels off in strips to produce an eye-catching feature in winter. Site where the tree will be well lit by winter sun. H and S 10m (33ft). Hardy/Z 6–8.

P. 'Shirofugen'
One of the best of the cherries, this makes a spreading tree. The abundant double white flowers, which open from pink buds and age to pink, are fragrant. They may not appear until early summer. H 8m (25ft), S 10m (33ft). Hardy/Z 6–8.

P. 'Spire'
(syn. P. 'Hillieri Spire')
This upright, vase-shaped tree is a good choice for a small garden, and a possible alternative to the roughly similar 'Amanogawa'. It has pale pink flowers, which appear with the leaves in mid-spring, and good autumn colour. H 10m (33ft), S 7m (23ft). Hardy/Z 6–8.

P. × subhirtella 'Autumnalis'
Autumn cherry
This cultivar, which was developed in Japan, is probably the finest winter-flowering tree, producing flushes of pink-tinged white flowers throughout winter, during mild spells. The peak display usually occurs right at the end of winter, shortly before the equinox. The leaves turn yellow in autumn. H and S to 8m (25ft). Hardy/Z 6–8.

Prunus × *subhirtella* 'Autumnalis'

PTEROCARYA
Wingnut

This Asiatic genus consists of towering trees that make handsome specimens where there is lots of space. The common name relates to the winged seeds, which dangle in strings from the branches in autumn.
Cultivation Wingnuts need fertile, well-drained soil in sun, in a position where they will not be exposed to late frosts, which can damage young foliage.

P. stenoptera
Chinese wingnut

A fast-growing tree, this is particularly happy near water. Once mature, it produces greenish-yellow catkins (pussy willows) in early summer. The glossy green leaves turn yellow in autumn at the same time as the winged nuts develop. H 30m (100ft), S 15m (50ft). Hardy/Z 7–9.

PYRUS
Pear

"Pears for your heirs" is a familiar saying among the gardening fraternity – in other words, fruiting varieties will not produce any worthwhile crops until some years after you have planted them. Apart from the fact that this is not strictly true, the genus does include a number of attractive ornamental trees, which reward the gardener from the word go.
Cultivation Grow in fertile, well-drained soil in sun or light shade.

Pyrus calleryana 'Chanticleer'

Pyrus elaeagnifolia

P. calleryana
Chinese pear, callery pear

This Chinese species is usually represented in cultivation by the selection **'Chanticleer'**, a conical ornamental tree with white flowers in spring followed by inedible brown fruits. The leaves redden attractively in autumn. H 15m (50ft), S 6m (20ft). Hardy/Z 5–8.

P. elaeagnifolia

A dainty specimen when young, this is an unusual species from Asia Minor that deserves to be better known. Its thorny branches are covered with attractive, grey-felted leaves. White flowers in spring are followed by green fruits. H 12m (40ft), S 8m (25ft). Hardy/Z 5–9.

P. salicifolia 'Pendula'
Weeping willow-leaved pear

This is the form of the species that is, deservedly, most commonly encountered, and it makes a delightful and elegant specimen in a small garden. The narrow, silver-grey leaves are borne on pendulous branches, and creamy white flowers appear in spring. H 5m (16ft), S 4m (13ft). Hardy/Z 5–9.

QUERCUS
Oak

All the oaks are magnificent trees, and you shouldn't be put off by their final size. They stay small for quite a long time and can be pollarded to keep them within bounds, even if this prevents them from achieving their full

Quercus ilex

splendour. Oak trees are also important for wildlife, providing shelter for an enormous range of insects, birds and small mammals.
Cultivation Oaks should be grown in ordinary, well-drained soil, preferably in a sunny, open site. They tolerate light shade, but need space to expand.

Q. ilex
Holm oak

This majestic evergreen does particularly well in coastal situations. The variable leaves, often lance-shaped are silver-grey when young, darkening to a glossy green as they age. H 25m (80ft), S 20m (65ft). Borderline hardy/Z 7–9.

Q. robur
(syn. Q. pedunculata)
Common oak, English oak

The large species has the characteristically lobed leaves and

clusters of acorns in autumn. H 35m (120ft), S 25m (80ft). Hardy/Z 5–8. More manageable in smaller gardens are some of the selections, including the shrubby **'Compacta'**, which is very slow growing. H 5m (16ft), S 4m (13ft). Also slow growing is **'Concordia'** (golden oak), a small, rounded form carrying bright yellow-green leaves in spring. H and S 10m (33ft). The neatly upright **'Hungaria'** resembles *Populus nigra* 'Italica' (Lombardy poplar) in outline. H 9m (30ft), S 1.5m (5ft).

ROBINIA

These handsome trees are often, rather ill-advisedly, recommended for small gardens. Most make quite large plants and grow rapidly. A safer bet if space is at a premium is the shrubby *R. hispida* (rose acacia) at 2.5m (8ft) in height.
Cultivation These trees need well-drained soil in a sunny, sheltered spot. Avoid excessively windy sites: the branches are brittle and snap easily.

R. pseudoacacia
False acacia, black locust

The species from the United States is less widely grown than the selected form **'Frisia'**, a golden-leaved variety, which has become one of the most popular of all garden trees, although it

Quercus robur

can eventually grow quite large. Unlike other yellow-leaved trees and shrubs, it holds its colour well through the summer, making a splendid foil for purple-leaved shrubs. The shoots are very thorny and brittle. H 15m (50ft), S 8m (25ft). Hardy/Z 4–9. At the other end of the scale, **'Lace Lady'** is a compact, even bonsai-like form, which is good for a container. H and S 45cm (18in).

SALIX
Willow

The genus contains creeping shrubs as well as some quite large trees. Willows offer a variety of attractions for the garden. Many are grown for their catkins (pussy willows) or brightly coloured young shoots – regular annual or biennial hard pruning ensures a good supply of these – and weeping varieties look attractive growing at the water's edge. Some willows are also prized for their handsome summer foliage. *Cultivation* Willows need reliably moist soil, ideally in full sun.

S. alba
White willow

The fast-growing species, from Europe and western Asia, is a spreading tree with a large number of garden forms, some with coloured stems, which are best coppiced or pollarded. H 25m (80ft), S 10m (33ft), but considerably less if cut back hard annually. Hardy/Z 2–8. **'Hutchinson's Yellow'** has clear golden-yellow stems. *S. alba* subsp. *vitellina* **'Britzensis'** (scarlet willow, coral-bank willow) has brilliant orange-scarlet shoots. *S. alba* var. *sericea* (syn. *S. alba* 'Splendens'; silver willow) is also best if cut back hard, but in this case to create a vase-like clump of silvery foliage.

S. babylonica var. pekinensis 'Tortuosa'
(syn. *S. matsudana* 'Tortuosa')

This bizarre tree is grown exclusively for the interest of its twisted stems, at their most striking in winter. H 15m (50ft), S 8m (25ft). Hardy/Z 5–8.

S. caprea 'Kilmarnock'
(syn. *S. caprea* var. *pendula*)
Kilmarnock willow

This is a weeping miniature, with cascades of silver-white catkins in late winter. The tree is created artificially by grafting a prostrate plant on to rootstocks of varying height. H 1.5–2m (4–6ft), S 2m (6ft). Hardy/Z 5–8.

S. daphnoides
Violet willow

The species, an upright, fast-growing tree, is found from

Robinia pseudoacacia 'Frisia'

Europe to central Asia. The young shoots are purple. H 8m (25ft), S 6m (20ft). Hardy/Z 5–9. The superior selection **'Aglaia'** has bright red shoots and silvery catkins before the dark green leaves appear. H 8m (26ft), S 6m (20ft).

S. 'Erythroflexuosa'
(syn. *S.* 'Golden Curls', *S. matsudana* 'Tortuosa Aureopendula')

This spreading tree has twisting stems and leaves, which are useful in flower arrangements. Pale yellow catkins appear in spring. It can be kept smaller by regular cutting. H and S 5m (16ft). Hardy/Z 5–9.

S. integra 'Hakuro-nishiki'
(syn. *S.* 'Albomaculata')

This willow is actually a shrub that is usually sold grafted on to a clear stem to create a round-headed miniature tree. The leaves, which follow the slender catkins, are strikingly variegated with pink and cream. They keep a good colour well into summer. This graceful tree is a good choice for a container. The height varies according to the rootstock. H to 1.5m (5ft), S to 1m (3ft). Hardy/Z 5–8.

S. × sepulcralis var. chrysocoma
(syn. *S.* 'Chrysocoma')
Golden weeping willow

The fast-growing weeping willow is possibly the most familiar of all willows, and it is an evocative sight when the tips of its arching branches trail in water. It is equally attractive when bare in winter as when it is clothed in its bright green, lance-shaped leaves in summer. H and S 15m (50ft). Hardy/Z 6–8.

Salix integra 'Hakuro-nishiki'

Sophora microphylla

SOPHORA

An interesting genus, *Sophora* contains both deciduous and evergreen trees and shrubs and some perennials. In many ways they are plants for the connoisseur, and they do look rather exotic with their wisteria-like flowers. They are good as specimens or, in cold areas, trained against a warm wall.
Cultivation Grow sophoras in fertile, well-drained soil in a sunny, sheltered spot.

S. japonica
Japanese pagoda tree, Chinese scholar tree

The tree, which is native to China and Korea, is grown for its late summer flowers, which are white and scented, although these appear only after a hot summer and on mature trees. The leaves turn yellow in autumn. H 30m (100ft), S 20m (65ft). Hardy/Z 5–9.

S. microphylla
(syn. *Edwardsia chilensis*)
Kowhai

A spreading species from New Zealand and Chile, this evergreen tree bears rich yellow, pea-like flowers in mid- to late spring, followed by dangling seed pods. Train against a warm wall in frost-prone areas. H and S 8m (25ft). Borderline hardy/Z 8–10.

SORBUS
Rowan

The rowans are splendid plants for cold gardens. They are hardy and provide a valuable food source of berries for birds in winter. Attractive flowers and outstanding autumn colour add to their appeal.
Cultivation Grow in any well-drained soil in sun or light shade. Most rowans tolerate winds and urban pollution.

S. aria
Whitebeam

A large number of cultivars have been developed from this European species. 'Lutescens' has a more conical habit than the species and is thus better suited to small gardens. The leaves are covered in creamy-white hairs and are particularly brilliant as they emerge in spring. The heads of white flowers that appear in late spring are followed by dark red berries. H 10m (33ft), S 8m (25ft). Hardy/Z 6–8.

Sorbus aria 'Lutescens'

Sorbus mougeotii

S. aucuparia
Mountain ash, rowan

The species, which is a conical to rounded tree with good autumn colour, is found in Europe and Asia. 'Sheerwater Seedling' is a narrowly upright selection with white flowers in spring followed by orange berries. The leaves turn red or yellow in autumn. H 10m (33ft), S 5m (16ft). Hardy/Z 4–7.

S. cashmiriana
Kashmir rowan

Native to the western Himalayas, this is a light, airy tree with finely toothed greyish-green leaves. The pink-flushed flowers are followed by round white berries, which remain on the tree after the leaves have fallen. H 4m (13ft), S 3m (10ft). Hardy/Z 5–7.

S. commixta

This compact tree, from Korea and Japan, is generally grown in the form 'Embley', which fruits

Sorbus cashmiriana

Sorbus scalaris

rather more freely. The white spring flowers are followed by an abundance of brilliant orange-red berries at the same time as the leaves turn red. H 10m (33ft), S 7m (23ft). Hardy/Z 6–8.

S. 'Joseph Rock'

This upright hybrid has white flowers in spring followed by bright yellow fruits in autumn as the leaves colour brilliant red. This is the best yellow-fruited variety, but is susceptible to fireblight. H 10m (33ft), S 7m (23ft). Hardy/Z 7–8.

S. mougeotii

This unusual small tree or shrub is native to mountainous regions of northern Europe. The broad leaves have greyish hairs on their undersides. The fruits, sometimes lightly speckled, turn red in autumn. H 4m (13ft), S 3m (10ft). Hardy/Z 6–7.

S. 'Pearly King'

The glossy dark green foliage of this spreading hybrid colours yellow or red in autumn. White flowers in spring are followed by pinkish berries. H and S 6m (20ft). Hardy/Z 6–8.

S. sargentiana
Sargent's rowan

Native to south-western China, this rowan is one of the most outstanding members of the genus. The large, crimson, sticky leaf buds make a strong statement in late winter, emerging as matt green, feathery leaves that turn brilliant orange-red in autumn. Masses of red berries develop from the clusters of white spring flowers. H and S 10m (33ft). Hardy/Z 7–8.

Sorbus thibetica 'John Mitchell'

S. scalaris
(syn. *S. aucuparia* var. *pluripinnata*)
Ladder-leaf rowan
This Chinese species makes a spreading tree or large shrub, with glossy green leaflets that turn red and purple before they fall in autumn. The white flowers, which appear in late spring to early summer, are followed by red berries. H and S to 10m (33ft). Hardy/Z 6–8.

S. thibetica 'John Mitchell'
(syn. *S. aria* 'Mitchellii')
A notable selection of a Chinese species, this has leaves that are covered with white hairs on their undersides in spring, making a brilliant effect in the wind. They turn yellow in autumn, when the green berries ripen to red. H 20m (65ft), S 3m (10ft). Hardy/Z 5–7.

S. vilmorinii
Vilmorin's rowan
An outstanding specimen for a small garden, this tree is native to south-western China. Arching branches carry glossy green, fern-like leaves, which turn red and purple in autumn. The white flowers, produced in late spring to early summer, are succeeded by berries that are initially red but turn to white flushed with pink as winter advances. H and S 5m (16ft). Hardy/Z 6–8.

STYRAX
These graceful trees are delightful, but the cultivation requirements restrict their use to woodland gardens.
Cultivation These trees need fertile, well-drained, humus-rich, lime-free soil in light shade with shelter from wind and late frosts.

Sorbus vilmorinii

S. japonicus
Japanese snowbell
An elegant species from China, Korea and Japan, this bears fragrant, bell-shaped white flowers in summer. The leaves turn yellow or red in autumn. H 10m (33ft), S 8m (25ft). Hardy/Z 6–8.
'Pink Chimes', with pink flowers with yellow stamens, is rare and worth looking out for. H 9m (30ft), S 7m (23ft).

S. obassia
Fragrant snowbell
The species, from China, Korea and Japan, has bell-shaped white flowers in summer amid dark green leaves that turn yellow in autumn. H 12m (40ft), S 7m (23ft). Hardy/Z 6–9.

TILIA
Lime, linden
Avenues of these long-lived trees are often a feature of stately homes and they were also commonly planted in town squares. Although the scent of the inconspicuous flowers is incomparable, their suckering habit made them unpopular for a while. The following selections

are improvements that make excellent garden plants. Pollard or pleach them to restrict their size, albeit at the expense of the flowers.
Cultivation Grow lime trees in any moderately fertile, well-drained soil (preferably alkaline), in sun or light shade.

T. cordata
Small-leaved lime
The upright European species flowers in midsummer, and the heart-shaped leaves turn yellow in autumn. H 25m (80ft), S 15m (50ft). Hardy/Z 4–8.
'Winter Orange' is a desirable selection with golden-orange young stems that are a feature in winter. Cut back hard for the best winter display. H 25m (80ft), S 15m (50ft) (unpollarded).

T. × europea
(syn. *T. intermedia*, *T. × vulgaris*)
Common lime
This long-lived and vigorous tree is a hybrid of *T. cordata* (small-leaved lime) and *T. platyphyllos* (large-leaved lime) and is too large for most gardens. It has dark green leaves and, in midsummer, clusters of pale yellow flowers. H 35m (120ft), S 15m (50ft). Hardy/Z 4–7. **'Wratislaviensis'** is a more modest size, but its distinction is obvious only at

maturity, when the bright yellow young leaves contrast vividly with the older green ones, creating a spectacular golden halo effect. H 20m (65ft), S 12m (40ft). Hardy/Z 5.

TRACHYCARPUS
Chusan palm, windmill palm
The hardiest of all palm trees, this remarkably tough evergreen makes an exotic-looking specimen.
Cultivation These palms will grow in any well-drained soil in sun or light dappled shade. It is important to provide shelter from strong winds.

T. fortunei
(syn. *Chamaerops excelsa* of gardens)
This evergreen is the only palm hardy enough to be grown outside in northern Europe. Its exact origins are unknown, but it is widely naturalized in China and Japan. It is grown for its stiff, pleated, fan-like leaves and, on mature specimens, its fibrous bark. It needs a position sheltered from cold winds, and young plants should be protected from the worst winter weather with horticultural fleece. In favourable situations it can grow larger than the dimensions indicated. H 4m (13ft), S 2.5m (8ft). Borderline hardy/Z 8–10.

Trachycarpus fortunei

Conifers

The backbone of the garden, conifers are a diverse group of plants ranging from mighty giants such as the redwoods to dwarfs suitable for rock and scree gardens, troughs and window boxes. Mainly evergreen, tough and hardy, they give year-round pleasure, providing backdrops to the transient flowers of summer and coming into their own in autumn and winter as their firm outlines begin to dominate the scene. Conifers embrace a wide range of colours, from blue-grey through many shades of green to vivid golden yellow.

This collection of conifers indicates something of the variety of textures and forms to be found in this fascinating plant group.

Conifers for your garden

Conifers are a fascinating group of plants. Within the plant kingdom, they belong to a division called gymnosperms – plants that produce naked seed. The word conifer itself means "cone-bearing". Other gymnosperms include palms and cycads. Conifers are assumed to be "lower" or more primitive plants than the angiosperms (all flowering plants), which produce covered seed.

Conifers do not flower in the conventional sense. In spring, male and female cones, not necessarily conspicuous at this stage, appear together with new shoots and leaves. Male and female cones can be borne on separate plants (such species are described botanically as dioecious) or on the same plant (monoecious). The cones are either held erect on the branches or hang down; in many cases, the female cones are a conspicuous and decorative feature. The males ripen and shed their pollen grains then wither and drop. The pollen adheres to the sticky surface of the female cone's ovule (the structure on which fertilization takes place). The female cone develops as a woody structure, whose scales part to release the ripe seed, between a few months to two and a half years after pollination, depending on the species. Conifer seed usually has a papery "wing" attached to it and is wind-borne.

A few conifer genera, however, generally assumed to be younger in evolutionary terms for this reason, have fleshy berries instead of cones, notably yew (*Taxus*), juniper (*Juniperus*) and the nutmeg yew (*Torreya*). Seed dispersal is through the gut of whatever animal feeds on the berries. Included here is the maidenhair tree (*Ginkgo biloba*), not strictly a conifer, but the sole survivor of a prehistoric division of plants.

Dwarf conifers planted close will gradually merge with one another to create a living sculpture. A spiky phormium provides strong contrast.

What distinguishes conifers from other plants in most people's eyes are the leaves, which are usually needle-like (botanically, linear or acicular) or scale-like. Most are stiff and hard and have a waxy surface that stops water evaporating – essential to the survival of the plant in freezing conditions. The needles are usually mid- to dark green, but some are yellowish and others have a glaucous bloom that makes them appear blue (extreme cold usually intensifies the blue). The leaves can be carried in two ranks opposite each other on the stem in a comb-like arrangement; alternative arrangements include whorls (three or more arising from a single point), spirals or loose bundles. Spruces (*Picea*) have leaves that are set singly, but densely; some species have decidedly bristly branches.

Most conifers grow strongly upright, naturally forming tall, slim obelisks or cone shapes, good examples being the Serbian spruce (*Picea omorika*) and the Japanese cedar

(*Cryptomeria japonica*). A few, such as the Kashmir cypress (*Cupressus torulosa* 'Cashmeriana'), have pendulous, "weeping" branches. Many, such as the Scots pine (*Pinus sylvestris*), become spreading with age, developing a characteristic broad crown. A few conifers, however, are prostrate plants that hug the ground. Some dwarf forms make dense mounds or cone shapes.

Many conifers are resinous and have sticky, aromatic stems. Though some are so well-clothed with foliage that the central trunk is barely visible, if at all, others shed their lower branches as they mature. This can reveal striking bark. The black pine (*Pinus jeffreyi*), for instance, has black bark that is deeply fissured (split) and greyish shoots.

Changes in the names given to conifers down the years have resulted in some potential confusion. Certain common names have remained in use in spite of revisions to the botanical name. Not all conifers commonly referred to as cedars belong to the genus *Cedrus*: botanically, the Japanese cedar is *Cryptomeria japonica*, and the white cedar *Thuja occidentalis*. The swamp cypress belongs to the genus *Taxodium*, not *Cupressus*. Nor are all firs *Abies*: some belong to *Pseudotsuga*.

Conifers in the garden

These plants are – or can be – a mainstay of the garden, providing solid masses of colour (in rather subdued tones it is true) throughout the year. They earn their keep as a backdrop to showier but transitory spring- and summer-flowering plants, but come into their own when the earth is bare in winter and their shapes, textures and colours dominate. With heights ranging from 1m (3ft) or less for a dwarf conifer such as *Picea pungens* 'Globosa' to the 90m (300ft) of the giant redwood, there is a conifer for every garden. When choosing a small conifer, however, make sure that dwarf really does mean dwarf. Some varieties sold as dwarfs are actually better described as slow-growing: they stay reasonably compact for a number of years, but eventually make huge trees, and are a viable option only provided that you are prepared to discard them once they outgrow their allotted space.

Some of the bigger conifers make dramatic specimens provided there is adequate room for them. Many of the cedars (*Cedrus*) are excellent for this purpose, as also are the spruces (*Picea*) and cryptomerias. For a deciduous tree, the maidenhair tree (*Ginkgo biloba*) would take some beating, with its unique fanlike leaves that turn butter yellow in autumn, as well as its fissured bark.

Dwarf conifers planted close together will grow into each other, like a living sculpture, besides making excellent ground cover. Some

Conifers and heathers are a classic combination, and can provide welcome colour during the coldest months of the year.

form dense mats, particularly the prostrate junipers (*Juniperus*). In such plantings, they are often combined with heathers, a combination that should not be dismissed, despite its ubiquity: subtle effects can be achieved through a judicious mix of foliage and flower colours. Dwarf conifers are also excellent in rock gardens, providing height and structure among mat-forming

alpines, and are also suitable for troughs and containers, either with other dwarf plants or on their own.

Certain conifers, such as yew (*Taxus*), *Thuja* and false cypress (× *Cupressocyparis*), make excellent hedging plants that provide thick, impenetrable screens. The deciduous larch (*Larix*), however, makes a very effective windbreak, filtering the wind when the branches are bare.

Dramatically lit by the winter sun, this group of conifers exhibit a great variety of subtle colours at a time when the showier plants have finished their display.

Abies amabilis 'Spreading Star'

Abies balsamea 'Nana'

Abies grandis

Abies koreana

ABIES
Silver fir

These trees are found in Europe, North Africa, Asia and North America. Most grow too large for the average garden, but there are some dwarf and slow-growing forms. *A. koreana* is very popular, and there are compact forms of that which can be planted in borders and rock gardens. Most silver firs are conical.
Cultivation Silver firs will grow in most fertile soils, but not in shallow chalk or excessively dry soil. They like a reasonably open situation as long as it is not exposed to harsh winds.

A. amabilis
Pacific silver fir, beautiful fir

The species is not widely grown, but the selection '**Spreading Star**' makes excellent ground cover, as its name implies. The glossy dark green needles smell of oranges when they are crushed, and the cones are deep purple. H 50cm (20in), S to 5m (16ft). Hardy/Z 6–8.

A. balsamea
Balsam fir, balm of Gilead

Although this, too, is unfamiliar in gardens, it has a number of notable cultivars. All are hardy/Z 4–7. Those classified as **Hudsonia Group** are dwarf trees, usually compact and rounded in form, although there is some variation. H to 60cm (2ft), S 1m (3ft). '**Nana**', a good rock garden conifer, makes a dome-shaped

bush, which is tolerant of some shade. The aromatic, shiny green, needle-like leaves, shorter than those on the species, are arranged in two ranks on the stems; the cones are purplish-blue. H and S 1m (3ft).

A. cephalonica
Greek fir

This rare tree is, at 30m (100ft) in height, unsuitable for most gardens, but the selection '**Meyer's Dwarf**' (syn. 'Nana') is more manageable, forming a low, spreading, flat-topped, shade-tolerant mound that is good in a rock garden. The needle-like leaves are glossy green and are shorter than on the species; the cones are greenish-brown and resinous. H 50cm (20in), S 1.5m (5ft) or more. Hardy/Z 6–8.

A. forrestii
Forrest fir

This medium-sized to large conifer is from Yunnan, China, and it forms a narrow, cone-

shaped tree. The needles, carried in a comb-like arrangement, are dark green above and silvery white beneath; the cones are violet blue. This is a quick-growing tree, but it can be unreliable in areas where prolonged cold spells occur. H 10–20m (33–65ft), S 3–6m (10–20ft). Hardy/Z 7.

A. grandis
Giant fir, grand fir

Native to western North America, this is one of the most majestic of the species, making a tall, slim, cone-shaped tree. The needle-like leaves smell of oranges when they are crushed; the cones ripen from green to reddish brown. Vigorous and quick-growing, this makes a handsome specimen tree. H to 80m (270ft), S to 8m (25ft). Hardy/Z 7–9.

A. koreana
Korean fir

This is one of the most attractive of the silver firs, notably for its impressive violet cones that age to brown, which are produced even by young specimens. The needles are dark green with white undersides. Use it as a specimen tree or in mixed planting; it associates well with a wide range of garden plants. H 10m (33ft), S 6m (20ft). Hardy/Z 6–8.

A. procera
(syn. *A. nobilis*)
Noble fir

From the western United States, this forms a cone-shaped tree, which matures to a broader, irregular obelisk. The greyish-green needles, sometimes with a bluish cast, are arranged in

Abies cephalonica 'Meyer's Dwarf'

Abies procera

two ranks. Mature trees have silvery-grey, fissured bark; the cones are green. The noble fir makes an attractive specimen, particularly when young; it is sometimes used as a Christmas tree. It is wind-tolerant and reliable at high altitudes. H to 45m (150ft), S to 9m (30ft). Hardy/Z 6–8.

ARAUCARIA

The southern hemisphere is the main home of these striking trees, which have, triangular leaves that are larger than those of most conifers. Only *A. araucana* is in general cultivation, and mature specimens are often found in the gardens of Victorian houses, to which they bring an exotic flavour. Other species are well worth considering for a warm climate or as conservatory (porch) plants.
Cultivation Araucarias do well in a fertile soil in a sunny but sheltered position.

A. araucana
(syn. *A. imbricata*)
Chile pine, monkey-puzzle-tree
This tree, which comes originally from Chile and Argentina, is slow growing at first but accelerates as it approaches maturity. It develops a broad, dome shaped crown on a tall trunk. The female trees have impressive spiky cones, almost pineapple-like in appearance: large and rounded, they take up to three years to ripen. H 25m (80ft), S 10m (33ft). Hardy/Z 7–10.

A. heterophylla
(syn. *A. excelsa*)
Norfolk Island pine
A good conservatory (porch) plant when young, this will eventually outgrow most conservatories. It has an appealing tiered habit and fan-like branches. It occasionally serves as a Christmas tree in Latin countries. H to 45m (150ft), S 8m (25ft). Tender/Z 9–10.

CALOCEDRUS
Incense cedar
Incense cedars are a small genus of large conifers from the Far East and parts of western North America. Only the species described is widely grown.

Cultivation Any good soil in sun or light shade is suitable, but avoid exposed positions.

C. decurrens
(syn. *Heyderia decurrens, Libocedrus decurrens*)
Native to the western United States, this tree tends to vary in habit in gardens. In Europe it forms a tall, elegant spire, whereas specimens in the wild are often more spreading, since the habit influenced by climatic differences. The needles are glossy dark green. The maroon bark is fissured and flakes off, and the cones are yellowish-brown, aging to red-brown. It is resistant to honey fungus. H 30m (100ft) or more, S 6m (20ft) or more. Hardy/Z 6–9.

CEDRUS
Cedar
A small genus, but perhaps containing the most magnificent of all conifers when mature. They are generally suitable only for large gardens but are worth considering if you are prepared to remove them once they start to get too large. They make ideal lawn specimens.
Cultivation Cedars are tolerant of most soils, including chalk (alkaline), and do best in a sunny open site.

C. atlantica
Atlas cedar
Originating from the Atlas Mountains in North Africa, this species is less common in gardens than some of the following selections. All are hardy/Z 7–9. 'Aurea' has bright, golden-yellow leaves. H 40m (130ft), S 10m (33ft). *C. atlantica* f. *glauca* (blue Atlas cedar) is one of the most handsome forms. Initially cone-shaped, it develops a more spreading crown. The needles, white when young but becoming bright glaucous blue, are arranged in clusters; the cones are light green. H 40m (130ft), S to 10m (33ft). Plants in cultivation are normally sold under the name Glauca Group (indicating that they may vary). 'Glauca Pendula', also glaucous blue, has an arching leader and pendulous branches,

Cedrus atlantica 'Aurea'

Cedrus atlantica f. *glauca*

and it develops as a tent-like structure. It can be kept small by cutting back the central leader, which will persuade the horizontal branches to spread more widely (they may need support as a result). H and S to 15m (50ft), more or less.

C. deodara
Deodar cedar
This graceful, though potentially large, conifer originating from the Himalayas has a weeping habit. H 40m (130ft), S 10m (33ft). Hardy/Z 7–9. The more modestly sized 'Aurea' is an improvement, having the same broadly conical outline, with weeping branches,

but with the added distinction of bright yellow needles. A slow-growing tree, it is a good choice for a specimen in a small garden. H 5m (16ft), S 2.5m (8ft).

C. libani
Cedar of Lebanon
A tree for a stately home, this species originates from the near Middle East. It forms a conical tree that spreads with age, making a dramatic outline. The needle-like leaves are dark greyish-green; the cones are greyish-brown. Heavy snowfalls can cause problems to mature specimens, which may need surgery. H and S to 30m (100ft). Hardy/Z 7–9.

Cedrus atlantica 'Glauca Pendula'

Chamaecyparis lawsoniana 'Aurea Densa'

CHAMAECYPARIS
False cypress

This is a useful genus, from East
Asia and North America, with a
huge range of cultivars. There is a
cypress for every garden, and the
range includes giant forest trees
as well as smaller forms that can
be used as specimen trees, for
hedging and as dwarf plants for
the rock or scree garden.
Cultivation The soil should ideally
be neutral to acid, but cypresses
tolerate chalk. An open, sunny
site is best.

C. lawsoniana
(syn. *Cupressus lawsoniana*)
Lawson cypress
Although this conical tree, native
to North America, is too large for
most gardens, it has given rise to
a bewildering number of cultivars
of widely diverging habits. All are
hardy/Z 6–9. Among the best
dwarfs is **'Aurea Densa'**, which
is ultimately rounded and one of
the outstanding golden-leaved
cultivars. H 2m (6ft), S to 1m
(3ft). **'Bleu Nantais'** is another
good blue-green, slow-growing,
cone-shaped, dwarf cultivar.
H and S to 1.5m (5ft). Both
these have needle-like leaves that
become scale-like. Taller varieties
include the conical **'Ellwoodii'**,
which is one of the most popular
grey-green varieties. H 3m (10ft).

Chamaecyparis obtusa 'Nana Gracilis'

'Fletcheri' forms a dense, greyish-
green column. H to 12m (40ft).
The weeping **'Pembury Blue'** has
striking bluish-grey foliage. H to
15m (50ft).

C. obtusa
(syn. *Cupressus obtusa*)
Hinoki cypress
This Japanese species is less tolerant of lime than some species,
and it is not widely planted, yield-
ing to its many attractive cultivars.
All are hardy/Z 4–8. **'Crippsii'**
(syn. 'Crippsii Aurea') is a rich
gold when grown in full sun,

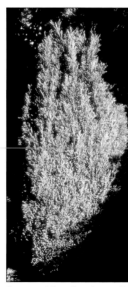

Chamaecyparis lawsoniana 'Bleu Nantais'

making a fine specimen. H 15m
(50ft), S 8m (25ft). **'Nana
Gracilis'** is a dwarf, forming a
rough pyramid. The scale-like,
glossy green leaves are held in
plates. H and S 2m (6ft) or more.

C. pisifera
(syn. *Cupressus pisifera*)
Sawara cypress
Seldom found in cultivation,
this Japanese species has given
rise to a number of useful
cultivars, all of which are hardy/
Z 5–8. **'Boulevard'** is a popular
selection, which will thrive in
moist soil, and has bright silver-
blue, feathery leaves. H 10m
(33ft), S 4m (12ft). **'Filifera
Aurea'** is a delightful conifer, with
elegant, drooping, whippy branches.
It is a good choice for a small plot
because it is too slow-growing to
pose a problem in most gardens,
despite its eventual height.
H 12m (40ft), S 5m (15ft).

CRYPTOMERIA
Japanese cedar

Despite the common name, this
monotypic genus (there is only
one species) is found in China
as well as Japan, albeit in two
distinct forms. Unusually among
the conifers, Japanese cedars will
tolerate pruning and can even be
coppiced or trained. They look
good in a Japanese-style garden,
especially when they are grown to
develop a gnarled trunk. Japanese
cedars are among the most
beautiful of all conifers.
Cultivation These trees will grow
in any well-drained, preferably
fertile, soil in sun or light shade.

C. japonica
The species can reach a height
of 25m (80ft) and is roughly
columnar in shape. There are a
huge number of cultivars available,
suitable either as specimens or
for use in rock gardens. All are
hardy/Z 6–9. **'Bandai-Sugi'** is a
slow-growing rounded dwarf
form with blue-green foliage that
bronzes well in cold winters. H
and S 2m (6ft). The intriguing
'Cristata' (syn. 'Sekka-sugi') has
leaves that are curiously fused
together, so that they resemble
coral. H 8m (25ft), S 5m (15ft).
'Elegans' is potentially large and

Cryptomeria japonica

will form a broad obelisk; the
trunk is often attractively curved.
The wedge-shaped leaves are soft
and bluish-green when young,
turning a rich, glowing bronze in
autumn. Plants sold as **Elegans
Group** may vary. H 20m (65ft),
S 6m (20ft). **'Lobbii'** makes a
handsome specimen in a large
garden, forming a tall, slender,
conical tree. The needle-like leaves
are arranged in spirals. On mature
specimens the thick, fibrous bark
peels away. The cones age to
brown. H 25m (80ft) or more,
S to 6m (20ft).

Cryptomeria japonica 'Lobbii'

× *Cupressocyparis leylandii*
'Golconda'

× *Cupressocyparis leylandii*
'Leighton Green'

smooth, reddish-purple and flaking; it thickens and turns to greyish-brown on older trees. The scale-like leaves are glaucous bluish-grey and aromatic; the cones are dark brown. H to 15m (50ft), S to 5m (15ft). Hardy/ Z 7–9.

C. macrocarpa
Monterey cypress
From Monterey Bay, California, this was once widely used for hedging, but it has largely been superseded by × *Cupressocyparis leylandii*. Excellent cultivars have been developed from the species, however. Both those listed here are borderline hardy/Z 7–10. **'Donard Gold'** forms an elegant obelisk that gradually becomes conical. The bright yellowish-green leaves are aromatic when crushed; the cones are rounded and maroon- to dark-brown. H to 30m (100ft), S to 12m (40ft). **'Goldcrest'** is a highly desirable smaller version. H 5m (16ft), S 2.5m (8ft).

GINKGO
Maidenhair tree
This deciduous tree is a living fossil, the sole survivor of a family of trees from 200 million years ago, once serving as a food source for dinosaurs during the Mesozoic era.
Cultivation Ginkgos are easy to grow in any moderately fertile soil in sun. They are also tolerant of urban pollution.

G. biloba
This long-lived, ornamental deciduous tree makes an eye-catching specimen. Initially upright in habit, it becomes more spreading on maturity. Its distinction lies in its unique, fan-shaped, light green leaves, which turn butter yellow before falling in autumn. The fruits (not cones) are plum-like. H to 30m (100ft), S to 8m (25ft). Hardy/Z 5–9. The selection **'Fastigiata'** (sentinel ginkgo) is narrower and more column-like. H 30m (100ft), S 5m (16ft).

× CUPRESSOCYPARIS
The chief value of this much maligned hybrid genus between *Chamaecyparis nootkatensis* and *Cupressus macrocarpa* lies in the trees' speed of growth. They are often planted as hedging where a pollution-resistant screen is needed quickly, and they do in fact make a splendid, tough, tight hedge, but only if cut regularly. Allowed to grow freely, they can soon get out of hand.
Cultivation Grow in any well-drained soil in sun or light shade.

× Cupressocyparis leylandii
Leyland cypress
This is the hybrid most common-ly sold as hedging, but it has a number of named varieties that can fulfil other purposes. All are hardy/Z 6–9. **'Golconda'**, one of the most decorative, forms a narrow cone shape. The scale-like leaves, carried in flattened sprays, are brilliant golden yellow; the cones are rounded. H to 35m (120ft), S to 5m (16ft), but tolerant of clipping. **'Leighton Green'** develops as a tall, narrow, cone-shaped tree with bright green foliage. Although it is no less

suitable for hedging than other cultivars, it is perhaps best as a specimen because it produces a stronger central leader than the other cultivars and thus makes a slimmer, more elegant tree. The cones are freely produced. H to 35m (120ft), S to 5m (16ft).

CUPRESSUS
Cypress
The characteristic tree of the Mediterranean, these are among the stateliest of conifers. They are not always easy to grow away from their native habitat, but they can be used as fine specimens or for hedging. They resent transplanting, so always look for young specimens rather than mature trees. The broadly similar *Chamaecyparis* is more reliable.
Cultivation Grow in any fertile, well-drained soil in full sun.

Cupressus arizonica var. glabra
(syn. C. glabra)
Smooth cypress
From the south-west United States, this is a good specimen where space in a garden is limited. It forms a regular cone shape. On young specimens the bark is

Cupressus arizonica var. *glabra*

Cupressus macrocarpa 'Donard Gold'

Juniperus chinensis 'Aurea'

JUNIPERUS
Juniper

Junipers are usually represented in gardens by the cultivars and hybrids rather than by the species. Many are rock garden plants, while others look good grouped in island beds. They also do well in troughs and containers. On female plants, berry-like fruits develop and are used in the production of gin or to flavour game dishes.
Cultivation Any well-drained soil in sun or light shade is suitable. Junipers tolerate pruning.

J. chinensis
Chinese juniper

The species is not notable in itself, but has given rise to many attractive cultivars. **'Aurea'** (Young's golden juniper), a slow-growing male selection that forms a narrow obelisk, has aromatic, dull golden-yellow leaves, which are wedge-shaped initially, but become scale-like as they mature. Many cones appear in spring, and the tree produces its best colour in sun. H to 20m (65ft), S to 6m (20ft). Hardy/Z 5–9.

J. communis
Common juniper

This variable species is found throughout the northern hemisphere. Selections include **'Hibernica'** (Irish juniper), which makes a distinctive, narrow cone-shape, the foliage having a bluish-green cast; the berries, initially green, ripen to black over three years. H 3–5m (10–15ft), S 30cm (1ft). Hardy/Z 3–7.

J. 'Grey Owl'
(syn. *J. virginiana* 'Grey Owl')

This is a splendid, spreading conifer, with silver-grey leaves and violet berries. H 3m (10ft), S 4m (13ft). Hardy/Z 3–9.

J. horizontalis
Creeping juniper

A ground-hugging conifer from North America, the species forms a mat of greyish-green leaves, which are needle-like when young, becoming scale-like with age, with dark blue berries. H to 30cm (1ft), S 2m (6ft) or more. Hardy/Z 3–9. There are many attractive cultivars, all suitable for ground cover. **'Blue Chip'** (syn. 'Blue Moon') is glaucous blue. H 50cm (20in), S 3m (10ft). **'Douglasii'** is bluish-green, turning rich purple in autumn. H 30cm (1ft), S 3m (10ft). **'Golden Carpet'** is bright yellowish-green. H 30cm (1ft), spread 3m (10ft).

Juniperus × pfitzeriana
(syn. *J. × media*)

This dwarf conifer is a hybrid probabl between *J. chinensis* and

Juniperus communis 'Hibernica'

J. sabina (the hybrid is thought to occur wild in Inner Mongolia). The cultivars listed are hardy/Z 4–9. **'Pfitzeriana Glauca'** forms a spreading, flat-topped bush clothed in glaucous blue to silver foliage. The berries are dark purple initially, developing a paler bloom as they ripen. The natural habit develops best if the plant is given sufficient space. H 1m (3ft), S 2m (6ft). **'Sulphur Spray'**, which has yellowish-green

Juniperus horizontalis

foliage, can become table-like on maturity. The dark purple berries develop a bluish bloom as they ripen. This is one of several plants in this hybrid group that are more or less indistinguishable from one another, including the widely grown **'Pfitzeriana Aurea'**. H 1m (3ft), S 2m (6ft).

LARIX
Larch

A genus of deciduous conifers with often brilliant autumn colour. Larches are usually grown as forestry trees but are useful for windbreaks.
Cultivation Grow in any moist garden soil in an open situation.

L. decidua
European larch

As the common name implies, this is a European species, which develops a spreading crown with age. The pale green leaves turn red and yellow before falling in autumn. H to 30m (100ft), S to 6m (20ft). Hardy/Z 3–6.

L. kaempferi
Japanese larch

Largely similar to *L. decidua*, this has purplish-red shoots that are conspicuous in winter, making it more garden-worthy. Both have a number of cultivars. H 30m (100ft) or more, S to 6m (20ft). Hardy/Z 5–7.

METASEQUOIA
Dawn redwood

The genus consists of a single species, one of the few deciduous conifers. It is a remarkable tree, known until 1941 only from fossilised remains. It is best by water, appreciating damp conditions, but is also tolerant of drier soils. It can be used as a specimen in a lawn.
Cultivation Fertile, preferably moist soil, in sun or light shade, suits the dawn redwood. On drier soils it is usually less vigorous.

M. glyptostroboides

Native to China, this rapidly grows into a narrow cone-shaped, almost columnar tree. The feathery leaves are light green in spring, turning pink, red, then brown in autumn, the best colour

Metasequoia glyptostroboides

being produced on mature trees. H to 40m (130ft), S to 5m (16ft). Hardy/Z 5–10.

PICEA
Spruce
Found throughout the northern hemisphere, spruces are widely planted as Christmas trees, *P. abies* being the usual choice. There is a wide range of garden varieties, some with grey, yellow or blue foliage. Most are symmetrical in shape, and there are many dwarf forms suitable for rock gardens.
Cultivation Neutral to acid, slightly moist soil is the ideal, in an open site. Late frosts can cause damage.

Picea abies 'Gregoryana'

P. abies
Christmas tree, Norway spruce
The species, which is native to Scandinavia, is a conical tree and the traditional choice for Christmas trees in Europe. H 40m (130ft), S 6m (20ft). Hardy/Z 3–8. **'Gregoryana'** is an attractive dwarf selection that makes an impenetrable mound of dark green foliage. It is one of the most compact of all dwarf conifers. H and S 60cm (2ft).

P. glauca
White spruce
Although the species, which comes from North America, is rarely grown in gardens, it is represented in cultivation by its many cultivars. Those listed here are hardy/Z 3–6. *P. glauca* var. *albertiana* **'Conica'** is a dwarf selection of a naturally occurring variant from the Canadian Rocky Mountains. As its name suggests, it makes a tight cone of bluish-green, seldom bearing cones. H to 4m (13ft), S 2m (6ft). The slow-growing **'Alberta Globe'** is another, even smaller clone, also bluish-green but making a dome. H and S 1m (3ft).

P. omorika
Serbian spruce
This large conifer comes from Bosnia and Serbia. Initially narrowly conical, it matures to a broad obelisk. The dark green foliage sometimes has a bluish cast; the bark cracks in squares on maturity. The cones are purple, ripening to brown. It tolerates alkaline soils and urban pollution. H 20m (65ft), S to 3m (10ft). Hardy/Z 5–8.

P. pungens
Colorado spruce
Originating in the United States, the species is the parent of many notable garden plants. All are hardy/Z 3–8. **'Globosa'** forms a dome or mound shape and has bristle-like, glaucous green foliage, arranged radially. H and S 1m (3ft). **'Montgomery'** is silver-blue, making a broad-based cone. Slow-growing, it should be among the first choices for a specimen tree in a small garden. H 1.5m (5ft), S 1m (3ft).

Picea pungens 'Globosa'

PINUS
Pine
Most of the straight species are unsuitable as garden plants, magnificent though they are, since they are nearly all too large for the average plot. Selection by nurserymen has produced a number of useful clones that are more manageable, however. The needles, which are sometimes quite long, are held in characteristic bundles. Dwarf pines associate well with heathers in a border display.
Cultivation Any well-drained soil in sun is suitable, but pines are not tolerant of pollution.

P. mugo
Dwarf mountain pine
This useful conifer from central Europe is less widely grown than its many garden-worthy clones, many of them dwarf and ideal for

Picea pungens 'Montgomery'

Pinus mugo 'Corley's Mat'

a rock garden. H to 3.5m (11ft), S to 5m (16ft). Hardy/Z 3–7. **'Corley's Mat'**, as its name suggests, makes a prostrate, spreading carpet. H 1m (3ft), S 2m (6ft). The slow-growing **'Mops'** is almost spherical. Resinous brown buds are borne in winter. H and S 1m (3ft).

P. sylvestris subsp. scotica
Scots pine
A majestic conifer, this is widely distributed throughout northern Europe and eastern Asia. It grows as a cone-shape but develops a characteristic spreading crown with age. A distinguishing feature is its grey-green, twisted needles. An exceptionally hardy conifer, it is effective when planted in stands in exposed sites. H to 30m (100ft), S to 9m (30ft). Hardy/Z 3–7.

Pinus sylvestris subsp. scotica

Sequoia sempervirens 'Adpressa'

SEQUOIA
Californian redwood

The single member of this genus is one of the tallest and oldest living things on the planet, with specimens dating back 2000 years and achieving heights of more than 100m (325ft). There are a few more modest selections, but even these need space.
Cultivation Well-drained, fertile soil is needed, in sun or light dappled shade. Growth is slower in shade.

S. sempervirens

This is a gigantic conifer from coastal California and Oregon. The smaller **'Adpressa'** develops a broadly conical habit, with horizontal upper branches and lower ones that sweep down to the ground. The foliage is creamy white at first, aging to grey-green. This selection is slow growing and may with time exceed the dimensions given here; it does best in a damp climate. H 9m (30ft) or more, S to 6m (20ft). Hardy/Z 7–9.

SEQUOIADENDRON
Giant redwood, big tree, Sierra redwood, wellingtonia

A close relative of *Sequoia*, the giant redwood is also a genus of one species. Although less tall than the Californian redwood, it is the world's largest tree by mass.
Cultivation Grow in fertile, well-drained soil in a sunny, open site.

S. giganteum

Native to California, this forms a cone shape, more spreading with age; the lower branches sweep down, then curve upwards. The scale-like leaves, arranged spirally, are awl-shaped, suffused with grey and aromatic when crushed. The bark is thick and fissured. A magnificent specimen tree, although it is obviously suitable for large gardens only, it can achieve a great age. H 80m (260ft) or more, S to 10m (33ft). Hardy/Z 6–9.

Sequoiadendron giganteum

Taxodium distichum

TAXODIUM
Swamp cypress

Swamp cypresses are among the most beautiful and elegant of all conifers. Unfortunately, their eventual size rules them out for all but the largest gardens.
Cultivation These trees need reliably moist or even wet soil, ideally acid, and a shaded spot.

T. distichum
Swamp cypress, bald cypress

This large, deciduous (though sometimes semi-evergreen) conifer comes from the south-eastern United States. It forms a tall cone shape that becomes untidy as it matures. The needle-like leaves, which redden in autumn, are carried in two ranks, as on yew. Mature plants produce the best colour. Purple male cones hang down and are a feature in winter; the female cones are inconspicuous. Near water it produces special breathing roots, which look like knees emerging from the ground around the trunk. H to 40m (130ft), S to 9m (30ft). Hardy/ Z 5–10. The slender *T. distichum* var. *imbricatum* **'Nutans'** is more modest. H to 20m (70ft), S to 6m (20ft).

TAXUS
Yew

This is an extremely valuable genus of conifers for the garden, with a range of foliage colour and habit. Yew is widely used for

hedging and topiary work, since, unlike most other conifers, it tolerates pruning and even seems to thrive on it. Even mature specimens will recover well if cut back hard. A further distinction is that these conifers produce fleshy berries (usually red) rather than woody cones, helping to brighten up the winter garden. All parts of the conifer are toxic; in some areas, there are restrictions on planting, particularly where cattle are grazed.
Cultivation These tolerant conifers can be grown in any but swampy ground, in sun or shade.

T. baccata
Common yew

A long-lived conifer, this is widely found in Europe and also in North Africa and Iran. Typically, it has blackish-green leaves, carried in a comb-like arrangement on the stems; male and female flowers are produced on separate plants, with berries, each containing a single seed, following on the females. Uncut, the yew forms a broad, spreading cone shape with dense horizontal branches. H to 20m (65ft), S to 10m (33ft), if unpruned. Hardy/Z 6–7. **'Fastigiata'** (Irish yew), a female (and hence berry-producing) selection, is a familiar graveyard tree, forming an obelisk, pointed at the crown, but spreading with age. The stems are

Taxus baccata 'Fastigiata'

Taxus baccata 'Repandens'

strongly upright. It can be kept within bounds by pruning and can also be wired into a narrower, more formal shape. H to 10m (33ft), S to 6m (20ft). The selection **'Fastigiata Aureomarginata'**, also strongly upright, is a golden-foliaged female, which forms a broad obelisk. The leaves are actually dark green; only the margins are yellow. H to 5m (16ft), S to 2.5m (8ft). **'Repandens'** does not produce a strong vertical leader but forms a mat of spreading branches near ground level. It makes good ground cover and is best without extensive pruning that might affect its natural habit.

Taxus baccata 'Standishii'

H to 60cm (2ft), S to 5m (16ft). **'Standishii'** forms a slim, tightly packed column of yellowish-green, needle-like leaves carried on strongly upright stems. It is one of the most decorative of all yews and, due to its limited size, is an excellent choice for a small garden. It requires full sun and makes a good container plant. H 1.5m (5ft), S 60cm (2ft).

THUJA
Arborvitae

These excellent conifers are similar to *Chamaecyparis* and are often mistaken for them, a distinction being that *Thuja* has aromatic foliage. They are just as good for hedging. Varieties include a number of coloured foliage forms.
Cultivation Any but waterlogged soil is suitable, in full sun or light shade, although yellow forms are best in full sun.

T. occidentalis
Eastern thuja, northern white cedar

Although this species is not widely grown, it is the parent of a vast number of cultivars. **'Ericoides'** is a dwarf form, growing into a broad, sometimes rounded, obelisk. The spreading, scale-like leaves are green in summer, turning rich brown, sometimes purple, in autumn. As the name suggests, it combines well with heathers and is good in a rock garden. H and S 1.2m (4ft). Hardy/Z 3–8.

T. orientalis 'Aurea Nana'
(syn. *Platycladus orientalis* 'Aurea Nana')

This is an appealing dwarf selection of a much larger species from China and Iran. It makes an egg-shaped plant, with yellowish-green, scale-like leaves held in irregular, vertical, fan-like plates; they tinge bronze in cold weather in autumn. The cones are flagon-like and bluish-green, maturing to grey. An excellent choice for a small garden, it associates well with heathers and other yellow-leaved shrubs. H and S to 60cm (2ft). Hardy/Z 6–9. **'Sieboldii'** (syn. *Platycladus orientalis* 'Sieboldii') also makes an egg-shaped plant and holds its mid-green, aromatic leaves in similar fashion. It combines well with heathers or other low-growing conifers. H and S 2m (6ft).

T. plicata
Western red cedar

A large conifer originating from western North America, the species forms a cone-shaped tree, broadening at the crown with age. It is an excellent specimen for a large garden. The scale-like leaves are carried in two ranks on stems that hang downwards at their tips. The spread of the Western red cedar can exceed the dimensions shown because where the stems

Thuja occidentalis 'Ericoides'

trail on the ground, they can self-layer, a habit that has produced some vast specimens in the wild. It is suitable for planting as a hedge. H to 35m (120ft), S 9m (30ft) or more. Hardy/Z 6–8. The conical **'Atrovirens'** is slightly slower growing than the species. H 8m (25ft), S 2m (6ft). **'Irish Gold'** usually stays fairly dwarf. The foliage is bright yellow-green with lighter patches. H and S 2m (6ft), although it can reach a height of 20m (65ft).

Thuja orientalis 'Aurea Nana'

Thuja plicata 'Irish Gold'

Shrubs

Shrubs encompass a wide range, from tree-like plants (which can substitute for trees in small gardens) to more diminutive ones that can be used in rock gardens or as ground cover. Most are grown for their often spectacular flowers, but others have less obvious attractions — showy berries or good leaf colour in autumn, attractive winter stems, or an appealing habit. Judiciously chosen, shrubs give an air of permanence to any planting.

Shrubs are the mainstay of any garden and this large garden of trees and shrubs will virtually look after itself.

Shrubs for your garden

Shrubs are woody plants and can be evergreen or deciduous. That definition also applies to trees, but most gardeners would never confuse the two. In general, shrubs are usually compact plants with a height and spread no greater than 3m (10ft), and usually branching from the base. This habit, however, can also be observed in trees; equally there are some shrubs that can be grown with a single upright trunk and look to all intents and purposes like miniature trees. Some slow-growing plants, such as hollies (*Ilex*) and bay (*Laurus*), will be shrubby initially (and can be treated as shrubs in gardens) but will end up as trees in the fullness of time.

In the wild, shrubs are found in a huge range of habitats, from coastal areas to high altitudes, open plains to woodland: hence the need to consider carefully any plant's cultural preferences when making a choice. The different habits of growth represent a response to climate. Plants from coastal areas, for instance, tend to be tough,

Magnolias can be either be classified as trees or shrubs depending on the species. This *Magnolia × loebneri* 'Leonard Messel' in bloom is however a shrub, and here combines well with the flowers of a Camellia japonica hybrid.

stunted-looking and scrubby, the better to weather salt-laden winds, while woodland shrubs are more rangy, as they crane their necks towards the available light. You do not need to imitate nature slavishly in your garden, however, since many seem to perform well in a variety of conditions.

The shrubs grown in gardens today comprise both species and hybrids. Some genera have been extensively hybridized to produce a vast range of plants, most notably roses – dealt with in their own chapter in this section – and rhododendrons, which include dwarf plants suitable for a rock garden as well as others that end up as huge tree-like specimens. Shrubs such as *Fuchsia* and – to a lesser extent – *Hydrangea* and *Ceanothus* are other genera that have attracted the attention of hybridizers.

Shrubs in the garden

These useful plants are the backbone of many a planting, particularly in a small garden, where there is

frequently little or no space to grow trees.

A shrub border can be a low-maintenance option for a driveway, or indeed any area of the garden where there is space to be filled. A mixture of evergreens and deciduous shrubs will provide a shifting focus of interest; apart from the seasonal flowers and berries for which most shrubs are grown, variegated evergreens will provide year-round interest. Be sure to include some winter-flowering shrubs, such as *Viburnum tinus*, *Mahonia × media* and *Lonicera fragrantissima*. There are too many spring-flowering shrubs to mention, but for interest after midsummer, you could look to the hydrangeas, fuchsias, *Buddleja davidii* and *Ceratostigma willmottianum* (of modest size, but a real eye-catcher when starred with its sky blue flowers). *Parrotia persica* has vivid autumn leaf colour.

Many shrubs are utility plants and make ideal hedging material, the shrubby honeysuckle (*Lonicera nitida*)

Massed heathers need little attention, and provide weed-suppressing ground-cover besides making a sea of colour.

and privet (*Ligustrum*) both providing good dense screens. *Aucuba* and Portugal laurel (*Prunus lusitanica*) have larger, more handsome leaves, but cannot be clipped quite so tightly. Some camellias make excellent flowering hedges, and it is also possible to mix plants for an informal look appropriate to rural gardens (such hedges will also attract wildlife).

There is a whole host of shrubs suitable for planting in light woodland. If you have acid soil, a rhododendron garden can be spectacular (perhaps also including other acid lovers such as *Pieris* and camellias), but there are plenty of lime-tolerant alternatives, such as *Photinia*, if you garden on alkaline soil. On a very open, windswept site, heathers are the obvious choice.

For a specimen, choose architectural plants such as a yucca or those with spectacular flowers, such as a tree peony (provided the site is reasonably sheltered). Forms

Rhododendrons, combining well here with conifers and other evergreens, have flowers that range from small and delicate to magnificent and gloriously coloured, along with exquisite foliage.

of *Viburnum plicatum* have a striking tiered habit that is appealing even when the plant is bare in winter.

Prostrate shrubs can be used as ground cover, particularly those with stems that will root where they touch the ground. *Ceanothus*

thyrsiflorus var. *repens* would be a delight when smothered with its clear blue flowers in early summer, but is not so long-lived or as shade-tolerant as such humbler alternatives as cotoneasters and periwinkle (*Vinca*).

Some shrubs lend themselves to pruning and training, and these are ideal in a formal scheme, either to punctuate geometrically shaped borders or to line the edge of a path. Box is the classic choice for a low formal hedge, and larger specimens can be clipped to ball, cone or cube shapes. Rather faster growing is privet – a coarser plant, it is true, but of surprising elegance when trained as a standard. *Viburnum tinus* and *Prunus lusitanicus* are comparably stylish alternatives.

All of these shrubs are also excellent in containers, as are the spotted laurel (*Aucuba japonica* 'Crotonifolia') and hydrangeas. Many others will also thrive in pots, and this gives you the opportunity to grow any that would not thrive otherwise in the soil type in the open garden.

Pruning

Many woody plants benefit from pruning occasionally, but few actually need it regularly, and a good many are best with minimum intervention. You should be guided by the way the plant is performing in your garden.

If necessary, winter- and spring-flowering shrubs can be pruned immediately after flowering, which gives them ample time to produce sufficient new growth for flowering the following year. Summer-flowering shrubs (which generally flower on wood made in the current season) can be pruned in early spring. All deciduous shrubs can also be pruned in winter, often a good time, since the stems are bare then and it is easy to see what you are doing.

As a matter of routine, cut out all diseased, damaged or obviously dead wood. You should also remove entirely any plain green shoots on variegated shrubs. You can then trim the rest of the growth, but be selective. Cut out some of the older wood to the base (this is always less productive and more disease-prone than younger growth) and shorten the remaining stems, cutting weak shoots back hard, but vigorous ones only lightly. You will probably be able to leave some shoots unpruned.

In cold districts the topgrowth of some shrubs (for instance some fuchsias) will die in winter, and this should be cut back hard in spring. Certain other shrubs, notably *Buddleja davidii*, can also be cut back hard annually, though this is by no means essential.

Abelia × grandiflora

ABELIA

These evergreens are greatly valued for their graceful habit and late flowers, which last from summer to late autumn.
Cultivation Grow in any well-drained soil in full sun or light shade. In cold areas, they prefer a warm, sheltered site, ideally against a wall.

A. × grandiflora

Of garden origin, this shrub has slightly scented, white flowers from midsummer to autumn. H and S 2m (6ft). Borderline hardy/Z 6–9. **'Gold Spot'** (syn. 'Aurea', 'Gold Strike', 'Goldsport') has golden-yellow leaves. H and S 2m (6ft).

Abelia × grandiflora 'Gold Spot'

ABELIOPHYLLUM

There is only one species in the genus, and it is a real connoisseur's plant and something of a rarity in gardens. It is slow-growing, takes some years to settle down to reliable flower production and is difficult to propagate. Like wisteria, it is hardy but needs a hot spot to ripen the wood sufficiently for good flowering. Left to its own devices, it is a sprawling shrub, seen to best advantage when wall-trained. Frost can damage the flowers.
Cultivation Grow in fertile, well-drained soil in a sheltered site, ideally trained against a warm wall.

A. distichum

In late winter to early spring this deciduous Chinese species has dainty, sweetly fragrant white flowers, something like forsythia but much smaller. H and S to 1.5m (5ft). Hardy/Z 5–9.

ABUTILON
Flowering maple, Indian mallow

These elegant shrubs produce appealing lampshade-like flowers from late summer into autumn. They are sometimes trained as standards and used as dot plants in park bedding schemes. They are also good in containers, either on their own or as the central feature in a mixed planting.
Cultivation Grow in any fertile, well-drained soil in full sun in a

sheltered spot. In cold areas, wall-training is an effective way of improving their hardiness. The species described is a very lax grower, needing the support of wires or of other shrubs.

A. megapotanicum
Trailing abutilon

The evergreen or semi-evergreen species has orange-red and yellow, lantern-like flowers and maple-like leaves. H and S 2m (6ft). Borderline hardy/Z 8–9. The leaves of **'Variegatum'** are mottled with yellow. This makes a good standard.

ARTEMISIA
Wormwood

These aromatic subshrubs are ideal for mixed borders, white and grey gardens and herb gardens. They make excellent 'fillers' in rose gardens or, indeed, anywhere where you need to fill space in summer. The genus also includes a number of perennials.
Cultivation Artemisias will grow in poor, dry, well-drained soil in full sun. Prune in spring to keep plants neat.

Abutilon megapotanicum 'Variegatum'

A. abrotanum
Southernwood, lad's love, old man

This deciduous or semi-evergreen species is an effective filler in a number of situations. The aromatic, silvery-grey leaves are very finely divided. The grey-yellow flowers borne in late summer are insignificant. H 70cm (28in), S 50cm (20in). Hardy/Z 6–9.

Artemisia abrotanum

Aucuba japonica

AUCUBA

Tough, tolerant evergreens, aucubas thrive in quite deep shade and make excellent hedging. Female plants have red berries in autumn, but there are also self-fertile forms. It is easy to take them for granted, but few shrubs look so stylish in containers, which is, perhaps, the best way of growing them.
Cultivation Aucubas grow in any soil that is not waterlogged, in sun or shade.

A. japonica
Spotted laurel
To all intents and purposes, this is the only species grown, generally in one of its variegated

Ballota pseudodictamnus

forms. **'Crotonifolia'** (female) is the best, with leaves generously mottled with yellow. H and S 2m (6ft). The plain green *A. japonica* f. *longifolia* (female) is worth looking out for, however and has elegant, narrow, glossy leaves with wavy edges. H and S 2m (6ft). Hardy/Z 7–10.

BALLOTA

These often sub-shrubby plants are excellent in a Mediterranean-style garden or as an edging to a border, where they are a good foil to more flamboyant plants. They look their best in hot, dry conditions and revel in the reflected heat of a gravel garden.
Cultivation Grow in sharply drained soil in full sun.

B. pseudodictamnus
This woolly-leaved species is of greatest interest when it is in flower in summer. The individual flowers, tiny and lilac-purple, are not striking in themselves, but they are held in woolly, beige-green calyces in 'bobbles' on the stem and complement the grey-green evergreen leaves. H 45cm (18in), S 60cm (2ft). Borderline hardy/Z 7–9.

BERBERIS
Barberry
An important genus, tough and hardy, that includes both evergreens and deciduous species, all with spiny stems. Although some are almost too familiar as hedging, there are also some very choice species that are well worth seeking out. The forms with coloured leaves make excellent specimens.
Cultivation Any soil is suitable. The evergreens are shade-tolerant. Deciduous types grown for their leaf colour are best in sun or only light shade. Overgrown and straggly plants can be cut back hard in spring.

B. darwinii
This evergreen species from Chile is one of the best for hedging. Showers of rich orange flowers are produced in mid- to late spring, followed by blue-black fruits. H 2m (6ft), S 1.2m (4ft). Hardy/Z 7–9.

B. 'Goldilocks'
One of the best evergreens, this slow-growing hybrid has drooping racemes of glowing orange flowers in spring (and sometimes in mid-summer). The flowers are followed by blue-black fruits. H 4m (13ft), S 3m (10ft). Hardy/Z 7–10.

B. temolaica
A very handsome deciduous berberis, this slow-growing plant is difficult to propagate but is well worth looking out for. It has glaucous green leaves on whitened stems, lemon-yellow spring flowers and egg-shaped autumn fruits. Plants can be cut back hard annually or every two years for the interest of its winter stems. H and S 1.5m (5ft). Hardy/Z 5.

B. thunbergii
This variable deciduous shrub has a number of interesting selections, all of which do best in fertile soil. The purple leaves of *B. thunbergii* f. *atropurpurea* turn orange in autumn. H and S 1.5m (5ft). **'Aurea'** has soft yellow leaves and is best in some shade. H and S 1m (3ft). **'Helmond Pillar'** is a

Berberis temolaica

distinctive upright selection with dark purple-red leaves. H 1.5m (5ft), S 45cm (18in). The popular and distinctive **'Rose Glow'** has purple leaves swirled with pink and cream turning lipstick red in autumn. H 1.5m (5ft), S 1.2m (4ft). On **'Silver Beauty'**, the leaves are mottled with creamy white. H 60cm (2ft), S 1m (3ft). Hardy/Z 5–9.

Berberis thunbergii f. *atropurpurea*

Buddleja alternifolia

BUDDLEJA

The heavily fragranced flowers of these medium-to-large deciduous shrubs are irresistible to butterflies. *B. davidii* is almost a weed in some gardens, seeding itself freely even in cracks in walls, paving and gravel drives, but there are also other species, many beautiful. They are reliable plants for the back of a border.
Cultivation Grow in any, even poor, soil in full sun. Buddlejas thrive in alkaline soil. Some species can be pruned hard in late winter to early spring, but this is not essential.

B. alternifolia
This handsome plant, originally from China, has pendent racemes of deliciously scented mauve flowers in early summer. Its size is easily controlled by pruning. H and S 4m (13ft). Hardy/Z 6–9. The form **'Argentea'** is even more desirable. It has silver-grey

leaves and is very effective both as a standard and as a specimen. H and S 2.4m (8ft).

B. crispa
(syn. *B. sterniana*, *B. tibetica*)
This handsome Chinese species makes a fine subject for a warm wall, the additional heat enhancing the woolliness of its grey leaves. The lilac-coloured flowers are scented. H and S 3m (10ft). Borderline hardy/Z 9.

B. davidii
Butterfly bush
The most familiar of all the buddlejas, this bears long spikes of fragrant, usually mauve flowers in mid- to late summer. It is essential in a wild or ecological garden, because of its attraction to butterflies. H and S 3m (10ft), if unpruned. Hardy/Z 7–9. There are several selections, all of which can be pruned hard in late winter to early spring, including **'Black Knight'**, which has rich reddish-purple flowers; **'Nanho Blue'** with rich lavender-blue flowers; and **'Peace'**, which is a reliable white selection.

B. × weyeriana
A curious hybrid of *B. globosa* and *B. davidii*, this plant bears flowers that show the characteristics of both parents, being arranged in tapering, ball-shaped clusters. The flowers are a muted orange flushed with mauve, a refreshing addition to any mixed planting in high summer. H 4m (13ft), S 3m (10ft), but less if pruned hard annually. Hardy/Z 6–8.

BUXUS
Box
These are indispensable evergreen plants in the garden for dwarf hedging. New plants can be easily raised from cuttings. Box thrives in containers.
Cultivation Grow in any reasonable soil in full sun or light shade. Clip hedges in mid-spring and late summer.

B. sempervirens
Common box
The species most commonly used for hedging, this would eventually make a tree if left unpruned (albeit over several generations), although the plants seen in gardens are usually considerably smaller than the dimensions indicated. H and S 4m (13ft). Hardy/Z 6–9. **'Elegantissima'** is a delightful selection, with small leaves that are variegated with cream. H and S 1.5m (5ft). **'Suffruticosa'** is a very slow-growing dwarf form, also with small leaves and a tight habit. It is the traditional choice for knot gardens. H 1m (3ft), S 1.5m (5ft).

CALLISTEMON
Bottlebrush
Native to Australia, the evergreen bottlebrushes bring a quirky, exotic touch to gardens with their vivid, brush-like flowers. In general, callistemons are not reliably hardy and are best grown in only fairly mild climates or in sheltered spots in frost-prone gardens.
Cultivation Grow callistemons in lime-free, preferably acid, well-drained soil in full sun, against a warm wall in cold areas. They are suitable for growing in containers under glass.

C. citrinus
Crimson bottlebrush
This species has a profusion of spikes of red flowers from early to midsummer. H and S 5m (16ft). Half-hardy/Z 9–10. **'Splendens'** has flowers of a more vivid scarlet. H and S 2m (6ft).

C. viminalis 'Captain Cook'
This low-growing form produces an abundance of large red flowers from spring to summer. H and S 1.2m (4ft). Half-hardy/Z 10.

Buxus sempervirens 'Suffruticosa'

CALLUNA
Heather, ling
This genus of heathers consists of a single species, but there are a huge number of cultivars, all evergreen and producing their spikes of bell-shaped flowers between midsummer and late autumn (some have a shorter flowering season within that overall period). Some also have coloured foliage, which provides interest over a longer period. Grow them on their own in heather beds or combine them with dwarf conifers or the other heath genera, *Daboecia* and *Erica*. Heathers are good in containers.
Cultivation Grow in a sunny, open site in well-drained, humus-rich, acid soil. Clip after flowering.

C. vulgaris
The following selection indicates something of the scope of the hybrids now available. All are hardy/Z 5–7. **'Alba Rigida'**

Buddleja davidii 'Black Knight'

Buddleja davidii 'Nanho Blue'

Callistemon citrinus

Calluna vulgaris 'Alison Yates'

Calluna vulgaris 'Dark Beauty'

Calluna vulgaris 'Darkness'

(syn. 'Rigida Prostrata') has white flowers. H 15cm (6in), S 30cm (12in). **'Alison Yates'** has white flowers and silver-grey foliage. H 45cm (18in), S 60cm (24in). **'Annemarie'** has double, rose pink flowers. H 50cm (20in), S 60cm (24in). **'Anthony Davis'** has white flowers and grey-green foliage. H 45cm (18in), S 50cm (20in). **'Arran Gold'** has purple flowers and bright golden-yellow foliage, which turns lime green flecked with red in winter. H 15cm (6in), S 25cm (10in). **'Beoley Gold'** has white flowers and bright golden-yellow foliage. H 35cm (14in), S 60cm (24in). **'County Wicklow'** has double, pale pink flowers. H 25cm (10in), S 35cm (14in). **'Dark Beauty'** has blood-red flowers and grey-green foliage. H 25cm (10in), S 35cm (14in). **'Darkness'** has bright crimson flowers and dark green foliage. H 25cm (10in), S 35cm (14in). **'Elsie Purnell'** has double, pale

pink flowers and greyish-green foliage. H 40cm (16in), S 75cm (30in). **'Firefly'** has pinkish-lilac flowers and orange-red summer foliage, darkening to brick red in winter. H 45cm (18in), S 50cm (20in). **'Foxii Nana'** has mauve flowers. H 15cm (6in), S 30cm (12in). **'H.E. Beale'** (syn. 'Pink Beale') has double, pink flowers. H and S 60cm (24in). 'Hammondii' has white flowers. H and S 75cm (30in). **'Hammondii Aureifolia'** has white flowers and foliage tipped with yellow in spring. H 30cm (12in), S 40cm (16in). **'J.H. Hamilton'** has double, dark pink flowers. H 10cm (4in), S 25cm (10in). **'Joy Vanstone'** has pink flowers and yellow-gold foliage, which turns orange in winter. H 50cm (20in), S 60cm (24in). **'Kerstin'** has mauve flowers and greyish-lilac foliage, the new growth tipped with light yellow and red in spring. H 50cm (20in), S 45cm (18in). **'Kinlochruel'** has double, white flowers. H 25cm (10in), S 40cm (16in). **'Mair's Variety'** (syn. 'Alba Elongata') has white flowers. H 40cm (16in), S 60cm (24in). **'Mullion'** has lilac-pink flowers and dark green foliage. H 20cm (8in), S 50cm (20in). **'Multicolor'** has mauve flowers and copper foliage flecked with orange and red. H 10cm (4in), S 25cm (10in). **'My Dream'** (syn. 'Snowball') has double, white flowers, which are good for cutting. H 45cm (18in), S 75cm (30in). **'Orange Queen'** has lavender flowers and golden-yellow foliage, which turns bronze in autumn and orange in winter. H 30cm (12in), S 50cm (20in). **'Peter Sparkes'** has double, pink flowers. H 25cm (10in), S 55cm (22in). **'Red Carpet'** (syn. 'Marinka') has mauve-pink flowers and golden-yellow foliage, reddening after hard frosts in winter. H 20cm (8in), S 45cm (18in). **'Red Favorit'** has double, crimson flowers and dark green foliage. H 20cm (8in), S 70cm (28in). **'Red Pimpernel'** has crimson flowers. H 20cm (8in), S 45cm (18in). **'Red Star'** has double, deep lilac-pink flowers and dark green foliage. H 40cm (16in), S 60cm (24in). **'Robert Chapman'**

has lavender flowers and golden-yellow summer foliage, which turns orange in autumn and red in winter and spring. H 25cm (10in), S 65cm (26in). **'Roland Haagen'** has mauve flowers and golden-yellow foliage, turning bright orange with darker tips in winter. H 15cm (6in), S 35cm (14in). **'Serlei Aurea'** has white flowers and yellowish-green foliage, tipped with yellow in summer and autumn. H 50cm (20in), S 40cm (16in). **'Silver Queen'** has pale mauve flowers and silver-grey foliage. H 40cm (16in), S 55cm (22in). **'Silver Rose'** has lilac-pink flowers and hairy, silver-grey foliage. H 40cm (16in), S 50cm (20in). **'Sir John Charrington'** has mauve-pink flowers and golden-yellow summer foliage, which turns orange and red in winter. H 40cm (16in), S 50cm (24in). **'Sister Anne'** has mauve flowers and grey-green foliage, turning bronze in winter. H 10cm

(4in), S 25cm (10in). **'Spring Cream'** has white flowers and foliage tipped with cream in spring, and yellow in autumn and winter. H 35cm (14in), S 45cm (18in). **'Spring Torch'** (syn. 'Spring Charm') has mauve flowers and foliage tipped with cream orange and red in spring. H 40cm (16in), S 60cm (24in). **'Sunset'** has lilac-pink flowers and golden-yellow summer foliage, turning red in autumn and winter. H 20cm (8in), S 45cm (18in). **'Tib'** has cyclamen purple flowers and dark green foliage. H 30cm (12in), S 40cm (16in). **'White Coral'** has white flowers. H 30cm (12in), S 40cm (16in). **'White Lawn'** has white flowers. H 5cm (2in), S 40cm (16in). **'Wickwar Flame'** has mauve-pink flowers and flame-orange foliage, deepening to brilliant orange-red in winter. H 50cm (20in), S 60cm (24in).

Calluna vulgaris 'Arran Gold'

Calluna vulgaris 'Hammondii Aureifolia'

Calluna vulgaris 'Wickwar Flame'

Camellia 'Cornish Snow'

Camellia 'Inspiration'

Camellia japonica 'Elizabeth Hawkins'

CAMELLIA

This is a large genus, containing about 250 species of superb evergreen shrubs and small trees, made larger by the number of hybrids. Unfortunately for many gardens, they must have acid soil. On the credit side, they thrive in containers, so it is possible to enjoy these aristocrats of spring whatever your soil type. There are an increasing number of autumn-flowering camellias, which have been bred from *C. sasanqua*. Few of the species are in general cultivation: on the whole, they are not very hardy and are too large for most conservatories (porches). Hybrids can be divided into two large groups: cultivars of *C. japonica* and of *C. × williamsii*, although from the gardener's point of view, there is no appreciable difference between the two. There are two smaller groups: cultivars of *C. sasanqua* (which flower in autumn) and of *C. reticulata* (which flower in late winter to spring). Use camellias as specimens or in shrub borders. All have lustrous green leaves, making them splendid backdrops to other plants when out of flower. Some camellias

have flexible stems and can be wall-trained, to breathtaking effect once they are mature. *Cultivation* Camellias must have lime-free soil (although they do not demand such a low pH as rhododendrons). The soil should be fertile and well-drained and, ideally, incorporate leaf mould. Camellias are best in light shade where early morning sun will not strike emerging flower buds in early spring. Make sure they do not dry out in late summer to early autumn, when plants are building the following season's flowers. They can be pruned after flowering.

C. 'Cornish Snow'
This medium-sized shrub produces dainty, single white flowers opening from pink-tinted buds from midwinter to late spring. It needs a sheltered spot. H 3m (10ft), S 1.5m (5ft). Hardy/Z 7–9.

C. 'Doctor Clifford Parks'
This desirable camellia bears semi-double, loose peony- or anemone-form deep red flowers in mid-spring. H 4m (13ft), S 2.5m (8ft). Half-hardy/Z 7–9.

C. 'Inspiration'
A reliable, upright plant that has semi-double, deep pink flowers from midwinter to late spring. This is good when trained as a wall shrub. H 4m (13ft), S 2m (6ft). Hardy/Z 7–9.

C. japonica cultivars
The following flower from mid- to late spring. All are hardy/Z 7–9 unless otherwise stated. '**Adolphe**

Audusson' has semi-double, dark red flowers with white stamens in early to mid-spring. H 5m (16ft), S 4m (13ft). '**Akashigata**' (syn. 'Lady Clare') has very large, semi-double, deep salmon-pink flowers from early to late spring. It is suitable for wall training. H 1.5m (5ft), S 3m (10ft). '**Apollo**' (syn. 'Paul's Apollo') has semi-double, red flowers (sometimes marbled with white) with yellow stamens from early to late spring. H and S 3m (10ft). '**Ave Maria**' has formal double, pale pink flowers from early to late spring. This is a slow-growing plant, which is an excellent choice for a container. H and S 3m (10ft). '**Berenice Boddy**' has semi-double, pale pink flowers from late winter to late spring. It is exceptionally hardy and wind-tolerant. H and S 3m (10ft). '**Bob Hope**' has semi-double or peony-form blackish-red flowers. It is a good choice for a container. H and S 3m (10ft). The choice and unusual '**Bob's Tinsie**' has anemone-form flowers, the outer petals deep crimson, the inner petals crimson and white, from early to late spring. H 2m (6ft), S 1m (3ft). The compact and upright '**Doctor Tinsley**' has peony-form or formal double, pale pink flowers. H and S 3m (10ft). '**Elegans**' (syn. 'Chandler's Elegans') has anemone-form, soft pink flowers, sometimes spotted with white. It is slow-growing and best with minimal pruning. H and S 3m (10ft). '**Elizabeth Hawkins**' has anemone-form, bright red flowers in mid-spring. H and S 2m (6ft). '**Gloire de Nantes**' has semi-double, rich rose-pink flowers from late autumn to late spring, one of the longest flowering

seasons of any camellia. H and S 3m (10ft). '**Grand Prix**' has semi-double, brilliant clear red flowers with yellow stamens. This looks magnificent when wall-trained. H and S 5m (16ft). '**Janet Waterhouse**' has semi-double or formal double, white flowers. H and S 3m (10ft). The reliably hardy '**Jupiter**' (syn. 'Paul's Jupiter') has single, bright red flowers with golden stamens. H 3m (10ft), S 2m (6ft). '**Kramer's Supreme**' has beautiful peony-form, bright red flowers in late autumn and in early to mid-spring. H 3m (10ft), S 2m (6ft). Borderline hardy/Z 8. '**Lady Loch**' has peony-form, pink flowers. H 3m (10ft), S 2m (6ft). '**Lavinia Maggi**' (syn. 'Contessa Lavinia Maggi') has formal double, white to pale pink flowers striped with pink and red from early to mid-spring. H and S 2m (6ft) or more. '**Nuccio's Jewel**' has peony-form, white flowers, flushed pink. This is a slow-growing camellia and a good choice for a container. H and S 3m (10ft). The dense and compact '**Rubescens Major**' has formal double or rose-form double, pinkish-crimson flowers with attractive darker veins in mid-spring. H and S 2.5m (8ft). '**Tricolor**' (syn. 'Sieboldii') has single or semi-double flowers striped in shades of red, pink or white in early spring. H and S 2m (6ft).

C. 'Leonard Messel'
Semi-double to peony-form, pink flowers, veined with darker pink, are borne in early to late spring. H 4m (13ft), S 3m (10ft). Hardy/Z 7–9.

Camellia 'Doctor Clifford Parks'

Camellia japonica 'Ave Maria'

Camellia × *williamsii* 'Jury's Yellow'

C. reticulata

This species has a number of desirable cultivars, suitable for training against a warm wall. H and S to 4m (13ft) or more. Half-hardy/Z 9–10. **'Captain Rawes'** has large, semi-double flowers in mid-spring. **'Mandalay Queen'** has deep, rose-pink, semi-double flowers.

C. sasanqua

This species is distinguished by its fragrant flowers, produced from late autumn to late winter. H and S to 3m (10ft). Borderline hardy/Z 7–9. The upright selection **'Narumigata'** has single, pink-tinted white flowers.

C. 'Spring Festival'

This charming camellia has dainty, formal double, pale pink flowers from mid- to late spring. H 4m (13ft), S 2m (6ft). Borderline hardy/Z 8.

C. × williamsii hybrids

The following is just a selection of the large number of fine hybrids available in this group. All are hardy/Z 7–9. The slow-growing **'Anticipation'** has very large, peony-form, deep rose-pink flowers from late winter to early spring. H 4m (13ft), S 2m (6ft). The exceptionally hardy **'Brigadoon'** has semi-double, soft silver-pink flowers with golden stamens in mid- to late spring. H 2.5m (8ft), S 2m (6ft). The prolific **'Debbie'** has peony-form, clear deep pink flowers from late winter to late spring. H 3m (10ft), S 2m (6ft). **'Donation'** has semi-double, pink flowers veined darker pink and with yellow stamens from late winter to late spring. It is deservedly one of the most popular of all camellias. H 5m (16ft), S 2.5m (8ft). One of the best whites, **'E.T.R. Carlyon'** has semi-double to rose-form white flowers in mid- and late spring. H 2.5m (8ft), S 2m (6ft). **'Golden Spangles'** has single, pinkish red flowers from mid- to late spring, but it is grown primarily for its leaves, which are generously splashed with yellow. H 2.5m (8ft), S 2m (6ft). **'J.C. Williams'** bears single, pale blush pink flowers in profusion in mid- to late spring. This is suitable for wall training. H and S 5m (16ft). **'Joan Trehane'** has rose-form, clear pink flowers from mid- to late spring. H 2.5m (8ft), S 2m (6ft). **'Jury's Yellow'** has anemone- to peony-form flowers, with creamy-white outer petals and creamy-yellow inner ones, from mid- to late spring. This is the nearest to a yellow camellia. H 2.5m (8ft), S 2m (6ft). **'Muskoka'** has semi-double, pink flowers veined darker pink, the number one camellia for a container. H 2.5m (8ft), S 2m (6ft). **'Rose Parade'** has formal double, rich deep rose pink flowers from early to late spring. H and S 3m (10ft). **'St Ewe'** has single, bright rose pink flowers with golden stamens in early to mid-spring. H 2.5m (8ft), S 2m (6ft).

CEANOTHUS
California lilac

No shrub has flowers of so true a blue as the *Ceanothus*. When the early forms burst into flower, it is a sure sign that summer is only just around the corner. There is also a valuable second group that flowers in late summer. There are deciduous and evergreen species, the evergreens being slightly more tender. In cold areas all are best grown as wall shrubs, but in more favoured spots they make truly spectacular specimens. The pink- and white-flowered types are of interest but less popular.
Cultivation Grow in any fertile, well-drained soil in full sun. They tolerate lime, but dislike shallow soils over chalk. In cold areas most do best as wall shrubs. Prune after flowering if necessary.

C. 'Autumnal Blue'

A late-flowering plant, with clusters of powder blue flowers from late summer to autumn. One of the hardiest evergreens and ideal for wall training. H and S 3m (10ft). Hardy/Z 8–9.

C. 'Cascade'

This evergreen is seen at its best when loosely tied to a wall, so that the arching stems, smothered in powder-blue flowers in late spring, can billow forwards. H and S to 2m (6ft). Half-hardy/Z 9.

C. 'Dark Star'

Dark purplish blue flowers are carried in spring on this arching evergreen. H 2m (6ft), S 3m (10ft). Half-hardy/Z 8.

C. 'Delight'

This evergreen variety, which has clusters of rich blue flowers in late spring, makes a good wall shrub. H and S 3m (10ft). Half-hardy/Z 9.

C. × delileanus 'Gloire de Versailles'

An open, deciduous ceanothus, this would make a fine specimen in a sheltered spot. The pale blue

Ceanothus 'Delight'

flowers appear from midsummer to early autumn. H and S 1.5m (5ft). Hardy/Z 7. **'Topaze'** is more compact and has richer blue flowers. H and S 1.5m (5ft). Hardy/Z 7.

C. × pallidus 'Marie Simon'

One of the few pink-flowered hybrids, this is a deciduous variety with pale pink flowers from midsummer to autumn. H and S 1.5m (5ft). Hardy/Z 9.

C. 'Puget Blue'

This evergreen hybrid has masses of brilliant blue flowers appearing in early summer. H and S 2.1m (7ft). Borderline hardy/Z 8–10.

C. thyrsiflorus var. repens Blueblossom

The species, one of the hardiest evergreens, is usually grown in this prostrate form, which is a wonderful carpeter for banks and large rockeries. Rich blue flowers cover the plant in late spring to early summer. It is shade-tolerant and looks splendid as groundcover under such airy, deciduous trees as gleditsias. H 1m (3ft), S 2.5m (8ft). Hardy/Z 8–9.

Camellia 'Leonard Messel'

Camellia 'Spring Festival'

Ceanothus 'Dark Star'

Ceratostigma willmottianum

Cestrum elegans

Chaenomeles × superba 'Crimson and Gold'

CERATOSTIGMA

A diminutive shrub, but of great significance, for this is probably the only late-flowering shrub that can provide flowers of this shade of blue. It tends to die back in hard winters but generally recovers. The species described should have a place in every garden. Its low habit makes it suitable for a mixed planting including perennials, annuals and grasses. The genus also includes the perennial *C. plumbaginoides*.
Cultivation Grow in any well-drained soil in full sun. In cold areas, cut back hard annually in spring.

C. willmottianum

This deciduous Chinese species, which makes a twiggy bush, has small, vivid blue flowers in late summer to early autumn. H and S 60cm (2ft). Hardy/Z 7–10.

CESTRUM

This small genus of generally tender plants contains one species that is hardy enough to be grown outdoors in cool gardens. The others make good conservatory (porch) plants in cold areas.
Cultivation Any fertile, well-drained soil is suitable. Grow in full sun, ideally in the shelter of a warm wall, and cut back hard annually in spring if the topgrowth dies back.

C. elegans
(syn. C. purpureum)

An evergreen species originally from Mexico, this has clusters of reddish-purple flowers that appear throughout summer. H 1.2m (4ft), S 1m (3ft). Tender/Z 10.

C. parqui
Willow-leaved jessamine

This deciduous species from Chile has pyramid-like clusters of lime-green, star-shaped flowers, unspectacular in themselves but releasing a unique bubblegum-like fragrance at night in late summer. H 1.2m (4ft), S 1m (3ft). Borderline hardy/Z 7–10.

CHAENOMELES
Ornamental quince, japonica

Essential shrubs for late-winter interest, these plants are charming as free-standing specimens and spectacular when trained against a wall. Selections with white, pink and red flowers are available, but the red-flowered types are the most popular.
Cultivation These plants are tolerant of any but waterlogged soil. They will grow in sun or shade and can be trained against north-facing walls.

C. × superba

This multi-stemmed, deciduous hybrid group is usually represented in gardens by its selections, all of which flower on the bare wood in late winter. H and S 1.5m (5ft). All are hardy/Z 5–8. 'Crimson and Gold' has red flowers with eye-catching yellow stamens. 'Knap Hill Scarlet', has large, bright red flowers. 'Nicoline' has scarlet, sometimes semi-double flowers. 'Pink Lady' has dark pink flowers.

CHOISYA

A small genus of evergreens that have a neat, rounded habit making them excellent for creating a topiary effect without pruning, though older plants can become untidy. The leaves are highly aromatic, and they also bear fragrant white flowers in spring.

Cultivation Grow in any fertile, well-drained soil. Choisyas will tolerate some shade and are good for growing against a wall, but flower best in full sun.

C. 'Aztec Pearl'

This compact shrub has fairly narrow, elegant dark green leaves

Choisya ternata

Choisya ternata 'Sundance'

and pink-tinged, white flowers that have a scent of almonds. H and S 1.5m (5ft). Hardy/Z 7.

C. ternata
Mexican orange blossom
A handsome evergreen with glossy green leaves, this flowers mostly in spring with, often, a second flush in late summer or autumn. H and S 2.4m (8ft). Hardy/Z 7–9. The selection **'Sundance'** (syn. 'Lich') has bright yellow leaves. H and S 2m (6ft).

CISTUS
Sun rose, rock rose
In Mediterranean countries these scrubby evergreen shrubs fulfil the same function as heathers in northern Europe. The flowers, which have a papery texture, like poppies, are short-lived, but

Cistus × skanbergii

follow one another in quick succession at the height of summer. A hot spot enhances the resinous quality of the stems, and hence the plant's aromatic property. They are perfect in a scree or gravel garden, basking in the reflected heat from the stones, combining well with shrubby herbs and *Genista*.
Cultivation Cistus need very well-drained soil of low to moderate fertility in full sun. Dead-head regularly to maintain flower production. In cold areas they may need winter protection.

C. × hybridus
(syn. *C. coeris, C. × corbariensis*)
This tough hybrid has crinkled, papery, white flowers with a yellow blotch at the base of each petal in summer. H 1m (3ft), S 1.5m (5ft). Borderline hardy/Z 7–9.

C. ladanifer
Gum cistus
This species has large white summer flowers, each petal of which is blotched with maroon at the base. H 2.4m (8ft), S 1m (3ft). Borderline hardy/Z 8.

C. × pulverulentus
A hybrid cistus with pale pinkish-purple flowers. H and S 60cm (2ft). Borderline hardy/Z 7–9. The compact, spreading **'Sunset'** has glowing magenta flowers. H 60cm (2ft), S 1m (3ft).

C. × skanbergii
A hybrid with small green leaves and pale pink flowers from early to midsummer. H and S 1m (3ft). Hardy/Z 8–9.

CORNUS
Dogwood, cornel
These mainly deciduous shrubs and trees, native to northern temperate areas around the world, are excellent in cold, damp sites, associating very well with water features. Many can be cut back hard annually, which not only keeps them well within bounds but improves their winter stem colour, for which most are grown. They are highly effective in groups, a feast for the eye when lit up by low shafts of winter sun.

Cistus × pulverulentus 'Sunset'

Cultivation Dogwoods are tolerant of most soil types. They prefer sun but will do reasonably well in shade.

C. alba
(syn. *Swida alba, Thelycrania alba*)
Red-barked dogwood
This suckering, deciduous species has clusters of small yellow-white flowers in early summer and good autumn leaf colour (red and purple). H and S 3m (10ft). Hardy/Z 2–7. **'Aurea'** has golden leaves and glowing red winter stems. H and S 3m (10ft).

'Sibirica Variegata' has leaves boldly variegated with creamy-white, excellent autumn leaf colour and red winter stems. H and S 3m (10ft).

C. stolonifera
Red osier dogwood
This deciduous species is mainly seen in the form **'Flaviramea'**, which has mustard-yellow winter stems. H and S 1.5m (5ft). **'Kelseyi'** is a dwarf form with blackish-red winter stems. H 75cm (30in), S 1.5m (5ft). Hardy/Z 2–8.

Cornus alba 'Sibirica Variegata'

Cotinus 'Grace'

Cotoneaster lacteus

COTINUS
Smoke bush

The two species of impressive deciduous shrubs in the genus are usually grown in their purple-leaved forms, which also make spectacular autumn colour. They make large, rangy shrubs, but can be cut back hard for larger leaves, albeit at the expense of the flowers. The flowers are tiny, but carried in large panicles, looking like smoke from a distance – hence the common name. They are produced reliably only in hot summers. In cold areas it is better to cut the plant back hard annually for an improved foliage display. The purple-leaved forms are indispensable in a red or purple border.
Cultivation Grow in reasonably fertile soil in full sun. Hard pruning in spring produces the best leaves, but this can be at the expense of good autumn colour.

C. coggygria
Smoke bush, smoke tree

The plain green species is seldom grown. Far better known is the selection **'Royal Purple'**, grown principally for its coin-like, dramatic purple leaves, which turn vivid red in autumn. H and S 1.2m (4ft). Hardy/Z 5–9.

C. 'Grace'

This familiar hybrid is similar to *C. coggygria* 'Royal Purple', but is larger and has oval leaves, which turn dark brownish-red in autumn. H 6m (20ft), S 5m (16ft). Hardy/Z 5–9.

COTONEASTER

This is one of the most important shrub genera, containing both evergreen and deciduous species. Cotoneasters are tough, hardy, tolerant plants, which make excellent foils to a huge range of other showier plants. Some have sufficient distinction to work as specimens, but on the whole it is best to think of these as companions to other plants. Bees appreciate their creamy-white flowers in that bloom in early summer, and birds enjoy their autumn berries.
Cultivation Cotoneasters will do well in any reasonable soil in sun or light shade (evergreens cope with deep shade) and are tolerant of pruning.

C. dammeri

This evergreen or semi-evergreen species is an outstanding ground-cover plant, carpeting the ground and thriving in many difficult garden situations. The plant flowers in early summer and bears scarlet berries in autumn. H 5cm (2in), S 1.2m (4ft). Hardy/Z 5.

C. frigidus

This semi-evergreen species has the outstanding cultivar **'Cornubia'**, a tree-like shrub, bearing bright red fruit in autumn, that is good enough to use as a specimen in a small garden. H and S 5m (16ft). Hardy/Z 7–8.

C. horizontalis
Fishbone cotoneaster

A versatile deciduous species, this can be grown as a wall shrub (or even up a tree trunk) or allowed to cascade over a bank, both of which methods display its unusual 'herringbone' habit, or it can be clipped to a table-like shape. It has excellent autumn leaf colour, along with an impressive display of vivid red berries. H 1m (3ft), S 2m (6ft). Hardy/Z 5–9.

C. lacteus

This evergreen or semi-evergreen species is a dense shrub with an abundant crop of early summer flowers followed by orange-red berries. It is excellent hedging material. H and S 1.5m (5ft). Hardy/Z 7–9.

Cytisus battandieri

C. salicifolius
Willowleaf cotoneaster

The species is seldom grown, but its excellent selections include **'Rothschildianus'**, a large evergreen notable for its abundant autumn crop of creamy-yellow berries. H and S 5m (16ft). Hardy/Z 7–8.

C. × suecicus 'Coral Beauty' (syn. C. 'Royal Beauty')

This small evergreen with arching branches is covered with masses of bright red fruits in autumn. It is good for groundcover. H 60cm (2ft), S 1.2m (4ft). Hardy/Z 6–8.

CYTISUS
Broom

The genus contains about 50 species, found mainly in Europe, but also northern Africa and western Asia. These desirable, if usually short-lived, deciduous shrubs seem to pour out their pealike flowers in late spring to early summer. These are fragrant, usually yellow, and are followed by green seedpods. The brooms are excellent in gravel gardens or on any hot, dry site.
Cultivation Full sun and well-drained soil is essential, as is wall-training in cold districts. Brooms do not respond well to pruning or being transplanted.

C. battandieri
Pineapple broom

A fascinating plant, this is beautiful in all its parts. The yellow flowers, which both look and smell like pineapples, appear in midsummer among the silky textured, silver-grey leaves. H and S 4m (13ft). Borderline hardy/Z 7–9.

C. × beanii

Golden-yellow, pea-like flowers smother this sprawling hybrid in late spring or early summer. H 30cm (1ft), S 60cm (2ft). Hardy/Z 7–8.

C. × praecox

This hybrid group has generally pale yellow flowers. H and S 1m (3ft). Hardy/Z 6–9. The form **'Warminster'** (Warminster broom) has masses of long-lasting, rich cream-coloured flowers.

Daboecia cantabrica 'Alba'

Daboecia cantabrica 'Rainbow'

Daphne bholua

DABOECIA
Heather

This genus contains two evergreen species, but only one is hardy, and most of the plants in cultivation are selected forms of this or hybrids with the other. They are best grown en masse in an open situation or in island beds with other heathers or conifers.
Cultivation Grow in preferably sandy, well-drained, acid soil in full sun. An open, scrubby site is preferable.

D. cantabrica
Cantabrian heath, St Dabeoc's heath

This plant is normally represented in gardens by one of its many cultivars, all producing their urn-shaped flowers from early summer to mid-autumn. The following are all hardy/Z 5–8. **'Alba'** has white flowers; plants sold under this name can vary. H 40cm (16in), S 70cm (28in). **'Atropurpurea'** makes glowing colonies of bronze-tinged foliage and has dark pinkish-purple flowers. H 40cm (16in), S 70cm (28in). The flowers of **'Bicolor'** can be white, pink or beetroot red (or streaked), different colours appearing simultaneously on the same stem. H 25cm (10in), S 65cm (26in). The purple flowers of **'Hookstone Purple'** appear only from midsummer. H 25cm (10in), S 65cm (26in). **'Rainbow'** is less eye-catching for its purple flowers than its colourful foliage, variegated with red and yellow. H 25cm (10in), S 65cm (26in). **'Waley's Red'** (syn. 'Whaley') has deep magenta flowers. H 35cm (14in), S 50cm (20in).

D. × scotica

There are several outstanding members of this hybrid group. **'Silverwells'** has white flowers in summer and mid-green foliage. H 15cm (6in), S 35cm (14in). **'William Buchanan'** has purplish-crimson flowers which appear in mid- to late summer. H 35cm (14in), S 55cm (22in). Both are borderline hardy/Z 4–7.

DAPHNE

Evergreen, semi-evergreen or deciduous, these delightful shrubs bear flowers with an exquisite fragrance. Some are rock garden plants, but the ones described here work well in mixed or shrub borders. Winter-flowering types are best sited near a door where their fragrance can be appreciated to the full without the need to go too far outdoors.
Cultivation Grow these plants in any moist but well-drained soil in sun or light shade, ideally in a sheltered spot.

D. bholua

This semi-evergreen species bears deliciously scented clusters of pink and white flowers in late winter. H 3m (10ft), S 1.2m (4ft). Borderline hardy/Z 8–9. The deciduous and hardiest variety **D. bholua var. glacialis 'Gurkha'** bears purplish-pink flowers from mid- to late winter. Hardy/Z 8. **'Jacqueline Postill'** is evergreen and has deep purplish-pink flowers. H 3m (10ft), S 1.2m (4ft). Borderline hardy/Z 8–9.

D. mezereum
Mezereon

A deciduous species, which suits a woodland garden, this produces pink or reddish, highly scented flowers in late winter. The red summer berries are poisonous, but equally attractive. H 1.2m (4ft), S 1m (3ft). Hardy/Z 5–8.

D. tangutica

This small, evergreen species originates from western China. The fragrant white flowers, which are tinged with rose-purple, appear in late winter to early spring. H 60cm (2ft), S 45cm (18in). Hardy/Z 7–9.

DESFONTAINEA

This genus of evergreen shrubs is usually represented in gardens by the species described here. When they appear, the flowers are something of a surprise, because in all other respects the plant looks just like a holly. This is an excellent specimen.
Cultivation Any well-drained, fertile soil suits these plants, but they need light shade and a sheltered spot. They do well in a mild, damp, maritime climate and will not thrive in dry conditions. In cold areas, grow against a warm wall.

D. spinosa

Narrow, tubular scarlet and orange flowers hang among the branches in late summer. H and S 2m (6ft). Borderline hardy/ Z 9–10.

Daboecia cantabrica 'Atropurpurea'

Daphne tangutica

Desfontainea spinosa

Deutzia longifolia

Elaeagnus × ebbingei 'Limelight'

Erica carnea 'Eileen Porter'

DEUTZIA

These elegant deciduous shrubs are grown for their dainty flowers in late spring and early summer. They are ideal plants for a cottage garden-style planting or for a small garden.
Cultivation Grow in any moderately fertile soil in sun or light shade.

D. × elegantissima

This hybrid has fragrant pink flowers. H and S 1.5m (5ft). Hardy/Z 5–8. Selections include the upright 'Rosealind', which has deep carmine pink flowers; 'Rosea Plena' with double flowers that open pink and age to white and 'Strawberry Fields', which has large deep red-pink flowers. H 2m (6ft), S 1.2m (4ft).

D. × hybrida

The hybrids in this group have clusters of star-shaped flowers. H 1.2m (4ft), S 1m (3ft). Hardy/Z 5–9. 'Mont Rose' has deep pink flowers borne on arching stems. H 1.2m (4ft), S 1m (3ft).

D. longifolia

The straight species has white flowers (usually striped purple on the back) in early to midsummer, but is better known through the selected form 'Veitchii', which has purple flowers on purple stems. H 2m (6ft), S 3m (10ft). Hardy/Z 7–9.

ELAEAGNUS

The genus contains handsome evergreen and deciduous shrubs with a number of uses in the garden, either as specimens or as hedging. Some seem to prefer acid soil. Some also have the benefit of late autumn flowers, which are inconspicuous and parchment-textured, but highly fragrant.
Cultivation They suit any well-drained soil except shallow soil over chalk (alkaline soil).

E. × ebbingei

A good plant for coastal gardens, this has evergreen leaves that seem to tolerate salt-laden winds, making it excellent hedging material. The leaves appear speckled with pewter grey. The autumn flowers are inconspicuous but ravishingly scented. H and S 3m (10ft). Hardy/Z 7–9. 'Limelight' has leaves that are marked golden yellow in the centre. H and S 3m (10ft).

E. pungens

This large evergreen species is seldom seen and is usually represented in gardens by 'Maculata', an excellent shrub for the winter garden, with leaves that are splashed with bright yellow. It has a tendency to revert to the plain green of the species. H and S 3m (10ft). Hardy/Z 7–9.

Elaeagnus 'Quicksilver'

E. 'Quicksilver'

A truly outstanding deciduous hybrid, in time virtually a tree, this has narrow, silvery leaves, which are especially striking in spring. H and S 1m (3ft), ultimately larger. Hardy/Z 2–9.

ERICA
Heath

Also known as heathers, these are the familiar heaths, scrubby plants that can be used to carpet large tracts of land. They form the largest genus of heaths (the other two are *Calluna* and *Daboecia*), with some 700 or more evergreen species, and are particularly valued in the winter garden, although there are species that flower at other times of year. In smaller gardens ericas are excellent in island beds, either on their own (or with *Calluna* and *Daboecia*) or with dwarf conifers, with which they associate happily. They are also ideal container plants.
Cultivation Most heaths need acid soil, preferably sandy and well-drained, but *E. vagans* will tolerate alkaline conditions. If necessary, clip plants lightly after flowering. Tree heathers withstand hard pruning.

E. australis
Spanish heath

These are the shrublike tree heaths, straggly in growth but outstanding in flower. The species has lilac-pink flowers from mid- to late spring. H 2m (6ft), S 1m (3ft). Borderline hardy/Z 7–10. Selections include the more compact 'Riverslea', which has bright pinkish flowers, mostly in clusters of four. H 1.2m (4ft), S 1m (3ft).

E. carnea
Alpine heath, winter heath

This is an important species of carpeting heaths. The flowering season is from late autumn to mid-spring, with plants in milder climates being as much as two months earlier than those in colder areas. Generally they are in flower for six to eight weeks. The following selection of cultivars are all hardy/Z 5–8. 'Adrienne Duncan' has lilac-pink flowers and dark green foliage tinged bronze. H 15cm (6in), S 35cm (14in). 'Ann Sparkes' has rose-pink flowers deepening to lilac-pink from late winter to late spring and orange, bronze-tipped foliage, which turns crimson in winter. H 15cm (6in), S 25cm (10in). 'Aurea' has pink flowers and gold foliage tipped with orange in spring. H 15cm (6in), S 35cm (14in). 'Challenger' has magenta and crimson flowers and dark green foliage. H 15cm (6in), S 45cm (18in). The slow-growing 'Eileen Porter' has magenta flowers. H and S 20cm (8in). 'Golden Starlet' has white flowers and glowing yellow foliage, which turns lime green in winter. H 15cm (6in), S 40cm (16in). 'King George' has pink flowers and dark green foliage. H 15cm (6in), S 25cm (10in). 'Myretoun Ruby' (syn. 'Myreton Ruby') has pink flowers, which turn magenta then crimson, and dark green foliage. H 15cm (6in), S 45cm (18in). 'Praecox Rubra' has lilac-pink flowers and foliage that is sometimes tinged with brown. H 15cm (6in), S 40cm (16in).

Erica carnea 'Rosy Gem'

'**Rosy Gem**' has lilac-pink flowers and dark green foliage. H 20cm (8in), S 45cm (18in). The vigorous '**Springwood White**' has white flowers. H 15cm (6in), S 45cm (18in). '**Vivellii**' (syn. 'Urville') has lilac-pink flowers, which deepen to magenta, from late winter to early spring and dark green, bronze-tinged foliage. H 15cm (6in), S 35cm (14in). '**Westwood Yellow**' has shell-pink flowers initially that darken to lilac-pink, and yellow foliage throughout the year. H 15cm (6in), S 30cm (12in).

E. cinerea
Bell heather, twisted heather
These are the summer-flowering heathers, although some will continue well into autumn. The bell heather is typical of the genus and requires acid soil. The cultivars listed are all hardy/Z 6–8. '**Alfred Bowerman**' has magenta flowers. H 35cm (14in), S 45cm (18in). '**Blossom Time**' has also magenta flowers. H 30cm (12in), S 55cm (22in). '**C.D. Eason**' has bright magenta-pink flowers and dark green foliage. H 25cm (10in), S 50cm (20in). '**C.G. Best**' (syn. 'Graham Thomas') has salmon pink flowers. H 30cm (12in), S 70cm (28in). '**Champs Hill**' has dusky rose-pink flowers. H 35cm (14in), S 45cm (18in). Hardy/Z 5. '**Eden Valley**' has lavender-pink flowers with white bases. H 20cm (8in), S 50cm (20in). '**Fiddler's Gold**' has lilac-pink flowers and bright golden-yellow foliage, which is best in spring. H 25cm (10in), S 45cm (18in). '**Golden**

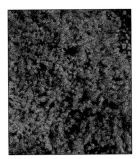

Erica cinerea 'Golden Drop'

Drop' has lilac-pink flowers and bright golden-yellow foliage, which is tinged copper in spring and turns copper red in winter. H 20cm (8in), S 60cm (24in). '**Golden Hue**' has amethyst flowers and pale yellow foliage, tipped with orange in winter. H 35cm (14in), S 70cm (28in). '**Golden Sport**' has deep carmine pink flowers and bright golden-yellow foliage. H 15cm (6in), S 30cm (12in). '**Heidebrand**' has flaming pink flowers. H 20cm (8in), S 30cm (12in). '**Hookstone White**' has white flowers. H 35cm (14in), S 65cm (26in). '**Lady Skelton**' has ruby red flowers. H 10cm (4in), S 15cm (6in). '**P.S. Patrick**' has bright reddish-purple flowers and dark glossy green foliage. H 30cm (12in), S 45cm (18in). '**Pentreath**' has rich reddish-purple flowers. H 30cm (12in), S 55cm (22in). '**Pink Ice**' (syn. 'Pink Lace') has rose-pink flowers and foliage that is tinged bronze when young and in winter. H 20cm (8in), S 35cm (14in). '**Stephen Davis**' has luminous red flowers. H 25cm (10in), S 45cm (18in). '**Summer Gold**' has magenta-pink flowers and bright golden-yellow foliage. H 30cm (12in), S 45cm (18in).

E. × darleyensis
Darley heath, Darley Dale heath
These easy-to-grow hybrids have coloured young foliage and a long flowering period, usually from midwinter (sometimes earlier) until well into spring. Darly Dale heaths tolerate lime reasonably. The following selection of cultivars are all hardy/Z 7–8.

Erica × darleyensis 'Kramer's Rote'

'**Archie Graham**' has lilac-pink flowers. H 50cm (20in), S 60cm (24in). '**Arthur Johnson**' (syn. 'Dunwood Splendour') has pink flowers, which deepen to lilac-pink, and foliage tipped with cream in spring. H 60cm (24in), S 75cm (30in). '**Jack H. Brummage**' has lilac-pink flowers and foliage that is yellow-orange throughout the year. H 30cm (1ft), S 60cm (2ft). '**Kramer's Rote**' has magenta flowers and bronze-tinged foliage. H 35cm (14in), S 60cm (24in). '**Silberschmelze**' (syn. 'Molten Silver') has ash-white flowers and foliage faintly tipped with cream in spring. H 35cm (14in), S 80cm (32in). '**White Perfection**' has pure white flowers. H 40cm (16in), S 70cm (28in).

E. lusitanica
Portuguese heath
This has the longest flowering period of any tree heath. The straight species has pink buds opening to white flowers from midwinter to late spring. H 1m

(3ft), S 70cm (28in). Borderline hardy/Z 8–10. The selection '**George Hunt**' is smaller, with white flowers in mid-spring. Its chief merit lies in its yellow foliage, which lasts all year, making it an outstanding specimen plant. It is a frost hardy heath but needs a sheltered position. H and S 60cm (24in).

E. vagans
Cornish heath, wandering heath
A vigorous, evergreen, bushy species that provides flowers in autumn (some selections coming into flower in late summer). Tolerates some lime and responds well to pruning. The faded flowers (if left on the plant) turn an attractive russet brown in winter. All are hardy/Z 6–8. '**Birch Glow**' has glowing rose-pink flowers. H 30cm (12in), S 50cm (20in). '**Hookstone Rosea**' has pale rose-pink flowers. H 35cm (14in), S 70cm (28in). '**Kervensis Alba**' has white flowers. H 30cm (12in), S 50cm (20in). '**Lyonesse**' has white flowers. H 25cm (10in), S 50cm (20in). '**Mrs D.F. Maxwell**' has deep rose-pink flowers and dark green foliage. H 30cm (12in), S 45cm (18in). '**Saint Keverne**' has bright pink flowers. H 30cm (12in), S 50cm (20in). '**Summertime**' has shell-pink flowers. H 15cm (5in), S 35cm (14in). '**Valerie Proudley**' has sparse, white flowers and bright lemon-yellow foliage. H 15cm (6in), S 30cm (12in). '**Viridiflora**' has small bluish-green or mauve flowers encased in green bracts. H 30cm (12in), S 55cm (22in).

Erica cinerea 'Alfred Bowerman'

Erica lusitanica 'George Hunt'

Erica vagans 'Valerie Proudley'

Euonymus fortunei 'Emerald and Gold'

Exochorda × macrantha 'The Bride'

Fremontodendron 'California Glory'

EUONYMUS
Spindle tree
This is a large genus of about 175 species of deciduous, semi-evergreen and evergreen shrubs, trees and climbers. The evergreen shrubs make excellent ground-cover and some can even be persuaded to climb walls. Deciduous types are among the best plants for autumn interest, having both spectacular leaf colour and showy fruits.
Cultivation Grow these shrubs in any reasonable garden soil, including chalk (alkaline soil). The evergreens tolerate shade.

E. alatus
Winged spindle tree
The autumn fruits are the distinguishing feature of this deciduous shrub: bluish-purple, they split to reveal bright orange seeds, at the same time as the leaves redden but persisting on the branches for a while after the leaves have fallen. It is suitable for a wild garden or can be used in a hedgerow-type planting and will ultimately make a fine specimen. H 2m (6ft), S 3m (10ft). Hardy/Z 4–9.

E. fortunei
This evergreen is exclusively grown in its variegated forms, of which there are a great many. The following are all hardy/Z 5–9. **'Emerald and Gold'** has leaves edged yellow. H 1m (3ft), S 1.5m (5ft). **'Harlequin'** is a dwarf plant, with mottled white and green leaves, useful as ground-cover if planted in groups. H and S 1m (3ft). Most handsome of all is **'Silver Queen'**, which has

leaves broadly edged with creamy white. It is slow-growing but worthwhile and spectacular as a climber. H and S 1.5m (5ft), more if wall-trained.

EXOCHORDA
Pearl bush
A genus usually represented in gardens in the form described here, a lovely, fresh-looking plant for late spring, associating happily with late-flowering white or cream daffodils.
Cultivation This is tolerant of all except waterlogged soils in sun or light shade.

E. × macrantha 'The Bride'
The deciduous hybrid is only ever seen in this form, which is wreathed in white flowers in late spring, as its name implies. H and S 1m (3ft). Hardy/Z 5–9.

FORSYTHIA
Indispensable spring-flowering shrubs, these deciduous plants bear bright yellow flowers before the leaves appear. They can be grown as specimens, and are also

Forsythia suspensa

excellent in a shrub or mixed border, especially with spring bulbs. The stems are good for cutting, which is a good method of keeping plants within bounds. Eye-catching when in full flower, but of less interest the rest of the time, plant them as unobtrusive backdrops to perennials or as a support for summer-flowering climbers such as clematis.
Cultivation Grow in any reasonable soil in sun or light shade. Remove older wood after flowering if necessary and shorten the previous year's growth by about one-third.

F. × intermedia 'Lynwood'
This ungainly shrub is the best-known form, with rich yellow flowers on arching stems in early to mid-spring. H to 3m (10ft), S 1.5m (5ft). Hardy/Z 5–9.

F. suspensa
Golden bell
An arching shrub with branches covered in bright yellow flowers in early to mid-spring. H and S 2m (6ft) or more. Hardy/Z 6–8.

FOTHERGILLA
This small but interesting genus, containing only two deciduous species, is related to *Hamamelis*.
Cultivation Fothergillas need neutral or lime-free soil in sun or light shade.

F. major
The pussywillow-like, fragrant flowers are a delight in early spring. Good leaf colour in autumn provides a second season of interest. H and S 2m (6ft). Hardy/Z 5–9.

FREMONTODENDRON
Flannel bush
A superb plant for a favoured spot in the garden, these Californian plants will reward you with a magnificent display of gleaming yellow flowers in summer. Contact with the stems and leaves can cause allergies.
Cultivation Fremontodendrons tolerate all soil types (except those that are waterlogged) but need a very warm position, such as against a heat-reflecting wall in cold areas. Some winter protection may also be necessary.

F. 'California Glory'
This hybrid, which is evergreen in all but the hardest winters, covers itself with gleaming buttercup-yellow flowers in summer. It is a fast-growing plant, but can be short-lived. H 3m (10ft), S 2m (6ft). Borderline hardy/Z 8–9.

FUCHSIA
Thousands of hybrids have made this deservedly popular genus of evergreen or deciduous shrubs huge. They flower over a long period (from summer until the first frosts). Some have small, dainty flowers, like the species, but others are more flamboyant. They have a number of uses: in beds and borders, as wall shrubs, and in containers and hanging baskets (particularly pendent varieties). So-called hardy types can be cut back by hard frosts but will recover. From the gardener's point of view, fuchsias can be divided into two broad groups: hardy and tender. Hardy varieties (here defined as those that tolerate temperatures of -5°C/ 23°F or below) are excellent for cool borders. Smaller ones work well as edging plants and in rock gardens. Larger types can be used as specimens, trained against a wall or used for an informal flowering hedge, *F. magellanica* being especially effective for all these purposes. Tender varieties can be used as summer bedding and in containers planted for seasonal interest; those with trailing stems are ideal for hanging baskets. All are suitable for training as standards (trailing fuchsias will produce weeping standards). Most can be

Fuchsia 'Army Nurse'

Fuchsia 'Prosperity'

Fuchsia 'Dark Eyes'

Fuchsia 'Igloo Maid'

successfully overwintered if allowed to dry off at the end of summer before storage in a cool, bright, frost-free place. (The beautiful triphylla types, however, cannot always be relied upon to regenerate the next year.) *Cultivation* Grow fuchsias in any well-drained soil in sun or light shade in not too cold a position. Protect hardy types over winter with a dry mulch. Cut back to ground level in spring.

F. magellanica
Lady's eardrops

This elegant species comes from South America and is one of the most reliable of all the fuchsias. From late summer until well into autumn, the red and bluish-purple flowers hang from the stems in a most appealing way. H 1.2m (4ft), S 45cm (18in), but considerably more where it overwinters successfully. Borderline hardy/Z 7–8. Desirable selections include *F. magellanica* var. *gracilis*, which is more slender in all its parts, with leaves daintily margined with

cream; *F. magellanica* var. *molinae*, which has smaller, pale pink flowers; and **'Versicolor'**, which has the advantage of beautiful leaves, coppery pink on emergence in spring, becoming grey-green.

Hardy hybrids

These hybrids are all frost hardy/Z 7–9. **'Army Nurse'** has semi-double, blue-violet and deep carmine red flowers. It makes an excellent standard. H 1.5m (5ft), S 1m (3ft). **'Brutus'** is vigorous and has single, rich dark purple and cerise-red flowers. H and S 1m (3ft). The upright and bushy **'Genii'** has single violet-purple and cerise-red flowers among yellow-green leaves. H 1.5m (5ft), S 75cm (30in). **'Hawkshead'** is a popular cultivar, with single, pinkish-white flowers, which are tinged green. H 60cm (2ft), S 45cm (18in). **'Mrs Popple'** has single, deep violet and scarlet flowers. It is good as a hedge. H and S 1m (3ft). **'Prosperity'** has double, pale rose-pink and crimson flowers. H 1.5m (5ft),

S 1m (3ft). **'Riccartonii'** (syn. *F. magellanica* 'Riccartonii'), a good hedging fuchsia, has small purple and red flowers. H and S 1m (3ft). **'Tom Thumb'**, a compact form and good for a rock garden, produces masses of small, single, mauve-purple and carmine-red flowers. H and S 50cm (20in).

Tender hybrids

These are all half-hardy to frost tender/Z 9–10. **'Alf Thornley'** has double, white and rose-pink flowers. H and S 1m (3ft). **'Chang'** has unusual, single, orange-red flowers, the sepals tipped green. H 1m (3ft), S 75cm (30in). **'Cotton Candy'** is an upright form with double, pale pink and blush-white flowers. H 1m (3ft), S 60cm (2ft). The trailing **'Dark Eyes'** has an abundance of perfectly formed, double, deep violet-blue and red flowers. H and S 1m (3ft). The trailing **'Frosted Flame'** produces large, single, barrel-shaped, bright red and white flowers over a long period. H 30cm (1ft), S 1m

(3ft). **'Gay Parasol'** has dramatic, dark red-purple and ivory-white flowers that open like a parasol. H 1m (3ft), S 45cm (18in). **'Golden Eden Lady'** has single, violet and pink flowers among yellow-green leaves. H 1m (3ft), S 75cm (30in). The trailing **'Igloo Maid'** is initially upright, then spreading, with double, white, pink-tinged flowers among yellow-green leaves. H 1m (3ft), S 60cm (2ft). **'Lord Lonsdale'** is unique, with single, salmon-orange and apricot-pink flowers and curled and crinkled foliage. H 1.5m (5ft), S 1m (3ft). **'Mantilla'**, a trailing, triphylla type, has long, single, rich carmine-pink flowers among bronze-tinged leaves. H 15cm (6in), S 75cm (30in). **'Monterey'** has elegant, long, single, salmon-orange flowers. H and S 1m (3ft). **'Royal Velvet'** has large, double, luminous deep purple and crimson flowers. H 75cm (30in), S 1m (3ft). **'Thalia'** is a triphylla type, with long, single, rich orange-red flowers among velvety leaves. H 45cm (18in), S 1m (3ft).

Fuchsia 'Brutus'

Fuchsia 'Chang'

Fuchsia 'Golden Eden Lady'

Fuchsia 'Mantilla'

Genista aetnensis

× Halimiocistus sahucii

GENISTA
Broom

These largely deciduous, airy plants, native to the Mediterranean, have showers of yellow pea flowers in spring or summer. The stems are leafless, giving a twiggy, even dead appearance in winter. They are not long-lived but are easily raised from seed. Essential plants for a Mediterranean garden or any planting in gravel. *G. aetnensis* can be a tree.
Cultivation Brooms thrive in well-drained soils of low fertility in full sun. They do not respond well to hard pruning.

G. aetnensis
Mount Etna broom

A delightful deciduous shrub or small tree for a hot, dry garden, showering golden-yellow flowers over lower plants in mid- to late summer. H and S 6m (20ft). Borderline hardy/Z 9–10.

G. lydia

This deciduous species produces a mass of twiggy branches that are covered in deep yellow flowers in late spring and early summer. H 30cm (12in), S to 1m (3ft). Hardy/Z 6–9.

× HALIMIOCISTUS

A group of usually evergreen hybrids, crosses between the genera *Halimium* and *Cistus*, both of which hybridize naturally in the wild. They have papery flowers that are saucer-shaped, and are excellent in a Mediterranean garden.
Cultivation Grow in any free-draining soil, ideally gritty and of low fertility, in full sun.

× H. sahucii

A shrub with a long flowering season. The chalk-white flowers can be produced from early summer into autumn. H 45cm (18in), S 1m (3ft). Hardy/Z 7–9.

× H. wintonensis

A compact shrub, with white flowers marked with yellow and maroon at the base of the petals. H 60cm (2ft), S 1m (3ft). Borderline hardy/Z 7–9.

HAMAMELIS
Witch hazel

The genus contains some of the finest winter-flowering shrubs, which would no doubt be more widely grown were it not for their specific cultivation needs. Propagation is also difficult, and plants are slow-growing, so those offered for sale tend to be small and expensive. Besides their spidery, scented winter flowers, they also have outstanding autumn leaf colour.
Cultivation Witch hazels need rich, ideally lime-free soil in a sunny site that is sheltered from strong winds.

H. × intermedia

This is a group of variable hybrids. H and S 4m (13ft), but only after many years. Hardy/Z 5–9. Selections include 'Arnold Promise', which has bright yellow winter flowers and splendid autumn leaf colour; 'Diane', which has red flowers and rich autumn tints; and the rare 'Vesna', with pale copper-coloured flowers and superb autumn leaf colour.

H. mollis
Chinese witch hazel

One of the best of the witch hazels, this slow-growing species has scented yellow flowers in mid-winter. H and S 4m (13ft), for mature plants. Hardy/Z 5–9.

HEBE

The large genus of scrubby evergreen plants from Australia and New Zealand contains about 100 species. They are grown for their (mainly) summer flowers, which are highly attractive to bees, and for their foliage. All hebes are excellent in seaside areas. Some have small leaves that cling to the stems almost like scales; these are the so-called whipcord hebes. The species with large, fleshy leaves are less hardy than others. Compact types are good in containers.
Cultivation Grow in any reasonable soil in full sun. Some of the taller hebes are remarkably tolerant of dry shade. The larger-leaved species can be pruned hard.

H. 'Blue Clouds'

This excellent hybrid has long spikes of bluish-mauve flowers from early summer until well into autumn. H 1m (3ft), S 1.2m (4ft). Hardy/Z 8.

H. cupressoides

This whipcord hebe has grey-green leaves and pale lilac-blue

Genista lydia

Hamamelis mollis

Hebe 'Blue Clouds'

Hebe cupressoides

flowers which appear in early
summer. H and S 1.2m (4ft).
Borderline hardy/Z 8–9. The
selection **'Boughton Dome'** is
unique. It looks like a conifer,
seldom if ever flowers and makes
a neat bun shape without pruning.
H 30cm (12in), S 60cm (24in).
Hardy/Z 8–9.

H. 'Great Orme'
An elegant hybrid, this has narrow
green leaves and spikes of pale
pink flowers, aging to white, from
summer to autumn. H 1.5m
(5ft), S 1m (3ft). Borderline
hardy/Z 9–10.

H. hulkeana
A species quite unlike any other,
this has red-edged, toothed leaves
and lilac-like flowers, which may
be white, blue or mauve, in early

summer. H and S 60cm (2ft).
Borderline hardy/Z 9–10.

H. 'Mrs Winder'
(syn. H. 'Waikiki',
H. 'Warlyensis')
This hebe has violet-blue flowers
in autumn. The leaves often
flush purple in cold weather. H
and S 1m (3ft). Borderline
hardy/Z 8.

H. pinguifolia 'Pagei'
A dainty, spreading shrub, this has
thick, silver-grey leaves and spikes
of white flowers towards the end of
spring. H 20cm (8in), S 60cm
(2ft). Hardy/Z 8–9.

H. rakaiensis
This small, green-leaved species
grows in a compact bun-shape
and produces its white flowers in
early to midsummer. H 60cm
(2ft), S 1m (3ft). Hardy/
Z 8–10.

H. speciosa 'La Séduisante'
This upright hybrid is aptly
named. The rich, purplish-red
flowers, carried on stems of the
same colour, open from midsummer to late autumn. The
leaves also have a purplish finish.
H and S 60cm (2ft). Borderline
hardy/Z 8.

HELIANTHEMUM
Rock rose, sun rose
The genus contains about 110
species of evergreen or semi-
evergreen shrubs and subshrubs
with brightly coloured flowers

Hebe pinguifolia 'Pagei'

from late spring to summer.
Cultivation Grow in any free-
draining soil in full sun. They
thrive on soils of low fertility.

H. hybrids
Most rock roses are of garden
origin, varying in habit but
generally hummock-forming.
The following are hardy/Z 6–8.
'Ben Nevis' has yellow flowers
with red centres. H and S 20cm
(8in). **'Rhodanthe Carneum'**
(syn. 'Wisley Pink') has pink
flowers. H 25cm (10in), S to
45cm (18in). **'Wisley White'** has
white flowers with yellow stamens.
H 25cm (10in), S 45cm (18in).

HIBISCUS
Rose mallow
These shrubs have mallow-like
flowers in late summer. The

deciduous types described here
are among the last woody plants
to come into leaf, which happens
in late spring. The genus also
includes perennials and annuals.
Cultivation Grow in any well-
drained soil in a sunny,
sheltered position.

H. syriacus
A large number of cultivars have
been developed from this upright
deciduous species. The following
are all hardy/Z 6–9. H 2.5m
(8ft), S 2m (6ft). **'Oiseau Bleu'**
(syn. 'Blue Bird') is among the
best known. It has violet-blue
flowers with darker eyes. **'Totus
Albus'** is a rarity in having pure
white flowers. It will add late
interest to a white border.
'Woodbridge' has warm rose-
pink flowers.

Hebe 'Great Orme'

Helianthemum 'Rhodanthe Carneum'

Hibiscus syriacus 'Oiseau Bleu'

Hydrangea arborescens 'Annabelle'

Hydrangea macrophylla 'Ayesha'

Hydrangea quercifolia 'Snow Flake'

HYDRANGEA

The genus contains medium to large, mainly deciduous shrubs. Late-flowering shrubs are few, and hydrangeas fill the gap nicely. They are also some of the few deciduous shrubs that thrive in containers. Planted in half-barrels, they give distinction to any garden. Hydrangea flower heads take a number of forms: lacecaps have a central mass of tiny fertile flowers surrounded by larger sterile flowers only; mopheads (hortensias) have domed heads of sterile flowers only; others have flowers in conical panicles. *Cultivation* All hydrangeas need rich, moisture-retentive soil. The larger, soft-leaved varieties need shelter from strong winds and hot sun, thriving in woodland conditions. Soil pH affects the colour of some hybrids: acid soil enhances blue flowers, while alkaline soil enhances pink flowers. Some selected forms of *H. paniculata* can be pruned hard annually for larger flowers.

H. arborescens
Sevenbark
The species is less widely grown than its named selections, the loveliest of which is '**Annabelle**', which produces large, cream-coloured flowerheads in late summer. H and S 1.5m (5ft). Hardy/Z 4–9.

H. aspera
A rangy shrub, this has velvety stems and blue and white flowers in late summer. Best in lime-free soil in light woodland. H 3m (10ft), S 1.5m (5ft). Hardy/Z 7–9. The **Villosa Group** (syn. *H. villosa*) hybrids are characterized by pale purple flowers and make more rounded shrubs. H and S 1.2m (4ft) or more.

H. macrophylla
Common hydrangea
The Japanese species is rarely seen in cultivation, but it is widely represented by many selected forms. The following are all hardy/Z 6–9. '**Altona**' (mophead) is a stiffly growing shrub, with flowers that are cerise pink on alkaline soils and mid-blue on acid soils. H and S 1m (3ft). '**Ayesha**' (mophead) has pale mauve or pale blue flowers. H and S 1.5m (5ft). '**Mariesii Perfecta**' (syn. 'Blue Wave'; lacecap) has blue (or mauve, depending on the soil pH) outer flowers surrounding pink central ones. H and S 2m (6ft).

H. paniculata
This species makes an upright, vase-shaped shrub and has conical flowerheads. It can be pruned annually to keep it within bounds. H 2m (6ft), S 1.2m (4ft), less if pruned annually. Hardy/Z 4–8. There are a number of fine cultivars, including '**Burgundy Lace**', which has white flowers, aging to dull pink; '**Kyushu**', which has pure white flowers; and '**Limelight**', which has cool lime green flowers, the best colour being in shade.

H. quercifolia
This species has conical flower-heads, like those of *H. paniculata*, but is distinguished by its oak-like leaves. H 2m (6ft), S 1.5m (5ft). Hardy/Z 5–9. '**Snow Flake**' has pure white flowers.

H. serrata
(syn. *H. macrophylla* subsp. *serrata*)
The straight deciduous species seldom finds a place in gardens, but the named forms include some splendid plants for late summer-autumn interest, all hardy/Z 6–9. '**Bluebird**' (syn. 'Acuminata'; lacecap) has pale pink, pale purple or rich blue flowers and leaves that assume rich red autumn tints. H 80cm (32in), S 1m (3ft). '**Grayswood**' (lacecap) produces mauve central flowers surrounded by large white flowers that redden as they age. H and S 2m (6ft). '**Preziosa**' (syn. *H.* 'Preziosa'; hortensia) is outstanding, with rich red, mauve or blue flowers, depending on the soil pH. H and S 1.5m (5ft). '**Rosalba**' (lacecap) has a row of white sterile flowers surrounding the central pink ones. H and S 1.2 m (4ft).

Hydrangea aspera

Hydrangea macrophylla 'Altona'

Hypericum 'Hidcote'

HYPERICUM
St John's wort
These valuable shrubs can be difficult to place in the garden because of the uncompromising yellow of the flowers. Try growing them in association with white groundcover roses. *H. olympicum* makes good groundcover.
Cultivation Grow hypericums in any well-drained soil in sun or light shade.

H. 'Hidcote'
This is probably the most significant member of the genus. It has large, shining yellow flowers from midsummer onwards. H and S 1m (3ft). Hardy/Z 6–9.

H. olympicum
The best species for groundcover, this is a sprawling shrub with golden-yellow flowers from midsummer onwards. Trim it with shears. It can also be grown in rock gardens. H 25cm (10in), S 30cm (12in). Hardy/Z 6–8.

H. 'Rowallane'
This elegant hybrid needs a sheltered spot. Large, golden-yellow flowers are produced from early summer to autumn. H 2m (6ft), S 1.2m (4ft). Borderline hardy/Z 7–9.

ILEX
Holly
Hollies become trees eventually, but they are slow-growing plants and can be treated as shrubs in the garden, particularly if they are cut back regularly, a practice to which they generally respond well. Male and female flowers are carried on separate plants, so if

Hypericum olympicum

you are growing hollies for berry production, make sure there is a male nearby. Conversely, if you grow only males, don't expect any berries. Hollies make excellent hedges (given time) and can be clipped to shape.
Cultivation Hollies are tolerant of most sites and soils and will grow in sun or light shade.

I. × altaclerensis
This is a large hybrid group. The heights and spreads shown are the ultimate size if plants are not pruned, but all can be controlled by regular pruning. Hardy/Z 7–9. The female **'Belgica Aurea'** has leaves that are irregularly variegated with creamy yellow.

Ilex × altaclerensis 'Golden King'

H and S 3m (10ft). **'Camelliifolia'** is a handsome plain green, free-berrying form. It has smooth leaves that develop a bronze hue in cold weather, and it is one of the best for hedging. H and S 5m (16ft). **'Golden King'**, a female form, bears large red berries and has gold-edged leaves. H and S 6m (20ft). **'Lawsoniana'**, a female, is unusual in that the leaf edges are green and the centres are splashed with yellow. H 2.4m (8ft), S 1m (3ft). **'Wilsonii'** is a female that is grown for its abundant scarlet berries, rather than its plain green leaves. It will eventually reach tree proportions. H to 9m (29ft), S 5m (16ft).

I. crenata
Japanese holly
The species has small, rounded leaves, similar to those of box, and plants can be used for the same purposes. H 2.5m (8ft), S 2m (6ft). Hardy/Z 6–8. **'Mariesii'**, a female form, is very slow-growing, with black berries. H and S 1m (3ft).

ITEA
These elegant rather than showy shrubs have fragrant flowers and handsome leaves. The species described here repays careful cultivation and makes a superb wall shrub.
Cultivation Grow in fertile, well-drained but not too dry soil in a sunny, sheltered site.

Itea ilicifolia

I. ilicifolia
This beautiful evergreen shrub from China has shining, holly-like leaves and racemes of greenish flowers in late summer. It is an excellent support for yellow-flowered clematis. H and S 3m (10ft). Borderline hardy/Z 7–9.

KALMIA
The genus contains seven species of hardy, evergreen shrubs for an acid site. Kalmias are excellent used in conjunction with heathers or in light woodland.
Cultivation Grow in reliably moist, lime-free soil in either sun or light shade.

K. latifolia
Calico bush, mountain laurel
The species bears white, pink, purple or red flowers in midsummer, which provide a fine contrast to the glossy leaves. H and S 3m (10ft). Hardy/Z 5–9.

Kalmia latifolia

KERRIA
Jew's mallow
These spring-flowering, deciduous shrubs, bearing desirable yellow flowers, have a curious, upright, suckering habit. Not the most winsome plants, they are tough and reliable, equally good with daffodils and in a shrub border. There is only one species.
Cultivation Kerrias are tolerant of all but waterlogged soils in sun or light shade.

K. japonica
The species from China and Japan is seldom seen in gardens. It has single yellow flowers from mid- to late spring. H and S 2m (6ft). Hardy/Z 5–9. **'Golden Guinea'** is a rare but worthwhile single form with larger flowers than the species. H 1.5m (5ft), S 1m (3ft). Much more often grown is **'Pleniflora'**, which has double, button-like flowers. H to 2m (6ft), S 1m (3ft).

KOLKWITZIA
Beauty bush
The single species in the genus was given its common name for good reason. Its beautiful pink flowers make a stunning sight.
Cultivation Kolkwitzias are suitable for all except waterlogged soils in sun or light shade.

K. amabilis
This elegant, arching deciduous shrub is normally seen in the selected form **'Pink Cloud'**, which

Kerria japonica 'Pleniflora'

is festooned with pink, bell-shaped flowers in late spring to early summer. H 3m (10ft), S 4m (12ft). Hardy/Z 5–9.

LAVANDULA
Lavender
Lavenders are well-known herb garden plants, but they have a number of other uses, principally as flowering hedging. When they are in flower, these evergreen shrubs and subshrubs will be alive with bees. They make a classic combination with old roses and can also be trained as standards.
Cultivation Lavenders will grow in all soil types but must have good drainage and a position in full sun. Clip hedging lightly in spring.

L. angustifolia
(syn. *L. officinalis*)
Old English lavender
The species has grey-green leaves and scented blue-grey flowers all summer long. H and S 60cm (2ft). Hardy/Z 6–9. There are many selections, including **'Hidcote'** (syn. *L.* 'Hidcote Blue'), which has rich deep lavender-blue flowers; **'Munstead'**, which has soft, lilac-blue flowers; and the strong-growing **'Rosea'**, with pink flowers. H and S 60cm (2ft).

L. stoechas
French lavender
Essential in any herb garden, this species has distinctive flower spikes, with bright purple, erect bracts at the top of each flower-head. It has a long flowering period. H and S 45cm (18in). Borderline hardy/Z 7–9.

LAVATERA
Tree mallow
A genus of evergreen, semi-evergreen and deciduous shrubs, perennials and annuals, which are highly valued for their late-season flowers. The species described is widely grown but is rather harsh in colour. The various hybrids are all improvements on the species and integrate better into mixed borders planned for late-summer interest.
Cultivation Grow lavateras in any well-drained soil in full sun.

L. 'Barnsley'
One of the best-known hybrids, this semi-evergreen plant bears very pale pink mallow flowers with warm pinkish-red eyes towards the end of summer. It has a tendency to revert to type over time. H and S 2m (6ft). Hardy/Z 8.

L. thuringiaca
Tree lavatera
The species bears deep pink flowers in profusion in late summer to autumn. H 2m (6ft), S 1.5m (5ft). Hardy/Z 8. The superior selection **'Ice Cool'** is similar to 'Barnsley', but the flowers do not have the red maskings. H and S 1.5m (5ft).

× LEDODENDRON
This hybrid genus consists of a single shrub, which is a cross between *Rhododendron trichosomum* and *Ledum glandulosum* var. *columbianum*.
Cultivation Grow in acid, well-drained soil in partial shade.

Kolkwitzia amabilis 'Pink Cloud'

Lavandula stoechas

Lavandula angustifolia 'Hidcote'

× *Ledodendron* 'Arctic Tern'
(syn. *Rhododendron* 'Arctic Tern')
This compact, vigorous, evergreen
shrub bears white flowers in late
spring to early summer. H and S
60cm (2ft). Hardy/Z 8.

LEPTOSPERMUM
Tea tree
The genus contains about 80
species of evergreen trees and
shrubs from Australia, New
Zealand and South-east Asia
grown for their foliage and small
flowers. Not for all gardens, these
plants are not reliably hardy and
have specific soil requirements,
although in the right conditions
they make charming specimens.
Cultivation Grow in lime-free,
reliably moist, well-drained soil in
full sun with some shelter,
particularly in cold areas.

L. lanigerum
Woolly tea tree
This erect species from Australia
has white flowers in early summer.
H 1.5m (5ft), S 1m (3ft).
Borderline hardy/Z 8.

L. scoparium
Manuka, New Zealand tea-tree
This is a variable species, which
is rarely seen in cultivation, but
there are many cultivars. The
following are half-hardy/Z 9–10.
The dwarf **'Kiwi'** has pinkish-red
flowers and reddish-purple leaves.
H and S 1m (3ft). The rarer
'Lyndon' has white flowers. H
and S 3m (10ft).

Lavatera 'Barnsley'

LEUCOTHOE
These compact and dainty shrubs
are grown for their evergreen
foliage and flowers. They are not
reliably hardy in all situations and
have specific soil requirements.
They are good in peat beds or in
light woodland.
Cultivation Grow in fertile, acid
soil in sun or light shade, with
shelter from cold winds. They will
not tolerate dry conditions.

L. 'Scarletta'
(syn. *L. axillaris* 'Scarletta',
L. 'Zeblid')
This evergreen shrub bears small,
white, pitcher-shaped flowers in
late spring. The foliage reddens in
late summer, but is not shed. H
and S 60cm (2ft). Hardy/Z 5.

L. walteri
(syn. *L. fonanesiana*)
The form of the species most
generally seen is **'Rainbow'**, a
spreading evergreen with striking
leaves variegated with pink and
cream. The white, lily-of-the-
valley-like flowers seem incidental
when they appear in summer. H
and S 60cm (2ft). Hardy/Z 5–8.

LEYCESTERIA
These sombre, deciduous shrubs
are grown for their late-summer
flowers and autumn fruits.
The genus, which contains six
species, is generally represented in
cultivation by the single species
described here.
Cultivation It is suitable for most
soils in sun or light shade.

L. formosa
Pheasant berry, Himalayan
honeysuckle
The first common name derives
from the appeal of the dark
purple autumn fruits to
pheasants. These follow the
drooping panicles of white and
claret-purple summer flowers.
H 2m (6ft), S 1m (3ft).
Borderline hardy/Z 7–9.

LIGUSTRUM
Privet
An unnecessarily maligned genus,
Ligustrum is usually seen in
gardens as hedging, for which
purpose it is inferior to some
other plants. It is put to best use
in a mixed or shrub border as an

Leucothoe 'Scarletta'

unassuming backdrop to other
more flamboyant plants, but
privets are also surprisingly good
as specimens. Variegated forms
are highly effective when trained
as standards.
Cultivation Privets are tolerant
of any ordinary garden soil in sun
or shade.

L. ovalifolium
This is the privet most widely used
as hedging, when it is clipped to
keep it to size. The species, which
is usually evergreen, has plain green
leaves and white flowers in summer.
H and S 4m (13ft). Hardy/Z
6–10. The selection **'Aureum'**
(syn. 'Aureomarginatum') is
variegated with yellow and is less
vigorous. H and S 3m (10ft).

Leptospermum scoparium 'Lyndon'

Leycesteria formosa

Ligustrum tschonoskii

L. tschonoskii

This handsome deciduous species is a rarity in gardens. The leaves and flowers are somewhat larger than those of most other privets. H and S 2m (6ft), but eventually tree-like. Hardy/Z 6.

LONICERA
Honeysuckle

Most honeysuckles are climbers, but the genus also includes the following shrubs, many of them excellent for the winter garden and extremely hardy. The deciduous species described here can be wall-trained if you choose, which can sometimes lead to more abundant flowering. *L. nitida* is useful for hedging and also for small-scale topiary.

Lonicera nitida 'Baggesen's Gold'

Cultivation Honeysuckles will grow in any, preferably humus-rich, soil in sun or light shade. Cut back some of the oldest stems every year after flowering.

L. fragrantissima

A good plant for winter interest, this deciduous or semi-evergreen Chinese species has small, fragrant, white and pink flowers in midwinter. Unfortunately, it is rather dull the rest of the time, unless used as a support for annual climbers, such as sweet peas. H and S 1.5m (5ft). Hardy/ Z 5–8.

L. nitida

This dense evergreen shrub has neat, oval, dark green leaves. Both the species and the cultivar described below are ideal for hedging and may be easily controlled by pruning. H 2m (6ft), S 1.5m (5ft). Hardy/Z 7–9. The form usually seen is '**Baggesen's Gold**', which has yellow-green leaves.

L. × purpusii

This deciduous hybrid produces fragrant, white flowers on the bare stems in winter. Both this and the selected form described here are almost indistinguishable from *L. fragrantissima*, leading to confusion in the nursery trade. H and S 1.5m (5ft). Hardy/Z 7–9. '**Winter Beauty**' has creamy-white flowers from early winter until spring. H and S 1.2m (4ft).

MAGNOLIA

Many magnolias are trees, but there are a few shrubs in the genus that are delightful and easy to cultivate, if a little slow to get into their stride. The deciduous spring-flowerers make ideal central features in spring borders planted with dwarf narcissi, *Anemone blanda*, species tulips and crocuses.
Cultivation Grow in fertile, well-drained soil in sun, although in frost-prone areas early flowering magnolias benefit from some shade from morning sun at flowering times.

M. × loebneri 'Leonard Messel'

This delightful deciduous hybrid has pale pink, spidery flowers in mid-spring. H 3m (10ft), S 2.5m (8ft). Hardy/Z 5–9.

M. stellata
Star magnolia

This slow-growing, deciduous species is indispensable, with masses of spidery white flowers in mid-spring. It requires a sheltered spot. H 1.2m (4ft), S 1.5m (5ft). Hardy/Z 5–9.

MAHONIA

The genus contains about 70 species of evergreen shrubs, which are rather similar to *Berberis* – in fact, some botanists would like to unite the genera. Most have deliciously scented flowers, but their prime use is to fill inhospitable sites.

Magnolia × *loebneri* 'Leonard Messel'

Cultivation Mahonias are happy in all well-drained soils, including chalk (alkaline soil). Large-leaved species benefit from shelter from strong winds. Pruning plants when young can encourage bushiness, but some forms are naturally rangy.

M. aquifolium
Mountain grape holly, Oregon grape

The species has glossy green leaves and yellow flowers in late winter to early spring. H 1m (3ft), S 1.5m (5ft). Hardy/Z 6–9. There are a number of cultivars, including the vigorous and low-growing '**Apollo**'; and '**Smaragd**', which has bronze, netted foliage. H 60cm (2ft), S 1m (3ft).

Magnolia stellata

Mahonia trifolia

Mahonia aquifolium

Mahonia × media 'Lionel Fortescue'

M. japonica

This erect species produces its arching racemes of scented yellow flowers from late autumn to early spring, followed by blue-purple berries. H 2m (6ft), S 3m (10ft). Hardy/Z 7–9. The selection 'Bealei' has more compact flower spikes.

M. lomariifolia

This elegant species is one of the parents of M. × media (the other is M. japonica), which it resembles in some respects, though it is more rangy in habit and slightly less resistant to extreme cold. The racemes of flowers, which smell like lily-of-the-valley, appear from autumn to late winter and are followed by bluish, grape-like fruits. H 3m (10ft), S 2m (6ft). Hardy/Z 8–10.

M. × media

This hybrid group includes a number of notable named garden selections, all similar and equally effective and all with long racemes of fragrant yellow flowers in winter. Leggy specimens can be pruned hard in spring. They include 'Charity', which has slender, upright, later-spreading spikes of very fragrant yellow flowers; 'Lionel Fortescue', which has upright plumes of bright yellow, slightly less fragrant flowers; and 'Winter Sun', which has dense clusters of yellow flowers. H 2m (6ft), S 1.2m (4ft). Hardy/Z 7–9.

M. trifolia
(syn. M. eutriphylla)

This unusual species is variable, existing in both prostrate and more upright forms. The short spikes of yellow flowers appear in spring, and the leaves flush purple-red in cold weather. H and S 2m (6ft). Hardy/Z 7.

M. × wagneri

This hybrid group contains a number of excellent garden plants. The notable 'Undulata' (syn. M. 'Undulata') bears yellow flowers in spring and has hollylike leaves that, in addition to having wavy edges, turn rich plum-purple in cold weather. The rich yellow flowers appear in spring. H and S 2m (6ft). Hardy/Z 8–9.

MYRTUS
Myrtle

Myrtles are rich in historical associations and were traditionally used in royal wedding bouquets. In cold areas, they need to be tucked under a sheltering wall.
Cultivation They will grow in most soils, including chalk (alkaline), but they need a warm, sunny site. Young plants benefit from some protection in winter until they are well established.

M. communis
Common myrtle

This slow-growing evergreen bushy shrub has dark green foliage and fragrant white flowers in summer, followed by purple-black berries. H and S 3m (10ft).

Borderline hardy/Z 9–10. The more compact and wind-resistant M. communis subsp. tarentina (syn. 'Jenny Reitenbach', 'Microphylla', 'Nana') has pink-flushed, white flowers and white berries. H and S 2m (6ft).

NANDINA
Sacred bamboo, Heavenly bamboo

The only species in the genus is this elegant evergreen or semi-evergreen shrub, which is grown for its overall appearance and summer flowers. Although related to Berberis, it looks nothing like it. The sacred bamboo combines well with grasses and is a good choice where a true bamboo would be too large.
Cultivation Grow in any well-drained but not too dry, reasonably fertile soil in sun, preferably with some shelter. Young plants may need winter protection in cold areas.

N. domestica

The large panicles of white, starry, summer flowers are followed by red autumn berries. The leaves start purplish-red when young, turn dark green, redden again in autumn and hold their colour into winter. H 2m (6ft), S 1m (3ft). Borderline hardy/Z 7–10. 'Fire Power' is a more compact form. H 1.2m (4ft), S 60cm (2ft). 'Richmond' bears a mass of scarlet berries in autumn. H 2m (6ft), S 1.2m (4ft).

Myrtus communis

Nandina domestica 'Fire Power'

Nerium oleander 'Roseum Plenum'

Osmanthus delavayi

Olearia 'Waikariensis'

NERIUM
Oleander
This is a typical plant of the Mediterranean (although it also appears in China), where it is widely planted as a kerbside shrub. Not hardy enough to be grown outdoors in frost-prone climates, it makes an excellent conservatory (porch) plant. There is only one species, of which all parts are poisonous.
Cultivation Grow in moderately fertile, well-drained soil in full sun. Conservatory plants can be pruned hard to keep them compact.

N. oleander
Rose bay
The evergreen species has fragrant, pink, red, apricot, yellow

or white flowers throughout the summer among the upright, lance-shaped leaves. When grown in a container it will be smaller than the dimensions indicated. H to 3m (10ft), S 2m (6ft). Tender/Z 10. Selections include **'Peach Blossom'**, which has pink flowers; **'Roseum Plenum'**, which has double, pink flowers; and **'Variegatum'**, which has variegated leaves and pink flowers. H and S to 2m (6ft).

OLEARIA
Daisy bush
The daisy bushes, mainly from Australia and New Zealand, are fine shrubs, valued for their daisy-like summer flowers and evergreen foliage. They are good in island beds and also make very good wind-resistant shelter.
Cultivation Grow olearias in any well-drained, reasonably fertile soil in full sun.

O. × haastii
This hybrid has clusters of flowers in mid- to late summer and makes a dense, rounded bush. H 2m (6ft), S 3m (10ft). Hardy/Z 8–10.

O. macrodonta
New Zealand holly
This species is one of the most impressive of the genus, with large, pewter grey, holly-like leaves and daisy-like flowers in summer. H 6m (20ft), S 5m (16ft). Borderline hardy/Z 9–10.

O. 'Waikariensis'
(syn. *O. oleifolia*)
This hybrid has felted stems and the characteristic grey leaves and daisy-like summer flowers. H and S 2m (6ft). Hardy/Z 8.

OSMANTHUS
These shrubs with handsome, evergreen leaves are related to the olive. Plant in mixed or shrub borders or in light woodland. They also make an unusual hedge.
Cultivation Almost any soil is tolerated in sun or shade, but some shelter from cold winds is desirable to avoid leaf scorch.

O. decorus
(syn. *Phillyrea decora*)
This fine species from western

Asia is grown for its overall appearance. The white flowers, which appear in spring, are small but sweetly scented. It takes kindly to pruning. H 3m (10ft), S 4m (13ft). Hardy/Z 6–9.

O. delavayi
(syn. *Siphonosmanthus delavayi*)
A slow-growing species from China, this has tiny leaves and fragrant, white flowers in mid-spring. H 2m (6ft), S 2.4m (8ft). Hardy/Z 7–9.

OZOTHAMNUS
The genus of summer-flowering, evergreen shrubs, which look like *Rosmarinus*, contains about 50 species. They are good in mixed or shrub borders but are not

Olearia × *haastii*

Ozothamnus rosmarinifolius 'Silver Jubilee'

Paeonia suffruticosa subsp. rockii

Paeonia delavayi var. lutea

Philadelphus 'Belle Etoile'

hardy enough for all gardens. They are excellent in summer borders.
Cultivation Grow in any well-drained soil in sun. Some protection may be necessary in cold winters.

O. rosmarinifolius
(syn. *Helichrysum rosmarinifolium*)
This species has an erect habit and dark green foliage. Pinkish buds open to heads of white flowers in early summer. H 3m (10ft), S 1.5m (5ft). Borderline hardy/Z 8–9. The leaves of 'Silver Jubilee' are silvery green. H 2m (6ft), S 1.2m (4ft).

PAEONIA
Peony
This is a genus primarily of perennials, but it also includes some magnificent deciduous shrubs, the so-called tree peonies. The hybrids are usually expensive, but the outlay should not put off the committed gardener, for these are long-lived plants that reward careful cultivation. All tree peonies make splendid specimens, while the species are probably best grown in light woodland.
Cultivation Tree peonies need rich, fertile soil in sun or light dappled shade. Some protection from late frost, which can damage leaves and flowers, is desirable.

P. delavayi
This species has rich dark red, bowl-shaped flowers in late

spring. H 2m (6ft), S 1m (3ft). Hardy/Z 5–8. The variety *P. delavayi* var. *lutea* (syn. *P. lutea*) has golden-yellow flowers and deeply divided glossy foliage.

P. suffruticosa
Moutan
This is the species that has engendered the huge range of hybrids (many of Japanese origin). All are hardy/Z 4–8. 'Banksii' has double, carmine flowers; 'Reine Elizabeth' has double, salmon-orange flowers with ruffled margins; and 'Renkaku' (syn. 'Flight of Cranes') has dense, double, white flowers. *P. suffruticosa* subsp. *rockii* (syn. 'Joseph Rock', 'Rock's Variety') is the ultimate connoisseur's plant, with huge, double white flowers marked with maroon at the base. This rare plant is not variable in cultivation. H 2m (6ft), S 1.5m (5ft).

PEROVSKIA
Russian sage
A good shrub for late-summer flowers, this tough plant comes

Perovskia 'Blue Spire'

from Siberia. It produces a sheaf of whitened stems covered in small, mauve-blue flowers. It is excellent in a Mediterranean or gravel garden, hot sun only enhancing its aromatic properties. The genus is normally represented in gardens by hybrids.
Cultivation Grow perovskias in any free-draining soil in full sun. They tolerate stony soil. Prune hard each year in spring.

P. 'Blue Spire'
This hybrid has silver-blue, deeply cut leaves and spires of rich blue flowers in late summer. H and S to 1m (3ft). Hardy/Z 6–9.

PHILADELPHUS
Mock orange
The scent of the mock orange is unmistakable and almost cloyingly sweet when it hangs in the air in early summer. Most of the plants in cultivation are hybrids of garden origin. Grow them as a fragrant backdrop to a mixed border. *P. coronarius* 'Aureus' can be grown exclusively for its foliage.
Cultivation Mock oranges do well in most reasonable garden soil in sun or light shade.

P. 'Avalanche'
This aptly named plant has masses of scented white flowers. H and S 1.5m (5ft). Hardy/Z 5–8.

P. 'Beauclerk'
The flowers of this distinctive, arching shrub are characterized by

central cerise blotches. H and S 1.5m (5ft). Hardy/Z 5–8.

P. 'Belle Etoile'
This hybrid has delicious, fragrant single white flowers. H 1.5m (5ft), S 1.2m (4ft). Hardy/Z 5–8.

P. coronarius
The species is grown less than its lovely cultivars, which are hardy/Z 5–9. 'Aureus' has soft gold-green leaves. It needs shelter from hot sun, but lights up a dark corner when the light strikes it. Pruning just before flowering results in a fresh crop of lime-green leaves (at the expense of the flowers). 'Variegatus' (syn. 'Bowles' Variety') has leaves that are edged in cream and white flowers. H and S 1.2m (4ft).

P. 'Manteau d'Hermine'
One of the daintiest of the mock oranges, this hybrid smothers itself in double, creamy-white flowers. H and S 45cm (18in). Hardy/Z 5–8.

P. microphyllus
This elegant species produces a mass of fragrant, single, pure white flowers. H and S to 1m (3ft). Hardy/Z 6.

P. 'Virginal'
This well-known and justly popular cultivar has double, white flowers. This is a grand plant. Old specimens tend to become bare at the base. H to 3m (10ft), S 2m (6ft). Hardy/Z 5–9.

Philadelphus 'Manteau d'Hermine'

Phillyrea angustifolia

PHILLYREA
Jasmine box

This classy evergreen shrub was widely grown in the 17th century but is nowadays increasingly rare. It is a good alternative to box and rather faster-growing. It is suitable for a maritime garden. On the debit side, it is difficult to propagate, so stocks tend to be low.
Cultivation They will grow in any fertile, well-drained soil in sun or light shade.

P. angustifolia
The flame-like, hard, dark green leaves always excite comment. The flowers, produced in spring, are insignificant. This species responds well to pruning. H and S to 3m (10ft), but usually less in gardens. Hardy/Z 7–9.

PHLOMIS
These evergreen shrubs and perennials have woolly grey leaves. They are well-suited to a Mediterranean border, grown in association with plants such as *Cistus* and *Halimium* and woody herbs such as rosemary and lavender.
Cultivation Phlomis need very well-drained, only moderately fertile soil and a position in full sun.

P. fruticosa
Jerusalem sage
The best-known species, with whorls of sulphur-yellow flowers appearing in summer among the grey leaves. H and S 1.2m (4ft). Hardy/Z 8–10.

Phlomis italica

P. italica
Daintier than *P. fruticosa*, this choice species has pink or pale purple flowers. H and S 60cm (2ft). Borderline hardy/Z 8–9.

PHOTINIA
These excellent shrubs are grown mainly for the brilliance of their spring foliage. They suit a mixed or shrub border and make a good alternative to *Pieris* in gardens with alkaline soil.
Cultivation Grow in any well-drained soil in sun or light shade.

P. davidiana
(**syn.** *Stranvaesia davidiana*)
This handsome shrub, semi-evergreen in all but the coldest areas, has as its main feature long-lasting crimson berries, which ripen in autumn. Some of the leaves turn bright red at the same time, while others remain green. H and S 2.4m (8ft). Hardy/Z 7–9.

P. × fraseri
This hybrid group includes a number of excellent selected forms. Hardy/Z 8–9. The new growth of the spreading form 'Birmingham' is deep coppery red. 'Red Robin' has spectacular bright red young stems and leaves in vivid contrast to the glossy green older leaves. H and S 1.5m (5ft).

PHYGELIUS
The subshrubs in this genus will be evergreen in mild winters, but may die back in periods of prolonged cold, although they often reshoot from ground level. In cold areas, they are best in the lee of a wall.
Cultivation Phygelius need well-cultivated, rich soil and a warm, sheltered site. Cut back hard annually in spring if the top-growth is killed by frost.

P. aequalis
The species, a compact shrub, has dusky red-pink tubular flowers. H 1m (3ft), S 60cm (2ft). Borderline hardy/Z 7–9. The species is less often seen than the cultivar 'Yellow Trumpet', which has light green leaves and, as the name suggests, yellow flowers. H 1m (3ft), S 60cm (2ft).

P. × rectus
A group of hybrids normally represented in gardens by one of the several available cultivars, such as 'African Queen', which has red flowers; and 'Moonraker', which has creamy yellow flowers. H 1m (3ft), S 60cm (2ft). Borderline hardy/Z 8–9.

Phygelius × rectus 'Moonraker'

PIERIS
These elegant evergreen woodland shrubs bear racemes of lily-of-the-valley-like flowers in spring. Some forms have eye-catching young foliage as well.
Cultivation Acid soil, preferably enriched with leaf mould, is essential. Shelter from early morning sun and strong winds is also desirable. They do best in dappled light or a site with afternoon sun only.

P. 'Forest Flame'
This fine hybrid is grown for its foliage rather than for its flowers, which are not reliably produced. The flush of young leafy growth in spring is brilliant red, fading to green. H 2.2m (7ft), S 1m (3ft). Borderline hardy/Z 7–9.

Photinia x fraseri

Phygelius × rectus 'African Queen'

Pieris 'Forest Flame'

Pieris japonica

Potentilla fruticosa 'Medicine Wheel Mountain'

Potentilla fruticosa 'Abbotswood'

P. formosa

The young leaves are red, turning bronze and maturing to dark green. Sprays of white flowers are borne in spring. H and S 2m (6ft). Borderline hardy/Z 7–9. The species is normally represented in gardens in the form *P. formosa* var. *forrestii* 'Wakehurst', which has vivid red young leaves and sprays of white flowers that open from red buds.

P. japonica
Lily-of-the-valley bush

This bushy shrub has glossy green leaves and cascading sprays of white flowers in spring. H and S 3m (10ft). Hardy/Z 6–8. Selected forms include 'Pink Delight', which has masses of pink flowers; 'Valley Rose', which has pale pink flowers; and the prolific 'Valley Valentine', which has cherry red flowers.

PITTOSPORUM

These evergreen shrubs are grown for the interest of their leaves. Not only do some forms have coloured foliage, but the leaves also have wavy edges. Most thrive in coastal areas.
Cultivation These plants are suitable for most well-drained soil in sun, but they will not tolerate very cold spots.

P. tenuifolium

This, the most popular species, is usually grown in its coloured leaf forms, which all make excellent container plants. Borderline hardy/Z 9–10. 'Irene Paterson' has very pale green leaves heavily

marked with white. It is slower growing than the species. H 1.2m (4ft), S 60cm (2ft). The young leaves of 'Purpureum' are green but age to purple. H 1.2m (4ft), S 60cm (2ft). The leaves of the dwarf 'Tom Thumb' turn rich purple in cold weather. H and S 1m (3ft).

POTENTILLA

These neat, very hardy, deciduous shrubs bear masses of rose-like flowers in summer. They are a good choice for the front of a border or to mark the turn in a path. They can also be grown in rock gardens.
Cultivation Potentillas will grow in most well-drained soils is sun or light shade.

P. 'Blazeaway'

This hybrid has dark green leaves and fiery orange-red flowers. H and S to 1m (3ft). Hardy/Z 5–8.

Potentilla 'Blazeaway'

P. fruticosa
Shrubby cinquefoil

This is the best-known species, and a huge range of garden varieties have been developed from it, including 'Abbotswood', which has white flowers over a long period; 'Medicine Wheel Mountain', which has yellow flowers; 'Pretty Polly', which has pink flowers; and 'Snowbird', an unusual variety, which has double, pure white flowers. H 1m (3ft), S 1.2m (4ft). Hardy/Z 3–8.

PRUNUS
Ornamental cherry

This genus contains over 200 species and ornamental cherries are well known, but the genus also includes a couple of fine evergreen shrubs, which are good for hedging and for clipping to formal shapes or as standards.
Cultivation These grow in most soils but may not do well on shallow soil over chalk (alkaline soil).

P. laurocerasus
Cherry laurel

This useful evergreen shrub is much used for hedging, the large glossy leaves making a welcome contrast to most other hedging plants. Spikes of white flowers in spring and black autumn berries are bonuses. It can easily be kept under control by pruning. H 3m (10ft), S 2m (6ft). Hardy/Z

7–9. 'Camelliifolia' has curiously twisted leaves. H 3m (10ft), S 4m (13ft). The diseased-looking 'Marbled White' (syn. 'Castlewellan') has leaves that are heavily mottled with creamy white. H and S 5m (16ft). The well-known 'Otto Luyken' is a low-growing form with handsome, narrow leaves. H 1m (3ft), S 1.5m (5ft).

P. lusitanica
Portugal laurel

Less familiar, but more refined than *P. laurocerasus*, this evergreen species carries glossy leaves and spikes of white flowers in early to midsummer. It makes a beautiful large standard. H 2.7m (9ft), S 2m (6ft). Borderline hardy/Z 7–9.

Prunus laurocerasus 'Marbled White'

Rhamnus alaternus 'Argenteovariegata'

PYRACANTHA
Firethorn
An important genus of tough, hardy, spiny, evergreen plants that tolerate exposure. The cream-coloured flowers cascading from the branches in summer are followed by equally impressive yellow, orange or red berries that last all winter. An unexpected but highly effective use for pyracanthas is as a hedge.
Cultivation Grow in any fertile, well-drained soil in sun or shade.

P. coccinea 'Red Column'
This upright shrub has reddish shoots and vivid red berries in autumn, and shows good resistance to fireblight. H 1.5m (5ft), S 1m (3ft). Hardy/Z 7–8.

P. 'Knap Hill Lemon'
An unusual variety, worth growing for its clear yellow berries in autumn. H 1.5m (5ft), S 1m (3ft). Hardy/Z 7.

P. 'Soleil d'Or'
This popular hybrid has hawthorn-like white flowers in late spring succeeded by golden-yellow berries in autumn. H and S 1.5m (5ft). Hardy/Z 7.

RHAMNUS
Buckthorn
Fine foliage plants, sometimes evergreen, these shrubs are excellent as hedging or in a shrub border. The berries are poisonous.
Cultivation Grow in any reasonable garden soil in sun or light shade.

R. alaternus 'Argenteovariegata' (syn. *R. alaternus* 'Variegata')
Probably the most familiar of the genus, the leaves of this evergreen are handsomely variegated with grey marbling and irregular white leaf margins. It appreciates a warm, sheltered site. H and S 1.5m (5ft). Borderline hardy/Z 7–9.

RHODODENDRON
This large and complex genus includes plants that range from huge, tree-like shrubs to diminutive specimens for a rock garden or alpine trough. There would be a rhododendron for every garden were it not for the fact that they must have acid soil, which rules them out for some gardeners. Some are happy in containers, however, bringing them within reach for gardeners on alkaline soil. Essentially, most are wood-landers and look good in that setting, but modern varieties (especially those related to *R. yakushimanum*) are compact, dwarf plants that cope with more open situations. Rhododendrons combine well with other acid-loving shrubs, such as pieris and camellias, as well as with heathers. Deciduous rhododendrons, which are often more rangy and open in habit, are good with spring bulbs.
Cultivation Rhododendrons must have acid soil that is high in nutrients and well-drained. Most prefer light, dappled shade.

Species and selected forms
R. augustinii Electra Group
An evergreen shrub with funnel-shaped, violet-blue flowers in mid-spring. H 4m (13ft), S 2.5m (8ft). Hardy/Z 7–8.

Rhododendron decorum

R. charitopes
This compact evergreen species, which is good in a rock garden, comes from southern Tibet. Trusses of waxy, bell-shaped, pale pink or violet flowers are borne in late spring to early summer. H and S 1m (3ft). Hardy/Z 6–8.

R. cinnabarinum subsp. *cinnabarinum* Roylei Group
These evergreen hybrids have deep coppery plum to crimson, funnel-shaped flowers, which appear between mid-spring and early summer. H to 6m (20ft), S 2m (6ft). Hardy/Z 7–8.

R. decorum
This tree-like evergreen species from China bears loose trusses of fragrant, white or pink flowers in early summer. It tolerates warm dry conditions. H to 6m (20ft), S 2.5m (8ft). Hardy/Z 6–8.

R. impeditum
This dwarf evergreen, which is ideal for a rock garden or trough, comes from the mountains of Yunnan and Sichuan. The scaly leaves are aromatic. The blue-purple flowers open almost flat,

Rhododendron impeditum

like stars, in mid- to late spring. H and S to 60cm (2ft). Hardy/Z 6–8.

R. luteum
A dazzling deciduous species, this elegant rhododendron bears highly fragrant, clear yellow flowers in late spring and early summer. It is the parent of many more compact hybrids. H and S to 4m (13ft). Hardy/Z 6–9.

R. hybrids
There are a huge number of hybrid rhododendrons of garden origin of widely diverging size. The following gives an indication of the range available; all are evergreen unless otherwise stated. Hardy/Z 4–9. Plants of the **Alison Johnstone Group** have dainty, peach-pink flowers in late spring to early summer. H and S 2m (6ft). **'Bashful'** (Yakushimanum hybrid) has pink flowers aging white in spring; sun-tolerant. H and S 2m (6ft). The deciduous **'Berryrose'** has salmon-pink flowers with yellow flares in late spring; sun-tolerant. H and S 1.5m (5ft). **'Blue Peter'** has lavender-blue, frilled flowers in late spring and early summer;

Rhododendron charitopes

Rhododendron luteum

Rhododendron 'Bruce Brechtbill'

Rhododendron 'Cary Ann'

Rhododendron 'Dopey'

Rhododendron 'Exbury White'

Rhododendron 'Persil'

sun-tolerant. H and S 3m (10ft). **'Bruce Brechtbill'** has a dense habit and pale pink flowers in late spring and early summer. H 2m (6ft), S 2.5m (8ft). **Carita Group** rhododendrons have trusses of pale lemon-yellow flowers in mid-spring; they are best with some shelter. H and S 2.5m (8ft). **'Cary Ann'**, which is good for small gardens, has coral pink flowers in late spring to early summer. H and S 1.5m (5ft). The deciduous **'Cecile'** has salmon pink flowers over a long period in late spring. H and S 2m (6ft). **'Chanticleer'** has spectacular maroon-purple flowers in late spring and early summer. H and S 1.5m (5ft). The old deciduous cultivar **'Corneille'** has double, creamy-pink flowers in early summer. H and S 1.5–2.5m (5–8ft). **'Curlew'** has large, pale yellow flowers in mid-spring; it does best in a cool spot. H and S 60cm (2ft). **'Cynthia'**, an old, sun-tolerant cultivar, bears huge trusses of rich crimson pink flowers in late spring. H and S 6m (20ft). The deciduous **'Daviesii'** has scented cream flowers in late spring to early summer and good autumn leaf

colour. H and S 1.5m (5ft). The compact and upright **'Dopey'** (Yakushimanum hybrid) bears rounded trusses of satiny orange-red flowers in late spring. H and S 2m (6ft). The deciduous **'Exbury White'** has large white flowers with yellow eyes in late spring and early summer and good autumn leaf colour; it makes an elegant specimen. H and S 2m (6ft). **'Fastuosum Flore Pleno'** has deep mauve flowers in late spring and early summer. H and S 4m (13ft). The free-flowering **'Golden Torch'** has pale yellow flowers fading to cream in late spring and early summer. H and S 1.5m (5ft). **'Grace Seabrook'** is a robust and vigorous form bearing conical trusses of deep pink flowers in early to mid-spring. H and S 2m (6ft). The dwarf and compact **'Hatsugiri'** bears masses of funnel-shaped, glowing crimson flowers in spring. H and S 60cm (2ft). **'Hinomayo'** has clear pink flowers in mid-spring and early summer. H and S 60cm (2ft). The deciduous **'Homebush'** has trusses of rose pink flowers in late spring. H and S 1.5m (5ft). **'Hydon Dawn'** has globular trusses of pale pink

flowers in mid-spring and early summer. H and S 1.5m (5ft). **'Hydon Hunter'** has deep pink flowers spotted with orange in mid-spring and early summer; sun-tolerant. H and S 1.5m (5ft). The robust, vigorous and sun-tolerant **'Loder's White'** gives a sumptuous display of fragrant white flowers in midsummer. H and S 3m (10ft). **'May Day'** has funnel-shaped, glowing red flowers in late spring; sun-tolerant. H and S 1.5m (5ft). **'Mrs Charles E. Pearson'** has pale mauve-pink flowers spotted with brown in late spring and early summer. H and S 2m (6ft). **'Naomi'**, which has lilac-mauve flowers in mid-spring, is the parent of **'Naomi Exbury'** (yellow-tinted flowers) and **'Naomi Pink Beauty'** (deep satin pink). H and S 5m (16ft). The deciduous **'Narcissiflorum'** has fragrant soft-yellow flowers in late spring and early summer. H and S 2.5m (8ft). **'Palestrina'**, which has pure white flowers in late spring, is an excellent choice for a small garden. H and S 1.2m (4ft). **'Penheale Blue'** has star-like, glowing deep violet flowers in early spring; sun-tolerant. H

and S 1.2m (4ft). The compact and hardy **'Percy Wiseman'** has peach-pink flowers fading to white in late spring and early summer. H and S 2.5m (8ft). The deciduous **'Persil'** has glistening white flowers with golden-orange central blotches. H and S 2m (6ft). **'Pink Pearl'** has huge trusses of soft pink flowers in mid- to late spring; sun-tolerant. H and S 4m (13ft). **'Polar Bear'** produces headily scented, lily-like, white flowers in mid- to late summer, produced freely only once the plant is mature. H and S 5m (16ft). **'Sappho'** has funnel-shaped, white flowers liberally sprinkled on the inside with dark purple-maroon in early summer. H and S 3m (10ft). The deciduous **'Strawberry Ice'** has strawberry pink flowers in mid- to late spring. H and S 2m (6ft). **'Vuyk's Rosy Red'**, which has deep rose-pink flowers in mid-spring, is excellent for a sunny rock garden. H 75cm (30in), S 1.2m (4ft). **'Wombat'**, which has small pink flowers in profusion in early summer, makes excellent groundcover, even in sun. H 25cm (10in), S 1.2m (4ft).

Rhododendron 'Curlew'

Rhododendron 'Fastuosum Flore Pleno'

Rhododendron 'Narcissiflorum'

Rhododendron 'Strawberry Ice'

Rosmarinus officinalis

ROSMARINUS
Rosemary

The evergreen, aromatic rosemary is an essential element of any herb garden, but prostrate forms make good groundcover and also work well when planted at the tops of walls. There are also some suitable for hedging, and all can be clipped to shape. Rosemaries are not long-lived but are easily raised from cuttings.
Cultivation Rosemary does best in free-draining, light soil in full sun. Trim hedges after flowering.

R. officinalis

To all intents and purposes this is the only species widely cultivated. It has dark green, narrow leaves and mauve-blue flowers in summer. H and S to 1.5m (5ft). Borderline hardy/Z 7–9. There is a huge range of cultivars. 'Lady in White' has white flowers. H and S 1m (3ft). 'Miss Jessop's Upright' (syn.

'Fastigiatus') is an upright form with light purplish-blue flowers. H 2m (6ft), S 60cm (2ft). Plants in the **Prostratus Group** are spreading, and less hardy than the straight species. H 60cm (2ft), S 1m (3ft). 'Sissinghurst Blue' is upright with deep blue flowers and one of the best for culinary purposes. H 1.2m (4ft), S 1m (3ft).

RUBUS
Bramble

In addition to a huge range of soft fruits (raspberries, blackberries and a number of hybrids), this genus also includes a few ornamental plants.
Cultivation Grow in well-drained, fertile soil in sun or partial shade.

R. 'Benenden'
(syn. R. tridel 'Benenden')

This beautiful deciduous hybrid has masses of large, saucer-shaped, white flowers in late spring to early summer. H and S 2m (6ft). Hardy/Z 5–9.

R. cockburnianus

Glistening white stems make this one of the finest of deciduous winter plants, an effect improved by annual hard pruning in spring. H 2m (6ft), S 1.2m (4ft). Hardy/Z 5–9.

R. odoratus
Flowering raspberry

An erect, vigorous deciduous species with fragrant, pinkish-purple flowers in summer followed by orange-red fruits. H and S 2m (6ft). Hardy/Z 4–9.

Ruta graveolens

R. thibetanus

This semi-erect species has small, purplish-red summer flowers and furry leaves, but it is grown principally for the winter interest of its stems, which are covered in a whitish bloom. Cut back hard annually for the best display. H and S to 2.4m (8ft), less with regular pruning. Hardy/Z 7–9.

RUTA
Rue

These subshrubs have aromatic, glaucous blue leaves. Only the species described is widely grown. Contact with the plant can cause allergic reactions in some people.
Cultivation Grow in well-drained soil in a sunny site. Clip plants in summer for a fresh crop of leaves.

R. graveolens
Common rue

This evergreen species has bluish-green, much divided leaves. Yellowish flowers appear in

Salvia officinalis Purpurascens Group

summer. H 1m (3ft), S 75cm (30in). Hardy/Z 5–9. The form generally found in gardens is 'Jackman's Blue', which has leaves of a more pronounced bluish-grey and is more compact. H and S 30cm (12in).

SALVIA
Sage

This large genus contains annuals and perennials as well as a number of shrubby plants, which are the familiar sages, widely used as a culinary herb. They are also good enough to use in borders, with roses or in a mixed planting.
Cultivation Grow in any well-drained soil in full sun.

S. officinalis
Common sage

The species has dull pewter-green leaves and blue and purple flowers. H 60cm (2ft), S 1m (3ft). Hardy/Z 6–9. Attractive selections include 'Icterina', which

Rubus odoratus

Rubus thibetanus

Salvia officinalis 'Icterina'

Santolina chamaecyparis

Skimmia japonica 'Tansley Gem'

has leaves marked with yellow and gold; **Purpurascens Group**, which has soft purple leaves; and 'Tricolor', with leaves marked with pink, cream and purple.

SANTOLINA
Curry plant
The species described is a useful evergreen, which can be used in the rock garden, as dwarf hedging or in combination with other plants, to which it offers a good foil. It is ideal for filling gaps in a border.
Cultivation Grow santolinas in any well-drained soil in full sun.

S. chamaecyparis
(syn. *S. incana*)
Cotton lavender
This is the best-known species, a mound-forming shrub with finely dissected silvery leaves. It has lemon-yellow flowers in mid-summer, but is principally valued as a foliage plant. Clip over in

spring to neaten, if necessary, but old, straggly plants are best replaced. H and S 60cm (2ft). Borderline hardy/Z 6–9.

SARCOCOCCA
Christmas box, sweet box
These choice plants for the winter garden have small but highly scented flowers among the shiny evergreen leaves. Use them with snowdrops, *Arum italicum* subsp. *italicum* 'Marmoratun' and early hellebores. They make excellent groundcover under deciduous trees, and flowering stems can be cut for use in winter flower arrangements.
Cultivation Grow in any fertile, well-drained soil in sun or light shade. They tolerate deeper shade.

S. confusa
This is an excellent dwarf shrub, which is useful as groundcover if planted en masse. Very fragrant, creamy white flowers are produced in midwinter. H and S 1m (3ft). Hardy/Z 6–9.

S. hookeriana var. digyna
This naturally occurring form has deliciously scented white flowers with pink stamens in winter. H and S 1.2m (4ft). Hardy/Z 6–9.

SKIMMIA
This small genus includes several attractive shrubs, which bear scented flowers in spring and (on female plants) crops of red berries in autumn, a fine contrast to the handsome, evergreen leaves. They are excellent in shrub or mixed borders and also work well in

containers. Young specimens of the male *S. japonica* 'Rubella' can be used in winter windowboxes.
Cultivation Most soils in sun or shade are suitable, but some yellowing of the older leaves can occur in alkaline conditions because of magnesium deficiency.

S. × confusa 'Kew Green'
This male selection has fragrant, cream flowers in early spring among the narrow leaves. H and S to 1m (3ft). Hardy/Z 7.

S. japonica
This, the most widely grown species, has distinctive narrow, glossy foliage and panicles of cream buds throughout winter that open to fragrant creamy-white flowers in spring. H and S to 1.2m (4ft). Hardy/Z 7–9. 'Rubella' is a male form with clusters of red buds through winter that open to dingy white flowers in early spring. 'Tansley

Gem' is a female form, with a good crop of red berries. 'Wakehurst White' (syn. 'Fructo-alba'), a female form, has creamy-white berries. H 50cm (20in), S 1m (3ft).

SPIRAEA
These easy deciduous shrubs are cultivated for their flowers and leaves. Most stay reasonably compact and are suitable for small gardens. For maximum impact plant in groups of three or more, but solo plants work well with a wide range of perennials in mixed borders.
Cultivation These shrubs are easy to grow in most soils, in sun or light shade.

S. japonica
The species is usually grown in one of the following forms, both of which are hardy/Z 4–9. H and S 1m (3ft). 'Anthony Waterer' is a charming selection, with dark leaves and rich pink flowers from mid- to late summer. 'Goldflame' has yellowish-green leaves, which are sometimes marked with red. The dull pink summer flowers make a strange combination, but pleasing when positioned next to a purple-leaved plant.

S. nipponica 'Snowmound'
This outstanding form is smothered in creamy-white flowers in late spring or early summer. The plant tolerates hard pruning and can be kept smaller than the dimensions indicated. H and S 2m (6ft). Hardy/Z 4–9.

Sarcococca confusa

Skimmia japonica 'Rubella'

Spiraea japonica 'Goldflame'

Syringa emodi

Syringa vulgaris 'Firmament'

Viburnum × bodnantense 'Dawn'

SYRINGA
Lilac

Late spring can almost be defined as 'lilac time': a season easily recognized by that unmistakable scent in the air. Unfortunately, most of the hybrids, which are so impressive in flower, end up as unwieldy, rangy shrubs of small interest during the rest of the year. If you have the space, grow them in stands in a rough part of the garden. In a restricted area, choose from the species, many of which are more compact, with daintier flowers.
Cultivation Lilacs will grow in any well-drained soil and are especially useful on chalk (alkaline soil). They prefer sun but tolerate light shade. They can be pruned back hard.

S. emodi
Himalayan lilac
This vigorous species with dark green oval leaves has very pale flowers in late spring to early summer. H 5m (15ft), S 4m (13ft). Hardy/Z 7–8.

S. meyeri var. spontanea 'Palibin' (syn. S. palibiana, S. patula of gardens)
A most rewarding small lilac, this has very fragrant, pale lilac-coloured flowers, produced freely in late spring to early summer. H and S 1.5m (5ft). Hardy/Z 4–7.

S. vulgaris
Common lilac
This is the parent of a huge range of garden forms, all heavily scented, and including **'Andenken an Ludwig Späth'**, which has wine red flowers; **'Charles Joly'**, which has double, purplish-red flowers; 'Congo', with rich pink flowers opening from darker buds; **'Firmament'**, which has pink buds opening to lilac-coloured flowers; **'Madame Lemoine'**, with double, white flowers; and **'Primrose'**, the closest to yellow, with rich cream-coloured buds opening to creamy-white flowers. H and S 3.5m (12ft). Hardy/Z 3–9.

TEUCRIUM
Germander

These evergreen shrubs or subshrubs have aromatic foliage. Germanders are often included in herb gardens, but are also effective as rock garden plants or in mixed borders.
Cultivation Grow in free-draining, light soil in full sun. Winter protection may be necessary in cold areas. Prune lightly in spring to keep plants in shape.

T. chamaedrys
This species has glossy, holly-like leaves and purple flowers in summer. H and S 30cm (12in). Borderline hardy/Z 5.

T. fruticans
This elegant plant has pale blue summer flowers, making a cool complement to the pewter-green leaves, which are covered in a soft silvery down. It looks beautiful billowing out at the front of a border. H 1.2m (4ft), S 4m (13ft). Borderline hardy/Z 7–10. 'Azureum' is even more desirable, with darker blue flowers.

VIBURNUM

This large and important genus consists of both evergreen and deciduous shrubs that, between them, provide interest throughout the year. Some are grown for their flowers (winter or spring), others for their berries, and some for both. They are essential plants. Native species are excellent in wild gardens, providing food for birds in winter. Others are good in winter gardens or mixed borders. A select few make good specimens. V. tinus can be trained as a standard.
Cultivation Grow viburnums in any reasonably fertile, well-drained soil in sun or light shade.

V. × bodnantense 'Dawn'
One of the stars of the winter garden, this upright, deciduous, vase-shaped shrub has richly scented, pink flowers opening in mild spells from autumn to spring. H 2m (6ft), S 1.2m (4ft). Hardy/Z 7–9.

V. carlesii
This deciduous species from Japan and Korea is almost unmatched for the scent of its white spring flowers, pink in bud and carried in rounded clusters.

Teucrium fruticans

Viburnum carlesii 'Diana'

Viburnum plicatum 'Mariesii'

Viburnum tinus 'Eve Price'

Weigela 'Candida'

YUCCA

These dramatic, architectural evergreens add a touch of the exotic to any garden. They are often sold as houseplants, but the species described here are hardy enough to survive (and flower) outdoors. In their native habitat (North American desert) yuccas become trees. In gardens they are excellent when planted as focal points or sited at the corner of a border, and they make splendid permanent plantings for large containers.
Cultivation Grow in any well-drained soil in full sun.

H and S 1.5m (5ft). Hardy/Z 6–9. **'Diana'** has purplish-pink flowers that fade to white.

V. plicatum
Japanese snowball bush
A grand deciduous shrub with an architectural, tiered habit that makes a breathtaking specimen when in flower. Hardy/Z 5–8. **'Mariesii'** (syn. *V. mariesii*) is one of the most distinctive selections, with tabulated branches carrying flattened lacecap heads of white flowers in late spring. H 3m (10ft), S 4m (13ft). *V. plicatum* f. *tomentosum* produces blue-black berries in autumn as the leaves redden. H 3m (10ft), S 4m (13ft).

V. tinus
Laurustinus
An important winter shrub, this evergreen has a rounded habit and white flowers in late winter or early spring. Bluish-black berries follow the flowers. H and S 3m

(10ft). Hardy/Z 7–9. The flowers of **'Eve Price'** open from rich eye-catching pink buds.

VINCA
Periwinkle
These valuable trailing evergreen subshrubs make excellent ground-cover, particularly in the dry soil under trees. They are also good in containers. A large pot planted solely with *V. major* 'Variegata' will provide material for flower arranging throughout the year.
Cultivation Grow in any well-drained soil in sun or shade. Mulching in dry soils will accelerate growth. Stems can root wherever they touch the ground.

V. major
The species is not worth growing, but it has several worthy cultivars, the best of which is probably **'Variegata'** (syn. 'Elegantissima'), which has leaves with pale yellow margins. The periwinkle-blue flowers are produced mainly in early summer but never in sufficient quantities to smother the plant. H 20cm (8in), S indefinite. Hardy/Z 7–9.

V. minor
This species, which has small leaves, is more worthwhile than *V. major* and has many more cultivars, including **'Aureovariegata'**, which has leaves edged with creamy yellow and blue summer flowers; **'Burgundy'**, which has wine-purple flowers; and **'Gertrude Jekyll'**, which has white flowers. H 15cm (6in), S indefinite. Hardy/Z 4–8.

WEIGELA
The genus contains 12 species of deciduous shrubs with interesting leaves and trumpet-shaped flowers in early summer. They work well in a shrub border or a mixed planting, where, after flowering, they make effective backdrops to later-flowering perennials, annuals and bulbs.
Cultivation They do well in most soils, in sun or light shade.

W. 'Candida'
This is an unusual garden form with pure white flowers. H and S 1.5m (5ft). Hardy/Z 5–9.

W. florida
This is one of the less-appealing species in its wild form, but some of the selections are of great value. The following are hardy/Z 5–9. **'Aureovariegata'** is one of the prettiest. The leaves are edged with white in spring, making a fine combination with the pink flowers. The variegation deepens to yellow later on. H and S 1.2m (4ft). **'Foliis Purpureis'**, which needs careful siting, has rich purple leaves and deep pink flowers. H and S 1m (3ft).

W. 'Looymansii Aurea'
This hybrid has yellowish-green leaves and pink flowers. It needs shelter from strong, hot sun. H and S 1.5m (5ft). Hardy/Z 5–9.

W. middendorffiana
This superior species has sulphur-yellow flowers marked with dark orange in mid- to late spring. H and S 1.5m (5ft). Hardy/Z 5–9.

Y. filamentosa
Adam's needle
The species forms a rosette of stiff, upright, lance-shaped leaves. The distinguishing feature is the curly threads on the edges of the leaves. Established plants produce upright spikes, to 2m (6ft) tall, of white, tulip-shaped flowers in late summer to autumn, but not necessarily every year. H and S 1m (3ft). Hardy/Z 5–10. The leaves of **'Bright Edge'** have broad yellow edges.

Y. gloriosa
Spanish dagger
This plant has a thick stem topped by a rosette of hard, spiny, upright blue-green to dark-green leaves, through the middle of which the flowering spikes emerge in late summer (the flowers are similar to those of *Y. filamentosa*). Mature plants are multi-stemmed. H and S 2m (6ft) or more. Hardy/Z 7–10.

Vinca minor 'Aureovariegata'

Yucca filamentosa

Perennials

For many, a garden just would not be a garden without the contribution of perennials, often long-lived plants that provide interest year on year, usually with very little maintenance required. A herbaceous border can provide interest for many weeks in summer, but perennials also encompass many early-flowering plants (usually low-growing) that are delightful with spring bulbs, as well as plants that carry the flowering season into autumn and continue to provide colour in the garden as the days grow shorter and cooler.

Most perennials are easy to care for and provide colour for many weeks during the summer months.

Perennials for your garden

Perennials are leafy, soft-stemmed plants, distinguished from annuals and biennials in being longer lived, persisting for at least three years, usually rather longer. Most spread by sending out shoots from their roots that develop into new stems, usually soon after flowering. Over several years, the offshoots from only one plant may cover a wide area. Granted that stems (in principle at least) remain soft throughout the life of a plant, that places a restriction on how tall they can grow without falling over. Hence the majority are under 1m (3ft) in height. In some cases, the stem itself spreads sideways, usually at ground level, with the leaves and flower stems emerging from it at right angles. Such stems, which act as storage organs, are referred to as rhizomes. Many of the irises exhibit this growth pattern.

Strictly speaking, bulbs are also perennials, since they also persist from year to year, but they are treated separately in this book, as are certain other groups of plants that

Achilleas spin their heads of flowers like plates behind an exotic planting of cannas and *Crocosmia* 'Lucifer'.

have very specific cultivation requirements or garden use, such as grasses, aquatics, alpines, ferns and orchids. Some climbers are also soft-stemmed (though the majority are woody, and thus technically shrubs).

Many perennials are deciduous or herbaceous: the topgrowth dies back completely in winter, when conditions are unfavourable for growth, and the plant stays dormant underground. Fresh leafy growth reappears when the weather warms up in spring. Such popular garden perennials as bleeding hearts (*Dicentra*), columbines (*Aquilegia*), daylilies (*Hemerocallis*), delphiniums, peonies (*Paeonia*) and poppies (*Papaver*) need an annual cool season for the growth of new buds. They therefore do not grow well in tropical climates.

A precious few perennials are evergreen, and these include the splendid hellebores (*Helleborus*) and bergenias, both invaluable for winter interest, as well as some irises.

Some evergreens tend to become woody at the base with age, and are sometimes referred to as subshrubs, a characteristic that can be observed in many of the Mediterranean herbs such as the artemisias and sages (*Salvia*). Chrysanthemums and Michaelmas daisies (*Aster*) also tend to become woody, as do penstemons and pelargoniums.

Slow-growing perennials such as hellebores and peonies are best left to get on with it, but others tend to die off in the middle or form congested mats. To maintain the flower power, they should be dug up every three years or so and divided, replanting the youngest, healthiest-looking bits and composting the remainder. Those that become woody also tend to become bare at the base, but can be replaced by younger, softer-stemmed plants raised from cuttings. Rhizomatous plants can be increased by cutting up the rhizome, making sure that each section has growth buds and roots. Properly cared for, many perennials can be maintained virtually indefinitely, even as the successive generations die off over the years.

In this subtle scheme, arching, swordlike leaves are almost as important a feature as the bright blue agapanthus and orange crocosmia flowers.

A large percentage of the perennials grown in gardens today are hybrids, such as the stately peonies, phlox, chrysanthemums and delphiniums. They have often been bred to produce large flowers that are too heavy for the stems, and thus require staking. Species grown in gardens (and their forms) tend to be more modest in appearance, though of no lesser value, generally have the advantage of excellent health and do not need staking. Such plants as geraniums, thalictrums and euphorbias, which have not been extensively hybridized, are increasingly valued by gardeners for their ease of cultivation besides the charm of their flowers.

These sun-loving perennials, in a vibrant combination of reds and yellows, are basking in the summer heat reflected by the gravel path.

Perennials in the garden

Gardeners value perennials mainly for their flowers. Nearly all flower in spring or summer, and this is when the most dramatic effects can be created. They are traditionally the star performers of the garden and in the past were often grown in dedicated borders (the so-called herbaceous border), planned for interest over a long period. Gertrude Jekyll was the progenitor of the archetypal colour border, presenting a dramatic sweep with pale pink at one end and pale blue at the other, with "hot" oranges, reds and yellows at the centre. Typically, taller plants would be placed to the back of the border, with shorter ones in front and the real ground-huggers to the fore. She also planned single colour borders, though never a white garden, a concept that skipped a generation, only emerging in the gardens of Laurence Johnstone at Hidcote and Vita Sackville-West at Sissinghurst. Breathtaking as they are, such plantings are labour-intensive, and most gardeners

nowadays favour an informal mix of perennials, grasses and shrubs.

Where there is room, the most satisfactory effects are achieved by planting in drifts or interlocking groups of three or more. A solitary large-leaved plant, such as a hosta or a rheum, can be used for impact. To avoid a spotty effect, group together plants that flower at the same time, but remember also that many perennials have interesting foliage that adds value to the border at times when they are not in flower. Peonies, hellebores and bergenias, which make satisfying clumps of foliage, are all effective partners to later-flowering plants.

Winter-flowering perennials include the essential hellebores and *Iris unguicularis.* At the other end of the year, interest focuses on the daisy tribe: chrysanthemums, Michaelmas daisies and heleniums, many continuing until the first frosts. *Schizostylis* and toad lilies (*Tricyrtis*) should on no account be overlooked for late interest.

Many of the early flowerers will flower a second time if cut back after the first flush, albeit usually less impressively. In nearly all cases, deadheading is advisable (unless you wish to gather seed for propagation). This diverts the plant's energies away from seed production and into vegetative growth instead, which will result in a larger plant for next year.

A few perennials have a very restricted use, true woodlanders such as trilliums, for instance, but most like a fairly open, sunny site in fertile, well-drained soil, and combine happily with one another. A good many provide ample material for cutting. Ground-cover plants, usually low-growing, that spread to create dense mats are useful for suppressing weeds and filling a large area of bare soil quickly. These include *Lamium* and *Alchemilla mollis,* though at times they can be almost too effective, colonizing areas of the garden to the point of becoming weeds themselves.

Acanthus mollis

Achillea filipendulina 'Gold Plate'

Aconitum 'Stainless Steel'

ACANTHUS
Bear's breeches

These stately, hardy perennials, mostly from Mediterranean countries, are of unquestioned value in the garden, in sun or shade, although they have rather sinister-looking hooded flowers. They are colonizing plants, which can be difficult to eradicate once they are established, so choose where you plant them with care. The flowers can be dried for winter arrangements.
Cultivation Grow in any well-drained fertile soil in sun or light shade. Flowering is best in sun.

A. mollis
Tall spikes of hooded mauve and white flowers appear in early summer above the large, handsome, glossy green leaves. H 1.2m (4ft), S 1m (3ft). Hardy/Z 7–9.

A. spinosus
A species that resembles *A. mollis* in all respects but for its deeply cut leaves. H 1.2m (4ft), S 60cm (2ft). Hardy/Z 6–10.

ACHILLEA
Yarrow
More than 80 species are included in this genus. Yarrows are tough plants, with flat heads of flowers in mid- to late summer on stout stems. The majority of them have feathery, aromatic foliage. They are indispensable for providing colour – if not vibrant – in the late summer border, working well with grasses, but some tend to be

short-lived. The flowers can be dried and hold their colour well.
Cultivation Grow in free-draining, preferably moist, soil in full sun.

A. filipendulina
(syn. *A. eupatorium*)
This species has flat heads of sulphur-yellow flowers in late summer. H 1.5m (5ft), S 1m (3ft). Hardy/Z 3–9. The selection **'Gold Plate'**, which bears slightly domed flowerheads, is more robust. H 1.2m (4ft), S 60cm (2ft).

A. 'Moonshine'
This hybrid is grown as much for its ferny, grey-green leaves as its pale yellow flowerheads. H and S 60cm (2ft). Hardy/Z 4–8.

A. ptarmica 'The Pearl'
A dainty plant, with heads of button-like, white flowers in summer. Plants sold under this name probably belong to The Pearl Group – in other words they have been seed-raised and thus may differ in some respects. H and S 60cm (2ft). Hardy/Z 4–9.

ACONITUM
Monkshood, wolf's bane
These tall plants with hooded flowers are a useful shade of rich blue. All species in the genus are poisonous.
Cultivation Any soil is suitable, but they do best in moisture-retentive soil in full sun, although they will also do well in shade.

A. 'Spark's Variety'
Of all the available hybrids, this is probably the best known, with spires of rich, dark violet-blue flowers from early to midsummer. H 1.5m (5ft), S 45cm (18in). Hardy/Z 5–8.

A. 'Stainless Steel'
This cultivar has subtly coloured, beautiful pewter grey flowers. H 1.5m (5ft), S 45cm (18in). Hardy/Z 6.

AGAPANTHUS
African lily
These elegant and desirable plants produce umbels of refreshing blue or white flowers in late summer. They contrast well with yellow flowers, of which there will be many at flowering time, as well as blending easily with softer tones. They also thrive in containers, in

which they look very handsome. Overcrowding seems to intensify the flower power, so divide them only when absolutely necessary. They are easily raised from seed.
Cultivation Grow in fertile, reliably moist (but not boggy) soil in full sun.

A. 'Ben Hope'
This hybrid has umbels of rich blue flowers from mid- to late summer. H 1.2m (4ft), S 60cm (2ft). Hardy/Z 7–10.

A. 'Castle of Mey'
This is one of the daintier hybrids, producing rich dark blue flowers on erect stems in late summer. H 60cm (2ft), S 30cm (1ft). Hardy/Z 7.

AJUGA
Bugle
Useful as groundcover, these plants are grown mostly for their evergreen leaves, although the blue spring flowers make an attractive bonus. They spread by runners and will colonize any area where the conditions suit them.
Cultivation Grow in moisture-retentive soil in sun or light shade.

A. reptans
This is the most widely grown bugle, although it is seldom seen in its typical form in gardens. H 10cm (5in), S 1m (3ft). Hardy/Z 3–9. Selections available include **'Atropurpurea'** (syn. 'Purpurea'), which has rich burgundy-purple leaves; **'Jungle Beauty'** (syn. 'Jumbo'), with large

Agapanthus 'Castle of Mey'

Ajuga reptans 'Jungle Beauty'

Alchemilla mollis

Alstroemeria 'Apollo'

Anemone × hybrida 'Königin Charlotte'

green leaves that turn warm brown in winter; and **'Variegata'** (syn. 'Argentea'), which has leaves splashed with cream and grey.

ALCHEMILLA
Lady's mantle
The species described, which comes from Turkey and the Caucasus, is an essential garden plant. It is an excellent filler for gaps in borders and the frothy, lime-green flowers, also good for cutting, blend with almost anything else. It makes excellent groundcover but can be invasive, and its habit of self-seeding everywhere makes it a menace in some gardens. To prevent this from happening, cut off the flowers as they fade (this will also encourage further flowers). It makes a marvellous foil to old roses and looks charming where allowed to seed in the cracks between paving.
Cultivation These extremely tolerant plants will grow in almost any soil in sun or light shade.

A. mollis
The soft, almost felted, pleated, fan-like leaves emerge in early spring, followed by masses of tiny, star-like, lime green flowers throughout summer. H and S 50cm (20in). Hardy/Z 3–7.

ALSTROEMERIA
Peruvian lily, lily of the Incas
These exquisite plants, long associated with cottage gardens, are of undoubted distinction. The newer hybrids may be hardier and have a longer flowering season than some of the older ones, but

they have not supplanted them. Excellent in a warm, sunny border, in cold areas they need the shelter of a wall. Leave them undisturbed after planting; they may take some years to establish, but thereafter are extremely reliable plants.
Cultivation Peruvian lilies need reasonably fertile, well-drained soil in sun, with some shelter in cold areas. Most are best when staked, but they can be supported by neighbouring plants.

A. 'Apollo'
This outstanding hybrid has large, white flowers marked with yellow within and flecked with brown appearing from mid-summer to autumn. H and S 60cm (2ft). Borderline hardy/Z 8.

A. ligtu hybrids
This group of hybrids includes plants with varying flower colour, including pink, coral and salmon orange, but all are desirable. They

flower in early to midsummer. They are seed-raised, so buy plants in flower to ensure getting the desired colour. The plants can be invasive. H and S 60cm (2ft). Borderline hardy/Z 7–10.

A. 'Morning Star'
A hybrid with rich purplish-pink flowers fading to yellow and flecked with brown from midsummer to autumn. H and S 45cm (18in). Borderline hardy/Z 8.

ANEMONE
Windflower
This large genus includes a few perennials of undoubted merit. Their late season and tolerance of a range of conditions make them essential plants for any garden, to say nothing of the beauty of the flowers, carried on tall, elegant, wiry stems. They are ravishing in drifts under

deciduous trees, or they can be used more formally in borders planned for late interest. They are sometimes informally referred to as Japanese anemones.
Cultivation These anemones do best on moisture-retentive soil in sun or shade, although they do tolerate drier, lighter soils.

A. hupehensis
This elegant species, with white or pink, bowl-shaped flowers that seem to float at the tops of wiry stems, is rare in cultivation. H 75cm (30in), S 45cm (18in). Hardy/Z 5–8. More common is the distinguished selection **'Hadspen Abundance'**, which has rich deep pink flowers. H and S 1m (3ft).

A. × hybrida
(syn. A. japonica of gardens)
This large group of hybrids are the true Japanese anemones (the plant sometimes referred to as *A. japonica* does not seem to exist). Seedlings often appear in gardens, and all are worth growing, but named forms worthy of note include **'Honorine Jobert'**, which has white flowers; **'Königin Charlotte'** (syn. 'Queen Charlotte'), which has semi-double, purplish-pink flowers with frilly petals; **'Luise Uhink'**, which has chalk-white flowers; and **'Whirlwind'**, which has semi-double, green-tinged, white flowers with twisted petals. H 1.5m (5ft), S 60cm (2ft). Hardy/Z 5–8.

Alstroemeria 'Morning Star'

Anemone × hybrida 'Luise Uhink'

Anthemis tinctoria

Argyranthemum 'Mary Wootton'

Artemisia absinthium

ANTHEMIS

These cheerful plants with their daisy-like flowers are indispensable for the flower gardener because of the length of their flowering season and the freedom with which blooms are produced. Although the plants will provide endless material for cutting, they may be short-lived.

Cultivation Grow in well-drained soil in full sun. Regular division in spring helps maintain health.

A. tinctoria

The species has parsley-like leaves with masses of yellow daisies in summer. H and S 60cm (2ft). Hardy/Z 4–8. The selection **'E.C. Buxton'** is widely available. This essential plant has lemon-yellow flowers throughout summer that look good with blue flowers (especially campanulas) and border phlox. H and S 1m (3ft).

AQUILEGIA
Columbine

These short-lived perennials are notorious for seeding themselves in the garden. Unfortunately, not all seedlings develop into attractive plants, as they sometimes produce flowers of an indifferent pink or murky purple, but the best ones make elegant additions to the border, with their distinctive, spurred flowers, and usefully fill the flowering gap between spring bulbs and summer perennials. They are probably at their best when grown in informal clumps in light woodland but also blend well with irises, catmint and poppies in

cottage garden-style plantings. The genus also includes some alpines.

Cultivation Grow in any well-drained soil in sun or light shade.

A. 'Lavender and White'

This hybrid has distinctive bi-coloured flowers in early summer, in lavender and creamy white, as the name suggests. H 60cm (24in), S 45cm (18in). Hardy/Z 4.

A. vulgaris
Granny's bonnets

This is one of the most familiar garden plants, with its dumpy purple, pink, crimson or white flowers appearing in late spring to early summer. Some of the many selections available include **'Nivea'** (syn. 'Munstead's White'), which has bright white flowers; and the distinctive *A. vulgaris* var. *stellata* **'Norah Barlow'**, which

Aquilegia 'Lavender and White'

has pompon-like pink, green and white double flowers. H 60cm (24in), S 45cm (18in). Hardy/Z 4–9.

ARGYRANTHEMUM
Marguerite, Paris daisy

These plants are in flower for longer than any other perennial – almost throughout the growing season. They are woody plants and, as well as their obvious value in borders, they can also be grown as standards.

Cultivation Argyranthemums will grow in sun in most well-drained, reasonably fertile soils. Pinching out the tips of the shoots in early spring can encourage bushiness and extra flowers.

A. gracile 'Chelsea Girl'

One of the best known cultivars, this has attractive, ferny grey leaves and an abundance of

Artemisia absinthium 'Lambrook Silver'

yellow-centred, white daisies from spring to autumn. H and S 60cm (2ft). Half-hardy/Z 9.

A. 'Jamaica Primrose'

An equally valuable hybrid, this bears long-stalked, cool lemon-yellow daisies throughout the growing season. H and S 1m (3ft). Half-hardy/Z 9.

A. 'Mary Wootton'

This fine hybrid has double, pompon-like, peach pink flowers. H and S 1m (3ft). Half-hardy/Z 9.

A. 'Snow Storm'
(syn. 'Jamaica Snowstorm')

This compact form has blue-green leaves and yellow-centred, white flowers. H and S 30cm (1ft). Borderline hardy/Z 9.

ARTEMISIA
Wormwood, mugwort

These are excellent foliage plants for borders, particularly hot, dry ones. The silvery foliage blends well with roses as well as with a range of herbaceous perennials. Artemisias, some of which are shrubby, also have aromatic foliage which has herbal applications.

Cultivation Grow artemisias in any well-drained, preferably gritty, soil in full sun. Prune straggly plants in spring.

A. absinthium
Absinthe, wormwood

This is the plant from which the spirit absinthe is distilled. In the garden it is valued chiefly for its silky-grey, divided leaves. The daisy-like flowers, produced in late summer, are insignificant. H and S 1m (3ft). Hardy/Z 5–8.

Asphodeline lutea

'Lambrook Silver' is more compact and has more finely dissected foliage. It is an excellent foil to purple-leaved plants. H and S 75cm (30in).

A. ludoviciana
(syn. *A. palmeri, A. purshiana*)
Western mugwort
This species has dissected silver grey leaves that look as if they are lightly dusted with powder. H 1.2m (4ft), S 60cm (2ft). Hardy/Z 4–8. *A. lucoviciana* var. *latiloba* is shorter growing, and, like the species, looks well grown in association with pink or crimson flowering plants. H and S 60cm (2ft).

ASPHODELINE
Jacob's rod
These stately plants, native to Mediterranean countries, are ideal for giving structure to a border. *Cultivation* Grow in any well-drained soil in full sun.

A. lutea
(syn. *Asphodelus luteus*)
Spires of fragrant, bright yellow flowers appear from spring to early summer above clusters of bluish-grey leaves. After flowering, the developing bead-like, green seeds continue to provide interest. H 1.2m (4ft), S 30cm (1ft). Hardy/Z 6–8.

ASTER
This large genus includes the well-known Michaelmas daisies, essential plants for the autumn garden, many of which flower from late summer until the first frosts. Most also last well as cut flowers. The species are as worthy of consideration as the hybrids, some of which have an annoying tendency towards mildew (although all those described are trouble-free). The genus also includes annuals.
Cultivation Asters will grow in any reasonably fertile soil, in sun or light shade. Some will do well in poor soil. The taller forms often benefit from staking.

A. ericoides
The species, which is native to North America, has given rise to several garden-worthy forms. These have wiry stems that are starred with flowers, all with yellow centres, in autumn. H 75cm (30in), S 30cm (12in). Hardy/Z 5–8. **'Blue Star'** has pale blue flowers; **'Golden Spray'** has white flowers; **'Pink Cloud'** has light mauve-pink flowers.

A. × frikartii
This group of vigorous hybrids includes some of the best of the Michaelmas daisies, all with a long flowering season. H 75cm (30in), S 38cm (15in). Hardy/Z 5–8. **'Mönch'** is an outstanding selection, which has large, lavender-blue flowers carried freely on branching stems; it is an excellent companion to shrubby lavateras. **'Wunder von Stäfa'** (syn. 'Wonder of Stafa') usually needs staking and has pinkish-blue flowers. H 1m (3ft), S 75cm (30in).

Aster × frikartii 'Mönch'

A. lateriflorus
(syn. *A. diffusus*)
The species has an unusual habit in that the erect stems produce flowering sideshoots, almost at right angles, giving a tiered effect. The flowers are white to pale lilac. H 1m (3ft), S 30cm (1ft). Hardy/Z 4–8. **'Horizontalis'**, which is rather more spreading, has pale lilac flowers. The coppery tinges acquired by its dainty leaves as the weather turns colder enhance its appeal. H 60cm (2ft), S 30cm (1ft).

A. novae-angliae
New England aster
The tough, tolerant species flowers from late summer to early autumn, and is rarer in gardens than its many progeny. Hardy/Z 5–8. **'Andenken an Alma Pötschke'** (syn. 'Alma Pötschke') has rich pink flowers. H 1.2m (4ft),

S 60cm (2ft). **'Harrington's Pink'** has clear pink flowers. H 1m (3ft), S 60cm (2ft). **'Herbstschnee'** (syn. 'Autumn Snow') has white, yellow-centred flowers. H 1.2m (4ft), S 60cm (2ft).

A. novi-belgii
Michaelmas daisy
Although generally applied to the whole genus, strictly the common name belongs to this species alone, the parent of a bewildering number of garden forms. It is often found growing as a weed, brightening up railway cuttings and areas of rough land with its violet-blue flowers in early autumn, which suggests a use in a wild garden or grass. The colours of the garden forms range from white, through all shades of pink, to pale and dark lavender-blue and some purples. They vary in height from dwarf forms, which are good at the edge of a border, to more substantial plants. All are hardy/Z 4–8. One of the best of the taller varieties is **'Climax'**, which has pale lavender-blue flowers in early autumn. H 1.2m (4ft), S 60cm (2ft). Among the good dwarf forms are **'Jenny'**, which has purplish-red flowers, and **'Lady in Blue'**, which has lavender-blue flowers. H 30cm (12in), S 45cm (18in).

A. turbinellus
A refined-looking species from the United States, this has wiry stems that carry violet-blue daisies in autumn. H 1.2m (4ft), S 2ft (60cm). Hardy/Z 4–8.

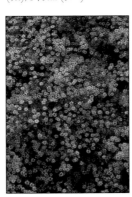

Aster ericoides 'Pink Cloud'

Aster lateriflorus

Aster turbinellus

Astilbe × arendsii 'Elizabeth Bloom'

ASTILBE

These sturdy border plants, which have striking feathery plumes of flowers in mid- to late summer, have been bred to produce a range of plants of different sizes. Since the plants appreciate damp conditions, they associate well with hostas (to which they provide a strong contrast with their attractive, ferny foliage) and *Iris sibirica*. Leave the faded flowers on the plant: they will turn a rich brown, providing continued interest through the winter months. Most of the astilbes grown in gardens are hybrids.
Cultivation Grow in fertile, reliably moist soil in sun or light shade. However, they will tolerate dry soil if they are grown in shade.

A. × *arendsii*

This large hybrid group includes the following outstanding forms. H and S to 1m (3ft) unless otherwise indicated. All are hardy/Z 6. **'Bergkristall'** has white flowers. The late-flowering **'Elizabeth Bloom'** (syn. 'Eliblo') has pale pink flowers and bronze leaves. **'Fanal'** has long-lasting, dark crimson flowers. **'Glut'** (syn.

'Glow') is rich ruby red and flowers late. The white flowers of **'Irrlicht'** are a dramatic contrast to the dark green leaves. H and S 45cm (18in). **'Weisse Gloria'** (syn. 'White Gloria') is also white, but is bigger and early flowering. H and S 60cm (2ft).

A. **'Bronce Elegans'**
(syn. *A.* **'Bronze Elegance'**)
This hybrid bears plumes of pinkish-red flowers above bronze foliage. H and S 45cm (18in). Hardy/Z 6.

Astilbe × arendsii 'Fanal'

A. × *crispa* **'Perkeo'**
This is the outstanding member of this hybrid group with deep pink flowers borne in pyramidal spires. The young leaves are tinged with bronze as they emerge. H and S to 45cm (18in). Hardy/Z 4–8.

ASTILBOIDES

Despite the name, the single species in this genus bears little resemblance to *Astilbe*. In fact, it looks more like a dwarf gunnera, for which it makes a good substitute in small gardens. It is a dramatic-looking foliage plant for a waterside location.
Cultivation This needs fertile, reliably moist soil in sun or light shade.

A. tabularis
(syn. *Rodgersia tabularis*)
The large, light green leaves, which can be up to 1m (3ft) across, are held flat on upright stems. Small star-like white flowers appear in midsummer. H 1.5m (5ft), S 1.2m (4ft). Hardy/Z 5–7.

ASTRANTIA
Hattie's pincushion, masterwort
These perennials are not especially showy in their own right, but they combine well with other more eye-catching performers. They self-seed freely, which may become a nuisance.
Cultivation Astrantias are easy to grow in most soils in sun or light shade, and prefer fertile, well-drained ground. The species *A. major* however tolerates drier soil.

A. major
Greater masterwort
The species has straw-textured, green and pink, posy-like flowers in summer. Selections are worth growing with martagon lilies, which have similarly subdued flowers. H 60cm (24in), S 45cm (18in). Hardy/Z 5–7. The best forms include *A. major* subsp. *involucrata* **'Shaggy'**, which has clear pinkish-white flowers; *A. major* var. *rubra*, with purplish-red flowers; and **'Sunningdale Variegated'** (syn. 'Variegata'), which is a charming foliage plant with leaves generously splashed with green.

BERGENIA
Elephant's ears
These tough, hardy evergreens have stout rhizomes and leathery leaves. Most flower in early spring (some as early as late winter), producing spikes of weather-resistant, bell-shaped flowers, but they can also flower intermittently at other times of year. On some, the leaves turn beetroot (beet) purple in cold weather, retaining this colour through the winter. They look best planted en masse in an informal group near woodland and are excellent with flowering cherries. They make excellent filling for 'problem' areas of the garden, providing ideal groundcover in dry, windy sites. Most are hybrids of garden origin.
Cultivation Any soil is suitable for bergenias, which will grow in sun or shade. For the best winter leaf colour, plant in not too fertile

Astrantia major

Bergenia 'Bressingham White'

soil in an open situation. Remove damaged leaves regularly to keep plants looking their best.

B. cordifolia
This species has pink flowers among puckered leaves. H and S 30cm (12in). Hardy/Z 4–8. The selection **'Purpurea'** has rich purple flowers in spring and also later in the year. The leaves flush purple in winter.

B. hybrids
Among the best of the many forms now available are **'Baby Doll'**, which has pale pink flowers; **'Bressingham White'**, with white flowers and dark green leaves; **'Silberlicht'** (syn. 'Silverlight'), which has white flowers that fade to pink; and **'Wintermärchen'**, with deep rose-pink flowers and leaves that turn scarlet in winter. H and S to 45cm (18in). Hardy/Z 3–8.

Bergenia 'Silberlicht'

BIDENS
Ideal hanging basket plants (and therefore often treated as annuals), these plants produce an apparently unending succession of bright yellow flowers throughout summer. **Cultivation** Grow in any well-drained soil in full sun.

B. aurea
A loosely branching, sprawling plant, this bears masses of bright yellow flowers. H 50cm (20in), S 40cm (16in). Half-hardy/Z 8–9.

CAMPANULA
Bellflower
This is a huge genus that includes choice rock plants and biennials as well as the sturdy perennials described here. Stalwarts of the border, they combine easily with a huge range of plants, especially roses. Tough and easy to grow, they are often used to introduce their refreshing blue tones to any scheme, although other colours also occur. The common name is a perfect description of the flower shape.
Cultivation Campanulas tolerate a range of soils, provided they are well drained, and will grow in sun or light shade.

C. 'Burghaltii'
One of the subtlest campanulas, the smoky-lilac flowers are borne on erect stems in summer. Cutting back the stems after flowering can result in a second, albeit less impressive, crop of flowers. H 60cm (2ft), S 30cm (1ft). Hardy/Z 4–8.

Campanula lactiflora

C. glomerata
Clustered bellflower
This summer-flowering species is invasive in its natural form and can be troublesome, but there are several desirable cultivars. Hardy/Z 4–8. **C. glomerata var. alba 'Schneekrone'** (syn. 'Crown of Snow') is a good white form. H 50cm (20in), S 60cm (2ft). **'Joan Elliott'** bears large violet flowers in early summer. H 40cm (16in), S 45cm (18in). **'Purple Pixie'** produces smaller, deep violet flowers late in the season. H 30cm (1ft), S 60cm (2ft). Possibly the best is **'Superba'**, which bears dense clusters of violet-purple flowers, ideal for adding a deeper note to plantings of red roses and peonies. H and S 60cm (2ft).

C. lactiflora
Milky bellflower
There are a number of desirable forms of this Caucasian species, all flowering in summer and early autumn. The tall, sturdy stems (taller varieties will need staking in a windy location) make them excellent for giving height to a border, and they are good as companions for shrub roses and lilies. They are also tough enough to plant in rough grass. Hardy/Z 4–8. **'Loddon Anna'** has soft lilac-pink flowers. H to 1m (3ft), S 45cm (18in). The dwarf form **'Pouffe'** makes mounds of pale blue flowers. H and S 45cm (18in). One of the grandest cultivars is **'Prichard's Variety'**, which has violet-blue flowers. H 1.5m (5ft), S 60cm (2ft).

Campanula latiloba 'Percy Piper'

C. latiloba
(syn. *C. persicifolia* subsp. *sessiiflora*) In summer this occasionally evergreen species throws up erect stems, thickly set with rich lavender-blue flowers, from the basal rosettes of leaves. H 1m (3ft), S 45cm (18in). Hardy/Z 4–8. **'Highcliffe Variety'** and **'Percy Piper'**, both of which bear stalkless lavender-blue flowers, are similar. H 70cm (30in), S 45cm (18in).

C. punctata
This species from Russia and Japan does best in a sandy (but fertile) soil in sun. Low-growing and somewhat spreading, it flowers in mid- to late summer. The flowers are white or mauve (usually with a pink flush) and spotted inside with red. H 30cm (12in), S 45cm (18in). Hardy/Z 5–8. **C. punctata var. hondoensis** has greyish-pink flowers.

Campanula punctata var. hondoensis

Chysanthemum 'Curtain Call'

Chrysanthemum 'Southway Swan'

Chrysanthemum 'Taffy'

CHRYSANTHEMUM

This large – formerly much larger – genus has been the subject of much controversy in recent years. Strictly speaking, the name is now applied only to annual species, but it is so deeply entrenched in gardening lore that it is retained here for a range of perennials that are now sometimes assigned to the genus *Dendranthema*. Many are for enthusiasts only, bred for exhibition and requiring a good deal of care under glass if they are to produce their stunning flowers. The plants described here, while of no lesser value, are reliable garden performers that, along with Michaelmas daisies, provide a welcome warmth of colour as the days grow cooler at the end of summer and into autumn (some continue into early winter). They are effective with late-flowering grasses.

Cultivation The plants described here do best in fertile, well-drained soil in full sun. Taller varieties need staking. Dividing plants every two years or so will help to keep them fresh.

C. hybrids

There are a vast number of named chrysanthemums available in a range of colours to suit every possible garden scheme, and flowering in late summer into autumn. The following is just a small selection. All are hardy/Z 4–9 unless otherwise stated. **'Bronze Elegance'** has light bronze, pompon flowers. H and S 60cm (2ft). **'Curtain Call'** has anemone-centred, orange flowers. H and S 60cm (2ft). **'Emperor of China'** is an old variety, with double, silvery pink flowers; the leaves are tinged with red in autumn. H 1.2m (4ft),

S 60cm (2ft). **'George Griffiths'** is an early-flowering form, with large, deep red, fully reflexed flowers; it is often grown for exhibition. H 1.5m (5ft), S 75cm (30in). Half-hardy/Z 7–9. **'Glamour'** has warm, reddish-pink pompon flowers. H and S 1m (3ft). As the name suggests, **'Goldengreenheart'** has single, gold flowers with green centres; it is late flowering. H and S 60cm (2ft). **'Mei-kyo'** is an early-flowering plant with pink pompon flowers. H and S 60cm (2ft). **'Pennine Oriel'**, an early-flowering plant, has anemone-centred, white flowers. H 1.2m (4ft), S 75cm (30in). **'Primrose Allouise'** is an early-flowering sport of 'White Allouise', with weather-resistant, incurving, soft yellow flowers. H 1.2 (4ft), S 75cm (30in). Half-hardy/Z 7–9. **'Southway Swan'**

has single flowers, with silvery pink petals surrounding yellow-green centres. H 1.2 (4ft), S 75cm (30in). **'Taffy'** has rich bronze-orange flowers. H 1.2 (4ft), S 75cm (30in).

CIMICIFUGA
Bugbane, cohash

The imposing perennials in this genus are useful for the back of a border. The upright spikes of flowers do not need staking. *Cultivation* Bugbanes do best when planted in reliably moist soil in a cool position.

C. racemosa
Black snake root

This excellent plant has elegant, ferny foliage and tall bottlebrush-like spikes of white flowers throughout summer. H 2m (6ft), S 60cm (2ft). Hardy/Z 4–8.

C. simplex

This species is similar to *C. racemosa* but is more compact and flowers rather later in the year, from late summer into autumn. H 1.2m (4ft), S 60cm (2ft). Hardy/Z 3–8. Good garden forms include **C. simplex var. matsumurae 'Elstead'**, which has purplish stems and creamy-white flowers; and **'White Pearl'**, which has pure white flowers and pale green leaves. H and S 60cm (2ft).

CLEMATIS

Most familiar in gardens are the many climbers belonging to this genus, but there are also a few perennials, worth growing for

Chysanthemum 'George Griffiths'

Chysanthemum 'Primrose Allouise'

Cimicifuga simplex

Convallaria majalis

their quiet charm. All need staking.
Cultivation Grow in any fertile,
preferably alkaline, soil in sun or
light shade.

C. integrifolia
This weak-growing species has
noticeably hairy leaves and stems.
The indigo-violet flowers, borne in
midsummer, have recurving petals
like a turkscap lily. H and S 60cm
(2ft). Hardy/Z 3–9.

C. recta
One of the best of the herbaceous
clematis, this bears masses of
scented, star-like, white flowers in
mid- to late summer, and is an
excellent foil to blue delphiniums.
H 1.2m (4ft), S 1m (3ft).
Hardy/Z 3–9. **'Purpurea'** is more
dramatic, with dark purple stems
and purple-flushed leaves, but
plants sold under this name can
vary, some being more intensely

coloured than others. H 1.2m
(4ft), S 75cm (30in).

CONVALLARIA
Lily-of-the-valley
With flowers of unsurpassed and
instantly recognizable fragrance,
you would think that these would
be in every garden. They can be
troublesome, however: difficult
to establish in some cases and
annoyingly rampant if they find
situations they like. The flowers
are excellent for cutting. The
plants can also be potted up and
forced under glass for early
flowers. All are toxic.
Cultivation Lily-of-the-valley is
best grown in fertile soil in light
shade, but it also tolerates sun.

C. majalis
This species spreads by means of
branching underground rhizomes.
The handsome leaves emerge
in spring and are followed in late
spring by elegant sprays of bell-
shaped, fragrant, white flowers.
H 23cm (9in), S indefinite.
Hardy/Z 2–9. **'Albostriata'** is a
choice selection, with leaves striped
with silvery white. **'Fortin's Giant'**
is larger altogether and later
flowering. H and S 30cm (1ft).

COREOPSIS
Tickseed
The genus includes perennials and
annuals with daisy-like flowers in
summer, all excellent in borders
and ideal for cutting.
Cultivation Coreopsis does best in
fertile, well-drained soil in sun.
Tall varieties benefit from staking.

Coreopsis verticillata 'Moonbeam'

C. grandiflora 'Mayfield Giant'
This selection has large, single,
yellow flowers in mid- to late
summer. H 1m (3ft), S 60cm
(2ft) Hardy/Z 4–9.

C. verticillata
The best-known species in the
genus, with a number of selected
forms, this is a bushy plant with
star-shaped, bright yellow flowers
in early summer. H 45cm (18in),
S 30cm (12in). Hardy/Z 4–9.
'Golden Gain' has golden-yellow
flowers from early to midsummer.
Flowering later in the year,
'Grandiflora' (syn. 'Golden
Shower') has rich yellow daisies
and filigree foliage. H 60cm

(24in), S 45cm (18in). Also late-
flowering is the versatile
'Moonbeam', which has pale
yellow flowers. H 40cm (16in),
S 30cm (12in).

CRAMBE
These large, rather coarse but
undeniably dramatic plants are
excellent for giving height and
structure to borders. They are
magnificent as the dominant
feature of a white garden. After
flowering, leave the flower stem
intact and use it as a support for
a late climbing annual such as
sweet peas.
Cultivation Crambes will do well in
any well-drained soil in full sun.

C. cordifolia
This species makes a mound of
rough, cabbage-like, green leaves.
In early to midsummer the flower
stem carries a gypsophila-like
cloud of scented, white flowers.
H 2.5m (8ft), S 1.2m (4ft).
Hardy/Z 6–9.

C. maritima
Sea kale
This tolerant species, found wild
in coastal areas, has tough,
glaucous green leaves and large
panicles of white flowers in
summer. The young stems are
edible. H 75cm (30in), S 1m
(3ft). Hardy/Z 6–9.

Clematis recta 'Purpurea'

Crambe cordifolia

Delphinium 'Clifford Sky'

Delphinium 'Fenella'

Dianthus 'Riccardo'

Dianthus 'Uncle Teddy'

DELPHINIUM

These are grand plants but are now somewhat less popular than previously, probably because they require staking from early in the season and are susceptible to slug and snail damage, which means that a certain amount of work is necessary if they are to reach their full glory. That said, few other summer perennials can equal the colour range of these stately plants: primrose-yellow, cream, white, pale and dark blue, mauve, pink and deep purple. Recent breeding programmes (mainly in the Netherlands and the United States) have also introduced orange and red into the range, making pink strains possible. A traditional, Jekyllian-style herbaceous border would be unthinkable without them, the stronger blues associating well with *Thalictrum flavum* subsp.

glaucum. The method of propagation (cuttings) has weakened the stocks of many older selections over the years, but a revival of interest in the genus has resulted in a number of vigorous plants. All parts of the plant are harmful if eaten, and the leaves can cause irritation.
Cultivation Delphiniums need fertile, well-drained, preferably limy soil in sun. Tall varieties need staking. Cutting back stems after flowering can result in further (though much less impressive) flowers later on.

D. hybrids

While some of the species make good garden plants, they have not achieved the popularity of the many hybrids, only a few of which can be described here. **Elatum Group** plants have almost flat flowers in dense, upright spikes; **Belladonna Group** plants have branched stems and loose sprays of flowers. All cultivars are hardy/Z 2–7. **'Blue Nile'** (Elatum) is a classic pale blue delphinium, with flowers, each with a white eye, densely set on the spikes. H 1.5m (5ft), S 60cm (2ft). **'Casablanca'** (Belladonna), which has pure white flowers with yellow centres, is an excellent choice for a pale planting. H 1.2m (4ft), S 60cm (2ft). **'Clifford Sky'** (Elatum) has Wedgwood-blue flowers. H 1.5m (5ft), S 60cm (2ft). **'Fenella'** (Elatum) has stems densely set with semi-double, blue flowers, each with a black centre. H 1.5m

(5ft), S 60cm (2ft). **'Finsteraarhorn'** (Elatum) has cobalt-blue flowers touched with purple, each flower having a black eye. H 1.7m (5ft 6in), S 60cm (2ft). **'Langdon's Royal Flush'** (Elatum), a good choice among pink delphiniums, has conical spires of semi-double, purplish-pink flowers. H 1.5m (5ft), S 60cm (2ft). **'Mighty Atom'** (Elatum) has solidly packed spikes of semi-double, lavender-blue flowers with brown eyes. H 2m (6ft), S 1m (3ft). The charming **'Sandpiper'** (Elatum) is a compact plant, the pure white of its flowers enhanced by their dark brown eyes. H 1.2m (4ft), S 45cm (18in).

DIANTHUS
Carnation, pink

These appealing plants are justly popular as florist's flowers, but the genus is actually a large and complex one, simplified here as border carnations, perpetual-flowering carnations, Malmaison carnations and garden pinks. Perpetual-flowering and Malmaison carnations, which are half-hardy and can be forced into flower at any time of year, are generally grown commercially under glass.

The genus also includes many alpines, the biennial *D. barbatus* (sweet William) and some annuals. Many of the species are real enthusiasts' plants, and will not do well in all gardens. Where suited, however, they are splendid additions to any border, particularly in cottage garden-style plantings. The evergreen, bluish-grey leaves provide interest over a long period, making a particularly gracious picture when combined with old-fashioned roses. They are splendid edging plants, softening the lines of any path. Dianthus are not long-lived plants, but they are easily increased by cuttings or layering late in the season.

Border carnations, which are summer-flowering, are further divided by flower type as: selfs (a single colour); fancies (one colour spotted, flecked, blotched or striped with another); and picotees (one colour edged with another). They can also be clove-scented.

Garden pinks (sometimes just referred to as 'pinks') can be further divided into: old-fashioned pinks, which flower in early summer (they can be selfs; bicolours, with the central part of

Delphinium 'Sandpiper'

Dianthus 'Spinfield Red'

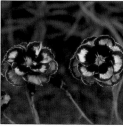

Dianthus 'Louise's Choice'

Dianthus 'Letitia Wyatt'

Dianthus 'Dawlish Joy'

Dicentra formosa

the flower a different colour; or laced, with each petal edged in a contrasting colour); and modern pinks, which can have a longer season, from early summer to autumn (these can be selfs, bicolours, fancies or laced, and can also be clove-scented). **Cultivation** The plants described need well-drained, neutral or alkaline soil in sun. They will tolerate some shade if it is not directly overhead.

Border carnations

All the following border carnations are hardy/Z 4–8. H to 60cm (24in), S to 40cm (16in). Among recommended varieties are the vigorous **'Bookham Fancy'**, which has yellow flowers edged and marked with carmine-purple. **'Bookham Perfume'** has scented, deep burgundy flowers. **'Lavender Clove'** has clove-scented, lavender-pink flowers. **'Orange Maid'** has apricot flowers flecked with bronze. The flowers of **'Riccardo'** combine red and white. **'Spinfield Red'** has red flowers. **'Uncle Teddy'** is red and white.

Dianthus 'Mendlesham Maid'

Garden pinks

All the following are hardy/Z 4–8. H to 45cm (18in), S to 30cm (12in). **'Bovey Belle'** has double purple flowers. **'Brympton Red'** has fragrant, crimson flowers with darker marbling. The scented flowers of **'Dad's Favourite'** are white laced with maroon, with dark centres. **'Dawlish Joy'** has variegated pink flowers. **'Devon Dove'** is pure white. **'Doris'**, a bicolour, has pale pink flowers with maroon centres. **'Excelsior'** has large-petalled, pink flowers; the flowers of **'Freckles'** are salmon-pink, delicately blotched with red. **'Gran's Favourite'** has clove-scented, white flowers laced with maroon; **'Joy'** has salmon-pink flowers. **'Letitia Wyatt'** has pale pink flowers. The semi-double **'London Brocade'** has pale pink flowers laced with dark red. **'Louise's Choice'** has crimson laced pink flowers; the miniature **'Mendlesham Maid'** has white flowers with frilly petal edges. The bicolour **'Monica Wyatt'** has phlox-pink flowers with ruby centres; **'Mrs Sinkins'** is fragrant, with double, white, fringed flowers; **'Musgrave's Pink'**, also fragrant, has double, white flowers with green centres. **'White Ladies'** has clove-scented, double, white flowers, purer in colour than 'Mrs Sinkins'.

DIASCIA

These interesting perennials (the genus name is pronounced with a hard 'c') bear nemesia-like flowers in a range of subtle colours, centring around coppery pink, throughout summer. They are not reliably hardy in cold areas, but, as with penstemons, cuttings are easily overwintered. They tend to

sprawl and look good at the base of a warm wall or in containers. **Cultivation** Grow in any fertile (but not too dry) soil in full sun. Cutting the flowered stems back in summer results in further flowers in autumn.

D. barberae 'Blackthorn Apricot'
Spires of warm apricot-pink flowers are borne from summer to autumn above the mats of dark green foliage. H 25cm (10in), S 50cm (20in). Borderline hardy/Z 8.

D. rigescens
Of the several species, this is the best for general garden use. It is a shrubby South African native, with dense spikes of coppery-pink flowers in early and late summer. H and S 45cm (18in). Borderline hardy/Z 7–9.

D. hybrids
There are many excellent garden forms, including **'Lilac Belle'**, which has purplish-pink flowers; **'Rupert Lambert'**, which has pink flowers; and **'Twinkle'**, which has purplish-pink flowers. H 45cm (18in), S 40cm (16in). Borderline hardy/Z 8.

DICENTRA
Bleeding heart
This genus contains elegant perennials with arching, glassy stems clothed with ferny foliage. The heart-shaped flowers are unique. Dicentras are excellent in shady rock gardens or light woodland, but they also tolerate more open conditions, combining

Diascia 'Rupert Lambert'

well with simple cottage garden plants, such as aquilegias, and flowering at around the same time in late spring to early summer. **Cultivation** Grow in humus-rich, fertile soil in sun or light shade; they appreciate cool conditions.

D. eximia
This species is similar in appearance to *D. formosa*, and there is some confusion between the two within the nursery trade, but this is daintier with typically furry foliage and tubular, pink, purple or white flowers. H 30cm (1ft), S 45cm (18in). Hardy/Z 4–8.

D. formosa
A species with deeply divided foliage and drooping sprays of tubular, pinkish-mauve flowers. H 45cm (18in), S 60cm (24in). Hardy/Z 3–8. *D. formosa* var. *alba* is the desirable white form.

D. spectabilis
Dutchman's breeches
The best-known species and deservedly popular, this produces fern-like foliage and masses of heart-shaped, rose-pink flowers that dangle appealingly from the arching stems. H 75cm (30in), S 60cm (24in). Hardy/Z 3–8. The selection **'Alba'** is if anything even more desirable, with white flowers and a slightly more compact habit. Both are good for cutting. H 60cm (24in), S 45cm (18in).

D. 'Stuart Boothman'
(syn. *D.* 'Boothman's Variety')
This hybrid has flesh-pink flowers on arching stems amid the bluish-grey leaves. H 30cm (12in), S 40cm (16in). Hardy/Z 4–8.

Dierama pulcherrimum

Digitalis lutea

Doronicum 'Miss Mason'

DIERAMA

Angel's fishing rods, wandflower
The common name is apt: these are plants of almost unearthly beauty, with tall, arching stems of elegant bell-shaped flowers that look well near water.
Cultivation Grow in reliably moist soil in full sun. Winter protection may be necessary in cold areas.

D. pulcherrimum

Venus' fishing rod, wandflower
From among the grassy, evergreen leaves, wiry stems emerge in mid-summer, dangling bell-shaped pink to lilac flowers. H 1.5m (5ft), S 30cm (1ft). Borderline hardy/Z 8–10. **'Blackbird'** has deep violet-mauve flowers.

DIGITALIS

Foxglove
Typical woodlanders, foxgloves also do well in more open conditions. The species described are all subtly attractive and will seed themselves where suited. They suit any cottage garden-style planting. All have spikes of charac-teristic, thimble-like flowers in early summer and occasionally produce lesser spikes later on, even into autumn. Poisonous.
Cultivation Foxgloves will grow in any fertile soil, but they do best in humus-rich soil, in partial shade. They will tolerate full sun.

D. lutea

(syn. D. eriostachya)
This species has small, pale yellow flowers and smooth green leaves. H 60cm (2ft), S 30cm (1ft). Hardy/Z 5–9.

D. × mertonensis

The hybrid has downward-pointing, tubular flowers the colour of crushed strawberries, a curious coppery, buff pink. The leaves are greyish-green. H 60cm (2ft), S 30cm (1ft). Hardy/Z 5–9.

D. purpurea

Common foxglove
This is the foxglove familiar in woodlands, but it makes a good garden plant, with mounds of soft, grey-green leaves, flushed purple towards the base. It is a variable species, both in flower colour, coming in shades of pink, red and purple, and height. H 1.5m (5ft), S 45cm (18in). Hardy/Z 4–8. **D. purpurea f. albiflora** is the delightful white-flowered form, luminous in shade. The leaves are unmarked green. The form **'Suttons Apricot'** is also desirable, with apricot-coloured flowers.

DORONICUM

Leopard's bane
These cheerful perennials have bright yellow, daisy-like flowers in spring. The species described is easily pleased and can be invasive. It is poisonous.
Cultivation Grow in any reasonable soil in sun or light shade.

D. 'Miss Mason'

This old hybrid holds its bright-yellow daisies well above the heart-shaped leaves in spring. H 45cm (18in), S 60cm (2ft). Hardy/Z 6.

D. pardalianches

Great leopard's bane
A rather coarse plant, this is suitable for colonizing light woodland and is tough enough to fill areas under deciduous trees and shrubs. The yellow, daisy-like flowers are produced in mid- to late spring. H 1m (3ft), S 60cm (2ft). Hardy/Z 4–8.

ECHINACEA

Coneflower
Sturdy border plants, echinaceas are essential for providing interest from midsummer into autumn. The prominent central boss of stamens and the backwards sweeping outer petals distinguish them from all other daisy flowers.
Cultivation Grow in any fertile, ideally humus-rich, well-drained soil in sun.

E. purpurea

This is the most widely grown species. The flowers have rich purple-crimson outer petals surrounding the prominent orange-brown centre. H 1.2m (4ft), S 45cm (18in). Hardy/Z 3–9. **'Robert Bloom'** has intense cerise-mauve flowers. **'White Swan'** is not clear white as the name suggests, but is touched with fresh pale green. H 75cm (30in), S 45cm (18in).

ECHINOPS

Globe thistle
Tolerant and undemanding, echinops are excellent in an ecological garden, since they attract bees and butterflies.
Cultivation They will grow in any, even poor, soil in an open, sunny situation.

E. ritro

The jagged leaves are grey underneath; the ball-like flowerheads show their colour (steely blue) before the flowers open in late summer, giving a long period of interest. H 60cm (2ft), S 45cm (18in). Hardy/Z 3.

Digitalis purpurea f. albiflora

Echinacea purpurea 'White Swan'

Echinops ritro 'Veitch's Blue'

Erigeron 'Quakeress'

'Veitch's Blue' is taller, to 90cm (3ft), with darker flowerheads.

EPILOBIUM
Willowherb
These mainly tall plants are good for providing height in a border, and they flower over a long period.
Cultivation Grow in any well-drained soil that is not too rich; excessive fertility encourages leafy growth at the expense of flowers.

E. angustifolium
Rosebay willowherb
The species, attractive as it is, tends to be an invasive weed in gardens so is best confined to a wild area. H 1.5m (5ft), S 1m (3ft). Hardy/Z 3–7. 'Album', with spires of pure white flowers in late summer, is less rampant.

EREMURUS
Foxtail lily
Stately perennials, foxtail lilies produce tall spikes of star-shaped flowers that rise above other plants in late spring to early summer. Grow them among lower plants for maximum impact. They die back after flowering, so plant near something that will cover the gap they leave, such as *Gypsophila paniculata* or late-sown annuals. The plants may need staking in windy weather.
Cultivation Grow in any well-drained soil in sun. They tolerate dry soil.

E. × isabellinus Shelford hybrids
Under this name is a range of garden-worthy plants with tall spikes of yellow, orange, pink or white flowers. H 2m (6ft), S 1m (3ft). Hardy/Z 5.

E. stenophyllus
This lovely species has slender spikes of yellow flowers, which fade to orange-brown, giving a bicolour effect. H 1.5m (5ft), S 60cm (2ft). Hardy/Z 5.

ERIGERON
Fleabane
Useful daisy plants, suitable for a sunny border, these suit cottage garden-style plantings. There are a large number of hybrids; only the species described is well-represented in gardens.
Cultivation Best in fertile, moist but well-drained soil in sun. Taller varieties may benefit from light staking.

E. karvinskianus
(syn. E. muconatus)
Wall daisy
This spreading species has dainty white flowers from late spring to autumn. H to 30cm (1ft), S 1m (3ft). Hardy/Z 8–9.

E. hybrids
The following hybrids flower throughout summer but can also flower intermittently at other times. They are all hardy/Z 2–7. 'Dignity' has violet-blue flowers.

H and S 45cm (18in). 'Dunkelste Aller' (syn. 'Darkest of All') has deep purple flowers with yellow eyes. H 60cm (2ft), S 45cm (18in). 'Gaiety' has mid-pink flowers. H 60cm (2ft), S 45cm (18in). The deservedly popular 'Quakeress' has white flowers flushed with pale lilac-pink. H 60cm (2ft), S 45cm (18in). 'Schneewittchen' (syn. 'Snow White') has pure white flowers, which turn pink as they age. H 60cm (2ft), S 45cm (18in).

ERYNGIUM
Eryngo, sea holly
Spiky, stiffly branched, architectural plants, eryngiums are perhaps best given space to make their own statement, ideally in a gravel garden, but they will also integrate into mixed borders, providing an excellent contrast to softer plants. Some are biennials.
Cultivation Grow in any well-drained soil in full sun. They thrive in poor, gritty soils.

E. bourgatii
This striking plant has deeply cut, bluish-grey leaves, veined white, and spiky steel-blue cones of flowers in early to midsummer. H 60cm (2ft), S 50cm (20in). Hardy/Z 5–8.

E. × tripartitum
This hybrid has wiry stems that branch freely, carrying many metallic-blue flowerheads throughout summer. It looks particularly striking with *Crambe maritima*. H 1m (3ft), S 50cm (20in). Hardy/Z 5–8.

Epilobium angustifolium 'Album'

Eremurus stenophyllus

Eryngium × tripartitum

Erysimum 'Bowles' Mauve'

ERYSIMUM
Wallflower

Wallflowers and tulips are a classic cottage garden combination, although bedding plants sold for this purpose are usually treated as biennials. The plants described here are all true evergreen perennials, and although they are often short-lived, they are easily increased by cuttings. All are of hybrid origin.
Cultivation Grow wallflowers in any well-drained, not too rich soil in sun, in a sheltered position. Dead-heading encourages further flowering.

E. 'Bowles' Mauve'
This truly remarkable perennial belongs in every garden. Officially it produces its four-petalled, fragrant, rich mauve flowers from

Eupatorium album 'Braunlaub'

late winter to early summer, but it is seldom without flowers at any time of year. H 75cm (30in), S 60cm (2ft). Hardy/Z 5–9.

E. cheiri
(syn. *Cheiranthus cheiri*)
This species is the parent of the many seed strains that are sold for raising bedding plants. The reliably perennial 'Harpur Crewe' has double, rich yellow flowers from late spring to midsummer. H 30cm (12in), S 60cm (2ft). Hardy/Z 6–7.

E. 'Constant Cheer'
From mid-spring to early summer this hybrid has orange-yellow flowers that fade to purple. H 60cm (2ft), S 40cm (16in). Hardy/Z 7–10.

E. 'Parish's'
The flowers of this hybrid, produced from early spring to midsummer, open brick-red and mature to purplish-crimson. H and S 30cm (12in). Hardy/Z 7–10.

EUPATORIUM
Hemp agrimony

Somewhat coarse, but easily grown, these perennials are suitable for a wild garden or an informal border. They are valuable for their height and late season. Some are weeds.
Cultivation Any reasonable soil in sun is suitable.

E. album
(syn. *E. rugosum* var. *album*)
This species, with hairy stems and

Euphorbia cornigera

leaves, has domed heads of white flowers in late summer. H 1m (3ft), S 45cm (18in). Hardy/Z 4–9. The variant 'Braunlaub' is similar but has brownish flowers and brown-tinged young foliage. H 1m (3ft), S 45cm (18in).

E. purpureum
Joe Pye weed, gravel root, queen of the meadow
This imposing species has characteristically rough leaves and clusters of dull pinkish-purple flowers in late summer. H 2m (6ft), S 1m (3ft). Hardy/Z 3–8. E. purpureum subsp. maculatum 'Atropurpureum' is a superior form, with purple-flushed leaves and stems and light purple flowers. H 2m (6ft), S 1m (3ft).

EUPHORBIA
A hugely significant genus, many members of which provide interest over a long period. The true flowers are insignificant, but are surrounded by showy bracts (referred to as 'flowers' below) that continue to attract attention after the true flowers have faded. The genus encompasses a vast range of perennial plants that are at home in any garden as well as shrubs, trees, exotic succulents and annuals, in addition to the popular Christmas houseplant, *E. pulcherrima*, sold as poinsettia. Euphorbias combine happily in the border with a range of other plants. The species described here are all easy to grow, but care needs to be taken when handling them: when cut or broken, the stems

exude a milky sap that can cause skin irritations.
Cultivation The euphorbias described below will grow in any well-drained fertile soil in sun. Any preferences of individual species are included in the relevant entry. To keep plants looking neat, cut back the flower stems of evergreen forms to ground level when the blooms have faded.

E. amygdaloides var. robbiae
(syn. *E. robbiae*)
Mrs Robb's bonnet
A good plant for a shady position under trees or for poor soil, this plant has rosettes of dark green leaves and dull green flowers in spring. H and S 60cm (2ft). Hardy/Z 5–9.

E. characias
This is a variable evergreen, rather shrubby species, happy in sun or shade, but probably better in sun. It is splendid against a warm wall, when it will send out tall, billowing shoots from ground level, clothed in narrow, grey-green leaves and topped, from early spring into summer, by lime-green flowers. H and S 1.2m (4ft). Hardy/Z 7–9. Worthwhile variants include E. characias subsp. wulfenii, which has more brilliant yellow-green flowers; and subsp. wulfenii 'Lambrook Gold', which has rich golden-green flowers. H and S 1.2m (4ft).

E. cornigera
(syn. *E. longifolia*, *E. wallichii*)
An excellent border plant, this

Euphorbia myrsinites

Euphorbia schillingii

Galega × hartlandii 'Alba'

species has dark green leaves striped centrally with paler green and, throughout summer, typical euphorbia lime-green flowers. H 50cm (20in), S 30cm (12in). Hardy/Z 7–9.

E. dulcis
This species can be invasive but makes good groundcover in shade. It has dark green leaves, sometimes tinged with bronze, and greenish-yellow flowers in early summer. H and S 30cm (12in). Hardy/Z 6. The form 'Chameleon' is a more interesting and coveted plant than the species. It has rich purple leaves and purple-tinted flowers.

E. griffithii
This notable early summer-flowering species is invasive but desirable as groundcover in sun or light shade, especially in one

of its named varieties. It is excellent with yellow-flowered azaleas. The species has dark green, red-ribbed leaves and colourful red, yellow and orange flowerheads. H 1m (3ft), S 60cm (2ft). Hardy/Z 5–9. Among the best cultivars are 'Dixter', which has orange flowers and red-tinged leaves; and 'Fireglow', which has tomato-red flowers. H 75cm (30in), S 1m (3ft).

E. myrsinites
Myrtle euphorbia
This succulent-looking species is good in gravel gardens in full sun or in troughs, where its trailing stems are especially effective. The thick, almost triangular leaves are blue-green. The long-lasting, greenish-yellow flowers that fade to pink appear in early summer. H 15cm (6in), S 30cm (12in). Hardy/Z 6–8.

E. polychroma
(syn. E. epithymoides)
A must for the spring garden, this herbaceous perennial makes a mound of foliage that in late spring becomes a mass of brilliant yellow-green as the flowers open. It is excellent with late-flowering daffodils or Tulipa praestans. H and S 30cm (12in). Hardy/Z 4–9.

E. schillingii
A robust plant, this has dark green leaves and long-lasting, yellow-green flowers from midsummer to mid-autumn. It does best in light shade in reliably moist soil. H 1m (3ft), S 60cm (2ft). Hardy/Z 5–8.

FRAGARIA
Strawberry
Strawberries are usually grown exclusively in kitchen gardens for their edible fruit. The plant

described here has ornamental value, however, and makes an excellent edging plant as well as providing good groundcover. *Cultivation* Grow in any moist but well-drained soil, preferably alkaline, in sun or light shade.

F. 'Pink Panda'
(syn. 'Frel')
Like the edible strawberries, this plant spreads by runners and can be invasive. It has dark green leaves and, from late spring to mid-autumn, bright pink flowers but seldom fruits. H 15cm (6in), S indefinite. Hardy/Z 4.

GALEGA
Goat's rue
This genus of large summer-flowering perennials deserve to be better known. They resemble a giant vetch with masses of pea-like flowers and are excellent for filling gaps in large borders, associating well with a wide range of other plants.
Cultivation Grow in any soil, poor or fertile, in sun or shade. Tall forms may need staking.

G. × hartlandii
This hybrid group consists of a number of worthwhile forms, usually with flowers in shades of lilac, lavender, pink or pinkish-mauve. H to 1.5m (5ft), S 1m (3ft). Hardy/Z 3–8. 'Alba' has white flowers; 'His Majesty' has pinkish-mauve and white flowers; and 'Lady Wilson' is a similar bicolour, but the flowers are a more bluish-mauve.

Euphorbia polychroma

Galega × hartlandii 'Lady Wilson'

Galium odoratum

Geranium 'Ann Folkard'

Geranium macrorrhizum

GALIUM
Bedstraw

These are useful plants for filling gaps in borders, and the star-like flowers are a good foil for other, more flamboyant plants. The species described is the best known and is often included in herb gardens for its historical associations.
Cultivation Grow in any well-drained soil in sun or light shade. *G. odoratum* is one of the few plants that positively thrives in dry shade.

G. odoratum
(syn. *Asperula odorata*)
Sweet woodruff
This species cultivated as ground cover produces masses of fragrant, star-like white flowers in late spring. H 30cm (12in), S indefinite. Hardy/Z 5–8.

GERANIUM
Cranesbill

It would be difficult to over-estimate the value of these plants, which have rightly gained in popularity over recent years. Easy to grow, spreading easily and combining happily with a range of other plants, they are excellent in fairly informal, cottage-garden schemes, associating particularly well with most roses. They make excellent groundcover without being invasive. Smaller types are good in rock gardens.
Cultivation Grow hardy geraniums in any reasonable (but not boggy) soil in sun or light shade. *G. phaeum* prefers shade.

G. 'Ann Folkard'
A fine plant, this bears a succession of magenta flowers, with blackish centres and veining, throughout summer. Early in the season the flowers are pleasingly offset by yellowish leaves, but these usually turn green by midsummer. This is a good plant for growing through small shrubs in shade. H 30cm (12in), S 60cm (2ft). Hardy/Z 5–8.

G. clarkei
The spreading species, which is from India, has saucer-shaped flowers in shades of purplish-blue or white with purplish veining from early to late summer. H 50cm (20in), S indefinite. Hardy/Z 4–8. The species is usually represented in gardens by its selected forms, outstanding among which is **'Kashmir White'** (syn. *G. pratense* 'Rectum Album'),

whose white summer flowers are delicately veined with lilac-pink. H and S 45cm (18in).

G. 'Johnson's Blue'
A plant for every garden, this hybrid has clear blue flowers in late spring over the mounds of copious green leaves. Cutting the plant back to ground level after flowering results in a fresh crop of leaves and (in a good year) a second flush of flowers. H 30cm (1ft), S 60cm (2ft). Hardy/Z 4–8.

G. macrorrhizum
(syn. *G. macrorrhizum* var. *roseum*)
The species, which spreads by means of thick rhizomes, has gummy, aromatic leaves, which assume red tinges in autumn. The liverish magenta flowers are small in relation to the size of the plant and appear in late spring. H 25cm

(10in), S 50cm (20in). Hardy/Z 3–8. The flowers of the species yield in beauty to those of **'Album'**, which are not clear white, but a delicate, pale shell pink. H 30cm (1ft), S 60cm (2ft).

G. × magnificum
This robust but sterile hybrid has handsome, slightly hairy leaves, which often redden attractively in autumn. Sticky flower stalks carry rich purple flowers, heavily pencilled with a darker shade, in late spring to early summer. H and S 60cm (2ft). Hardy/Z 4–8.

G. phaeum
Mourning widow, dusky cranesbill
The common names are appropriate: the dusky purple flowers that hang from elegant, wiry stems in mid-spring have a slightly plangent air. H 60cm (2ft), S 45cm (18in). Hardy/Z 4–9. The form **'Album'** is also desirable; it has pure white flowers and golden-yellow anthers. Where grown in proximity with the species, the two will hybridize to produce plants with pleasing soft mauve flowers. **'Lily Lovell'** is a selected form with large, mauve flowers with paler centres.

GEUM
Avens

Simple, cottage-garden-style plants, geums provide strong colour and borders for many weeks in early summer; they are good at the front of borders.
Cultivation Grow geums in any reasonable soil in sun or light shade. They benefit from division every two to three years.

G. 'Lady Stratheden'
(syn. *G.* 'Goldball')
This is one of the best known of the hybrids, with semi-double yellow flowers from late spring to midsummer. H 45cm (18in), S 30cm (12in). Hardy/Z 5–8.

G. 'Mrs J. Bradshaw'
(syn. *G.* 'Feuerball', *G.* 'Mrs Bradshaw')
The semi-double, coppery red flowers of this hybrid can be produced at any time during the summer. H 45cm (18in), S 30cm (12in). Hardy/Z 5–9.

Geranium 'Johnson's Blue'

Geranium phaeum

Geum 'Mrs J. Bradshaw'

HELENIUM
Sneezeweed, Helen's flower
These valuable daisy-like flowers are easily grown and merit a place in any border planned for late summer and autumn interest. Together with dahlias and chrysanthemums, they bring a warm glow to the garden at the end of the season, and they look good with a range of grasses and purple-leaved plants or with the strong foliage of bergenias. Most garden forms are hybrids that have been developed in Germany.
Cultivation Grow in any reasonable soil in sun. Tall forms may need staking. Regular division also prevents congestion.

H. hybrids
The following hybrids all flower from late summer to mid-autumn. All are hardy/Z 3–8. H and S 1m

(3ft). **'Gartensonne'** has light yellow flowers with dark centres; **'Indianersommer'** has rich golden-yellow flowers; **'Moerheim Beauty'**, one of the best known, has rich brownish-red flowers that age lighter brown; **'The Bishop'** has yellow flowers with dark eyes.

HELICHRYSUM
The plants in this genus are distinguished by their daisy-like, straw-textured flowers, some of which hold their colour well when dried. Some are primarily foliage plants, useful in summer bedding schemes, or in large pots or hanging baskets.
Cultivation Grow in any well-drained soil in full sun. This will not tolerate wet conditions.

H. petiolare
(syn. *H. petiolatum*)
This sprawling, evergreen subshrub is essential for hanging baskets or for trailing over the edges of a large container of seasonal plants. The typical plant has silvery, woolly leaves. H and S 1m (3ft). Half-hardy/Z 10. Selections include **'Limelight'** (syn. 'Aureum'), which has lime-green leaves; and **'Variegatum'**, which has grey-green leaves variegated with cream.

H. 'Schweffellicht'
(syn. *H.* 'Sulphur Light')
This hybrid provides interest over a long period. The white-woolly leaves are themselves a feature before the sulphur, tawny-orange daisy-like flowers appear in mid-

Helichrysum 'Schweffellicht'

to late summer. H and S 35cm (14in). Hardy/Z 5–9.

HELLEBORUS
Hellebore
An important genus from the gardener's point of view, with many desirable plants, all with nodding flowers (some a little sinister-looking, it is true) and handsome, more or less evergreen leaves. They are indispensable in the winter garden. Hellebores thrive in the shade of deciduous trees and shrubs and will even tolerate heavy shade next to a wall. All are poisonous.
Cultivation Easy to grow in any fertile, well-drained (although most prefer heavy and alkaline) soil in sun or shade.

H. argutifolius
(syn. *H. corsicus, H. lividus* subsp. *corsicus*)
Corsican hellebore
This handsome species tolerates drier conditions than most other hellebores. The firm, jade-green leaves are attractive throughout the year. The clusters of apple-green, bell-shaped flowers appear in mid-spring and last until early summer. It is a splendid foil for *Iris reticulata*. H and S 1m (3ft). Hardy/Z 6–8.

H. foetidus
Bear's foot, stinking hellebore
A dramatic species that makes a clump of blackish-green leaves. Strong stems carrying many bell-shaped, apple-green flowers (usually edged with maroon)

appear in late winter to early spring. It looks good with snowdrops. H 75cm (30in), S 60cm (2ft). Hardy/Z 4–9. Plants of the **Wester Flisk Group** have red-tinged stems and leaf and flower stalks. H 60cm (2ft), S 45cm (18in).

H. niger
Christmas rose
This is one of the most desirable of the hellebores, but unfortunately it is also one of the trickiest to grow. It has dark green, leathery leaves and large glistening white flowers in mid- to late winter. It is slow to establish and needs fertile sticky soil that does not dry out. H 30cm (12in), S 45cm (18in). Hardy/Z 4–7. **'Potter's Wheel'** is a desirable selection with larger flowers.

H. orientalis
Lenten rose
One of the easiest hellebores to grow, this is also one of the most variable species. The flowers, which appear from late winter into spring, can be white, yellowish-cream, dusky-pink, clear glowing red or plum-purple, and can also be spotted inside with a different colour to varying degrees. All are flushed green inside and out. The leaves are also handsome: firm and with serrated edges, and of varying shades of green, paler leaves being associated with paler flower colours. Blackened leaves should be removed. H 45cm (18in), S 60cm (2ft). Hardy/Z 5–9.

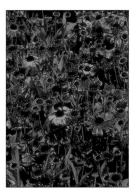

Helenium 'Indianersommer'

Helichrysum petiolare

Helleborus foetidus

Hemerocallis 'Golden Chimes'

Hemerocallis 'Jake Russell'

Hemerocallis 'Joan Senior'

Hemerocallis 'Ruffled Apricot'

HEMEROCALLIS
Daylily

These almost indestructible plants, with their usually trumpet-like flowers, are of increasing value in gardens. Breeding programmes (particularly in the United States) have greatly increased the number of hybrids and the length of flowering season. The colour range is also greater, but centres around yellow and orange. They make excellent border plants, rapidly forming vigorous clumps. Although the individual flowers last only a day (hence the common name), they are freely produced over a long period, and the grassy foliage is always appealing, a refreshing sight when emerging in spring and a good foil for early bulbs. Small daylilies are excellent for edging a border; the larger kinds consort happily with hostas and peonies, as well as with roses of all kinds. The species are tough enough for a wild garden or for growing in grass.

Cultivation Daylilies seem to thrive in any soil but preferably one that is not too dry. Grow in sun or light shade. Lift and divide the plants every two or three years to prevent congestion.

H. citrina
Broader leaves than average distinguish this species, whose fragrant, lemon-yellow flowers open in the evening in midsummer. H 1m (3ft), S 60cm (2ft). Hardy/Z 3–9.

H. fulva
This species is usually grown in one of its double forms. Hardy/Z 3–9. 'Flore Pleno' has sometimes muddled, rich orange flowers in summer. H and S to 1m (3ft).

'Kwans Variegata' has similar flowers but is less robust, with leaves narrowly margined with white. H and S 75cm (30in).

H. lilioasphodelus (syn. *H. flava*)
Late spring to early summer is the season of this semi-evergreen, evening-flowering species with scented, lemon-yellow flowers. H 75cm (30in), S 45cm (18in). Hardy/Z 3–9.

H. hybrids
There are many named hybrids, with colours and heights to fit into every garden scheme. The following, all of which are evergreen and hardy/Z 3–9 unless otherwise indicated, are just a selection. 'Cartwheels' has freely borne, orange, nocturnal flowers in midsummer. H and S 75cm (30in). The compact 'Corky' has clear yellow flowers in midsummer. H 70cm (28in), S 40cm (16in). 'Eenie Weenie', one of the first dwarfs raised, has rounded yellow flowers in early to midsummer. H 25cm (10in), S 40cm (16in). The intriguing, semi-evergreen 'Gingerbread Man' has butterscotch-orange flowers in early summer. H 70cm (28in), S 1m (3ft). Borderline hardy/Z 8–9. 'Golden Chimes' has deep yellow flowers in early summer. H 1m (3ft), S 45cm (18in). 'Green Flutter' has light yellow flowers with green throats over a long period. H 50cm (20in), S 1m (3ft). 'Jake Russell' has golden-yellow flowers with a velvety sheen in mid- to late summer. H 1m (3ft), S 45cm (18in). The semi-evergreen 'Joan Senior', the closest to a white cultivar, has pinkish-white flowers with yellow-green throats in mid- to late summer. H 60cm (2ft), S 75cm (30in). The vigorous 'Little Grapette' has deep purple flowers in midsummer. H 30cm (12in), S 45cm (18in). 'Lusty Leland' produces an abundance of scarlet and yellow flowers over a long period in summer. H 70cm (28in), S 1m (3ft). The outstanding and prolific 'Marion Vaughn' has fragrant, lemon-yellow flowers in mid- to late summer. H 85cm (34in), S 75cm (30in). 'Maura Loa' has brilliant orange flowers in summer. H 55cm (22in), S 1m (3ft). 'Prairie Blue Eyes' is semi-evergreen with lavender-purple flowers in midsummer. H 70cm (28in), S 75cm (30in). 'Ruffled Apricot' has characteristically crimped-edged, apricot flowers in early to midsummer. H 70cm (28in), S 1m (3ft). 'Scarlet Orbit' has bright red flowers with yellow-green throats in midsummer. H 50cm (20in), S 1m (3ft). 'Stafford', one of the best of its colour range, has rich scarlet flowers in midsummer. H 70cm (28in), S 1m (3ft). The vigorous 'Stella de Oro' is a dwarf selection, with rounded, bright yellow flowers in early summer, sometimes repeating in autumn. H 30cm (12in), S 45cm (18in).

HEUCHERA
Alum bell, coral bells

Invaluable plants for ground-cover, heucheras have handsome leaves, often tinted or marbled

Hemerocallis 'Little Grapette'

Hemerocallis 'Stafford'

Heuchera 'Pewter Moon'

with silver-grey. There are a large number of hybrids, all making excellent companions for border carnations and pinks (*Dianthus*).
Cultivation Grow in any reasonable soil in sun or light shade. Plants benefit from regular division.

H. micrantha var. diversifolia 'Palace Purple'

The species is most often represented in cultivation by this form, although plants sold under this name can vary. It is a striking plant with large, purple, maple-like leaves and sprays of tiny white flowers in midsummer. H 60cm (2ft), S 45cm (18in). Hardy/Z 4–8.

H. 'Pewter Moon'

This hybrid is grown primarily for the appeal of its heavily silver-marbled leaves rather than for its sprays of pink summer flowers. H 45cm (18in), S 30cm (12in). Hardy/Z 4.

H. 'Strawberry Swirl'

The hybrid has ruffled green leaves, overlaid with silver, and pale pink flowers in early summer. H 45cm (18in), S 30cm (12in). Hardy/Z 4.

× HEUCHERELLA

These dainty evergreen woodland plants, hybrids of *Heuchera* and *Tiarella*, have an old-fashioned look to them. They are clump-forming and make excellent groundcover.
Cultivation Grow in partial shade in any soil that does not dry out completely in summer.

Hosta nigrescens

Hosta sieboldiana var. elegans

× H. tiarelloides

This beautiful evergreen ground-cover plant makes dense clusters of short leaves. The sprays of appealing, salmon-pink flowers appear in late spring. H and S 45cm (18in). Hardy/Z 4–8.

HOSTA
Funkia, plantain lily

This is an enormous genus, made larger by a huge number of hybrids, mostly of American origin. They are the ultimate foliage plants, combining handsomely with roses and a whole range of herbaceous perennials. They make good groundcover and look good with filigree ferns in shade gardens. They are also stylish in containers, although, being herbaceous, they do not provide year-round interest. The flowers, which are carried on tall 'scapes' in mid- to late summer, are of secondary interest, and some gardeners go as far as cutting them off.

Although of undoubted distinction, hostas are not universally popular, as many gardeners object to the slug and snail control that is necessary to guarantee perfect leaves. Apart from poisons, a good frog, toad and bird population or a hedgehog will control but not eradicate the pests. The parasitic nematode is effective on slugs only. An eco-friendly method that defies the cultivation hints given below is to restrict your choice to thick-leaved types and grow them in poor, gritty soil. This results in smaller but tougher leaves that

are less palatable to pests.
Cultivation Most hostas do best in fertile, humus-rich, moist soil in partial to full shade. Some will tolerate sun, but for the best leaves, the more sun, the moister the soil should be.

H. nigrescens

This large species has broadly oval, puckered leaves that are glaucous blue when mature (the emerging shoots in spring are almost black, hence the name). The near white flowers open from pale purple buds. H and S 70cm (28in). Hardy/Z 4–9.

H. sieboldiana

An impressive species with almost quilted, waxy, bluish-green leaves and almost white flowers. H 1m (3ft), S 1.2m (4ft). Hardy/Z 3–9. While of evident distinction, the species usually gives ground in gardens to **H. sieboldiana var. elegans** (syn. *H.* 'Elegans', *H. glauca*, *H.* 'Robusta'). This has even more thickly puckered and glaucous leaves.

H. sieboldii

One of the few naturally occurring variegated species, this should not be confused with *H. sieboldiana*, which is quite different. This has oval or lance-shaped leaves with white margins and pale mauve flowers streaked with violet. H and S 60cm (2ft). Hardy/Z 4–9.

H. ventricosa

This species has shiny green leaves with pointed tips and striking,

Hosta ventricosa

bell-shaped, deep violet flowers. H 50cm (20in), S 1m (3ft). Hardy/Z 4–9.

H. venusta

This vigorous dwarf species is suitable for a rock garden. It has oval to lance-shaped green leaves and violet flowers, borne on scapes up to 35cm (14in) tall. H 5cm (2in), S 25cm (10in). Hardy/Z 4–9.

H. hybrids

For convenience, the following hybrids are divided into three groups: large, measuring 64cm (25in) or more from leaf tip to opposite leaf tip; medium, 40–60cm (16–24in) from leaf tip to opposite leaf tip; and small, 38cm (15in) or less from leaf tip to opposite leaf tip. All hybrids are hardy/Z 3–9 unless otherwise stated.

Hosta sieboldii

Hosta venusta

Hosta 'Antioch'

Large hybrids

'Antioch', an elegant plant, has oval leaves irregularly margined with cream or creamy white and lavender-coloured flowers. It is best in full shade. 'August Moon' has soft yellow leaves that develop a faint greyish-blue bloom and pale greyish-lavender to white flowers. It does best in sun. 'Blue Angel' has thick, glaucous-blue leaves (although less puckered than many of its type) and pale mauve to white flowers. 'Francee' has leaves that are narrowly edged with white and funnel-shaped, lavender-purple flowers. 'Frances Williams' (syn. 'Eldorado', 'Golden Circles', *H. sieboldiana* 'Frances Williams', *H. sieboldiana* 'Yellow Edge') is a famous hosta and one of the most beautiful, with deep glaucous blue leaves, margined with creamy-beige, and lavender-coloured flowers. 'Gold Standard' has striking leaves that are generously splashed with greenish yellow, the colour becoming brighter before fading to buff beige. The flowers are greyish purple. 'Green Acres' has oval green, deeply ribbed leaves on tall petioles and near-white flowers. It is a striking plant when mature. 'Krossa Regal', a sumptuous, urn-shaped hosta, has waxy-bloomed, bluish-green leaves and lavender-coloured flowers. 'Pearl Lake', which has small, grey-green leaves carried on tall petioles and masses of pale lavender-coloured flowers, makes excellent groundcover. 'Piedmont Gold' is aptly named. It has thick-textured, yellowish-green leaves with a distinct whitish bloom. The flowers are pale lavender-white. 'Sagae' (syn. *H. fluctuans* 'Sagae', *H. fluctuans* 'Variegated') is a truly dramatic hosta with thick, blackish-green leaves margined with cream or creamy-yellow. The funnel-shaped flowers are pale lavender overlaid with purple. Sun-tolerant 'Sum and Substance' has puckered leaves that are pointed at the tip, greenish to bright yellow in colour, depending on the amount of sun, and pale mauve flowers. 'Sun Power' has oval to heart-shaped, yellow-green leaves and lavender flowers. 'Tall Boy', almost uniquely among hostas, is grown for its pale purple, funnel-shaped flowers, which are carried on unusually tall scapes. The leaves are glossy mid-green. 'Wide Brim' has puckered, bluish-green leaves that are broadly and irregularly margined with creamy white and near-white flowers. 'Zounds' has heavily puckered, golden-yellow leaves, which develop a metallic sheen as they mature, and pale lavender-white flowers.

Medium hybrids

'Blue Wedgwood', an elegant plant, produces heavily puckered, intense glaucous blue leaves and pale lavender to white flowers. 'Devon Green', a beautiful plant, has shiny dark green leaves and greyish-lavender to white flowers. 'Golden Prayers' is a vigorous hosta, with puckered, vivid golden-yellow leaves that are held erect and almost white flowers. 'Hadspen Blue' has substantial, glaucous-blue leaves and lavender-coloured flowers. 'Hadspen Heron' has substantial, oval to lance-shaped, glaucous blue-green leaves and near-white flowers. 'Halcyon', a good choice for a container, has intensely blue leaves and near-white flowers. 'June', an unusual hosta, has bluish-green leaves that have a strong yellow central splash, which darkens to greenish yellow. The flowers are pale lavender-grey. The sun-tolerant 'Midas Touch' has, deeply puckered, heart-shaped, bright yellowish-green leaves and near white flowers. 'Shade Fanfare' has yellowish-green leaves broadly margined with creamy white (both colours brighter in sun) and lavender flowers.

Small hybrids

'Blue Cadet' has thick, rounded, puckered leaves, which are intense glaucous blue, and purple flowers. 'Blue Moon', which is suitable for a rock garden, has thick, puckered, dark blue leaves and pale lavender to white flowers. 'Brim Cup' has small leaves, broadly edged with creamy white, that pucker as they age and pale lavender to white flowers. 'Ginko Craig' has lance-shaped green leaves, crisply edged with white, and deep mauve flowers.

INULA

These robust plants have cheerful, golden-yellow daisy flowers in summer. They are undemanding cottage garden plants.

Cultivation Grow in any reasonable soil in sun. Tall species may need staking.

I. hookeri

Probably the best-known species, this coarse plant rapidly makes clumps that produce masses of acid yellow daisies in summer. H

Hosta 'Shade Fanfare'

75cm (30in), S 60cm (2ft). Hardy/Z 4–8.

I. magnifica

As magnificent as its name implies, this is an ideal plant for a grand border, with masses of rich yellow daisies on stout stems in late summer. It combines superbly with orange-red roses and purple-leaved plants. H 2m (6ft), S 1m (3ft). Hardy/Z 5–8.

IRIS

This large genus also includes bulbs. The plants described here are rhizomatous perennials – that is, they have a fleshy rootstock (actually a modified stem) at ground level – but they represent a vast number of plants that are generally divided further as described. Irises are grown for their beautiful flowers. The combination of richness and purity of colour (in all shades except red) and elegance of form is unmatched by any other garden plant. Larger border irises are magnificent, flowering at the same time as peonies. Later on, their

Hosta 'Gold Standard'

Hosta 'Devon Green'

Hosta 'Blue Cadet'

Inula magnifica

Iris 'Blue-Eyed Brunette'

Iris unguicularis

sword-like leaves are a good foil to other perennials and annuals. A few are best with their feet in water, in nature helping to bind the banks of streams and ponds. The winter-flowering *I. unguicularis* is unique and should be included in every garden.

Cultivation Bearded irises need well-drained soil, preferably neutral or alkaline, and a position in sun. The upper surface of the rhizome should be above ground level for a good summer baking, which promotes good flowering the next year. Beardless irises have varying requirements, as detailed in the individual entries below; the rhizomes are usually best planted below the soil surface. Crested irises (some of which are tender and excluded here) need fertile soil in a lightly shaded situation. All irises are of indefinite spread.

Bearded irises

These deciduous plants have sword-like leaves arranged like a fan; the flowers have distinctive hairs (the beard) on the falls (the three petals that hang down). The

group encompasses an enormous number of hybrids, all richly coloured, of which the following are a small selection.

I. 'Blue-Eyed Brunette'

An iris with distinctive rich red-brown flowers with gold beards in late spring to early summer. H 1m (3ft). Hardy/Z 4–9.

I. 'Bold Print'

This iris has impressive flowers, basically white but heavily marked with rich purple. H 55cm (22in). Hardy/Z 4–9.

I. 'Chantilly'

An iris with pale lavender flowers in late spring to early summer. H 1m (3ft). Hardy/Z 4–9.

I. pallida

This iris, sometimes evergreen, is one of the best species for general use in the border. The warm lavender-blue flowers, good as a cut flower, open in late spring and early summer. H 1m (3ft) or more. Hardy/Z 6–9.

I. 'Peach Frost'

An iris with peach-pink standards and rich golden-orange falls in late spring to early summer. H to 1.2m (4ft). Hardy/Z 4–9.

Beardless irises

These irises, some of which are evergreen, have no hairs on the falls and generally have slimmer rhizomes than those of the bearded irises.

I. 'Arnold Sunrise'

This early spring-flowering iris has white flowers marked with

orange. It needs neutral or slightly acid soil in sun or light shade. H 25cm (10in). Hardy/Z 5–9.

I. ensata
(syn. *I. kaempferi*)
Japanese water iris

This species is the parent of a large number of irises, all suitable for growing in moist, neutral to acid soil at the water's edge in full sun. Flowering is in midsummer. H to 1m (3ft). Hardy/Z 5–9. 'Ayasegawa' has white flowers edged with blue; and 'Variegata' has white markings on the leaves and deep purple flowers.

I. sibirica

This iris is a parent of a huge range of hybrids, referred to as Siberian irises, all good plants for sunny borders, but seeming to prefer damp soil. The species is an elegant plant, with narrow, grassy leaves and exquisite butterfly-like, rich violet-blue flowers, pencilled with white and gold, in early summer. H 1m (3ft). Hardy/Z 4–9. The following can be usefully grouped under this species, but are actually hybrids with other species and are therefore sometimes listed separately: 'Butter and Sugar' has white and yellow flowers. H 70cm (28in). 'Ruffled Velvet' has rich reddish-purple flowers with ruffled edges. H 55cm (22in). 'White Swirl' is a good white variety. H 1m (3ft).

I. unguicularis
(syn. *I. stylosa*)
Algerian iris

One of the harbingers of spring, this iris is unique in the genus.

Among the copious grassy foliage, elegant lilac-mauve flowers with yellow markings unfurl from scrolled buds as early as midwinter, the main flowering being in late winter to early spring. This plant needs a hot spot in very well-drained soil: at the foot of a warm wall is ideal. For reliable flowering, the upper surface of the rhizome should be exposed to the sun and plants should be left undisturbed once established. H 23–30cm (9–12in).

Crested irises

These resemble bearded irises except that the beard is replaced by a raised ridge.

I. japonica

This iris has glossy green leaves and pale lavender to white flowers in mid- to late spring that are exquisitely marked with orange and purple. H to 1m (3ft). Borderline hardy/Z 8–9. In cold gardens the reputedly hardier 'Ledger's Variety', similar in all other respects, is to be preferred. H to 1m (3ft).

Iris 'Chantilly'

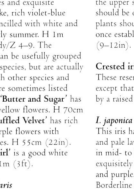

Iris pallida

Iris sibirica

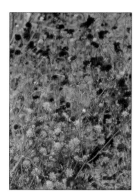

Knautia macedonica

Kniphofia 'Alcazar'

Kniphofia 'Toffee Nosed'

KNAUTIA

The genus contains around 40 species of plants with scabious-like flowers, but only a few are widely grown. The flowers are attractive to bees, and the plants make excellent edging for the front of a border.
Cultivation Grow in any well-drained soil in sun.

K. macedonica

The best-known species, this has crimson, pincushion-like flowers on curving stems from mid- to late summer. It makes good infill in rose gardens. H and S 60cm (2ft). Hardy/Z 5–9.

KNIPHOFIA
Red hot poker, torch lily

Considered vulgar by some, there is no denying the impact that red hot pokers can have in a garden with their luminous torch-like

flowers. Unfortunately, their coarse clumps of grassy foliage do not integrate well with other plants, and they tend to look best grown in isolation, for example at the foot of a warm wall. Some modern hybrids are more gently coloured and smaller, and can be grown at the front of a border. Not all kniphofias are reliably hardy, which again limits their appeal to some gardeners, but their long flowering season makes them desirable. Nearly all the plants in cultivation are hybrids of garden origin.
Cultivation Kniphofias need soil that does not dry out in summer and a position in full sun. Excessive winter wet is undesirable.

K. hybrids

There are a large number of hybrids available, ranging in size, colour and flowering time. The

following are all hardy/Z 6–9.
'Alcazar', an archetypal poker, is a substantial plant with bright red flowers in midsummer. H 1.5m (5ft), S 50cm (20in).
'Candlelight' is an elegant plant, bearing slender spikes of clear yellow flowers in midsummer among long, narrow leaves. H to 50cm (20in), S 30cm (12in).
'Forncett Harvest', an autumn-flowering hybrid, has spikes of small, greenish-yellow flowers. H 1m (3ft), S 45cm (18in). One of the daintiest of recent introductions, 'Little Maid' has soft lemon-yellow flowers in summer. H 60cm (2ft), S 45cm (18in). 'Prince Igor' is a dramatic and vigorous plant, with large spikes of brick-red flowers that develop yellow touches at the base. It flowers from late summer to autumn. H 1.8m (6ft), S 1m (3ft). 'Samuel's Sensation' is a

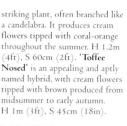

striking plant, often branched like a candelabra. It produces cream flowers tipped with coral-orange throughout the summer. H 1.2m (4ft), S 60cm (2ft). 'Toffee Nosed' is an appealing and aptly named hybrid, with cream flowers tipped with brown produced from midsummer to early autumn. H 1m (3ft), S 45cm (18in).

LAMIUM
Deadnettle

Invaluable as groundcover, these plants are considered weeds by some gardeners, but some varieties are pretty and useful for filling space under trees and shrubs.
Cultivation Grow in any well-drained soil in sun or shade.

L. maculatum

The species has mid-green leaves striped centrally with silver and whorls of reddish-purple, pink or white flowers in summer. H 20cm (8in), S 1m (3ft) or more. Hardy/Z 4–8. It is attractive enough but yields in appeal to the selections 'Beacon Silver', which has silver leaves edged in green; 'Pink Pewter', with grey-green leaves and pink flowers; and 'White Nancy', which has silver foliage and white flowers.

LEUCANTHEMUM

These daisy flowers have been included in *Chrysanthemum*. Whatever controversy may rage over their correct names, they are superb garden plants, reliably producing a show of robust daisy flowers in summer. Undemanding, they are excellent when cut, if not the most fragrant of flowers.
Cultivation Most soils are suitable, although some alkalinity seems desirable. Grow in full sun.

L. × superbum
(syn. *Chrysanthemum maximum*)
Shasta daisy

Once considered a species, this group of sturdy perennials are now known to be hybrids. All produce white flowers with yellow centres, but there are variations among the many cultivars. All are hardy/Z 5–9. 'Aglaia' has semi-double flowers. H and S 60cm (2ft). 'Everest' (syn. 'Mount Everest') has large, single flowers.

Kniphofia 'Candlelight'

Lamium maculatum 'White Nancy'

Leucanthemum × superbum 'Everest'

H to 1m (3ft), S 60cm (2ft). **'Phyllis Smith'** has charming flowers, with narrow outer petals giving a dainty, feathery appearance. H to 1m (3ft), S 60cm (2ft). **'Wirral Supreme'** has double flowers. H to 75cm (30in), S 60cm (2ft).

LIATRIS
Gay feather, blazing star
The feathery flowers of these perennials are unique and eye-catching, if not to all tastes. They are particularly effective as cut flowers.
Cultivation Grow in any soil that does not dry out and in a position in full sun.

Liatris spicata

L. spicata
This is the most widely grown species, with long, upright spikes of luminous mauve flowers throughout summer. H 1m (3ft), S 30cm (1ft). Hardy/Z 4–9. **'Alba'** is an excellent white form.

LUPINUS
Lupin
With their tall spires of pea flowers in a range of bright colours (some being bicoloured), lupins are essential for giving height to borders in early to midsummer. Cutting them down after flowering (before they have time to set seed) can result in a second crop of (smaller) flowers in late summer, but this cannot be guaranteed so it is best to plant them behind other plants that will provide late interest. Lupins are not long-lived plants and need to be replaced regularly. They work best in groups of a single colour.
Cultivation Lupins need to grow in well-drained, lime-free soil and require a position in full sun.

L. hybrids
There are a vast number of hybrids, all of which are hardy/Z 4–8, including the following. H 1m (3ft), S 75cm (30in). The flowers of **'Blushing Bride'** are white, flushed with pink; **'Catherine of York'** has pinkish-

Lupinus 'The Governor'

orange and yellow flowers; **'Chandelier'** has pale yellow flowers; **'Deborah Woodfield'** is an unusual creamy pink. **'Esmerelder'** has lilac flowers; **'Pope John Paul'** is a good white selection; **'The Chatelaine'** has pink and white flowers; **'The Governor'** has blue and white flowers; **'The Page'** is red.

LYCHNIS
Catchfly
These plants, with their attractive foliage, are easily grown. They look best planted en masse and blend particularly well with old roses and all cottage-garden plants.
Cultivation Grow in any well-drained soil in sun or light shade.

L. chalcedonica
Maltese cross, Jerusalem cross
This cottage-garden plant has vivid scarlet flowers in midsummer. H to 1.2m (4ft), S 40cm (16in). Hardy/Z 4–8.

L. coronaria
Dusty miller, rose campion
This species has felted grey leaves, a charming foil to the magenta flowers, which appear in midsummer. H 60cm (2ft), S 45cm (18in). Hardy/Z 4–8. The white-flowered form **'Alba'** is even more desirable.

LYSIMACHIA
Loosestrife
Some of these plants are almost weed-like in their toughness and vigour, but all are useful as ground-cover, particularly in rough parts of the garden.

Lychnis coronaria 'Alba'

Lysimachia nummularia 'Aurea'

Cultivation Grow in sun in moist, well-drained, rich soil.

L. nummularia 'Aurea'
Golden creeping Jenny
The species is generally represented in cultivation by this selection, a spreading, mat-forming perennial with yellow leaves. The cup-shaped, yellow flowers, which appear throughout summer, are a bonus. In addition to its use as ground-cover, it is effective in hanging baskets or trailing over the edge of a large container. H 5cm (2in), S indefinite. Hardy/Z 4–8.

L. punctata
Dotted loosestrife
This invasive plant is almost a weed, particularly in the boggy soil in which it thrives. The bright yellow, cup-shaped flowers are carried in whorls on the upright stems in summer. H 1m (3ft), S 60cm (2ft). Hardy/Z 5–8.

Lysimachia punctata

Lythrum salicaria 'Feuerkerze'

Macleaya cordata

Melianthus major

Melissa officinalis 'All Gold'

LYTHRUM
Loosestrife

These plants, which are suitable for a bog garden, have two seasons of interest. Not only do they attract attention when in flower in midsummer, but the whole plant often turns a vivid yellow in autumn before dying back. They self-seed prolifically unless dead-headed.
Cultivation Grow in reliably moist soil in sun. Staking may be necessary on windy sites.

L. salicaria
Purple loosestrife

This familiar plant produces tall spikes of reddish-purple flowers in summer. H 1.2m (4ft), S 45cm (18in). Hardy/Z 4–9. It has several named forms, the best of which is **'Feuerkerze'** (syn. 'Firecandle'), whose flowers are a more intense purple. H 1m (3ft), S 45cm (18in). The similar sized **'Robert'** is bright pink.

MACLEAYA
Plume poppy

These are plants for a large border. Despite their size, their overall splendour suggests that they should be grown near the front of a border, where their handsome leaves can be appreciated to the full. They work well with phlox, which flowers at around the same time, as well as helping to cool down 'hot' schemes.
Cultivation Any fertile, well-drained soil in sun or light shade is suitable. Although tall, they never need staking.

M. cordata
(syn. *Bocconia cordata*)

This is the best-known species, with plumes of cream-coloured flowers in summer. H 2m (6ft), S 60cm (2ft). Hardy/Z 4–9.

M. microcarpa

The species is broadly similar to *M. cordata*, with plumes of creamy-white flowers, but is less desirable on account of its invasive habit. The selection **'Kelway's Coral Plume'** is worthwhile, with rich pink flowers in summer. H 2m (6ft), S 1m (3ft). Hardy/Z 4–9.

MECONOPSIS

The genus includes annuals and biennials as well as the perennial described here, which is a useful addition to a wild garden.
Cultivation Grow the species described in reliably moist soil in partial shade.

M. cambrica
Welsh poppy

This European species forms clumps of dissected, bright green foliage. From spring until autumn solitary poppy flowers in yellow or orange are borne on slender stems. H 45cm (18in), S 30cm (12in). Hardy/Z 6–8.

MELIANTHUS

One of the grandest of all foliage plants, the species described becomes shrubby in warm areas where it can overwinter successfully. In cold gardens it behaves as a herbaceous perennial and is cut down by hard frosts, usually regenerating from below ground level the following spring. It is excellent for adding height to an 'exotic' planting of cannas, dahlias and half-hardy annuals.
Cultivation Grow in any fertile, well-drained soil in full sun. In cold areas, protect the base of the plant with a dry mulch in winter.

M. major
Honey bush

Large, soft, grey divided leaves, with serrated edges, are the principal ornamental feature. In a good year plumes of brownish-red flowers can appear in summer. H 2.4m (8ft), S 2m (6ft). Half-hardy/Z 9–10.

MELISSA
Lemon balm, bee balm

An essential plant for the herb garden, lemon balm is also decorative enough for use as a foliage plant in mixed plantings. The leaves have a distinct citrus scent when crushed and can be used in herb teas.
Cultivation Grow in any well-drained soil in sun or light shade. Alkaline soil is particularly suitable.

M. officinalis 'Aurea'
(syn. *M. officinalis* 'Variegata')

The straight species bears pale yellow flowers in summer, but is of limited ornamental value. More interesting are **'All gold'**, with golden yellow leaves and lilac-tinged white flowers; and **'Aurea'** (syn *M. officinalis* 'Variegata'), with green leaves splashed with gold. H 60cm (2ft), S 45cm (18in). Hardy/Z 4–9.

MENTHA
Mint

Most mints are grown for their culinary rather than for their ornamental use, and they are indispensable in the herb garden, although they can be invasive. The flowers are of scant interest.
Cultivation Unlike most other herbs, mints prefer moist soil, but they will grow in almost any garden soil, in sun or shade. Some

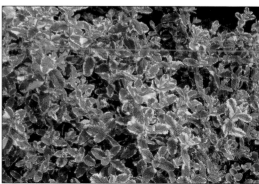

Mentha suaveolens 'Variegata'

Monarda didyma

Morina longifolia

means of restraining the roots is advisable (for instance by growing them in pots sunk in the ground).

M. × gracilis
(syn. M. × gentilis)
Ginger mint, red mint
Apart from its culinary use, this hybrid, with upright, red-tinged stems and lilac-pink flowers, is of little ornamental value. Hardy/Z 4–9. More interesting is the selection 'Variegata' (syn. 'Aurea'), which has bright green leaves speckled and striped with yellow. The best leaf colour is produced in sun. H and S 60cm (2ft).

M. suaveolens
Apple mint
This invasive mint, sometimes wrongly known as M. rotundifolia, has apple-scented leaves and pink to white flowers. H 1m (3ft), S indefinite. Hardy/Z 5–9.

'Variegata' (apple mint, pineapple mint) is a more attractive form. The leaves are marked with creamy-white, and it has a sharper fragrance (of apples) than the species. It sometimes produces plain cream leaves.

MONARDA
Bergamot
These excellent border plants bear showy heads of hooded flowers from mid- to late summer in a range of clear colours. The leaves are similar to those of mint. The stems are square in cross-section. They are ideal for a mixed or herbaceous border. Most of the plants in cultivation are hybrids.
Cultivation Monardas, particularly those with purplish flowers, prefer reliably moist soils in sun, but they will grow in most soils if improved with organic matter.

M. didyma
Oswego tea, sweet bergamot
This species, which is often included in herb gardens, has dense heads of pinkish-red flowers in mid- to late summer. H 1m (3ft), S 45cm (18in). Hardy/Z 4–9. 'Alba' has white flowers.

M. hybrids
The garden hybrids, all flowering from midsummer to early autumn, and all hardy/Z 4–9, include the following. 'Beauty of Cobham' has pale pink flowers held in purple calyces and leaves that are flushed purple. H 1m (3ft), S 45cm (18in). 'Cambridge Scarlet', the most widely grown cultivar, has rich red flowers held in plum red calyces. H 1m (3ft), S 45cm (18in). 'Croftway Pink' has rose-pink flowers. H 1m (3ft), S 45cm (18in). 'Mahogany' has purplish-red flowers. H 1m (3ft), S 45cm (18in). The tall 'Mohawk' has light mauve flowers with paler bracts. H 1.2m (4ft), S 45cm (18in). 'Prärienacht' (syn. 'Prairie Night') has dark lilac flowers. H 1m (3ft), S 45cm (18in). 'Snow Queen' has pale pinkish-white flowers. H 1m (3ft), S 45cm (18in). The vigorous 'Squaw' has scarlet flowers. H 1m (3ft), S 45cm (18in).

MORINA
Whorlflower
Elegant rather than showy, these plants need a fairly prominent position in borders among low-growing plants for their distinction to be apparent. Only the species

described is generally grown.
Cultivation Grow in fertile, well-drained but moist soil in sun. Although hardy, cold, wet conditions in winter can kill it.

M. longifolia
The species forms a rosette of thistle-like leaves, from which the flower spikes emerge in summer. These carry whorls of tubular flowers set in thorny collars that open white, turn to clear rose pink, then darken to crimson after they have been fertilized. H 1m (3ft), S 30cm (1ft). Hardy/Z 5–8.

MUSA
Banana
These exotic-looking plants are grown for their lush, tropical leaves – in cold climates, fruit is hardly likely to appear, let alone ripen. They can be used as bedding plants with cannas, dahlias and tender perennials and also look dramatic in containers. The species described is more or less hardy and can survive cold winters if given adequate protection.
Cultivation Grow in any fertile soil in full sun. Protect plants over winter with a mulch of straw or other dry material.

M. basjoo
(syn. M. japonica)
Japanese banana
This species has huge, simple, bright green leaves that tend to split horizontally and fold over. H and S 1.5m (5ft) (more in favourable conditions). Borderline hardy/Z 9–10.

Monarda 'Snow Queen'

Musa basjoo

Myrrhis odorata

Oenothera fruticosa subsp. *glauca*

MYRRHIS
Sweet cicely

A genus of one species, this is a fragrant cow-parsley-like plant that seeds itself willingly throughout the garden. It is especially effective near water or in a wild garden, and the flowers will light up any dark corner. It makes a delicate contrast to more dramatic plants such as rheums.
Cultivation Grow in any reasonable soil in sun or light shade. It prefers cool, damp situations.

M. odorata
The ferny leaves are aniseed-(anise seed-) scented and can be used in salads when young. The fluffy heads of flowers appear in early summer. H and S 1m (3ft). Hardy/Z 4–8.

NEPETA
Catmint

The catmints are essential in any garden, especially cottage gardens. They make excellent edging plants, effectively softening the hard edges of paths with their billowing habit, and are an excellent foil to herbaceous perennials and old roses. Plants become woody with age.
Cultivation Grow in any well-drained soil in full sun.

N. × faassenii
(syn. *N. mussinii*)
This hybrid is the commonly grown catmint, making mounds of aromatic, soft sage green leaves. The lavender-coloured flowers will

appear in succession throughout the summer if regularly cut back as they fade. H and S 45cm (18in). Hardy/Z 4–9.

N. racemosa
A spreading catmint with soft grey-green leaves and lavender-coloured summer flowers. H 30cm (1ft), S 60cm (2ft). Hardy/Z 4–9. There are several cultivars, including **'Snowflake'**, which has white flowers; and **'Walker's Low'**, which has an arching habit and is somewhat taller. H 30–45cm (12–18in), S 60cm (2ft).

N. 'Six Hills Giant'
Generally considered the most distinguished of the catmints, this hybrid is bigger than the species

in all its parts. It has the typical soft grey-green leaves and masses of lavender-coloured flowers on upright stems in summer. It can be used as a low – albeit floppy – hedge. H and S to 1m (3ft). Hardy/Z 4–9.

OENOTHERA
Evening primrose

Plants of unique charm, evening primroses have large, cool lemon-yellow flowers that open in the evening – hence the common name. They are excellent for adding dots of colour among lower-growing plants, and, because they are attractive to butterflies, are ideal for a wild garden.
Cultivation Grow in any well-drained soil in sun. Tall plants may need staking.

O. fruticosa
(syn. *O. linearis*)
Sundrops
This species is sometimes grown as a biennial and is distinct in that the flowers are open during the day. H 60cm (2ft), S 40cm (16in). Hardy/Z 4–8. On **'Fyrverkeri'** (syn. 'Fireworks') the stems and leaves are flushed with brown, and the yellow flowers open from red buds. H 45cm (18in), S 30cm (12in). *O. fruticosa* **subsp. glauca** (syn. *O. tetragona*, *O. tetragona var. fraseri*) has greyish-green leaves and pale yellow flowers. H 60cm (2ft), S 40cm (16in).

O. macrocarpa
(syn. *O missouriensis*)
Ozark sundrops
This prostrate species produces a

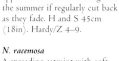

Nepeta racemosa 'Walker's Low'

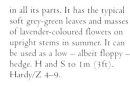

Ophiopogon planiscapus 'Nigrescens'

Origanum vulgare 'Aureum'

Osteospermum 'Lady Leitrim'

long succession of bright yellow flowers that open from red calyces throughout summer and into autumn. It is an ideal plant for the front of a sunny border. H 23cm (9in), S 60cm (2ft). Hardy/Z 4–8.

OPHIOPOGON
Lilyturf

A genus normally represented in gardens by the form described here, which is more a conversation piece as a 'black' plant than a thing of beauty. For the most impact, grow it in gravel. It is especially effective in a Japanese-style planting.
Cultivation Grow in fertile, preferably lime-free or slightly acid soil in sun or light shade.

O. planiscapus
The straight species, an evergreen, grass-like plant with deep green leaves and small, bell-shaped pale pinkish-purple flowers, is of small distinction. Hardy/Z 6–9. Of greater interest are its cultivars, especially **'Nigrescens'** (syn. *O.* 'Arabiscus'; 'Black Dragon'; 'Ebony Knight'), with black-purple leaves and small, purplish, bell-shaped flowers. The plant spreads slowly by stolons. H and S 20cm (8in).

ORIGANUM
Oregano, marjoram

Apart from their value as culinary herbs, marjorams are of great value in the ornamental garden. In many cases the small flowers are carried in coloured bracts that persist for several weeks, making these plants of long-lasting appeal.
Cultivation Grow in any well-drained soil in sun.

O. laevigatum
This species has dark green leaves that are less aromatic than those of some other marjorams. Its principal interest lies in its late-summer, purplish-pink flowers. It looks good with grey-leaved plants. H and S 45cm (18in). Hardy/Z 5–8.

O. vulgare
Oregano, wild marjoram
This is the species most widely grown in herb gardens, but its tiny mauve flowers in late summer are also appealing in a modest way.

Origanum vulgare

H and S 60cm (2ft). Hardy/Z 6–9. **'Aureum'** is more compact, and grown mainly for its golden-yellow leaves, which become progressively greener during the season. It flowers only sparsely. H and S 30cm (12in).

OSTEOSPERMUM

These attractive, evergreen daisies, scarcely without a flower throughout the growing season, are of borderline hardiness and are thus often treated as summer bedding, in borders, containers and hanging baskets. However, they are reliably perennial given some shelter or can easily be overwintered as cuttings. Most of the plants sold commercially are hybrids.
Cultivation Grow in well-drained soil in full sun. To ensure winter survival in cold areas, grow them in the shelter of a warm wall. Protecting them with a dry mulch during the cold months will further increase their chances of overwintering safely.

O. hybrids
In recent years many new cultivars have been developed, extending the colour range and style of the petals. All have daisy-like flowers. **'Buttermilk'** is upright, with primrose yellow flowers. H and S 60cm (2ft). Borderline hardy/Z 9–10. **'Lady Leitrim'** has white flowers that age to pink. H and S 35cm (14in). Half-hardy/Z 9. **'Whirligig'** (syn. 'Tauranga') has flowers with distinctive, spoon-

shaped, white petals, which are mauve on the reverse, and with white centres. H and S 60cm (2ft). Half-hardy/Z 9–10. **'White Pim'** (syn. *O. ecklonis* var. *prostratum*) is low-growing. The flowers have white petals and purplish-blue centres. H 10cm (4in), S 30cm (12in). Half-hardy/Z 9.

PAEONIA
Peony

Gorgeous flowers and lustrous foliage characterize this genus. The hybrids – of which there are many – are sumptuous, but the species are equally beautiful in a different way, with simple, bowl-shaped flowers. The fact that the hybrids need staking is unlikely to deter many gardeners, for peonies are essential garden plants, either as soloists, perhaps offset by hostas or other plants with bold, simple leaves, or, where there is room, in grand groups. The species work well in light woodland. Plant spring bulbs around them, which will flower as the red peony buds appear from ground level. Peonies are usually slow to establish, but reward patience and are generally long-lived and trouble-free. The genus also includes a number of highly desirable shrubs.
Cultivation Peonies need fertile, humus-rich, well-drained soil, ideally in sun. Peonies will grow in light shade, but the flowering will be delayed and possibly impaired. They do not like being transplanted.

Papaver orientale 'Effendi'

Papaver orientale 'Khedive'

Paeonia lactiflora 'Alice Harding'

P. cambessedesii
Majorcan peony
This beautiful species has single, poppy-like, deep rose-pink flowers in spring, a glowing complement to the striking foliage, which is deep green suffused with crimson-purple. Unfortunately, it is not reliably hardy in cold gardens. H and S 45cm (18in). Borderline hardy/Z 7–8.

P. lactiflora
(syn. P. albiflora, P. japonica of gardens)
The species, from Russia, China and Tibet, has handsome, dark green leaves and fragrant, single, white to pale pink flowers. It has given rise to many fine cultivars. Hardy/Z 3–7. 'Adolphe Rousseau' has rich red, double flowers. H and S 60cm (2ft). 'Alice Harding' has creamy-white, double flowers. H and S to 1m (3ft). 'Bowl of Beauty', an aptly named plant, has glowing satin-pink petals, which open to reveal a central boss of cream-coloured petaloids in mid- to late spring. H and S 1m (3ft). 'Duchesse de

Nemours' (syn. 'Mrs Gwyn Lewis') has globe-shaped, double flowers in early to mid-spring. The outer petals are white, the inner creamy-yellow. H and S 60cm (2ft). 'Félix Crousse' produces a profusion of silky, clear cerise pink flowers over a long period in mid-spring. H and S 75cm (30in). The pleasingly scented 'Laura Dessert' is a ravishing plant, if rather slow to establish. It has cream or pale lemon-yellow flowers that open from pink-tinged buds to reveal a central mass of creamy-yellow inner petals. H and S 1m (3ft). 'Président Poincaré' is a tall, vigorous variety, with dark, red-veined leaves and semi-double, garnet-red flowers in mid-spring. H and S 1m (3ft). A deservedly popular cultivar with a good track record, 'Sarah Bernhardt' has large, double, soft silvery pink flowers in late spring. Strong flower stems make this a good peony for cutting. H and S 1m (3ft). 'White Wings', a cultivar flowering in late spring, has deliciously fragrant single flowers with glistening white petals surrounding golden-yellow stamens. H and S 75cm (30in).

P. mlokosewitschii
Caucasian peony
This is one of the most desirable of all the species, even if its moment of glory is all too brief. The pewter green foliage is attractive throughout the season, a splendid foil to its cool lemon-yellow flowers, which are open for no more than a week in spring.

A massed planting creates a breathtaking sight. H and S 60cm (2ft). Hardy/Z 5–8.

P. officinalis
The true species has single pink or red flowers and is seldom seen in cultivation. Unnamed hybrids with fully double, white, red or pink flowers are often sold under this name, all fragrant and flowering in mid- to late spring. H and S 60cm (2ft). Hardy/Z 4–8.

PAPAVER
Poppy
Simple, beautiful plants for late spring, the flowers have silk-textured petals of unique appeal. In borders, poppies are superb curtain-raisers to the rose season. Most will have died back by midsummer, but it is possible to cover their traces with a planting of Gypsophila paniculata or late-flowering annuals. Many have attractive seedheads, which are

good for drying for indoor decoration. Some poppies are annuals and self-seed generously. *Cultivation* Poppies do best in poor, dry soil in sun.

P. orientale
Most of the perennial poppies grown in gardens are descended from this species, although some are manifestly hybrids involving other species. They are usually grouped under P. orientale for practical reasons; they all produce their large, bowl-shaped flowers in late spring. All are hardy/Z 3–7. 'Beauty of Livermore' has scarlet flowers, each petal blotched with black at the base. H and S 1m (3ft). 'Black and White' has white petals blotched with black at the base. H and S 1m (3ft). 'Cedric Morris' (syn. 'Cedric's Pink') has subtly coloured greyish-pink flowers. H and S 1m (3ft). 'Effendi' has orange-red flowers. H and S 1m (3ft). 'Karine' has pale pink, flat flowers with maroon centres. H and S 80cm (32in). 'Khedive' has pale pink flowers. H and S 1m (3ft). 'Picotee' has frilly-edged flowers that are white flushed with salmon pink. H and S 1m (3ft).

PELARGONIUM
With a seemingly endless succession of cheerful flowers, in shades of white, pink and crimson, pelargoniums are the archetypal summer plant. These (usually) evergreen perennials are infinitely versatile: whether they are grown in hanging baskets, containers, windowboxes or as bedding, they belong in every

Paeonia lactiflora 'Bowl of Beauty'

Paeonia lactiflora 'Adolphe Rousseau'

Pelargonium inquinans

Pelargonium triste

Pelargonium 'Schöne Helena'

Pelargonium 'Ashley Stephenson'

summer planting, either on their own or with other bedding plants such as lobelias, alyssums and *Helichrysum petiolare*.

The genus is huge. The large number of species (native mainly to South Africa) and the sheer quantities of named varieties can seem bewildering. Breeders have devised various categories for subdividing them, as described. *Cultivation* All the plants described here are tender and are best grown in containers. Most potting composts (soil mixes) are suitable, though it is wise to add grit or perlite to the mixture to improve the drainage. Feed with a high-potassium feed when in growth to prolong flowering. Most are best in full sun, but will also tolerate light shade. Plants can be overwintered in bright, frost-free conditions. Keep the compost barely moist.

P. betulinum
This decorative plant is probably a parent to both the regal and

unique pelargoniums. It has large, pink or purplish-pink (occasionally white) flowers that are heavily veined with purple-red. H and S 30–60cm (1–2ft). Tender/Z 10.

P. inquinans
This branching species has red-hairy stems, soft, almost circular leaves and scarlet, pink or white flowers. H to 1m (3ft), S 50cm (20in). Tender/Z 10.

P. triste
This appealing species has hairy, carrot-like leaves on short stems. The flowers are brownish-purple or (sometimes) yellow or brown and are remarkable in releasing a strong freesia-like scent at night. H 15cm (6in), S 45cm (18in). Tender/Z 10.

Zonal pelargoniums
The leaves are banded (or 'zoned') with a darker colour, and for most gardeners these are the typical pelargonium. This very large group is sometimes further sub-

divided. All are tender/Z 10. 'Appleblossom Rosebud' has tightly clustered, double, pale pink flowers that are flushed deeper pink. H and S 35cm (14in). 'Happy Thought' has rounded leaves, with pale cream or yellow-green centres, a pale brown zone, and a broad, bright green margin. The small flowers are crimson. H and S 40–45cm (16–18in). 'Irene' has generous clusters of crimson, semi-double flowers. H and S 45cm (18in). 'Joan Fontaine', a good bedding plant, is branching and bushy, with dark green leaves and pale salmon pink flowers with small white eyes. H and S 25–30cm (10–12in). 'Lass o' Gowrie' has tri-coloured leaves, green margined with silver-green overlaid with a dark, reddish band, and bright scarlet flowers. H and S 25–30cm (10–12in). 'Mr Everaarts' is a neat, bushy plant that is ideal for windowboxes, with double, rose pink flowers. H and S to 20cm (8in). 'Mr Henry Cox' has strongly tri-coloured foliage, with a brilliant golden margin surrounding a green centre, overlaid by a deep red-black zone, and single, salmon-pink flowers. H and S 30cm (12in). 'Plum Rambler' has unusual, double, plum-red flowers. H and S 40cm (16in). 'Red Black Vesuvius' (syn. 'Black Vesuvius') has blackish-green leaves with an even darker zone and an abundance of rich scarlet flowers. H and S 13cm (5in). 'Scarlet Rambler' has clusters of eye-catching, double, brilliant scarlet flowers. H and S 40cm (16in). 'Schöne Helena' is erect

and stocky, with semi-double, large, clear salmon flowers carried in large heads. H and S 40cm (16in). 'Silver Kewense' has leaves variegated silver and green and crimson flowers. H and S 13cm (5in). 'Wallis Friesdorf' has dark, blackish-green leaves and narrow-petalled, semi-double, deep rose pink to scarlet flowers. H and S to 20cm (8in).

Regal pelargoniums
These have large, richly coloured flowers. All are tender/Z 10. 'Ashley Stephenson' is compact, with creamy-pink flowers blotched and pencilled with mahogany red. H and S to 35cm (14in). 'Black Magic' produces rich blackish-red, velvety flowers. H and S to 35cm (14in). 'Fleur d'Amour' has pale leaves and soft pink and white frilly-edged flowers. H and S to 35cm (14in). 'Sunrise' has large, salmon-orange flowers that have white throats and are strikingly blazed with magenta. H and S to 40cm (16in).

Pelargonium betulinum

Pelargonium 'Irene'

Pelargonium 'Black Magic'

Pelargonium 'Moon Maiden'

Angel pelargoniums
These pelargoniums are derived from regals and are similar to them but smaller. All are tender/ Z 10. 'Catford Belle' is compact, producing an abundance of small, mauve-purple flowers that are frilled and marked with purple. H and S 30cm (12in). 'Jer'Rey' has masses of deep red-purple flowers edged with crimson over an extended period. H and S to 35cm (14in). 'Moon Maiden' has almost circular, pale pink flowers, which are marked with rich deep pink, and neat, dark green leaves. H and S 45–50cm (18–20in).

Decorative pelargoniums
Similar to regal pelargoniums, these have smaller leaves and flowers. All are tender/Z 10. 'Black Knight' has masses of small, purple-black flowers that are edged with lavender. H and S 40cm (16in). 'Madame Layal' has bicoloured flowers: deep plum-purple upper petals edged

white and white lower petals marked dark purple. H and S 45cm (18in). 'Sancho Panza', which does well in light shade, has deep purple flowers with paler, lavender-coloured borders that are attractive to bees. H and S to 45cm (18in).

Scented-leaf pelargoniums
As the name suggests, these have aromatic leaves, and it is for these that they are grown: the flowers are small and simple, like those of the species. They are popular as houseplants. All are tender/Z 10. Members of the **Fragrans Group** make lax, open plants with pine-scented, grey-green leaves and small white flowers on trailing stems. H and S to 20–25cm (8–10in). 'Lady Scarborough' makes a loose mound of lemon-scented foliage, above which appear small, pale pink flowers with dark purple veining. H and S to 50cm (20in). 'Little Gem' has soft leaves that release a warm rose-lemon scent and an abundance of small mauve flowers. H and S to 45cm (18in).

Unique pelargoniums
These make large, shrubby plants with soft, aromatic leaves; the flowers usually bear some mauve coloration. All are tender/Z 10. 'Pink Aurore' has warm pink flowers, the upper petals strongly marked with a burgundy blaze. H and S to 50cm (20in). 'Rollisson's Unique', a lax variety, has magenta-purple flowers marked darker purple, and rose-scented leaves. H and S 40–45cm (16–18in).

Pelargonium 'Pink Aurore'

Stellar pelargoniums
Both the flowers and leaves are roughly star shaped. All are tender/ Z 10. 'Bird Dancer', a neat plant, has spidery, narrow-petalled, pale pink flowers. H and S to 20cm (8in). 'Fandango' (syn. 'Stellar Fandango') has flowers in a clear shade of salmon-pink. H and S to 18cm (7in). 'Meadowside Midnight' has blackish-green leaves edged with paler green and orange-red flowers. H and S 18cm (7in). 'Rads Star' has clear rose pink flowers with white eyes. H and S to 20cm (8in). 'Strawberry Fayre' produces single to double, coral-red flowers with white eyes reliably throughout the summer. H and S to 25cm (10in).

Ivy-leaved pelargoniums
Thick, shield-like leaves are borne on trailing stems; these are ideal for hanging baskets. All are tender/Z 10. 'Eclipse' produces large, open heads of salmon-pink flowers. S 60cm (2ft). 'Giro Fly'

Pelargonium 'Strawberry Fayre'

has rosebud-like, double, bright purple-red flowers that are crowded together in balls. S 60cm (2ft). 'Golden Lilac Gem' is very ornamental, with golden-green leaves and double lilac flowers. S 60cm (2ft). 'Harvard' has semi-double, deep wine red flowers on long-jointed stems. S 60cm (2ft). 'Rigi' is strong-growing, with semi-double, cerise pink flowers, which are feathered with burgundy red. S 60cm (2ft). 'Rio Grande' has double, blackish-maroon flowers and shiny green leaves. S 60cm (2ft).

PENSTEMON
Penstemons are becoming increasingly popular, both for their spikes of foxglove-like flowers that appear throughout the summer and for their ease of cultivation. They make excellent border plants, but need a sheltered spot in cold areas. As a rule, the larger the flowers and leaves, the more tender the plant. Taking cuttings in late summer to autumn will ensure continuing stocks, although plants cut back by frost often regenerate from ground level. Smaller types are good in rock gardens.
Cultivation Grow in fertile, well-drained soil in full sun.

P. hybrids
The following hybrids are suitable for borders. 'Andenken an Friedrich Hahn' (syn. 'Garnet') is useful in borders for providing the elusive clear claret red over a long period. H 75cm (30in), S 60cm (2ft). Borderline hardy/Z 7-9. 'Apple Blossom' has soft

Pelargonium 'Black Knight'

Pelargonium 'Little Gem'

Penstemon 'Sour Grapes'

Penstemon 'Pennington Gem'

Penstemon 'Russian River'

Persicaria bistorta 'Superba'

pink flowers from midsummer until autumn. H and S 45cm (18in). Borderline hardy/Z 5–8. **'Evelyn'** is a neat-growing penstemon with slim, warm rose pink flowers striped inside with paler pink. H 45cm (18in), S 30cm (12in). Hardy/Z 6–9. **'Pennington Gem'** is a popular hybrid with large, soft pink flowers from midsummer to mid-autumn. H 75cm (30in), S 45cm (18in). Borderline hardy/Z 5–8. At its dramatic best when grown en masse, **'Russian River'** has small, dark purple flowers over a long period. H 45cm (18in), S 30cm (12in). Borderline hardy/Z 6–9. A well-known penstemon, **'Sour Grapes'** has large flowers of a rich violet-purple hue, with the characteristic white insides, striped with purple. H 60cm (2ft), S 45cm (18in). Borderline hardy/Z 6–9. An appealing plant, **'Stapleford Gem'** produces flowers that combine two colours: lilac-blue and cream. H 60cm (2ft), S 45cm (18in). Hardy/ Z 6–9. **'White Bedder'** (syn. 'Snow Storm') is a beautiful plant, which is essential in a white garden. It has pure white flowers that acquire pink tints as they age. H 60cm (2ft), S 45cm (18in). Borderline hardy/Z 6–9.

PERSICARIA
Knotweed

A genus of rampant plants that includes annuals as well as perennials, which are good for mass planting in damp soil. Most have a long flowering season. *Cultivation* Grow in reliably moist soil in full sun or light shade.

P. affinis
(**syn.** *Polygonum affine*)
The species is seldom grown in its typical form, being represented in cultivation usually by the excellent **'Darjeeling Red'**, which has drumstick-like heads of pinkish-red flowers in summer and autumn. H 25cm (10in), S 50cm (20in). **'Dimity'** is shorter with light pink flowers. H 10cm (4in), S 48cm (18in). **'Superba'**, a vigorous plant, has pale pink flowers. H 25cm (10in), S 50cm (20in). Hardy/Z 3–9. All turn rich reddish-brown in autumn, and are effective for a long time in winter.

P. amplexicaulis
(**syn.** *Bistorta amplexicaulis*, *Polygonum amplexicaule*)
Bistort
This semi-evergreen species has erect, lavender-like spires of pink flowers from summer to autumn. It is particularly effective with Michaelmas daisies. H and S 1.2m (4ft). Hardy/Z 5. The robust **'Firetail'** is bright red.

P. bistorta
(**syn.** *Polygonum bistorta*)
Bistort
The semi-evergreen species is almost always encountered in the form **'Superba'**, in some ways similar to *P. affinis* 'Superba' but not to be confused with it. It forms strong clumps that produce bottlebrush-like spikes of cool pink flowers on stiff stems in late spring to early summer. The damper the soil, the longer the flowering period. H and S 60cm (2ft). Hardy/Z 4.

P. virginiana
(**syn.** *Polygonum virginianum*, *Tovara virginiana*)
The species is seldom grown, but the following selection is a beautiful foliage plant. **'Painter's Palette'** has green-and-cream marbled leaves generously blotched with brown and touched with pink. H and S 60cm (2ft). Hardy/Z 5.

PHLOX

This is a large genus of popular evergreen and herbaceous perennials, which give an air of grandeur to borders from midsummer onwards with their pyramid-shaped heads of flowers. They are useful for providing soft colours at a time when orange and yellow are predominant in the garden, as well as being richly scented. There is a huge number of cultivars, mostly developed from *P. maculata* and *P. paniculata*, plants belonging to the former species being generally slighter and more elegant. The genus includes alpines.

Cultivation The phlox described here need humus-rich soil and a position in sun.

P. maculata
Meadow phlox
The species is characterized by hairy, often red-spotted stems. The cultivars, hardy/Z 4–8, all have flowers in the white–pink–lilac range and include **'Alpha'** with soft pink flowers; the excellent **'Omega'**, which has white flowers with violet eyes; and **'Schneelawine'** (syn. 'Avalanche') with white flowers. H 1m (3ft), S 45cm (18in).

P. paniculata
Perennial phlox
The species has smaller flowers than the many cultivars developed from it. The fragrant flowers are white or lilac. It is excellent in a wild garden. H 1.2m (4ft), S 60cm (2ft). Hardy/Z 4–8. More garden forms have been derived from this species than from *P. maculata*, all making slightly more imposing plants. **'Blue Ice'** has white flowers opening from pink buds. H 75cm (30in), S 60cm (2ft). The free-flowering **'Eve Cullum'** has rich pink flowers with deeper pink eyes. H 1.2m (4ft), S 60cm (2ft). **'Fujiyama'** has white flowers. H 75cm (30in), S 60cm (2ft). **'Little Laura'** is a compact selection with purple flowers. H 65cm (26in), S 45cm (18in). **'Mother of Pearl'** has white, pink-tinted flowers. H 1.2m (4ft), S 60cm (2ft). **'Prince of Orange'** has orange-red flowers. H 80cm (32in), S 45cm (18in).

Persicaria virginiana 'Painter's Palette'

Phlox paniculata 'Mother of Pearl'

Phormium cookianum 'Cream Delight'

PHORMIUM
Flax lily, New Zealand flax

These architectural foliage plants form imposing clumps of stiff, upright leaves, giving style and substance to borders and making an effective contrast to rounded shrubs and any plant with soft or filigree leaves. They are equally effective in containers. Be careful when handling them: the leaf tips are sharply pointed and can cause injuries. There are many selected forms with dramatically coloured leaves. The robust flowering spikes, which appear in summer, are also eye-catching.

Cultivation Grow phormiums in any, preferably reliably moist, soil in full sun or light shade. A winter mulch of straw or other dry material may be necessary in cold districts. Remove damaged leaves regularly.

P. 'Bronze Baby'

This dramatic hybrid (sometimes listed as a form of *P. tenax*) has bronze-purple, arching leaves and is useful where there is not enough room for larger forms. H and S 60cm (2ft). Borderline hardy/Z 8–10.

P. cookianum
Mountain flax

This distinguished species has plain, light green leaves and is effective where a dramatic stroke is needed. H 2m (6ft), S 1.2m (4ft). Borderline hardy/Z 8–10. *P. cookianum* 'Cream Delight' is less vigorous. The leaves have a broad cream band along the centre. H and S 1.2m (4ft).

P. 'Sundowner'

This handsome plant has erect bronze-green leaves with deep pink edges. H and S to 2m (6ft). Borderline hardy/Z 8–10.

P. tenax
New Zealand flax

The species has smooth, grey-green, sword-shaped leaves. H 4m (13ft), S 2m (6ft). Borderline hardy/Z 8–10. Plants in the **Purpureum Group** have leaves overlaid with various shades of bronze-purple. H 2.4m (8ft), S 2m (6ft).

PHYSOSTEGIA
Obedient plant

This small genus of perennials exhibits a unique characteristic: the stems can be moved to any position, hence the common name. The species described makes a good border plant but can be invasive.

Cultivation Grow in reliably moist, humus-rich soil in sun or light shade.

Polygonatum × hybridum

P. virginiana
(syn. *P. speciosa*)

The species has spikes of white, red or pink flowers in late summer. H 1m (3ft), S 60cm (2ft). Hardy/Z 3–9. *P. virginiana* subsp. *speciosa* 'Variegata' is a neater-growing form, with white-edged leaves and deep pink flowers. 'Summer Snow' (syn. 'Snow Queen') is a good white variety. H and S 60cm (2ft).

POLYGONATUM
Solomon's seal

These quietly elegant plants are related to lily-of-the-valley and enjoy similar conditions. Their arching stems and beautiful leaves make them ideal companions for hostas and ferns, especially in woodland gardens. Sawfly caterpillars often decimate the leaves after flowering, but without affecting the plant's longevity.

Cultivation They are best in humus-rich, heavy, moisture retentive soil in shade but will tolerate most other conditions, apart from hot and dry situations.

P. × hybridum
(syn. *P. multiflorum* of gardens)

This, the best-known member of the genus, is a hybrid of *P. multiflorum* and *P. odoratum*. The arching stems appear in spring and bear small, lightly fragrant, bell-shaped flowers, which are white tipped with green, in late spring. H 1m (3ft), S 30cm (1ft). Hardy/Z 4–8. 'Striatum' (syn. 'Variegatum') is a less vigorous form with cream-edged leaves. H 60cm (2ft), S 30cm (1ft).

PRIMULA
Primrose

This large and complex genus contains about 400 species of perennials, some suitable for mixed plantings, others for bedding, while a few are happiest in a rock garden. Charming though they are, they are not for all gardens, many having highly specific cultivation needs, and some particularly choice species (excluded here) are definitely best grown under glass. The plants described below do well in cool, damp atmospheres and may even seed themselves to the point of becoming a nuisance where suited. All have characteristic rosettes of spoon-shaped leaves from which the flowering stems arise. Another characteristic (but not of all) is 'farina', a flour-like bloom on the stems and leaves, which can provoke an allergic reaction.

Phormium tenax Purpureum Group

Physostegia virginiana

Physostegia virginiana 'Summer Snow'

Primula beesiana

Shorter growing primulas are delightful with dwarf spring bulbs and are good in windowboxes; primroses and polyanthus are archetypal cottage-garden plants; moisture-lovers are effective near water (preferably running water); and they are among the few plants that combine happily with rhododendrons as well as being good companions for the smaller hostas. So-called candelabra types are distinctive and graceful plants, with flowers carried in whorls up the stems.
Cultivation The plants described here are best in moisture-retentive, preferably neutral soil in sun or light shade (the more sun, the damper the soil should be). Candelabra types need moist soil.

P. beesiana

This candelabra primula, which is deciduous or semi-evergreen, produces whorls of magenta flowers from late spring to early summer. H 45cm (18in), S 30cm (12in). Hardy/Z 5–8.

P. bulleyana

The semi-evergreen species, a candelabra primula, is valued for its sharp orange flowers, which are produced throughout summer. H and S 60cm (2ft). Hardy/Z 6–8.

P. denticulata
Drumstick primula

This distinctive species has golfball-like heads of purple flowers on stout stems in spring. H and S 30cm (1ft). Hardy/Z 4–7. **P. denticulata var. alba** is a desirable form with white flowers. 'Rubra' is one of many selections with reddish-purple flowers.

P. florindae
Giant cowslip

One of the largest species, this candelabra primula will produce satisfying mounds of foliage in damp soil, above which the erect stems carry mealy, deliciously fragrant, soft yellow flowers in early summer. It looks best planted en masse. H 1.2m (4ft), S 1m (3ft). Hardy/Z 5–8.

P. 'Inverewe'

A well-known candelabra hybrid, this has bright red flowers in summer. H 75cm (30in), S 60cm (2ft). Hardy/Z 6–8.

P. Polyanthus Group

This large hybrid group is understood here to include primroses (with flowers carried singly) and polyanthus (with clusters of flowers on upright

Primula Polyanthus Group

stems). The so-called 'hose-in-hose' polyanthus apparently have one flower emerging from the inside of another and are much sought after. Seed mixtures are available, and seed-raised plants in a range of jewel-like colours (some appealingly combining two or more) are often sold unnamed for use in bedding schemes. Depending on how they have been raised, they can flower from late winter to mid-spring in their first year. Most lose vigour the season after planting, but the following are reliably perennial and will flower in spring once established. They will grow in most garden soils that have been improved with organic matter. All are hardy/Z 6–8. Flowers of the evergreen plants in the **Gold-laced Group** (polyanthus) have an old-fashioned look, with purple-brown flowers margined with golden-yellow. H 25cm (10in), S 30cm (12in). **'Guinevere'** (syn. 'Garryarde Guinevere'; polyanthus) is distinctive, with pink flowers on red stalks and evergreen leaves suffused with bronze. H 13cm (5in), S 25cm (10in). The evergreen or semi-evergreen **'Lady Greer'** (polyanthus) has small, pale yellow flowers. H 15cm (6in), S 30cm (12in). The evergreen **'Schneekissen'** (syn. 'Snow Cushion'; primrose) has white flowers. H 10cm (4in), S 20cm (8in). Plants in the **Wanda Group** (primrose) are evergreen or semi-evergreen and have warm

bluish-purple flowers. H to 15cm (6in), S 30cm (12in).

P. pulverulenta

A vigorous species, this candelabra primula has very mealy stems carrying rich pinkish-red flowers with darker eyes over a long period in summer. H 1m (3ft), S 60cm (2ft). Hardy/Z 6–8. Plants grouped as **Bartley Hybrids** vary in colour from pink to pinkish-purple and have contrasting eyes. H 1m (3ft), S 60cm (2ft).

P. veris
Cowslip

A familiar sight in damp meadows, this dainty species can be established in grass, as long as the ground is damp. The small, fragrant, yellow flowers hang from the stems in late spring. H and S 25cm (10in). Hardy/Z 6–8.

Primula denticulata

Primula pulverulenta

Primula veris

Pulmonaria saccharata

Rheum palmatum

PULMONARIA
Lungwort
Pretty plants for the spring garden, pulmonarias provide a long season of interest as the rough-textured, grey-spotted leaves expand in size. Some are more or less evergreen. Plant them with dwarf bulbs in areas around deciduous trees or shrubs. They make a good alternative to hostas for those gardeners reluctant to use slug pellets, and they are worth trying in conditions inhospitable to most other plants.
Cultivation Grow these easily pleased plants in any reasonably fertile, well-drained soil in light (or even full) shade.

P. angustifolia
Blue cowslip
This species differs from most other pulmonarias in having small, unspotted, deciduous

leaves. The flowers, which open in spring, are rich blue, an effective contrast to yellow forsythias. H 23cm (9in), S 45cm (18in). Hardy/Z 4–8. Selections include **'Munstead Blue'**, which has violet flowers that age to blue. H 23cm (9in), S 45cm (18in).

P. officinalis
Jerusalem cowslip, spotted dog
This evergreen species has pink flowers, which age to violet-blue. The mid-green leaves are spotted with white. H 30cm (12in), S 45cm (18in). Hardy/Z 4–8.

P. rubra
This evergreen species, which makes excellent groundcover, has coral-red flowers that hold their colour, opening in late winter in a good year. The leaves are plain green. H 40cm (16in), S 60cm (2ft). Hardy/Z 4–8.

P. saccharata
Jerusalem sage
This species has the most heavily marked leaves – sometimes the whole leaf is silver. The spring flowers are pink, aging to blue. H 30cm (1ft), S 60cm (2ft). Hardy/Z 3–7. Plants of the **Argentea Group** have narrow leaves that are almost all silver. The flowers are red, aging to violet.

P. 'Sissinghurst White'
This outstanding hybrid, developed from *P. officinalis*, has white flowers and leaves spotted with silver. H 25cm (10in), S 45cm (18in). Essential in a white garden. Hardy/Z 4–8.

RHEUM
These are fine plants for the water's edge or for a large border. The genus includes the edible rhubarb, a handsome foliage plant in its own right. The plants described below are strictly ornamental and are especially effective as 'accent' plants in a large border but will lend an exotic touch to any garden.
Cultivation Rheums need fertile, reliably moist soil in sun or light shade.

R. 'Ace of Hearts'
(syn. R. 'Ace of Spades')
This hybrid is especially effective if placed where the crimson undersides of its large, heart-shaped, dark green leaves will be lit up by

the sun. The plumes of tiny, pinkish-white flowers that rise up in summer are an added – if not the principal – attraction. H 1.2m (4ft), S 1m (3ft). Hardy/Z 6.

R. alexandrae
Unlike other members of the genus, this species is grown less for its glossy dark green leaves (smaller than on other species) than for its flowers, which are hooded by conspicuous cream bracts and carried on tall stems in early summer – a ghostly apparition in the twilight. It does not do well in all gardens, seeming to prefer cool, moist climates. H 1.2m (4ft), S 60cm (2ft). Hardy/Z 6–8.

R. palmatum
Chinese rhubarb
Probably the grandest rheum, this plant will command any planting. Above its mound of large, deeply cut, red-veined leaves, spires of starry, greenish flowers arise in early summer. H and S 2m (6ft). Hardy/Z 5–9. The leaves of **'Atrosanguineum'** (syn. 'Atropurpureum') are vivid red on emergence in spring, retaining that colour until the deep pinkish-red flowers appear.

ROMNEYA
Californian tree poppy, matilija poppy
The tree poppy is both beautiful and maddening in equal measure.

Pulmonaria 'Sissinghurst White'

Rudbeckia fulgida

Their deeply divided, grey foliage and huge, glistening white flowers make these plants highly desirable, but they are difficult to establish and, once at home, become aggressively rampant rapidly. Grow them in large borders and keep them well away from paths and house walls: they have been known to penetrate bricks and mortar.
Cultivation These plants do best in sun in deep, fertile, slightly heavy soil, although most types of soil are tolerated as long as it is not boggy.

R. coulteri
This striking species has large, fragrant, poppy-like flowers with crumpled white petals surrounding a central boss of deep yellow stamens. H 2.1m (7ft), S 1m (3ft). Borderline hardy/Z 6–9.

RUDBECKIA
Coneflower
Essential plants for borders in late summer, rudbeckias are sturdy and easy to grow. The petals of the daisy-like flowers droop away from the contrasting centres in a most appealing way. They combine well with grasses.
Cultivation Grow in any reasonable soil in sun. Tall varieties may need staking.

R. fulgida
Black-eyed Susan
This species makes for an excellent garden plant. The vivid yellow flowerheads with striking black centres appear from summer to autumn. H 75cm (30in), S 30cm (12in). Hardy/Z 3–9. **R. fulgida** var. **sullivantii 'Goldsturm'** has large, richer yellow flowerheads. H 60cm (2ft), S 30cm (12in).

R. 'Goldquelle'
This hybrid has double flowers with yellow petals surrounding greenish centres. It associates well with *Artemisia lactiflora*. H 1m (3ft), S 60cm (2ft). Hardy/Z 4–9.

SALVIA
Sage
In addition to important shrubby plants for the herb garden, this genus includes a number of fascinating perennials (as well as some annuals). These are becoming better known and exert a subtle attraction.
Cultivation Grow in any well-drained soil in full sun. *S. uliginosa* needs damp soil.

S. candelabrum
This woody based, almost shrubby species is rare in cultivation but of undoubted garden merit. It has wrinkled, somewhat hairy leaves and blue to violet flowers, flecked with white, in summer. H and S 1m (3ft). Borderline hardy/Z 7.

S. uliginosa
Bog sage
This full, graceful species, which sometimes needs staking, has sprays of clear blue flowers from late summer to mid-autumn. It makes a fine companion to cannas. H 1.5m (5ft), S 45cm (18in). Borderline hardy/Z 6–10.

SCHIZOSTYLIS
Kaffir lily
These plants will brighten up the autumn (and winter) garden with

Schizostylis coccinea 'Major'

their elegant spikes of fresh-looking flowers. Kaffir lilies spread rapidly, so regular division is advisable. Although there is only one species, there are a number of desirable selections.
Cultivation Grow in any but dry soil in sun. Plants will not thrive in soil that dries out in summer.

S. coccinea
The whole plant looks like a miniature gladiolus, with slender, grassy leaves and spikes of cup-shaped, bright red flowers. H 60cm (2ft), S 23cm (9in). Borderline hardy/Z 6–9. Among the many cultivars are **'Major'** (syn. 'Grandiflora'), which has bright clear red flowers; **'Sunrise'** (syn. 'Sunset'), which has salmon pink flowers; and **'Viscountess Byng'**, one of the last to flower, with pale pink flowers. H 60cm (2ft), S 23cm (9in).

Romneya coulteri

Salvia candelabrum

Schizostylis coccinea

Sedum aizoon

SEDUM
Stonecrop

These tough, hardy plants are not immediately appealing, but their merits slowly become obvious: fleshy, healthy leaves that tolerate drought and late flowers that attract bees and butterflies. They are good plants for 'problem' areas of the garden. The genus also includes small species for the rock garden and tender species, which are usually grown as houseplants.
Cultivation Sedums thrive in any well-drained, even poor, soil in full sun.

S. aizoon
(syn. *S. maximowiczii*)
One of the first sedums to flower, the star-shaped yellow flowers, held in flat heads, begin to open in midsummer. The leaves are green and toothed at the edges. H and S 45cm (18in). Hardy/Z 4–9. **'Euphorbioides'** (syn. 'Aurantiacum') is more dramatic, with red stems, darker leaves and richer yellow flowers. H 35cm (14in), S 30cm (12in).

S. 'Herbstfreude'
(syn. *S.* 'Autumn Joy')
This robust hybrid is probably the best known of all sedums. It has large, fleshy grey-green leaves and heads of scented flowers in autumn, deep pink at first, turning to salmon-pink and aging to a rich brick-red. H and S 60cm (2ft). Hardy/Z 3–9.

S. spectabile
Iceplant
Probably one of the parents of 'Herbstfreude', this species is roughly similar to the hybrid but is smaller and has pinkish-mauve flowers. H and S 45cm (18in). Hardy/Z 4–9. Among the many cultivars are **'Brilliant'**, which has bright pink flowers; and **'Iceberg'**, which is a good white.

S. 'Vera Jameson'
One of the most dramatic of the sedums, this hybrid has glaucous, purple leaves and heads of dusky-pink flowers in late summer. H 30cm (12in), S 45cm (18in). Hardy/Z 4–9.

SIDALCEA
False mallow, prairie mallow

Mallow-like flowers, like miniature hollyhocks, characterize this genus, which, from the gardener's point of view, consists mainly of hybrids. They are excellent additions to the mixed or herbaceous border and work well in cottage gardens.
Cultivation Grow in any reasonable soil in sun or light shade. Tall varieties may need staking. Cutting down the stems after flowering can result in further flowers.

S. hybrids
There are several fine hybrids, mostly developed from *S. malviflora* (checkerbloom) and flowering in early to midsummer. **'Elsie Heugh'**, one of the palest, has spikes of fringed, pink flowers. H 1m (3ft), S 45cm (18in).

Sidalcea 'Elsie Heugh'

'Oberon' has clear pink flowers. H 1m (3ft), S 45cm (18in). **'Puck'**, which is more compact and robust, has deep pink flowers. H 40cm (16in), S 30cm (12in). Hardy/Z 5–7.

SISYRINCHIUM

These plants, which have iris-like leaves, have a happy knack of seeding themselves around – generally to good effect. They are excellent in gravel gardens, their stiffly upright habit providing effective contrast to mat-forming plants. They can also be grown in borders. The genus includes annuals as well as the perennials described here.
Cultivation Grow in sun in any well-drained soil that is not too fertile and preferably gritty and alkaline.

Sisyrinchium striatum

S. striatum
(syn. *Phaiophleps nigricans*)
The best-known species, this has compact tufts of sword-shaped, grey-green leaves and, in summer, slender spikes of straw yellow flowers, striped purple on the reverse of the petals. H 75cm (30in), S 23cm (9in). Hardy/Z 6–9. **'Aunt May'** (syn. 'Variegatum') has leaves edged creamy-yellow. H 50cm (20in), S 20cm (8in).

STACHYS
Betony, hedge nettle

A group of charming edging plants for a border or for a Mediterranean scheme – the hotter and drier it is, the more they like it.
Cultivation Grow in any well-drained soil in full sun.
S. macrantha will take some shade.

S. byzantina
(syn. *S. lanata*)
Lamb's ears, bunny's ears
Softly furry, silvery leaves, enhanced by hot sun, characterize the plants of this low-growing species. The flower spikes appear in summer and are also furry, swaddling the tiny pinkish-purple flowers. H 45cm (18in), S indefinite. Hardy/Z 4–8. There are a large number of selections, all of which make good edging plants to rose beds, including **'Cotton Boll'** (syn. 'Sheila McQueen'), which has flowers that look like balls of cotton wool; **'Primrose Heron'**, which

Sedum 'Herbstfreude'

Stachys byzantina 'Silver Carpet'

Tradescantia Andersonia Group 'Innocence'

Thalictrum flavum subsp. *glaucum*   *Tradescantia* Andersoniana Group 'Isis'

has leaves with a pronounced soft yellow flush; and **'Silver Carpet'**, a valuable non-flowering form, which is useful where a low mat of foliage is required.

S. macrantha
(syn. *S. grandiflora*)
This slightly coarse plant has corrugated, dark green, hairy leaves and rich rose-mauve flowers in summer, which combine in a particularly pleasing fashion with old-fashioned roses. H 60cm (2ft), S 23cm (9in). Hardy/Z 4–8.

THALICTRUM
Meadow rue
Still all too rare in gardens, these are plants of considerable style. They combine delicacy with stature and bring a touch of freshness to borders with their frothy flowers at the height of summer. Use them as a contrast to plants that have bolder, showier flowers or combine them with the foaming *Gypsophila paniculata* for a romantic billowing cloud of blossom.
Cultivation Grow in any fertile, well-drained soil in sun or light shade.

T. aquilegiifolium
This species is distinguished by its aquilegia-like foliage, although it is much taller and the flowers are far from similar. Appearing in early summer, these are a fluffy mass of warm pinkish-lilac. H 1m (3ft), S 60cm (2ft). Hardy/Z

5–8. Also worth growing are *T. aquilegiifolium* **var. album**, which has white flowers, and **'Thundercloud'**, which has dramatic dark purple flowers.

T. flavum
Yellow meadow rue
The species has glaucous grey leaves and masses of fluffy yellow flowers in summer. H 1m (3ft), S 45cm (18in). Hardy/Z 5–9. The leaves of *T. flavum* **subsp. glaucum** (syn. *T. speciosissimum*) are more pronouncedly glaucous.

TIARELLA
Foam flower
Dainty woodland plants, tiarellas are useful as groundcover in shady areas of the garden. They are grown primarily for the appeal of their leaves; the pretty flowers are an attractive bonus.

Tiarella cordifolia

Cultivation Tiarellas do best in humus-rich, fertile soil in shade; they prefer cool conditions.

T. cordifolia
The heart-shaped leaves of this species take on bronze tints in cold weather. Upright spikes of creamy white flowers appear in summer. H and S to 30cm (12in). Hardy/Z 3–8.

T. wherryi
(syn. *T. cordifolia* **var. collina**)
Although it is broadly similar to *T. cordifolia*, this is more compact and has white or pink flowers. H and S 20cm (8in). Hardy/Z 3–8. **'Bronze Beauty'** has bronze-tinged leaves and pink flowers. H and S 20cm (8in). Hardy/Z 3–8.

TRADESCANTIA
The flowers are unusual in having only three petals, which gives them a distinctive appearance. Tradescantias are easy to grow and look good towards the front of mixed or herbaceous borders, providing thick cover and flowering reliably. The genus also includes some well-known house-plants, grown mainly for their variegated leaves.
Cultivation Grow in any well-drained soil in sun.

T. Andersoniana Group
This hybrid group includes a number of worthy garden plants, all of which are hardy/Z 4–9, including **'Innocence'**, which has

pure white flowers; **'Isis'**, with rich indigo-blue flowers; and **'J.C. Weguelin'**, with pale blue flowers. H and S 45cm (18in).

TRICYRTIS
Toad lily
These are gracious little flowers for the end of the season. They need a prominent position in borders, where their unique appeal can be appreciated. They are also effective in light woodland.
Cultivation Grow in any fertile soil in light shade.

T. formosana
This species sends up tall, thin, branching flower stems with glossy oval leaves in early autumn. The small, lily-like flowers are mauve, heavily spotted with darker mauve. H to 1m (3ft), S 45cm (18in). Hardy/Z 7.

Tricyrtis formosana

Trifolium repens 'Purpurascens Quadrifolium'

TRIFOLIUM
Clover

With the exception of the plant described, most clovers are generally considered to be weeds. Nevertheless, selected forms are effective at the front of a border and are essential in wildflower gardens, the flowers being especially attractive to bees.
Cultivation Grow clover in moist, neutral soil in sun.

T. repens
Dutch clover, shamrock
The species is normally encountered as a lawn weed but the form **'Purpurascens Quadrifolium'** has attractive maroon-purple leaves edged with green and typical white clover flowers in summer. H 10cm (4in), S indefinite. Hardy/Z 4–7.

TRILLIUM
Trinity flower, wood lily

These dramatic woodlanders are among the most desirable of spring-flowering plants, but unfortunately they are not always easy to please. Where they are happy, a massed planting can be breathtaking (although isolated clumps are also effective), but they are best appreciated when kept away from daintier flowers.
Cultivation Grow in fertile soil, preferably enriched with leaf mould, in shade, ideally beneath overhanging deciduous trees.

T. grandiflorum
Wake robin
One of the grandest of the genus, this is also the best-known species. The flowers, which have three curving, pure white petals, open in spring above the large, simple leaves. H 38cm (15in), S 30cm (12in). Hardy/Z 4–9.
'Flore Pleno', which has double white flowers, is if anything even more sumptuous.

TROLLIUS
Globe flower

Pleasing perennials for the spring garden, globe flowers are good in borders with tulips, although they really prefer damp conditions and are ideal for a streamside planting or bog garden. They are also good companions to rhododendrons.
Cultivation Grow in reliably moist soil in sun or light shade. Also worth trying in ordinary soils provided they are not in full sun.

Trillium grandiflorum 'Flore Pleno'

T. × cultorum
The hybrid group contains a large number of selections, all of which are hardy/Z 3–7, flowering from mid-spring to midsummer. The unique **'Alabaster'** has pleasing soft ivory-yellow flowers, but is none too vigorous. H 60cm (2ft), S 40cm (16in). The early-flowering **'Earliest of All'** has yellow flowers. H 50cm (20in), S 40cm (16in). **'Orange Princess'** is vigorous and has orange-yellow flowers. H to 60cm (2ft), S 45cm (18in).

VERBASCUM
Mullein

A genus of stately plants, many of which are grown as biennials, but including a number of perennials. They are excellent for giving height to summer borders.

Cultivation Grow in any well-drained soil in sun. Tall plants may need staking.

V. chaixii
Nettle-leaved mullein
This sturdy semi-evergreen species has woolly, upright stems, which are densely set with buttercup-like yellow flowers in summer. H 1m (3ft), S 45cm (18in). Hardy/Z 5–9. The selected form **'Album'** has white flowers.

V. 'Helen Johnson'
A very desirable hybrid, this is difficult to propagate – hence the high price of plants in the nursery trade. The spikes of pinkish-brown flowers bring a unique colour into the garden. H 1m (3ft), S 45cm (18in). Hardy/Z 5–8.

V. 'Mont Blanc'
This hybrid has pure white flowers, so has an honoured place in white gardens, the grey-green leaves adding to its value. H 1m (3ft), S 30cm (1ft). Hardy/Z 6.

VERBENA
Not all verbenas are reliably hardy, and that has probably kept them out of many gardens, but the ones described here are all worth taking a chance on. They provide a long season of colour and for that reason deserve their place, even if they behave as annuals and succumb to winter frost (the

Trollius × cultorum 'Earliest of All'

Verbascum chaixii 'Album'

Verbena bonariensis

Viola 'Jackanapes'

V. 'Jackanapes'

A delightful hybrid with a cheeky look to its yellow and brown flowers, the yellow petals streaked with purple. It tends to be short-lived. H 12cm (5in), S 30cm (12in). Hardy/Z 5–7.

V. labradorica
Labrador violet

This species is a prolific self-seeder in conditions that suit it, and charming where allowed to naturalize beneath shrubs. Its dainty, apple purple flowers appear above the bronze-tinged leaves in spring. H to 8cm (3in), S indefinite. Hardy/Z 4–8.

ZAUSCHNERIA
Californian fuchsia

This genus of sun-loving perennials provides brilliant material for the front of a border, the funnel-shaped flowers being a vivid scarlet in most cases.
Cultivation Good drainage is essential, as is a position in full sun. They are best with the shelter of a warm wall in cold areas, where they are not reliably hardy.

Z. californica

This, the best-known species, has attractive, lance-shaped, grey-green leaves, the perfect foil to the luminous scarlet flowers, produced from late summer to early autumn. H and S 45cm (18in). Hardy/Z 6–9. 'Dublin' has slightly longer, bright orange-red flowers. H 25cm (10in), S 30cm (12in).

genus also includes true annuals). Verbenas are delightful in borders, popular as bedding, and short varieties also work well in containers (including window-boxes) and hanging baskets.
Cultivation Grow in any well-drained soil in full sun. In cold areas a dry mulch can help them overwinter.

V. bonariensis

This is a plant that should be in every garden. The tall stems (square in cross-section) are much-branched and have a profusion of heads of small, luminous violet flowers from summer until well into autumn. It combines happily with almost every other plant in the garden, as well as adding an airy charm all of its own. Even where not hardy, it

tends to seed itself freely. For the best effect, plant in groups. H to 1.5m (5ft), S 30cm (1ft). Borderline hardy/Z 7–10.

V. 'Sissinghurst'
(syn. V. 'Saint Paul')

This is one of a number of hybrids with a low, spreading habit, and it is, therefore, ideal for the front of a border. It has heads of glowing magenta flowers throughout the growing season. H 20cm (8in), S 60cm (2ft). Borderline hardy/Z 5–9.

VERONICA
Speedwell

These easy-to-grow plants are excellent in mixed and herbaceous borders, and the spikes of flowers are produced over a long season. Mostly in the violet-blue-lilac range, they provide an excellent contrast to orange and yellow daylilies. Small species are good in rock gardens.
Cultivation Grow in any ordinary garden soil in sun or light shade.

V. longifolia

This species has hebe-like spikes of lavender-blue flowers in late summer and autumn. H 1m (3ft), S 30cm (1ft). Hardy/Z 4–8. 'Blauer Sommer' is more compact and has clear blue flowers. H 50cm (20in), S 30cm (12in).

VIOLA
Violet

This huge genus containing about 500 species includes annuals

(pansies), biennials and alpines as well as a number of perennials. They are excellent for carpeting large areas, especially under trees and shrubs. There are also a huge number of hybrids, omitted here, developed for exhibiting.
Cultivation Grow in any well-drained soil in sun or light shade.

V. biflora
Twin flowered violet

This dwarf rhizomatous species is found in Europe to Northern Asia and North America. Kidney-to heart-shaped pale green leaves are borne on thin stems and lemon-yellow flowers, veined dark purple-brown on the lower petals, appear either solitary or in pairs in late spring to summer. H 5-15cm (2-6in), S 15cm (6in). Hardy/Z 4-8.

Veronica longifolia

Zauschneria californica

Annuals

Annuals are unrivalled for bringing colour into the garden throughout the warmer months. They bring any border to vivid life within a matter of weeks, and give an established air to even a new garden. Besides their use in the larger garden, they are also excellent in tubs, hanging baskets and all manner of containers. Many bring other rewards, being deliciously scented or attractive to beneficial insects, or providing cut flowers for the house.

Few plants provide the gardener with such a wide range of colour and form as the annuals.

Annuals for your garden

An annual is a plant that completes its life cycle within one growing season: the seed germinates, grows, flowers, sets seed and dies all within the space of a year. The seed is dormant until the return of conditions favourable to germination, usually the next spring. In the case of biennials, the seed usually germinates as soon as it is set, in summer or autumn, and the young plantlet overwinters to flower the following year (but the entire process is still completed within the twelve months).

As with the rest of gardening, these definitions are by no means hard and fast. Many annuals can be treated as biennials, and vice versa. Some supposed annuals often survive the winter to flower again the following year, but, since their powers are greatly reduced, are best weeded out and replaced with new stock. There are also a number of plants that are usually described as "short-lived perennials": in other words, they can overwinter and survive a number of years, but since their health and strength cannot be relied on, they too are best replaced annually.

Another group of plants (which includes the popular tobacco plant *Nicotiana*) are truly perennial in their country of origin, but, since they will flower in the same year that they are sown, can be treated as annuals in cold areas where they cannot be expected to overwinter. Theoretically, of course, it is possible to overwinter them under glass, though it is hardly worth it, considering the high heating costs involved against the cheapness of a packet of seeds.

Bearing in mind that seed-raised plants always carry the potential for variation, the seed of most annuals is

This traditional annuals border consists of begonias and ageratum planted to provide strong blocks of colour for interest.

sold as mixtures or strains. The basic charateristics of the plants raised will be the same but some aspect (usually flower colour) will vary. Occasionally it is possible to isolate an individual colour through careful selection.

Annuals in the garden

There are countless uses for annuals, and they are particularly valuable in a new garden to create an impact quickly or to fill in the gaps before more permanent plants such as trees, shrubs and perennials have grown to fill their allotted space. Few gardeners these days embark on the elaborate bedding schemes still to be seen in public parks and gardens – such plantings are labour-intensive – but it is nevertheless possible to indulge in such fantasies on a smaller scale, in large tubs, window-boxes or hanging baskets planted for seasonal appeal. You can also use annuals in the open garden to try out a particular colour scheme before investing in longer-lived plants, but some gardeners are quite happy to ring the changes annually, and areas of the garden are left

unplanted specifically for growing a different selection of annuals each year.

The key to their appeal is that they provide such solid blocks of colour over a long period. Many cover themselves in flower to the extent that the leaves are completely hidden, and these are the plants that are traditionally chosen for jazzy schemes designed to make an impact at flower shows. Some annuals, such as *Eschscholzia*, can be used more informally: simply scatter the seed over a gappy border in late spring, and by summer you will be enjoying a sea of colour.

With their length of flowering season, annuals are also unmatched for attracting a range of beneficial insects into the garden. French marigolds (*Tagetes*) and nasturtiums (*Tropaeolum*) are often planted in vegetable plots, since they attract hoverflies, which feed on aphids. It is worth including a few of these among your roses (or among any other ornamental plants prone to aphid attack).

All annuals thrive in containers. For hanging baskets or to cascade down the sides of a large container, those with trailing stems are the most suitable. Certain strains of *Petunia* and *Lobelia* have been specially developed for this very purpose. Compact annuals on the other hand, such as *Lobularia* and *Ageratum*, are ideal for windowboxes.

Growing annuals from seed

For the widest choice, order seed from a seed merchant: their catalogues are often very extensive and also provide useful growing tips. Otherwise, buy seed from a garden centre, nursery or hardware store.

Easiest to raise from seed are those with large seeds (such as nasturtiums) that can be sown in situ where they are to flower. Others are also suitable for sowing in situ, but if the seed is very fine and has to be scattered, it may be necessary to thin seedlings later on. Some hardies are best sown in containers (either pots or seed trays). These should be kept outdoors in a cold frame and covered in cold weather (keep the covers on during the day if the temperature is below freezing). All seedlings in containers should be

This very modern style of planting relies on a wide range of annuals that flower simultaneously to create a beautifully informal border.

pricked out as they grow and potted on to prevent overcrowding.

Half-hardy annuals need to be started off in the protected environment of a propagator. Bottom heat will speed up germination, but is by no means essential, especially as the days lengthen and warm up in spring. Seedlings should be hardened off before being planted outdoors (when there is no longer any danger of frost). Remove the cover from the propagator for increasingly long

periods during the day over a number of weeks until you can leave it off entirely. As the temperature warms up from mid-spring, place the seedlings outdoors during the day, again for increasingly long periods. By late spring they should be ready for planting out in their flowering positions.

With a few notable exceptions (principally sweet peas), little is to be gained by sowing early – later sowings will catch up. For an extended display, it is often worth staggering sowings. Some hardy annuals can be sown in autumn for flowers the following spring. When the plants are exhausted, replace them with spring sowings. Conversely, it is possible to make late sowings of half-hardies (up to early summer) for a late summer to early autumn display, replacing a spring sowing. For this reason, precise flowering times are not given in the descriptions to follow.

If you do not have time to raise your own seedlings, buy young plants from garden centres in spring – though you may not have as wide a choice as you would like.

Annuals come in a wide variety of flower forms and colours, which many gardeners make use of for interesting combinations each year.

Ageratum houstonianum 'Blue Danube'

AGERATUM
Floss flower

These fluffy half-hardy annuals, mostly in shades of blue, are ideal for edging a border. They are also excellent in windowboxes.
Cultivation Grow in any soil in full sun. Sow from late winter onwards in a propagator.

A. houstonianum

Most seed and hybrid strains are listed under this species, although they may result from crosses with other species. **'Blue Danube'** forms compact hummocks of rich lavender-blue flowers; **'Blue Mink'** has powder-blue flowers; **'North Star'** has warm purplish-blue flowers; **'Pinky Improved'** is an unusual dusky pink variety; and **'Summer Snow'** is a good white form. H and S 15cm (6in) or more. Half-hardy/Z 8.

ALCEA
Hollyhock

Hollyhocks are quintessential cottage-garden plants, such that most gardeners are prepared to put up with their tendency to develop rust for the sake of their spires of mallow-like flowers. Although they can be perennial, their propensity to disease makes it advisable to treat them as biennials and discard plants that have flowered. Plant them towards the back or middle of a border. The flowers attract butterflies.
Cultivation Grow in any soil in sun. Sow in summer for flowering the following year and transplant in autumn, if necessary.

Ageratum houstonianum 'North Star'

A. rosea
(syn. *Althaea rosea*)

The papery-textured flowers, carried the length of tall, felted stems, are characteristic of this Turkish species. Named forms and strains include plants in **Chater's Double Group**, which have peony-like, double flowers in a range of colours; and the impressive **'Nigra'**, which has dramatic, rich chocolate-maroon flowers. H 2m (6ft), S 60cm (2ft). Hardy/Z 6–9.

AMARANTHUS
Love-lies-bleeding

The unusual tassel-like flowers of these half-hardy annuals are not to all tastes, although they are indispensable in a 'hot' scheme of reds, oranges and purples.
Cultivation Grow in any soil in sun or light shade. Sow in containers in early spring.

A. caudatus

The species produces pale green leaves and dangles its tassels of

Amaranthus caudatus

Antirrhinum majus 'Double Madam Butterfly Mixed'

tiny blood-red flowers from mid-to late summer. H and S to 1.2m (4ft). Half-hardy. **'Viridis'** has electric green flowers that fade to cream. H and S 60cm (2ft). **'Pygmy Torch'** has purple-flushed leaves and red flowers. H and S 45cm (18in).

ANGELICA

These stately biennials are well known in herb gardens, but they can also be effectively deployed in ornamental mixed borders, where they will add height and structure.
Cultivation Grow in any fertile soil in sun or light shade. Sow the seed as soon as it is ripe.

A. archangelica
(syn. *A. officinalis*)
Archangel

In its first year this species produces fresh green leaves with

Angelica archangelica

serrated edges. In the second year tall, ribbed stems carry domed heads of tiny greenish flowers. H 2m (6ft), S 1m (3ft). Hardy/Z 4–9.

ANTIRRHINUM
Snapdragon

The unique "snapping" lips of the flowers of snapdragon gives them a certain appeal to children. These half-hardy annuals provide strong blocks of colour – white, yellow, orange, pink and red (some flowers being bicoloured) – in beds and borders.
Cultivation Any soil in full sun is suitable. Sow in a propagator from midwinter.

A. majus

The many hybrids are often ascribed to this species. They are characterized by upright spikes of richly coloured flowers over a long period from summer to the first frosts. All are half-hardy. **'Black Prince'** has deep crimson flowers and bronze foliage. H 45cm (18in). **'Brazilian Carnival'** has bicoloured flowers in a combination of colours. H 60–90cm (2–3ft). **'Double Madam Butterfly Mixed'** has rather muddled, double flowers in a range of colours. The flowers are excellent for cutting. H 60–90cm (2–3ft). **'Kim Orange Bicolor'** has dazzling flowers, combining brilliant orange and yellow. H 25–30cm (10–12in). Plants from the **Royal Carpet Series** are vigorous and ideal for bedding, with flowers in a range

Antirrhinum majus 'Black Prince'

Bellis perennis 'Dresden China'

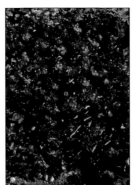

Begonia semperflorens Cocktail Series

BRACTEANTHA

These Australian annuals have daisy-like flowers with distinctive papery petals. They are excellent for filling gaps in summer borders, holding their colour well in hot sun.
Cultivation Grow in any well-drained soil in sun. Sow in a propagator in spring.

B. bracteata
(syn. *Helichrysum bracteatum*)
Golden everlasting, strawflower
Most of the seed strains and cultivars are included within this species. Tender/Z 9–10. **Bright Bikinis Series** is a dwarf strain with double, pompon-like flowers in white or shades of red, pink and yellow. H 30–45cm (12–18in), S to 30cm (12in). **'Coco'** (syn. *Helichrysum* 'Coco') has straw white flowers with yellow centres. H 1m (3ft), S 30cm (12in). **'Silvery Rose'** has clear pink flowers with yellow centres. H to 75cm (30in), S 30cm (12in).

CALCEOLARIA
Slipper flower
This is a large genus containing about 300 species, although only a few are widely available. Selected forms are grown as half-hardy annuals for summer bedding. The common name refers to the shape of the inflated flowers.
Cultivation Grow in well-drained soil in sun. Sow in a propagator in spring or, for earlier flowers the following year, in summer.

Bracteantha bracteata 'Coco'

C. Herbeohybrida Group
Most of the strains grown in gardens belong to this complex hybrid group, which involves a number of species. Besides their garden use, they can also be grown as flowering pot plants for conservatories. Half-hardy/Z 9. The **Anytime Series** produces dwarf plants in a range of colours that are good for growing in containers under glass. H and S to 20cm (8in). **'Bright Bikinis'** has dense heads of yellow, orange or red flowers. H and S 20cm (8in). **'Kentish Hero'** has vivid yellow flowers marked with orange-red to maroon. H and S to 30cm (12in). **'Sunset Mixed'** is a strain of bushy plants that produce clustered flowers in shades of red, including some bicoloured with yellow or orange. H and S to 30cm (12in).

of colours. H 25–30cm (10–12in). Plants raised from the **Sonnet Series**, which are also in mixed colours, show good weather resistance. H 45cm (18in).

BEGONIA
In addition to the tuberous species and houseplants, this large genus includes a number of tender annuals, which are useful for bedding or for growing in hanging baskets.
Cultivation Grow in any soil in sun or light shade. Sow in a propagator from midwinter (this is not always successful and it can be advisable to buy in young plants as plugs for growing on).

B. semperflorens
These versatile plants, with pink, red, white or bicoloured flowers, can also be used as summer houseplants. All are tender/Z 10. The single flowers in the **Cocktail Series** are set off by round, bronze leaves. H 20–30cm (8–12in), S 30cm (12in). Flowers in the **Coco Mixed Series** are also offset by rich bronze leaves. H 20–30cm (8–12in), S 30cm (12in). Plants in the **Options Mixed** series can have green or bronze leaves. H 20–30cm (8–12in), S 30cm (12in).

BELLIS
The genus includes the attractive lawn daisies that generally appear unannounced in all gardens, but the hardy biennials described here are appealing bedding plants for early in the season. They are also

delightful in windowboxes.
Cultivation Grow in any soil in full sun. Sow in summer for planting out in autumn.

B. perennis
This species, which is native to Europe, is the parent of a number of seed strains, all producing rosettes of leaves and flowers in shades of red, pink or white. All are hardy/Z 4–8. **'Dresden China'**, a dwarf form, has small, pink, double flowers with quilled petals. H and S to 10cm (4in). Plants in the **Habanera Series** have flowers with long petals, each flower to 5cm (2in) across. H and S to 20cm (8in). The **Pomponette Series** produces double, tightly quilled, pompon flowers, each to 4cm (1½in) across. H and S 15cm (6in).

BIDENS
These plants are actually perennial in frost-free conditions but are usually treated as annuals. Their trailing habit and dainty, fern-like foliage make them ideal for hanging baskets or to soften the edge of a large container.
Cultivation Grow in any soil in sun or light shade. Sow in a propagator in early spring.

B. aurea 'Sunshine'
This form is the one most commonly seen. It has bright yellow flowers over a long period from early summer until the first frosts. H 50cm (20in), S 40cm (16in). Half-hardy/Z 8.

Bellis perennis Pomponette Series

Calceolaria 'Kentish Hero'

Calendula officinalis 'Fiesta Gitana'

Cerinthe major

Cleome hassleriana 'Helen Campbell'

Cleome hassleriana 'Pink Queen'

CALENDULA
Pot marigold

The common name refers to the culinary use of these hardy annuals, not to their suitability for containers. They are rather coarse plants of easy cultivation (often seeding themselves indiscriminately), but valued for their cheery flowers.
Cultivation Grow in any soil in full sun. Sow in situ from autumn onwards.

C. officinalis
The straight species has single orange flowers and aromatic, light green leaves. H and S to 60cm (2ft). Hardy/Z 6. There are several named selections. Plants in the **Art Shades Mixed Series** have flowers in shades of orange, apricot or cream. H and S 60cm (2ft). **'Fiesta Gitana'** is a more compact form, which has orange or yellow (sometimes bicoloured) flowers. H and S 30cm (1ft). The flowers of **'Pacific Apricot'** have pale apricot petals, tipped in a deeper shade. H and S to 30cm (12in).

CENTAUREA
Knapweed, hardheads
The genus contains about 450 species of annuals and perennials, of which the species described is an indispensable plant for a wild-flower meadow, attracting bees and butterflies into the garden. Selected forms are good for cutting.
Cultivation Grow in any well-drained soil in sun. Sow in containers in late winter to early spring.

C. cyanus
Cornflower
The species can have blue, pink, purple or white flowers throughout summer and into autumn. H to 1m (3ft), S 30cm (1ft). Hardy/Z 7. **'Blue Diadem'** has double, rich blue flowers and is more compact. H 75cm (30in), S 30cm (12in).

CERINTHE
Honeywort
Until recently, these hardy annuals were little known, but gardeners have slowly become more aware of their subtle charms. They are grown for their coloured bracts, of interest over a long period in summer, rather than the true flowers, which are insignificant.
Cultivation Grow in any well-drained soil in sun. Sow in spring in containers or in situ.

C. major
The species, from southern Europe, has sea-green bracts tinged with yellow and purple.

H to 60cm (2ft), S 30cm (1ft). Hardy/Z 5. The flowers of the more compact **'Kiwi Blue'** are shaded more blue-purple. H 45cm (18in), S 30cm (12in). **'Purpurascens'** has rich purple-blue flowers with cream insides. H to 45cm (18in), S 30cm (12in).

CLEOME
Spider flower
These beautiful plants, with airy domed heads of scented flowers, lend elegance to any planting. They are among the tallest of the half-hardy annuals.
Cultivation Grow in any well-drained soil in sun. Sow in a propagator from late winter.

C. hassleriana
(syn. *C. pungens*, *C. spinosa* of gardens)
Most of the garden forms are grouped under this species. H 1.2m (4ft), S 45cm (18in). Half-hardy/Z 1–11. **'Colour Fountain'** has flowers in shades of pink, lilac, purple and white. Single-

colour selections include **'Cherry Queen'**, with reddish flowers; **'Helen Campbell'** (syn. 'White Queen'), with pure white flowers; **'Pink Queen'**, with pinkish-white flowers; and **'Violet Queen'**, with mauve flowers.

COBAEA
Cathedral bell,
cup-and-saucer vine
The common name is descriptive: the large flowers really are like cups and saucers. This tender annual (a perennial in its native Mexico) is an ideal plant for adding seasonal interest to a pergola or can be grown on a tripod to give height to a border.
Cultivation Grow in any moderately fertile soil in sun, preferably with some shelter. Sow in a propagator in spring.

C. scandens
Where grown as an annual this species, which climbs by means of tendrils, will produce large, fragrant, velvety-purple and green

Cerinthe major 'Kiwi Blue'

Cerinthe major 'Purpurascens'

Cobaea scandens

Convolvulus tricolor 'Royal Ensign'

Coreopsis grandiflora 'Early Sunrise'

Cosmos bipinnatus 'Versailles Tetra'

flowers from summer to autumn.
H to 3m (10ft), more in
favourable conditions. Tender/Z
9–10. The attractive **C. scandens f.
alba** has white flowers aging to
yellowish-cream.

CONVOLVULUS
In addition to the pernicious
bindweed, this genus includes
some highly desirable hardy
annuals that, with their spreading
habit, make excellent hanging
basket plants.
Cultivation Grow in any well-
drained soil in sun. Sow in situ in
spring or in summer for flowers
the following year.

C. tricolor
(**syn. C. minor**)
This species is actually a short-
lived perennial, but is best treated
as an annual. It has short-lived,
blue, funnel-shaped flowers, borne
in succession all summer long. H
40cm (16in), S 30cm (12in).
Hardy/Z 8. Strains in single
colour and mixtures are also
available, of which one of the best
is **'Royal Ensign'**. It has rich, deep
blue, trumpet-shaped flowers with
yellow and white centres. H and S
35–50cm (14–20in).

COREOPSIS
Tickseed
These plants produce cheerful,
usually bright yellow daisy flowers
over a long period in summer.
Cultivation Grow in any well-
drained soil in sun or light shade.
Sow in situ from late winter, or
from midsummer to autumn for
early flowers the following season.

C. californica
This erect annual produces a vivid
show of yellow daisies over grassy
foliage. H to 45cm (18in), S to
30cm (12in). Hardy/Z 1–11.

C. grandiflora
This perennial species is parent
to a number of strains that are
invariably grown as annuals. All
are hardy/Z 4–9. **'Early Sunrise'**
bears masses of semi-double, yellow
flowers, which are excellent for
cutting. H 45cm (18in), S 38cm
(15in). **'Mayfield Giant'** has
large, single, bright yellow flowers.
H 1m (3ft), S 45cm (18in).

COSMOS
With one of the longest flowering
seasons of any annual, these half-
hardies are of unquestioned value,
quite apart from the distinction
of the glistening flowers and
feathery foliage. They are also
excellent for cutting.
Cultivation Grow in any soil in
sun. Sow in situ after all danger
of frost has passed.

C. bipinnatus
Most of the available seed strains
are ascribed to this species. All are
half-hardy/Z 1–11. **'Sea Shells'**
has distinctive flowers, with
rolled, almost tubular florets in
shades of crimson, pink and
white, some being bicolours. H to
1m (3ft), S 45cm (18in). The
compact plants in the **Sonata
Series** produce carmine, pink or
white, bowl-shaped flowers.
Single-colour selections include
'Sonata White', which has pure
white flowers and grows to 60cm
(2ft), and **'Sonata Pink'**, which
has all-pink flowers. H 45cm
(18in), S 30cm (12in).
'Versailles Tetra' has greyish-pink
flowers with a darker area towards
the golden-yellow centres. H 1m
(3ft), S 45cm (18in).

DIANTHUS
Pink
Most dianthus are perennials or
rock garden plants, but there
are also a few annuals and the
appealing biennial, sweet William,

a plant of old-fashioned charm
that is essential for any cottage-
style planting.
Cultivation Grow in any well-
drained soil in sun. Sow sweet
Williams in midwinter, in containers, for flowers in late summer, or
in summer, in situ, for flowers the
following spring. Sow annuals in
containers in early spring.

D. barbatus
Sweet William
Uniquely in the genus, this
biennial produces flowers in dense
rounded heads. The deliciously
scented flowers can be red, pink
or white; some are bicoloured.
Selected strains are available. H
to 70cm (28in), S 30cm (12in).
Hardy/Z 4. **Indian Carpet Mixed**
is a dwarf strain. H and
S 15cm (6in).

D. chinensis
(**syn. D. sinensis**)
Chinese pink, Indian pink
The annual pinks are usually
grouped under this species. They
are all excellent in containers or
for edging borders. Hardy/Z 7.
Plants in the **Carpet Series** have
flowers in a range of colours and
are good in exposed situations. H
and S to 20cm (8in). **'Fire Carpet'**
is bright red. The **Heddewigii
Group** includes **'Black and White
Minstrels'**, an eye-catching strain,
with flowers in various colours,
highlighted with white. H
30–38cm (12–15in), S to 30cm
(12in). Plants in the compact
Princess Series have masses of
scarlet, white, crimson or salmon-
pink flowers, and usually bloom
early. H and S 20cm (8in).

Cosmos bipinnatus 'Sonata Pink'

Dianthus barbatus

Echium vulgare

Eschscholzia californica

GAZANIA
Treasure flower
These half-hardy annuals would be perennials in a warm climate. Needing heat, they are ideal candidates for growing along the foot of a wall. The flowers open fully only in sunshine.
Cultivation Most soils in full sun are suitable, but a sheltered spot is desirable in cool areas. Sow in a propagator from late winter.

G. varieties
Chansonette Series, a prolific strain, produces exotic-looking flowers in shades of lemon-yellow, rich golden-yellow, apricot, orange, bronze, lavender-pink or carmine red, all zoned with a contrasting colour. H and S 23–30cm (9–12in). Plants in the **Daybreak Series** produce bronze, orange, pink, yellow or white flowers, usually with a contrasting central zone. **'Daybreak Orange'**, a perennial grown as an annual, has orange flowers only, which stay open longer than other varieties. H to 20cm (8in), S to 25cm (10in). Half-hardy/Z 8–10.

GLAUCIUM
Horned poppy
The species described here is a short-lived perennial best treated as a biennial. Thriving in dry spots, it is ideal for sowing in the cracks in paving or in a gravel garden. The common name refers to the curved, horn-shaped seedcases.
Cultivation Grow in well-drained, preferably dry and not too fertile soil in sun. Sow in situ in spring or autumn.

Glaucium flavum

G. flavum
Yellow horned poppy
The species forms a rosette of blue-green leaves from which arise hairy stems carrying clear yellow, poppy-like flowers in summer. H 60cm (2ft), S 30cm (1ft). Hardy/Z 7.

HELIANTHUS
Sunflower
Most sunflowers are coarse plants, although they can be very effective in splendid isolation. The seeds are a valuable food source for birds in winter, suggesting use in an ecological garden, and the temptation to cut the plants down after the flowers have faded should be resisted if possible. Shorter types are good in mixed borders. The genus includes some useful perennials, as well as the hardy annuals described here.
Cultivation Most soils are suitable (although heavy, lime clays seem to be preferred) in sun. Sow in situ in spring. Tall plants may need staking.

H. annuus
This species sends up a stout stem at the top of which is a solitary, although huge, daisy-like yellow flower with a brown or purple centre. H 2.5m (8ft), S 60cm (2ft). Hardy/Z 4–7. There are many selections. **'Moonwalker'** has lemon-yellow petals surrounding chocolate brown centres. H 1.2m–1.5m (4–5ft), S 60cm (2ft). **'Music Box'**, a good dwarf, has a mixture of cream, yellow to dark red flowers, some being bicolours. H to 70cm (28in), S 45cm (18in).

ECHIUM
The genus includes perennials and shrubs as well as the hardy annuals described here. They are easy to grow and the upward-facing flowers will attract bees and butterflies into the garden, making them a good choice for a wildlife border. They can also be treated as biennials. The plants contain a skin irritant.
Cultivation Grow in any soil in full sun. Sow in spring for flowers the same year, or in late summer for flowering the following spring.

E. vulgare
Viper's bugloss
This annual or biennial produces tall spikes of bell-shaped, blue, pink or white flowers over a long period. H to 1m (3ft), S 30cm (12in). Selected forms are more compact. H to 30cm (12in). **'Blue Bedder'** has blue flowers; those of the **Dwarf Hybrids** can be blue, lavender, pink or white. Hardy/Z 1–11.

Echium vulgare 'Blue Bedder'

ESCHSCHOLZIA
California poppy
These hardy annuals are gratifyingly easy to grow, and it is possible to develop your own strains by weeding out unwanted colours as the flowers appear and letting the remainder self-seed.
Cultivation Any well-drained soil in full sun is suitable. Sow in situ from spring onwards. Late sowings will flower the following year.

E. californica
The species typically produces satiny, yellow-orange flowers (although they can also be red, yellow or white). H to 30cm (12in), S 15cm (6in). Hardy/Z 6. Plants in the **Thai Silk Series** have fluted petals (giving a double appearance) in scarlet, orange, pink-orange, yellow, cream and white, while the **Thai Lemon Silk Series** has yellow flowers only. H to 20cm (8in), S 10cm (4in).

FELICIA
Kingfisher daisy
The delightful plants described are actually tender perennials, which are ideal for use in summer hanging baskets or at the edges of large containers.
Cultivation Grow in any soil in sun. Sow in a propagator in spring; named forms are best increased by cuttings.

F. amelloides
This species has lax stems with an abundance of vivid blue, yellow-centred, daisy flowers throughout summer. H and S 30cm (12in). Tender/Z 10. **'Santa Anita'** has large, deep blue flowers.

Gazania 'Daybreak Orange'

Helianthus annuus

'**Teddy Bear**', very dwarf, has rounded, very double, powder-puff flowers in golden-yellow. H 45cm (18in), S 30cm (12in).

HELIOTROPIUM
Heliotrope
The species described is actually an evergreen shrub in its native Peru but is treated as a half-hardy annual in colder climates. The wrinkled leaves and fragrant, richly coloured flowers make it a distinctive bedding plant. It is also suitable for windowboxes and other containers.
Cultivation Grow in most soils in full sun. Sow in a propagator in spring. Named varieties are best raised from cuttings, although 'Marine' and its variants, such as 'Mini Marine', can be raised from seed.

H. arborescens
(syn. *H. peruvianum*)
Cherry pie
The species has rich green leaves and domed heads of violet, purple or white flowers throughout summer. H and S to 45cm (18in). Half-hardy/Z 10. Many cultivars

have been developed, including the strongly growing '**Chatsworth**', which has purple flowers; '**Marine**', which is a dramatic and highly desirable form with very dark green leaves and deep purple flowers; and '**Mini Marine**', which is roughly similar but more compact. H and S 35cm (14in).

HESPERIS
Dame's violet, sweet rocket
This cottage-garden favourite produces phlox-like flowers, which are fragrant in the evening. Perennial in favourable conditions, this is best treated as a biennial in most gardens and is indispensable in a border planned for scent.
Cultivation Grow these plants in any well-drained soil (preferably neutral to alkaline) in sun or light shade. Sow in situ in spring.

H. matronalis
The species, a good butterfly plant, produces domed heads of flowers in shades of purple (usually pale, but darker and white flowers are also possible) from late spring to midsummer. H 60cm (2ft), S 30cm (1ft). Hardy/Z 4–9. *H. matronalis* var. *albiflora* has white flowers only.

IMPATIENS
Busy Lizzie
These annuals are invaluable for providing colour in shady borders. Use them in borders, containers, windowboxes or – especially – hanging baskets for a long period of interest. Packed tightly, they will produce a ball of flowers.
Cultivation Grow in any soil in

Ipomoea tricolor 'Purpurea'

light to full shade. Sow in a propagator in late winter. Seed can be tricky to germinate and it may be more practical to buy in young plants as seedlings or plugs.

I. New Guinea Group
These striking plants have the added attraction of exotic-looking red, bronze or rich green leaves, sometimes marked with yellow and pink. The flowers can be pink, red, purple, orange or white. H 45cm (18in), S 40cm (16in). Tender/Z 10. '**Tango**' is a superb selection, with deep orange flowers offset by rich bronze leaves. H 35cm (14in), S 30cm (12in).

I. walleriana
Most of the seed strains are grouped under this species. **Double Carousel Mixed** produces well-branched plants with double, rose-like flowers in orange, pink, red and white, with some bicolours. H and S 23–30cm (9–12in). Plants of the **Super Elfin Series** are free-flowering and compact, with flowers in a range of dazzling colours. H and S 15cm (6in). '**Tempo Peach Frost**' has pink flowers edged scarlet. H and S to 25cm (10in). '**Victoria Rose**' has pink flowers. H and S 23–30cm (9–12in). Tender/Z 10.

Ipomoea lobata

IPOMOEA
Morning glory
With their trumpet-shaped, convolvulus-like flowers, these tender plants are true glories of the garden, with a shade of blue probably unmatched by any other summer flowers. The species described here are twining climbers, which look charming when they are allowed to wander through other plants, but they can also be more formally trained on vertical wires or other supports.
Cultivation Morning glories need well-drained soil in sun, preferably in a sheltered site. Sow in a propagator from late winter.

I. lobata
(syn. *Mina lobata*)
Spanish flag
This climber is grown for its variety of beak-like flowers. Initially scarlet, they age to orange, yellow and finally white, all colours appearing simultaneously. H and S 1.2–2m (4–6ft) or more. Tender/Z 10.

I. tricolor
The straight species is well worth growing, for the joy of its clear blue, white-throated flowers. H to 4m (13ft), but probably less in cool gardens. Tender/Z 8. Selected forms include '**Flying Saucers**', which has larger flowers striped blue and white; and '**Heavenly Blue**', which has richer blue flowers with white throats and '**Purpurea**', with rich purple, white-throated flowers.

Heliotropium arborescens 'Marine'

Hesperis matronalis var. *albiflora*

Impatiens walleriana 'Victoria Rose'

Lathyrus odoratus 'White Supreme'

LATHYRUS

For many gardeners, summer would not be summer without the delicious scent of these tendril climbers. Cutting the flowers for arrangements is actually to the benefit of the plant, since it will greatly extend the flowering season. Some gardeners like to grow them for this purpose alone and relegate them to the vegetable plot trained on cordons, which seems a pity, because their flower colours blend so happily with other plants. In borders they have great charm if allowed to climb over wigwams of peasticks or trellis obelisks.

Cultivation Grow in any soil in full sun. Sweet peas need a long growing season, so sow from late autumn in special sweet pea tubes, which will minimize disturbance to the roots on planting out.

L. odoratus
Sweet pea

Both the specific name and common name are slightly misleading. Not all strains are scented, and some are distinctly more fragrant than others (the sweet peas described are all richly scented unless otherwise indicated). H to 2m (6ft) unless otherwise stated. Hardy/Z 1–11. **'Cream Southborne'** produces large, frilled, cream flowers. The prolific **'Firecrest'** has unusual bicoloured flowers of fiery red and orange. **'King Size Navy Blue'**, one of the darkest blues, has wavy-edged flowers on long slender stems. **'Orange Dragon'**

has startling orange (only lightly scented) flowers, which hold their colour best in a position that is sheltered from hot sun. Plants of the **Snoopea Group** are compact and have no tendrils. The flowers can be white, pink, red or purple. H to 60cm (2ft). One of the best white varieties available is **'White Supreme'** with outstandingly fragrant flowers produced on long, strong stems.

LAVATERA

Among the 25 species in the genus are a number of perennials. The annuals are easy and resilient hardy plants, which are ideal for plugging summer gaps in borders.
Cultivation Any soil in full sun is suitable. Sow in containers from late winter or in situ in mid-spring.

L. trimestris
Most of the annual lavateras are listed under this species. They make bushy plants with mallow flowers. Selections include **'Mont Blanc'**, which has dark leaves and glistening white flowers; and **'Silver Cup'**, a very weather-resistant form, which has glowing silvery pink flowers with darker veins. H to 1m (3ft), S 45cm (18in). Hardy/Z 5–9.

LIMNANTHES
Poached egg plant

These hardy annuals, with their simple white and yellow flowers, will attract a wide range of beneficial insects (especially bees) into the garden. They seed themselves readily, particularly in gravel.

Limnanthes douglasii

Cultivation Most well-drained soils in full sun are suitable. Sow in situ in spring or in early autumn for early flowers the following year.

L. douglasii
This easily grown species has gleaming yellow, buttercup-like flowers, with white edges to the petals, throughout summer. H 15cm (6in), S 20cm (8in). Hardy/Z 8.

LOBELIA

Given the chance, these half-hardy annuals would be perennial, but they are usually raised annually from seed. Compact forms are the mainstay of park bedding schemes, while a hanging basket would be virtually unthinkable without the trailing kinds. Lobelias are among the precious few shade-tolerant annuals. Most are blue, although there are also selections in other

Lobelia erinus 'Cambridge Blue'

colours. The genus also includes true perennials and shrubs.
Cultivation Grow in any soil in sun or light shade. Sow in a propagator from late winter.

L. erinus
The annuals are usually usefully grouped under this species. All are hardy/Z 5–8. The compact **'Cambridge Blue'**, which is suitable for bedding, has clear sky-blue flowers. H and S 10cm (4in). Trailing varieties suitable for hanging baskets include those in the **Cascade Series**. Individual colour selections are **'Blue Cascade'**, **'Crimson Cascade'**, **'Lilac Cascade'**, **'Red Cascade'** and **'White Cascade'**. H 15cm (6in), S 30cm (12in). **'Crystal Palace'**, a compact form suitable for bedding, has dark blue flowers. H and S 10cm (4in). **'Sapphire'** has rich blue flowers with white eyes. H and S 15cm (6in).

LOBULARIA
Sweet alyssum

These tough little hardy annuals are very useful. They will seed themselves in various nooks and crannies around the garden, generally to good effect. Easy to grow, they are excellent for edging a path or border and are especially tolerant of coastal conditions. They also work well in containers and windowboxes. The flowers are scented.
Cultivation Alyssums will grow in any well-drained soil in sun. Sow in containers in late winter or in situ in spring.

Lavatera trimestris 'Mont Blanc'

Lobularia maritima 'Carpet of Snow'

L. maritima
(syn. *Alyssum maritimum*)
This species, native to the Canary Islands, has a huge range of selections. Most make compact hummocks. All are hardy/Z 1–11. **'Carpet of Snow'**, which is neat-growing and ground-hugging, has white flowers. H 10cm (4in), S 30cm (12in). **'Oriental Night'** has rich purple flowers. H 10cm (4in), S 30cm (12in). The flowers of **'Sweet White'** are white and smell of honey. H 10cm (4in), S 30cm (12in). **'Trailing Rosy Red'**, which has pinkish-purple flowers, is less compact than the others; its trailing habit makes it ideal for hanging baskets. H 10cm (4in), S 40cm (16in).

LUNARIA
Honesty, satin flower
These modest biennials (sometimes persisting a bit longer) have two seasons of interest. The pretty spring flowers are followed by distinctive, papery, oval seedheads, which are excellent in dried arrangements. Honesty often appears unbidden in gardens and once established is unlikely to die out.
Cultivation Honesty tolerates most soil, in sun or light shade. Sow in situ from late spring to early summer.

L. annua
(syn. *L. biennis*)
This European species has usually purple, sometimes white, flowers in spring followed by translucent white seedheads in autumn. H 1m (3ft), S 30cm (1ft). Hardy. For white flowers only, sow seeds of **L. annua var. albiflora**. 'Alba Variegata' is a desirable garden form with white variegated leaves and white flowers. 'Variegata' has similar leaves but flowers in shades of purple.

MATTHIOLA
Stock, gillyflower
Among the most fragrant of all flowers, these beautiful, hardy biennials (which can also be treated as annuals) can be sown in succession for an extended season. The flowers, which are white, pink, lavender, lilac or crimson, blend well with virtually all others. Night-scented stock, the most fragrant of all, has rather insignificant looking flowers of light mauve. Seed can usefully be scattered among showier but scentless plants.

Cultivation Any soil in sun is suitable. Sow seed from summer onwards for flowers the following year and from late winter for flowers the same year.

M. incana
Most strains are usefully gathered within this species and include Brompton stocks and Ten Week stocks. So-called Brompton stocks, which are biennials, are available in a wide colour range. H 50cm (20in), S 30cm (12in). There are many dwarf strains including the **Cinderella Series**, plants of which produce multiple spikes of double flowers. H 30cm (12in), S 10cm (4in). **'Cinderella Antique Pink'** is a selection with flowers in a unique shade of bronze-pink. **Ten Week Mixed** are annuals, with branching spikes of usually double flowers in a range of colours. H 30cm (12in), S 20cm (8in). Hardy/Z 6.

M. longipetala subsp. *bicornis*
(syn. *M. bicornis*)
Night-scented stock
This annual species is grown for the power of its scent alone. The lilac-mauve flowers open, modest in appearance and sparsely scattered up the stems, in the evening. H 30cm (1ft), S 23cm (9in). Hardy/Z 5.

MYOSOTIS
Forget-me-not
Although they will seed on their own freely, it is worth sowing these biennials afresh every season – the named forms always have flowers of a more intense colour than their natural progeny. Indispensable for most spring bedding schemes, forget-me-nots make a classic cottage-garden combination with pink tulips.
Cultivation Forget-me-nots will grow in most well-drained soils in sun or, preferably, light shade. Sow outdoors in early summer.

M. sylvatica
The straight species has mid-blue, yellow-eyed flowers in spring and early summer and grey-green leaves. H 30cm (12in), S 15cm, (6in). All forms are hardy/Z 5–8. **'Blue Ball'** is a more compact form with indigo flowers. H and

S 15–20cm (6–8in). The flowers of **'Compindi'**, another dwarf form, are even darker. H and S 15–20cm (6–8in). **'Rosylva'** is something of a novelty, with large flowers of clear pink. H 30cm (12in), S 15cm (6in).

NEMOPHILA
These hardy annuals have delightfully marked, cup-shaped flowers. They should be planted near the edge of a border or in a container or windowbox where this feature can be fully appreciated best.
Cultivation Most soils are suitable, although it should ideally be reliably moist. Plant in sun or light shade. Sow in situ in spring, or in autumn for larger plants that will flower earlier the following year.

N. maculata
Five spot
The common name is descriptive. Each pale blue petal is marked at the edge with a dark blue spot. This is a charming plant for a hanging basket. H and S to 30cm (12in). Hardy/Z 1–11.

N. menziesii
Baby blue eyes
In summer, this carpeting species is smothered in sky-blue flowers with paler centres. It is excellent for adding late colour to a rock garden. H 15cm (6in), S 30cm (12in). Hardy/Z 1–11. **'Pennie Black'** has blackish-purple flowers with scalloped, silvery edges and is more ground hugging. H 10cm (4in), S 30cm (12in).

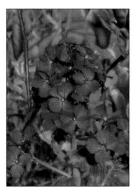

Lunaria annua

Matthiola longipetala subsp. bicornis

Nemophila menziesii

Nicotiana 'Lime Green'

NICOTIANA
Tobacco plant

These sticky, half-hardy annuals (actually tender perennials) bear flowers that remain closed at daytime but perk up at dusk and give off an incense-like fragrance. Modern selections are more compact and floriferous, but have not displaced older varieties.
Cultivation Grow in any soil in full sun or light shade. Sow in a propagator in spring.

N. langsdorfii
This distinctive annual is one of few species grown in its straight form. The branching stems carry drooping, pale, lime-green flowers. It combines well with a wide variety of border plants. H 1.5m (5ft), S 35cm (14in). Half-hardy/Z 7.

Nicotiana langsdorfii

N. 'Lime Green'
Blending with all other flowers, this popular selection produces lime sherbet flowers throughout the summer. H 60cm (2ft), S 20cm (8in). Half-hardy/Z 7.

N. × sanderae
Most of the annual strains are considered to belong to this hybrid group. All are half-hardy/Z 7. Plants of the **Domino Series** are branching and bushy, with red, white, pink or green flowers. Domino Series **'Salmon Pink'** is only lightly scented but produces unique salmon-pink flowers. H 30–45cm (12–18in), S 25cm (10in). Plants in the **Havana Series** are compact. The selection **'Apple Blossom'** has unusually coloured flowers: pale pink with darker pink reverses, giving a two-tone effect. H 30cm (12in), S 20cm (8in). Plants in the **Merlin Series** are compact and bushy, ideal for containers or the front of a border. The flowers can be purple, crimson, lime green or white (bicolours being a possibility). Seed is also often sold as single colour selections; the white-flowered ones are usually the most potently scented. H and S 23–25cm (9–10in).

N. sylvestris
This beautiful Argentinean species, which is actually a short-lived perennial, sometimes behaves as a biennial, surviving winter cold and flowering only in its second year. The fragrant, white flowers are carried in a candelabra-like arrangement on tall plants in summer, making this an excellent 'dot' plant. H 1–1.2m (3–4ft), S 60cm (2ft). Half-hardy/Z 9–10.

NIGELLA
Love-in-a-mist

These charming and elegant annuals are dainty cottage-garden stalwarts, almost as attractive when the seedheads develop as when they are in flower; the feathery foliage is a definite bonus. They are easy to grow.
Cultivation Grow in any soil in sun. Sow in situ from spring onwards.

N. damascena
The species is the parent of the garden strains, all of which are hardy/Z 1–11. **'Dwarf Moody Blue'** is a compact form, which can be used to make a temporary low hedge at the margin of a border. The flowers are sky blue. H 15–20cm (6–8in), S 10cm (4in). The popular and widely grown **'Miss Jekyll'** has bright blue, semi-double flowers. H 45cm (18in), S 15cm (6in). The rarer and desirable **'Miss Jekyll Alba'** is white. H 45cm (18in), S 15cm (6in). Plants in the **Persian Jewel Series** have flowers in a range of colours: pink, blue, violet and white. H 38cm (15in), S 15cm (6in).

OENOTHERA
Evening primrose

These stately annuals and biennials produce a succession of

Nigella damascena 'Miss Jekyll'

Oenothera biennis

flowers over the summer months that are valuable for attracting butterflies and other beneficial insects into the garden. Some open only in the evening – hence the plant's common name. All have a cool beauty. The genus includes some perennials.
Cultivation Evening primroses will grow in any well-drained soil in sun. Sow in situ in autumn; annuals can also be sown in containers in spring.

O. biennis
This species can be treated as an annual or a biennial and will usually seed itself. From basal rosettes of leaves emerge tall stems carrying shorter leaves and the large, cup-shaped, scented yellow flowers. H 1m (3ft), S 40cm (16in). Hardy/Z 4.

Papaver rhoeas

Papaver somniferum

PAPAVER
Poppy

Annual and biennial poppies, all hardy and easy to grow, are as valuable in gardens as their perennial cousins. Some will seed themselves, often to good effect, but sometimes to the point of becoming weeds. All have characteristically silky-textured flowers and are excellent in wildflower gardens as well as in borders.
Cultivation Any soil in sun is suitable. Sow annuals in situ in early spring, or in autumn for earlier flowers the following season. Biennials can be sown in situ in summer.

P. croceum
(syn. *P. nudicaule* of gardens)
Arctic poppy, Icelandic poppy
The species, usually grown as a biennial, has blue-grey leaves and fragrant, yellow, white or pale orange flowers. H to 30cm (12in), S 15cm (6in). Hardy/Z 4–8. Some ravishing strains, all with glistening flowers, including some doubles, have been developed. **Meadow Pastels** is a mixture that produces large, single flowers in shades of white, pink, rose pink, yellow and orange on sturdy stems. Early sowings can flower the same year. They are excellent for cutting. H to 30cm (12in), S 15cm (6in). **Oregon Rainbows** produces smaller plants, with flower colours including apricot, pink, soft cream and lemon-yellow. H to 25cm (10in), S 10cm (4in).

P. rhoeas
Corn poppy, field poppy
This is the annual species that appears on arable land that has been recently cultivated, the soil disturbance effectively breaking the seed's dormancy. The typically red flowers are a familiar sight, blanketing entire fields in summer. H to 1m (3ft), S to 30cm (1ft). Hardy/Z 5. Selected strains include the well-known **Shirley Series**, which produces semi-double or double flowers in red, pink, lilac and white, some flowers uniting two colours. Self-sown seedlings that revert to type should be weeded out if the characteristics of the strain are to be maintained. H 60cm (2ft), S 30cm (1ft).

P. somniferum
Opium poppy
The species, which has blue-green leaves, produces pink, purplish, red or white flowers, followed by striking seedheads. H 1m (3ft), S 30cm (1ft). Hardy/Z 7. Double forms have distinctive ruffled petals. **'Hen and Chickens'** has pink flowers, but is really grown for its larger than average seedheads, which can he dried for winter decoration. H 30cm (12in), S 20cm (4in). Plants raised from the **Peony Flowered** group live up to their name and have double flowers in red, purplish-pink, pink or white. H 1m (3ft), S 30cm (1ft). **'White Cloud'** has large, double white flowers. H 1m (3ft), S 30cm (1ft).

PETUNIA

The trumpet flowers of these sticky, half-hardy annuals have an immediate appeal. Most are ideal bedding plants, but recent introductions with trailing stems are best in hanging baskets. Blue-flowered plants are often heavily scented. All petunias grown in gardens are hybrids (sometimes lumped under the catch-all name *P. × hybrida*). According to flower size, they are usually grouped among the three groups specified below (some seed merchants have created other divisions).
Cultivation Petunias need well-drained soil in sun. Sow in a propagator from late winter.

Petunia 'Blue Daddy'

P. Grandiflora Group
Plants in this group produce the largest flowers. The **Aladdin Series** has wavy-edged flowers in an impressive colour range, including blue, red, burgundy, pink, lilac and white. H to 30cm (12in), S to 1m (3ft). The **Daddy Series** has flowers in unique shades of plum burgundy, orchid lavender, pink, blue and red, all with a velvety texture and darker veins. **'Blue Daddy'** has silver-blue flowers with darker veins and is early-flowering. H to 35cm (14in), S 1m (3ft). The well-known **Surfinia Series** produces vigorous plants of trailing habit that makes them ideal for hanging baskets. Flower colours include pink, red and blue. H 40cm (16in), S 1m (3ft). Half-hardy/Z 7.

P. Milliflora Group
Plants in this group produce quantities of small flowers. H and S to 30cm (12in). **Fantasy Series** plants are smothered with flowers in a range of colours throughout summer. They are ideal for containers and hanging baskets. H 15cm (6in), S to 30cm (12in). Half-hardy/Z 7.

P. Multiflora Group
This, the largest group, is characterized by medium-sized flowers on bushy plants. Plants in this group are the most weather resistant. **Carpet Mixed** produce low-growing, spreading plants that flower early in shades of pink, red, plum purple, rich blue and white. **'Carpet Buttercream'** is a selection that has creamy-yellow flowers only. H to 25cm (10in), S to 1m (3ft). Petunias belonging to the **Duo Series** have double flowers in a range of colours, including some strongly veined flowers and some bicolours. H to 30cm (1ft), S to 1m (3ft). The **Mirage Series** has plants with red, pink, blue and lavender flowers, all attractively veined with darker shades. H to 30cm (1ft), S to 1m (3ft). **Storm Mixed** petunias produce rain-resistant flowers in shades of salmon, white, pink and lavender. Single colour selections are available. **'Lavender Storm'** is vigorous, with pale yellow-throated lavender flowers. H 20–30cm (8–12in), S to 1m (3ft). Half-hardy/Z 7.

Petunia 'Lavender Storm'

Salvia fulgens

SALVIA
Sage

In addition to the well-known culinary herb, this large genus includes several annuals, as well as some perennials and subshrubs that can be treated as annuals or biennials in cool climates. Most have spikes of vivid flowers, while some are grown more for the appeal of the conspicuous bracts that surround them.
Cultivation Salvias prefer light, well-drained soil and a position in sun. Sow even hardy varieties in a propagator in mid-spring, or in situ once all danger of frost has passed; late sowings flower later.

S. fulgens
(syn. *S. cardinalis*)

A woody-based perennial or sub-shrub in its native Mexico, this upright plant produces spikes of vivid red flowers in summer. It is electric with *Verbena bonariensis*. H 1.2m (4ft), S 75cm (30in). Half-hardy/Z 9–10.

S. patens

This species is of borderline hardiness, but most gardeners are prepared to persevere with it for the sake of the very vivid blue flowers produced from summer to autumn. H 60cm (2ft), S 45cm (18in). It sometimes survives as a perennial. Borderline hardy/Z 7–9. Among the cultivars are **'Cambridge Blue'**, which has paler blue flowers; and **'White Trophy'**, which has white flowers.

S. sclarea var. turkestanica

The species is most often seen in this naturally occurring form. It is a hardy perennial best treated as a biennial. The plant is branching, with erect, pink stems and pink-flecked white flowers held in purple bracts. A choice plant for the border. H to 1m (3ft), S 30cm (1ft). Hardy/Z 4–7.

S. splendens
Scarlet sage

This includes the vivid red cultivars familiar in park bedding schemes, although other colours also occur. **'Blaze of Fire'** is a compact and early-flowering form. H 30cm (12in), S 20cm (8in). Plants belonging to the **Phoenix Series** can have pink, purple, white, red or lilac flowers. H 25–30cm (10–12in), S 20cm (8in). **'Red Arrows'** has the advantage of deep green leaves to set off the scarlet flowers. H 30cm (12in), S 20cm (8in). The flowers of **'Sizzler Burgundy'**, also red, are long-lasting. H 30cm (12in), S 20cm (8in).

S. viridis
(syn. *S. horminum*)
Annual clary

This species is grown for its pink, purple or white bracts. The stems can be dried for winter decoration. H to 50cm (20in), S 23cm (9in). Hardy/Z 4–7. **'Claryssa'** is a dwarf form with somewhat more brightly coloured bracts. H to 40cm (16in), S 20cm (8in).

Salvia sclarea var. turkestanica

Tagetes erecta Jubilee Series 'Golden'

Tagetes erecta Gold 'n' Vanilla Series

TAGETES
Marigold

These are among the easiest of half-hardy annuals to grow, and provide a reliable, long-lasting display throughout summer. There are two large groups, African marigolds and French marigolds, African marigolds tending to be taller and less spreading than the French. Hybrids between the two groups also exist, as well as a range deriving from *T. tenuifolia*. Single-flowered French marigolds make good companions for plants that are attacked by aphids: they attract hoverflies, which will help control the pests.
Cultivation Any fertile soil in sun is suitable. Sow in a propagator in spring.

T. erecta
African marigold

These plants have fully double, daisy-like flowers, in shades of cream, yellow and orange. Half-hardy/Z 9. **Crackerjack Mixed** plants have bold, double flowers in orange, golden-yellow and lemon-yellow. H 60cm (2ft), S 30cm (1ft). The **Gold 'n' Vanilla Series** includes creamy white flowers. H 50–75cm (20–30in), S 30cm (1ft). **Jubilee Series 'Golden'** is a single

colour selection with golden-yellow flowers. H 50cm (20in), S 30cm (1ft).

T. patula
French marigold

The flowers of these marigolds can include more than one colour. Plants of the **Boy O' Boy Series** are neat and compact, making them very suitable for window-boxes. The double flowers, with crested centres, can be yellow, orange or rich brownish-red. H and S 15cm (6in). **'Gypsy Sunshine'** bears a heavy crop of double butter-yellow flowers. H and S 15–20cm (6–8in). **'Naughty Marietta'** has single deep yellow flowers marked with maroon. H 30–40cm (12–16in), S 25cm (10in). Half-hardy/Z 9.

T. tenuifolia

These marigolds are bushy and produce domes of flowers. Half-hardy/Z 9. Plants of the **Gem Series** have single flowers in shades of yellow or orange, marked with darker colours. **'Golden Gem'** is a selection with golden-yellow flowers. H and S 15–23cm (6–9in). **Starfire Mixed** has red and yellow flowers, some dramatically bicoloured. H and S 15–23cm (6–9in).

Tagetes tenuifolia 'Golden Gem'

Tropaeolum majus Alaska Series

TROPAEOLUM
Nasturtium

These half-hardy annuals, which are perennials in warm climates, are gratifyingly easy to grow. Some strains make large plants with trailing stems, which are useful for providing quick cover, although the large leaves tend to mask the flowers. The more compact forms are good for bedding or, more informally, for slipping into the cracks in paving. The young leaves and the flowers are edible. The genus also includes some hardy perennials.
Cultivation Grow in any, but not too fertile, soil in sun. Sow in situ from mid-spring onwards.

T. majus
This is the species to which the annual strains are most usually ascribed. All are half-hardy/Z 8–9. The **Alaska Series** produces plants with leaves that are attractively marbled with cream and pink; the flowers can be brilliant orange, red or yellow. H 20–30cm (8–12in), S 45cm (18in). **'Empress of India'** is a compact form, with rich purplish-green leaves and bright scarlet flowers. H to 30cm (12in), S 45cm (18in). Plants raised from seed of the **Gleam Series** are trailing, with semi-double flowers in yellow, red or orange. H to 40cm (16in), S to 60cm (2ft). Plants in the **Whirlybird Series** make low mounds, with upward-facing yellow or red flowers. H to 25cm (10in), S to 40cm (16in).

VIOLA
Pansy

An endearing genus that includes perennials and rock garden plants as well as the charming hardy annuals and biennials described here. Attractive as the self-coloured strains are, most gardeners find the bicolours more appealing: the mask-like markings make the flowers look like faces. So-called winter pansies will flower intermittently from late autumn onwards, reaching their peak in spring. With successive sowings it is possible to produce flowering plants throughout the year. All pansies make ideal bedding and container plants; a winter windowbox is virtually unthinkable without them.
Cultivation Any soil in sun or light shade is suitable. Seed germinates best at low temperatures (maximum 10°C/50°F). Summer pansies are best treated as biennials and sown in containers in summer for flowering from the following spring, although they can also be sown from late winter for flowers the same year. Winter pansies should be sown in summer. Take care to keep summer sowings cool.

V. × wittrockiana
Seed strains are usually ascribed to this complex hybrid group, which has emerged from cross-breeding a number of species. All are hardy/Z 4–9.

Summer pansies
'Jolly Joker' has intense orange and purple flowers. H and S 15–23cm (6–9in). **'Lilac Frost'** has glistening lilac flowers that are blotched centrally with rich purple. H and S 15–20cm (6–8in). **Majestic Giants Mixed** plants produce huge bicoloured flowers in a range of iridescent colours; early-flowering, they show greater tolerance to extremes of weather than other strains. H and S 15cm (6in). **'Padparadja'** has intense, solid orange flowers. H and S 15cm (6in). **'Velour Purple Wings'** makes compact mounds that are smothered with miniature flowers with purple and cream petals. The cream petals are edged with mauve and shade to yellow at the centre. H and S 18cm (7in).

Winter pansies
Plants belonging to the **Floral Dance Series** are reliable and produce flowers in a range of colours. Selections in single colours are available. H and S 15–23cm (6–9in). **Universal Mixed** plants are compact, producing both self-coloured and bicoloured flowers in a colour range including red, purple, yellow, apricot and white. H and S 15–20cm (6–8in).

ZINNIA

These half-hardy annuals, with their dahlia-like flowers, bring an exotic touch to the garden.

Zinnia haageana 'Profusion White'

Unusually among half-hardy annuals, they are best sown where they are to flower, since they resent root disturbance.
Cultivation Grow in any soil in sun. Seed can be sown in containers in spring, but it is better to sow them in situ from late spring.

Z. elegans
This Mexican species encompasses a number of seed strains. Tender/10–11. Plants of the **Cactus-flowered Group** have large double flowers, similar to those of a cactus-flowered dahlia, in a range of colours. H to 1m (3ft), S 30cm (1ft). The **Desert Sun Series** produces large, pleated flowers in primrose yellow, ivory white and golden-yellow, which are excellent for cutting. H 1m (3ft), S 30cm (1ft). **'Double Dwarf Mixed'** is a compact strain, with fully double flowers in white, salmon, pink, yellow and scarlet. H 20cm (8in), S 15cm (6in). **'Envy'** has semi-double, chartreuse green flowers. H 75cm (30in), S 30cm (12in). **'Envy Double'** is fully double.

Z. haageana
(syn. *Z. angustifolia*)
Mexican zinnia
Strains allotted to this species are somewhat more compact than those of *Z. elegans*. Half-hardy/Z 9–10. Plants raised from **Persian Carpet Mixed** produce double, bicoloured flowers in shades of golden yellow, maroon, purple, chocolate, pink and cream. They are seemingly impervious to weather extremes. H 38cm (15in), S 30cm (12in). **'Profusion White'** has white flowers. H 30cm (12in), S 10cm (4in).

Tropaeolum majus 'Whirlybird Gold'

Viola 'Padparadja'

Climbers

Climbers are among the most dramatic and rewarding garden plants, lifting your eyes skywards as they reach towards the sun. They are ideal for beautifying walls, fences and ugly outbuildings and can also be draped over pergolas to provide welcome shade in summer or used to carpet banks. Some have spectacular flowers that can be deliciously scented. Others are grown for their leaves, while the evergreens provide year-round interest, being a good foil to other flowering plants in summer and supplying welcome greenery in winter.

Allowed to ramble through roses and perennials, this clematis lifts its flowers to the sun.

Climbers for your garden

Climbers are a fascinating group of plants. Typically, a climber is a woodland dweller, with its feet in the cool, leafy soil on the forest floor. Its long, flexible stems scamper up tree trunks and into their branches, usually with considerable vigour. On reaching the canopy, it spreads sideways and produces flowers that turn to face the sun. This natural habit is one that most gardeners spend considerable efforts on circumventing.

Most climbers have woody stems, and thus are essentially shrubs, but others are soft-stemmed perennials, and some are herbaceous, dying back completely in winter. There are also some annual climbers, sweet peas (*Lathyrus odoratus*) being the best-known.

Climbers have evolved various methods of attaching themselves to their host plant in the wild. Some have special suckering pads that adhere to the host, ivies (*Hedera*), Virginia creeper (*Vitis*) and the climbing hydrangea being notable

examples. Other climbers, such as honeysuckles (*Lonicera*), have twining stems that twist themselves around the host plant. A third group have specialized tendrils – for instance, passion flowers (*Passiflora*) – or twining leaf stalks (clematis being the best example), which cling to narrow stems. A fourth group, which includes roses (dealt with in their own section of this directory) and bougainvillea, have thorns that allow the plant to hook itself into tree bark as it ramps upwards.

A further group should not be overlooked. This comprises so-called scandent climbers, woody plants with long, flexible stems that have no means of supporting themselves. Some clematis come into this category, as well as the popular winter jasmine (*Jasminum nudiflorum*) and the beautiful potato vines (*Solanum*). Such plants can be treated like other climbers but have to be tied to their supports as they grow.

Climbers in the garden
While most plants present their flowers at eye level or below, climbers raise your gaze skywards, and thus bring a dynamism to the garden that is unmatched by any other group. They are high-value plants in that they can fill a large amount of space above ground, while actually only occupying a small area of soil.

In the artificial environment of a garden, climbers do not need to be grown into a host plant, but can be used to clothe a wall or fence, or to cover a pergola or trellis screen. In all these cases, you have to be careful to match the vigour of the plant to the structure that will support it. Many a climber has pulled down a fence, but it is an old wives' tale that suckering climbers will damage the

mortar on house walls: only if the mortar is unsound to begin with are you likely to experience problems. Perennial climbers and some of the less vigorous clematis are effective grown on trellis obelisks or pyramids in borders. A related, but highly effective, method is to train such plants on trellis panels set horizontally in the border on posts, to create a table of flowers that you can look down on.

You can imitate the way climbing plants behave in the wild by siting them near a suitable host plant and treating this as the support. You can plan for the two plants to flower simultaneously, in complementary, toning or even clashing colours, or for the one to follow the other, thus providing for a long season of interest. The summer-flowering perennial pea (*Lathyrus*) makes a good companion for a shrub rose such as 'Nevada' or 'Canary Bird', whose moment of glory comes earlier in season. The flame creeper (*Tropaeolum speciosum*) looks

Bougainvillea and *Trachelospermum jasminoides* make an entrancing combination in this Californian garden.

A tripod supports the vigorous hybrid clematis 'Jackmanii'. Once fully grown it will cover the support completely so it cannot be seen.

spectacular when its luminous crimson flowers light up a sombre yew hedge, and many clematis are suitable for growing into flowering shrubs. Such combinations are a matter of taste: an extreme example would be to grow *Clematis montana* into a mature conifer, a striking if bizarre sight, but honeysuckles and wisterias always strike a romantic note when allowed to ramble through mature deciduous trees.

Another use is as ground cover, a method of cultivation that is particularly effective on a bank or in a wild garden. Many climbers will actually root where the stems touch the ground (especially self-clingers such as ivy), thus creating a weed-suppressing carpet.

Many of the less rampant climbers can be grown in containers, provided these are deep enough to accommodate the root system. They can be trained on trellis panels in the same way as climbers in the open garden, or can simply be allowed to trail over the sides of the container. Ivies are very effective when grown in this way, as are some of the weaker-growing clematis.

Pruning and training climbers

Most climbers are vigorous plants that benefit from pruning occasionally to keep them under control. That said, it is generally impractical to prune climbers grown informally into trees and shrubs, and these can be given their head – hence the importance of choosing climbers that will not swamp the host.

On planting, cut out any dead, diseased or damaged stems and lightly trim back the remainder. Fan them out and tie them loosely to the support. If they are not long enough to reach the support, attach them to canes tied to the support. As the plant grows, train in the

The dainty *Clematis viticella* 'Purpurea Plena Elegans' supported by the pergola dangles its flowers in among the hanging basket's traditional mix of fuchsias and trailing annuals.

stems as near to the horizontal as possible to encourage even flowering. Thorny and scandent climbers will need to be tied in. If you are training the climber up a post (for instance, the upright of a pergola), wrap the stems around the support rather than tying them in vertically.

As a general rule, prune early-flowering climbers immediately after flowering, and late-flowering ones at the start of the growing season. Once the climber has filled

its allotted space, shorten overlong shoots and remove any crossing stems. Cut back thick, old stems to ground level. You can then shorten side shoots, if necessary. A plant that has really got out of hand can be given a new lease of life by renovative pruning. In late winter, cut back all the stems to near ground level. Feed the plant well, and new growth should be vigorous.

For pruning clematis and wisteria, see their own entries in this chapter.

Actinidia kolomikta

Akebia quinata

Campsis radicans

The plants listed are all deciduous unless otherwise indicated.

ACTINIDIA

In addition to the ornamental species described here, this genus of twining climbers also includes *A. deliciosa* (kiwi fruit, Chinese gooseberry).
Cultivation Grow actinidias in any reasonably fertile soil in sun or light shade.

A. kolomikta

This climber from eastern Asia is grown for its leaves, which look as if they have been splashed with cream and pink paint. The leaves show different colours each year (although they are always plain green on emergence, and will remain so in a very shaded site). The plant is not to everyone's taste, but it is attractive grown into the branches of a tree. H and S 3m (10ft). Hardy/Z 4–9.

AKEBIA
Chocolate vine

An interesting genus of five species of twining climbers, with several members that deserve wider recognition than they currently receive. Few are showy, but the plants have a subtle appeal.
Cultivation Grow in any fertile, well-drained soil in sun or light shade.

A. quinata

The dark purple-brown flowers that appear in mid-spring are not particularly conspicuous and can be lost among the compound, evergreen leaves, only the vanilla scent indicating their presence.

Where two plants are grown in proximity, sausage-shaped, purple fruits can develop in autumn. H and S 4m (13ft). Hardy/Z 4–9.

BOUGAINVILLEA

These half-hardy evergreen climbers are grown not for their flowers, which are inconspicuous, but for the brightly coloured bracts that surround them. The spiny stems have to be tied to a trellis. In a conservatory, plant with caution, because if the conditions are favourable they will be rampant. In warm climates they are impressive over large pergolas or allowed to cascade down banks. Combining them with *Trachelospermum jasminoides* will provide the scent they lack.
Cultivation In a conservatory use a loam-based compost and water freely when in active growth. A potash-based fertilizer, applied from spring to early summer, will boost flowering. Keep in full light and allow the temperature to drop no lower than 10°C (50°F).

Bougainvillea 'Miss Manila'

B. × buttiana

This large hybrid group contains a number of desirable plants, including **'Killie Campbell'**, which has large, coppery-orange bracts with ruffled edges. H and S to 10m (33ft) or more. Half-hardy/Z 10.

B. 'Miss Manila' (syn. B. 'Tango')

The bracts, to 5cm (2in) long, are reddish-pink. H and S to 10m (33ft) or more. Half-hardy/Z 10.

B. 'San Diego Red' (syn. B. 'Hawaiian Scarlet', 'Scarlett O'Hara')

The bracts are bright red shading to orange. H and S to 10m (33ft) or more. Half-hardy/Z 9–10.

CAMPSIS
Trumpet vine, trumpet creeper

These climbers with aerial roots are not as widely planted as you might expect, given the attraction of the trumpet-shaped flowers, which are produced from late summer to early autumn. Their lack of popularity is, perhaps, because the blooms are rarely produced in quantity.
Cultivation These climbers need any reasonably fertile, well-drained soil and a position in sun.

C. radicans (syn. Bignonia radicans, Tecoma radicans)
Common trumpet creeper

This species from the south-eastern United States has trumpet-shaped, orange-red flowers, which are borne in clusters in late summer. H and S to 10m (33ft). Borderline hardy/Z 5–9.

C. × tagliabuana 'Madame Galen'

A hybrid of considerable vigour, with deep apricot flowers, veined with salmon pink, and lightly hairy leaves. H and S to 10m (33ft). Borderline hardy/Z 4–10.

CELASTRUS
Bittersweet, staff vine

Unusually, this twining climber is grown for its autumn berries rather than for the flowers.
Cultivation Grow these climbers in fertile, well-drained soil in sun or light shade.

C. orbiculatus (syn. C. articulatus)
Oriental bittersweet

The starry, greenish summer flowers of this species from eastern Asia are succeeded by yellow berries, which split to reveal vivid red seeds. Both male and female plants are required to ensure good fruiting. **'Diana'** is female, **'Hercules'** is male, but if you have room for only one plant, look for one from the **Hermaphrodite Group**. H and S to 10m (33ft) or more. Hardy/Z 5–8.

CLEMATIS

This huge genus of leaf-stalk climbers includes a few herbaceous perennials, and there are also a few non-climbing, sprawling types. There is a clematis for virtually every season of the year. Both species and hybrids are usually divided into three groups, depending on the flowering season. Group 1 clematis flower from the start of the year to late spring on growth made during the previous season. Group 2 clematis flower twice: first in late spring on the previous season's growth and later, in mid- to late summer, on the current season's growth. This group includes some double-flowered hybrids, although only the flowers borne in the first flush are double. Group 3 clematis flower from midsummer to early autumn on the current season's growth.

Best known are the large-flowered hybrids, which are excellent for growing against walls and fences. Some have plate-like flowers, but the viticella hybrids have smaller flowers, and the texensis types are like miniature tulips. There are a number of hybrids that make an even daintier effect. The species are all effective over pergolas and when allowed to romp through trees. The non-climbing clematis described below do not twine but have long, flexible, sprawling stems. They can be used to flop into other plants, or they can be fan-trained against walls and fences. When planting clematis, always bury the stems to a depth of up to 15cm (6in) to encourage stem rooting, which will enhance the plant's overall vigour.

Cultivation Grow clematis in any well-drained soil (although they seem to do best in alkaline conditions) in sun or light shade, with shade at the roots.

Prune as follows. Group 1 clematis require no regular pruning, but congested plants can, if necessary, be thinned after flowering. Harder pruning is tolerated, but the next year's flowering will be impaired. On Group 2 clematis thin congested growth in late winter, cutting back old stems to the base and shortening others as necessary, bearing in mind that these will carry the current season's flowers. Deadhead after the first flush of flowers. For a single flush of late flowers, treat as for Group 3 (although double cultivars will produce single flowers only). Prune Group 3 clematis in late winter (early spring for texensis and viticella types), cutting back all stems to near ground level. Species and very vigorous hybrids can be also be left unpruned, depending on the effect required.

Clematis florida 'Sieboldii'

C. alpina (Group 1)
Alpine clematis
This dainty species has nodding, bell-shaped, blue flowers from spring to early summer. Selections include **'Frances Rivis'**, which has white-centred, mid-blue flowers with slightly twisted petals; and **'Helsinborg'**, which has deep purple-blue flowers. H 3m (10ft), S 1.5m (5ft). Hardy/Z 7–9.

C. armandii (Group 1)
This species, one of the few ever-green clematis, has long, leathery, dark green leaves and clusters of scented, white flowers in spring. A vigorous plant, it is best trained against a warm wall in cold areas. Selections include **'Apple Blossom'**, which has flowers that are initially pale pink; and **'Snowdrift'**, with pure white flowers that are larger than the type. H and S to 9m (30ft). Borderline hardy/Z 7–9.

C. cirrhosa (Group 1)
Fern-leaved clematis
This is usually the first of the

Clematis montana 'Continuity'

Clematis armandii 'Snowdrift'

clematis to flower: according to most books it begins to bloom in midwinter, but occasional flowers can be produced as early as autumn. These are bell-shaped, with a papery texture, and are creamy-white in colour, sometimes speckled with brownish-red inside. H 3m (10ft), S 1.5m (5ft). Hardy/Z 7–9, but best in a warm, sheltered position.

C. flammula (Group 3)
Masses of fragrant, star-like, white flowers cover the plant in late summer and early autumn. This is tolerant of poor soil and is excellent for growing through a tree. H 6m (20ft), S 3m (10ft). Borderline hardy/Z 7–9.

C. florida (Group 2)
This elegant species has two outstanding selections, both producing two flushes of passionflower-like flowers. **'Flore Pleno'** has double, greenish-white flowers; **'Sieboldii'** has creamy-white flowers with a central boss

Clematis montana 'Elizabeth'

of rich purple stamens. Both are weak-growing and need a warm, sheltered spot and fertile soil. H 2m (6ft), S 1m (3ft). Borderline hardy/Z 6–9.

C. macropetala (Group 1)
The bell-shaped flowers of this species, which appear in mid- to late spring, have only four petals, but appear to be double because some of the stamens are petal-like. They are blue or violet-blue. H 3m (10ft), S 1.5m (5ft). **'Blue Bird'** has semi-double, clear blue flowers. The charming **'White Moth'** (syn. *C. alpina* 'White Moth') has pure white flowers. Hardy/Z 6–9.

C. montana (Group 1)
The most vigorous of the early clematis, this is the last to flower, with white flowers appearing in late spring. H 5–8m (15–25ft), S 3m (10ft). Hardy/Z 6–9. Selections include the long flowering **'Continuity'** – hence the name – with creamy-white, pink-tinged flowers; **'Elizabeth'**, which has pale pink, richly scented flowers; and the vigorous *C. montana* f. *grandiflora*, which bears many white flowers.

C. rehderiana (Group 3)
This vigorous species produces a mass of bell-shaped, creamy yellow, cowslip-scented flowers in late summer. This is an excellent choice for growing into a sturdy tree. H 6m (20ft), S 3m (10ft). Hardy/Z 6–9.

C. tangutica (Group 3)
This species produces bright yellow, lantern-like flowers with pointed sepals and a prominent central boss of stamens, which are borne from midsummer to autumn and are followed by silky, silvery grey seedheads. There is much confusion between this species and the roughly similar *C. tibetana*, which will hybridize with it freely. H 6m (20ft), S 3m (10ft). Hardy/Z 6–9.

Hybrids
The following are large-flowered clematis, H and S around 2.4m (8ft) unless otherwise indicated. All are hardy/Z 4–9.

Clematis 'Allanah'

Group 2 clematis
'Barbara Dibley' has bright cerise-pink flowers with darker barring; 'Bees' Jubilee' is deep mauve-pink, aging lighter, and is best in shade; 'Duchess of Edinburgh' is weak-growing with double, dahlia-like, white flowers; the spectacular 'Fireworks' has luminous violet flowers with mauve-carmine bars; 'Gillian Blades' has large white flowers; 'Lasurstern' has mauve-blue flowers, fading to silvery mauve; 'John Warren' has pale greyish-pink flowers, which are veined and edged with deeper pink; 'Marie Boisselot' (syn. 'Mme le Coultre') is a free-flowering plant with pure white flowers with overlapping sepals; 'Mrs Cholmondeley' produces pale lavender-blue flowers over a long period; 'Mrs George Jackman' has creamy-white flowers, the first flush of which are semi-double; the well-known 'Nelly Moser' has pinkish-mauve flowers with carmine bars; 'Silver Moon' has

Clematis 'Gravetye Beauty'

gleaming lavender-white flowers; 'Royalty' has purplish-mauve flowers, the first flush of which are semi-double; 'Vyvyan Pennell' has rich lilac-blue flowers, the first flush of which are double.

Group 3 clematis
The sepals of the bright ruby red 'Allanah' do not overlap; the non-climbing *C. × aromatica* has small, fragrant, deep-violet flowers; 'Bill Mackenzie' has bright yellow, thick-textured, lantern-like flowers, which are followed by fluffy seedheads, H 7m (23ft), S 3m (10ft); 'Duchess of Albany' (texensis) has warm pink flowers banded with red; 'Gravetye Beauty' (texensis) produces red flowers with pink reverses to the sepals; the dainty 'Huldine' (viticella) has pearly white flowers with recurving sepals; 'Jackmanii', one of the most popular of all the hybrids, has purple flowers; the rich purple flowers of 'Jackmanii Superba' are darker than those of 'Jackmanii'; the non-climbing *C. × jouiana* 'Praecox' has small, pale purplish-blue flowers overlaid with silver; 'Kermesina' (viticella) has deep crimson flowers; 'Pagoda' (texensis) has warm pinkish-red flowers; the fully double, very distinctive flowers of 'Purpurea Plena Elegans' (viticella) are deep purplish-pink; 'Rouge Cardinal' has dusky red flowers; the flowers of 'Royal Velours' (viticella) are a deep velvety purplish-red; the young shoots of *C. × triternata* 'Rubromarginata', which has small, fragrant, pink flowers, are often decimated by slugs and snails; 'Victoria' has rose-purple flowers, fading to mauve; the flowers of 'Ville de Lyon' (viticella) are deep pinkish red.

CLIANTHUS
Hardy in only the most favoured spots, clianthus have intriguing, claw-like flowers. Though not strictly climbers, these plants have arching stems that are easily and effectively, if the flowers are to be enjoyed to the full, trained in a fan shape. They can also be grown in cool conservatories (porches).
Cultivation Grow in well-drained soil in sun, siting against a warm wall in cold areas.

Eccremocarpus scaber

C. puniceus
Lobster claw, parrot's bill, glory pea
This species, the commonest in cultivation, produces its flowers in late spring to early summer, usually in shades of gleaming red. Selections include 'Albus', which has exquisite ivory white flowers touched with green; and 'Roseus' (syn. 'Flamingo'), which has deep rose red flowers. H 4m (13ft), S 3m (10ft). Borderline hardy/Z 8.

ECCREMOCARPUS
Chilean glory vine
The species described is often grown as an annual, but it is a truly perennial plant, albeit not evergreen in cold winters, when it dies back to ground level. It looks effective when allowed to wander through a hedge.
Cultivation Grow in well-drained soil in sun. This species can also be grown in a container in an unheated conservatory.

E. scaber
The tubular orange flowers appear over a long period from summer right until the first frosts of autumn. H 3m (10ft), S 1m (3ft). Borderline hardy/Z 7–9.

FALLOPIA
The species described is one of the most rampant of all garden plants. Known as the mile-a-minute plant, it is recommended with caution. Nevertheless, it is unmatched for covering an unsightly outbuilding in record time, but any attempt to restrain its vigour is futile – it is a bottom-of-the-garden plant.

Hedera canariensis 'Gloire de Marengo'

Cultivation This will grow in any reasonable garden soil, in sun or light shade.

F. baldschuanicum
(syn. *Bilderdykia aubertii*, *Fallopia aubertii*, *Polygonum baldschuanicum*)
Russian vine, mile-a-minute plant
This species' chief claim to ornamental value lies in its generous sprays of tiny white flowers, borne in late summer. H and S 15m (50ft). Hardy/Z 5–9.

HEDERA
Ivy
These self-clinging climbers are among the most useful of garden plants, but their positive virtues are easily overlooked. *H. helix* is virtually a weed in some gardens, which should not blind you to the beauties of some of its cultivars. All ivies provide excellent evergreen cover for walls and fences, and can also do well as groundcover in the dry soil under trees where little else will grow. Another attractive use is trailing over banks with other plants, such as groundcover roses.
Cultivation Most ivies do well in any reasonable (preferably alkaline) soil in shade. Variegated ivies tend to produce plain green shoots in acid soil; large-leaved forms do best in sun.

H. canariensis
Canary Island ivy, North African ivy
Some confusion surrounds the naming of this species, which is variously listed as *H. algeriensis*, *H. canariensis* var. *algeriensis* or *H. canariensis* of gardens. No matter

what it is called, the plain green species is hardly a true garden plant, and it is usually represented by one of the following selections. **'Gloire de Marengo'** has green leaves irregularly margined with cream. H and S to 4m (13ft). **'Marginomaculata'** is a dramatic plant, if none too hardy, with leaves marbled and spotted with cream and green. It is sometimes grown as a houseplant. H and S to 4m (13ft). **'Ravensholst'** has very large, shiny, green leaves on red stems. H and S to 5m (16ft). Borderline hardy/Z 8.

H. colchica
Persian ivy
The species from northern Iran and the Caucasus is usually encountered in the form of one of the following. **'Dentata'** has enormous, dull green leaves, occasionally notched at the edges. H and S 5m (16ft) or more. The leaves of **'Sulphur Heart'** (syn. 'Paddy's Pride') are irregularly marked with yellowish-green at the centre. H and S 5m (16ft). Hardy/Z 6–9.

H. helix
Common ivy, English ivy
The species is common in hedgerows and on waste ground but is seldom cultivated as a garden plant. It has a huge number of cultivars. These ivies are easily controlled by pruning. All are hardy/Z 5–9 unless otherwise stated. **'Ambrosia'** has small, slightly curled and twisted leaves, lightly variegated with cream. H and S 1.2m (4ft). Hardy/Z 5. The young leaves of **'Angularis**

Hedera helix 'Buttercup'

Aurea' are bright golden yellow, becoming mottled with green as they age. H and S 4m (13ft). The leaves of **'Boskoop'**, a good houseplant, are claw-like. H and S 1m (3ft). Borderline hardy/Z 6. **'Bruder Ingobert'**, also good as a houseplant or in a hanging basket, has variably shaped leaves that are deep grey-green edged with creamy white. H and S 1m (3ft). Borderline hardy/Z 6. **'Buttercup'** produces its best leaf colour, a rich golden yellow, where it is in sun for at least half the day. H and S 2m (6ft). The mid-green leaves of **'Chicago Variegated'** are variegated with pale yellow. H and S 3m (10ft). The aptly named **'Curvaceous'** is a variegated sport of 'Manda's Crested', with wavy-edged, mid-green-grey leaves with cream margins. H and S 2m (6ft). **'Duckfoot'** has a bushy habit and is good for edging a border. H and S 1m (3ft). Among the variegated forms, **'Eva'** is outstanding, with leaves margined

with creamy yellow. It is good for hanging baskets and as a houseplant. H and S 1.2m (4ft). Borderline hardy/Z 8–9. The young leaves of **'Fantasia'** are cream, heavily speckled with green, turning plain green as they age. H and S 1.2m (4ft). Borderline hardy/Z 8. **'Glacier'** has grey-green leaves edged creamy white. H and S 2m (6ft). **'Green Ripple'** is a vigorous form suitable for groundcover. H and S 2m (6ft). The leaves of **'Jersey Doris'** emerge creamy white, developing green speckling before turning solid green. It is best grown in full light. H and S 1.2m (4ft). Hardy/Z 6. **'Little Luzii'** is excellent in flower arrangements and at the edge of a windowbox. The creamy gold leaves are mottled with green and hold their colour well. H and S 1m (3ft). Borderline hardy/Z 6. **'Manda's Crested'** was the first of the curly ivies. It has forked plain green leaves that turn bronze in winter. H and S 2m (6ft). The slow-growing **'Midas Touch'** has heart-shaped leaves that are basically dark green with patches of lighter green and irregularly blotched with yellow. It can scorch in an exposed site. H and S 1m (3ft). **'Oro di Bogliasco'** (syn. 'Goldheart') is very hardy, and the leaves retain their generous central golden-yellow blotch even in shade. H and S 2.2m (7ft) or more. **'Parsley Crested'** is an attractive ivy with rounded leaves that are crested at the edges and turn bronze in cold weather. It is good in a hanging basket. H and S 2m (6ft). **'Pedata'** (syn. 'Caenwoodiana') has distinctive, narrowly lobed, dark green leaves veined with greyish white. It is best against a wall. H and S 4m (13ft). **'Perkeo'** has unusual puckered leaves that are light green and turn red in cold weather. H and S 45cm (18in). Borderline hardy/Z 6–9. The leaves of **'Sagittifolia Variegata'** are variegated with golden yellow. This is a good ivy for the front of a windowbox, and it needs good light. H and S 1m (3ft). **'Spetchley'** is the smallest ivy available, with densely packed leaves that turn wine red in cold

Hedera colchica

weather. It is good as groundcover. H and S 30cm (1ft). Borderline hardy/Z 5. **'Triton'** (syn. 'Green Feather'), an eye-catching ivy, is a sprawling plant with deeply cut leaves. The three central lobes are elongated and twisted. H and S 45cm (18in).

HUMULUS
Hop
This is a commercially important genus, because hops are used to make beer, but providing one plant of interest to gardeners for its glowing foliage.
Cultivation Grow in any reasonably fertile, well-drained soil. The form described needs full sun for the best leaf colour.

H. lupulus
The straight species, a herbaceous twining climber, is not worth growing, but the selection **'Aureus'** is an outstanding plant wherever a curtain of foliage is needed. H and S to 6m (20ft). Hardy/Z 6–9.

Hedera helix 'Bruder Ingobert'

Hedera helix 'Pedata'

Humulus lupulus 'Aureus'

Lapageria rosea

Lonicera periclymenum 'Graham Thomas'

Jasminum officinale 'Aureum'

HYDRANGEA

This genus of shrubs also includes the outstanding climber described below, its single drawback being its reluctance to put on growth when young. Mature specimens are spectacular, grown either against walls or into trees.
Cultivation Hydrangeas tolerate a range of soil types, but the climbing species described does best in humus-rich, reliably moist soil in light shade.

H. anomala subsp. *petiolaris*
This self-clinging climber has creamy white 'lacecap' flowers in early summer. H and S 4m (13ft). Hardy/Z 4–9.

JASMINUM
Jasmine
For many gardeners, the heady scent of jasmine epitomizes summer; indeed, it can become almost overpowering. The winter jasmine has no scent, although the brilliant yellow flowers are undoubtedly welcome in the depths of winter.

Cultivation Grow in any well-drained soil in sun or light shade.

J. nudiflorum
Winter jasmine
Not strictly climbing, the stems of this Chinese species are lax and trailing. It can be trained against a wall or allowed to cascade down a bank. The cheery bright yellow flowers open during warm spells on the bare branches from late autumn to early spring. H and S 2m (6ft) or more. Hardy/Z 6–9.

J. officinale
Common white jasmine
This, the best-known species, is a twining climber with deliciously scented white flowers from midsummer to early autumn. 'Aureum' has leaves splashed with golden yellow. H and S to 5m (16ft). Borderline hardy/Z 9–10.

LAPAGERIA
A beautiful plant for a cool conservatory (porch) named after Empress Josephine, whose original name was Josephine de la Pagerie. There is only one species.
Cultivation Lapagerias need lime-free soil or potting compost (soil mix) in a lightly shaded position.

L. rosea
Chilean bellflower
This evergreen, twining climber has elongated bell-like, rich pinkish-red flowers that hang from the stems in late summer and autumn. H and S 3m (10ft), often less in a container. Half-hardy/Z 9–11. *L. rosea* var. *albiflora*, with white flowers, is possibly lovelier. H and S 3m (10ft). Borderline hardy/Z 10.

LATHYRUS
A large genus that includes many deliciously scented annuals and shrubs, as well as the delightful and easy-to-grow herbaceous tendril climbers described here. They are charming if allowed to wander through a hedge, but they can also be used more formally on tripods to give height to mixed borders. The flowers resemble those of the annual sweet peas.
Cultivation Grow in any well-drained soil in sun or light shade.

L. grandiflorus
Everlasting pea
This suckering species has glowing pinkish-purple flowers in summer and is good in a wild garden. H and S 2m (6ft). Hardy/Z 6–9.

L. latifolius
Everlasting pea
The species has vivid magenta flowers. Selections include the vigorous 'Rosa Pearl', which has pink flowers, and 'White Pearl', which has pure white flowers. H and S 3m (10ft). Hardy/Z 8–9.

LONICERA
Honeysuckle, woodbine
The scent of the honeysuckle is unmistakable, and fortunately can be enjoyed twice a year, since there are both early- and late-flowering varieties. These twining plants can make mounds and become congested with time. Although they can be used to cover walls and fences, they are at their best when grown more informally in a woodland or wild garden.
Cultivation Honeysuckles will do well in any soil that is not too dry, in a position where the roots are in shade.

L. periclymenum
Woodbine
This is a common woodlander throughout Europe and has deliciously scented, creamy-white flowers in summer. H and S 3m (10ft) or more. Hardy/Z 5–9. 'Belgica' (early Dutch honey-suckle) has pink and red flowers in midsummer, followed by red berries. 'Graham Thomas' bears

Hydrangea anomala subsp. petiolaris

Lathyrus latifolius 'White Pearl'

Lathyrus grandiflorus

Monstera deliciosa

copper-tinted, creamy flowers all summer long. **'Serotina'** (late Dutch honeysuckle) has purple and red flowers from midsummer to autumn. Hardy/Z 5–9.

L. × tellmanniana

This hybrid would no doubt be more widely appreciated were it not for the lack of the characteristic honeysuckle scent – a drawback in the eyes of some. This is more than compensated for by the large, rich amber-orange flowers that appear in early summer, lighting up shady areas of the garden. H and S 3m (10ft). Hardy/Z 7–9.

MONSTERA
Swiss cheese plant

Popular as a houseplant, the species described here is rarely given sufficient headroom to show what it is really made of. Although tolerant enough to withstand the central heating of most living rooms, it is at its superb best in a large conservatory or greenhouse and can be used to shade orchids.
Cultivation Grow in large pots of preferably loam-based compost in light shade and mist daily to simulate rainforest conditions.

M. deliciosa
Swiss cheese plant

The common name refers to the holes that develop in the large glossy leaves as they mature. This is a scrambling plant that needs tying to its support. As it climbs higher it develops aerial roots, which can trail down to the ground. It seldom flowers in

cultivation. H 3m (10ft), S 2m (6ft), but can be considerably more. **'Variegata'** is a desirable selection, the leaves of which are splashed with creamy white. Tender/Z 10.

MUTISIA

These tendril climbers are not reliably hardy in cold areas, but they can be grown in an unheated conservatory.
Cultivation Grow in almost any well-drained soil in a sunny, sheltered site. In cold areas, train against a warm wall or grow under glass.

M. decurrens

A real connoisseur's plant, this has brilliant orange, daisy flowers in summer. H 3m (10ft), S 2m (6ft). Borderline hardy/Z 9–10.

PARTHENOCISSUS

These foliage plants are grown mainly for their spectacular autumn colour. All the species described here cling by means of suckering pads and are excellent on walls.
Cultivation Grow in fertile, well-drained soil in sun or light shade.

P. henryana
(syn. Vitis henryana)
Chinese Virginia creeper

This species has dark green leaves that are distinctively marked with central silvery white veins; they turn red in autumn. H and S to 10m (30ft). Borderline hardy/Z 7–9.

P. quinquefolia
(syn. Vitis quinquefolia)
Virginia creeper

This species is well known by its common name, its claim to garden merit lying in its vivid red autumn leaf colour. Eye-catching as cover for a large wall, it can also be dramatic weaving through the branches of a large tree, such as a silver birch. H and S 15m (50ft). Hardy/Z 4–9.

P. tricuspidata
Boston ivy

This vigorous species has maple-like green leaves that turn rich orange-red in autumn. H and S 15m (50ft). **'Beverley Brook'** is less vigorous and has smaller

Parthenocissus quinquefolia

leaves. The leaves of **'Lowii'** are tinged with purple when they emerge. The leaves of **'Veitchii'** open purple, mature to green, then turn red-purple in autumn. Hardy/Z 5–9.

PASSIFLORA
Passionflower

The range of these tendril climbers has increased considerably over the past few years, and a number of new forms, mostly conservatory plants, have been introduced. The flowers are highly distinctive: ten outer petals surround a crown of central filaments, inside which are the prominent stamens and styles.
Cultivation The hardy *P. caerulea* can be grown in any well-drained soil in sun in a sheltered position. Conservatory plants need to be in large pots of fertile compost with some protection from hot sun.

P. caerulea

This species can be evergreen, but if cut down by frosts will usually

Passiflora caerulea 'Constance Elliot'

Passiflora caerulea

regenerate from ground level. The summer flowers are white, with filaments banded blue, white and purple. H and S to 10m (30ft), but generally much less in cool climates. **'Constance Elliot'** has fragrant, creamy white flowers with red stigmas. Borderline hardy/Z 7–9.

P. quadrangularis
Giant granadilla

This South American species produces large, fragrant flowers in summer, with striking, twisted, violet and white filaments. H and S 10m (30ft), less in a container. Tender/Z 10.

PHILODENDRON

Well known as houseplants, the two root-climbing, evergreen species described here are fine foliage plants, which look good trained up moss poles.
Cultivation Use standard potting compost and keep sheltered from direct bright sunlight. Winter temperatures should not fall below 15°C (59°F).

P. melanochrysum
(syn. P. andreasum)
Black-gold philodendron, velour philodendron

This Colombian species has velvety textured, heart-shaped leaves, with a pronounced coppery tint when young. They can be up to 1m (3ft) long and 30cm (1ft) across. H 3m (10ft), generally much less as a container plant. Tender/Z 10.

P. scandens
Sweetheart vine, heart leaf

This well-known houseplant has shiny, mid-green, heart-shaped leaves with pointed tips. H and S 3m (10ft), but easily restrained. Tender/Z 10.

Pileostegia viburnoides

Schisandra rubrifolia

Solanum crispum 'Glasnevin'

PILEOSTEGIA

The evergreen species described is a dramatic root climber related to *Hydrangea*. The fact that it is not reliably hardy has probably kept it out of most gardens, but it is well worth trying in a sheltered situation, either growing up a tree trunk or across a wall.
Cultivation Grow in any reasonably fertile soil in sun or light shade with some shelter from severe cold.

P. viburnoides
This self-clinging climber from China and India has glossy, leathery leaves and clusters of small creamy-white flowers in late summer and autumn. H and S to 6m (20ft). Borderline hardy/Z 7–10.

PLUMBAGO
Leadwort
These South African climbers are grown for their flowers, which are mostly an appealing clear blue, although there are also white forms. The plants do not climb unaided but need to be tied to some form of support.
Cultivation Grow in pots of high-fertility compost such as John Innes No. 3 (loam-based soil mix) and keep in a sunny or lightly shaded spot.

P. auriculata
(syn. *P. capensis*)
Cape leadwort
The clusters of pale sky-blue flowers are produced from summer to early winter. H and S 1.5m (5ft) or more in a favourable site. Tender/Z 9–10.

SCHISANDRA

These twining climbers are hardy but seem to do best in sheltered gardens. They are delightful when grown so that they can climb into trees in light woodland or against walls, but the species described has one drawback for owners of small gardens: for reliable fruiting, plants of both sexes must be grown in proximity.
Cultivation Grow in sun or light shade in fertile soil that does not dry out excessively.

S. rubrifolia
This twining species produces scarlet to dark red flowers in early summer, followed, on female plants, by red berries. H and S 10m (30ft). Hardy/Z 8–10.

SOLANUM

These delightful climbers deserve to be better known. They produce an abundance of potato flowers over a long period and are generally easy in cultivation. Both the species described are lax

Plumbago auriculata

climbers, which need to be tied to their supports.
Cultivation Grow solanums in any well-drained soil in full sun.

S. crispum
Chilean potato tree
This species, which can be evergreen, is usually represented in cultivation by the form 'Glasnevin', which is reputedly hardier. The deep blue flowers, with prominent central yellow 'beaks', are carried in clusters over many weeks in summer. H and S to 5m (16ft). Borderline hardy/Z 8–9.

S. jasminoides
Potato vine
The straight species has grubby, grey flowers, but the selection 'Album' is a real beauty, with yellow-centred, white flowers. In cold areas, this is best trained against a warm wall. A harsh winter may kill the topgrowth, but it should recover if the base of the plant is protected with a dry mulch. H and S 3m (10ft). Half-hardy/Z 8–10.

STEPHANOTIS

A lovely plant for a conservatory (porch) or as a houseplant, the species described has richly scented, waxy white flowers.
Cultivation Use standard potting compost and keep in good light, but not direct sunlight. In winter, the temperature should not drop below 13°C (55°F).

S. floribunda
Bridal wreath, floradora
This twining evergreen has thick,

glossy, pointed leaves and can flower at any time when in growth. H and S to 3m (10ft), but usually much less when container-grown. Tender/Z 10.

THUNBERGIA
Clock vine
These climbers are too tender to grow outdoors in any but frost-free gardens, but the twining species described can be treated as an annual. In addition to providing temporary cover against a small trellis, it is also effective on tripods in borders or containers or allowed to trail without support from a hanging basket or large trough.
Cultivation Thunbergias will grow in any reasonable garden soil – or standard potting compost (soil mix) for container-grown plants – in a warm, sunny spot.

T. alata
Black-eyed Susan
The simple yellow or orange flowers, produced over a long period during summer and into autumn, have pronounced dark purple-brown throats – hence the common name. H to 2m (6ft), S 25cm (10in) or more if grown as a perennial. Tender/Z 10.

TRACHELOSPERMUM
The genus contains about 20 species, and the one described is among the most worthwhile of all climbers, with attractive, evergreen leaves and a long succession of small but incomparably scented flowers from summer until autumn. It deserves a prime spot in any garden and makes an excellent companion to *Bougainvillea* in a frost-free climate.
Cultivation Grow in sun or light shade in any well-drained soil. In a cold climate, train against a warm wall.

T. jasminoides
Star jasmine, confederate jasmine
This species from China and Japan has leathery, pointed, glossy green leaves on twining stems, although these need tying to their support initially. The white flowers are curiously twisted. H to 9m (30ft), but usually much less in cold climates. Borderline hardy/Z 8–10.

Trachelospermum jasminoides

Tropaeolum speciosum

Vitis vinifera 'Purpurea'

framework. Shorten laterals to five or six leaves. In midwinter, cut these back further to two or three buds from the base of the stem. These are the spurs that will carry the flowers.

TROPAEOLUM

As well as the highly desirable climber described here, the genus includes the popular annual nasturtiums. A yew hedge festooned with this plant is an eye-catching sight in late summer, but it does not always prove easy to establish in gardens, a cool, damp climate appearing to suit it best.
Cultivation Grow in reliably moist, lime-free soil in sun or light shade. It does not like hot, dry conditions.

T. speciosum
Scottish flame flower, flame creeper
The common names of this herbaceous perennial make appropriate reference to the colour of the brilliant red flowers, which appear throughout the summer. H and S to 3m (10ft). Borderline hardy/ Z 7–9.

VITIS

This genus of tendril climbers is important commercially for the production of grapes, both for the

table and for wine-making. The plants described here are principally of ornamental value and are good for covering walls or clothing pergolas.
Cultivation Grow in poor soil in sun.

V. 'Brant'
This vigorous and attractive hybrid is a value-added plant in that its bloomy purple-black grapes are edible; these ripen in autumn as the leaves, which are veined yellow-green, turn dark purple-red. H and S to 12m (40ft) or more. Hardy/Z 5–9.

V. coignetiae
Crimson glory vine
This species from Japan and Korea is really valued for its spectacular autumn leaf colour – yellow, orange and deep scarlet – although it also produces crops of inedible, bloom-covered black grapes. H and S 15m (50ft). Hardy/Z 5–9.

V. vinifera
Tenturier grape
The species is the parent of the many varieties grown for edible crops and also of a number of purely ornamental selections. 'Purpurea' is one of the most widely grown. The leaves mature to purple, then develop even richer hues in autumn as the blackish, unpalatable fruits ripen. H and S 9m (30ft). Hardy/Z 6–9.

WISTERIA

Possibly the most desirable of all flowering climbers, wisterias bear dramatic racemes of scented pea flowers in late spring to early

summer. Old specimens trained against house walls are breathtaking, as are those trained to embrace arching bridges over water. They are also spectacular trained over arches, pergolas or – in a less formal garden – allowed to ramp into sturdy host trees. When shopping for wisterias, look for named varieties grafted on to vigorous rootstocks, expensive though these are. Seed-raised wisterias often have poor flowers, and plants raised from cuttings can lack vigour.
Cultivation Grow in any deep, fertile, well-drained soil in sun or light shade. Although fully hardy, they flower best when trained hard against a warm wall to ripen the stems. Prune young plants each year in late summer, cutting back any of the current year's growth that exceeds the allotted space and tying in suitably placed new stems to fill in the framework. Once the framework is established, in late summer cut back all stems that exceed the

W. floribunda
Japanese wisteria
The species has hanging racemes, up to 30cm (12in) long, of fragrant, violet-blue flowers in early summer. Selections include 'Alba' (syn. 'Snow Showers', *W. multijuga* 'Alba'), a desirable white-flowered form; **'Kuchi-beni'** (syn. 'Lipstick', 'Peaches and Cream'), which has lilac-pink and white flowers; and **'Multijuga'** (syn. 'Longissima', 'Macrobotrys'), which bears purple flowers in racemes to 60cm (2ft)long. H and S to 9m (30ft). Hardy/ Z 4–10.

W. × formosa
This hybrid group includes one of the most dramatic of all wisterias, **'Yae-kokuryû'** (syn. 'Black Dragon', 'Kokuryû'), which produces long, hanging racemes of rich purple, double flowers. H and S to 9m (30ft). Hardy/ Z 6–9.

W. sinensis
Chinese wisteria
This wisteria is somewhat more vigorous than the Japanese species. In its typical form, it has faintly-scented violet-blue flowers in late spring; **'Alba'** has white flowers; and **'Caroline'** has fragrant, deep blue-purple flowers. H 15m (50ft)or more, S 9m (30ft). Hardy/Z 5–9.

Vitis 'Brant'

Wisteria floribunda 'Kuchi-beni'

Wisteria sinensis

Roses

As a garden plant, the rose is unrivalled. Few other plants have attracted so much attention from breeders and down the ages they have epitomized the summer garden. From the uncomplicated charm of the species to the sophistication of the hybrid teas, there is a rose for virtually every purpose, as hedging, to give weight and substance to borders, as specimens or to provide cut flowers. The climbers provide magnificent cover for walls and pergolas, while nowadays the range has been extended to include tough, compact, disease-resistant plants that are excellent as ground cover or for growing in containers.

Elegant hybrid tea roses are esssential plants for any cottage garden scheme, here combining well with phlox and other border perennials.

Roses for your garden

Roses are a breed apart. No other plant genus has been so extensively hybridized to produce the wide range of plants that we enjoy in gardens today.

Roses are shrubs, mainly deciduous ones. In the wild, some make huge plants, colonizing vast areas and finding their way into trees, hooking themselves into the bark by means of their thorns.

Rose classification

The classification of roses represents an attempt to bring some order to a vast and diverse range of plants. However, in many cases, the distinctions are far from clear cut. Roses are generally classified as follows:

Wild roses

These comprise the species, their selections and certain hybrids. They usually have one flush of single flowers in early summer, often followed by decorative hips in autumn.

Old roses

- *Bourbon roses* are vigorous, and are usually repeat-flowering. They are often suitable for training as short climbers. *Portland roses* are similar, but repeat more reliably and generally make smaller plants.
- *Centifolia roses* (sometimes also called cabbage, Provence or Holland roses) make lax shrubs with large, many-petalled flowers that weigh down the arching canes. *Moss roses* are a closely allied group, distinguished by the characteristic mossy growth on their stems and calyces.
- *China roses* are dainty, repeat-flowering shrubs with small flowers and leaves. *Tea roses*, also repeat-flowering, are thin-stemmed with slender, pointed flower buds. Few are hardy enough to be grown outdoors in cold areas.

Correctly supported, many a climbing rose will reach the eaves of a house and be smothered in flowers in summer.

- *Damask roses* are lax, spreading shrubs, usually with fragrant flowers in clear colours. The leaves are typically greyish green and are downy underneath.

Flower shapes

Flat flowers are single (five petals) or semi-double (ten petals) and open flat.
Cupped flowers are single to fully double, with curving petals.
Rounded flowers have a rounded outline formed by overlapping petals.
Rosette flowers are low-centred and flat, with many short, crowded petals.
Quartered rosette flowers are similar to rosettes, but the petals are arranged in distinctive quarters.
Pointed and urn-shaped flowers, characteristic of Chinas, teas and hybrid teas, are high-centred and open from slender, elegant buds.
Pompon flowers are small and ball-like with many short petals, and are usually carried in clusters.

- *Gallica roses* are usually upright, compact shrubs with coarse leaves and flowers in shades of pink, rich crimson and purple. The group includes some striped roses.
- *Hybrid perpetuals* are vigorous and usually repeat-flowering. They tend to be leggy but this is a problem that can be overcome by pegging down the lax shoots.
- *Scotch roses* are dense shrubs with *R. pimpinellifolia* in their make-up.

Modern roses

- *Climbing roses* usually have long, stiff stems that make them suitable for training. The flowers, similar to those of hybrid teas and floribundas in appearance, are produced in one or – more usually – two flushes.
- *Floribunda* or *cluster-flowered roses* are repeat-flowering, with single to fully double flowers in clusters.
- *Ground-cover roses* have a lax, trailing habit, rather like miniature climbers. They typically have clusters of small flowers, produced over a long period.
- *Hybrid tea* or *large-flowered roses* are characterized by large, high-centred flowers carried singly (but sometimes in small clusters) that open from pointed buds. They are repeat-flowering. Some are of stiff, ungainly habit.
- *Miniature roses* are compact plants, usually under 30cm (12in) high, with sprays of tiny, usually scentless flowers. They are repeat-flowering.
- *Patio* or *dwarf cluster-flowered bush roses* are similar to floribundas but are much smaller, making them ideal container plants.
- *Polyanthas* are now more or less obsolete. Tough and repeat-flowering, with trusses of small flowers, they are the forebears of the modern floribundas.
- *Rambler roses* are large shrubs of exceptional vigour, with long flexible,

often trailing stems. Typically they flower early in the season on the previous season's wood.

- *Rugosa roses* are tough, hardy shrubs with characteristically wrinkled leaves and single to double flowers in succession throughout summer and autumn. Some have showy autumn hips.

- *Shrub roses* comprise a vast group of plants that do not fit into any of the above categories. They are usually larger than other modern roses and thus less suitable for bedding. Flowers can be single to double and can appear in one or two flushes. This group includes the so-called *English roses*, bred by David Austin, which combine the flower shape of the old roses with the repeat-flowering habit of modern roses.

Roses in the garden

Many people associate roses with bedding, and while it is true that many of the floribundas and hybrid teas are outstanding in a massed planting, the genus as a whole is much more versatile than that.

Many of the shrub roses are stylish plants that can be planted either as specimens or as elements of a mixed planting, combining happily with a range of other shrubs and perennials. The old roses earn their place in the garden largely on the merits of their sumptuous, usually deliciously scented flowers, as well as the romantic associations of their names – 'Cardinal de Richelieu', 'Duchesse de Montebello', 'Souvenir de la Malmaison', to mention just three.

A surprising number of roses are also excellent for hedging (though not providing an evergreen screen), thorny types making good barrier or boundary hedges. The rugosas are well suited for this purpose.

'Albertine' is an enduring favourite for its incomparable scent, trained here to allow the fragrance to waft through open windows.

The obvious way to grow the climbers and ramblers is by training them against a house wall, fence or over a pergola, but they can also be trained against trellis panels to screen one part of the garden from another. Shorter types can be grown over trellis obelisks or pillars to give height to a border. One of the most dramatic ways of growing climbers and ramblers is into the arms of a tree, but here you must make sure that the host is sturdy enough to bear the weight of the rose – some are vigorous plants that can swamp the tree. Among the most effective are those that bear a close resemblance to the species, such as 'Albéric Barbier' and 'Rambling Rector'.

Many of the more recent introductions make splendid ground cover, not just those defined as "groundcover roses". They are tough plants, handsome even when out of flower. Having been bred to be compact, to suit the modern garden, which tends to be smaller, they are also ideal plants for containers. Excellent health and length of flowering season only add to their merits.

Training the fragrant and long-flowering 'Dublin Bay' to climb up the wooden trellis is an effective and attractive way of screening one part of the garden from another.

'Agnes'

An upright, healthy rugosa of undoubted distinction, this bears double, scented, pale yellow flowers in summer, with only a few following in autumn. It combines the toughness of the rugosas with an old-rose look to the flowers. H 2m (6ft), S 1.2m (4ft). Hardy/Z 2–9.

R. × alba 'Alba Maxima' (syn. R. × alba 'Maxima')

This alba rose dates from the 15th century, or even earlier, and is sometimes assumed to be the white rose of York. It is also a beauty, with untidy, double, very fragrant flowers that are tinged pink on opening in summer, then fade to creamy white. Red hips follow. It is also known as the great white rose, the Jacobite rose or the Cheshire rose. H 2.1m (7ft), S 1.5m (5ft). Hardy/Z 4–9.

R. × alba 'Alba Semiplena' (syn. 'Semiplena')

An alba rose, this has been grown in gardens since the 16th century or before. It is a graceful shrub with clusters of semi-double, very fragrant, milky white flowers in summer. These open flat to display prominent golden stamens, with red hips making a second display in autumn. 'Alba Semiplena' is usually held to be the white rose of York, competing for that title with R. × alba 'Alba Maxima'. H 2.1m (7ft), S 1.5m (5ft). Hardy/Z 4–9.

'Alba Meidiland' (syn. 'Meiflopan')

This is a groundcover rose, and unusually for a rose in this group, the pure white, fully double flowers are good for cutting. H 1m (3ft), S 1.2m (4ft). Hardy/Z 4–9.

'Albéric Barbier'

This vigorous rambling rose is a good choice for brightening up a shady wall or a dull tree. In early to midsummer, masses of double, rosette, creamy white, scented flowers cover the plant. To compensate for the lack of further flowers, the glossy leaves often hang on through the winter. H 5m (16ft), S 3m (10ft). Hardy/Z 4–9.

'Albertine'

A vigorous rambling rose, this has fully double, light pink flowers, which appear in a single flush in midsummer, opening from copper-tinted buds; they become untidy as they age. The rich, distinctive scent of this rose has assured its continuing popularity, despite its all too obvious drawbacks: its talon-like thorns and propensity to mildew. Thinning the growth after flowering to improve air circulation can help the latter problem. H 5m (16ft), S 4m (12ft). Hardy/Z 4–9.

'Alec's Red' (syn. 'Cored')

This is a bushy hybrid tea with fully double, heavily scented, rich red flowers that open from pointed buds throughout summer and into autumn. A versatile rose,

Rosa 'Alec's Red'

it is suitable for cutting, bedding and as a hedge, but blackspot can be a problem. H 1m (3ft), S 60cm (2ft). Hardy/Z 4–9.

'Alexander' (syn. 'Harlex')

An upright hybrid tea, this has double, luminous red flowers opening from pointed buds from summer to autumn. The leaves are glossy dark green and show good resistance to disease. The flowers are produced on long stems, which means that this is a good rose for cutting as well as for planting in a tight hedge with little sideways spread. H to 2m (6ft), S 75cm (2ft 6in). Hardy/Z 4–9.

'Allgold'

A compact floribunda and an ideal bedding rose, this bears a succession of double, lightly scented, bright yellow flowers from summer to autumn. H 75cm (2ft 6in), S 50cm (20in). Hardy/Z 5–9.

'Aloha'

This climbing rose bears a succession of cupped, fully double, sweetly scented, light pink flowers from summer to autumn. The leaves are dark green, leathery and healthy. This is a rain-resistant variety, which is also good in a container. H 3m (10ft), S 2.5m (8ft). Hardy/Z 4–9.

Rosa × alba 'Alba Semiplena'

Rosa 'Albertine'

Rosa 'Anna Ford'

Rosa 'Apricot Nectar'

Rosa 'Avon'

Rosa 'Baby Masquerade'

'Amber Queen'
(syn. 'Harroony', 'Prinz Eugen van Savoyen')
A neat-growing floribunda, this rose bears clusters of fully double, heavily scented, rich amber-yellow flowers, which open from rounded buds. Its compact habit makes it a good choice for bedding, hedges and containers. H and S 50cm (20in). Hardy/Z 4–9.

'Anna Ford'
(syn. 'Harpiccolo')
This is a dense, low-growing patio rose. The warm orange-red flowers, produced freely from summer to autumn, open flat from pointed buds to reveal yellow centres. One of the earliest of its type, this remains a popular bedding or container rose. H 45cm (18in), S 38cm (15in). Hardy/Z 4–9.

'Anne Harkness'
(syn. 'Harkaramel')
An upright, branching floribunda, this bears large clusters of pointed, urn-shaped, double, soft buff-yellow flowers from late summer to autumn. Spectacular when in full flower, This is a disease-resistant rose that is suitable for bedding, hedging and cutting. H 1.2m (4ft), S 60cm (2ft). Hardy/Z 4–9.

'Apricot Nectar'
This bushy floribunda bears tight clusters of large, fully double, sweetly scented, pinkish-buff-apricot flowers from summer to autumn. It is a good hedging rose, but it can be susceptible to mildew from midsummer. H 80cm (32in), S 65cm (26in). Hardy/Z 4–9.

'Arthur Bell'
An upright, branching floribunda, this bears clusters of semi-double to double, bright yellow flowers that pale as they age. The scent is outstanding for a rose of this type. This is a versatile rose, suitable for bedding, hedging and containers; the autumn flowering is especially good, making it a good companion for annuals and late-flowering perennials and bulbs. H to 1m (3ft), S 60cm (2ft). Hardy/Z 4–9.

'Avon'
(syn. 'Fairy Lights', 'Poulmulti', 'Sunnyside')
From summer to autumn this compact, spreading groundcover rose bears clusters of small, semi-double, fragrant, pinkish-white flowers, which open flat to reveal golden stamens. Besides its obvious uses for massed planting and as a low hedge, this rose can also be grown successfully in containers. H 30cm (1ft), S 1m (3ft). Hardy/Z 4–9.

'Baby Masquerade'
(syn. 'Baby Carnival', 'Tanba', 'Tanbakede')
Many people believe that this miniature rose is more attractive than its full-sized equivalent. From summer to autumn it carries clusters of tiny, double, rosette-shaped flowers, which open yellow and fade to pink then to deeper red, so that all the colours are present at any one time. The rose is probably seen at its best when grown as a miniature standard. H and S 40cm (16in). Hardy/Z 4–9.

Rosa 'Anne Harkness'

Rosa 'Arthur Bell'

'Belle de Crécy'

The quartered-rosette, sweetly scented flowers of this gallica rose are produced in abundance in midsummer. They open rich purple-pink then fade to a greyish pale pink. It has a laxer habit than most other gallicas and its arching stems may require some support; alternatively, simply allow them to trail into neighbouring shrubs. It does not flower as well in poor, light soil. H 1.2m (4ft), S 1m (3ft). Hardy/Z 5.

'Blairii Number Two'

In midsummer, this strangely named bourbon, first raised in 1845, carries an abundance of large, cupped, fully double, sweetly scented flowers, which are pale silvery pink with deeper pink centres. However, unlike some other bourbon roses, it produces only a few further blooms in autumn, if any. Untrained, it will grow into an arching shrub about 2.1m (7ft) high and across. Its vigour and flexible canes make it suitable for growing as a pyramid, on a pergola or against a wall, where it can reach 5m (16ft). H 4m (12ft), S 2m (6ft). Hardy/Z 4–9.

'Blue Moon'
(syn. 'Blue Monday', 'Mainzer Fastnacht', 'Sissi', 'Tannacht')

An intriguing hybrid tea, this is not one of the best overall, but is worth growing for the individual

Rosa 'Belle de Crécy'

Rosa 'Blue Moon'

Rosa 'Buff Beauty'

flowers. Borne in summer and autumn, they are not blue, as the name implies, but silvery lilac, a colour associated with the old roses. However, the flower form is modern: high-centred and shapely. It is also one of the most sweetly scented of modern roses. 'Blue Moon' needs careful placing in the garden because of its curious colouring; it is perhaps best grown in isolation under glass. H 1m (3ft), S 60cm (2ft). Hardy/Z 4–9. The climbing form is also worth considering, but it needs good cultivation and a site where the flowers will not be bleached by too much sun.

'Bobbie James'

One of the most vigorous of ramblers, this rose looks like its wild antecedents. In summer it is covered with clusters of small, white, semi-double flowers that are also sweetly scented. It is a

good choice for growing into a large tree, and although it would be just as dramatic over a large pergola, its vigour could cause problems. H 10m (33ft), S 6m (20ft). Hardy/Z 5–9.

'Buff Beauty'

This is an excellent modern shrub rose or hybrid musk. The name refers to the colour of the cupped, fully double, sweetly scented flowers, which are pale buff-apricot, fading to creamy white in hot sun. They are carried in clusters in two distinct flushes, the autumn flowering being less profuse than the summer. 'Buff Beauty' can be used for hedging but needs the support of horizontal wires, since the canes are often bent down low by the weight of the flowers. Mildew may be a problem in late summer but need not deter you from growing this rose. H and S 1.5m (5ft). Hardy/Z 6–9.

'Cardinal de Richelieu'

This grandly named gallica – and one of the most sumptuous – was produced in 1840. It makes a

compact bush and will exceed its usual size if the flexible stems are supported. The clusters of scented, dark maroon flowers appear in midsummer; the petals are velvety in texture and reflex as the flowers age to form a ball shape. The stems are well-covered with healthy, dark green leaves. This rose needs fertile, well-drained soil and regular thinning of the old wood to give of its best. H 1m (3ft), S 1.2m (4ft). Hardy/Z 4–9.

'Cécile Brünner'

Sometimes identified as the sweetheart rose or Maltese rose, this is a dainty, airy cultivar, which is classified as either a China rose or a polyantha. It flowers over a long period from early summer to mid-autumn, when clusters of elegant, pointed buds open to urn-shaped, delicately scented, pale pink flowers, which become more untidy as as they age. H and S 1m (3ft). Hardy/Z 5–9. A climbing form is available, which is less restrained and easily reaches 6m (20ft) in all

Rosa 'Blairii Number Two'

Rosa 'Cardinal de Richelieu'

Rosa 'Cécile Brünner'

Rosa 'Céleste'

Rosa 'Charles de Mills'

Rosa 'Chinatown'

Rosa 'Complicata'

directions; it is ideal for growing into a tree. The white-flowered bush form 'White Cécile Brünner' is rare.

'Céleste'
(syn. *R.* × *alba* 'Celestial')
The date of the introduction of this Alba rose is unrecorded, but it is certainly a very old cultivar, perhaps dating back to ancient times. The semi-double, sweetly scented, shell-pink flowers, with petals that seem almost transparent, are borne in summer and open flat to reveal prominent golden stamens. Red hips succeed them in autumn. H and S 2m (6ft). Hardy/Z 4–9.

R. × *centifolia* 'Cristata'
(syn. 'Chapeau de Napoléon', 'Crested Moss')
This distinguished centifolia rose is sometimes included among the moss roses, though incorrectly, since only the calyces and not the stems are mossed. It makes a graceful, slender-stemmed shrub. In summer it produces drooping, cupped, fully double, richly scented, deep silvery-pink flowers that open flat and are sometimes quartered. The alternative name, 'Chapeau de Napoléon' (Napoleon's hat), refers to the unopened buds, which look like a tricorn hat. H 1.5m (5ft), S 1.2m (4ft). Hardy/Z 4–9.

'Charles de Mills'
(syn. 'Bizarre Triomphant')
This is a gallica rose of unknown origin. The fully double, quartered-rosette, moderately scented, rich crimson flowers, which appear in summer, fade with grey and purple tones as they mature. The

abundant foliage is matt dark green. It makes a compact shrub, but the slender stems may need staking to support the large flowers as they open. H 1.2m (4ft), S 1m (3ft). Hardy/Z 4–9.

'Chinatown'
(syn. 'Ville de Chine')
A floribunda rose, this is probably unmatched for size and overall vigour; indeed, it is sometimes justifiably classified as a shrub rose. The fragrant clusters of fully double, bright golden-yellow flowers are freely produced throughout summer and into autumn among glossy dark green leaves. It is ideal grown at the back of a border as a backdrop for smaller plants, as a hedge or as a specimen plant. H 1.5m (5ft), S 1m (3ft). Hardy/Z 5–9.

'City of London'
(syn. 'Harukfore')
A spreading floribunda, this shows some of the characteristics of one of its parents, 'New Dawn', notably its continuity (it flowers from summer to autumn), its scent and its appealing soft pink colour. More versatile than some other members of this group, if it is pruned fairly hard it can be used for bedding, but with minimum pruning it can also be treated as a specimen or trained as a short climber. It also associates well with old roses. H to 2m (6ft), S to 1.2m (4ft). Hardy/Z 4–9.

'Compassion'
From summer to autumn this climbing rose produces shapely, rounded, fully double, sweetly scented, warm apricot-pink flowers. It is an excellent choice

for a pillar or a sturdy garden fruit tree. H 3m (10ft), S 2.5m (8ft). Hardy/Z 4–9.

'Complicata'
(syn. *R. gallica* 'Complicata')
Although this is a gallica rose, it has few of the characteristics normally associated with the group and is of uncertain origin, its pedigree possibly including the vigorous species *R. canina*. Its name also implies double flowers; in fact, they are single but are produced in abundance all along the arching canes in summer. Bright porcelain pink, they are sweetly scented and open wide to reveal white centres and golden stamens. Unusually for a gallica, the matt greyish-green leaves are rather pointed. 'Complicata' tolerates light, sandy soils and can be used as a rambler among trees and shrubs in a wild garden

or it can be trained on a pillar; H and S 2.5m (8ft) if supported, probably more as a climber. Hardy/Z 4–9.

'Constance Spry'
(syn. 'Autance')
This was one of the first of David Austin's 'English' roses, and it is still one of the best, although it flowers once only, in midsummer. The large, cupped, fully double, peony-like flowers of this shrub rose are rich pink and heavily scented. It can also be grown as a climber on a pillar or against a wall, where it will tolerate some shade. Even as a shrub it is best given some support or pruned hard to keep it compact. Untrained, it will grow into a large, lax shrub. H and S to 2m (6ft), though the spread can sometimes exceed the height. Hardy/Z 4–9.

Rosa 'Constance Spry'

Rosa 'Duc de Guiche'

'Danse du Feu'

A stiffly branched climbing rose that, as far as the flower colour – luminous red – is concerned has not been surpassed, and it has retained its place in catalogues in spite of its tendency towards blackspot. The rounded, double flowers appear from summer to autumn, but the scent is not strong. H and S 2.5m (8ft). Hardy/Z 4–9.

'Desprez à Fleurs Jaunes'
(syn. 'Jaune Desprez')

This exquisite, vigorous climbing rose, introduced in 1830, should be planted more widely. The double flowers, borne throughout summer, are an unusual creamy buff-yellow and are also sweetly scented. The lax, flexible canes make this an excellent choice for training against a wall, preferably a sunny one. H and S 5m (16ft). Hardy/Z 6–9.

'Du Maître d'Ecole'

The date of origin of this gallica rose is in dispute, but some authorities say it was introduced in 1840. It makes a compact plant, and in summer the weight of blossom makes the stems arch over. The fragrant, fully double, quartered-rosette, carmine-pink flowers open flat and fade to lilac-pink and grey. H and S 1m (3ft). Hardy/Z 4–9.

'Dublin Bay'
(syn. 'Macdub')

A valuable red climber, this has almost fluorescent flowers. Double and lightly scented, they are carried in clusters from summer to autumn among glossy, healthy leaves. It is a good choice if space is limited, in a border on a tripod, for instance, since the growth tends to be upright. H and S 2.2m (7ft). Hardy/Z 4–9.

'Duc de Guiche'

The fully double, highly scented flowers of this outstanding gallica change colour as they age. Rich crimson initially, they develop purple veining before finally flushing purple. H and S 1.2m (4ft). Hardy/Z 4–8.

'Duchesse de Montebello'

This spreading gallica was bred before 1829. The open-cupped, fully double, sweetly fragrant flowers are soft blush pink. The foliage is light green. It is one of the daintiest and neatest growing of the gallicas. H and S 1.2m (4ft). Hardy/Z 4–8.

'Elina'
(syn. 'Dicjana', 'Peaudouce')

A bushy hybrid tea, this has fully double, lightly scented, creamy white flowers, which open to reveal lemon-yellow flushed centres. The flowering season lasts from summer to autumn. A versatile rose and easy to grow, it is generally healthy and can be used for bedding and cutting. H 1m (3ft), S 75cm (2ft 6in). Hardy/Z 4–9.

'Escapade'
(syn. 'Harpade')

This elegant floribunda has a freely branching habit, and it is also something of a novelty in being an outstanding garden plant. The semi-double, sweetly scented flowers, which are borne in clusters throughout summer into autumn, are of unusual coloration: they are soft lilac-pink, opening flat to reveal white centres and golden stamens. Unlike some other roses, it blends easily with other plants; it occasionally produces pure white flowers within the cluster, which adds to its charm. Shiny, light green foliage is borne in abundance. H to 1.2m (4ft), S 60cm (2ft). Hardy/Z 4–9.

Rosa 'Fantin-Latour'

'Fantin-Latour'

A centifolia rose, this makes a handsome, vase-shaped shrub, which is ideal as a specimen. The many-petalled, cup-shaped flowers are delicately scented. They are blush-pink and are borne in profusion over a long period in summer, their petals reflexing to reveal a green button eye. 'Fantin-Latour' was named in honour of the French painter, admired for his flower pieces, some of which include roses. Spraying against mildew may be necessary in summer. H and S to 2.2m (7ft). Hardy/Z 4–9.

'Félicité Parmentier'

This compact Alba rose bears a single crop of cup-shaped, highly scented, quartered, pale blush-pink flowers, which open from primrose yellow buds in midsummer. The densely packed petals fade to almost white in hot sun and reflex to form a ball

Rosa 'Du Maître d'Ecole'

Rosa 'Duchesse de Montebello'

Rosa 'Escapade'

Rosa 'Félicité Parmentier'

shape. The leaves are healthy and grey-green. One of the daintiest of its type, this is suitable for the smallest garden. H and S 1.2m (4ft). Hardy/Z 4–9.

'Fred Loads'
A strongly upright floribunda, this rose is ideal for the back of a border. Its generous clusters of semi-double, pleasantly scented, soft orange-vermilion flowers are produced from summer to autumn, making it invaluable for a long display in a mixed planting. Hard pruning can keep it in bounds, or it can be used for hedging. The flowers last well in water. H 2m (6ft), S 1m (3ft). Hardy/Z 5–9.

'Fru Dagmar Hastrup'
(syn. 'Frau Dagmar Hartopp')
This compact, spreading rugosa rose bears single, pale pink

summer flowers, which open almost flat to reveal prominent golden stamens; large, tomato-red hips develop in autumn as a second, sparser flush appears. This makes an excellent low hedge and can also be used for ground cover, possibly in light woodland. H 1m (3ft), S 1.2m (4ft). Hardy/Z 3–9.

'Frühlingsgold'
A Scotch hybrid rose, sometimes classified as a modern shrub rose, this makes a vigorous shrub, each arching cane reaching up to 2.2m (7ft) in length. The large, cupped, semi-double, fragrant, primrose-yellow flowers cover the stems in late spring to early summer, opening flat from long, pointed buds to display golden stamens. Its toughness and thorniness suggest that it might be used as a barrier plant at the end of the garden rather than in the border. H 2.5m (8ft), S 2.2m (7ft). Hardy/Z 4–8.

R. gallica var. _officinalis_
(syn. _R. officinalis_)
This is a bushy gallica rose, which has been recorded in gardens since the 13th century. In summer it produces an abundance of large, semi-double, sweetly fragrant, light crimson flowers, which open flat and reveal golden stamens. Rich in historical association both as the red rose of Lancaster and the medieval apothecary's rose, this remains a superb garden plant in its own right. H and S 1.2m (4ft). Hardy/Z 5–9.

Rosa 'Graham Thomas'

R. gallica 'Versicolor'
An eye-catching gallica rose, this old rose was first recorded in the 16th century but is probably much older. The lightly scented flowers, produced in midsummer, are semi-double, opening flat to reveal golden stamens. The pale pink petals are dramatically splashed and striped with red and crimson. The common name, Rosa Mundi, reputedly commemorates Fair Rosamund, the mistress of Henry II of England. H and S 1.2m (4ft). Hardy/Z 5–9.

'Gentle Touch'
(syn. 'Diclulu')
Neat and upright, this patio rose bears clusters of double, slightly fragrant, pale salmon-pink flowers, opening from urn-shaped buds, from summer to autumn. In addition to its suitability for containers and as groundcover, 'Gentle Touch' is excellent as a cut flower. H and S 40cm (16in). Hardy/Z 4–9.

'Gloire de Dijon'
One of the oldest climbing roses still in cultivation, this was introduced in 1853 and is usually one of the first climbers to flower. The striking, fully double, fragrant, quartered-rosette, buff-apricot flowers are produced over a long period from late spring to late summer. Its early flowering makes it susceptible to frosts, so grow it against a warm wall in cold areas. H 5m (16ft), S 4m (13ft). Hardy/Z 5–9.

'Golden Showers'
This climbing rose is a perennial favourite for many gardeners. It produces clusters of double, lightly scented, yellow flowers from summer to autumn. The flowers lack distinction, having few petals, but the reliability of this rose in a variety of situations, including light shade, has ensured its longevity. H 3m (10ft), S 2m (6ft). Hardy/Z 4–9.

'Graham Thomas'
A vigorous modern shrub or 'English' rose, this is one of the best of its type, combining the flower form of the old roses with a decidedly modern colour – rich orange-yellow – and a long season that lasts from summer to autumn. The rose is named in honour of the great rosarian, Graham Stuart Thomas. H and S 1.2m (4ft). Hardy/Z 4–9.

Rosa 'Frühlingsgold'

Rosa gallica var. officinalis

Rosa 'Gruss an Aachen'

Rosa 'Ingrid Bergman'

Rosa 'Just Joey'

'Gruss an Aachen'

Bred around 1909, this rose is variously described as a floribunda or a polyantha, but it has the air of an old rose. The shapely, deeply cupped, fully double, delicately scented flowers, which are carried in clusters from early summer to autumn, are tinged with pink on opening then fade to creamy white. A long flowering season and low habit of growth make 'Gruss an Aachen' an outstanding bedding rose. H and S 1m (3ft). Hardy/Z 4–9.

'Handel'

A vigorous climber, branching stiffly from the base, this bears double, urn-shaped, only lightly scented flowers from midsummer to autumn. These have cream petals, which are edged with pink, creating an unusual effect. With hard pruning it can be grown as a shrub; in any case its stiff canes make it a reluctant climber. Fan the stems against a wall or spiral them up a pillar. Blackspot may be a problem. H 3m (10ft), S 2.2m (7ft). Hardy/Z 4–9.

'Iceberg'
(syn. 'Fée des Neiges', 'Korbin', 'Schneewittchen')

One of the most successful roses ever produced, this deservedly popular floribunda has retained its place in the catalogues ever since its introduction in 1958. The double, ivory-white, lightly scented flowers open from tapering, pink-flushed buds and are produced in two very distinct flushes, with, unusually, the later, autumn display surpassing the summer one. An outstanding rose of its type, it can be used for bedding, hedging or cutting, but is best, with minimum pruning, as a specimen. H to 1.5m (5ft), S 1m (3ft). Hardy/Z 4–9. The climbing form, 'Climbing Iceberg', is equally valuable in the garden, suited to fences or trees.

'Ingrid Bergman'
(syn. 'Poulman')

This upright, branching hybrid tea bears fully double, only lightly scented, deep red flowers from summer to autumn. Good for cutting, bedding and in containers, this is one of the best roses in its colour range. H 75cm (2ft 6in), spread 60cm (2ft). Hardy/Z 4–9.

'Ispahan'

A compact damask rose, this was first recorded in 1832 but is quite probably much older and is possibly Persian in origin. Large clusters of cupped, loosely double, reflexing, richly scented, pink flowers appear throughout summer. The grey-green foliage is attractive. 'Ispahan' has a longer flowering season than most other damasks and is in bloom for up to six weeks. H 1.2–1.5m (4–5ft), S 1–1.2m (3–4ft). Hardy/Z 4–9.

'Just Joey'

The charm of the individual flowers makes this upright hybrid tea rose worth growing. Opening from long, shapely buds, throughout summer, the flowers are a warm coppery orange-pink with slightly ruffled petals, developing creamy buff tints as they age. Disease-resistance is another virtue. H 75cm (2ft 6in), S 60cm (2ft). Hardy/Z 4–9.

'Königin von Dänemark'
(syn. 'Queen of Denmark', 'Belle Courtisane')

This tall, elegant alba is thought by many to be one of the loveliest of all old roses. The luminous pink, fully double, quartered-rosette and richly scented flowers are borne in summer, and fade to rose-pink as they mature,. It also has one of the longest flowering seasons, up to six weeks, and the flowers have good resistance to wet weather. H to 1.5m (5ft), S 1.2m (4ft). Hardy/Z 4–9.

'Korresia'
(syn. 'Friesia', 'Sunsprite')

A neat, upright floribunda, this bears clusters of shapely buds, opening to fragrant, bright golden-yellow flowers, from summer to autumn. It can be used for bedding and for cut flowers; it is similar to 'Allgold' but has bigger flowers. H 75cm (30in), S 60cm (2ft). Hardy/Z 4–9.

'Laura Ford'

This miniature climber is unusual in that its dainty yellow double flowers are also scented. Borne from summer to autumn, they appear in clusters among small, shiny, dark green leaves. A good choice for a small garden, this rose is also suitable for growing in a container. H to 2.2m (7ft), S 1.2m (4ft). Hardy/Z 4–9.

'Madame Alfred Carrière'

This reliable, free-flowering, climbing rose was introduced

Rosa 'Iceberg'

Rosa 'Ispahan'

Rosa 'Königin von Dänemark'

Rosa 'Korresia'

Rosa 'Madame Hardy'

Rosa 'Madame Isaac Pereire'

in 1879. It bears creamy white, double, cupped, fragrant flowers from summer to autumn on almost thornless stems. Although the flowers are not of individual beauty, its many virtues – length of season, health, tolerance of shade – make this one of the best choices for growing against a house wall. H 5m (16ft), S 3m (10ft). Hardy/Z 5–9.

'Madame Grégoire Staechelin'
(syn. 'Spanish Beauty')
The sight of this vigorous climbing rose in full flower in early summer is unforgettable. The fully double, sweetly scented, warm pink flowers hang in clusters on arching stems. There is no repeat flowering. The large, showy hips redden in autumn, but not reliably. H 6m (20ft), S 4m (13ft). Hardy/Z 4–9.

'Madame Hardy'
An undoubted queen among roses, this damask dates from 1867. The fully double, quartered-rosette, strongly scented, white flowers are borne in profusion in summer, the petals reflexing to reveal a green button eye. It is generally considered to be one of the most sumptuous of old roses, though the flowers may be spoilt by rain. H and S 1.5m (5ft). Hardy/Z 4–9.

'Madame Isaac Pereire'
A bourbon rose, introduced in 1881, this retains its place in the catalogues on account of its strong scent, which is all but unsurpassed in a genus noted for exactly that attribute. The flower colour is also of note: a luminous, deep cerise pink. Produced throughout summer and into autumn, the flowers open as quartered-rosettes but become muddled as they mature, especially those of the first flush. A tendency towards mildew is its only drawback. H 2.5m (8ft), S 2m (6ft), possibly more if grown as a climber. Hardy/Z 4–9.

'Margaret Merril'
(syn. 'Harkuly')
An upright floribunda, this bears clusters of large, shapely, double, sweetly scented, pure white flowers from summer to autumn. In addition to its versatility in the garden, it can also be grown in

containers and is useful as a cut flower. Blackspot can be a problem, but the rose is worth persevering with for its delicious scent. H 1m (3ft), S 60cm (2ft). Hardy/Z 4–9.

'Marguerite Hilling'
(syn. 'Pink Nevada')
A sport of the popular 'Nevada', this shrub rose is similar in all respects apart from the colour of its semi-double flowers, which are pale pink and smother the arching canes in early summer. Healthy and vigorous, it makes an excellent specimen. H and S to 2.2m (7ft). Hardy/Z 4–9.

'Mermaid'
This beautiful climber is vigorous once established, but it can take some years to do this. The flowers are produced spasmodically from midsummer until autumn, with a handful later. The elegant, pointed buds open to reveal single, pale yellow, fragrant saucers with prominent golden stamens that

persist after the petals have dropped. The leaves are glossy and can be evergreen; the stems are viciously thorny. Tolerant of some shade, 'Mermaid' may be cut back by hard frost, so appreciates some shelter. H and S 6m (20ft). Hardy/Z 4–9.

'Mountbatten'
(syn. 'Harmantelle')
The clusters of mimosa yellow flowers are beautifully set off by the glossy dark green leaves on this shrub rose. With minimum pruning this makes an excellent specimen. H to 1.5m (5ft), S to 1m (3ft). Hardy/Z 4–9.

'Mrs Oakley Fisher'
This rather spindly hybrid tea has claims to attention on account of its unusual flowers. Not only are they subtle in colour – soft apricot-yellow flowers fading to pale buff yellow – but they are deliciously fragrant and, unusually for a rose in this group, single. H and S 1m (3ft). Hardy/Z 6–9.

Rosa 'Laura Ford'

Rosa 'Margaret Merril'

Rosa 'Mountbatten'

Rosa 'Orange Sunblaze'

'Nevada'

This vigorous shrub rose, which tolerates some shade, puts on a great show in early summer, when its arching, blackish canes are smothered in semi-double, creamy white flowers; their elusive fragrance seems to hang on the air. A few flowers are occasionally produced later in the season. It is best with light pruning. H and S to 3m (10ft). Hardy/Z 4–9.

'New Dawn'

This vigorous, healthy rambler is valued for its late flowering. From midsummer there is a great profusion of deliciously fragrant, silvery pink, semi-double flowers, which continue until well into autumn. Its thorny stems and occasional stiffness of habit need to be taken into consideration when planting. H and S to 5m (16ft). Hardy/Z 4–9.

'Nozomi'

This was one of the first ground-cover roses to be bred and is still one of the best, producing clusters

of single, only lightly scented, very pale pink to white flowers in midsummer. The trailing stems, which are covered in glossy dark green leaves, will root where they touch the ground. To maintain the creeping habit, cut back upward-growing shoots in winter. It can also be treated as a miniature climber. H 45cm (18in), S to 1.5m (5ft). Hardy/Z 4–9.

R. × *odorata* 'Mutabilis' (syn. *R. chinensis* 'Mutabilis')

A China rose, of uncertain age and parentage, this was evidently grown in China for many years before its introduction to Europe in 1894. The single flowers, produced over a long period from mid-spring to autumn, are unusual: flame orange in bud, they open to coppery yellow then fade to pink, the pink deepening to purple as they age. None too hardy, this rose is best grown in the shelter of a warm wall, where it can reach a height of 3m (10ft) with a spread of 2m (6ft). In the border it can also be trained on a tripod. H 1.2m (4ft), S 1m (3ft). Borderline hardy/Z 7–9.

R. × *odorata* 'Pallida'

Introduced to Europe around 1752 but undoubtedly much older, this China rose has one of the longest flowering seasons of all roses. From summer until the first winter frosts it produces double, cupped, sweetly fragrant, clear pink flowers amid elegant, pointed leaves. None too hardy, in some areas it will need growing against a warm wall to give of its best. It can also be trained as a climber. It is sometimes known as the old blush China rose or Parsons' pink China rose. H 1–3m (3–10ft), S 2m (6ft). Borderline hardy/Z 7–9.

'Orange Sunblaze' (syn. 'Meijikatar', 'Orange Meillandina', 'Sunblaze')

A neat and dainty miniature rose, this bears fully double, only lightly scented, bright vermilion-orange flowers from summer to autumn. It is an excellent choice where space is limited or for a container. H and S 30cm (12in). Hardy/Z 4–9. There is also a

Rosa 'Queen Mother'

climbing form, 'Climbing Orange Sunblaze' (syn. 'Meiji Katarsar'), which produces a dazzling display when grown on a sunny wall.

'Pascali'

This is one of the few pure white hybrid teas (albeit lightly touched with creamy buff). Shapely double, only lightly scented flowers are displayed from early summer into autumn. The rain-resistance of the flowers is unsurpassed in this colour range; they are also exceptionally long-lasting when cut. H 1m (3ft), S 75cm (2ft

6in). Hardy/Z 4–9. **'Climbing Pascali'**, a climbing form, shares the same qualities.

'Peace' (syn. 'Gioia', 'Gloria Dei', 'Madame A. Meilland')

One of the most popular hybrid teas ever produced, this rose is surely worthy of revival. The large, fully double, only lightly scented flowers are pale yellow with pink flushes, and they appear from midsummer to autumn. Its present lack of popularity is due to its supposed coarseness – that

Rosa 'Pascali'

Rosa 'Peace'

Rosa 'Président de Sèze'

Rosa 'Roseraie de l'Haÿ'

is, it is a vigorous, spreading, bushy rose that makes a fine specimen with light pruning. H 1.5m (5ft), S 1m (3ft). Hardy/Z 4–9.

'Président de Sèze'
Richly scented, large, quartered flowers appear on this sturdy gallica rose in summer. The centre petals are rich magenta-purple, the colour fading across the flower to soft lilac-pink, almost white, at the edges. The leaves are larger than is usual for a gallica rose. A well-grown specimen is a stunning sight when in full bloom. H 1.2m (4ft), S 1m (3ft). Hardy/Z 4–9.

'Queen Mother'
(syn. 'Korquemu')
This spreading patio rose deserves its popularity. The dainty buds open to semi-double, clear pink flowers from summer to autumn. It does well in a container and is sometimes available as a weeping standard. H 45cm (18in), S 60cm (2ft). Hardy/Z 4–9.

Rosa 'Royal William'

'Rambling Rector'
A vigorous rambling rose, this is covered with clusters of small, semi-double, fragrant, white flowers in summer. Small red hips follow in autumn. It is suitable for growing into a large tree, and a mature rose in full flower is an impressive sight, but it is not a rose suited to every garden. H and S 6m (20ft). Hardy/Z 5–9.

'Roseraie de l'Haÿ'
Despite its reluctance to produce the characteristic autumn hips, this is one of the best of the rugosa roses. Its value rests on its strongly scented, velvety, wine-red flowers, which open to reveal creamy stamens. The blooms are produced in abundance from summer to autumn. The wrinkled leaves redden in autumn. Dense and spreading, 'Roseraie de l'Haÿ' makes an excellent hedge and can also be planted in light woodland. H 2m (6ft), S 1.2m (4ft). Hardy/Z 4–9.

'Royal William'
(syn. 'Duftzauber '84', 'Fragrant Charm '84', 'Korzaun')
An upright hybrid tea, this rose is valued for its succession of large, fully double, fragrant, deep crimson flowers. The graceful blooms are carried on long stems from summer to autumn. This rose is excellent planted en masse for a stunning effect, or it can be grown to provide flowers for cutting. H 1m (3ft), S 75cm (2ft 6in). Hardy/Z 4–9.

'Savoy Hotel'
(syn. 'Harvintage', 'Integrity')
This bushy hybrid tea has strong stems that carry large, shapely, fully double, fragrant, light clear pink flowers from summer to autumn and with good repeat-flowering. It is a versatile rose, which provides excellent material for cutting, as long as you keep it well fed. H 1m (3ft), S 60cm (2ft). Hardy/Z 4–8.

'Schneezwerg'
(syn. 'Snow Dwarf')
A rugosa rose introduced in 1912, this has a dense, spreading habit. The anemone-like, semi-double, white flowers open flat to

Rosa 'Savoy Hotel'

reveal golden stamens. They are followed by small, orange-red, tomato-shaped hips. Although its flowers are unremarkable, this rose is perhaps at its best in autumn; the foliage does not change colour, but the flowers continue to appear alongside the reddening hips. In order to get the best of both worlds, therefore, deadhead selectively in summer. H 1.2m (4ft), S 1.5m (5ft). Hardy/Z 3–9.

'Sexy Rexy'
(syn. 'Heckenzauber', 'Macrexy')
This is an outstanding floribunda, of upright habit. It produces clusters of shapely, fully double, palest coral-pink flowers throughout summer and autumn. These are shown off by plentiful

Rosa 'Schneezwerg'

dark, glossy leaves. It is a versatile rose good for general garden use, growing in containers and for providing cut flowers. H and S 60cm (2ft). Hardy/Z 4–9.

'Sombreuil'
A distinctive and unusual rose, this is generally classified as a climbing tea, although it is not particularly vigorous, nor are its flowers tea-like, lacking a high centre. Borne from summer to autumn, the sweetly scented blooms are flat, quartered rosettes, creamy white in colour and acquiring pink tinges as they age. Wet weather will ruin them. H and S to 2.4m (8ft) when grown as a climber with support, but smaller if allowed to grow as a lax shrub. Hardy/Z 5–9.

Rosa 'Sexy Rexy'

Rosa 'Stanwell Perpetual'

Rosa 'The Queen Elizabeth'

'Southampton'
(syn. 'Susan Ann')
This is an excellent floribunda, with an upright, branching habit and shiny, dark green leaves. Clusters of large, double, soft apricot-orange flowers, which are flushed with scarlet, are carried from early summer into autumn; the petals are wavy-edged. The scent is not especially strong. H 1m (3ft), S 60cm (2ft). Hardy/Z 4–9.

'Souvenir de la Malmaison'
This beautiful, dense, spreading bourbon rose, produced in 1843, commemorates the famous garden created by Empress Josephine at Malmaison, although it is not clear whether it was actually grown there. Repeat-flowering throughout the summer, it bears very fragrant, fully double, soft pink flowers, which open to a quartered-rosette shape as they fade to blush-white. One major drawback is that the silk-textured flowers may be spoilt by wet weather. H and S 1.5m (5ft). Hardy/Z 4–9.

'Stanwell Perpetual'
This Scotch rose, raised in 1838, forms a dense, prickly shrub. The double, sweetly scented, attractive blush pink to white flowers open flat and are produced almost continuously throughout summer among the grey-green leaves. Tolerant of poor soil and some shade, this rose is ideal for growing in light woodland; it also makes a good hedge. H and S 1.5m (5ft). Hardy/Z 5–9.

'Sweet Dream'
(syn. 'Fryminicot')
One of the best of the patio roses, this produces an abundance of fully double, lightly scented, soft apricot-orange flowers from midsummer to autumn. It is usually well covered with glossy, healthy foliage. A good edging plant, 'Sweet Dream' is also suitable for growing in a container. H 40cm (16in), S 35cm (14in). Hardy/Z 4–9.

'Tango'
(syn. 'Macfirwal', 'Rock 'n' Roll', 'Stretch Johnson')
This upright floribunda is chiefly of interest to flower arrangers. From summer to autumn it produces clusters of semi-double flowers of some distinction: the petals, frilled at the edges, are orange-red with white rims, yellow at the base and on the reverse. H 75cm (2ft 6in), spread 60cm (2ft). Hardy/Z 4–8.

'The Fairy'
A dainty floribunda or polyantha, this has a dense, mounding habit and is well worth considering if you are planning an autumn border. It flowers later than almost any other rose, the clusters of small, double, light pink flowers appearing only from midsummer, but then continuing in profusion until the onset of winter. H and S 60cm (2ft). Hardy/Z 4–9.

'The Queen Elizabeth'
(syn. 'Queen Elizabeth', 'The Queen Elizabeth Rose')
This is one of the best of all the floribundas, but not especially characteristic of the group. Its vigour and strongly vertical habit really make it unsuitable for most of the purposes for which the floribundas were developed. It is best used at the back of a border or as a tall, informal hedge. Its fully double, china pink flowers, which are freely carried from summer to autumn, last well when cut. H 2.2m (7ft), S 1m (3ft); with minimal pruning it will easily top 3m (10ft). Hardy/Z 4–9. The climbing form, 'Climbing the Queen Elizabeth', is also well worth growing.

'Troika'
(syn. 'Royal Dane')
An outstanding hybrid tea, this has an upright, branching habit. The display of large, shapely, double, lightly scented, copper-orange flowers, sometimes veined scarlet, continues throughout summer and into autumn. Disease- and weather-resistant, this is a good choice for a massed planting and also provides good cut flowers. H 1m (3ft), S 75cm (2ft 6in). Hardy/Z 4–9.

'Tuscany Superb'
(syn. 'Double Velvet')
This erect gallica rose was raised before 1837. The large, semi-double, lightly scented, deep crimson flowers are produced in midsummer. They open flat, showing golden stamens, then fade to purple. Tolerant of poor

Rosa 'Souvenir de la Malmaison'

Rosa 'Sweet Dream'

Rosa 'The Fairy'

Rosa 'Tuscany Superb'

Rosa 'Veilchenblau'

Rosa 'Whisky Mac'

Rosa 'William Lobb'

soil, this is one of the few old roses that is suitable for hedging. It is not too thorny. H 1.5m (5ft), S 1m (3ft). Hardy/Z 4–9.

'Veilchenblau'
(syn. 'Blue Rambler',
'Violet Blue')
A vigorous rambling rose, this was introduced in 1909. In midsummer it bears clusters of sweetly scented, semi-double, violet-pink flowers with yellow stamens; the flowers fade to an unusual purplish grey as they mature. The leaves are glossy and light green. More modest than most ramblers, this rose is suitable for a small garden and is best grown with some shelter from the midday sun. H and S 4m (13ft). Hardy/Z 4–9.

'Whisky Mac'
(syn. 'Tanky', 'Whisky')
This famous hybrid tea has retained its popularity despite its propensity to die-back and fungal diseases. Its appeal lies in the unusual colouring of its sumptuous double flowers, which are a rich golden-orange of unrivalled intensity, and with a fragrance to match. Since it needs almost constant attention, this is really a plant for dedicated rose-growers only. H 75cm (2ft 6in), S 60cm (2ft). Hardy/Z 4–9.

'White Bells'
A dense, spreading groundcover rose, this bears a single, but abundant, crop of small, fully double, white flowers in summer. It is shade-tolerant, and thus useful for difficult areas of the

garden, but overall perhaps not as good as some other groundcover roses. H 60cm (2ft), S 1.2m (4ft). Hardy/Z 5–9.

'White Cockade'
This is one of the few white climbing roses. The perfectly shaped, fully double flowers appear almost continuously from summer to autumn, and the absence of a strong scent in no way detracts from its overall merit. Slow-growing, it is a good choice for growing in a container or on a short pillar. H 2.2m (7ft), S 1.5m (5ft). Hardy/Z 4–9.

'White Grootendorst'
A vigorous rugosa rose, with a dense, spreading habit, this produces clusters of small, double, scentless, white flowers, particularly notable for the frilly edges of the petals, which look like carnations. Like most of the rugosas, it tolerates some shade and poor soil, making it ideal for a wild garden. H 1.2m (4ft), S 1m (3ft). Hardy/Z 3–8.

'William Lobb'
(syn. 'Duchesse d'Istrie')
This rather sprawling moss rose is worth growing for its sumptuous rosette flowers. Richly scented, they open magenta-purple in midsummer from heavily mossed buds, then pass through a remarkable range of tones before fading to a subtle violet-grey. The ungainly habit makes it unsuitable as a specimen. Instead, try it wrapped around a tripod or as a short climber on a pillar or against a wall. H and S 2m (6ft). Hardy/Z 4–9.

***R. xanthina* 'Canary Bird'**
This wild rose is usually one of the first to flower in the garden, offering a burst of welcome colour in late spring. The single, cupped, scented, canary yellow flowers have prominent stamens. In a good year there will be a second, though lesser, flush of flowers in autumn. It makes an attractive arching shrub, although it is sometimes available as a grafted standard, when it makes a fine specimen. H and S 2.2m (7ft). Hardy/Z 5–9.

'Yellow Doll'
This spreading miniature rose has double, slightly scented, bright yellow flowers, which are produced singly or in clusters from summer to autumn. Rather unusually for a miniature, it is good for cutting; it can also be forced under glass for early weather conditions. H and S to 30cm (12in). Hardy/Z 3–8.

'Yesterday'
(syn. 'Tapis d'Orient')
A floribunda or polyantha rose, this has an elegant, open, spreading habit and a long flowering season, from summer to autumn. The clusters of semi-

double, fragrant, deep lilac-pink flowers open flat to reveal paler centres and golden stamens. It is good for cutting and, given lighter pruning than usual, makes an attractive specimen. H and S 1m (3ft). Hardy/Z 4–9.

'Zéphirine Drouhin'
This climbing rose is notable for its thornless stems, making it a good choice for an archway or pergola or for framing a doorway. In summer and autumn it produces clusters of double, cupped to flat, fragrant, magenta flowers. It can be prone to mildew. H 3m (10ft), S 2m (6ft). Hardy/Z 4–9. **'Kathleen Harrop'** is a pale pink sport.

Rosa 'Yesterday'

Bulbs

Few groups of plants provide the gardener with such a range of brilliant colours as the bulbs, and nearly all are easy to grow. There is scarcely a moment in the year when they do not make a contribution, from the diminutive harbingers of spring that brighten up the garden from late winter, the bold tulips and daffodils that epitomize spring, to the exotic, slightly tender dahlias and gladioli that carry on the interest into autumn, with a host of others in between. Hyacinths and hippeastrums can be forced to flower in the dead of winter indoors, ensuring that you need never be without flowers.

Easy and reliable, these alliums raise their heads of almost geometric precision above the lower-growing perennials.

Bulbs for your garden

Bulbs are perennials that have evolved a specialized mechanism, which allows them to survive periods of extreme heat or extreme cold, sometimes both. Essentially, a bulb is an energy store that enables the plant to return to a state of dormancy at times when conditions are unfavourable for growth. The bulb itself is an underground structure that is made up of scales fixed to a basal plate. The scales – actually modified leaves – surround a small piece of stem tissue, which produces a large bud near the centre of the bulb. In some cases, for instance daffodils (*Narcissus*) and tulips (*Tulipa*), the scales are tightly packed and are encased in a papery outer covering (the tunic). Lilies (*Lilium*), however, have fleshy, rather open scales. Roots grow from the bottom of the basal plate.

During the growing season, the plant builds a food supply through its leaves. As the winter or dry season approaches, the exposed parts of the plant die, but the bulb with its stored food remains alive underground. At the beginning of the next growing season, the bulb's central bud sends out a shoot, which produces a stem, leaves and flowers above the ground. Food stored in the bulb fuels the young shoot's rapid growth.

Typically (though not invariably) a bulb reproduces itself vegetatively by producing a number of bulblets around the basal plate. Eventually these split from the parent bulb, which then dies.

Corms and tubers are usually considered alongside bulbs, since their growth patterns are similar, and they have comparable garden uses. A corm is a modified stem with a bud on top, which produces shoots. After flowering, a new corm, formed at the

A wonderful matching display of spring-flowering tulips rising above lower-growing annual pansies in similar shades.

Here, tulips are used more informally and interplanted with bedding wallflowers to edge a path.

base of the old stem, grows on top of the old corm, which then dies. Smaller corms also develop around the base of the old corm. Gladioli, crocosmias and crocuses are corms.

Tubers are thickened fleshy roots or stems. They can be covered with scaly leaves or with fibrous roots. Growth buds develop on the top of the tuber, which gets larger with age and can persist for several years. Dahlias, begonias and cyclamen are good examples.

In the discussion to follow, all bulbs, corms and tubers are loosely referred to as bulbs.

Bulbs in the garden

Being mostly trouble-free and easy to grow, bulbs are essential garden plants. They are excellent for creating short bursts of colour, whether as a massed planting in beds or woodland, in drifts in grass, combined with other border plants or in containers.

In the dictionary section that follows, spreads are not given for those bulbs that have only a single growing point, for instance lilies and daffodils.

Nearly all bulbs need well-drained soil, either in full sun or light shade. None is adapted to deep shade. Bulbs from hot countries such as South Africa – this group includes many of the summer- and autumn-flowering bulbs – need baking conditions if the bulb is to survive and flower from year to year. At the foot of a wall that faces the midday or afternoon sun is often ideal. Woodland bulbs thrive in fertile, leafy soil, ideally in the dappled shade cast by deciduous trees.

Early bulbs are the delight of the spring garden, providing vivid colour before the perennials have begun to wake up. They are ideal additions to any mixed border. In a fairly informal, cottage-style planting, taller bulbs such as tulips, alliums and lilies can be planted to rise above lower-growing perennials. Bulbs can also be used more formally: tulips and hyacinths that grow to a uniform height are often effective where planted in blocks. The hyacinths have the advantage of an inimitable scent. Many of the later-flowering bulbs, such as dahlias and cannas, that are on the tender side, are best treated as bedding plants in colder areas, and these work well with annuals and other late-flowering tender perennials to bring the gardening season to a close with a blaze of colour.

Spring bulbs are excellent for naturalizing, a gardening principle that allows plants to build up colonies. Drifts of anemones in woodland are a breathtaking sight in spring, but many more are suitable for growing in more open situations in grass: a lawn studded with dwarf bulbs is a delight. It is important to choose robust selections that can compete with the grass, however, or the effect will be short-lived. *Crocus tommasinianus* is very useful for early flowers, and most of the so-called chrysanthus hybrids will be able to hold their own. Many of the daffodils can also be used. However, if the bulbs are to persist from year to year, they must be allowed to complete their growth cycle and die down completely before you mow the lawn, so early-flowering varieties are usually the ones recommended for this purpose. It is perfectly possible to use later-flowering types and mow around the clumps, but the grass will grow tall amid the clumps, resulting in a less tailored look. Snake's head fritillaries (*Fritillaria meleagris*) are excellent in a meadow garden where the ground is reliably moist, but here you do have to let the grass grow under your feet, as they are relatively late flowering. In a woodland garden, consider camassias, erythroniums and some of the lilies. Cyclamen are particularly valued, not only for their late season and ease of cultivation but also because they will thrive in the dry ground beneath deciduous trees and shrubs, a situation inhospitable to most other plants.

Although none is a true alpine, dwarf bulbs are excellent in the rock garden, relishing the superior drainage and the reflected heat from the rocks. Several of the species crocuses and tulips can be grown in this way, and look charming pushing through creeping or cushion plants, but again you have to be careful to match their vigour if one is not to put paid to the other.

Nearly all bulbs thrive in containers, especially those that benefit from a summer roasting. For the best effect, pack the bulbs in tightly. Include a few trailing ivies at the edge and a few bedding plants to cover the surface of the container for the best display.

Dahlias, such as this richly orange variety 'David Howard', are an ideal choice for bringing the summer to a colourful end.

Achimenes 'Prima Donna'

ACHIMENES
Hot water plant, cupid's bower
These tender plants are usually grown as houseplants. Nearly all plants sold commercially are hybrids, and they have short, trumpet-shaped flowers in shades of blue, peach, pink, red and orange and shiny, velvety leaves. The common name is misleading. When they are in growth the plants should be watered with barely tepid water, never hot water, which would kill them. The lax stems make them an excellent choice for hanging baskets. After they have died down the stunning bulbs, which look like miniature white pine cones, should be dried and stored over winter.
Cultivation These plants do best in containers in a light place but out of direct sun. Water them freely when in growth but keep them dry in winter at a temperature of 10°C (50°F).

A. hybrids
Hot water plants flower over a long period from early summer to autumn. There are many named varieties, including **'Blue Gown'**, which has blue flowers; **'Harry Williams'**, which has red flowers; **'Prima Donna'**, which has pink flowers; and **'Snow Princess'** with white flowers. H and S 30cm (12in) or more. Tender/Z 10.

ALLIUM
Ornamental onion
Only a few species of this large and important genus are grown in the flower garden. Some have the distinctive pungent, onion smell,

making them unsuitable for mass plantings. They combine well with old roses, and some, if grown in large quantities, will protect against aphids and fungal disease. Their bold, spherical heads of flowers make a strong statement, and they are the perfect foil for more flamboyant flowers. They look good dotted among lower growing perennials such as geraniums. The seedheads (which can be dried for winter decoration) are almost as attractive as the flowerheads. Small species can also be grown in rock gardens.
Cultivation Any well-drained soil in a sunny spot is suitable for alliums, although they will also tolerate semi-shade. Dead-head to prevent self-seeding.

A. cristophii
(syn. A. albopilosum, A. christophii)
Star of Persia
This species, originally from Turkey, has large flowerheads, up to 20cm (8in) across, of silver-purple, star-like flowers in late spring to early summer. These are attractive even after the flowers have faded. H 60cm (2ft), S 18cm (7in). Borderline hardy/Z 7–10.

A. giganteum
Giant onion
One of the tallest alliums, this dramatic plant, which is native to central Asia, has large purple flowerheads, up to 20cm (8in) across, carried at the top of the erect stems in late spring to early

Amaryllis belladonna

summer. H to 170cm (70in), S 15cm (6in). Hardy/Z 6–10.

A. hollandicum
(syn. A. aflatunense of gardens)
The species is native to central Asia. It bears globular heads, to 10cm (4in) across, of lilac-purple flowers from mid- to late spring. The blue-green leaves are also attractive. Plant in groups for the best display. H 1.2m (4ft), S 10cm (4in). **'Purple Sensation'** is a selection with deep purple flowers. H 1m (3ft), S 10cm (4in). Hardy/Z 4–10.

A. karataviense
This low-growing species from central Asia works well in containers as well as near the front a mixed border. It would be worth growing for its leaves alone, which are pewter-grey edged with maroon. The dull lilac-pink

flowers – interesting rather than beautiful – appear in late spring to early summer. H to 25cm (10in), S 10cm (4in). Hardy/Z 4–9.

A. moly
Golden garlic, lily leek
A species from southern Europe, suitable for a rock garden. It bears a profusion of yellow flowers in late spring to early summer. The grey-green leaves remain attractive over a long period. It is good for naturalizing in light shade and reliably damp soil. H to 30cm (12in), S 5cm (2in). Hardy/Z 3–9.

A. roseum
Rosy garlic
One of the most appealing alliums, the species is native to southern Europe and northern Africa. It has loose heads of scented pink flowers borne on sturdy stems in late spring to early summer. H 60cm (2ft), S 5cm (2in). Hardy/Z 8.

A. sphaerocephalon
Round-headed leek
A good allium for a massed planting, this species, native to Europe, northern Africa and western Asia, bears almost pear-shaped heads of reddish-purple flowers in late spring and early summer. It combines especially well with hostas, *Alchemilla mollis* and ornamental grasses. H 1m (3ft), S 8cm (3in). Hardy/Z 6–10.

Allium karataviense

Allium moly

Allium roseum

Anemone blanda

AMARYLLIS

There is only one species in this South African genus, which is related to *Hippeastrum* and is usually sold as 'amaryllis'. The true amaryllis can be a star of the autumn garden, with its trumpet-like flowers, which are rather small in relation to the size of the overall plant. They look best grown in isolation, revelling in the comfort of a sheltered spot at the base of a warm wall, with nothing to compete with their beauty.
Cultivation Full sun is essential for these plants, which should be grown in a sheltered spot in fertile, well-drained soil. Plant with the neck of the bulb just above soil level. The flower stems may need staking. In cold areas, cover with a dry mulch of straw or similar material in winter.

A. belladonna
Belladonna lily, Jersey lily
The leaves appear in spring, then die down in early summer. About two months later stems appear, carrying fragrant, bright pink, trumpet-like flowers. H 75cm (30in), S 10cm (4in). Borderline hardy/Z 7–10.

ANEMONE
Windflower
The genus contains both spring-flowering corms as well as some valuable autumn perennials. A major claim to distinction is that the corms include some with red flowers, a colour in short supply in the garden until the tulips make their mark.
Cultivation Different species have different light requirements, but any soil type is acceptable, as long as it is well drained. *A. apennina* prefers dappled shade, ideally beneath deciduous trees. *A. blanda* prefers full sun, but will also grow (although it will flower less freely) in light shade. *A. coronaria* needs sun.

A. apennina
Blue anemone
This species from southern Europe bears starry blue flowers, sometimes tinged with pink, in early spring. H 15cm (6in), S 30cm (12in). Hardy/Z 6–9.

A. blanda
One of the most worthwhile species, this plant is found in south-eastern Europe. It has daisy-like flowers in white or shades of pink, blue and mauve in mid-spring. It is an excellent choice for carpeting large areas under deciduous trees. H and S 15cm (6in). Selections include 'Blue Shades', which has light to dark blue flowers; 'Pink Star', which has pink flowers; 'Radar', with deep mauve-pink flowers, shading to white towards the centre; and 'White Splendour', which has white flowers.

A. coronaria
This species, seldom grown in its typical form, has two main hybrid groups, De Caen (with single flowers) and St Brigid (with double flowers). They flower from late spring to late summer, depending on when they were planted. They are often sold in mixtures, but there are also several selected forms, including 'Die Braut' (syn. 'The Bride'; De Caen Group), which has green-centred, white flowers; 'Hollandia' (syn. 'His Excellency'; De Caen Group), which has white-centred, red flowers; 'Lord Lieutenant' (St Brigid Group), which has dark blue flowers; 'Mister Fokker' (De Caen Group), which has violet-blue flowers; 'Mount Everest' (St Brigid Group), which has white flowers; 'The Admiral' (St Brigid Group), which has purple-pink flowers; and 'The Governor' (De Caen Group), which has red flowers. H 30–40cm (12–15in), S 15cm (6in). Hardy/Z 8–10.

A. nemorosa
Wood anemone
A graceful plant, which is native to Europe, this is ideal for naturalizing beneath shrubs and trees, where it benefits from the shade. The white, cup-shaped flowers are borne in spring. H 15cm (6in), S 20cm (8in). Hardy/Z 4–8.

ARUM
Lords and ladies, cuckoo pint
These tuberous perennials are quiet but handsome plants for a woodland garden. Lords and ladies is a common hedgerow plant in northern Europe; the plant described is a treasured garden form. It has two seasons of interest: the leaves emerge in late autumn and are at their best by late winter, when they make a splendid foil for snowdrops. The plant then dies down to ground level, but spikes of juicy-looking (but poisonous) red berries appear in late summer.
Cultivation Arums will grow in any, preferably fairly moisture-retentive soil in partial shade.

A. italicum
As its name suggests, this is an Italian species, but it also found elsewhere in the Mediterranean. The dark green leaves have white veins. A greenish-white spathe encloses the spike of orange-red berries. H 40cm (16in), S 20cm (8in). The leaves of **A. italicum** subsp. *italicum* **'Marmoratum'** (syn. 'Pictum') are beautifully marbled with cream and pink, appearing in autumn and lasting through the winter, dying back the following spring. Spikes of poisonous orange-red berries poke through the soil in autumn. Although frost flattens the leaves, they do stand up again as they thaw. It combines well with snowdrops. H to 45cm (18in), S 20cm (8in). Hardy/Z 7–9.

Anemone coronaria 'Die Braut'

Anemone nemorosa

Arum italicum subs. italicum 'Marmoratum'

Begonia × tuberhybrida 'Illumination Orange'

BEGONIA

This large genus contains about 900 species, including several annuals and a range of perennials that are usually grown as foliage houseplants. None of these plants are hardy, so in frost-prone climates they need to be lifted for overwintering or treated as annuals. Dwarf varieties make excellent bedding material for colour borders and are equally good in containers. Pendulous varieties are ideal subjects for a hanging basket. Some hybrid begonias have huge flowers and have been bred for enthusiasts. These, omitted here, must be grown in containers in controlled conditions under glass in order to give of their best.

Cultivation Tuberous begonias do best in a neutral soil or compost

Begonia × tuberhybrida 'Giant Flowered Pendula Yellow'

(soil mix) in light shade. Plants grown in containers should be lifted after the topgrowth has died back and stored dry in a frost-free place over winter. To coax them out of dormancy the following spring, repot the tubers into fresh compost, water and keep at a temperature of 16–18°C (61–64°F).

B. sutherlandii

This elegant, spreading species from South Africa is an ideal subject for a hanging basket and is perhaps best grown on its own with no competition from other plants. Its clear orange flowers are produced in succession throughout the summer. H 15–30cm (6–12in), S 30cm (12in). Half-hardy/Z 10.

B. × tuberhybrida

This vast hybrid group encompasses a range of different types and cultivars. They can be broadly divided into the Multiflora group (which are suitable for summer bedding) and the Pendula group (which have trailing stems and are suitable for hanging baskets). All are tender/Z 10. Flowers of the **Cascade Series** (Pendula) can be orange, pink, red or yellow. H and S to 30cm (12in). **'Giant Flowered Pendula Yellow'** (Pendula) has double yellow flowers. H and S to 20cm (8in). **'Helene Harms'** (Multiflora) has double yellow flowers. H and S to 45cm (18in). Flowers of the **Illumination Series** (Pendula) are pink or orange, **'Illumination Orange'** being a selected form. H 60cm (2ft), S 30cm (1ft). **'Madame Richard Galle'** (Multiflora) has double copper flowers. H and S 45cm (18in). Plants of the **Non Stop Series** (Multiflora) have double flowers in shades of orange, apricot, pink, yellow and red, and have a slightly more extended flowering period than the others. H and S 20cm (8in).

CAMASSIA
Quamash

This North American genus has not crossed the Atlantic very successfully, probably because it flowers at around the same time

Camassia leichtlinii

as bluebells, which most British gardeners seem to prefer. While nothing can match the blue of an English bluebell, camassias have a comparable distinction and should be more widely grown. They are best in drifts in light woodland or, as a prairie plant, in grass, but they can also be grown in borders.

Cultivation Any reliably moist garden soil is suitable, but these plants prefer humus-rich soil in sun that is not waterlogged in winter. They tolerate dappled shade but may flower less freely.

C. cusickii

This species flowers in late spring, its spikes of blue flowers combining well with *Dicentra spectabilis*. H 60–80cm (24–32in), S 10cm (4in). Borderline hardy/Z 3–8.

C. leichtlinii

This quamash readily forms compact groups. The star-like greyish-white or bluish purple flowers appear in late spring in tapering spikes. H 1m (3ft), S 10cm (4in). Borderline hardy/ Z 5–9. Among selected forms are **'Alba'**, which has white flowers, and plants in the **Caerulea Group**, with flowers in shades of blue.

CANNA
Indian shot plant, Indian reed flower

These are exotic plants for the autumn garden. Even if they did not flower, they would be worth

Canna 'President'

growing for their large, smooth leaves, which often have a bronze cast. Use them with grasses, brilliant annuals and dahlias to bring the season to a close with a flourish. They are also excellent in large containers.

Cultivation Grow cannas in fertile soil in full sun. In cold climates cannas need to be bedded out. Bring the rhizomes into growth in containers in late winter or early spring and keep them in a frost-free greenhouse or conservatory. When there is no further risk of frost plant them out just deep enough to cover with soil. In autumn, cut back the topgrowth, dig up the rhizomes and store them dry in a frost-free place over winter.

C. hybrids

The cannas grown in gardens are hybrids, of which there are many. All the following have green leaves unless otherwise indicated. All are half-hardy/Z 7–10. **'Black Knight'** has dark red flowers and bronze leaves. H 1.8m (6ft), S 50cm (20in). **'City of Portland'** has yellow-edged, rose pink flowers. H 1m (3ft), S 50cm (20in). **'Ingeborg'** has salmon pink flowers and bronze leaves. H 60cm (2ft), S 50cm (20in). The free-flowering **'Lucifer'** has yellow-edged crimson flowers. H 60cm (2ft), S 50cm (20in). **'Orchid'** has pink flowers. H 60cm (2ft), S 50cm (20in). **'President'** has bright red flowers. H 1m (3ft), S 50cm (20in). The

Canna 'Roi Humbert'

flowers of **'Primrose Yellow'** are pale yellow. H 60cm (2ft), S 50cm (20in). **'Richard Wallace'** has canary yellow flowers. H 80cm (32in), S 50cm (20in). **'Roi Humbert'** has orange-red flowers and bronze leaves. H 80cm (32in), S 50cm (20in). **'Rosemond Coles'** has yellow-edged, bright red flowers. H 1.5m (5ft), S 50cm (20in). The orange flowers of **'Wyoming'** are frilled and have darker orange edges; the leaves are bronze. H 1.8m (6ft), S 50cm (20in).

CARDIOCRINUM
Giant lily
The name giant lily is well deserved from the point of view of the flowers, which certainly are lily-like, but the plant itself is unlike any lily, having rounded

Cardiocrinum giganteum

leaves and a pyramidal habit. They are not plants for the average garden. They need to stand in splendid isolation, or in small groups, in woodland clearings, where their scale and majesty can be best appreciated. Patience is needed: they take up to seven years to reach flowering size, when they die off, leaving seedlings behind. For a regular display you need to build up a colony of various ages.
Cultivation Cardiocrinums need fertile soil (ideally enriched with leaf mould) in light, dappled shade.

C. giganteum
This imposing plant produces stout stalks clothed with immense leaves that are smaller towards the top, giving a narrowly pyramidal outline. The trumpet-shaped summer flowers are greenish-white with maroon red throats. H to 3m (10ft), S 1m (3ft). Hardy/Z 7–9.

CHIONODOXA
Glory of the snow
This small genus provides some delightful plants for early spring, typically with starry blue flowers. Grow them in a rock garden or in a border, or under deciduous trees and shrubs.
Cultivation Chionodoxas will grow in any but waterlogged soil in sun or light shade.

C. forbesii
(syn. C. luciliae of gardens)
The lavender-blue flowers, with white centres, appear in early spring – sometimes earlier, after a

Chionodoxa forbesii 'Pink Giant'

Colchicum 'The Giant'

mild winter. It is an excellent subject for naturalizing. H 15cm (6in), S 3cm (1in). Hardy/Z 3–9. There are several cultivars, including **'Alba'**, which has white flowers; and **'Pink Giant'**, which has slightly larger white-centred, pink flowers.

C. sardensis
This species is dwarfer than *C. forbesii*, but the deep blue flowers are more numerous. H 10cm (4in), S 4cm (1½in). Hardy/Z 5–9.

COLCHICUM
Autumn crocus, naked ladies
The flowers of colchicums are always a surprise when they appear in autumn – it is easy to forget that the corms are in the garden. The leaves, large and glossy, do not appear until the following spring (the best time to transplant them, if this is necessary). They are excellent in light woodland or planted around shrubs. In borders the leaves can be a nuisance in spring. Robust types are also excellent for naturalizing in grass.
Cultivation Grow in any good garden soil, ideally in light shade.

C. speciosum
This, the most widely grown member of the genus, produces

goblet-shaped, pink flowers in early autumn. H 25cm (10in), S 10cm (4in). Hardy/Z 4–9. **'Album'** has pure white flowers that are green at the base.

C. 'The Giant'
This is one of many hybrids, with the typical large, lilac-pink flowers. H to 20cm (8in), S 10cm (4in). Hardy/Z 4–9.

C. 'Waterlily'
This is a popular double form, with pinkish-purple flowers that, unfortunately, are not very weather-resistant. H 12cm (5in), S 10cm (4in). Hardy/Z 4–9.

Colchicum speciosum 'Album'

Crinum × powellii 'Album'

CRINUM
Swamp lily

This South African genus is similar to *Amaryllis*, and the plants enjoy similar conditions. In cold gardens, crinums need the hottest spot available, which will usually be at the base of a warm wall. They are best in splendid isolation, when the handsome, strap-shaped leaves and impressive trumpet-like flowers can be seen to advantage. Crinums take some years to adapt after planting, and by the time they are ready to flower, the bulbs will be almost as big as footballs. Left undisturbed, the display will improve year on year. They also do well in containers.
Cultivation Plant in fertile, humus-rich soil in full sun, with shelter from wind. In cold areas a dry mulch of straw in winter can help to protect the dormant bulbs from frost.

C. × powellii
This hybrid (of *C. bulbispermum* and *C. moorei*) is the plant most frequently offered for sale. In late summer to early autumn

Crocosmia 'Lucifer'

(sometimes earlier in favourable climates), it produces robust stems, topped with trumpet-like, pink flowers. H 1.2m (4ft), S 60cm (2ft). Borderline hardy/Z 7–10. **'Album'**, a distinguished selection, has white flowers. H 1m (3ft), S 60cm (2ft).

CROCOSMIA
Montbretia

This South African genus was not highly rated until Alan Bloom and others began to develop a range of hybrids, all with larger flowers than the plants previously seen in gardens, the most impressive of which, 'Lucifer', is an essential addition in any planting scheme. Excellent as they are as border plants, combining well with roses and annuals, they also look effective when grown in isolation in large groups, almost as a specimen.
Cultivation Crocosmias are tolerant of most garden soils in sun or light shade, but avoid sites that are too hot and dry.

C. × crocosmiiflora
The hybrid group includes many garden-worthy forms. **'Emily McKenzie'** has orange flowers with brown throats from midsummer to autumn. H 45cm (18in), S 8cm (3in). Also flowering from midsummer to autumn, **'Solfatare'**, which is sometimes sold as *C.* 'Solfaterre', produces a succession of apricot-yellow flowers among its grassy, bronze-tinged leaves. H 60cm (2ft), S 8cm (3in).

C. 'Lucifer'
This superb plant produces brilliant tomato red flowers in late summer and pleated, fan-shaped leaves. H 1.2m (4ft), S 8cm (3in). Borderline hardy/ Z 7–9.

CROCUS
Essential as they are in the spring garden, it is worth remembering that this large genus also includes some autumn-flowering forms – although confusingly colchicums are often sold under the common name 'autumn crocus'. Their bowl-shaped flowers are distinctive, as are their narrow,

Crocus chrysanthus 'Blue Pearl'

striped leaves. Almost every flower colour but pink is available, and some are attractively striped. A few have stamens in a contrasting colour. Robust hybrids are splendid for naturalizing in lawns, and can create a stunning effect, either in the traditional mixture of colours, or with a more subtle selection of just one or two shades. They can also be grown in shallow pans, bowls and alpine troughs, which is perhaps the best way of displaying some of the more choice and delicate species. Established bulbs tend to flower earlier than new plantings.
Cultivation Grow the larger species and hybrids in a position in full sun in any garden soil (as long as it is not waterlogged). If crocuses are naturalized in lawns, wait until six weeks after flowering before mowing to allow time for the new cormlets to reach flowering size. Dwarf species are best in very free-draining soil or in shallow pans of gritty compost in an alpine house or bulb frame.

Early-flowering crocuses
C. ancyrensis
Each corm of this Turkish species produces three golden-yellow flowers in late winter. H 8cm (3in), S 5cm (2in). Hardy/Z 5–8. The selection **'Golden Bunch'** is more robust, with up to five flowers per corm. H 5cm (2in), S 4cm (1in).

C. chrysanthus
This species, from Greece and Turkey, is seldom grown in its straight form but is usually

represented in cultivation by its many selections, all flowering in late winter to early spring and including **'Advance'**, yellow, with violet outer petals; **'Blue Pearl'**, which has silver-blue flowers; **'E.A. Bowles'**, which has golden-yellow flowers; **'Ladykiller'**, which has slender, pure white flowers marked with purple; **'Snow Bunting'**, pure white; and one of the most spectacular cultivars, **'Zwanenburg Bronze'**, which has rich yellow flowers marked with purple-brown. H 8cm (3in), S 5cm (2in). Hardy/Z 3–8.

C. sieberi
Flowering in late winter to early spring, this species from the Balkans and Crete has yellow-centred, light blue flowers with striking bright orange pistils. H 8cm (3in), S 5cm (2in). Among the worthwhile forms are the golden-throated, white **'Albus'** (syn. 'Bowles' White), which flowers in early spring; **'Firefly'**, which has unusual violet-red flowers; and the eye-catching *C. sieberi* subsp. *sublimis* **'Tricolor'**, which has flowers banded in the centre with purple, white and yellow. Hardy/Z 3–8.

C. tommasinianus
One of the best-loved species, this crocus, from the Balkans, Bulgaria, Hungary and Siberia, is also one of the best for naturalizing, producing gleaming lavender flowers in late winter. H 10cm (4in), S 2.5cm (1in). The different selections, which are

Crocus tommasinianus

Crocus sieberi subsp. *sublimis* 'Tricolor'

among the earliest crocuses to flower, are the cause of some confusion within the nursery trade. **'Ruby Giant'** has large, rich purplish-red flowers; **'Whitewell Purple'** also has purplish-red flowers, but with silvery mauve lining inside and more slender than those of 'Ruby Giant'. Hardy/Z 3–8.

C. vernus

The species, as found in Italy, Austria and Eastern Europe, is usually represented in gardens by its many selections, all of which are excellent for naturalizing and flower in late winter to early spring. These include **'Jeanne d'Arc'**, which has pure white flowers; **'Pickwick'**, which has greyish-white flowers, striped with violet; and **'Remembrance'**, which has violet flowers with a silvery sheen. H 10cm (4in), S 8cm (3in). Hardy/Z 3–8.

Crocus vernus 'Remembrance'

Autumn-flowering crocuses
C. banaticus

An unusual crocus from Central Europe, this has lilac flowers in early autumn, which look effective in drifts near the front of a border. It needs soil that stays moist in summer. H 10cm (4in), S 5cm (2in). Hardy/Z 3–8.

C. ochroleucus

This species from the Middle East has slender, creamy white flowers. It is excellent for naturalizing in grass or under deciduous shrubs and is one of the easiest of the late species to grow. H 5cm (2in), S 2.5cm (1in). Hardy/Z 3–8.

C. pulchellus

A species native to the Balkans and Turkey with pale lilac-blue flowers. A vigorous crocus that likes dry soil in full sun. H 12cm (5in), S 4cm (1½in). **'Zephyr'** has larger flowers. Hardy/Z 3–8.

CYCLAMEN
Sowbread

This delightful genus is native to the Mediterranean. The flowers are unique and distinctive, with their swept-back petals. Some cyclamen are not hardy and have been used to produce a range of houseplants with larger flowers. The hardy species are invaluable in the garden, as they belong to a select group of plants that thrive in dry shade and are therefore excellent for planting beneath trees, where in time they will build up large colonies. The leaves are usually beautifully marked. Make sure that any plants you buy are seed raised; wild populations have been decimated through over-collection.
Cultivation Hardy cyclamen prefer moderately fertile, moist but well-drained soil in partial shade, but they will tolerate drier soils. An annual mulch of leaf mould is beneficial. *C. persicum* hybrids grown as houseplants should be kept out of direct sunlight when in full growth. When watering, avoid wetting the upper surface of the tuber, which can collect water and rot. In winter keep the plants dry and place the pots in full light.

C. coum

This species flowers from late winter to mid-spring, in a variety of colours, from purple-violet to pink and white. H 8cm (3in), S 10cm (4in). Hardy/Z 5–9.

C. hederifolium
(syn. *C. neapolitanum*)

The name indicates that the leaves are ivy-like. The fact that they remain green when many other plants are below ground makes this a valuable plant for winter interest. The flowers, which may be deep pink, pale pink or pinkish-white, appear in late summer to mid-autumn. H 10cm (4in), S 15cm (6in). Hardy/Z 5–9.

C. persicum

This species is the parent of a large number of hybrids that are often sold unnamed. The scented flowers range in colour from white to a glowing cerise red and appear in winter and spring. Some combine two colours on the frilly petals. H and S to 15cm (6in). Tender/Z 9–10.

DAHLIA

These exotic-looking flowers are now enjoying something of a revival. They are the ideal plant for adding a splash of colour to the autumn garden, with their perfectly formed, almost geometric flowers. Flower colours include white, all shades of pink, red, orange, yellow and a warm rosy purple. Some combine more than one colour. For maximum impact,

Dahlia 'Small World'

plant dahlias in groups. Tall varieties are excellent for the back of a border.

Dahlias have been extensively hybridized, resulting in a range of flower shapes classified as described below.
Cultivation Dahlias need rich soil (although they do reasonably well in any ordinary, well-drained soil) in full sun. Pinch out the growing tips for bushiness and deadhead to keep the flowers coming. Tall varieties, particularly those with very large flowers, need staking. In cold areas the tubers should be lifted after the topgrowth has been blackened by frost, then dried off and stored over winter for planting out again the following spring. Alternatively, treat them as annuals and plant fresh tubers each year. For earlier flowers, start them into growth in containers under glass six weeks before planting out.

Cyclamen coum

Cyclamen hederifolium

Dahlia 'Ellen Huston'

All the following dahlias are half-hardy/all zones.

Single-flowered dahlias (Division 1)
One or two rows of petals surround a central disc. Mostly dwarf, these dahlias are suitable for bedding. **'Ellen Huston'** has orange-red flowers and contrasting purple-tinged foliage. H and S 30cm (12in). **'Moonfire'** has single, deep gold flowers with vermilion centres and dark bronze-green foliage. H 75cm (30in), S 30cm (12in). **'Tally Ho'** has red flowers with yellow centres and dark copper foliage. H and S 60cm (2ft).

Anemone-flowered dahlias (Division 2)
The flowers are double, with one or more rings of outer petals surrounding a central group of tubular florets. Those of **'Paso Doble'** have white outer petals and yellow centres. H 1m (3ft), S 60cm (2ft). **'Scarlet Comet'** has vivid red flowers with upright central petals. H 1.2m (4ft), S 60cm (2ft).

Collerette dahlias (Division 3)
The flowers have two rings of outer florets around a central group of disc florets.

Dahlia 'Hillcrest Regal'

'Chimborazo' has flowers with a yellow-tipped collar. H 1.2m (4ft), S 60cm (2ft). **'Hillcrest Regal'** has maroon flowers with a white-tipped collar. H 1.2m (4ft), S 60cm (2ft).

Waterlily dahlias (Division 4)
The flowers classified large, medium, small or miniature, are fully double and flattened. **'Figurine'** has small, pink and white flowers. H 1.2m (4ft), S 60cm (2ft). **'Glorie van Heemstede'** has small, orange-yellow flowers. H 1.2m (4ft or more, S 60cm (2ft). **'Lismore Willie'** has small, pale gold flowers. H 1.2m (4ft), S 60cm (2ft). **'Porcelain'** has small, white flowers flushed with lilac-pink. H 1.2m (4ft), S 60cm (2ft).

Decorative dahlias (Division 5)
The flowers, classified as giant, large, medium, small or miniature, are fully double, and the tips of the petals are bluntly pointed. **'Alva's Supreme'** has giant, soft yellow flowers. H 1.2m (4ft) or more, S 60cm (2ft). **'Charlie Two'** has medium, light yellow flowers. H 1.2m (4ft), S 60cm (2ft). **'David Howard'** has miniature, rich orange flowers and copper-tinged foliage. H 1m (3ft) or more, S 60cm (2ft). **'Fire Mountain'** has miniature, bright red flowers and very dark green foliage. H 1m (3ft) or more, S 60cm (2ft). **'Hamari Gold'** has giant, golden-bronze flowers. H 1.2m (4ft), S 60cm (2ft). **'Karenglen'** has miniature, orange-red flowers. H 1m (3ft), S 60cm (2ft). **'Kenora Valentine'** has large, brilliant red flowers. H 1.2m (4ft), S 60cm (2ft). **'Kidd's Climax'** has giant, yellow-flushed pink flowers. H 1m (3ft) or more, S 60cm (2ft). **'Phill's Pink'** has small, warm orange-pink flowers, the petals yellow at the base. H 1m (3ft), S 60cm (2ft). **'Skipley Spot'** has small, red flowers with white-tipped petals. H 1m (3ft), S 60cm (2ft).

Ball dahlias (Division 6)
The flowers, small or miniature, are fully double and globe-shaped. **'Cornel'** has small, rich red

Dahlia 'Figurine'

flowers. H 1.2m (4ft), S 60cm (2ft). **'Jomanda'** has miniature, terracotta-red flowers. H 1m (3ft) or more, S 60cm (2ft).

Pompon dahlias (Division 7)
The flowers are fully double and globe-shaped with petals that are round or blunt at the tips. **'Minley Carol'** has orange flowers with a hint of red at the tips of the petals. H 1m (3ft) or more, S 60cm (2ft). **'Small World'** (syn. 'Bowen') is one of the best white dahlias. The flowers are sometimes flecked with purple. H 1m (3ft) or more, S 60cm (2ft). **'Willo's Surprise'** has wine red flowers. H 1m (3ft) or more, S 60cm (2ft).

Cactus dahlias (Division 8)
The flowers, classified as giant, large, medium, small or miniature, are fully double and have rolled, pointed petals. **'Doris Day'** has small, cardinal red flowers. H 1m (3ft) or more, S 60cm (2ft). **'Kiwi Gloria'** has small, lilac-pink and white flowers. H 1m (3ft) or more, S 60cm (2ft).

Semi-cactus dahlias (Division 9)
As for cactus dahlias, but the petals are rolled to only half their length. **'Belle of the Ball'** has large, lavender-pink flowers. H 1.2m (4ft), S 60cm (2ft). **'Eastwood Moonlight'** has medium, pale yellow flowers. H 1m (3ft) or more, S 60cm (2ft). **'Fidalgo Climax'** has large, bright yellow flowers. H 1.2m (4ft), S 60cm (2ft). **'Hamari Accord'** has large, clear yellow flowers. H 1.2m (4ft), S 60cm (2ft). **'Hayley Jane'** has small, white flowers, the petals tipped with purple. H 1.2m (4ft) or more, S 60cm (2ft). **'Kenora Challenger'**

Dahlia 'Alva's Supreme'

has large, pure white flowers. H 1.2m (4ft), S 60cm (2ft). **'Kenora Sunset'** has medium, orange-red flowers with yellow centres. H 1.2m (4ft), S 60cm (2ft). **'Lemon Elegans'** has small, pure yellow flowers. H 1.2m (4ft), S 60cm (2ft). **'Match'** has small, white flowers, the petals tipped with purple. H 1.2m (4ft), S 60cm (2ft). **'Nargold'** has medium orange and gold flowers, with ragged petals. H 1.2m (4ft), S 60cm (2ft). **'Pink Pastelle'** has medium, bright pink flowers, with white centres. H 1.2m (4ft), S 60cm (2ft). **'Piper's Pink'** has small, glowing pink flowers. H and S 60cm (2ft). **'So Dainty'** has miniature, orange-bronze flowers. H 1m (3ft) or more, S 60cm (2ft). **'Tahiti Sunrise'** has medium, yellow flowers, the petals tipped with red. H 1.2m (4ft), S 60cm (2ft). **'Weston Pirate'** has miniature, dark red flowers. H 1m (3ft), S 60cm (2ft). **'White Moonlight'** has medium, white flowers. H 1.2m (4ft), S 60cm (2ft).

Miscellaneous (Division 10)
This designation covers a wide range of hybrids that are sometimes defined further as peony-flowered, orchid-flowered, mignon, gallery and so on, not all

Dahlia 'Jomanda'

Dahlia 'Art Deco'

Eranthis hyemalis

Erythronium dens-canis

Eucomis bicolor

of which are universally accepted. **'Art Deco'** (dwarf bedding) has orange flowers. H and S 25–30cm (10–12in). **'Bishop of Llandaff'** has semi-double bright red flowers with yellow centres and blackish-red foliage. H 60cm (2ft) or more, S 45cm (18in). **'Fascination'** (dwarf bedding) has pinkish-purple flowers and dark bronze foliage. H 60cm (2ft), S 45cm (18in). **'Rembrandt'** (dwarf bedding) has pink flowers, the petals tipped with darker pink. H and S 25–30cm (10–12in). **'Renoir'** (dwarf bedding) has deep pink flowers, more open than those of 'Rembrandt'. H and S 25–30cm (10–12in).

ERANTHIS
Winter aconite

These are one of the earliest bulbs to come into flower. They are robust enough to penetrate a light covering of snow, which is a charming effect when it occurs. Like snowdrops, they transplant best when putting on growth after flowering, so when buying them, look for plants 'in the green' rather than dormant tubers. They are excellent when planted to

carpet large areas beneath deciduous trees. The flowers, surrounded by a characteristic 'ruff' of green leaves, open only when the sun is shining.
Cultivation Grow in any well-drained soil, ideally humus-rich, in sun or light shade.

E. hyemalis
(syn. *Aconitum hyemale*)
The species has bright green leaves, forming a ruff beneath the lemon-yellow flowers. H 8cm (3in), S 5cm (2in). Hardy/Z 4–9. Plants in the **Cilica Group** (syn. *Aconitum cylicum*) have rather larger flowers thatn those of the species, and the leaves of the ruff are smaller. H 10cm (4in), S 5cm (2in).

ERYTHRONIUM
Dog's tooth violet

To those who grow them, these are one of the delights of the spring garden, although their presence is fleeting. The flowers, with their upswept petals, are of unique charm, and the leaves of some forms are attractively mottled. Grow them in clumps around deciduous trees and shrubs or on lightly shaded rock gardens.
Cultivation They will grow in most soils enriched with organic matter, and moisture retentive without being boggy. They prefer a cool spot, out of sun in summer: in the shade of deciduous trees is ideal. They must not be allowed to dry out. Plant them as soon after you buy them as possible and cover them with a mulch in dry summers.

E. californicum
The species is usually represented in cultivation by **'White Beauty'** (syn. *E. revolutum* 'White Beauty'),

which has large white flowers with brownish-yellow throats in mid- to late spring. The leaves are flecked with brown. H 20–25cm (8–10in), S 25cm (10in). Hardy/Z 3–9.

E. dens-canis
European dog's tooth violet
The beautiful species produces one flower, which may be white, pink or lilac, on each stem in early to mid-spring. H and S 25cm (10in). Hardy/Z 3–9. **'Rose Queen'** has pink flowers. H and S 25cm (10in).

E. 'Pagoda'
Probably the most popular of all the dog's tooth violets, 'Pagoda' has nodding, yellow flowers in late spring. The glossy, faintly mottled leaves are green. H 40cm (16in), S 15cm (6in). Hardy/Z 4–9.

EUCOMIS
Pineapple plant

So-called because of the pineapple-like flowers, which have a characteristic tuft of green leaves at the

top of the spike, these South African species do best in a sheltered spot (such as by a warm wall) and also thrive in containers. The flowers are attractive to bees.
Cultivation Grow in full sun in moderately fertile, well-drained soil. Protect in winter with a mulch of straw or other similar dry material.

E. bicolor
This species produces spikes of green flowers from mid- to late summer among the strap-shaped leaves. H 30–60cm (1–2ft), S 20cm (8in). **'Alba'** has white flowers. Borderline hardy/Z 8–10.

E. comosa
(syn. *E. punctata*)
A species with tall, narrow spikes of white flowers that are edged with purple. H 75cm (30in), S 20cm (8in). Borderline hardy/Z 8–10.

Dahlia 'Hayley Jane'

Erythronium 'Pagoda'

Fritillaria imperialis 'The Premier'

Fritillaria meleagris

FRITILLARIA
Fritillary

This is a variable genus, containing species that provide garden plants fit for a number of purposes. The imposing crown imperial is good for adding height to spring borders, while the snake's head fritillary is excellent for naturalizing in meadows or by the streamside. Others are connoisseurs' plants, needing special conditions but providing ample reward with their subtly coloured flowers. Only a few of the nearly 100 species are widely grown, all with pendent, bell-like flowers.
Cultivation Most fritillaries do well in any well-drained soil in sun. *F. meleagris* does best in heavier, moisture-retentive soil in sun or light shade but will tolerate ordinary soil. Bulbs of *F. imperialis* are prone to rotting. Planting them on their sides will help to prevent water collecting on the hollow upper surface.

F. imperialis
Crown imperial
These majestic plants are unmistakable. The yellow, orange-red or red flowers hang down from the tops of erect, sturdy stems in late spring. Plant the bare bulbs (which are unpleasantly scented) as soon after purchase as possible. H 1.2m (4ft) or more, S 30cm (1ft). Selections include 'Lutea', which has yellow flowers; 'Rubra', vermilion-red; and 'The Premier', which has orange-red flowers. Hardy/Z 5–9.

F. meleagris
Snake's head fritillary
This species is often found growing wild in damp European meadows. The flowers, which come in late spring, are appealingly chequered with dull purple. In the right conditions this species will self-seed. H 30cm (12in), S 5cm (2in). *F. meleagris* var. *unicolor* subvar. *alba* has white flowers that are delicately touched with green. Hardy/Z 3–8.

F. michailovskyi
Also flowering in late spring, this species has fascinating bell-like flowers that are a dusky reddish-purple edged with yellow. Grow in a shady rock garden or an alpine trough. H 20cm (8in), S 5cm (2in). Hardy/Z 5–8.

GALANTHUS
Snowdrop

Few plants have the charm of the snowdrop or are as welcome. They are usually among the first flowers to appear in the gardening year. Each flower has six petals, the outer three longer than the inner ones. Unusually among bulbs, snowdrops seem to prefer slightly damp soil. They are delightful in drifts in light woodland, or pushing through ivy.
Cultivation Most snowdrops do best in reliably moist soil, in a spot where they are in sun when in growth but lightly shaded when dormant; beneath deciduous trees and shrubs is usually an ideal spot.

G. elwesii
This species from Turkey and the Balkans is less well known than *G. nivalis* but possibly superior. It is a larger plant, with bright green, strap-shaped leaves and flowers with large green spots on the inner petals. H to 25cm (10in), S 8cm (3in). Hardy/Z 3–9.

G. nivalis
The best-known of the snowdrops and one that will naturalize very easily. The bell-shaped, pure white flowers hang downwards, the outer petals flaring outwards to reveal the green markings on the inner ones. H and S 10cm (4in). 'Flore Pleno', the double form, is no less charming. Hardy/Z 3–9.

GALTONIA
Cape hyacinth, summer hyacinth

These elegant plants, valued for their late season, provide a welcome freshness to summer borders where they are allowed to rise above annuals or late-flowering perennials. The flowers open in succession on the flower spike, from bottom to top, providing interest over a number of weeks.
Cultivation Galtonias need fertile, well-drained soil in a sunny spot.

G. candicans
The most popular species, this bears spikes of fragrant white flowers in late summer to early autumn. H 1–1.2m (3–4ft), S 10cm (4in). Hardy/Z 7–10.

G. viridiflora
The species is similar to *G. candicans* but has green flowers. H 1m (3ft), S 10cm (4in). Half-hardy/Z 7–9.

GLADIOLUS

Nowadays a less popular flower with gardeners than formerly, the gladiolus is still an excellent florist's flower. The ease with which it hybridizes has led to a huge number of selected forms.

The spikes can be picked while still in bud, and the flowers will open indoors. They do not combine well with other plants but can be used in a colour border in large groups. Otherwise, grow them in a picking border exclusively to provide flowers for the house. Shorter-growing forms are also effective in containers.
Cultivation Hardy gladioli will grow in any well-drained soil in full sun. The large-flowered hybrids need fertile soil that does not dry out in summer. Where these will not survive the winter, lift the corms in autumn and dry them off. Snap off the old corm and store the new one in a dry, frost-free place over winter for planting out again the following spring. Tall varieties need staking.

G. communis subsp. byzantinus (syn. G. byzantinus)
The exception to all other gladioli, this elegant species flowers in late spring. The rich magenta flowers (typical of gladioli but much smaller) are produced in long spikes. A superb plant for naturalizing, it is also effective in borders and large rock gardens. H 1m (3ft), S 8cm (3in). Borderline hardy/Z 7–10.

G. hybrids
Gladiolus hybrids, of which there are a vast number, are usually classified according to flower size: giant, large, medium, small and miniature. Butterfly gladioli are small-flowered, often with a contrasting patch of colour on the lower petals. Primulinus gladioli have funnel-shaped

Galtonia candicans

Gladiolus communis subsp. *byzantinus*

Gladiolus 'Seraphin'

Hippeastrum 'Christmas Star'

flowers that are less densely packed on the spike than with the other types. All flower from midsummer to early autumn and are half-hardy/Z 7–10. **'Aristocrat'** (medium) is late, with purple flowers. H 1m (3ft), S 10cm (4in). **'Bluebird'** (small) is early, with rich violet-blue flowers. H 1m (3ft), S 10cm (4in). The greenish-yellow flowers of **'Green Woodpecker'** (butterfly) are blotched with red. H 1.5m (5ft), S 12cm (5in). **'Lady Godiva'** (primulinus) is white. H 60cm (2ft), S 10cm (4in). **'Leonore'** (primulinus) has bright yellow flowers. H 1m (3ft), S 10cm (4in). The salmon pink and yellow flowers of **'Mykonos'** (butterfly) are marked with red. H 1m (3ft), S 10cm (4in). **'Peter Pears'** (large) is soft apricot-orange. H 1.2m (4ft), S 18cm (7in). **'Seraphin'** (butterfly) has muffled pink flowers with white throats. H 70cm (28in), S 10cm (4in). **'The Bride'** (miniature) is pure white. H 1m (3ft), S 10cm (4in). **'Trader Horn'** (giant) has deep, rich scarlet flowers. H 1.2m (4ft), S 18 cm (7in).

HIPPEASTRUM

Confusingly, these are usually sold under the name 'amaryllis'. Few of the species are grown, but there are a growing number of hybrids, all with huge, showy flowers, intended for growing exclusively as houseplants. They are often sold in packs with pots and compost (soil mix) for the Christmas gift market. Large bulbs produce more flowers (up to five) on each stem than smaller ones.

Cultivation Use any proprietary compost, with added grit (both for drainage and weight because these plants can be top-heavy). Plant with the neck of the bulb above the surface of the compost. Keep them well-watered and stand them in full light, but not directly next to a window. Stake the flower stem if necessary.

H. hybrids

There are many cultivars, with a wide range of flower forms and colours. All are tender/Z 10. **'Apple Blossom'** has white flowers with pink-edged petals. H 50cm (20in), S 30cm (12in). **'Christmas Star'** is an attractive, compact form with white flowers that are edged and striped with bright red. H to 45cm (18in), S 30cm (12in). **'Florida'** has bright red flowers. H to 60cm (2ft), S 30cm (12in). **'Snow Queen'** is one of several white-flowered amaryllis, others being **'White Dazzler'** and **'White Lady'**. H to 60cm (2ft), S 30cm (12in).

Hippeastrum 'Florida'

HYACINTHOIDES
Bluebell

This genus includes the well-known English bluebell, as well as the rather coarse Spanish species. Bluebells are excellent for colonizing areas beneath deciduous trees.
Cultivation Grow in any reasonable garden soil in light shade.

H. hispanica
(syn. *Scilla campanulata*)
Spanish bluebell

A rather more robust species than the English bluebell (with which it will hybridize), this sends up erect stems with blue, bell-shaped flowers in spring. H 60cm (2ft), S 10cm (4in). Hardy/Z 4–9.

H. non-scripta
English bluebell

Broadly similar to the Spanish bluebell, this species has daintier, somewhat darker blue flowers, which are also more tubular. They are borne in late spring. There are a number of pink and white forms. H to 60cm (2ft), S 8cm (3in). Hardy/Z 6–9.

HYACINTHUS
Hyacinth

Nothing can match the scent of hyacinths. In addition, they have one of the widest colour ranges of all the bulb genera, including the elusive blue. Only the hybrids are cultivated. Planted in blocks in beds, they are a little stiff and formal, and they do not integrate well with other plants. It is better to tuck them into odd corners and allow the scent to hit you as you wander around the garden. Otherwise, they are good in bowls and can be grown as houseplants. 'Forced' bulbs are sold from autumn onwards, and these will flower in the middle of winter, but all can be grown indoors initially. Planted in the garden after flowering, they will take a season or two to recover. The more compact forms are best for growing outdoors; larger ones are top-heavy and are best kept inside.
Cultivation Outdoors, grow in any well-drained soil in full sun. If treated as annuals, they can be planted in light shade. Indoors, grow in bowls of special bulb fibre. Bulbs for forcing should be

Hyacinthus 'Amethyst'

planted up and placed in a cool, dark place (such as a dry cellar or garage) for 8–10 weeks, then brought into a light, warm room for flowering 3–4 weeks later. Alternatively, they can be grown in special glass hyacinth vases that allow the roots to be in water while keeping the actual bulb dry.

H. hybrids

The following flower naturally in mid-spring but can be forced to flower at other times. All are hardy/Z 6–9. **'Amethyst'** has lilac-blue flowers; **'Anna Marie'** is bright pink; **'Blue Jacket'** is an arresting deep blue; **'Carnegie'** has pure white flowers; **'City of Haarlem'** is bright yellow; **'Gipsy Queen'** is a subtle salmon orange; the double flowers of **'Hollyhock'** are deep red; **'Jan Bos'** is carmine red; the well known **'L'Innocence'** is pure white; **'Ostara'** has deep violet-blue flowers; and **'Pink Pearl'** has pink flowers. H 20–30cm (8–12in), S 8cm (3in).

Hyacinthus 'City of Haarlem'

Iris reticulata 'George'

IRIS

Irises form a large genus that includes true bulbs (in the generally accepted sense of the term) as well as perennials (so-called rhizomatous irises are treated as perennials in this book). Some have very specific cultivation needs. Early-flowering species seldom last long in the garden and are best treated as annuals. So-called 'Dutch irises' are grown commercially for the cut flower market. Bulbous irises are excellent in borders, rock gardens and containers.
Cultivation Bulbous irises need a preferably well-drained, alkaline soil, in full sun.

I. bucharica

This species, native to central Asia, has fragrant, golden-yellow and white flowers in mid-spring, blotched with either green, brown or violet. It needs protection from winter wet and is probably best grown in an alpine house. H 40cm (16in). Hardy/Z 4–9.

I. danfordiae

This delightful dwarf species from Turkey, valued for its bright yellow flowers, blooms in late winter. It will tolerate some shade. H 10cm (4in). Hardy/Z 6–9.

I. reticulata

This dainty species from the Caucasus is one of the first bulbous plants to flower in the gardening calendar, producing its rich violet-blue, yellow-splashed flowers in late winter. It is excellent in rock gardens and shallow pans but unfortunately is not reliably perennial, so it is advisable to plant fresh stocks annually. H 15cm (6in). Hardy/Z 6–9. Selections include **'George'**,

which has deep purple flowers; **'Harmony'**, with deep blue flowers; **'Joyce'**, which has sky blue and orange flowers; and **'J.S. Dijt'**, with purple-violet flowers.

Xiphium irises

This large group, consisting mainly of robust hybrids that are easy to grow, includes irises sometimes referred to as 'Dutch irises', 'English irises' and 'Spanish irises'. They make excellent border plants that flower in late spring or early summer, but they are forced to flower at any time for the cut flower market. They are often sold as mixed colours, but there are several named selections, including **'Apollo'**, with yellow and white flowers; **'Casablanca'**, with white flowers; **'Imperator'**, which have blue and orange flowers; **'Professor Blaauw'**, deep blue; **'Symphony'**, with yellow and white flowers; and **'Telstar'**, deep blue. H 60–65cm (24–26in). Hardy/Z 5–8.

LEUCOJUM
Snowflake

These neglected bulbs look like large snowdrops, but differ in having six white petals of equal length, each one spotted with yellow-green at the tip. These plants appreciate damp soil and are at their most attractive when planted on the banks of a natural stream. They can also be grown in borders and rock gardens.
Cultivation The snowflakes described here need fertile soil that does not dry out and a position in full sun or light shade.

L. aestivum
Summer snowflake

This is the most commonly grown species. Despite the name,

it flowers in mid-spring, producing green-tipped white flowers and glossy green leaves. H 40cm (16in), S 8cm (3in). Hardy/Z 4–9.

L. vernum
Spring snowflake

The flowering period of this often coincides with the snowdrops (late winter to early spring). They need a fertile soil and are best left undisturbed after planting. H 35cm (14in). Hardy/Z 4–8.

LILIUM
Lily

This huge genus is also one of the most varied in terms of cultivation: there are lilies for sun, for shade, acid or alkaline soils. Lilies work well in mixed summer borders, appreciating the shade at their roots that the neighbouring plants provide. They are also excellent in pots. A few are delightful in woodland, but building up colonies of good size can take several years.
Cultivation All the lilies described here need well-drained soil and are better off where their flowers will be in sun while their roots are shaded. A few will tolerate light overhead shade. Most prefer acid to neutral soil, although some tolerate alkaline soil, with a few even preferring it. Many modern hybrids have been bred to thrive whatever the pH. Individual requirements are specified in the entries below.

Asiatic hybrids (Division 1)

Derived from Asiatic species and hybrids, these are sturdy stem-rooting lilies. There are three subdivisions: 1a, with upward-facing flowers; 1b, with outward-facing flowers; and 1c, with

Lilium 'Concorde'

pendent flowers. All are hardy/Z 4–8. **'Admiration'** (1a) has large, unscented, creamy yellow flowers spotted with maroon in early to midsummer. H to 40cm (16in). **'Bronwen North'** (1c) is striking with slightly scented, pale mauve-pink flowers heavily spotted and lined with purple in early summer. H to 1m (3ft). **'Concorde'** (1a), an excellent border plant, has unscented, lemon-yellow flowers, greenish at the base, that open from early to midsummer. H to 1m (3ft). **'Connecticut King'** (1a) is a popular hybrid, with unscented, rich deep yellow flowers in early summer. H to 1m (3ft). **'Côte d'Azur'** (1a) produces unscented, rich pink flowers in early to midsummer. H to 1m (3ft). **'Eros'** (1c) has nodding, fragrant, turkscap flowers in midsummer. The sepals are pinkish orange spotted with maroon. H to 1.2m (4ft). **'Karen North'** (1c) bears lightly scented turkscap flowers in midsummer. The sepals are orange-pink, lightly spotted with darker pink. H to 1.4m (55in). **'Mont Blanc'** (1a) produces unscented, brown-spotted, white flowers in early to midsummer. H to 70cm (28in). **'Orange Pixie'** (1a) has unscented, bright orange flowers in summer that are spotted with

Leucojum aestivum

Lilium 'Bronwen North'

Lilium 'Orange Pixie'

Lilium 'Roma'

chocolate-maroon. H to 40cm (16in). **'Peggy North'** (1c) is a good border lily, with lightly scented turkscap flowers in mid-summer. The sepals are glowing orange spotted with dark brown. H to 1.5m (5ft). **'Roma'** (1a) has fragrant creamy white flowers, lightly spotted with maroon, which open in early to midsummer. H to 1.2m (4ft).

Martagon hybrids (Division 2)
Derived mainly from *L. martagon* and *L. hansonii*, these are hardy, mainly stem-rooting lilies with turkscap flowers, suitable for light shade or woodland. All are hardy/Z 4–8. **'Mrs R.O. Backhouse'**, a famous lily, is one of the oldest still in cultivation. It has unscented, turkscap flowers that hang from the stems in early to midsummer. The sepals are orange-yellow with maroon spotting and are flushed pink on the outside. H 1.3m (52in).

Candidum hybrids (Division 3)
Derived from *L. chalcedonicum*, *L. candidum* and other European species (excluding *L. martagon*), this is a small group of lilies with sometimes scented, turkscap flowers. They are usually not stem-rooting. *L. × testaceum* (Nankeen lily) is a lime-tolerant

Lilium Bellingham Group

hybrid bearing fragrant, turkscap flowers in early to midsummer. The sepals are pale apricot-pink lightly spotted with red. H 1.2m (4ft). Hardy/Z 5–8.

American hybrids (Division 4)
Derived from American species, these are rhizomatous lilies, with sometimes scented, usually turkscap flowers. They are not stem-rooting. **Bellingham Group** have occasionally fragrant turkscap flowers that can vary in colour from yellow to orange and orange-red, all spotted deep brown and appearing in early and midsummer. They are excellent for naturalizing in light shade and need acid soil, preferably reliably moist. H to 1.5m (5ft). **'Shuksan'** is a selected form, with lightly scented, tangerine-yellow flowers tipped with red and spotted with black or reddish-brown. H to 1.2m (4ft). Hardy/Z 4–8.

Longiflorum hybrids (Division 5)
Derived from *L. formosanum* and *L. longiflorum*, this is a small but growing group of lilies with fragrant, trumpet- or funnel-shaped flowers, usually grown for the cut flower market.

Trumpet and Aurelian hybrids (Division 6)
Derived from Asiatic species (excluding *L. auratum*, *L. japonicum*, *L. rubellum* and *L. speciosum*), these are mostly hardy, fragrant, stem-rooting lilies. There are four subdivisions: 6a, with trumpet-shaped flowers; 6b, with usually outward-facing, bowl-shaped flowers; 6c, with shallowly bowl-shaped flowers that often open flat; and 6d, with sepals that are distinctly recurved. The lilies described are borderline hardy/Z 4–8. In mid- and late summer the beautiful lilies in the **African Queen Group** (6a) have heavily scented, tangerine-apricot flowers that are veined with deep purple on the outside. H 2m (6ft). **'White Henryi'** (6d) has large, fragrant flowers in midsummer that open flat. The sepals are white, flushed deep orange at the base and with rust-red papillae. H to 1.5m (5ft).

Lilium African Queen Group

Oriental hybrids (Division 7)
Derived from species from the Far East, these are late-flowering lilies, often with scented flowers. Most are lime-hating and need sun or partial shade. There are four subdivisions: 7a, with trumpet-shaped flowers; 7b, with bowl-shaped flowers; 7c, with flat flowers; and 7d, with sepals that are distinctly recurved. All are hardy/Z 4–8. **'Acapulco'** (7d) has fragrant, rich pink flowers with recurving sepals. H to 1m (3ft). **'Belle Epoque'** (7b), which flowers from midsummer to early autumn, has white to soft pink flowers, each sepal centrally banded with cream. H to 1m (3ft). **'Casa Blanca'** (7b) has heavily scented, pure white flowers in mid- to late summer. H to 1.2m (4ft). **'Little Joy'** (7d), bred for container growing, is a sturdy dwarf, with unscented flowers with recurved, pink to soft red sepals, spotted with dark maroon. H to 35cm (14in). From midsummer to early autumn **'Royal Class'** (7b) produces fragrant flowers, the sepals varying in colour from white to soft pink, with a central yellow band and prominent papillae. H to 1m (3ft). **'Star Gazer'** (7c) is a popular lily, albeit lime-hating. From midsummer it produces rich

Lilium 'Acapulco'

Lilium 'Royal Class'

crimson-pink, unscented flowers that are spotted with darker pink. H to 1.5m (5ft).

Other hybrids (Division 8)
This group includes all hybrids not accommodated by the other groups. **'Moneymaker'** produces up to six, sweetly scented, clear pink flowers in midsummer. H to 1m (3ft). Hardy/Z 4–8.

Species (Division 9)
This group includes all true species and their forms.

L. auratum
Golden-rayed lily
This species from Japan has the largest flowers of any lily. The heavily scented flowers open in late summer to autumn; the sepals are white, usually spotted with crimson, and banded with yellow and with fleshy papillae. It needs acid soil. H to 1.5m (5ft). Hardy/Z 5–8.

L. candidum
Madonna lily
This is a species from the Balkans and eastern Mediterranean with fragrant, trumpet-shaped, pure white flowers in summer. Grow in neutral to alkaline soil and plant the bulbs shallowly. H to 2m (6ft). Hardy/Z 4–9.

Lilium 'Moneymaker'

Lilium regale

Lilium speciosum var. album

Muscari armeniacum 'Blue Spike'

L. formosanum
This elegant but slightly tender species is native to Taiwan. In late summer and early autumn fragrant, trumpet-shaped, white flowers open from buds that are strongly flushed with wine purple. It needs moist, acid soil. H to 1.5m (5ft). Borderline hardy/ Z 5. The naturally occurring variant *L. formosanum* var. *pricei* is hardier and much smaller. H to 30cm (12in).

L. henryi
This Chinese species is clump-forming and easy to grow. In late summer elegant stems carry hanging, lightly scented, orange, turkscap flowers, spotted darker. It is best in neutral to alkaline soil in light shade. H to 3m (10ft). Hardy/Z 4–9.

L. martagon
Martagon lily, common turkscap lily
This species occurs in a range from northwest Europe to northwest Asia. The turkscap flowers, slightly unpleasant to smell, hang from the stems in early to midsummer. They are dull pink, spotted with maroon. It does well in almost any well-drained soil in sun or light shade. H to 2m (6ft). The naturally occurring *L. martagon* var. *album* is a desirable white form. Hardy/Z 4–8.

L. regale
Regal lily
An essential plant in any garden, this species is found growing wild in western China. Opening in midsummer, its richly scented,

white flowers have yellow bases and are heavily stained purple on the outside. It tolerates most well-drained soils. H to 2m (6ft). Hardy/Z 4–9. *L. regale* var. *album* has pure white flowers with golden yellow anthers.

L. speciosum
This attractive species from China, Japan and Taiwan needs moist, acid soil, preferably in light shade. The pale pink or white, fragrant, turkscap flowers are produced in late summer. H to 2m (6ft). There are a number of selected forms, including *L. speciosum* var. *album*, which has white flowers with prominent papillae; 'Krätzeri', which has white sepals striped green on the back; and 'Uchida', which has brilliant crimson flowers, spotted with green or darker red and tipped with white. Hardy/Z 5–8.

MUSCARI
Grape hyacinth
These flowers do indeed resemble miniature hyacinths, and their shape and deep purple-blue colour are also evocative of tiny grape bunches. They self-seed freely, making them a weed in some gardens, but can be of value for their unassuming charm. They are seen at their best when planted in large, river-like drifts among shrubs and trees.
Cultivation Grow in any well-drained soil in sun or light shade.

M. armeniacum
This is the most commonly grown species, with clusters of dull blue, bell-like flowers in spring. Try it in conjunction with

the yellow-flowered *Doronicum orientale*. H to 20cm (8in), S 5cm (2in). Hardy/Z 2–9. Selected forms include 'Blue Spike', which has double flowers; and 'Fantasy Creation', which has flowers that fade to green. H to 20cm (8in), S 5cm (2in).

M. botryoides
The straight species is rarely cultivated, but the selection 'Album' is becoming more popular. It has spikes of white flowers (less compact than those of *M. armeniacum*) in spring. Plant the bulbs in quantities, and close together, for the best display. H 20cm (8in), S 5cm (2in). Hardy/Z 3–9.

NARCISSUS
Daffodil
Spring would not be spring without daffodils, probably the largest of the bulb genera, with their distinctive central cups or trumpets. They have one of the longest flowering seasons of almost any bulb, with a few appearing as early as midwinter. Almost without exception, the daffodils grown in gardens today are artificial hybrids. The number of these is so vast that they are usefully categorized in a number of divisions (see right). Daffodils look best when planted en masse, in grass, on banks or beneath deciduous trees and shrubs. Smaller species and hybrids are excellent in sunny rock gardens or alpine troughs.
Cultivation Daffodils are tolerant bulbs that will grow in any reasonable garden soil so long as it is well drained. They should be

in sun when in growth, so if planting beneath deciduous trees, choose varieties that die down before the tree is in full leaf. Deadhead after flowering, where practicable, to ensure good flowering in subsequent seasons.

Trumpet daffodils (Division 1)
The trumpet is the same length as, or longer than, the petals. All are hardy/Z 3–9. The classic 'King Alfred' is a popular, sturdy hybrid, with bright yellow flowers in mid-spring. H 35cm (14in).

Large-cupped daffodils (Division 2)
The cup is longer than one-third of, but less than the length of, the petals. All are hardy/Z 3–9. 'Carlton' has soft yellow flowers with large cups with frilly edges in mid-spring. It is good for naturalizing. H 45cm (18in). One of the best-loved white daffodils, 'Ice Follies' has flowers, opening in early to mid-spring, with contrasting lemon-yellow coronas that fade to creamy white. It is excellent for naturalizing, especially where strong yellows are not wanted. H 40cm (16in). The strongly coloured 'Pinza' has rich yellow petals and deep red cups in mid-spring. It is an effective contrast to *Muscari armeniacum*. H 35cm (14in). The vigorous 'Rainbow', which flowers in late spring, is an unusual daffodil with white petals surrounding a pink cup. H 45cm (18in). 'Saint Patrick's Day' is an eye-catching daffodil, flowering in mid-spring, with lime green coronas surrounded by creamy-white petals. H 35cm (14in).

Narcissus 'Carlton'

Small-cupped daffodils (Division 3)

The cup is less than one-third the length of the petals. All are hardy/Z 3–9. **'Merlin'** has pure white petals and pale yellow cups. H 45cm (18in). **'Verona'** has white petals and a cream cup that fades to white. H 45cm (18in).

Double daffodils (Division 4)

The petals or the cup (or both) are doubled, sometimes leading to a muddled appearance. All are hardy/Z 3–9. One of the best-known, **'Rip van Winkle'** has bright yellow flowers in early spring. H 25cm (10in). **'White Lion'** has unusual flowers, with white outer petals and pale lemon-yellow central segments. Flowering in mid-spring, it is a good choice for naturalizing. H 40cm (16in). The fragrant **'Yellow Cheerfulness'** has golden-yellow flowers in mid-spring. It is a good border daffodil. H 45cm (18in).

Triandrus daffodils (Division 5)

Derived from *N. triandrus*, with usually between two and six flowers on each stem. All are hardy/Z 3–9. **'Hawera'** has dainty, canary yellow flowers in mid- to late spring. It is excellent in pots and can be brought indoors when in flower. H 25cm (10in). **'Thalia'** is technically a dwarf but is taller than most. It produces shining white flowers in mid-spring, combining well with *Fritillaria meleagris*. H 30cm (12in).

Cyclamineus daffodils (Division 6)

Derived from *N. cyclamineus*, these

Narcissus 'Jetfire'

have solitary flowers with characteristically swept-back petals. They are usually dwarf. All are hardy/Z 3–9. As its name suggests, **'February Gold'** produces bright yellow flowers in late winter. It is excellent in containers, windowboxes and in spring borders with primroses. H 30cm (12in). **'Jetfire'**, which flowers in early spring, has orange cups and rich yellow petals that flex back. It is a good contrast to *Muscari armeniacum*. H 20cm (8in). The vigorous **'Little Witch'** has bright yellow flowers. H 20cm (8in). **'Peeping Tom'** is sturdy, with golden-yellow flowers that have long trumpets and swept-back petals in early spring. It is an excellent border daffodil. H 25cm (10in).

Jonquilla daffodils (Division 7)

These have from one to five, usually fragrant, flowers on each stem. All are hardy/Z 3–9. **'Quail'** has appealing, clear yellow flowers in mid-spring. H 30cm (12in). **'Suzy'** is a strongly scented daffodil, which flowers

in mid-spring. Yellow petals surround flattened orange cups. H 40cm (16in).

Tazetta daffodils (Division 8)

These have from three to twenty flowers on each stem. Some are half-hardy but the following are both hardy/Z 3–9. The dainty **'Minnow'**, which flowers in early spring, has three to five flowers on each stem, with rounded, creamy-white petals and short primrose-yellow cups. H 18cm (7in). The fragrant **'Silver Chimes'** produces its silver-white flowers in mid- to late spring. It works well with *Fritillaria meleagris*. H 30cm (12in).

Poeticus daffodils (Division 9)

Related to *N. poeticus*, these have white petals and very shallow cups and are fragrant. They are usually late flowering. All are hardy/Z 3–9. One of the last to flower in late spring, **'Actaea'** has glistening white petals surrounding a brilliant orange corona. H 45cm (18in).

Species (Division 10)

The plants in this group are species and wild variants, few of which are suitable for general garden use. *N. bulbocodium* (hoop-petticoat daffodil) is a charming species from southern Europe and northern Africa. It has broad, funnel-like cups and pointed petals in mid-spring. Tricky to grow, it needs a site that is moist in spring and dry in summer, so is often easiest in an alpine house. H 10–15cm (4–6in). Hardy/Z 7–9.

N. cyclamineus is a distinctive species from Spain and Portugal. The bright yellow flowers, produced in early spring, have swept-back petals (like a cyclamen) and long, narrow cups. H 15–20cm (6–8in). Hardy/Z 3–9.
N. poeticus var. *recurvus* (old pheasant's eye) is fragrant and flowers in late spring. It has distinctive, glistening white petals and, short red-edged, yellow cups. It is a parent of **'Actaea'** and is excellent for naturalizing in grass. H 35cm (14in). Hardy/Z 3–9.

Split-corona daffodils (Division 11)

The flowers in this group are usually solitary with cups that are split for more than half their length. All are hardy/Z 3–9. **'Chanterelle'** has white petals and yellow cups. H 45cm (18in). **'Orangery'** has white petals and orange cups. H 45cm (18in).

Miscellaneous (Division 12)

Daffodils that do not fit easily into any of the above categories. The following are hardy/Z 3–9. **'Jumblie'** is a reliable dwarf for early spring display. Each stem carries several golden-yellow cups whose petals flex back slightly. It is a good choice for a hanging basket. H 20cm (8in). In early to mid-spring **'Quince'** has pale yellow petals that sweep back and surround darker yellow cups with frilly edges. H 15cm (6in). The popular **'Tête-à-Tête'** produces reliable crops of bright yellow flowers in early spring. It is good for a hanging basket or windowbox. H 15cm (6in).

Narcissus 'Rip van Winkle'

Narcissus 'Suzy'

Narcissus 'Actaea'

Narcissus bulbocodium

Nectaroscordum siculum

NECTAROSCORDUM

The small genus is related to *Allium*, but the flowers are distinctive. It is a quiet, elegant plant that combines well with the neater growing old roses.
Cultivation Grow in any reasonable, well-drained soil in sun or light shade.

N. siculum
(syn. *Allium siculum*)
This species from the eastern Mediterranean has pale greenish-cream flowers that hang from the tops of erect stems in summer; the outsides are flushed with plum red. H to 1.2m (4ft), S 10cm (4in). Hardy/Z 7–10.

NERINE
Guernsey lily
A well-established clump of nerines will be a focus of attention when the flowers appear in autumn. Each is trumpet-shaped, but the petals curve sharply backwards, giving a most elegant appearance. Usually a clear

Nerine bowdenii

pink, they look as if they have been lightly dusted with sugar.
Cultivation Nerines need a hot spot in well-drained soil. Plant the dormant bulbs with the necks just above soil level and leave them undisturbed unless they become very congested and stop flowering well.

N. bowdenii
The most commonly grown species, this has flowers that appear at the end of the growing season in late summer to autumn, when the foliage (which emerges in spring) has all but died down. H 45cm (18in) or more, S 8cm (3in). Hardy/Z 8–10. 'Alba' has white flowers, occasionally tinged with pink. H 45cm (18in) or more, S 8cm (3in).

ORNITHOGALUM
Star of Bethlehem
This is a large genus of about 80 species, which are found through Africa, Asia and Europe. Not all are hardy, but the species described are easy to grow. Hardy species naturalize readily. In cold areas, the less hardy species can be grown in containers or treated as annuals and planted in borders in spring. All make long-lasting cut flowers.
Cultivation Grow in well-drained soil in sun or light shade.

O. arabicum
This species produces cup-shaped, fragrant white flowers in early summer. H 30–80cm (12–32in), S 8cm (3in). Half-hardy/Z 7–10.

O. nutans
From 10 to 20 starry, white flowers, striped with green on the outside, hang from the stems in early to mid-spring. This does best in woodland. H 30–40cm (12–16in), S 5cm (2cm). Hardy/Z 6–10.

O. thyrsoides
Chincherinchee
This popular species has dense spikes of cup-shaped, white flowers from early spring to summer (depending on the planting time). H to 70cm (28in), S 10cm (4in). Half-hardy/Z 7–10.

Ornithogalum nutans

O. umbellatum
Later flowering than *O. nutans*, this has starry flowers that open only when the sun is shining, closing during dull weather and showing the green exteriors of their petals. It is excellent for naturalizing. H 20cm (8in), S 10cm (4in). Hardy/Z 7–10.

SCILLA
Squill
This is a large genus, although some of its species have now been transferred to *Hyacinthoides*. The species described is the best-known. It combines well with *Chionodoxa* (glory of the snow) in borders, rock gardens and under deciduous trees and shrubs.
Cultivation Grow in well-drained soil in sun or partial shade.

S. siberica
Siberian squill
This species, from central Russia, produces nodding, star- to bell-shaped, blue flowers in early spring. H 15cm (6in), S 5cm (2in). Among the selections are 'Alba', a rare white form; and 'Spring Beauty', which has larger flowers and is more robust. H to 20cm (8in), S 5cm (2in). Hardy/Z 1–8.

TIGRIDIA
Tiger flower, peacock flower
These exotic and distinctive flowers for late summer combine well with dahlias and cannas, and are also suitable for growing in containers. Treat them as annuals in cold areas, planting the bulbs only when all danger of frost has passed.

Tigridia pavonia

Cultivation Grow in well-drained, fertile soil in full sun. Alternatively, plant in containers of well-drained compost (soil mix).

T. pavonia
This is the species most generally grown. It produces several flowers on each spike, in shades of white, cream, yellow, pink or red, each lasting for one day only. The flowers are conspicuously spotted. Single-colour selections are seldom available. H 45–60cm (18–24in), S 10cm (4in). Tender/Z 8–10.

TULIPA
Tulip
Highly prized by many, but tulips are unlikely to achieve again the degree of popularity they enjoyed in the 17th century, when Tulipomania swept western Europe, bankrupting many. So vast is the number of hybrids, that the genus is split into divisions (see right).

All tulips can be grown in containers. Some of the species are dwarf, modest plants that are best in rock gardens, but the hybrids are more versatile. They should be grown en masse, the strikingly marked ones in isolation, but the self-coloureds combine well with a range of spring-flowering plants, including pulmonarias, winter pansies and polyanthus. Pink tulips with blue forget-me-nots is a classic cottage-garden combination, which also works well in containers. Tulips provide a memorable display, but most are

Tulipa 'Oranje Nassau'

Tulipa 'Golden Melody'

Tulipa 'Striped Bellona'

Tulipa 'Esther'

hard work from the gardener's point of view because they cannot simply be left in situ to flower every year – they need lifting. Many prefer to treat them as annual bedding plants, discarding them after flowering and buying in new stock each autumn – making it possible to try out new varieties. Growing tulips is an addictive but expensive hobby.
Cultivation Tulips do well in any ordinary garden soil, provided it is well drained. An open site in full sun is desirable, but some shelter from strong winds is advisable for taller varieties. Most of the hybrids, although perennial, do best if not left in the ground permanently. They should be lifted after they have died back, then cleaned and dried off for storage in a cool, well-ventilated place over summer. In autumn, replant the larger bulbs where they are to flower. Small bulbs will not flower but can be grown on in a nursery bed until they reach flowering size.

Single early tulips (Division 1)
The cup-shaped flowers are borne in early to mid-spring. These tulips are suitable for growing in borders or in mixed bedding. All are hardy/Z 3–8. **'Apricot Beauty'** has salmon-pink flowers. H 45cm (18in). **'Brilliant Star'** has scarlet flowers. H 30cm (12in). **'Yokohama'**, one of the best yellows, has lemon-yellow flowers. H 35cm (14in).

Double early tulips (Division 2)
These tulips have double, bowl-shaped flowers in mid-spring. They are suitable for bedding. All are hardy/Z 3–8. **'Carlton'** has blood-red flowers. H 40cm (16in). **'Monte Carlo'** has sulphur-yellow flowers. H 30cm (12in). **'Oranje Nassau'** is deep orange. H 25cm (10in). **'Schoonoord'** has pure white flowers. H 25cm (10cm). **'Stockholm'** is bright red. H 30cm (12in). **'Willem van Oranje'** has orange flowers, flushed with copper red. H 25cm (10in). **'Willemsoord'** has red flowers, edged with white. H 25cm (10in).

Triumph tulips (Division 3)
The single, cup-shaped flowers are produced from mid- to late spring. They are good for bedding and are rain resistant. All are hardy/Z 3–8. **'Abu Hassan'** has purple-brown flowers edged with yellow. H 50cm (20in). **'Attila'** has purple-violet flowers. H 50cm (20in). **'Barcelona'** has fuchsia-purple flowers. H 50cm (20in). **'Blue Ribbon'** has lilac-purple flowers. H 50cm (20in). **'Couleur Cardinal'** has violet-red

flowers. 35cm (14in). **'Don Quichotte'** is deep pink. H 50cm (20in). The violet flowers of **'Dreaming Maid'** are edged with white. H 55cm (22in). **'Garden Party'** has white and carmine red flowers. H 40cm (16in). **'Golden Melody'** has golden-yellow flowers. H 55cm (22in). **'Lustige Witwe'** (syn. 'Merry Widow') has red flowers, edged with white. H 40cm (16in). The yellow flowers of **'New Design'** fade to pinkish white. H 50cm (20in). **'Passionale'** has purple flowers. H 45cm (18in). **'Pax'** is pure white. H 45cm (18in). **'Prinses Irene'** has orange and red flowers. H 35cm (14in). **'Silver Dollar'** has yellow flowers. H 55cm (22in). **'Striped Bellona'** has yellow flowers striped with red. H 50cm (20in).

Darwin hybrids (Division 4)
The large, single, oval flowers are carried at the tops of tall, sturdy stems, making them excellent for cutting. (These should not be

confused with Darwin tulips, now included in division 5.) All are hardy/Z 3–8. **'Ad Rem'** has deep orange flowers. H 60cm (2ft). **'Apeldoorn'** has brilliant vermilion red flowers. H 55cm (22in). **'Golden Apeldoorn'** has lemon-yellow flowers. H 55cm (22in). **'Parade'** has bright red flowers. H 60cm (2ft).

Single late tulips (Division 5)
The flowers are cup- or goblet-shaped and are borne in late spring. (Darwin, Breeder and Cottage tulips belong to this group.) All are hardy/Z 3–8. **'Avignon'** has bright red flowers. H 50cm (20in). **'Electra'** has magenta flowers. H 25cm (10in). **'Esther'** has light magenta flowers. H 50cm (20in). **'Menton'** has rose-red flowers with pale orange stripes. H 65cm (26in). **'Pink Lady'** has pink flowers. H 50cm (20in). **'Queen of Night'** has purple-black flowers. H 60cm (2ft). **'Sorbet'** is pinkish-white. H 60cm (2ft).

Tulipa 'Attila'

Tulipa 'Apeldoorn'

Tulipa 'Queen of Night'

Tulipa 'Ballerina'

Tulipa 'West Point'

Tulipa 'Fantasy'

Lily-flowered tulips (Division 6)

The petals of the slender flowers are often pointed and curve backwards. They are late-flowering tulips and rather susceptible to wind damage. All are hardy/Z 3–8. **'Aladdin'** has deep red flowers edged with yellow. H 55cm (22in). **'Ballerina'** has blood-red flowers. H 55cm (22in). **'Mariette'** is pure pink. H 55cm (22in). **'Mona Lisa'** has yellow streaked with red flowers. H 55cm (22in). **'West Point'** has primrose-yellow flowers that look good with forget-me-nots. H 50cm (20in). **'White Triumphator'** has pure white flowers. H 60cm (2ft).

Fringed tulips (Division 7)

The petals of the cup-shaped flowers are fringed at the edges (sometimes in a different colour). The flowers appear in late spring. All are hardy/Z 3–8. **'Crystal**

Beauty'** has rose-pink flowers with an orange fringe. H 55cm (22in). **'Red Wing'** has rich red flowers. H 50cm (20in).

Viridiflora tulips (Division 8)

The flowers, which are produced in late spring, are touched with varying amounts of green. All are hardy/Z 3–8. **'Artist'** has deep orange and green flowers. H 30cm (12in). **'Groenland'** has pink and green flowers. H 55cm (22in). **'Spring Green'** has creamy white flowers with broad green stripes. H 50cm (20in).

Rembrandt tulips (Division 9)

The cup-shaped flowers, borne in late spring, are dramatically variegated with contrasting colours, usually brown, bronze, black, red, pink or purple on a white, yellow or red ground. (These are the tulips depicted in Dutch old master paintings. Unfortunately, since the breaking

of the flower colour is caused by a virus, few are nowadays produced commercially. The obsolete Bizarre and Bijbloemen tulips belonged to this division.) All are hardy/Z 3–8. **'Gala Beauty'** has red and yellow streaked flowers. H 60cm (2ft). **'Jack Laan'** has purple flowers shaded with brown and feathered with white and yellow. H 55cm (22in).

Parrot tulips (Division 10)

The cup-shaped flowers, borne in mid- to late spring, have twisted petals, which are irregularly cut and evenly banded with other colours. The flowers gradually open flat, exposing black centres and golden stamens. These tulips are sensitive to cold, wet weather and do best in a sheltered spot. These are sports of tulips from other divisions. All are hardy/Z 3–8. **'Black Parrot'** has violet-black flowers. H 55cm (22in). **'Blue Parrot'** is mauve-blue. H 55cm (22in). **'Estella Rijnveld'** has red and creamy white flowers. H 50cm (20in). **'Fantasy'** has pink flowers crested with green and irregularly crimped petals. H 55cm (22in). **'Texas Flame'** has yellow and red flowers. H 45cm (18in).

Double late tulips (Division 11)

Sometimes called peony-flowered tulips, these flower in late spring. They have fully double, bowl-shaped flowers and should be planted in a sheltered spot because they do not stand up well to bad weather. They do well in

areas with cold winters and late springs. All are hardy/Z 3–8. **'Allegretto'** has red flowers edged with yellow. H 35cm (14in). The pink flowers of **'Angelique'** are edged with white. H 45cm (18in). **'Casablanca'** has white flowers. H 45cm (18in).

Kaufmanniana tulips (Division 12)

These small, sturdy tulips are usually very early, often with bicoloured flowers and sometimes with spotted foliage. The flowers open flat in sunshine, hence the name 'waterlily tulips'. All are hardy/Z 3–8. **'Chopin'** has yellow flowers streaked with red and grey-green foliage mottled with brown. H 25cm (10in). **'Giuseppe Verdi'** has carmine-red flowers edged with yellow and mottled foliage. H 30cm (12in). **'Gluck'** has carmine-red flowers edged with bright yellow and spotted foliage. H 20cm (8in).

Tulipa 'Mona Lisa'

Tulipa 'Spring Green'

Tulipa 'Blue Parrot'

Tulipa 'Chopin'

Tulipa linifolia

The salmon-pink flowers of **'Shakespeare'** are flushed with orange and yellow. H 25cm (10in). **'Stresa'** has currant-red and yellow flowers and spotted foliage. H 25cm (10in).

Fosteriana tulips (Division 13)
The group includes *T. fosteriana* and hybrids developed from it. They are similar to the Kauffmanniana and Greigii tulips but have larger, slender flowers. The leaves are sometimes striped. They are suitable for naturalizing. The group includes many red tulips. All are hardy/Z 3–8. **'Madame Lefeber'** has bright red flowers. H 40cm (16in). **'Orange Emperor'** has bright orange flowers with a yellow base. H 40cm (16in). **'Purissima'** (syn. 'White Emperor') is pure white. H 45cm (18in).

Greigii tulips (Division 14)
The group includes *T. greigii* and hybrids developed from it. They

have blue-grey leaves, mottled to varying degrees with brownish purple. The flowers open wide in full sun. They are early flowering and good for naturalizing. All are hardy/Z 3–8. **'Ali Baba'** has deep pink flowers and spotted foliage. H 30cm (12in). **'Compostella'** has red flowers. H 30cm (12in). **'Ontario'** has magenta-pink flowers and spotted foliage. H 30cm (12in). **'Toronto'** has red flowers. H 30cm (12in).

Miscellaneous (Division 15)
The group includes the species, selected forms and hybrids that are not in the other divisions. All are hardy/Z 3–8.

T. clusiana var. _chrysantha_ (syn. _T. chrysantha, T. stellata_ var. _chrysantha_)
The species, which is from northern Afghanistan, has yellow flowers that open flat, like stars, in mid-spring. H 30–35cm (12–14in).

'Cynthia' has cream flowers, flushed with coral-red and edged with green.

T. linifolia
Native to Bukhara and the Pamir Alai mountains, this easy-to-grow species has fluorescent red flowers in late spring. H 20cm (8in).

T. praestans
A multi-flowered species from Central Asia, this is an excellent subject for naturalizing. It has orange-red flowers in early to mid-spring. H 20–25cm (8–10in). There are several cultivars, including **'Fusilier'**, which is a luminous vermilion red; and **'Unicum'**, which has bright red flowers and yellow-edged leaves.

T. saxatilis
This species, which is native to Crete, appreciates very well-drained soil. The flowers, which open wide in early spring, are soft lilac-pink with yellow centres and are lightly scented. H 30–40cm (12–16in).

T. tarda
Native to Central Asia, this is one of the best species for ordinary garden use. The star-shaped flowers, with yellow, white-tipped petals, appear in early spring. It naturalizes easily. H 12–15cm (5–6in).

T. turkestanica
This Turkish species is one of the first to bloom, the flowers appearing in late winter in a good year. The white flowers have bright yellow centres. H 25–30cm (10–12in).

ZANTEDESCHIA
Arum lily
South Africa is home to many fine bulbous plants, but few are as ravishing as this one, with its bold, glossy leaves and flowers of breathtaking purity. Planted en masse, arum lilies can be a breathtaking sight. For bulbs, they have a long flowering season. In cold gardens, the shelter of a warm wall will offer protection for many, but some selections are hardy enough to be grown in the

open border. Arum lilies can also be planted as an aquatic, but although plants undoubtedly look spectacular reflected in water, they are susceptible to rot. A number of tender hybrids have been bred for growing in containers under glass in cold areas.
Cultivation Arum lilies need soil that does not dry out in the growing season and a position in full sun. In cold areas, provide winter protection in the form of a mulch of straw or other dry material. When grown as an aquatic, plant in plastic baskets to a depth of 15–30cm (6–12in). Make sure that plants in containers do not dry out in winter.

Z. aethiopica
The best known species, this is also the hardiest, particularly in the form **'Crowborough'**. This produces pure white, funnel-shaped spathes on long stems, from early to midsummer among the glossy green leaves. H 85cm (33in), S 60cm (2ft). Borderline hardy/Z 8–10. **'Green Goddess'** has spathes splashed with green and is more susceptible to frost. Borderline hardy/Z 8–10.

Z. hybrids
Among the many hybrids are **'Black-eyed Beauty'**, which has deep creamy-yellow spathes, marked with black inside; **'Cameo'**, which has apricot-coloured spathes; **'Mango'**, with orange spathes; and **'Solfaterre'**, which has yellow and black spathes. H 30–40cm (12–16in), S 15–20cm (6–8in). Tender/Z 9–10.

Tulipa 'Shakespeare'

Tulipa saxatilis

Zantedeschia aethiopica 'Crowborough'

Alpines

Alpines are among the gems of the plant kingdom. Small but beautifully formed, they can be found producing their jewel-like blooms from the last days of winter to late autumn, providing a wealth of interest through the seasons. Since the majority are neat and compact-growing, alpines are eminently suited to gardens of restricted size, and are ideal for growing in troughs and containers, or, where space allows, in a dedicated rock garden or raised bed; but many can also be grown in mixed borders alongside bigger plants.

A rock garden is one of the most attractive ways of growing alpines. Here carpets of alpines create a tapestry of form and vivid colour.

Alpines for your garden

Botanically, alpines are no different from other plants, and a precise definition is elusive, since the term "alpine" can mean different things to different gardeners.

On the face of it, "alpine" implies mountain-dwelling plants, but most horticulturists understand it as applying to anything that grows above the tree line in harsh, exposed habitats, a definition in itself elastic. The tree line can be close to sea level in areas near the North and South Poles – if it exists at all – while in the Himalayas it can be at altitudes of up to 4,000m (13,000ft). The common feature is the plants' tolerance of open, exposed situations, on stony if not invariably rocky ground, conditions that invariably have a dwarfing effect. In other words, any small, tough, hardy plant may be considered as being "alpine", and this is the sense in which the word is used here. (However, conifer species that have dwarf variants in exposed situations are included with the rest of the conifers.)

The majority of alpines are perennials, and they are often long lived. (Dwarf bulbs, which are often planted to good effect alongside alpines in gardens, in rockeries and in troughs, are rarely found in alpine regions of the world.) Their compact habit is a response to climate. Alpines can be covered in snow for much of the year, during which time they are dormant. (No plant can survive in areas of permanent ice and snow.) When the snow melts, they burst into life: often their annual growth cycle is vastly accelerated compared to the majority of plants, since they often grow in areas with short summers. Their flowers are usually large in relation to the rest of the plant, and are often jewel-like in the vividness and clarity of their colours. They exhibit a number of characteristic habits.

Cushion Many alpines from high altitudes have a dense cushion or bun-like habit. The flowers are carried directly on the surface of the cushion or are held well above the foliage on long stalks. Cushion alpines are typical of high alpine habitats, especially rock slopes and cliffs as well as moraines (glaciated areas covered by rocks and other debris).

Mat In high, exposed regions, a creeping, mat-forming habit gives the plant considerable protection from strong winds. The mats, spreading outwards from the centre, consist of numerous low, leafy shoots. They can grow from a central rootstock or can root where the shoots touch the ground. Some have underground runners that throw up topgrowth here and there: in other words, what appears as a colony of separate plants can in fact be a single plant.

Rosette Some alpines form symmetrical rosettes, either solitary or bunched together, from the centre of which arise the flower stems.

Typically they occur on cliffs and other rocky ground, but occasionally also on high alpine meadows.

Shrubs What shrubs are found in alpine regions tend to be severely dwarfed by the bleak, exposed conditions and are therefore low and mounded or spreading.

Tuft This a common form and comprises a low, leafy tuft bearing flowers at the stem tips. The tufts are usually herbaceous, and the stems die down at the end of each season, to be replaced by new shoots the next spring that arise from the old base or from below ground level. Tufted alpines are characteristic of high-altitude alpine meadows and open scrub in the mountains, some occurring on more exposed rocky habitats.

Alpines in the garden

Many gardeners think of growing alpines as a spectator sport, imagining them to be difficult plants for the enthusiast only. While it is true that some alpines are best grown in a dedicated alpine house, a good many are suitable for growing

Dry-stone retaining walls, such as those at the edge of a lawn or patio, can act like an extra flower bed for alpine crevice dwellers.

This gently sloping gravel or scree garden is an ideal way of displaying some of the more spreading alpines.

in the open garden or in troughs, and it is these that form the basis for the following selections featured in this plant category.

What unites the majority of alpines is their need for good drainage (though some primulas prefer damper conditions). The best garden situation is an open, sunny site that is not shaded by overhanging trees or nearby walls or buildings. Exposure to strong winds, which can be detrimental to many other plants, is not a problem.

Some alpines will tolerate the typical conditions enjoyed by most other plants and can be grown in mixed borders: aubrieta *(Aubrieta deltoidea)* and rock soapwort *(Saponaria ocymoides)* are both excellent edging plants, while some of the sturdier bellflowers (notably the invasive *Campanula portenschlagiana)* and stonecrops *(Sedum)* can be planted alongside other border plants.

Ideally, however, create a rock garden, an artificial outcrop of rocks, preferably on a slope for good drainage. On gently sloping ground you could make an arroyo, in nature a dried-up stream bed or rocky ravine. Either will include numerous ledges, clefts and nooks for a wide variety of alpines. If your ground is flat, you can make what is effectively a rock garden on the horizontal, a scree (basically a gravel garden).

Alternatively, grow your alpines in raised beds, which give you all the advantages of improved drainage besides being of inestimable value to gardeners who experience difficulty in bending down. They can be made with a variety of materials. A dry-stone wall made from the local stone will be beautiful even before it is planted, and will allow you to plant in the gaps between the stones, while eco-friendly gardeners might

Each of these alpine stone troughs, enhanced with small rocky outcrops and dwarf shrubs, is a unique miniature garden of lasting interest over many months of the year.

prefer using reclaimed materials, such as railway sleepers (ties). Bricks and mortar can look uncompromisingly harsh initially, but will soon be softened by trailing plants, such as *Gypsophila repens,* that will cascade down the sides.

All alpines thrive in containers, either individually or as collections in troughs. These also offer you the opportunity of growing acid-loving plants (such as rhododendrons and some gentians) if the soil in the

open garden in alkaline. Really tiny alpines are best appreciated in small troughs; you could add a few dwarf conifers to make a miniature mountainscape. Plants such as houseleeks *(Sempervivum)* which in nature seem to grow in virtually no soil at all, are best in shallow pans.

Both raised beds and troughs should be filled with free-draining soil or special alpine compost (soil mix) and can be topdressed with grit and small stones.

Androsace sempervivoides

Aquilegia alpina

Aquilegia flabellata

ALCHEMILLA

This large genus contains many plants that are too large for the rock garden, but the species described here are neater and less prone to self-seeding than the familiar *Alchemilla mollis*.
Cultivation Grow in fertile, well-drained soil in sun or semi-shade.

A. alpina
Alpine lady's mantle
The dark green, deeply lobed leaves form mats, surmounted by tiny, yellow-green flowers in summer. H to 10cm (4in), S 45cm (18in). Hardy/Z 3–7.

A. conjuncta
The lobed leaves are blue-green. Clusters of tiny yellow-green flowers are borne in summer and autumn. H to 40cm (16in), S 30cm (12in). Hardy/Z 4–8.

ANDROSACE

This genus of about 100 species includes many mat-forming perennials that are ideal for rock gardens or alpine troughs.
Cultivation Grow in gritty, well-drained but reliably moist soil in sun.

A. carnea
The species from the Pyrenees and Alps has rosettes of evergreen, hairy leaves and, in spring, clusters of small, yellow-eyed, pink flowers. H to 5cm (2in), S to 15cm (6in). Hardy/Z 4–7.
A. carnea subsp. *laggeri* has pinkish-red flowers and is more densely tufted. H to 5cm (2in), S to 15cm (6in).

A. sempervivoides
(syn. *A. mucronifolia* of gardens)
This evergreen, mat-forming species, native to the western Himalayas, has small, neatly formed, deep-green rosettes, which produce further rosettes on short, strawberry-like runners. The clusters of small, mauve-pink to mid-pink flowers are held above the rosettes on short stalks. H 5–7.5cm (2–3in), S 15–30cm (6–12in). Hardy/Z 4–7.

AQUILEGIA
Columbine
The genus is best known for the herbaceous perennials grown in the border, but it also includes a number of species suitable for the rock garden.
Cultivation Grow in gritty but fertile, well-drained soil in full sun.

A. alpina
(syn. *A. montana*)
Alpine columbine
Too tall for all but the largest rock gardens, this has pretty blue flowers in late spring and blue-green, ferny foliage. H 45cm (18in), S to 30cm (12in). Hardy/Z 4–7.

A. flabellata
(syn. *A. akitensis*)
This delightful little alpine columbine has neat, grey-green, divided foliage. The typical flowers are purple-blue with white tips to the petals. They are borne in late spring and early summer and will seed around in the garden. H 40–50cm (16–20in), S 15–20cm (6–8in). Hardy/Z

4–9. *A. flabellata* var. *pumila* f. *alba* (syn. *A. flabellata* 'Nana Alba') has up to three white flowers on each stem. H and S 10–15cm (4–6in). Hardy/Z 3–9.

ARABIS
Rock cress
The genus contains more than 100 species of annuals and evergreen perennials with white or purple, four-petalled flowers.
Cultivation These plants need well-drained soil and a warm position in full sun.

A. alpina subsp. caucasica
(syn. *A. caucasica*)
The common arabis of gardens comes from the Balkans and western Asia. It is a mat-forming evergreen with close, rather coarse rosettes of greyish-green leaves and bears clusters of white flowers in spring and early summer. H to 15cm (6in), S 50cm (20in). Hardy/Z 4–8. Selected forms

include **'Flore-Pleno'**, which has double, pure white flowers; and **'Variegata'**, which has leaves variegated with creamy yellow. H 15–25cm (6–10in), S 20–40cm (8–16in). Hardy/Z 4–8.

ARMERIA
Sea pink, thrift
The genus of evergreen perennials and subshrubs is distributed across Europe, northern Africa and North America. All species produce the little spherical flowerheads.
Cultivation Grow in well-drained soil that is not too rich, in a position in full sun.

A. maritima
(syn. *A. vulgaris*)
The familiar, tough, evergreen hummocks of slender, deep green leaves bear long-stalked heads of pink to reddish-purple flowers in summer. H and S 15–25cm (6–10in). Hardy/Z 4–7.
'Vindictive' has large, rich pink flowerheads. H to 15cm (6in), S 25cm (10in). Hardy/Z 4–7.

AUBRIETA
These evergreen perennials are popular and reliable garden plants, ideal for sunny walls, scree beds and all manner of crevices. The forms grown in gardens are derived from *A. deltoidea*.
Cultivation Grow in well-drained, neutral to alkaline soil in sun. Shear over after flowering to maintain a neat shape.

A. deltoidea
This species is the familiar aubrieta of gardens, which is

Arabis alpina subsp. caucasica

Armeria maritima

Aubrieta 'Doctor Mules'

Campanula carpatica

native to south-eastern Europe. It is an evergreen, mat-forming plant with close, deep green or grey-green foliage in lax rosettes. The clusters of reddish-purple, violet, mauve or pink flowers are borne in spring and intermittently through summer. H 10–15cm (4–6in), S 15–50cm (6–20in). Hardy/Z 5–7. Among the many named forms are 'Argenteovariegata' (syn. A. albomarginata), which has single, silver-pink flowers and leaves variegated with cream; 'Doctor Mules', which has deep purple flowers; and 'Joy', which has single, mauve flowers.

AURINIA

The evergreen perennials in the genus are found in mountainous areas throughout southern and central Europe. The small yellow or white flowers have four petals. *Cultivation* Grow in a position in full sun in moderately fertile soil.

Plants will benefit from being sheared over after flowering to keep them neat.

A. saxatilis
(syn. *Alyssum saxatile*)
Gold dust
The familiar yellow alyssum of gardens is a subshrub with large tufts of greyish- or whitish-green leaves. In spring and through summer the plants produce sprays of tiny, yellow flowers. H 20–30cm (8–12in), S 30–50cm (12–20in). Hardy/Z 4–7.

BALLOTA

This genus includes shrubs and perennials. The species described here is a compact subshrub for a sunny spot in a scree garden or in a Mediterranean planting. *Cultivation* This needs well-drained soil, which need not be fertile. Grow in full sun and clip back in spring to keep plants neat.

B. acetabulosa
The grey-green leaves, the main attraction, are borne in pairs along the upright stems. Tiny purple-pink flowers appear in summer. H and S to 60cm (24in). Hardy/Z 5–9.

CAMPANULA
Bellflower
In addition to the many border perennials in this large genus, there are many species that can be grown in the rock garden. *Cultivation* Campanulas should be grown in fertile, well-drained soil, ideally neutral to alkaline. Grow in a position in full sun.

C. 'Birch Hybrid'
This prostrate, evergreen hybrid has mauve-blue, bell-shaped flowers in summer. H to 10cm (4in), S 50cm (20in). Hardy/Z 4–7.

C. carpatica
This widely grown, herbaceous plant, originally from the Carpathian mountains, forms small tufts with numerous, bright green, oval, sharply toothed leaves. The upright, broadly bell-shaped flowers are violet, purple, blue or white and are borne in summer and autumn. H 15cm (6in), S 30–45cm (12–18in). Hardy/Z 4–7.

C. cochleariifolia
(syn. *C. bellardii, C. pusilla*)
Fairies' thimbles
This dainty little bellflower, native to the mountains of Europe, forms spreading mats by means of underground rhizomes. The small leaves are bright, lustrous green, and the thin stems bear several small, nodding bells in blue, lilac, lavender or, occasionally, white. H 8–13cm (3–5in), S 15–40cm (6–16in). Hardy/Z 5–7.

C. portenschlagiana
Dalmatian bellflower
An excellent plant from Croatia for rock crevices or for colonizing old walls. The tufts of small leaves are bright green, and in early summer the numerous branched stems bear a profusion of lilac-blue, rather narrow, bell-shaped flowers. H 15–25cm (6–10in), S 15–50cm (6–20in). Hardy/Z 4–7.

C. saxatilis
The spreading species, found in rocky areas of Crete, has round leaves that form rosettes. In summer pale blue, tubular flowers are borne in spikes. H to 8cm (3in), S to 20cm (8in). Hardy/Z 5–8.

CERASTIUM

The species described, a vigorous, mat-forming plant, can be invasive, and the genus, in fact, includes some weeds. The popular perennial *C. tomentosum* is too vigorous and invasive for a rock garden and should be confined to areas of poor soil where nothing else will grow, or allowed to cascade over a wall or bank. *Cultivation* Grow in full sun in gritty, well-drained soil.

C. alpinum
Alpine chickweed
The grey-green, evergreen leaves of this European species form compact mats above which clusters of small white flowers are borne in late spring to early summer. H 10cm (4in), S 30cm (12in). Hardy Z 3–8.

Aurinia saxatilis

Campanula portenschlagiana

Campanula 'Birch Hybrid'

Corydalis flexuosa

CORYDALIS

There are some 300 species in the genus, including many attractive annuals and biennials and some perennials, suitable for shady, woodland gardens and herbaceous borders.
Cultivation Grow in a semi-shaded spot in moist, humus-rich but well-drained soil.

C. flexuosa

This widely available herbaceous perennial is native to China. The tufts of grey-green or bright green, fern-like, dissected leaves are present through most of the year except high summer. The sprays of blue or lilac-blue, spurred flowers are borne on wiry stems in spring and early summer. H 30cm (12in), S 20–50cm (8–20in). Hardy/Z 5–8.

C. lutea
(syn. *Pseudofumaria lutea*)
This tufted, evergreen perennial has rather fleshy, grey-green,

Daphne cneorum

dissected leaves. The pale stems bear small sprays of yellow, spurred flowers from spring until autumn. An excellent plant for crevices, it often self-sows profusely in the garden. H and S to 30cm (12in). Hardy/Z 5–8.

DAPHNE

The genus is possibly best known for its wonderfully fragrant shrubs, but it also includes some delightful small species, suitable for rock and scree gardens and alpine troughs. All parts of the plants are poisonous.
Cultivation Daphnes need moist but well-drained, fertile soil and a position in sun or partial shade.

D. alpina

This upright, deciduous, twiggy shrub with elliptical, greyish leaves bears clusters of fragrant white flowers in late spring and early summer. H and S 40cm (16in). Hardy/Z 6–8.

D. arbuscula

This very small, extremely slow-growing, twiggy, evergreen shrub has narrow, rather leathery, shiny, deep green leaves. The clusters of fragrant pink flowers appear in late spring. This is an excellent trough plant. H and S 15cm (6in). Hardy/Z 5–7.

D. blagayana

The trailing stems of this mat-forming, usually evergreen shrub can root where they touch the ground. Clusters of sweet-smelling, white flowers appear in spring. H 10cm (4in), S 30cm (12in) or more.

D. cneorum
(syn. *D. odorata*)
Garland flower
This branching and trailing evergreen shrub has fragrant pink flowers in spring and, occasionally, a second flush in autumn. The dark green leaves are greyish on the underside. H 20cm (8in), S 1m (3ft). Hardy/Z 5–8. **'Eximia'** is a vigorous cultivar, with narrow, grey-green leaves and small clusters of deep rose pink, sweetly fragrant flowers in late spring. H 20cm (8in), S 1m (3ft).

D. sericea Collina Group
(syn. *D. collina*)
Plants sold under this name are dense-growing, with elliptical, rather bristly, grey-green leaves. Pale to mid-pink flowers are borne in dense clusters in late spring and early summer. H and S 60cm (24in). Hardy/Z 7–8.

DIANTHUS
Pink
This huge genus includes many perennials as well as annuals and biennials. There are also several members of the genus that are ideally suited to raised beds, rock and scree gardens and to alpine troughs.
Cultivation Grow in fertile but gritty, well-drained soil (ideally neutral to alkaline) in full sun.

D. alpinus
Alpine pink
This delightful pink, which is native to the eastern Alps, forms a small, evergreen mat of deep green, narrow, blunt-tipped leaves. The relatively large, fringed flowers are pink to cerise or purplish-pink, with generous speckling above. H 10cm (4in), S 20cm (8in). Hardy/Z 5–8. **'Joan's Blood'** has very dark flowers with almost black centres. H 10cm (4in), S 20cm (8in).

D. deltoides
Maiden pink
This variable species, native to Europe and western Asia, is a mat-forming, evergreen perennial with numerous narrow, deep green leaves that are often flushed with

Dianthus deltoides

Dianthus alpinus

bronze or purple. The spreading, branched stems bear numerous small, fringed flowers in pink, cerise, crimson or white in summer and autumn. H 15–25cm (6–10in), S 30–50cm (12–20in). Hardy/Z 5–8.

DODECATHEON
American cowslip, shooting star
The perennial species that comprise this genus are native to North America, where they are found in meadows and woodland. They have cyclamen-like flowers, with swept-back petals.
Cultivation Grow in well-drained, reliably moist and fertile soil in sun or partial shade.

D. pulchellum
(syn. *D. radicatum*)
The dark green, oval leaves form rosettes above which the deep pink flowers are borne in mid- to late spring. H 35cm (14in), S 15cm (6in). Hardy/Z 3–8.

ERIGERON
Fleabane
This genus, which includes annuals and biennials, is best known for the perennial hybrids that bring colour to the summer border, but a number of species are suitable for rock gardens.
Cultivation Grow in well-drained but reliably moist soil in sun.

E. alpinus
Alpine fleabane
This species, native to central and southern Europe, has narrow, grey-green, hairy leaves. Yellow-centred, mauve, daisy-like flowers

are borne from mid- to late summer. H 25cm (10in), S 20cm (8in). Hardy/Z 5–8.

E. glaucus
Beach aster
This evergreen, leafy sub-shrub is native to western North America. It has rather coarse, pale bluish-green, oval leaves, and in summer numerous pale violet to lavender flowerheads are produced, each with an egg-yolk yellow centre. H to 50cm (20in), S 45–90cm (18–36in). Hardy/Z 5–8.

ERINUS
The two semi-evergreen or evergreen species that comprise this genus are native to rocky areas in central and southern Europe and northern Africa. Only the species described is in general cultivation.
Cultivation Grow in well-drained soil in sun or partial shade.

E. alpinus
Fairy foxglove
This species is found in rocky places in central and southern Europe, where it forms small, evergreen tufts. The neatly toothed foliage is mainly borne in small rosettes, and from late spring to summer the rosy-purple or white flowers are clustered at the ends of short leafy stems. H 15cm (6in), S 20cm (8in). Hardy/Z 4–7.

EURYOPS
Although there are about 100 species in the genus, only a few are widely grown. The species

Euryops acraeus

described is not reliably hardy and needs a sheltered position in a rock garden or raised bed.
Cultivation Grow in fairly rich, well-drained soil in full sun. Shear after flowering to keep plants neat.

E. acraeus
(**syn. E. evansii of gardens**)
This compact evergreen shrub, which is native to South Africa, has crowded, narrow, silver-grey leaves. The daisy-like flowers are acid-yellow and appear in summer. H and S 40cm (16in). Borderline hardy/Z 9–10.

GENTIANA
Gentian
The genus contains about 400 species of annuals, biennials and perennials, which may be evergreen, semi-evergreen or herbaceous. Some require the specialized cultural conditions best provided in an alpine house, but many other species are suitable for growing in a rock or scree garden or an alpine trough.
Cultivation Grow in moist but well-drained soil. Most summer-flowering gentians need a position in full sun and prefer neutral to alkaline soil; most autumn-flowering gentians need acid soil and shelter from hot sun.

G. acaulis
(**syn. G. excisa, G. kochiana**)
Trumpet gentian
One of the most beautiful of alpine plants, the species is from the mountains of central and southern Europe. It forms dense mats of evergreen, leathery leaves.

Gentiana acaulis

In spring, and sometimes also in autumn, large, bell-shaped flowers in rich kingfisher-blue appear. H 10cm (4in), S 40cm (16in). Hardy/Z 4–7.

G. asclepiadea
Willow gentian
This herbaceous perennial is from the mountains of southern and central Europe. In mid- to late summer it bears beautiful, trumpet-shaped, rich blue flowers. The narrow leaves are mid-green. H 75cm (30in) or more, S 45cm (18in). Hardy/Z 6–9.

G. septemfida
This herbaceous species is from the mountains of western Asia. It forms discreet tufts with spreading stems, which bear pairs of elliptical, deep green leaves. One or several deep blue, bell-shaped flowers are borne at the stem tips in late summer and autumn. H 10–25cm (4–10in), S 20–40cm (8–16in). Hardy/Z 6–8.

G. sino-ornata
Autumn gentian
This, the finest autumn-flowering gentian, comes from western China. It is a herbaceous perennial, forming small tufts of narrow, sharply pointed, deep green, rather glossy leaves. The solitary, deep blue, green- and purple-striped, bell-shaped flowers are held on the ends of the spreading stems. It needs humus-rich, acid soil. H 10–15cm (4–6in), S 15–25cm (6–10in). Hardy/Z 5–7.

G. verna
Spring gentian, star gentian
This evergreen perennial species from mountainous areas across Europe is one of the great delights of the alpine garden. It forms small tufts of bright green, oval foliage. The rich-blue, white-centred flowers appear in spring to early summer. H 8cm (3in), S 10–20cm (4–8in). Hardy/Z 4–7.

GERANIUM
Cranesbill
The large genus includes many perennials, but the dainty species described below are ideal for rock gardens and alpine troughs.
Cultivation Grow in any well-drained soil in full sun.

G. cinereum
The species, which is native to the Pyrenees, is an evergreen or semi-evergreen perennial with rounded, lobed, grey-green leaves. The paired, saucer-shaped flowers are pink with an elaborate network of purple veins and are produced in late spring and summer. H 15cm (6in), S 25cm (10in). Hardy/Z 4–9. **'Ballerina'** has grey leaves and purplish flowers with dark red-purple eyes.

G. dalmaticum
This clump-forming, evergreen perennial from the western Balkans has rounded, deeply lobed, glossy green leaves. The flowers, borne in masses in early and midsummer, are a rich pink with orange-red anthers. H 15cm (6in), S 50cm (20in). Hardy/Z 5–8.

Erinus alpinus

Geranium cinereum 'Ballerina'

GYPSOPHILA

The genus is best known for *G. paniculata*, which produces the familiar sprays of tiny white flowers, but the species described is a mat-forming plant, ideal for a rock or scree garden.
Cultivation Grow in well-drained, preferably alkaline soil in full sun.

G. repens

This mat-forming, semi-evergreen perennial is native to central and southern Europe. It has grey-green leaves and, in summer, clouds of tiny white, pink or purplish-pink flowers. H 20cm (8in), S 50cm (20in). Hardy/Z 4–7. **'Dorothy Teacher'** is a neat cultivar, with pale pink flowers. H 5cm (2in), S 40cm (16in). **'Fratensis'** has narrow, grey-green leaves, and the spreading stems bear sprays of small pink flowers. H 8cm (5in), S 30cm (12in).

G. tenuifolia
(syn. *G. gracilescens*)
This low-growing, hummock-forming, evergreen alpine is native to the Caucasus. It has a mass of grass-like, mid-green foliage, and the small white or pale pink flowers are borne aloft on delicate wiry stems in summer. H 10–15cm (4–6in), S 15–25cm (6–10in). Hardy/Z 5–9.

IBERIS
Candytuft
These easy-to-grow plants are ideal for sunny rock gardens or walls.
Cultivation Grow in any moist, well-drained soil, preferably neutral to alkaline, in sun.

I. saxatilis

This evergreen species from southern Europe has dark green leaves and clusters of small white (occasionally purplish) flowers in summer. H 15cm (6in), S 20cm (8in). Hardy/Z 4–8.

I. sempervirens
(syn. *I. commutata*)
A useful plant, this spreading, evergreen subshrub from southern Europe has dark green leaves carrying dense heads of brilliant white flowers in late spring and early summer. H 30cm (12in), S 60cm (24in). Hardy/Z 5–9.

Gypsophila repens 'Fratensis'

LEONTOPODIUM
Edelweiss
The genus contains species from the mountains of Europe and Asia. The insignificant flowers are surrounded by long, narrow bracts. Although some species require the specialized conditions of an alpine house, the species described will grow in rock gardens and raised beds.
Cultivation Grow in very well-drained, slightly alkaline soil in full sun. Protect from winter wet.

L. alpinum

This is the edelweiss of the European mountains. It is a small, short-lived, tufted perennial with narrow, greyish, felted foliage. The small, button-flowerheads are clustered and surrounded by white, woolly bracts, giving a daisy-like appearance. H and S 15cm (6in). Hardy/Z 4–6. **'Mignon'**, which is more mat-forming, has dark green leaves and smaller flowerheads than the species. H 10cm (4in), S 30cm (12in).

Leontopodium alpinum

Iberis sempervirens

LEWISIA

This genus of hardy perennials from North America form rosettes of strap-shaped leaves and showy, colourful flowers. Because they resent winter wet, they are often grown in alpine houses. Where they can be sheltered, they are ideal for rock gardens or walls.
Cultivation Grow in neutral to acid soil in light shade. Good drainage is essential.

L. cotyledon

This evergreen perennial is the most tolerant of the genus, and has spoon-shaped leaves, which form a tight rosette. The flowers, usually pinkish-purple but sometimes white, yellow or pinkish-yellow, are borne in clusters on upright stems. H 30cm (12in), S 25cm (10in). Hardy/Z 6–7. **Cotyledon Hybrids** have funnel-shaped flowers in shades of pink, magenta, orange and yellow. H to 30cm (12in), S to 40cm (16in). Flower colours of plants in the **Sunset Group** are in the yellow to red range.

Lychnis alpina

LYCHNIS
Campion, catchfly
The genus is familiar in cottage-garden plantings, but the species described here is better suited to an alpine trough or rock garden.

L. alpina
Alpine catchfly, alpine campion
This charming tufted perennial, which is native to a large part of northern and central Europe, has narrow, grassy foliage. Clusters of bright rose-purple flowers are held at the tops of short, leafy stems, each petal neatly notched. H and S 15cm (6in). Hardy/Z 4–7.

PENSTEMON

This large genus is often represented in gardens by the border perennials, but the species described here are ideal for rock and scree gardens.
Cultivation Grow in gritty, well-drained soil in sun.

P. alpinus

This clump-forming species from North America has broad leaves, which form dense rosettes, and blue or purplish, white-throated flowers from summer to autumn. H 25cm (10in), S 20cm (8in). Hardy/Z 5–9.

P. hirsutus var. pygmaeus

The typical species is an evergreen subshrub, large enough for a border, but this naturally occurring variety is compact and mat-forming. It has purple-tinged leaves and purplish flowers in summer. H and S 10cm (4in). Hardy/Z 5–8.

PHLOX

This is a large genus, which includes many perennials, some of which are semi-evergreen or evergreen, grown for summer colour in the border. There are also a number of low-growing, mat-forming species, which can be grown in rock gardens, raised beds and walls.
Cultivation The plants described here are best in fertile, moist but well-drained soil in light shade. *P. divaricata* and its forms and *P. subulata* can also be grown in full sun.

Penstemon hirsutus var. pygmaeus

P. divaricata subsp. laphamii 'Chattahoochee'
(syn. P. 'Chattahoochee')
This rather lax perennial, which is native to wooded areas in North America, has spreading stems bearing pairs of elliptical, deep green leaves, which are often flushed with purple. The saucer-shaped flowers, which are deep lavender with a crimson eye, are produced in summer over a long season. H 20cm (8in), S 30cm (12in). Hardy/Z 5–9.

P. douglasii
Also from North America, this low mat- or cushion-forming, evergreen perennial has small, tooth-like leaf-pairs. The fragrant, saucer-shaped flowers, borne in late spring and early summer, solitary or several, are clustered together close to the foliage, and they vary in colour from pink to lavender, purple, red or white. H 10cm (4in), S 20cm (8in). Hardy/Z 5–7. **'Boothman's Variety'** has violet-pink flowers with dark blue centres. H 8cm (3in), S 20cm (8in). **'Iceberg'** is white with a bluish coat.

P. subulata
Moss phlox
This species, which is native to the eastern United States, is a mat-forming, evergreen perennial with much-branched stems and numerous linear, pointed leaf-pairs. The saucer-shaped flowers, in shades of pink, purple, red or white, appear in late spring and early summer and are borne in clusters at the shoot-tips, close to the foliage. H 15cm (6in), S 50cm (20in). Hardy/Z 4–9.

PLATYCODON
Balloon flower
The single species in the genus comes from China, Korea and Japan. The common name derives from the shape of the buds from which the flowers open.
Cultivation Grow in fertile, moist but well-drained soil. These plants must have full sun.

P. grandiflorus
This clump-forming herbaceous perennial has erect, pale stems and oval to elliptical, toothed leaves. The deep blue flowers open from balloon-like buds. H 60cm (2ft), S 30cm (1ft). Hardy/Z 4–9. There are several selected forms, of which the dwarf **'Apoyama'** is particularly suitable for a rock garden. It has deep violet flowers. H and S 20cm (8in).

PRIMULA
Primrose
Besides the many valuable border perennials, the genus includes many species that are suitable for rock gardens or alpine houses.
Cultivation Grow in very well-drained, humus-rich soil in a sunny position.

Primula marginata

P. auricula
Bear's ear
The common auricula, native to the Alps, is a low, tufted perennial with rosettes of deep green, rather fleshy leaves. The scented, yellow flowers, up to 2.5cm (1in) across, are clustered at the stalk-tips in spring. H 7.5–15cm (3–6in), S 10–20cm (4–8in). Hardy/Z 5–7. There are many named forms, including **'Chocolate Soldier'**, which has double, brownish-purple flowers, the petals edged with golden-yellow; and **'Marie Crousse'**, which has double, violet flowers edged with white. H to 15cm (6in), S 25cm (10in).

P. marginata
This tufted, evergreen perennial from the Alps has rosettes of leathery, green or grey-green leaves, which are coarsely toothed and often have whitish powder along the margin. The pink to bluish-lavender, primrose flowers are clustered at the end of short stalks. H 13cm (5in), S 20cm (8in). Hardy/Z 4–7.

P. vulgaris
Common primrose
This more or less evergreen perennial, native to Europe and western Asia, has rough, elliptical, bright green leaves borne in lax basal rosettes. The fragrant, yellow flowers are borne in profusion in late winter and spring. H 10–20cm (4–8in), S 35cm (14in). Hardy/Z 3–8. Named selections include **'Alba Plena'**, with double white flowers, and **'Lilacina Plena'**, with double lilac flowers. Some plants sold under this name may be hybrids with other species.

PULSATILLA
Pasque flower
These lovely perennials have large, bell-shaped flowers, which are followed by silky seedheads. Plant in a raised bed or rock garden where the exquisite flowers can be appreciated.
Cultivation Grow in gritty, well-drained, chalky soil in full sun.

P. alpina
Alpine pasque flower
The species, which is native to mountainous areas of central Europe, has dark green, finely divided foliage. The white flowers, borne in spring, are tinged with bluish-mauve on the outside and have a central mass of bright yellow stamens. H 30cm (12in), S 20cm (8in). Hardy/Z 3–5.

P. vernalis
(syn. Anemone vernalis)
The leaves of this clump-forming species, which is native to Europe and Siberia, are dark green and finely divided. The beautiful white flowers, flushed with pale purplish-blue on the outside, have bright yellow centres. Protect from winter wet. H 10cm (4in), S 20cm (8in). Hardy/Z 5–8.

P. vulgaris
(syn. Anemone pulsatilla)
The species, found across Europe, has tufts of finely divided, deep green, rather feathery leaves. The solitary, half-nodding to erect, bell-shaped flowers, which are borne in spring, may be white, red, violet-blue or purple and have silky hairs on the outside. H 20cm (8in), S 30cm (12in). Hardy/Z 5–7. **'Alba'** is the white-flowered form.

Phlox divaricata subsp. laphamii 'Chattahoochee'

Platycodon grandiflorus

Pulsatilla vulgaris

Saponaria ocymoides

RAMONDA

The small genus includes three species of evergreen perennials. They are suitable for rock gardens, raised beds or walls, where they can be grown sideways on. They resent winter wet and for this reason are often grown in alpine houses.
Cultivation Grow in rich but very well-drained soil in partial shade.

R. myconi
(syn. *R. pyrenaica*)
The species is native to northern Spain. It has dark green, hairy leaves in neat rosettes above which dark purplish-blue, yellow-centred flowers are borne in late spring to early summer. H 10cm (4in), S 20cm (8in). Hardy/Z 5–7.

SALIX
Willow
Better known for its larger shrubs and trees, the genus also includes dwarf species, which are suitable

Salix 'Boydii'

for rock gardens or alpine troughs.
Cultivation Grow in gritty, well-drained soil in full sun.

S. 'Boydii'
(syn. *S. × boydii*)
This slow-growing, twiggy, deciduous shrub develops a thick trunk, which eventually looks rather gnarled. The rounded and crinkly leaves are grey-green, paler beneath. Small, brownish, upright catkins are produced in spring. H 30cm (12in), S 25cm (10in). Hardy/Z 4–7.

SAPONARIA
Soapwort
A genus of annuals and perennials from mountainous areas of Europe and south-western Asia. The well-known *S. officinalis* is suitable for a mixed border, but the plants described below can be grown in a rock garden, alpine trough or raised bed.
Cultivation Grow in gritty, well-drained soil in full sun.

S. 'Bressingham'
This mat-forming perennial hybrid has mid-green leaves and clusters of deep pink flowers in summer. H 8cm (3in), S 30cm (12in). Hardy/Z 4–8.

S. ocymoides
Rock soapwort, tumbling Ted
A mat-forming, evergreen perennial, this is native to central and south-eastern Europe. It has numerous, small, oval, deep green leaves. In late spring and summer, spreading clusters of pink or purplish flowers appear. Cut back

after flowering to keep plants neat. H 10cm (4in), S 30cm (12in). Hardy/Z 4–8.

SAXIFRAGA
Saxifrage
This is a large genus of more than 400 species of mat- or cushion-forming, evergreen or deciduous perennials that are widely distributed in the northern hemisphere, where they are found in mountainous regions. They show considerable variation in habit and leaf form and are widely grown in rock and scree gardens, raised beds and alpine troughs.
Cultivation Grow in rich, gritty, well-drained, neutral to alkaline soil in full sun.

S. cochlearis
A mound-forming, evergreen perennial from the south-western Alps, this has numerous, crowded rosettes of greyish, lime-encrusted leaf-rosettes. In summer, airy sprays of dainty, white flowers are produced on slender, reddish stems. H 25cm (10in), S 15cm (6in). Hardy/Z 6.

S. 'Kathleen Pinsent'
The spoon-shaped, silvery leaves form rosettes above which the pink flowers are borne in arching clusters. H and S 20cm (8in). Hardy/Z 5–7.

S. oppositifolia
Purple saxifrage
This saxifrage, native to many cold regions in the northern hemisphere, is a dense, mat-forming, evergreen alpine. It has

Saxifraga cochlearis

Saxifraga paniculata

deep green, scale-like leaves densely clothing the spreading stems. In late winter and early spring, solitary pale pink to rich purple flowers appear close to the foliage. H 2.5cm (1in), S 20cm (8in). Hardy/Z 2–6.

S. paniculata
(syn. *S. aizoon*)
This tufted, evergreen perennial, which is native to Europe, Canada and Greenland, has crowded rosettes of grey-green, lime-encrusted leaves. In summer, airy sprays of small, white or cream flowers are borne on stiff, arching stalks. H 15cm (6in), S 30cm (12in). Hardy/Z 4–6.

S. 'Tumbling Waters'
This slow-growing, mat-forming, evergreen hybrid grows in tight rosettes of narrow, lime-encrusted, silvery leaves. When the plant matures after several years, dense, arching, conical heads of small, open cup-shaped, white flowers are produced, after which the main rosette dies and the small offsets grow on. H 60cm (2ft), S 30cm (12in). Hardy/Z 5–7.

SEDUM
Stonecrop
The large and diverse genus contains around 400 species including perennials and succulents. They are from the northern hemisphere, where they are found in mountain and arid regions, and they are ideal plants for withstanding drought and strong sunshine. Some of the alpine types have a creeping,

scrambling habit, which will cover rock edges.
Cultivation Grow sedums in neutral to slightly alkaline, very well-drained soil in full sun.

S. acre
Wallpepper, biting stonecrop
This species, which is found in Europe, North Africa and western Asia, is a familiar little plant of old walls and rooftops. It is a bright green succulent with tiny, closely overlapping leaves. In summer, the shoot tips burst with flat-topped heads of tiny, star-shaped, yellow-green flowers. H 5cm (2in), S 60cm (2ft) or more. Hardy/Z 4–9.

S. pulchellum
Native to the south-eastern United States, this is a laxly tufted, succulent perennial with erect to ascending stems adorned with narrow leaves. The starry pink flowers are freely produced in summer. It is often grown as an annual. H 5cm (2in), S 25cm (10in). Hardy/Z 8.

S. spathulifolium
This compact species from western North America grows into rosettes. It is a mat-forming perennial with spoon-shaped, fleshy, brittle green or silvery leaves, often tinted with bronze and purple. In summer sprays of short-stemmed, tiny, star-shaped bright yellow flowers are produced. H 5cm (2in), S indefinite. Hardy/Z 5–9.

SEMPERVIVUM
Houseleek
The 40 species in the genus are mat-forming, evergreen succulents, largely from mountainous regions of Europe and Asia. There are many hybrids, some differing only slightly (if at all) from each other. They are ideal for rock and scree gardens, alpine troughs, walls and containers.
Cultivation Grow in gritty, very well-drained soil in full sun. Protect from winter wet.

S. arachnoideum
Cobweb houseleek
This mat- or mound-forming evergreen perennial is native to

Sempervivum montanum

central and south-west Europe. It has numerous, greyish leaf-rosettes, tipped with red and enveloped in a cobweb of whitish hairs. The starry, pinkish-red flowers are clustered at the top of a short, leafy stem in summer. H 10cm (4in), S 10cm (4in). Hardy/Z 5–9.

S. montanum
(syn. *S. helveticum*)
An evergreen perennial from central and southern Europe, this forms low mounds of dull green, downy, succulent leaf-rosettes. The wine-red, starry flowers are borne at the tips of erect flowering shoots in summer. H 10–20cm (4–8in), S 20–40cm (8–16in). Hardy/Z 5.

S. tectorum
Common houseleek
This rather coarse, evergreen perennial from mountainous areas of central and southern Europe has large, succulent leaf-rosettes, the leaves usually green or grey-green with reddish or purplish

Sempervivum arachnoideum

Veronica prostrata

tips. A mass of star-shaped, dull pink to purple flowers is borne on stout, leafy stems in summer. H 20cm (8in), S 50cm (20in). Hardy/Z 5–9.

VERONICA
Speedwell, brooklime
The genus contains about 250 species of diverse plants, originating mainly in Europe, where they are found in a range of habitats. Some are cushion-forming or mat-forming species, which are suitable for the rock garden, where they can be exploited to soften unsightly edges. Others are border perennials. They are easy to grow.
Cultivation Grow in fairly poor, well-drained soil in full sun.

V. prostrata
Prostrate speedwell
This mat-forming perennial, from the mountains of Europe, has deep green, narrow-oblong leaves. In summer, spikes of rich blue or purplish flowers are borne above the foliage on stiff, somewhat leafy, stems. 'Trehane' has lime green leaves, a sharp contrast to its darker blue flowers. H 15cm (6in), S 40cm (16in). Hardy/Z 4–7.

VIOLA
Pansy, violet
There are pansies and violas for every position in the garden, from the front of borders to alpine houses. They are ideal for summer bedding, and the smaller species are perfect for rock gardens, raised beds and containers.

V. cornuta
Horned violet, viola
This spreading plant, ideal for groundcover and growing with blue-leafed hostas, has deep violet flowers among the copious leaves in early summer. Shearing these off triggers a second crop in late summer. H 15cm (6in), S 60cm (24in). Hardy/Z 5–8. Plants belonging to the **Alba Group** have white flowers. H 15cm (6in), S 60cm (24in). '**Alba Minor**' is similar but more compact. **Lilacina Group** plants produce flowers in shades of lilac.

V. lutea
Mountain pansy
This tufted perennial, native to the mountains of central and western Europe, has bright green, oval leaves and pansy flowers, which are yellow, violet or bi-coloured and appear in spring and summer. H and S 15cm (6in). Hardy/Z 4–8.

Viola cornuta Alba Group

Water plants

Water is the most mysterious and beguiling of the four elements. There have been few more remarkable phenomena than the upsurge of interest in water features of all kinds in recent years. This is no doubt partly due to care for the environment, for any patch of water is bound to attract beneficial wildlife into the garden. Water plants – both those that grow in water and those that revel in the damp margins of a pool – are mostly easy to grow and maintain, and themselves do much to benefit the ecology of the garden at large.

This series of linked pools makes a calming feature, lushly planted with waterlilies and bordered by moisture-loving plants.

Water plants for your garden

Also called aquatics or hydrophytes, water plants are those plants that are specially adapted to live in water. Here the term is extended to include bog and marginal plants that grow in water-saturated soils.

Aquatics may be rooted in the mud and have their leaves and flowers above or at the surface of the water. Some kinds grow completely underwater. Submerged water plants often have air bladders or large air pores in their stems and leaves that help the plants stand upright or stay afloat.

Most aquatics are perennials. Only a few woody plants are adapted to thrive in permanently waterlogged conditions. A number of perennials, while thriving in soil that is reliably moist, seem equally happy in ordinary border soil, and in this book these are included with the rest of the perennials. Some of the grasses and bamboos also thrive in wet soil.

The water plants described here are adapted to varying depths of water. Bog plants need soil that is

Water lilies are the aristocrats of the water garden, here sharing the depths with the intriguing water soldier (*Stradiodes aloides*).

permanently wet, such as occurs on the edges of a natural pool or stream. Marginals are plants that like to have water around their ankles, usually to a depth of up to 15cm (6in) above the soil level. Deep-water plants have their roots in the mud at the bottom of the pond and (usually) leaves that float on the surface. This group includes the queen of all water plants, the water lily (*Nymphaea*), and no pond is complete without at least one of these beauties. Surface floaters also have floating leaves, but their roots hang unanchored, feeding on nutrients dissolved in the water. One important group is the so-called oxygenators, usually submerged plants that float just below the surface. These are seldom things of beauty in their own right but contribute much to the ecological balance of the pond.

An important consideration when choosing water plants is whether the water is still or moving. The majority are best in still water, though many of the oxygenators are adapted to tolerate moving water.

Water in the garden

A water feature brings an extra element into the garden, and for many people nowadays a garden would not be complete without one.

Water features can take many forms. A small bubble fountain or water spout mounted on a wall, attractive though these are, cannot support much plant life beyond the mosses and lichens that may ultimately take a hold. To grow the plants described in this chapter, you need a dedicated pond, ideally as big as possible, since most water plants are rampant growers. It is difficult to maintain an ecological balance in a very small, shallow pond, which will soon be colonized by duckweed and algae. Nevertheless, in a confined space, it is possible to make an attractive feature with a wooden half barrel, or similar deep container, which can be planted with a miniature water lily. Although most water plants are best in still rather than running water, it is perfectly acceptable for a pool to incorporate a fountain or other water-agitating device, provided this is not allowed to play continuously. In fact, it can

Most aquatics are rampant growers, but the water violet (*Hottonia palustris*) will deceive you with its dainty flowers.

be beneficial, helping to aerate and cool the water during hot weather.

Ponds are best sited in an open, sunny part of the garden, away from overhanging deciduous trees, which will not only shade the water, but drop their leaves in the pond in autumn, leading to a build-up of noxious gases as they decompose.

Water gardens should incorporate a variety of plant material. Submerged plants such as *Lagarosiphon major* provide the essential function of absorbing the nutrients that encourage algae and releasing oxygen, besides providing shelter for small aquatic invertebrates. Plants with floating leaves, such as water lilies, fulfil the valuable function of shading the surface of the water in summer – important if the water is not to overheat. The aim should be for the surface to be covered by between a half and one-third in summer. Marginals have less impact on water clarity, but soften the edges of the pool, besides providing shelter for wildlife.

In a formal pool, the proportions of which relate to other elements in the garden, it is usually best to keep the planting to the minimum, with perhaps a few well-chosen water lilies and some oxygenators to help keep the water clear. Judiciously placed containers around the edge can help to create symmetry and balance.

Informal pools that are more lushly planted will soon attract all manner of wildlife into the garden, which will mostly be of benefit to the garden at large besides being of interest in its own right. A pool is thus an essential element of any garden planned along ecological, environmentally friendly lines.

Water attracts a host of beneficial insects into the garden, as well as vertebrates that will feed on them. Frogs, toads, birds and hedgehogs, which will be attracted to the water, will help keep down slug and snail populations. If your intention is to maintain a breeding colony of frogs, keep fish out of the pond: they will eat frog spawn and attack tadpoles. It is perfectly possible to have two pools, of course, a strictly ornamental pool for fish and an environmental pool.

In a wild garden, this large pond is host to some of the more vigorous water lilies, with the lush and dense waterside plantings a haven for wildlife.

Aponogeton distachyos

Caltha palustris

ALISMA
Water plantain
There are nine species of aquatics in this genus found across the world, mainly in the northern hemisphere, growing on marsh and lake edges. The seeds, which provide valuable food for wildlife, are produced in abundance.
Cultivation Grow in a sunny position in water to 15cm (6in) deep.

A. plantago-aquatica
This deciduous perennial has rosettes of oval, grey-green, ribbed leaves, carried on tall stalks that emerge well above the water. Tiny, pinkish-white flowers appear in midsummer, with three petals arranged in whorls on a pyramidal spike. H 75cm (30in), S 45cm (18in). Hardy/Z 5–8.

APONOGETON
The genus contains some 44 species of rhizomatous perennials, mostly with floating leaves, which are found in mainly tropical and subtropical areas, but there is one hardy species, which is used extensively in cold water ponds. It is a tolerant plant, particularly of shade, which extends the flowering season.
Cultivation Grow in sun or shade in water to 60cm (2ft).

A. distachyos
Water hawthorn, Cape pondweed
This deep-water aquatic has oblong, bright green leaves, which can be semi-evergreen in mild winters. The white flowers, with purple-brown anthers, are held above the water. Scented, they can be produced in two flushes, in spring and autumn. S 1.2m (4ft). Borderline hardy/Z 9–10.

CALLA
A genus containing one species, a perennial marginal from the northern hemisphere, where it is found in swamps, bogs and wet woods. In mild winters it is semi-evergreen.
Cultivation Grow in full sun in water that is no deeper than 5cm (2in).

C. palustris
Bog arum
This has conspicuous, long, creeping surface roots and round to heart-shaped, glossy, mid-green leaves, which are firm and leathery. The flowers, which appear in spring, look like miniature arum lilies, and are followed by clusters

Calla palustris

of red or orange berries. H 25cm (10in), S 30cm (12in) or more. Hardy/Z 3–8.

CALLITRICHE
Water starwort
The 25 species in this genus are widely distributed throughout the world. They are small, slender plants, generally growing in a tight mass in a wide range of habitats, but mainly in temperate locations. The species described are valuable oxygenators.
Cultivation Grow in sun or partial shade in water to 50cm (20in) deep.

C. hermaphroditica
(syn. C. autumnalis)
Autumn starwort
This species has light green, linear leaves, held opposite each other on the thin, branching stems. The intertwined mass of stems is an important habitat for many smaller forms of plant life, and the young leaves are a particular delicacy for goldfish. This species is unique in not forming rosettes of floating leaves. S indefinite. Hardy/Z 4–9.

C. palustris
(syn. C. verna)
A submerged oxygenating plant from north Africa and Europe with cress-like leaves, which die back in winter. S indefinite. Hardy/Z 4–9.

CALTHA
This widespread and common genus contains ten species of temperate marginals, which are

extremely popular in both ornamental and wildlife ponds.
Cultivation Grow in sun or partial shade in water no deeper than 10–15cm (4–6in).

C. palustris
Marsh marigold, kingcup
Indispensable for the pond margins, the marsh marigold has long-stalked lower leaves and stalkless upper leaves, which grow longer at flowering. The glistening yellow, buttercup-like flowers can appear as early as late winter in a mild season but are generally at their peak in midspring. H 15–30cm (6–12in), S 45cm (18in). Hardy/Z 4–9.
'Flore Pleno' smothers itself in double yellow flowers in spring, often producing a second flush in the summer, and is more compact. H and S 25cm (10in).

EICHHORNIA
Water hyacinth, water orchid
There are seven species in this genus of tropical, mainly floating plants from South America, where they root in shallow mud and form huge colonies, which can swamp rivers and lakes, becoming a major problem. The species described will not survive winters outdoors in cool climates, but for a few months in hot weather it is a striking sight on the pond surface.
Cultivation Grow in full sun and warm water, preferably 18°C (64°F). Overwinter under glass at 10–13°C (50–55°F) on trays of moist soil.

E. crassipes
(syn. E. speciosa)
The shiny, pale green leaves have inflated bases, which act as floats.

Eichhornia crassipes

In very warm summers, spikes of pale lilac-blue hyacinth-like flowers appear. Long, feathery, dangling roots, purplish-black in colour, are perfect shelter for spawning goldfish. H 15–23cm (6–9in), S 15–30cm (6–12in), more in favourable conditions. Tender/Z 8–10.

FONTINALIS
Water moss
There are more than 50 species of submerged aquatic mosses in the genus, which are found throughout the world. They all form floating mats.
Cultivation Grow in sun or partial shade in water to about 40cm (16in) deep. Divide in spring. The species described here is suitable for growing in moving water.

F. antipyretica
Willow moss
The slender stems, to 80cm (32in) long, are covered with small, evergreen, dark green leaves. S indefinite. Hardy/Z 4–10.

GUNNERA
These perennials are widely distributed in the southern hemisphere. Some of them are gigantic plants, producing huge leaves. The sinister-looking *S. mamiata* has the largest of any hardy plant. Plenty of moisture and protection from wind are needed if they are to be seen at their best.
Cultivation Grow in sun or partial shade in fertile, moist soil. In cold climates, cover the resting crowns of *S. mamiata* with the old leaves.

G. magellanica
This mat-forming herbaceous perennial has dark green, rounded to kidney-shaped leaves, which are tinged bronze when young. H 15cm (6in), S 30cm (12in). Borderline hardy/Z 8–9.

G. manicata
(syn. G. brasiliensis)
Giant rhubarb
This dramatic species is the largest in the genus, with vast leaves, 2m (6ft) or more across, carried on bristly stalks. The flower spike is like a red-tinged

Houttuynia cordata 'Chameleon'

Houttuynia cordata 'Flore Pleno'

Hydrocharis morsus-ranae

bottlebrush to 1m (3ft) tall. H 2.4m (8ft), S 4m (13ft). Borderline hardy/Z 7–10.

HOTTONIA
The genus contains two species of submerged plants with delicate, primula-like flowers, which are held above the water. They are mainly found in clear ponds or slow-moving ditches in temperate areas of the northern hemisphere.
Cultivation Grow in full sun and clear water.

H. palustris
Water violet
In summer this oxygenator bears violet or white flowers with yellow throats, held well above the surface of the water. The submerged, bright green leaves are finely divided and are arranged like the teeth of a comb. S indefinite. Hardy/Z 5–9.

HOUTTUYNIA
The genus consists of a single species, which originates in eastern Asia. The plant flourishes in wet soil or the shallow margins of ponds and streams, creeping along pond margins and producing extensive mats of shallow rhizomes.
Cultivation Grow in full sun or partial shade in shallow water no deeper than 2.5–5cm (1–2in). This can be invasive and should be grown in a container in a small pond. It can also be grown in borders where the soil does not dry out.

H. cordata
The straight species has heart-shaped, metallic green leaves that smell of oranges when crushed. In full sun, they redden in autumn. The white flowers, with cone-like, green centres, appear in spring.

H 45–50cm (18–20in), S indefinite. Hardy/Z 5–9. The colourful leaves of **'Chameleon'** (syn. 'Tricolor') are splashed with crimson, green and cream. **'Flore Pleno'** has fragrant heart-shaped leaves and double flowers.

HYDROCHARIS
Frogbit
Frogbits are found in temperate and subtropical parts of Europe, Africa, Asia and Australia. Their short stems form mats just under the water surface.
Cultivation Grow in full sun in water to 30cm (12in) deep.

H. morsus-ranae
Rather like a tiny water lily, this species produces kidney-shaped, shiny green leaves that float on the surface and small white flowers with yellow centres. S indefinite. Hardy/Z 7–10.

LAGAROSIPHON
Curly water thyme
These submerged plants are native to central Africa and Madagascar but have established themselves in Europe and New Zealand. The species described is a first-rate oxygenator.
Cultivation Grow in full sun.

L. major
(syn. Elodea crispa)
This species produces long underwater stems set with thick dark green, recurring leaves. It can form dense masses but is easily reduced in summer. S indefinite. Hardy/Z 4–9.

Gunnera manicata

LIGULARIA

These imposing bog plants are excellent by the water's edge, but can also be included in mixed plantings where the soil doesn't dry out.
Cultivation Grow in reliably moist soil in full sun or partial shade. Divide in spring.

L. dentata

This handsome species produces its vivid orange daisy flowers in mid- to late summer. H 1.2m (4ft), S 60cm (2ft). Hardy/Z 4–8. **'Desdemona'** is more compact, and has richer orange flowers. **'Othello'** is similar but has leaves flushed with purple.

L. 'Gregynog Gold'

This hybrid has handsome, richly veined, heart-shaped leaves and huge, conical spires of large, vivid orange-yellow flowers. H 1.2m (4ft), S 1m (3ft). Hardy/Z 4–8.

L. przewalskii
(syn. *Senecio przewalskii*)

This species has very finely cut, dark green leaves, borne on nearly black stems, and spires of small, yellow daisy flowers in mid- to late summer. H 2m (6ft), S 1m (3ft). Hardy/Z 4–8.

LYSICHITON
Skunk cabbage

Grand, if rather coarse, plants for the waterside, these are good for colonizing tracts of wet ground. Site them where reflected light from the water will strike the glossy leaves. The common name

is a reference to the scent of the flowers.
Cultivation Grow in full sun in 2.5cm (1in) of water or in wet soil.

L. americanus
Yellow skunk cabbage

This impressive plant provides an early spring display of yellow, arum-like spathes. After flowering, the huge shining, cabbage-like leaves gradually lengthen. H 1.2m (4ft), S 1m (3ft). Hardy/Z 7–9.

L. camschatcensis
White skunk cabbage

This white-spathed species is less vigorous than the more common *L. americanus* and is therefore more suitable for the margins of a small pond. H and S 75cm (30in). Hardy/Z 7–9.

MENTHA
Mint

Aside from the culinary herbs, there is one species that will thrive in water.
Cultivation Grow in full sun or partial shade. It tolerates a wide range of water depths but does best in 15cm (6in) of water.

M. aquatica
Water mint

Common in ditches and alongside running water, this has deep lilac-coloured flowers above the mint scented leaves. H 15cm–1m (6in–3ft), S indefinite. Hardy/Z 6.

MYOSOTIS
Forget-me-not

With its characteristic blue flowers, the water forget-me-not is as appealing as the plants grown in borders.
Cultivation Grow in full sun or light dappled shade in no more than 8cm (3in) of water.

M. scorpioides
Water forget-me-not

This attractive species has a slightly looser and more delicate habit of growth than most of the more rampant marginals. It bears typical forget-me-not blue flowers with yellow centres in midsummer. H and S 30cm (12in). Hardy/Z 4–10.

Myosotis scorpioides 'Mermaid'

'Mermaid' is an improved, compact cultivar that is more free-flowering than the species.

NUPHAR
Cow lily, spatterdock

The 25 species of aquatics in the genus, found in temperate areas of the northern hemisphere, bear some resemblance to water lilies but have tougher floating leaves and will grow in conditions that are either too deep or too shaded for water lilies.
Cultivation Grow in sun or partial shade in water 30–60cm (1–2ft) deep.

N. lutea
(syn. *N. luteum*)
Yellow pond lily

The leathery floating leaves are large in relation to the bowl-shaped, buttercup yellow flowers that appear in summer. This plant

will survive in deep and slow-moving water. S 2m (6ft). Hardy/Z 5–10.

NYMPHAEA
Water lily

The aristocrats of the water garden, water lilies are among the most beautiful of all garden plants. Many fine cultivars have been raised, in every shade from white, through all the shades of pink to deepest red and yellow. Some have double flowers, and many are deliciously fragrant. Tropical water lilies extend the colour range into blue and orange, and although these plants are suitable only for frost-free gardens, they can be treated like summer bedding and the plants discarded after blooming. There are water lilies suitable for every size of pond, from barrels and tubs to lakes, but they will not thrive in moving water.
Cultivation All should be grown in a sunny position without any water turbulence. Water depths vary as detailed below.

N. hybrids

The spread refers to the average area that the leaves will eventually cover. All are hardy/Z 3–11. **'Amabilis'** has star-like flowers with pink petals with lighter tips surrounding deep yellow stamens. The nearly round leaves are reddish-purple when young. S 1.5–2.3m (5–7.5ft), planting depth 30–45cm (12–18in). The moderately vigorous **'Attraction'** has cup-shaped, red flowers,

Lysichiton americanus

Nymphaea 'Attraction'

Nymphaea 'Gladstoneana'

Nymphaea 'Pygmaea Helvola'

opening to a star shape and resting on the bronze-tinged leaves. S 2m (6ft), planting depth 15–45cm (6–18in).
'**Gladstoneana**' is a free-flowering water lily that does best in a larger pond. The starry flowers have white petals surrounding yellow stamens. Bronzed young leaves mature to almost round, wavy-edged green leaves, with crimped margins along the lobes. S 1.5–2.4m (5–8ft), planting depth 45–60cm (18–24in).
'**Hermine**' (syn. 'Albatross') is a moderately vigorous water lily for a medium-sized pond. The large white flowers have long petals surrounding deep yellow stamens. The red-tinged young leaves mature to dark green. S to 2m (6ft), planting depth 15–45cm (6–18in). The moderately vigorous '**Marliacea Rosea**' is suitable for a medium-sized pond. In summer the rose-red flowers appear among the leaves, which are flushed purple on emergence. S 2m (6ft), planting depth 15–45cm (6–18in). '**Mme Wilfron Gonmère**' has double

pink flowers that fade to white. S to 1.5m (5ft), planting depth 30–45cm (12–18in). '**Pygmaea Helvola**' (syn. *N. × helvola*) is a delightful miniature and the perfect water lily for a barrel or sink. The cup-shaped, later star-like flowers have pale yellow petals and darker yellow stamens. The leaves are heavily mottled and blotched with purple and have purple undersides. S 60cm (2ft), planting depth 15–23cm (6–9in).

ORONTIUM
Golden club
The genus comprises a single species from temperate areas of eastern North America, where it grows in bogs or shallow water.
Cultivation Grow in full sun in water 30–45cm (12–18in) deep. In water deeper than 30cm (12in) the leaves float on the surface.

O. aquaticum
This species produces large, bluish-green leaves with a silvery sheen on the undersides. The extraordinary flower spikes look like lighted cigarettes: yellow at the tip, white below. They appear from spring to early summer. H 45cm (18in), S 75cm (30in). Hardy/Z 7–10.

PONTEDERIA
This genus of shallow-water plants contains just five species. The plant described is the most widely grown.
Cultivation Grow in full sun with up to 13cm (5in) of water above the crown.

P. cordata
Pickerel weed
This perennial marginal has shiny, erect, heart-shaped, olive-green leaves, above which the purplish-blue, bottlebrush-like flowers appear in late summer. H 45–60cm (18–24in), S 75cm (30in). Hardy/Z 4–9.

POTAMOGETON
Pondweed
There are 80–100 species of submerged aquatic plants in this genus, but only the species described is of value to gardeners, as an oxygenator.
Cultivation Grow in full sun.

P. crispus
Curled pondweed
The stems, which are capable of growing to 4m (13ft) or more, bear narrow, stalkless, green to

reddish brown leaves, the whole plant looking like seaweed. S indefinite. Hardy/Z 7–10.

RANUNCULUS
Buttercup
Among the many garden plants provided by this genus is the species described, one of the precious few flowering oxygenators.
Cultivation Grow in full sun in still or running water to a depth of 15–60cm (6–24in).

R. aquatilis
Water crowfoot
This submerged perennial has flat, kidney-shaped, floating leaves and thread-like submerged leaves. The buttercup-shaped, white flowers, which are held above the water, have a yellow base to the petals and appear in spring and summer. S indefinite. Hardy/Z 4–8.

STRATIOTES
This genus comprises a single species, an intriguing plant that behaves both as an oxygenator and a surface floater.
Cultivation Grow in full sun in water over 30cm (12in) deep.

S. aloides
Water soldier
Rosettes of sword-shaped leaves are produced on runners. These are usually submerged but rise to the surface in early summer, when the white flowers are produced. Dormant buds rest on the bottom of the pond over winter. S indefinite. Hardy/Z 6–9.

Nymphaea 'Hermine'

Stratiotes aloides

Cacti and succulents

Cacti and succulents are mostly undemanding plants that are adapted to certain extremes of climate. The range encompasses small, button-like plants to larger, tree-like plants, though they rarely reach unmanageable proportions in cultivation. Though many have spectacular flowers, most are grown for their often bizarre appearance — some hardly look like plants at all. From barrel-shaped cacti, often ribbed like a concertina, to the huge rosettes of agaves, with their thick, fleshy, often boldly marked leaves, and not forgetting the twining hoyas, with their waxy, scented flowers, there is bound to be one amongst them that catches your eye.

Cacti and succulents provide some of the most arresting plant forms in the plant kingdom.

Cacti and succulents for your garden

This section could as well be called simply "Succulents". The term "succulent" actually includes the cacti, and what distinguishes cacti from the rest is not, as might be imagined, the spines, but the presence of areoles, modified axillary buds from which all growth arises. The spines do in fact arise from the areoles, but not all cacti are spiny. Equally, some succulents are distinctly cactus-like in appearance, but lack the tell-tale areoles.

In evolutionary terms, cacti and succulents are the youngest plants on the planet and are uniquely adapted to thrive in conditions that are hostile to nearly all other forms of plant life. They have evolved to cope with low rainfall by growing slowly, and can survive periods of drought by conserving as much moisture as possible in their leaves, stems and roots. Hence their fleshy, bloated appearance. The waxy coatings of the leaves also guard against moisture loss.

Succulents are found throughout much of the world. Many are found in deserts, a habitat that is actually

In a hot, dry climate, succulents can play their part as true garden plants.

surprisingly diverse. Some desert areas experience winter rainfall, while in others it tends to rain in the summer only, and plants from such regions will be active in winter and summer respectively and dormant the rest of the time. Some of the maritime regions where succulents occur are subject to cold Antarctic tidal currents, as on the west coast of Africa and South America, and these plants are therefore hardier than those found further inland. To all intents and purposes, cacti are found exclusively in the New World (colonies of *Rhipsalis baccifera* in Africa and Madagascar seem to have been introduced by migratory birds).

Cacti can be split into two main groups: those from the desert and those from the rainforest. They occur in a range from Canada (where they can be covered in snow in winter) down to Chile and Argentina, including offshore islands. They are prevalent in the southern USA, down to northern and central South America.

The shape of desert cacti is a response to climatic conditions. Being spherical or globular

minimizes the surface area and thus the amount of moisture that will be lost in transpiration. The characteristic ribbing of some species enables them to expand as moisture becomes available and then contract, like an accordion, without splitting the outer skin. Nearly all have spines, which are usually quite sharp, presumably as a defence against browsing animals. In some species, however (notably the old man cactus, *Cephalocereus senilis*), they look like hair.

Rainforest cacti can easily be mistaken for succulents, since spines are often absent or are replaced by bristles, only the presence of areoles betraying their true allegiance. They generally have flattened, leaf-like stems. In the wild, they often grow epiphytically in places where dead leaves collect, usually in the hollows or forks of trees.

Most cacti and succulents are grown for the sheer fascination of their shape: they are quite unlike any other group of plants. Some, however, have spectacular, if usually short-lived, flowers. One of the most reliable for flower production is the

The round pads of opuntia contrast well with the spiky, steel blue leaves of the agave behind it.

well-known Christmas cactus (*Schlumbergera*), widely grown as a houseplant.

Cacti and succulents have not been heavily hybridized, and the plants grown are mainly species or naturally occurring forms of the species.

How to grow cacti and succulents

Most cacti and succulents can be grown outdoors only in frost-free, arid climates. Elsewhere, they have to be grown in containers under glass or as houseplants; in fact, they thrive in the warm dry conditions created by most modern central heating systems. Good light is usually essential for all except rainforest cacti, which are adapted to lower light levels. These can be placed in more humid parts of the house, such as a kitchen or bathroom, in a light position but out of direct sunlight. They can be brought into a position in full light in winter. All can be stood outside during the summer months, or even sunk in their pots into borders to make a temporary succulent garden. In a greenhouse, a

winter minimum temperature of 5°C (41°F) is necessary for most species, rising to 10°C (50°F) for most rainforest cacti. Good air circulation is important for all but rainforest cacti (and even these should not be grown in stagnant conditions).

Globular and low-growing plants are best in shallow containers. Large bonsai bowls are excellent and can be planted up with a range of different species. Tall-growing plants are better in correspondingly deeper pots. Epiphytic cacti and any others with trailing stems are effective in hanging baskets.

All cacti and succulents need to be grown in a free-draining medium. Specially formulated composts for cacti are available, and it is best to use these. Alternatively, mix your own by adding one part grit to three parts loam-based compost (soil mix) or two parts loamless compost. Epiphytes need a compost that is moisture-retentive without becoming waterlogged, and the best mix is made up of three parts potting compost, two parts grit and one part leaf mould. Some succulents can be

Indoor cacti and succulent container plants can benefit from a holiday outdoors over the summer months.

grown in conventional potting compost, provided you add grit or sharp sand to improve the drainage. A top-dressing of grit can help prevent water from collecting around the collar of the plant.

Soils where cacti grow in the wild are actually nutrient-high (though humus-low), so you should feed your plants, either with a cactus fertilizer or with a tomato feed at half strength.

Plants should be watered when in active growth, less frequently when dormant. Dormancy occurs not only during winter but also when the temperature rises above a certain level at the height of summer, so you should take care not to over-water during this period. In a cool situation, most can be kept dry from late winter to early spring, but in a centrally heated room, they may need watering every couple of weeks to prevent the compost from drying out completely. Rainforest plants need more water than desert plants. Water them freely when in active growth and give them enough in winter to prevent them from shrivelling.

This impressive collection of mature cacti and succulents in a dedicated greenhouse features several cacti from the popular *Mammilaria* group, which includes many easy-to-cultivate species.

The heights and spreads indicated relate to five-year-old, container-grown plants.

AEONIUM
These succulents from the Mediterranean, northern Africa and the Canary Islands are grown for their rosettes of fleshy leaves. *Cultivation* Grow in standard cactus compost (soil mix); in winter, maintain a temperature no lower than 5°C (41°F). The maroon-leaved varieties turn green if overwatered.

A. arboreum
At the end of each branching stem there is a rosette of shiny, glaucous green leaves. Small, star-shaped yellow flowers appear in spring on 2–3 year old stems. H 1m (3ft), S 60cm (2ft). Tender/Z 9–10. 'Arnold Schwarzkopff' has dark maroon (almost black) and bright green leaves. The glossy leaves of 'Atropurpureum' are flushed with dark purplish-red and maroon.

A. haworthii
Pinwheel
This species from the Canary Islands has bluish-green rosettes, often edged with red in summer. Clusters of cream flowers are produced in spring. H and S 30cm (12in). Tender/Z 10.

AGAVE
There are more than 200 species of dramatic succulents in the genus. They make virtually stemless, usually solitary, rosettes of leaves from ground level. These usually die after flowering, but a cluster of new rosettes generally develops around the base. *Cultivation* Grow in standard cactus compost (soil mix). The

Aporocactus flagelliformis

species described require a minimum winter temperature of 5°C (41°F), but as a rule blue-leaved types are hardier than those with pale green leaves.

A. americana
(syn. *A. altissima*)
Century plant, maguey
This handsome Mexican species is often used in landscaping in warm climates, where it will make a dramatic rosette of spiny edged, sharply pointed, pewter grey leaves up to 2.5m (8ft) long (less if grown as a container plant). H and S 2m (6ft). Tender/Z 9–10. 'Mediopicta Alba' is slower growing and less hardy. The leaves are centrally striped with creamy-white. H and S 30cm (12in).

ALOE
There are about 35 species of succulents in this genus. They are important plants in the cosmetics industry and are widespread from Africa to the Middle East. *Cultivation* Grow aloes in standard potting compost (soil mix) with added grit. The minimum winter temperature varies across the genus.

Cephalocereus senilis

A. vera
Medicine plant, burn plant
This species has been used for its medicinal properties since the time of the pharaohs. The rosettes of dull green leaves are spotted with red on young plants. A winter minimum temperature of 10°C (50°F) is best, although plants have been reported to withstand light frosts. H 30cm (12in), S 10cm (4in). Tender/ Z 10.

APOROCACTUS
Rat's tail cactus
These Mexican epiphytic cacti have trailing stems, which make them ideal for growing in hanging baskets. They are one of the first cacti to flower, their red or lilac flowers appearing in spring. *Cultivation* Grow in epiphytic cactus compost (soil mix). In summer water regularly as the compost begins to dry out and keep lightly shaded; in winter keep at 6°C (43°F) and water occasionally.

A. flagelliformis
(syn. *Cereus flagelliformis*)
One of the easiest species to grow, this has slender, cylindrical,

trailing stems to 2m (6ft) long and double, cerise flowers in spring. S 25cm (10in). Tender/Z 10.

ASTROPHYTUM
The six or so species of slow-growing cacti in the genus are from Mexico. They are globular at first, becoming columnar as they mature. Large, funnel-shaped, yellow flowers appear in summer. *Cultivation* Use standard cactus compost (soil mix) with added calcium. Take care not to over-water in summer and keep dry in winter, at 6°C (43°F), otherwise they can rot.

A. myriostigma
(syn. *Echinocactus myriostigma*)
Bishop's cap
These squat cacti have ribbed, virtually spineless, grey bodies (although some variants show shades of green). H and S 5cm (2in). Tender/Z 10.

A. ornatum
(syn. *Echinocactus ornatus*)
The ribs of this species, one of the easiest to grow, have clusters of straw-coloured spines. H and S 5cm (2in). Tender/Z 10.

CEPHALOCEREUS
Only one species, the distinctive old man cactus from Mexico, is commonly found in collections. *Cultivation* Grow in standard cactus compost (soil mix); *C. senilis* benefits from added calcium. Allow plants to dry out between waterings in summer and keep them completely dry between autumn and spring. Grow in full light and maintain a minimum temperature of 7°C (45°F) in winter.

Aeonium haworthii

Agave americana 'Mediopicta Alba'

Aloe vera

Astrophytum myriostigma

Crassula ovata

Echinocactus grusonii

Epiphyllum anguliger

C. senilis
(syn. *Cereus senilis, Pilocereus senilis*)
Old man cactus
The long white hairs that cover the plant are the distinctive characteristic of this popular species, which is long lived and can reach a height of 2m (6ft) after 50 years. H 8cm (3in), S 2cm (¾in). Tender/Z 10.

CRASSULA
This extremely diverse genus of succulents includes both small species as well as tree-like plants. On some, the leaves are shiny and glossy; on others they are rough and waxy.
Cultivation Grow crassulas in standard cactus compost (soil mix). They need a minimum winter temperature of 5°C (41°F).

C. ovata
(syn. *C. argentea*)
Money plant, jade plant
This species from southern Africa is widely grown as a houseplant, being tolerant of a range of conditions. Mature plants sometimes bear small white flowers in autumn. Ideally, keep at a temperature no lower than 7°C (45°F) in winter, although plants will tolerate short spells at 3°C (37°F). H 45cm (18in), S 30cm (12in). Tender/Z 10.

ECHEVERIA
With their rosettes of fleshy leaves, these succulents from Central and South America make handsome houseplants and can also be used in summer bedding.
Cultivation Standard cactus compost (soil mix) is suitable. The species described needs a minimum winter temperature of 5°C (41°F).

E. agavoides
The broad, pointed leaves of this distinctive, slow-growing species are pale olive-green, sometimes tinged with red. The flowers, which appear from spring to early summer, are of small ornamental value. H 15cm (6in), S 30cm (12in). Tender/Z 10.

ECHINOCACTUS
These slow-growing cacti are difficult to grow but are included here because mature specimens are often seen in gardens in California and Mexico and in other hot, dry gardens.
Cultivation Use standard cactus compost (soil mix) and maintain a minimum winter temperature of 10°C (50°F).

E. grusonii
Golden barrel cactus, mother-in-law's cushion
The mid-green body of this cactus is covered in distinctive golden spines which shine in full sun. Golden-yellow flowers appear in the crown of mature plants in summer. H 5cm (2in), S 8cm (3in). Tender/Z 10.

ECHINOPSIS
The easy-to-grow cacti in this genus vary from small, globular plants to tall, columnar ones and are usually free-flowering.

Cultivation Grow in standard cactus compost (soil mix). Minimum winter temperature requirements vary; most will endure near-freezing temperatures.

E. aurea
(syn. *Lobivia echinopsis*)
Golden lily cactus
Small, bright yellow flowers are carried on this densely spined species in summer. It needs a minimum winter temperature of 6°C (43°F). H 5cm (2in), S 2.5cm (1in). Tender/Z 10.

E. 'Gloria'
This hybrid has large scarlet flowers. A minimum winter temperature of 4°C (39°F) is required. H 25cm (10in), S 10cm (4in). Tender/Z 9–10.

E. smrziana
(syn. *Trichocereus smrziana*)
Mature plants of this Argentinian species bear nocturnal white flowers on thick sturdy stems at various times of year. A minimum winter temperature of 3°C (37°F) is required. H 25cm (10in), S 8cm (3in). Tender/Z 9.

EPIPHYLLUM
On some species of these rain-forest cacti the flowers, which can be scented, open at night.
Cultivation Grow in epiphytic cactus compost (soil mix), in pots or hanging baskets. Keep lightly shaded in summer and in full light in winter with a minimum temperature of 10°C (50°F). Water throughout the year, but sparingly in winter.

E. anguliger
Herringbone cactus
This species from southern Mexico has characteristic notched

stems and small, scented flowers in summer. H 60cm (2ft), S 15cm (6in). Tender/Z 10.

E. hybrids
Named selections include 'Jennifer Ann' with yellow flowers; 'King Midas' with golden-yellow flowers; and 'Wendy May' with long, pink flowers. H 60cm (2ft), S 15cm (6in). Tender/Z 10.

ESPOSTOA
These cylindrical cacti from South America have typically woolly stems. The flowers sometimes emit a horrible smell.
Cultivation Grow in standard cactus compost (soil mix) with a minimum winter temperature of 7°C (45°F). They are sensitive to overwatering.

E. lanata
Snowball cactus
This is one of the least hairy species in the genus and one of the quickest and easiest to grow. H 10cm (4in), S 2.5cm (1in). Tender/Z 10.

Echeveria agavoides

Echinopsis 'Gloria'

Espostoa lanata

Euphorbia milii

EUPHORBIA

This huge genus is generally represented in gardens by its hardy perennials, but it also includes many succulents, which are diverse in character, some being distinctly cactus-like.
Cultivation Use standard potting compost (soil mix) with added grit for the species listed here. The minimum winter temperatures required vary.

E. milii
Crown of thorns
Popular as a houseplant, this species from Madagascar has thorny stems, which are hexagonal in cross-section. It can produce bright red flowers at any time of year. Ideally keep no lower than 16°C (61°F) in winter; at lower temperatures it tends to drop its leaves, although it generally returns to health in spring. H 60cm (2ft), S 30cm (12in). Tender/Z 9–10.

FEROCACTUS

These large, barbarously armed plants from the southern USA, Mexico and Guatemala are sometimes referred to as barrel cacti, and they can indeed grow to 3m (10ft) in diameter. They usually flower only when they are 25cm (10in) across or more.
Cultivation Grow in standard cactus compost. Winter temperature requirements vary.

F. glaucescens
This species has a ribbed, blue-green body and straight, golden-yellow spines. It needs a minimum winter temperature of 7°C (45°F). H and S 8cm (3in). Tender/Z 10.

Ferocactus glaucescens

F. herrerae
(syn. F. wislizeni var. herrerae)
Candy barrel cactus
Ultimately a large cactus, to 2m (6ft) tall, this globular species has fishhook-like spines. It flowers only when 30cm (12in) in diameter. Minimum winter temperature 6°C (42°F). H 10cm (4in), S 2.5cm (1in). Tender/Z 10.

HOYA
Wax flower
These succulents, popular as houseplants, have thick, glossy leaves and attractive, sometimes scented, flowers.
Cultivation Grow in standard potting compost (soil mix), with added grit or perlite for improved drainage. The temperature should be no lower than 10°C (50°F) in winter, although lows of 5°C (41°F) are tolerated for short periods.

H. carnosa
Probably the easiest of the hoyas to grow, this climber is however seldom free-flowering in cultivation. The thick, waxy leaves are pointed and bright green; the nectar-rich, highly fragrant flowers appear in summer and can be white or pale pink. H to 3m (10ft), S to 2m (6ft). Tender/Z 10.

H. lanceolata subsp. bella
(syn. H. bandaensis)
This hoya is also easy to grow. Daintier in all its parts than H. carnosa, it has sprawling stems set with pointed green leaves and produces quantities of waxy white flowers in hanging clusters in late summer. Its trailing habit makes it ideal for a hanging basket. H and S 30cm (12in). Tender/Z 10.

KALANCHOE

These perennial succulents, which are widely distributed in the tropics, are grown as houseplants for their foliage and bell-shaped to tubular flowers. They are easy to grow and usually flower readily. There are many hybrids, and not all plants offered for sale are named.
Cultivation Grow in standard potting compost (soil mix) with added grit. Winter temperature requirements vary according to species, but the plants described here need a minimum winter temperature of 12°C (54°F).

K. blossfeldiana
Flaming Katy
This familiar species has dark green leaves with scalloped edges, and it can produce its (typically) red flowers at almost any time of year. Short day length triggers flowering, and this can be simulated by keeping the plant in the dark for a few hours a day during the warmer months. Plants sold under this name can have pink, yellow or white flowers. H and S to 30cm (12in). Tender/Z 10.

LAMPRANTHUS

Originating from South Africa, the succulents in this genus of over 180 species are grown for their profusion of appealing, daisy-like flowers, which make carpets of colour in areas where they can be grown outdoors.
Cultivation Grow in standard cactus compost (soil mix) and keep no lower than 1°C (34°F) in winter. Flowers open only in full sun.

Lampranthus haworthii

L. haworthii
Deep pink flowers are borne in late spring. Eventually it can make a large bush, but can be clipped to shape. H 60cm (2ft), S 1m (3ft). Tender/Z 10.

LITHOPS
Living stone, pebble plants
These intriguing succulents look just like small stones, an impression entirely destroyed when their spectacular flowers appear. Each plant is composed of a pair of swollen leaves.
Cultivation Grow in standard cactus compost (soil mix). Position in a very bright spot and take care not to over-water. In winter keep plants completely dry at a temperature no lower than 1°C (34°F), but preferably 7°C (45°F).

L. aucampiae
One of the larger species and native to South Africa, this has chocolate-brown leaves with flat upper surfaces. The bright yellow, daisy-like flowers appear in early autumn. H and S 3cm (1in). Tender/Z 10.

MAMMILLARIA

This genus contains some of the largest and most popular of the globular cacti, since they are easy to grow and to bring into flower. The flowers are carried in rings around the crown of the plant in spring, often with a second (and even third) flush appearing later on.
Cultivation Grow in standard cactus compost (soil mix) and maintain a minimum temperature of 6°C (43°F) in winter.

Lithops aucampiae

Mammillaria bombycina

Opuntia microdasys

Rebutia minuscula f. senilis

M. bombycina
This Mexican species produces pink flowers after about four years. The spines can be red, brown or yellow. H and S 8cm (3in). Tender/Z 10.

M. hahniana
Old lady cactus
This globular species from Mexico is densely covered with long, curly, hair-like spines, which sometimes grow long and wrap themselves around the body of the plant. The bright red flowers can be followed by even brighter red seedpods. H 5cm (2in), S 8cm (3in). Tender/Z 10.

OPUNTIA
Prickly pear
These fast-growing cacti, widespread from Canada to southern South America, are also a familiar sight in the Mediterranean area, where they have escaped from gardens and become naturalized.
Cultivation Grow in standard cactus compost (soil mix). Minimum winter temperatures vary. Take care when handling the plants because the glochids (bristles) are easily embedded in the skin.

O. microdasys
Bunny ears
The flattened pads of this species from Mexico are more or less spineless, but regularly dotted with white areoles filled with glochids. Flowers are produced only on mature plants. This requires a minimum winter temperature of 10°C (50°F). H 15cm (6in), S 10cm (4in). Tender/Z 10.

OREOCEREUS
Old man of the Andes
These slow-growing cacti are found throughout the Andes, where they survive in lower temperatures than they will tolerate in cultivation, probably because of low humidity.
Cultivation Grow in standard cactus compost (soil mix). Water with care in summer and keep them dry in winter, allowing the temperature to fall no lower than 6°C (43°F).

O. celsianus
(syn. *Borzicactus celsianus, Oreocereus neocelsianus, Pilocereus celsianus*)
Old man of the mountains
This makes sturdy, upright stems with both thick, straight spines and woolly, white ones. Pale purplish-pink flowers are borne in summer. H 8cm (3in), S 2.5cm (1in). Tender/Z 10.

PARODIA
Originating from South America, these are some of the easiest cacti to bring into flower.
Cultivation Grow in standard cactus compost (soil mix). In winter they are best at a temperature no lower than 10°C (50°F); water occasionally to prevent them from drying out completely.

P. leninghausii
(syn. *Eriocactus leninghausii*)
This distinctive species produces a single stem at first, offsets from the base appearing only as it gets larger. Yellow flowers are produced on plants taller than 15cm (6in). It will tolerate a winter low of 5°C (41°F). H 10cm (4in), S 5cm (2in). Tender/Z 10.

REBUTIA
These easy-to-grow cacti from South America are among the first to flower in spring.
Cultivation Use standard cactus compost (soil mix). They will tolerate temperatures down to near freezing in winter if they are kept dry.

R. arenacea
(syn. *Sulcorebutia arenacea*)
This has a small, rounded body and numerous short spines. The golden-yellow flowers appear in late spring. H 2cm (¼in), S 5cm (2in). Tender/Z 10.

R. minuscula f. senilis
Fire crown cactus
The form differs from the species in having longer, white, hairy spines and brighter red flowers. The squat green body produces offsets slowly, ultimately making clumps. H 2.5cm (1in), S 5cm (2in). Tender/Z 10.

SCHLUMBERGERA
Christmas cactus
These popular rainforest cacti from Brazil have been extensively

hybridized to produce a range of easy-to-grow plants. Not all are named. They are valued for their winter flowers, usually produced in abundance.
Cultivation Use epiphytic cactus compost (soil mix), and maintain a minimum winter temperature of 5°C (41°F), preferably warmer. Keep out of direct sunlight. Water and feed when in active growth (summer and autumn), but keep the compost barely moist after flowering and for the rest of the year.

S. hybrids
The arching stems are made up of flattened, bright green segments. At their tips, they produce flowers in winter, the colour range including red ('**Firecracker**', '**Joanne**'), pale pinkish-orange ('**Gold Charm**'), and lilac ('**Lilac Beauty**'). H 15cm (6in), S 30cm (12in). Tender/Z 10.

SEDUM
A large genus of succulents which also includes many popular hardy perennials. Sedums range from tiny mats to large, shrubby or even tree-like plants.
Cultivation Use standard potting compost (soil mix) with added grit and leaf mould.

S. rubrotinctum
Short, blunt, fleshy leaves are carried on this arching succulent subshrub. Maintain a minimum winter temperature of 1°C (34°F). H 25cm (10in), S 20cm (8in). Tender/Z 9. The form '**Aurora**' has leaves that are pink to yellow, the colour being more intense in sun. H 20cm (8in), S 1m (3ft).

Parodia leninghausii

Sedum rubrotinctum

Orchids

Beautiful, flamboyant, sometimes bizarre: orchids exert a unique appeal. Everything about them is fascinating, from their strange habit of growth, nestling on fallen tree trunks or among rocks or clambering skywards to the tree canopy, to their striking, often intoxicatingly scented flowers. Formerly considered plants for the connoisseur only, nowadays there is a huge range of hybrids that are easy to grow and well within the scope of any gardener. Through careful choice it is possible to make a collection that provides flowers virtually year-round.

Many orchids provide a succesion of impressive flowers over a long period, making them among the most desirable of all plants.

Orchids for your garden

Forming a huge plant family, orchids are primarily herbaceous or evergreen perennials, distinguished from other plant families by the structure of their flowers. Orchids are found throughout the world, in every continent except Antarctica.

Terrestrial orchids, native mainly to temperate regions, are rooted in the ground like most other plants and have either a rhizome (a swollen, horizontal stem) or an underground tuber (a structure with a similar function but without the tendency to grow laterally). Most of these orchids experience a period of dormancy, usually in winter for herbaceous species with rhizomes, while tuberous species are dormant in summer. Evergreens rest either in winter or just after flowering.

Epiphytic orchids, most of which are evergreen, spend their lives above ground and have special aerial roots that allow them to cling to trees or rocks (the latter are more correctly referred to as lithophytic). The roots can absorb nutrients and minerals from any matter that washes down the tree, but do not derive nourishment from the tree itself, so are not parasites. They are usually dormant in winter, when growth slows down or stops altogether, but tropical species that have their home near the equator will grow and flower virtually continuously. The difference between terrestrial and epiphytic orchids is not as marked as you might think: epiphytes are often to be found with their roots nestling in as deep a layer of leaf litter and other plant debris as is ever to be found on the forest floor, and some terrestrials are quite capable of living epiphytically.

Orchid flowers are composed of six segments, collectively referred to as the perianth. The unopened flower is enclosed by three sepals. These open to reveal three petals. In most other plant families, the sepals are green and are hidden by the open flower. In the case of orchids, they are usually petal-like and are marked and coloured in a similar fashion to the true petals. The lowest of the three petals, called the lip or labellum, is modified in shape and serves as a landing platform for pollinating insects. This structure represents a peak in plant adaptation to specific pollinators. In some orchids, the lip is inflated and forms a pouch or "slipper", as in the case of *Paphiopedilum*.

Orchid flowers are distinct (though not unique) in that they are symmetrical only from side to side and not from top to bottom. They are produced singly or in a spray (sometimes referred to as a raceme) or on a branched spike.

Different orchids flower at different seasons of the year. Some, however, can flower at any time of year, while others will flower on and off throughout the year. The flower spikes are mostly long-lasting, but in a few species the flowers last for only a day.

Flower size varies. The smallest can be no more than 2mm (0.1in) across, while *Brassia* for instance can be up to 38cm (15in).

How to grow orchids

All the orchids described on the following pages are suitable for growing indoors, and most of the hybrids have been developed for that very purpose, so in no way can they be described as conventional garden plants. They are usually divided into three broad groups depending on the climate in which the parent species is found.

Cool-growing orchids originate from high altitudes where nights are cool, often dropping to 10°C (50°F). They need a minimum temperature range of 10–13°C (50–55°F) and a maximum of 21–24°C (70–75°F).

Intermediate-growing orchids, from slightly warmer areas, need a minimum temperature of 14–19°C

This *Dendrobium* species is a member of a huge genus, widely distributed in India, south-east Asia, Australia and the Pacific islands.

Cattleyas provide the enthusiast with some of the most flamboyant of all orchid flowers. These orchids show just some of the variations to be found within the genus.

(57–66°F) with a maximum of 30–33°C (86–91°F).

Warm-growing orchids, originating from steamy rainforests, have a minimum requirement of 20–24°C (68–75°F) and a maximum of 30–33°C (86–91°F).

Light is also an important factor. Orchids from near the equator are adapted to light levels that remain more or less constant throughout the year. In temperate zones, day length fluctuates widely between summer and winter. To persuade the plants that they are nearer home than they are, it is usually necessary to shade them in summer to protect them from hot sun and from scorch: under glass, temperatures can soar much higher than they would in the plants' natural habitat. Conversely, in winter most orchids need maximum light, and the shading should be removed.

Most orchids – even epiphytes – can be grown successfully in containers. Epiphytes are also commonly grown in special wooden or plastic baskets, and this is an especially effective way of displaying those with trailing flower stems,

such as *Stanhopea*. An alternative, for smaller epiphytes, is to tie them to pieces of bark or tree fern fibre, usually with some coconut fibre wrapped around the roots to retain moisture. Bark can be wall mounted or suspended horizontally to make a raft.

Orchids need special composts (soil mix) that are swift-draining; some are specially formulated to suit particular genera. Humidity is also important, and the plants should be misted twice daily when in growth, orchids on bark particularly thoroughly, as this is the only means of watering them. Alternatively, stand the pots on trays of special expanded clay pellets. The trays are filled with water, which is then allowed to evaporate.

Water orchids freely during the growing season, but make sure that the containers drain properly and that the plants do not have their feet in water. Water less in winter or when the plants are resting, just enough to keep the growing medium barely moist. Orchids that are more or less permanently in growth can be watered year-round, though less in winter, when growth tends to slow down. Always water directly into the compost, not on to the plant itself – water that collects in the leaves can lead to rotting.

Orchids seem to thrive in collections with others of their kind, so grow as many as you can in the space available.

Growing orchids in special slatted wooden baskets allows roots access to the air they need, as well as being an effective way of displaying the plants.

BRASSIA

The mainly epiphytic evergreen orchids in this genus are found in the tropical Americas. They have been much used in hybridizing.
Cultivation Grow the orchids described below epiphytically in baskets or on bark. Provide light shade in summer and full light in winter.

B. Rex

Spidery flowers, up to 20cm (8in) long and smelling of musk, appear in summer. The sepals and petals are elongated and are sulphur yellow to lime green, spotted and marked with red-brown to black. The lips are white and are similarly spotted. Flower spike 30cm (12in). Cool-growing/Z 10.

B. verrucosa
(syn. *B. brachiata*)
Spider orchid

The species occurs in a range from southern Mexico to Venezuela. 'Sea Mist' is a selection with spidery, musky smelling, greenish-yellow flowers in summer, arranged alternately on arching stems. This is an ideal orchid for a growing case. Flower spike to 75cm (30in). Cool-growing/Z 10.

× BRASSOLAELIO-CATTLEYA

For many growers, these plants, with their huge, dramatic flowers, are the archetypal orchid. They

Brassia verrucosa 'Sea Mist'

are also easy to grow. The plants are complex hybrids, involving *Brassavola*, *Cattleya* and *Laelia*.
Cultivation Grow these orchids in containers in free-draining compost (soil mix).

× B. Enid Moore × *Laeliocattleya* Starting Point

One of the showiest of the group, this bears large, creamy-white flowers with ruffled petal edges. The lips are heavily stained with rich rosy purple and have yellow centres lined with purple. Flower spike to 20cm (8in). Cool-growing to intermediate/Z 10.

× B. Yellow Imp 'Golden Grail'

Bright yellow flowers are borne in spring or autumn. Flower spike to 20cm (8in). Cool-growing to intermediate/Z 10.

BULBOPHYLLUM

The plants in this large genus of epiphytic orchids, found in a wide range of habitats throughout the tropics, are for the enthusiast rather than for the general grower.
Cultivation Grow in epiphytic orchid compost (soil mix) in slatted baskets or on bark.

B. lobbii

This creeping species is found in tropical regions of north-eastern India, south-eastern Asia and the Philippines. The solitary, pale yellow, red-yellow or ochre flowers appear in summer. They are conspicuously lined with red and brown and can be speckled

Brassia Rex

× Brassolaeliocattleya Enid Moore × *Laeliocattleya* Starting Point

with pink and yellow. Flower spike to 13cm (5in). Intermediate/Z 10.

B. ornatissimum
(syn. *Cirrhopetalum ornatissimum*)

In autumn this orchid, which is native to India, produces sprays of short-lipped, straw yellow flowers, three to a stem. Each flower is dotted and striped with purple. Flower spike to 10cm (4in). Cool-growing/Z 10.

CATTLEYA

There are about 40 species in all in the genus, which is possibly the most important to orchid-lovers and probably the most commonly grown. In the wild cattleyas grow epiphytically in Central and South America, but in cultivation they are generally represented by their complex hybrids, which have huge, flamboyant flowers, often with petals with ruffled edges. Cattleyas are familiar flowers, much used by florists.

Bulbophyllum lobbii

Cultivation Grow in epiphytic orchid compost (soil mix) in containers.

C. Carla × *Brassolaeliocattleya* Nickie Holguin

In late summer and autumn this hybrid has large, showy, creamy white flowers with lips stained yellow in the centre. Flower spike to 20cm (8in). Cool-growing to intermediate/Z 10.

C. Enid × *Brassolaeliocattleya* Holiday Inn

Huge, white flowers with pale greenish-yellow centres and lips that are stained rich rosy purple are borne in late summer to autumn. The petal edges are ruffled. Flower spike to 20cm (8in). Cool-growing to intermediate/Z 10.

C. harrisoniana × Penny Karoda

This desirable and distinctive orchid produces solitary, luminous pink flowers in summer and autumn. The trumpet-like lips are light violet-pink, shading to rich purplish-pink at the edges and with yellow centres. Flower spike to 20cm (8in). Cool-growing to intermediate/Z 10.

C. labiata × *Brassocattleya* Cutty Sark

The white, yellow-centred flowers appear in summer to autumn. Flower spike to 20cm (8in). Cool-growing to intermediate/Z 10.

C. loddigesii 'Alba' × Old Whitey

This is a stunning orchid, bearing large, solitary, luminous violet flowers, with ruffled petal edges, in late summer to autumn. The lips are elongated, are marked with rosy purple and have yellow centres. Flower spike 20cm (8in). Cool-growing to intermediate/Z 10.

C. loddigesii × *Sophrolaeliocattleya* Jeweller's Art 'Carved Coral'

The flowers, which are produced from autumn to spring, are a warm rose-purple with darker purple lips. Flower spike to 20cm (8in). Cool-growing to intermediate/Z 10.

Cattleya loddigesii 'Alba' × Old Whitey

Coelogyne Memoria William Micholitz

Cymbidium erythrostylum

C. Louis × Carla × *Brassolaeliocattleya* Nickie Holguin
Almost entirely pure white, the flowers, borne from summer to autumn, are stained yellow only at the centre of the lips. Flower spike to 20cm (8in). Cool-growing to intermediate/Z 10.

COELOGYNE
The genus contains about 200 evergreen, epiphytic orchids, which are found in the mountainous regions of India, south-eastern Asia and the Pacific islands. In spite of their wide spread in the wild, they are not generally well represented in growers' collections. They are easy to grow, but some of the species take up a lot of room. The ones described are modest in size and would make worthwhile additions to any collection, particularly winter-flowering types.
Cultivation These are suitable for containers or hanging baskets, unless otherwise indicated.

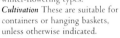

C. cristata
In spring this species, which is native to the eastern Himalayas, has dangling stems of fragrant, frosty white flowers, streaked yellow in the throat in spring. It needs a winter rest. Flower spike to 30cm (12in). Cool-growing to intermediate/Z 10.

C. fimbriata (syn. *Broughtonia linearis*)
This species grows wild in northern India and in a range from Vietnam to Hong Kong. Its solitary, buff yellow flowers, which appear in summer, have white or pale yellow lips marked with dark brown. Flower spike to 5cm (2in). Cool-growing/Z 10.

C. massangeana
In early spring to summer hanging stems carry up to 20 scented, pale yellow flowers with brown and yellow lips. Native to Malaysia, Sumatra and Java, this orchid needs to be kept dry over winter and is seen at its best when grown hanging from an orchid raft. Flower spike to 45cm (18in). Intermediate/Z 10.

C. Memoria William Micholitz
The flowers on this hybrid are larger – at 9cm (3½in) across – than those of most coelogynes. Appearing from spring to summer, they are creamy-white and have lips spotted with red and yellow. Flower spike to 45cm (18in). Cool-growing/Z 10.

CYMBIDIUM
The ideal beginner's orchid, cymbidiums are virtually indestructible plants, bearing impressive spikes of long-lasting, waxy flowers. Unfortunately, they are not the most consistent

Cattleya Louis × Carla × *Brassolaeliocattleya* Nickie Holguin

flowerers, and the best way to guarantee reliable flowering is to provide temperatures that fluctuate between night and day in summer and autumn. This is most easily achieved by placing the plants outdoors until as late in the season as possible (in other words, before the first frosts) so that they experience the drop in temperature necessary to trigger flower production. In frost-free climates they are best grown out of doors all year round. The genus, which contains both epiphytes and terrestrials, is found in both temperate and tropical areas of India, the Far East and parts of Australia.
Cultivation Grow in epiphytic or

Cymbidium Summer Pearl 'Sonya'

terrestrial orchid compost (growing medium) in containers.

C. erythrostylum
This compact epiphyte hails from Vietnam and has brilliant white flowers with red striping on the lips in spring and summer. This may also be grown on bark. Flower spike to 60cm (2ft). Cool-growing/Z 9.

C. Maureen Grapes 'Marilyn'
Erect spikes of greenish-yellow flowers appear mainly in summer on this hybrid. The lips are spotted red towards the edge. Flower spike 60cm (2ft) or more. Cool-growing/Z 9.

C. nitida (syn. *C. ochracea*)
This epiphyte has very fragrant white flowers, marked with orange and yellow, from spring to early summer. Flower spike to 20cm (8in). Cool-growing/Z 9

C. Summer Pearl 'Senna'
Similar in overall appearance and flowering time to *C.* Maureen Grapes 'Marilyn', this hybrid has more greenish, acid-yellow flowers spotted with darker red. Flower spike to 60cm (2ft). Cool-growing/Z 9. The miniature 'Sonya' is a greenish-pink selection from the same hybrid group. The flowers of both orchids stay on the plant for six to eight weeks.

Dendrobium Mousmée

DENDROBIUM

There are both epiphytes and terrestrials in this large genus of deciduous, semi-evergreen and evergreen orchids. In the wild they occur across a huge area: India, China, south-eastern Asia, Japan, Malaysia, the Philippines, New Guinea, the Pacific islands, Australia and New Zealand. Many are easy to grow, while others need more specialist care. The most popular are hybrids derived from *D. nobile*.
Cultivation Grow the following orchids in small pots to restrict the roots or epiphytically on bark. All like bright light; lack of light is usually the cause of failure to produce flowers.

D. 'Emma Gold'

From summer to autumn the hybrid has tall, upright stems bearing small, greenish-yellow flowers with maroon lips. Support the flower stems with canes if necessary. Flower spike to 60cm (2ft). Cool-growing/Z 10.

D. loddigesii

This miniature orchid is an epiphyte found in south-western China. The fragrant, rose-pink flowers, with lips lined and fringed yellow, appear in early summer. Flower spike to 15cm (6in). Cool-growing/Z 10.

D. Mousmée

This is one of the oldest hybrid orchids, but it is still well worth growing. In summer, trusses of

white flowers with rich yellow lips hang from strong, upright canes. Flower spike to 40cm (16in). Cool-growing/Z 10.

D. nobile

An epiphytic species from the Himalayas, southern China and Taiwan, in spring this bears large, pale pink flowers with maroon lips. It needs a winter rest. Flower spike to 45cm (18in). Cool-growing/Z 10.

ENCYCLIA

The genus, from Central America, contains about 150 species, and the ones in cultivation are mainly from Mexico. These are collector's orchids, rather than for the general grower, but they are highly rewarding. The flowers are often brightly coloured and can be scented. Compact and freely branching, encyclias are suitable for growing outdoors in frost-free areas.
Cultivation Good drainage is essential, so grow these orchids in slatted baskets and keep them dry in winter.

E. brassavolae

This is an evergreen species originating from southern Mexico to western Panama, where it grows epiphytically in forested areas. The racemes of yellowish-green to brown flowers have purple-tipped, white lips and appear from summer to autumn. Flower spike 50cm (25in) or more. Cool-growing/Z 10.

Encyclia fragrans

E. cochleata
Cockleshell orchid, clamshell orchid

The curious, ribbon-like flowers, which are pale green with deep purple lips, can be produced at any time of year on this species, which is distributed from Florida to Mexico, Colombia and Venezuela. Flower spike to 50cm (25in). Cool-growing/Z 10.

E. fragrans

As its Latin name suggests, this species, from southern Mexico, Central America to Brazil and Greater Antilles, has scented flowers. Cream to greenish-white, with dark maroon striped lips, they are produced in racemes from spring to summer. Flower spike to 20cm (8in). Cool-growing/Z 10.

E. 'Sunburst'

Racemes of light greenish-yellow flowers with white lips appear in late summer. Flower spike to 15cm (6in). Cool-growing/Z 10.

E. vitellina 'Burnham Star'

This is a selected form of a species from Mexico and Guatemala. Panicles of vermilion to scarlet flowers with orange to yellow lips are borne from spring to summer. Flower spike to 15cm (6in). Cool-growing/Z 10.

EPIDENDRUM

This is one of the largest of orchid genera, containing more than 500 species, which are found throughout the tropical Americas, some at high altitudes. A noteworthy feature is that the flowers, sometimes on branching stems, open a few at a time so that individual plants can be in flower for several months. They are all evergreen, some being epiphytes, others terrestrials. They are best displayed so that the flowers are at eye-level.
Cultivation These orchids do best in containers. Either provide support for the long stems or allow them to trail down.

E. 'Pink Cascade'

As befits its name, this hybrid has tall, arching stems with hanging clusters of small, mauve, long-lasting flowers, which are tinged with pink. Flower spike to 60cm (2ft). Cool-growing to intermediate/Z 10.

Encyclia brassavolae

Encyclia vitellina 'Burnham Star'

Epidendrum 'Pink Cascade'

Epidendrum 'Plastic Doll'

E. 'Plastic Doll'
An unfortunate name, but this is a pretty plant, with hanging clusters of small, pale green flowers, sometimes marked pink in the centre, with yellow lips. These are carried over a long period in summer. It will flower as a small plant, so it makes a good introduction to the genus for new enthusiasts. Flower spike to 1m (3ft). Cool-growing to intermediate/Z 10.

LAELIA
This is an important genus, although not many of the 70 species find their way into amateur collections. Their value as parents to intergeneric hybrids (mostly with *Cattleya*) can hardly be overestimated, however. In the wild laelias are found growing both epiphytically and as terrestrials in much of Central and South America from coastal regions to high altitudes. *L. purpurata* is the national flower of Brazil.
Cultivation See individual descriptions for the plants listed.

L. anceps
This elegant species is an epiphyte originating from central Mexico. The soft lilac flowers have deep mauve, yellow-centred lips veined purple and are produced on tall stems in autumn to winter. Grow in a container or on bark. Rest the plant in winter after flowering. Flower spike to 60cm (2ft). Cool-growing/Z 10.

L. Pulcherrima 'Alba'
This beautiful hybrid has large, pure white, fragrant flowers in summer. It should be grown in a container. Flower spike to 60cm (2ft). Cool-growing/Z 10.

× LAELIOCATTLEYA
This hybrid genus consists of crosses between *Laelia* and *Cattleya*, sometimes referred to as cattleyas. It includes some of the most glamorous orchids, which should be represented in any collection.
Cultivation Grow in containers or slatted baskets.

× L. Callistoglossa
From summer to autumn this orchid has very large, pure white flowers that have ruffled petal edges and lips stained yellow at the centre. Flower spike to 30cm (12in). Cool-growing to intermediate/Z 10.

× L. Canhamiana 'Caerulea'
An orchid that bears large, showy blue flowers with darker lips from winter to spring. Flower spike to 30cm (12in). Cool-growing/Z 10.

× L. Gila Wilderness 'Majestic'
The large, reddish-purple flowers, which appear in summer, have flared petals. Flower spike to 30cm (12in). Cool-growing/Z 10.

× L. Love Fantasy 'Sweet Dreams'
From late summer to autumn this orchid produces racemes of sumptuous white flowers with lips that are splashed rosy purple and have yellow centres. Flower spike to 30cm (12in). Cool-growing/Z 10.

Laelia Pulcherrima 'Alba'

× L. Mini Purple 'Pinafore'
An orchid of luminous beauty, this bears large, rosy purple flowers, which have trumpet-like lips stained darker at the tips and yellow at the centre. They are produced from late summer to autumn. Flower spike to 20cm (8in). Cool-growing/Z 10.

× L. Tiny Treasure × Lake Casitas
Spectacular white flowers, with ruffled petal edges and lips that are stained reddish-purple at the edge and yellow towards the centre, appear in summer and autumn. Flower spike to 20cm (8in). Cool-growing/Z 10.

MASDEVALLIA
These fascinating orchids have a unique flower structure. They differ from other orchids in that the sepals are very large in comparison with the other parts of the flower, which are so small that they are almost invisible. The 300 or so species occur in the

× *Laeliocattleya* Tiny Treasure × Lake Casitas

wild at high altitudes (mostly in cloud forest) in Mexico, Brazil and Colombia, growing both epiphytically and as terrestrials. They are all evergreen. In the home the hybrids are easier to grow than the species. They do well if underpotted, to restrict the roots.
Cultivation Grow in containers of epiphytic compost (soil mix) and do not allow to dry out in winter. They are vulnerable to pesticides and fertilizers, so make sure these are well diluted before applying them.

M. Whiskers
This unique and distinctive hybrid is notable for the elongated 'tails' that extend from the tips of its sepals. The background colour of these is yellow-orange, but the heavy red spotting predominates. Flower spike to 15cm (6in). Cool-growing/Z 10.

Laelia anceps

× *Laeliocattleya* Mini Purple 'Pinafore'

Masdevallia Whiskers

Miltonia clowesii

Miltonia warsewiczii 'Alba'

Miltoniopsis Storm

MILTONIA
Pansy orchid
Although this is a small genus, the orchids are deservedly popular because of their ease of cultivation. There has been some confusion with the genus *Miltoniopsis*, which it resembles in some ways. There are about 20 species in the genus, and in the wild they are found in forested areas, mainly in Brazil, where they grow epiphytically. (Species found outside Brazil are sometimes included in other genera.) They like to be kept a little pot-bound.
Cultivation Grow these orchids in containers or slatted baskets or mounted on bark.

M. clowesii
In autumn, each erect stem carries from six to ten greenish-yellow,

Miltoniopsis St Mary

star-shaped flowers, which are heavily blotched and barred brown. The lips are white, with a pinkish-mauve blotch on the upper part. Misting in summer can mark the foliage, so provide humidity by other means. It is suitable for growing on a windowsill. Flower spike 60cm (2ft). Cool-growing/Z 10.

M. warsewiczii 'Alba'
This is a selection of a species from Peru, Colombia and Costa Rica. In summer it produces fragrant, yellow and white flowers. Flower spike to 50cm (20in). Intermediate/Z 10.

MILTONIOPSIS
These orchids are also sometimes called pansy orchids because the flowers look like pansies. Their

flat faces, usually with a contrasting 'mask', are just as appealing. Flower colours include white, pink, purple, red and yellow as well as a dramatic blackish-maroon. The five species in the genus are mainly epiphytes, found in the mountains of Central and South America. The hybrids are desirable plants in every respect: vividly coloured, scented, often with two flowering periods a year, and easy to grow.
Cultivation Grow in containers. Like miltonias, with which they are often grouped, they like to be kept a little pot-bound and appreciate high humidity.

M. Bremen × Lilac Surprise
This hybrid has white flowers, marked deep maroon, which appear mainly in summer but also occasionally at other times. Flower spike to 23cm (9in). Cool-growing/Z 10.

M. St Mary
The white flowers are appealingly marked with red and yellow at the centre. As with the other hybrids described, flowering is mainly in summer but can also occur at other times. Flower spike to 23cm (9in). Cool-growing/Z 10.

M. Storm
The eye-catching, rich red flowers appear mainly in summer but also at other times. They are blotched with yellow and pink at the base of the lips. Flower spike to 23cm (9in). Cool-growing/Z 10.

× ODONTIODA
This hybrid group was created by crossing *Odontoglossum* with *Cochlioda*, and in many respects they look like odontoglossums. They do not have a specific flowering season, but can flower at any time when the current season's pseudobulb is mature. The flowers are very showy.
Cultivation Grow in containers of epiphytic orchid compost (soil mix).

× O. Honiton Lace 'Burnham'
This orchid has tall sprays of large mauve and pink flowers. Flower spike to 45cm (18in). Cool-growing/Z 10.

× O. Mont Felard × St Aubin's Bay
A neat-growing orchid, this bears spikes of white flowers spotted with rich pink. The lips are stained the same colour towards the edge and have yellow centres. The petal edges are ruffled and frilled. Flower spike to 45cm (18in). Cool-growing/Z 10.

× O. Rialto × Odontocidium Panse
This orchid has sprays of creamy-white flowers, blotched with yellow, and frilled petal edges. Flower spike to 45cm (18in). Cool-growing Z 10.

× ODONTOCIDIUM
A hybrid group produced by crossing *Odontoglossum* with *Oncidium*. The flowers are often distinctively mottled. Some have definite flowering seasons, while others will flower all year in the right conditions.
Cultivation Grow in containers of epiphytic orchid compost (soil mix).

× O. Purbeck Gold
Rich yellow flowers mottled with brown are borne mainly in autumn but also occasionally at other times. Flower spike to 50cm (20in). Cool-growing/Z 10.

× O. Tiger Hambühren 'Butterfly'
An orchid with impressive spikes of rich yellow flowers mottled with chestnut brown. They appear

× *Odontocidium* Tiger Hambühren 'Butterfly'

mainly in autumn but also at other times. Flower spike to 45cm (18in). Cool-growing/Z 10.

ODONTOGLOSSUM

This is an important genus for hybridists and plants from it have been used to create a vast number of excellent, easy-to-grow hybrids. In the wild they are found growing epiphytically, mainly in cool mountain regions of Central and South America. Many of the hybrids can flower at any time of year.
Cultivation Grow in containers of epiphytic orchid compost (soil mix).

O. Geyser Gold

The showy flowers of this orchid, which are carried on upright

stems, are rich yellow overlaid with darker gold markings. They can be produced at any time of year. Flower spike to 50cm (20in). Cool-growing/Z 10.

ONCIDIUM

There are about 450 species of mainly epiphytic orchids in this genus from South America and the West Indies.
Cultivation These orchids do best in containers of epiphytic orchid compost (soil mix).

O. longipes

This small species, from south-eastern Brazil, produces an abundance of short racemes of yellow flowers, spotted and streaked with reddish-brown, in spring and summer. Flower spike to 15cm (6in). Cool-growing to intermediate/Z 10.

O. macranthum
(syn. *Cyrtolichum macranthum*)

In summer this species, from Colombia, Ecuador and Peru, bears tall, spreading panicles of golden-yellow flowers with lips edged in purple. Flower spike to 1m (3ft). Cool-growing to intermediate/Z 10.

O. Sharry Baby

From summer to autumn tall, branching stems carry an abundance of dainty, maroon and white flowers that are chocolate-scented. Support the flower stems with canes. Flower spike to 60cm (2ft). Cool-growing/Z 10.

PAPHIOPEDILUM
Slipper orchid, Venus' slipper

Paphiopedilums are the well-known slipper orchids, so called because of the flowers' inflated, pouch-like lips (actually designed to trap pollinating insects). Predominantly in shades of green and brown, the flowers can add a rather sinister touch to any orchid collection. The 60 or so evergreen species in the genus are Asian in origin and are mostly terrestrial. There are many hybrids, which are often more sympathetically coloured in white, pink or cream. The leaves can be mottled. Paphiopedilums are robust plants, which tolerate low light levels, making them ideal houseplants. The flowers mainly appear in winter and can last for up to ten weeks on the plant. However, the plants are often slow-growing and reluctant to flower, so they are not the ideal beginner's orchid.
Cultivation Grow in terrestrial orchid compost (soil mix) in containers that restrict the roots. Do not mist.

P. Avalon Mist

Yellowish-green flowers appear from spring to summer on this hybrid. Flower spike to 23cm (9in). Cool-growing to intermediate/Z 10.

P. Calloso-Argus

This hybrid, which blooms from spring to summer, produces solitary flowers. They are green, striped and spotted with maroon.

Paphiopedilum Avalon Mist

The leaves are attractively mottled. Flower spike to 23cm (9in). Cool-growing to intermediate/Z 10.

P. insigne

From autumn to spring, this species, originating in the eastern Himalayas, carries slipper-like, copper-brown, solitary flowers with yellow dorsal petals. They are spotted with brown. Flower spike to 30cm (12in). Cool-growing to intermediate/Z 10.

P. philippinense × ciliolare

In autumn and winter, greenish-brown flowers appear on this hybrid. These are heavily spotted and striped with darker brown and have deep pouches. Flower spike to 30cm (12in). Cool-growing to intermediate/Z 10.

Odontoglossum Geyser Gold

Oncidium Sharry Baby

Paphiopedilum Calloso-Argus

Phalaenopsis Lady Sakhara

PHALAENOPSIS
Moth orchid

To the orchid-growing community, phalaenopsis hybrids have become as important as laelias once were, largely because of their tolerance of central heating – that is, they will grow in a drier atmosphere than suits most other orchids. This makes them suitable as houseplants. In the wild, they are found growing epiphytically in tropical areas of the Far East, almost always in deep shade. They are of unmatched elegance, which has recently made them a popular choice for bridal bouquets.

Cultivation Unless otherwise indicated, these orchids are best grown in slatted baskets or on bark, but they are also suitable for containers if they are free-draining.

P. equestris
A compact species from the Philippines and Taiwan, this orchid bears significantly smaller flowers than most of the hybrids. From spring to winter gracefully arching stems carry small, soft pink flowers with darker lips, which are streaked with red. Flower spike to 30cm (12in). Warm-growing/Z 10.

P. Lady Sakhara
This gorgeous hybrid has racemes of pink flowers, veined with darker pink and with glowing cerise pink lips. They are produced

on arching stems throughout the year. Flower spike 45cm (18in). Warm-growing/Z 10.

P. Mystic Golden Leopard
This hybrid can flower throughout the year, producing racemes of soft yellow flowers spotted with maroon. The lips are bright orange. Flower spike 30cm (12in). Warm-growing/Z 10.

P. Paifang's Golden Lion
The striking orchid has white flowers that are heavily spotted with rich violet-pink and have glowing pink lips. Flower spike 30cm (12in). Warm-growing/ Z 10.

PHRAGMIPEDIUM
Lady slipper

Phragmipediums are similar to paphiopedilums, both having the characteristic pouches, but they are less often found in collections because of the difficulty of finding plants in the wild. (Many species are officially designated as endangered, and their importation is prohibited.) The lateral petals are considerably extended and are also twisted. The species are mainly terrestrials, which die back in winter, and are found at low altitudes in Central and South America. There are relatively few hybrids, making them plants for the connoisseur, although they are easy to grow.

Cultivation Grow in containers of terrestrial orchid compost (growing medium). Good drainage is essential.

P. Eric Young
This hybrid produces a succession of orange-yellow flowers from summer to autumn. Flower spike 45cm (18in). Intermediate/Z 10.

P. longifolium
The species comes from Costa Rica, Panama, Colombia and Ecuador. In autumn it produces racemes of light yellowish-green flowers with twisted petal edges margined with purple and sepals veined dark green. The lips are flushed purple. Flower spike to 2m (6ft). Cool-growing/Z 10.

× Sophrolaeliocattleya Marion Fitch 'La Tuilerie'

P. schlimmii 'Wilcox'
A selected form of a Colombian species, in summer this produces a succession of white flowers, flushed pink and shading to yellowish green at the centre, with darker lips. Flower spike 45cm (18in). Intermediate/Z 10.

× SOPHROLAELIO-CATTLEYA

These orchids are of complex parentage, involving *Sophronitis*, *Laelia* and *Cattleya*. The flamboyant flowers, typical of all the cattleyas, can be produced at any time of year.

Cultivation Grow in containers of terrestrial orchid compost (soil mix).

Phalaenopsis Mystic Golden Leopard

Phragmipedium Eric Young

Phragmipedium longifolium

× _S._ Jewel Box 'Dark Waters'
As befits its name, this orchid
produces rich deep red flowers
that have trumpet-like lips. These
are usually borne from autumn
to spring. Flower spike to 30cm
(12in). Cool-growing to
intermediate/Z 10.

× _S._ Marion Fitch 'La Tuilerie'
This orchid can flower at any
time of year. The solitary flowers
are an eye-catching luminous
pinkish-red and have lips that
are ruffled at the edges. Flower
spike 30cm (12in).
Intermediate/Z 10.

**× _S._ Rocket Burst 'Deep
Enamel'**
The brilliant orange-red
flowers usually appear in spring
and last for a month or so.
Flower spike 30cm (12in).
Intermediate/Z 10.

STANHOPEA

These epiphytic evergreens from
Central and South America are
orchids for real enthusiasts. The
flowers, which are some of the
most strongly scented of all
orchids, last for only about three
days (in some species only one
day). It is essential to grow
stanhopeas in baskets, because
the flowering stems emerge
from the base of the pseudobulbs
and grow downwards. The species
described is the one most
frequently found in collections.
The shortness of the flowering
season means that the seed (and
hence new plants) are always in
short supply.
Cultivation Grow in epiphytic
orchid compost (soil mix) in
special baskets or on bark.

**_S._ tigrina
(syn. _S. hernandezii_)**
From late summer to autumn
this Mexican species produces
downward-growing stems carrying
substantial, waxy, yellow flowers
splashed with deep red, which are
strongly scented. They last for
only about three days. The plant
sometimes experiences a slow-
down in growth in early summer
before flowering. Flower spike to
45cm (18in). Cool-growing to
intermediate/Z 10.

× _Vuylstekeara_ Cambria 'Plush'

VANDA

Among the most dramatic of all
orchids, these evergreen epiphytes
are widely distributed in China,
the Himalayas, New Guinea and
northern Australia, where they
clamber through tree branches
to reach heights of 2.2m (7ft).
Although usually more modest in
domestic settings, they will still
need plenty of room vertically.
They are, nevertheless, among the
most rewarding orchids, with
flowers produced two or three
times a year (mostly in winter),
and these can last up to four
weeks on the plant. In cold areas
they can be placed outside in the
summer months.
Cultivation Grow in slatted
baskets of epiphytic orchid
compost (soil mix).

× _Vuylstekeara_ Linda Isler

_V._ Rothschildiana
This remarkable hybrid can
flower at any time of year. The
flowers, carried on long racemes,
are violet-blue with darker veining.
Flower spike 60cm (2ft).
Intermediate/Z 10.

× VUYLSTEKEARA

These hybridized orchids are
crosses of _Cochlioda_, _Miltonia_ and
Odontoglossum. The spikes of showy
flowers appear when the
pseudobulb is mature, usually in
autumn. They are easy to grow
and make ideal beginner's orchids.
Cultivation Grow these orchids in
containers of epiphytic compost
(soil mix).

× _V._ Cambria 'Plush'
At varying times of the year, when
the pseudobulb is mature, this
hybrid produces long sprays of
vivid crimson flowers, up to 10cm
(4in) across, with large red and
white lips. Flower spike to 50cm
(20in). Cool-growing/Z 10 (but
tolerates warmer conditions).

× _V._ Linda Isler
The tall, sometimes branching
spikes of this orchid carry rust
red flowers, with lips that have
contrasting white borders. Flower
spike to 60cm (2ft). Cool-
growing/Z 10 (but tolerates
warmer conditions).

× WILSONARA

These hybrids are evergreens,
derived by crossing _Cochlioda_,
Odontoglossum and _Oncidium_. The
star-like flowers are generally
produced in large quantities.
Cultivation Grow in containers
that constrict the roots, filled
with epiphytic compost
(soil mix).

× _W._ Bonne Nuit
When the pseudobulbs are
mature, this orchid produces
tall, branching spikes that carry
masses of showy, yellow flowers
spotted with brown and with
white lips. Flower spike to 60cm
(2ft). Cool-growing/Z 10.

**× _W._ Hambühren Stern
'Cheam'**
This epiphytic orchid bears spikes
of warm brown flowers with

× _Wilsonara_ Bonne Nuit

yellow lips, which can be
produced at any time of year
when the pseudobulb is mature.
Flower spike to 60cm (2ft).
Cool-growing/Z 10.

**× _W._ Widecombe Fair
'Burnham'**
This orchid makes an excellent
houseplant, since it tolerates
fluctuating temperatures, and is
therefore suitable for a mixed
collection. When the pseudobulbs
are mature, they produce long
spikes of white and pink flowers.
Flower spike to 60cm (2ft).
Cool-growing/Z 10 (but tolerates
warmer conditions).

× _Wilsonara_ Widecombe Fair
'Burnham'

Ferns

Ferns are a fascinating group of
plants, increasingly valued for their
architectural form, ease of cultivation
and tolerance of conditions
inhospitable to many other plants.
They have a welcome freshness as
their fronds begin to unfurl in
spring, and then develop a
considerable elegance, adding a
subtle, understated note to the
garden. Ravishing in light woodland,
they are also effective near water
or in any other damp, shady part
of the garden.

This mixture of ferns and other perennials brings interest to a shady
corner of the garden.

Ferns for your garden

Ferns are primitive plants. The lowest form of plant life grown in gardens, they evolved long before seed-producing plants, some being as old as the Carboniferous Period (beginning 360 million years ago). They belong to the pteridophytes, a class that includes horsetails, club mosses and ground pines. Fossil remains indicate that prehistoric pteridophytes reached the size of large trees, but those that have survived to the present day – apart from the tree ferns of the tropics – are much more modest.

Ferns occur in a variety of habitats. Profuse in the tropics, they are also found – albeit in lesser numbers – as far north as Greenland and as far south as Antarctica, from sea level to high altitudes, but not in deserts or very cold areas. Most – though by no means all – are shade- and moisture-loving. In humid climates, some are epiphytic, clinging to trees like orchids. A few are aquatics.

A few species are widespread to an extraordinary degree: common bracken (*Pteridium aquilinum*), though hardly a garden plant, is found throughout the temperate regions as well as some areas of the tropics, while the maidenhair fern occurs in western Europe, parts of Asia, the Americas and Polynesia.

Like other plants, ferns have well-developed stems, roots and leaves. They can be evergreen or deciduous, and some can be either, depending on the climate. Though they can be long-lived plants, the leaves, or fronds, survive for only one or two years and are replaced by fresh leaves that emerge from the tip of the stem annually.

Ferns do not flower, and thus cannot reproduce in the conventional way by pollination. In fact, the

Few gardening sights are more dramatic than the unfurling fronds of ferns, lit up by early morning sun in spring.

plants we recognize as ferns are actually asexual, and reproduction takes place in two stages. Spores form on the undersides of the mature fronds. These are shed and develop as prothalli, tiny heart-

Here, ferns are used to line a path of stepping stones, strewn with fir cones and decorative masks, through a shady woodland area.

shaped plants that look like liverworts, bearing separate male and female germ cells. Male gametes are able to migrate across the surface of the prothallium to unite with the female gametes, and a new embryo fern is then produced. This absorbs nutrients from the prothallium until its roots penetrate the soil and it is able to survive on its own. The prothallium then dies. Some species are able to reproduce by bulbils that form on the fronds. Hybridization does not seem to occur, but many species show astonishing variation. Some have developed a variety of forms, the fronds being crisped, crested or dwarfed, and these are found both in the wild and in gardens.

Ferns exhibit a wide diversity of size. The tree ferns can reach 15m (50ft) – growing slowly, it is true, often at a rate of no more than 2.5cm (1in) a year – while others are tiny. They can be symmetrical, with the fronds erect and arranged like a shuttlecock, or spread by rhizomes. Some have long stems that twine into trees and other plants, pulling the plants skywards.

The fronds are usually roughly triangular or arrow- or strap-shaped. They can be entire or divided, often very finely, giving a filigree effect. Sometimes they divide like a fish tail or have a feathery appearance. The fronds of all ferns are basically green, but some show red, yellow or grey coloration and have a metallic sheen. Variegation does not occur.

Ferns in the garden

Formerly very popular, then dismissed as drab and dreary, ferns are finally experiencing a renaissance in gardens. They are unrivalled for bringing dank, dark corners of the garden to life, but it would be a serious underestimation of their value to make that their sole use. Gardeners averse to slug and snail control much prefer them to hostas, which enjoy roughly similar conditions: once established, ferns are virtually indestructible. Gertrude Jekyll was fond of combining hostas and ferns in shady courtyards – an elegant and simple solution to what can be a problem area of the garden.

Ferns can be tricky to place in the open garden, most needing soil that is consistently moist without being waterlogged. Find a cool spot for them, ideally in the shade of deciduous trees, where they are protected from direct sunlight and strong winds – both equally detrimental to most ferns. The traditional fernery – perhaps incorporating a water feature – was essentially a large rockery in shade (sometimes under glass to accommodate tender species), providing conditions that also suit the mosses and lichens that would soon take hold unbidden.

Some of the more architectural ferns, such as the tree fern (*Dicksonia antarctica*), the royal fern (*Osmunda regalis*) and forms of *Polystichum setiferum*, make striking specimens, but are also supremely effective in a massed planting (space permitting) of five or more. Site them where light will filter down on them through the tree canopy above. Many ferns, particularly those with rhizomes, are ideal as ground cover in a shady site or in light woodland. Evergreens can be outstanding features of the winter garden, and even the deciduous species are of value then, as the foliage dies back much later than does that of most other plants.

Unusual but interesting effects can be created by combining some of the sun-tolerant ferns with the usual inhabitants of the mixed border. Forms of the golden male fern (*Dryopteris affinis*) or polypodys (*Polypodium*) would be well worth trying with roses, for example, provided the site is not too open. *Asplenium, Dryopteris* and *Polypodium* are invaluable in so far as they are among the few plants that will tolerate dry shade. Very pleasing effects could be created by combining them with variegated periwinkles (*Vinca*), small-leaved ivies (a form of *Hedera helix*) or hardy cyclamen.

The rhythm of the paving slabs is reflected in the subtle border plantings of ferns and pulmonarias.

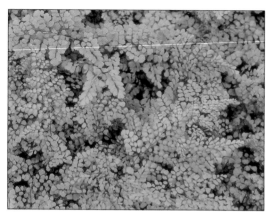

Adiantum venustum

ADIANTUM
Maidenhair fern

A genus of deciduous, semi-evergreen and evergreen ferns with an elegant overall appearance. The plants described here are hardy, but the genus also includes some tender varieties that can be grown indoors.
Cultivation Leafy soil in a shaded spot suits these woodlanders.

A. aculeatum subsp. subpumilum (syn. A. aculeatum subsp. aleuticum) Asiatic maidenhair fern

Originally found in North America and eastern Asia, this is a beautiful fern with a creeping rootstock. It has slender, purplish-black stems with fingered, fan-like blades. It needs fertile, humus-rich soil. H and S 30cm (12in). Hardy/Z 3–8.

A. venustum Himalayan maidenhair fern

The triangular fronds of this evergreen native of China are pink when they first appear in spring, turn soft green and then develop a bluish tinge as they mature. H and S 15–30cm (6–12in). Hardy/Z 3–8.

ASPLENIUM
Spleenwort

These evergreen ferns are found worldwide, except in Antarctica. They are ideal for a rock garden.
Cultivation Good drainage is essential. Plant them in light shade in crevices between rocks or in gritty soil.

A. scolopendrium (syn. Phyllitis scolopendrium, Scolopendrium phyllitis) Hart's tongue fern

This fern, which is native to western Asia, Europe and North America, is easy to grow and has smooth, leathery, strap-like fronds. H and S 45–60cm (18–24in). Hardy/Z 4–8. It has a number of interesting variants, including **Cristatum Group**, in

which the final third of the frond is divided, giving a tassel-like or crested appearance. H 60cm (2ft), S 80cm (32in).

ATHYRIUM
Lady fern

A genus of deciduous, occasionally semi-evergreen, ferns, whose common name apparently relates to their overall elegance and grace. The species are all highly variable, and no two plants are ever quite identical.
Cultivation Grow in a moist, shady site, in neutral to acid soil.

A. filix-femina Lady fern

Found throughout the northern hemisphere, this has fine, lacy fronds. There are many selected forms. H 50cm (20in), S 30cm (12in). Hardy/Z 4–9. **'Fieldii'** has long, narrow fronds. H 90cm (3ft), S 30cm (1ft). **'Frizelliae'** (tatting fern) has massed pinnae that are contracted into balls, giving the appearance of a necklace of green beads. H 20cm (8in), S 30cm (12in).

A. niponicum var. pictum (syn. A. niponicum 'Pictum') Japanese painted fern

This beautiful and unusual fern is native to Japan. The broadly triangular fronds are wine red, merging with grey-green. It needs a moist, shady, sheltered position. H and S 45–60cm (18–24in). Hardy/Z 3–8.

Athyrium niponicum var. pictum

A. otophorum

Originating from eastern Asia, this distinctive fern has fairly broad, triangular fronds, which have dark green segments with purple-red stalks. It does best in a moist, shady, sheltered position. H and S 45–75cm (18–30in). Hardy/Z 3–8.

CYRTOMIUM

This genus, which was formerly known as *Phanerophlebia*, contains both evergreen and deciduous ferns with distinctive fronds that make an effective contrast to other daintier species in a fernery or a shady rock garden.
Cultivation These woodland plants need fertile, moist but well-drained soil in shade.

Asplenium scolopendrium Cristatum Group

Athyrium filix-femina 'Fieldii'

Athyrium filix-femina 'Frizelliae'

Athyrium otophorum

Cyrtomium fortunei

C. fortunei
Holly fern
This upright, architectural evergreen from eastern Asia has mid-green, leathery fronds with smooth margins. H and S 30–60cm (1–2ft). Hardy/ Z 6–9.

DICKSONIA

These dramatic tree-like ferns, originating from the temperate and tropical highland forests of Australasia and South America, are ideal as specimens. They can be grown in containers and overwintered indoors.
Cultivation Grow in fertile, acid soil in deep to light shade.

D. antarctica
Tree fern
This fern, which originates in Australia, is an increasingly popular choice for gardens where a dramatic, exotic-looking feature is wanted. The fronds will reach 2m (6ft) in length on mature specimens. It needs a mild, moist climate. In cool areas it is usually deciduous. Packing the crown loosely with dry straw can help it survive cold winters. H 6m (20ft), S 4m (13ft). Half-hardy/Z 10.

DRYOPTERIS
Buckler fern
A genus of (usually) deciduous ferns found by streams and lakes. The common name derives from the kidney-shaped spore covers. They are robust plants, useful for providing large, trouble-free clumps of greenery among flowering perennials.
Cultivation Plant in fertile soil in partial shade, although *D. affinis* is tolerant of sun.

D. affinis
Golden male fern
The leathery, golden-green fronds of this European fern become progressively darker through the season. H and S up to 1m (3ft). Hardy/Z 4–9. **'Congesta'** is a very pretty dwarf form. H and S 15–23cm (6–9in). **'Cristata'**, rightly known as the king fern, is

Dryopteris erythrosora

a truly magnificent plant that makes a bold statement in the garden. The fronds are symmetrically crested. H and S 0.6–1.2m (2–4ft). **'Cristata Angustata'** is less robust, with narrower fronds and a neater habit. H and S 45–60cm (18–24in). **'Polydactyla Mapplebeck'** is equally noteworthy, with crested fronds divided into two terminal crests. H and S 0.6–1.5m (2–5ft).

D. erythrosora
This fern, which comes from China and Japan, has broadly triangular fronds. They are glossy coppery pink when young,

Dryopteris filix-mas 'Crispa Cristata'

maturing to plain green. This may be evergreen in mild winters. H and S 45–60cm (18–24in). Hardy/Z 5–9.

D. filix-mas
Male fern
This woodlander, found in Europe and North America, is a good choice for a wild garden. It has tall, upright, lance-shaped but feathery, light green fronds. Although technically deciduous, the male fern does not die back completely in autumn. H and S 1m (3ft). Hardy/Z 4–8. **'Crispa Cristata'** has well-crisped and neatly crested fronds. H 60cm (2ft), S 1m (3ft).

Dicksonia antarctica

Dryopteris affinis 'Polydactyla Mapplebeck'

Dryopteris affinis 'Cristata'

Gymnocarpium dryopteris 'Plumosum'

GYMNOCARPIUM

This group of deciduous, rhizomatous ferns make excellent groundcover plants.
Cultivation Grow in leafy, fertile soil, preferably neutral to acid, in shade.

G. dryopteris
Oak fern

This fern, which is found throughout Europe, Asia and in Canada, has soft, golden-green fronds that arise from a creeping rootstock, forming a dense mat. Oak ferns are a good choice for the front of a border in a shady rock garden or in stony soil in woodland. H 23–30cm (9–12in), S indefinite. Hardy/Z 3–8.
'Plumosum' has even lovelier foliage, with triple-headed fronds opening into three delicately laced triangles of vivid green. H 23cm (9in), S indefinite.

MATTEUCCIA

The moisture-loving deciduous, rhizomatous ferns in this genus, native to the woodlands of North America, eastern Asia and Europe, have a characteristic 'shuttlecock' appearance. They look graceful at the margins of a pond or in damp woodland.
Cultivation These ferns need moist, ideally slightly acid, soil in light shade.

M. struthiopteris
Shuttlecock fern, ostrich feather fern

This native of Europe, Asia and North America is well known. It

Matteuccia struthiopteris

has tapering fronds – up to 1.5m (5ft) long – that create an elegant, vase-like structure around a stout rootstock. The creeping rootstock spreads rapidly. H to 1.5m (5ft), S to 1m (3ft) in moist conditions. Hardy/Z 2–8.

ONOCLEA

This lush deciduous fern makes a good subject for pond margins. An effective use is to stabilize the edges of natural streams. There is only one species in the genus.
Cultivation These ferns do best in slightly acid, fertile, moist soil in light shade.

O. sensibilis
Sensitive fern, bead fern

This moisture-loving fern, which is native to eastern North America and eastern Asia, bears upright pink-bronze fronds that later become mid-green and arching, with the spores enclosed in bead-like pinnules. It has a creeping rootstock and rapidly colonizes wet areas. H and S 1.2–1.5m (4–5ft). Hardy/Z 4–8.

OSMUNDA

These large deciduous ferns with upright fronds are widely distributed in the wild. They are distinctive plants for a shady bog garden or for planting at the water's edge.
Cultivation They do best in moist, preferably acid, soil in light shade.

O. regalis
Royal fern

Found in temperate and subtropical regions around the world, this species does best in very wet conditions, making for a magnificent specimen for a water-side planting. The deep green fronds, with a tough, leathery texture, appear from aerial roots. The tips of the fronds change into long, narrow masses of brownish spore capsules. Royal ferns also make handsome container plants. H and S 0.9–2m/3–6ft. Hardy/Z 3–9.

PELLAEA

This genus of deciduous, semi-evergreen or evergreen ferns make excellent rock garden plants in sheltered areas.

Onoclea sensibilis

Cultivation The species described needs well-drained, alkaline soil in sun, but shaded at midday.

P. atropurpurea
Purple cliff brake

Native to North America, this evergreen fern has glaucous green fronds. H and S 30–40cm (12–16in). It makes a good container plant for an alpine house or cool conservatory. Borderline hardy/Z 9–10.

PLATYCERIUM
Staghorn fern

The common name of these intriguing tender ferns relates to the shape of the leathery fronds. In the wild, they are rainforest epiphytes.
Cultivation Grow in slatted baskets in an epiphytic compost (soil mix) consisting of equal parts leaf mould, perlite or vermiculite, and charcoal. Keep in a lightly shaded spot and mist frequently. In frost-free climates, they can be grown epiphytically in trees.

P. bifurcatum
Elkhorn fern

The stiff, antler-like fronds emerge from among heart-shaped basal fronds, which turn brown. H and S 60cm (2ft). Tender/Z 10.

POLYPODIUM
Polypody

These evergreen ferns with fleshy rhizomes are good for year-round groundcover.

Polypodium vulgare

Polypodium vulgare 'Longicaudatum'

Polystichum setiferum 'Pulcherrimum Bevis'

Cultivation They do best in stony, but humus-rich soil, in sun or light shade and with protection from cold, dry winds.

P. vulgare
Common polypody, wall fern
This evergreen fern, which is found in Europe and Asia, is a useful plant in the garden, adapting to a range of conditions but preferring stony soil. It has smooth, leathery, deeply cut, lance-shaped green fronds set on either side of a central stem. H 10–45cm (4–18in), S indefinite. Hardy/Z 5–8. The vigorous **'Cornubiense'** is a curious cultivar, with three distinct forms of frond: some are like those of the species; others are very finely cut, consisting of very narrow

segments; and some are coarser versions of these. Sometimes all three are incorporated in one frond. H 30–40cm (12–16in), S indefinite. Hardy/Z 5–8. **'Longicaudatum'** (syn. *P. glycyrrhiza* 'Longicaudatum') has more elongated fronds than the species. H and S 23–60cm (9–24in). Hardy/Z 5–8.

POLYSTICHUM
Holly fern, shield fern
This genus of elegant evergreen, semi-evergreen or deciduous ferns usually have a shuttlecock-like appearance. They make good plants for a shady border or a rock garden.
Cultivation Grow in preferably alkaline, humus-rich soil in light to deep shade.

P. setiferum
Soft shield fern
This elegant fern, which is native to Europe, has gracefully arching fronds. An evergreen, it is easy to grow, producing large clumps if given shade and moisture. H and S 60cm (2ft), but it can reach 1.5m (5ft). Hardy/Z 5–8. **Acutilobum Group 'Othello'** has extra-long, elegant fronds, which spread out horizontally. H and S 0.9–1.2m (3–4ft). Hardy/Z 5–8. Plants of the **Divisilobum Group** are variable, but all have large, finely cut fronds. The new growth in spring is densely covered in white scales, which creates an attractive effect. H and S to 1.5m (5ft), but only after several years. Hardy/Z 5–8. **Lineare Group** ferns are prostrate, with long, slender, light green fronds. H and S 0.9–1.2m (3–4ft). **'Pulcherrimum Bevis'** is an architectural, finely divided fern, with tall, arching fronds. H and S to 1m (3ft). Hardy/Z 5–8.

THELYPTERIS
This small genus of deciduous ferns is usually represented in gardens by the species described. It is an invasive plant but useful at the margins of a natural pool or stream; it does well at the edge of water.
Cultivation Grow in moist or very moist, ideally acid soil in a sunny or lightly shaded spot.

T. palustris
Marsh fern
This fern, which spreads by means of creeping rhizomes, has dainty, erect, finely divided, light green fronds. It is an unassuming plant, but useful to fill damp ground. H and S 50cm–1.5m (20in–5ft). Hardy/Z 5–8.

Polypodium vulgare 'Cornubiense'

Polystichum setiferum Acutilobum Group

Grasses and bamboos

This group of plants is becoming increasingly popular with gardeners as their potential is being realized. There is a grass suitable for every soil type and virtually every location in the garden. Some are grand, imposing plants that give height to borders or provide accents, while others are more feathery and can be used in drifts to soften any colour scheme. Some bamboos make good barrier plants, besides providing a wealth of material for use as stakes. Most grasses and bamboos retain their structure over winter, continuing to provide interest during the coldest months.

Grasses add a delicate, feathery texture, in strong contrast to the more formal shape of the dahlias.

Grasses and bamboos for your garden

Though they look quite different, grasses and bamboos both belong to the same family, Gramineae (or Poaceae). In fact, close inspection readily reveals the similarities, and it is only the difference in scale that distinguishes them. In the discussion that follows, general references to "grasses" should be understood as including bamboos.

Grasses are among the most important plants on the planet and make up one of the largest and most varied of all the plant families. They are mainly perennial (both evergreen and herbaceous), though there are some annual species. They are found in both swamps and deserts, in the polar regions as well as in the tropics, from coastal areas to near the tops of snow-covered mountains.

Grasses have roots, stems, leaves and flowers like other plants. The stems (called culms, particularly in descriptions of bamboos) are jointed; while the joints are always

solid, the part of the stem in between can be solid or, more usually, hollow. Some have stems that spread sideways. Such stems below ground are referred to as rhizomes, while those above ground are called stolons. Both habits allow many species to colonize great tracts of open ground. In the wild (and indeed in gardens) grasses fulfil the valuable function of preventing soil erosion.

Aside from the important lawn grasses and the ornamentals described in the following pages, grasses encompass food crops such as wheat, oats, barley, corn and cane sugar, while the leaves of some are used in paper manufacture. Others are grown to provide a food source for grazing animals.

Bamboos, generally considered the most primitive of the grasses, are found only in the tropics and warm areas of the temperate zones. Prized for the strength and durability of their hard, woody stems, they have been widely used throughout Asia to make furniture (and even houses), as well as cooking utensils and fishing rods. An interesting feature of bamboos is that the individual culms do not thicken with age once they are mature (as do the stems of other woody plants). Equally extraordinary is the infrequency with which they flower. While other grasses flower annually, bamboos flower only every ten to twenty years (with even longer gaps recorded). After flowering, the plant either dies or is severely weakened, taking some years to recover. (The infrequency of flowering causes botanists difficulties in classification, since relationships among the different species can be established only by studying the inflorescences. This has resulted in a comprehensive revision

of the genera in recent years. Certain genera have been amalgamated, and some species have been reassigned.)

Sedges are similar to grasses in appearance but are distinct in having solid triangular or round stems. They thrive in marshes, swamps, shallow water and water meadows.

Grasses and bamboos in the garden

Considering the diversity of their natural habitats, it follows that there is a grass for virtually every garden situation. Nothing has been more remarkable than the surge of interest in this group of plants in recent years.

Bamboos have traditionally been regarded as utility plants, but an increasing awareness of their beauty and architectural merits has resulted in more extended use. Excellent for filling "problem" areas of the garden such as ditches or rough, stony ground too difficult to cultivate,

The feathery plums of *Cortaderia selloana* 'Sunningdale Silver' brings interest late in season, along with the sedum and cosmos.

The arching leaves of *Carex elata* 'Aurea' and *Miscanthus sinensis* 'Zebrinus' make for an attractive waterside planting.

they are also valued for providing culms for cutting to make plant supports and screens. As an extension of the latter use, they can themselves be planted to screen one part of the garden from another. They are entirely to the point in a Japanese-style garden and strangely, despite their size (or perhaps because of it), they look superb when planted in a small enclosed town garden. For strictly ornamental use (particularly where space is at a premium), stick to clump-forming species rather than the invasive kinds, or restrict their spread by planting them in large containers sunk in the ground.

Ornamental grasses are grown for the long-lasting appeal both of their leaves and of their plumes of flowers. Beds devoted to grasses alone can be highly effective in a quiet, understated way, but on the whole they are best in mixed company. None are vividly coloured, but they provide an admirable foil for a range of more flamboyant plants. They are especially effective planted in drifts with traditional border perennials and bedding plants, helping to soften potential colour clashes. Many are ideal for a low-maintenance garden, since the tufts of foliage they create are virtually impenetrable to weeds. Larger kinds can be used to "punctuate" borders, used as accent plants as an alternative to yuccas and phormiums, or can be planted as specimens, pampas grass (*Cortaderia selloana*) and *Arundo donax* being among the best. They can also lighten the impression created by the solid lumps of conifers and evergreen shrubs. Both bamboos and the larger grasses are highly effective near water, adding to the calming effect of that element in contrast to

A variety of tufty grasses make an excellent combination in a low-maintenance border scheme such as this one.

busier schemes you may have devised elsewhere. The smaller clump-forming types, such as forms of *Festuca glauca*, are excellent for edging.

Grasses add much to the winter garden. Even though the topgrowth

may be technically dead, they often show pleasing beige coloration and retain their elegant outline, a feature only enhanced by a riming of frost on the bitterest days. The purple moor grass (*Molinia caerulea*) and *Pennisetum alopecuroides* are well worth including in a border for this effect alone.

A highly successful method of growing grasses and bamboos is in containers – in fact this is often the only practical way of enjoying handsome but invasive species. Gardeners with limited time especially appreciate the drought-tolerant ones, since these will withstand a certain amount of neglect. Make sure to keep moisture-loving kinds well watered.

Flower arrangers also value the grasses: not only are they long-lasting and ideal for adding bulk and substance to arrangements, but they can also be dried and used during winter when there is precious little other plant material available.

A fine collection of grasses with mixed planting creates a variety of form and texture, and provides interest over a long period of the year.

Arundo donax

ARUNDO
Giant reed

The genus of three evergreen grasses is generally represented in gardens by the species described below, which is a plant with bamboo-like foliage that is good in mixed borders and bog gardens.
Cultivation Grow this in any reasonable soil, preferably reliably moist, in sun.

A. donax

One of the most imposing of the grasses, the species, which is native to southern Europe, has stout stems with broad, bluish-green leaves, each about 60cm (2ft) long, that hang down. It seldom flowers in cool climates. H 5m (16ft), S 2m (6ft). Hardy/Z 7–10. *A donax* var. *versicolor* (syn. *A. donax* 'Variegata') has white-striped leaves. H 2m (6ft), S 60cm (2ft). Half-hardy/Z 7–10.

BRIZA
Quaking grass

This attractive genus of grasses includes both annuals and perennials suitable for mixed borders. They provide excellent material for drying.
Cultivation Grow quaking grass in any well-drained soil in sun or light shade.

B. minor
Lesser quaking grass

This annual species, found across Europe and into western Asia, is easily raised from seed. It produces airy, branching stems of bead-like flowers, which are useful

for cutting and drying to use in winter arrangements. H 60cm (2ft), S 30cm (12in). Hardy/Z 5–8.

CAREX
Sedge

This is a large and important genus of sedges, containing about 1000 species, which are distinguished by their triangular stems. They are ideal bog garden plants, but some are also worth trying in mixed borders for their attractive mounds of leaves.
Cultivation Sedges have varying needs, but most are best in reliably moist soil in sun or light shade.

C. comans 'Frosted Curls'

This evergreen hybrid is a compact plant, which makes dense clumps of narrow, pale green leaves that curl at the tips. It is equally tolerant of sun and light shade, but it prefers moist soil, although it is worth trying in drier sites. H and S to 45cm (18in). Hardy/Z 5–9.

C. conica 'Snowline' (syn. *C. conica* 'Hime-kan-suge')

The evergreen species, which is from Japan and South Korea, is usually seen in gardens in this attractive form, which makes neat clumps of dark green leaves strikingly margined with white. This does well in ordinary garden soil and is useful for providing long-term interest at the front of a border; it is also effective in

Briza minor

Carex elata 'Aurea'

gravel. H 30cm (1ft), S 35cm (14in). Hardy/Z 6–8.

C. elata 'Aurea' (syn. *C. stricta* 'Aurea', *C. riparia* 'Bowles' Golden')
Bowles' golden sedge

This well-known cultivar is a herbaceous sedge with slender, arching, yellowish-green leaves. It is especially effective near water but can also be grown in a container if kept well watered. H 70cm (28in), S 45cm (18in). Hardy/Z 5–9.

C. flagellifera

This species, native to New Zealand, makes a clump of arching, bronze-brown leaves, which are an excellent foil to green-, silver- or yellow-leaved plants. It will grow in almost any soil. H 2m (6ft), S 1m (3ft). Borderline hardy/Z 8–9.

C. oshimensis 'Evergold' (syn. *C. morrowii* 'Evergold')

This outstanding evergreen sedge has arching leaves, centrally banded with cream. It is an excellent plant for lighting up a winter garden. It prefers well-drained soil but will grow in sun or semi-shade. H and S 45cm (18in). Hardy/Z 4–9.

C. pendula
Pendulous sedge, weeping sedge

This is an elegant sedge, found in Europe and northern Africa, which is ideal for a water-side planting. The tall stems, from which the brown, catkin- (pussy willow-) like flowers dangle,

appear in spring and early summer. It will tolerate shade. H 1.2m (4ft), S 1.5m (5ft). Hardy/Z 5–9.

C. testacea

This evergreen sedge from New Zealand has a subtle appeal. The arching, slender, pale olive-green leaves are tinged with bronze. It will grow in most soils and is effective in containers. H 1.2m (4ft), S 60cm (2ft). Half-hardy/Z 7.

CHUSQUEA

The genus contains about 120 species of evergreen bamboos from South and Central America. They are handsome plants but many are tender, and only the hardy species described is in general cultivation.
Cultivation The species described needs fertile, well-drained soil in sun or light shade.

C. culeou

One of the most dramatic of all bamboos, this species from Chile makes a splendid specimen. Generally slow-growing, it makes a clump of upright stems with small evergreen leaves. The canes, which are unusual in being solid, are pale olive-green when young, maturing to darker green. H 6m (20ft), S 2.5m (8ft). Hardy/Z 6–9.

CORTADERIA
Pampas grass, tussock grass

There are about 24 species of

Chusquea culeou

evergreen, tussock-forming grasses in the genus, and some forms are so well known that they have become clichés of suburban gardens. They are, nevertheless, handsome plants, with their richly coloured, glistening plumes. They can be an outstanding feature of the winter garden when rimed with frost. Take care when cutting back the plants in spring: the leaves are lethally sharp.
Cultivation Grow pampas grasses in fertile, well-drained soil in sun. Remove dead foliage in early spring.

C. selloana
Pampas grass
Widely grown as a specimen, this perennial species is also excellent for use in mixed borders, where its feathery plumes will tower over lower growing plants in late summer. H 3m (10ft), S 1.5m (5ft). Hardy/Z 7–9. Choose carefully among the many selections, because seed-raised plants are often undistinguished. **'Pumila'** is a desirable compact form, with mid-green leaves and yellow plumes of flowers. H 1.5m (5ft), S 1m (3ft). **'Sunningdale Silver'** is an outstanding form, with generous plumes of silver-cream flowers in late summer and autumn. H 3m (10ft), S 2.5m (8ft). Hardy/Z 7–10.

CYPERUS
Technically, the 600 or so species belonging to this genus (which includes both annuals and perennials) are sedges not grasses, much though they resemble them in outward appearance. Tender species can be grown as houseplants or 'bedded out' in containers at the margins of a pond. All are good in bog gardens or at the margins of a pool.
Cultivation Grow in reliably moist soil or in shallow water in sun or light shade.

C. involucratus
(**syn.** *C. alternifolius, C. flabelliformis*)
Umbrella grass
This plant, originally from Africa, is widely grown as a houseplant, but it also makes an effective marginal aquatic in warm areas. The tall stems are topped with

sprays of small, pale green flowers surrounded by bracts, which look like the spokes of an umbrella. H 70cm (28in), S 40cm (16in). Tender/ Z 9–10. The dwarf form **'Nanus'** is similar in every respect to the species type but grows to about half its height. H 30cm (12in), S 20cm (8in).

C. longus
Galingale
One of the hardier members of the genus, this species, which is native to Europe and North America, has umbrella-like, greenish-brown flowerheads. It makes an effective marginal aquatic. H 1.5m (5ft), S 1m (3ft). Hardy/Z 7–10.

DESCHAMPSIA
Hair grass
There are about 50 species of evergreen tufted grasses in the genus. They make good border plants and provide a wealth of material for cutting.
Cultivation Grow in lime-free soil in sun or light shade.

D. cespitosa
Tufted hair grass, tussock grass
This elegant grass from Europe and Asia and the mountains of Africa makes a fountain of leaves. Stems carrying silky, pale green flowerheads, developing as buff-yellow seedheads, arch gracefully and are effective in flower arrangements, both fresh and dried. H 2m (6ft), S 1.2m (4ft). Hardy/Z 4–7.

Cyperus involucratus

ELYMUS
Wild rye, lyme grass
Most of the 150 species of easily pleased grasses in the genus are perennials that are excellent as infill in mixed or herbaceous borders.
Cultivation Grow these grasses in any ordinary garden soil in sun or light shade.

E. magellanicus
This clump-forming species, which is native to Chile and Argentina, has spiky, steel-blue leaves. It is a good container plant. H 15cm (6in), S 45cm (18in).

FARGESIA
The four species of evergreen bamboos in the genus are native to China and the north-eastern Himalayas. They make fine specimens.

Cultivation Grow the species described in reliably moist soil in light shade.

F. nitida
(**syn.** *Arundinaria nitida, Sinarundinaria nitida*)
Fountain bamboo
The appropriate common name of this evergreen bamboo derives from its arching habit. The canes are generously clothed with narrow green leaves on purplish stems, making an elegant plant despite its size. It can also be grown in a large container, if kept well watered. H 5m (16ft), S 1.5m (5ft). Hardy/Z 4–9.

FESTUCA
Fescue
The genus contains about 300 perennial grasses, which produce attractive tufts of foliage. They are ideal for placing at the front of borders or among rock plants.
Cultivation Fescues will grow in garden soils that are well-drained. They prefer a position in sun.

F. glauca
Blue fescue, grey fescue
Rightly one of the most popular of grasses, this evergreen species makes tufts of steely blue leaves. The summer flowers are an added bonus. It can also be grown in containers. H and S 30cm (1ft). Hardy/Z 4–8. The many selections include **'Blaufuchs'** (syn. 'Blue Fox'), which has bright blue leaves. The blue-green leaves of **'Harz'** are tipped purple.

Cortaderia selloana 'Pumila'

Deschampsia cespitosa

Festuca glauca

GLYCERIA
Sweet grass, manna grass
The 16 species of perennial grass in the genus are usually grown at the margins of a pond – in the wild, they are found in water to 75cm (30in) deep – but they can also be used to fill gaps in large borders, provided you take measures to restrict their spread. *Cultivation* Grow in shallow water or in any reliably moist soil in a border in sun. To restrict spread, plant in pots or aquatic baskets sunk in the soil.

G. maxima
(syn. *G. aquatica*)
Reed meadow grass, reed sweet grass
This rampant species from temperate regions of Europe and Asia produces deep green leaves, which are flushed with pink when they emerge, and panicles of greenish-purple flowers. H 1m (3ft), S indefinite. Hardy/Z 5–9. The species is generally represented in gardens by the slightly less vigorous *G. maxima* var. *variegata* (syn. *G. aquatica* var. *variegata*, *G. spectabilis* 'Variegata'), which has broad, arching leaves striped creamy white and green. Tinted pink in spring, they die back in winter. Pale green flowers are produced in summer. Excellent near water if space is not a problem but, in some cases, a beautiful menace.

HAKONECHLOA
Hakone grass
This genus consists of a single deciduous species, which is native to Japan. It is one of the most desirable of all grasses, equally effective in woodland, in borders and in containers.
Cultivation Grow hakone grass in fertile, well-drained soil in sun or light shade.

H. macra 'Aureola'
Hakone is generally represented in gardens by this cultivar, which has broad, arching, yellow leaves narrowly striped with green and flushed with pink or red. The best leaf colour is produced when plants are in a lightly shaded situation. It is an excellent choice for a container. H and S to 45cm (18in). Hardy/Z 5–8.

HELICTOTRICHON
The 50 or so species of deciduous and evergreen grasses in the genus make excellent border plants and are an effective foil to both grey- and silver-leaved plants.
Cultivation These grasses will grow in most reasonable, preferably alkaline, soils in sun.

H. sempervirens
(syn. *Avena candida*, *A. sempervirens*)
Blue oat grass
This evergreen species, from central and south-western Europe, is a truly outstanding grass from the gardener's point of view: it has steel-blue, evergreen leaves and loose panicles of straw-coloured flowers in early summer. It is a good choice for a container. H 1.2m (4ft), S 60cm (2ft). Hardy/Z 5–8.

Hordeum jubatum

HORDEUM
Barley
The genus contains 20 species of annuals and perennials, including *H. vulgare*, the well-known cereal crop, which are mainly of interest to the gardener because of their flowers. They are splendid additions to late summer and autumn borders, combining well with dahlias and Michaelmas daisies.
Cultivation Grow these grasses in any well-drained soil in sun.

H. jubatum
Foxtail barley, squirrel-tail barley
This attractive grass, from north-eastern Asia and North America, is an annual, easily raised from seed. The showy plumes of straw-coloured flowers appear in late summer and autumn, making this excellent for filling gaps in borders towards the end of the season. The flowers can be cut and used in both fresh and dried arrangements. H 50cm (20in), S 30cm (12in). Hardy/Z 5–8.

IMPERATA
The six species of grass in the genus are grown for the simple beauty of their leaves rather than for their flowers, which appear only in areas with long hot summers. They make a good foil to a range of flowering plants in mixed and herbaceous borders.
Cultivation Grow in any reasonable soil in sun or light shade. Some winter protection – a dry mulch of straw, for instance – is advisable in cold climates.

Imperata cylindrica 'Rubra'

I. cylindrica 'Rubra'
(syn. 'Red Baron')
Japanese blood grass
The upright species is usually found in the form of this attractive cultivar, whose common name refers to the red colouring that the leaves develop from the tip downwards. For the best effect, site it where the sun will shine through the glowing foliage. Remove seedheads to prevent self-seeding because seedlings will almost invariably revert to the plain green of the species. H 1m (3ft), S 60cm (2ft) or more. Half-hardy/Z 5–10.

LAGURUS
Hare's tail
The single species in the genus, which is native to the Mediterranean, is a real flower arranger's plant that is also effective in beds and borders.

Glyceria maxima var. *variegata*

Helictotrichon sempervirens

Lagurus ovatus

Cultivation This grass needs sharply drained, not too fertile soil in sun.

L. ovatus
Hare's tail grass
The familiar species is an annual, making compact clumps of long, narrow and flat leaves but valued principally for its fluffy white oval flowerheads, which are produced throughout summer. These are excellent for drying. H 60cm (2ft), S 15cm (6in). Hardy/Z 6–9.

LEYMUS
The 40 perennial grasses in the genus are of very striking appearance, but they tend to be invasive. Although they are excellent running through large borders, they can become a menace if not regularly thinned. On the credit side, they are excellent in containers.
Cultivation Grow these grasses in any reasonable well-drained soil in sun.

L. arenarius
(syn. Elymus arenarius)
Lyme grass, European dune grass
This rhizomatous perennial species, native to north and west Europe and western Asia, is one of the most attractive of all grasses, but unfortunately it is too invasive for most gardens. It has arching blue-grey leaves, and, in summer, spikes of blue-grey flowers, which fade to straw yellow. H 1.5m (5ft), S indefinite. Hardy/Z 4–9.

Melica ciliata

MELICA
Melick
The 70 species of grasses in the genus are widespread in temperate areas. The species described are dainty, elegant grasses, which are good in shady gardens, although they take on their best colour in sun.
Cultivation Grow melicks in fertile, well-drained soil in sun or light shade.

M. altissima
Siberian melick
This evergreen perennial species, native to Eastern and Central Europe, has slender upright stems and broad leaves. Spikelets in narrow panicles of pale green flowers are produced during summer. It is useful for flower arrangements and for drying. H 1.2m (4ft), S 60cm (2ft). Hardy/Z 6–9.

M. ciliata
Silky spike melick
This charming species, which is suitable for most soil types, produces a mound of grey-green leaves and has heads of pale straw-coloured flowers in early summer. H 45cm (18in), S 60cm (2ft). Hardy/Z 6–9.

MILIUM
There are six species in the genus, all from western Asia, but the grass described below is one of the best of all garden plants, providing a vivid patch of colour throughout the growing season. Use it in mixed beds and borders, in light woodland or in a container.
Cultivation This grass will grow in any reasonably fertile, well-drained soil, in sun or (preferably) light shade.

M. effusum 'Aureum'
Bowles' golden grass
This is an outstanding grass that should be in every garden. The fresh, bright yellow leaves are at their best as they emerge in spring, making a charming picture with daffodils and other early bulbs, but maintaining a good colour throughout the season. The yellow flowers in summer are a welcome bonus. H (in flower) 60cm (2ft), S 45cm (18in). Hardy/Z 5–8.

MISCANTHUS
The 17 species of elegant perennial grasses in the genus are handsome enough to serve as specimens, besides their other uses in beds and borders and for cutting. They sometimes develop pleasing russet tints in autumn.
Cultivation These grasses like a sunny site and succeed in both dry and moist soils, although extremes are best avoided.

M. sinensis
This clump-forming species from eastern Asia has bluish-green leaves and attractive pale grey spikelets, tinged with purple, in autumn. It has given rise to many fine cultivars. H to 4m (13ft), S 1.2m (4ft). Hardy/Z 5–9. 'Gracillimus' (maiden grass) is tall, with narrow leaves, which curl

Molinia caerulea

at the tips, and plumes of buff-yellow flowers in autumn. H 1.5m (5ft), S 60cm (2ft). One of the most attractive of the selections from the species is 'Kleine Fontäne', which produces upright clumps of leaves and heads of pale pink flowers in late summer. It is an excellent choice in borders with late summer perennials. H 1m (3ft), S 45cm (18in). 'Zebrinus' is an eye-catching form, with narrow green leaves, banded horizontally with yellow, and silky brown flowers. H 1.5m (5ft), S 60cm (2ft).

MOLINIA
There are only two or three species in the genus, but these are graceful perennial grasses, which look delightful in herbaceous and mixed borders.
Cultivation Molinias need neutral to acid, well-drained soil in sun or light shade.

M. caerulea
Purple moor grass
This species from Europe and south-western Asia has green foliage that turns yellow in autumn. Upright stems are topped with light purplish flowerheads from late summer to autumn. H 1.2m (4ft), S 60cm (2ft). Hardy/Z 5–8. *M. caerulea* subsp. *caerulea* 'Variegata' is an elegant form, with green and white striped leaves, which are sometimes tinged pink, and loose purple-grey flowers on arching stems in late summer and autumn. H and S 60cm (2ft).

Leymus arenarius

Miscanthus sinensis 'Zebrinus'

Pennisetum alopecuroides

Phalaris arundinacea var. *picta* 'Picta'

PENNISETUM

This large genus of about 80 grasses includes annuals as well as the perennials described here. All make excellent border plants and provide material for cutting.
Cultivation Grow in well-drained, preferably light, soil in sun.

P. alopecuroides
(syn. *P. compressum*)
Fountain grass, swamp foxtail grass
This species, from western Australia and eastern Asia, makes airy clumps of narrow leaves, which turn reddish-orange in autumn and fade to buff in winter. Purple-brown, bottlebrush-like flowerheads emerge in autumn. H and S 1.2m (4ft). Hardy/Z 5–9.

P. orientale
Sadly, this beautiful species from Asia and northern India is not reliably hardy in cold areas, where it needs winter protection. It makes clumps of narrow leaves, and bears spikes of soft pinkish-grey summer flowers, which are excellent in arrangements both fresh and dried. H and S 60cm (2ft). Half-hardy/Z 7–9.

P. villosum
Feathertop
This African species is grown principally for its beige-white flowerheads, which are produced from summer to autumn and are much valued by flower arrangers. The leaves are narrow. This species is not fully hardy in cold

climates, where it will need winter protection. H and S 60cm (2ft). Half-hardy/Z 7–9.

PHALARIS

Although there are about 15 annual and perennial grasses in the genus, to all intents and purposes the species described is the only member of the genus that is generally seen. It can be grown in borders, but is happiest near water.
Cultivation The species will grow in any ordinary garden soil, but does best in moist or even boggy ground in sun or light shade.

P. arundinacea
Reed canary grass, ribbon grass
This invasive evergreen species, which is found in the wild in western Asia, southern Africa and North America, has upright, mid-green leaves and, in summer, pale green spikelets, which turn buff. H 1.5m (5ft), S indefinite. Hardy/Z 4–9. The species is usually seen in gardens in the vigorous form *P. arundinacea* var. *picta* 'Picta' (gardener's garters),

which has green and white striped, arching leaves. The flower spikes, which appear in summer, can be 1.5m (5ft) high. H 60cm (2ft), S indefinite. 'Tricolor' is similar except that the leaves have a pink tinge. H 60cm (2ft), S indefinite.

PHYLLOSTACHYS

The 80 or so evergreen bamboos in the genus are elegant enough for use as specimens in large gardens or at the backs of large borders as a backdrop to other plants. They are also good screening material.
Cultivation Grow these bamboos in fertile, well-drained soil in sun or light shade.

P. bambusoides
Giant timber bamboo
Mature specimens of this imposing Chinese bamboo have thick green canes that can be used for building. It has copious, broad, glossy, dark green leaves. H and S 5m (16ft) or more. Hardy/Z 7–10. 'Allgold' (syn. 'Holochrysa', 'Sulphurea') has golden-yellow canes, sometimes striped with green.

P. nigra
Black bamboo
This dramatic Chinese species has canes that become black with age, a good contrast to the abundant green leaves. It makes an impressive specimen, particularly in an eastern-style garden. H 5m (16ft), S 2m (6ft). Hardy/Z 7–10. The selection 'Boryana' is shorter and has characteristic brown mottling on its canes once mature. H 4m (13ft), S 2m(6ft).

P. viridiglaucescens
(syn. *P. edulis* f. *subconvexa*)
This vigorous, elegant species has

smooth, green canes that bend outwards under the weight of the dense, bright green leaves. H and S 4m (13ft). Hardy/Z 7–10.

PLEIOBLASTUS

The 20 species of dwarf to medium-sized evergreen bamboos in the genus can be rampant and are best used to colonize woodland.
Cultivation Grow in moist soil in sun or light shade.

P. auricomus
(syn. *Arundinaria auricoma*, *A. viridistriata*, *P. viridistriatus*)
This modest species from Japan is useful for small gardens. The leaves are striped with golden yellow and green. It is suitable for growing in containers, provided it is kept well watered. H and S 1m (3ft). Hardy/Z 5–10.

P. simonii f. *variegatus*
This attractive form of the Japanese species makes an imposing stand, with broad leaves narrowly striped with green and white, the best colours being on the young leaves. It combines well with other large-leaved plants in an open setting. H and S 4m (13ft). Hardy/Z 7–10.

POA

Meadow grass, spear grass
Some of the 500 species in this genus are lawn grasses, but the one described is a good border plant.
Cultivation This grass will grow in most well-drained soils, preferably light ones, in sun or light shade.

P. labillardieri
This evergreen species from Australia makes dense mounds of fine blue-grey leaves, above which arching stems carry purplish flowerheads in summer. It associates well with red- and purple-leaved plants. H 1.2m (4ft), S 1m (3ft). Hardy/Z 6–9.

PSEUDOSASA

The six evergreen bamboos in the genus, being very invasive, are principally used as screening material or in a wild garden.
Cultivation Grow in fertile, well-drained soil in sun or light shade.

Pleioblastus simonii f. *variegatus*

Poa labillardieri

Pseudosasa japonica

P. japonica
(syn. *Arundinaria japonica*)
Arrow bamboo, metake
This robust evergreen species
from Japan makes a good backdrop to other plants. Its tall, erect
canes arch over under the weight
of its abundant large, broad,
bright green leaves. H and S 4m
(13ft) or more. Hardy/Z 7–10.

SASA

The roughly 40 small to medium-
sized bamboos in this genus
spread by means of running
rootstocks and are potentially far
too invasive for general garden
use. Provided room, they are
excellent for filling large areas and
will tolerate deep shade.
Cultivation Grow in any reasonable
garden soil, in sun or shade.

S. palmata
(syn. *Arundinaria palmata*)
This attractive, clump-forming
evergreen species from Japan has
very broad, green leaves. A good
plant for colonizing rough areas
in a large garden. H 4m (13ft),
S indefinite. Hardy/Z 6–10.

Sasa palmata

S. veitchii
(syn. *Arundinaria veitchii*)
An evergreen species from Japan,
this has broad green leaves that
appear variegated but actually are
not. They are solid green when
young, but as they age the green
retreats from the edges of the leaf,
leaving an irregular, creamy buff
margin. It is good for creating a
thicket. H 1.5m (5ft), S
indefinite. Hardy/Z 6–10.

SCIRPOIDES
Round-headed clubrush
This genus consists of a single
species, a sedge that is ideal for a
bog or stream-side planting.
Cultivation This plant needs
permanently moist soil (or
shallow water) in sun.

S. holoschoenus
(syn. *Holoschoenus vulgaris,
Scirpus holoschoenus*)
This dramatic plant has narrow,
grass-like foliage that turns tawny
brown in autumn and small brown
flowers. It is suitable for larger
gardens only, where it is most
effective when planted at the
water's edge. H 1m (3ft), S
indefinite. Hardy/Z 7.

SEMIARUNDINARIA

There are between 10 and 20
species of upright bamboos in the
genus, all from China and Japan.
They tend to be clumpforming in
gardens and as such make fine
specimens. Alternatively, use them
for screening.
Cultivation Reasonably fertile soil
is suitable, in sun or light shade.

S. fastuosa
(syn. *Arundinaria fastuosa*)
Narihira bamboo
This imposing bamboo has tall,
erect green canes (turning reddish
on maturity), topped with masses
of airy leaves. This is one of the
hardiest bamboos. H 5m (15ft),
S indefinite. Hardy/Z 7–10.

SHIBATAEA
The genus contains eight species
of the most manageable evergreen
bamboos. The species described
can be grown in borders and looks
wonderful in gravel. It is also a
good container plant.
Cultivation Grow in ideally reliably

Shibataea kumasasa

moist soil in sun or light shade;
the more sun, the wetter the soil
should be.

S. kumasasa
(syn. *Sasa ruscifolia*)
A compact species from Japan,
this is suitable for small gardens.
H 1m (3ft), S 60cm (2ft).
Hardy/Z 6–10.

STIPA
Feather grass, needle grass
There are about 300 species, in
the genus. They are lovely grasses
that make fine border plants,
either in a position of prominence
or used in conjunction with
summer flowers. Stipas also
provide good material for arrangements, both fresh and dried.
Cultivation Grow in any reasonably
fertile, soil in sun.

S. arundinacea
Pheasant's tail grass
An excellent grass for the autumn
garden, this New Zealand species
has long, tawny-beige foliage that
intensifies in colour as the
temperature drops. Thin stems
carry brownish flowers in late
summer. H and S 1m (3ft).
Hardy/Z 7–10.

Stipa calamagrostis

S. calamagrostis
(syn. *S. lasiogrostis*)
This grass, from southern Europe,
is good for planting in drifts, and
with its narrow, arching leaves, it
blends happily with a range of
plants. The silky flowerheads,
which appear in summer, are
initially green with a reddish
tinge, fading to pale golden-
yellow in late summer. H and S
1m (3ft). Hardy/Z 7–10.

S. gigantea
Giant feather grass, golden oats
Native to Spain and Portugal, this
is a large plant, very effective in
borders when combined with
lower growing plants. It forms
tough mounds of leaves from
which arise tall stems topped with
long-lasting oat-like flowers in
summer and autumn. They
become golden yellow as they age.
H to 2m (6ft), S indefinite.
Hardy/Z 7–9.

S. tenuissima
This well-known species from the
southern United States is one of
the more handsome of the smaller
grasses and is a good choice for
use as a specimen in a restricted
space. The delicate stems and
leaves, which turn blond in
summer, move in the slightest
breeze, a charming effect when
the silky, cream flowers appear in
summer. H and S 60cm (2ft).
Hardy/Z 6–9.

TYPHA
Bulrush, reedmace
There are 10 species in the genus,
which are familiar plants around
natural pools and lakes in many
parts of the world. Few are of
sufficient distinction to find a
place in gardens, but the species
described is of some merit.
Cultivation Grow in shallow water
or in the moist soil at the margins
of a pond in sun.

T. latifolia
Great reedmace, cat's tail
This invasive species is best used
as a marginal aquatic. It has erect
stems topped by compact, velvety,
brown flowerheads in summer,
much valued in flower
arrangements. H to 2m (6ft), S
indefinite. Hardy/Z 3–10.

Recommended planting lists

The following lists offer a guide to plants adapted to certain conditions. Most of the entries relate to entire genera. For more detailed information as to preferences of individual species, refer to the relevant entry. Remember that some plants are tolerant of a range of conditions, hence their presence in more than one list.

PLANTS FOR DRY SOIL IN SUN

TREES
Cercis
Gleditsia

CONIFERS
Juniperus
Pinus
Thuja

SHRUBS
Artemisia
Ballota
Buddleja
Ceanothus
Cistus
Genista
× Halimiocistus
Helianthemum
Hibiscus
Lavandula
Lavatera
Olearia
Perovskia
Phlomis
Potentilla
Rosmarinus
Ruta
Salvia
Santolina

Teucrium
Thymus
Yucca

PERENNIALS
Achillea
Anthemis
Artemisia
Aster
Dianthus
Eryngium
Euphorbia
Helichrysum
Kniphofia
Lychnis
Nepeta
Osteospermum
Papaver
Salvia
Sedum
Stachys
Verbascum
Verbena
Zauschneria

ANNUALS AND BIENNIALS
Calendula
Cleome
Cosmos
Eschscholtzia
Limnanthes
Oenothera

Papaver
Salvia
Tagetes

BULBS, CORMS AND TUBERS
Allium
Crocus
Nerine
Tulipa

ALPINES
Aubrieta
Cerastium
Dianthus
Gypsophila

PLANTS FOR DRY SOIL IN SHADE

SHRUBS
Buxus
Elaeagnus
Hypericum
Kerria
Sarcococca
Vinca

ANNUALS AND BIENNIALS
Lunaria

CLIMBERS
Hedera

BULBS, CORMS AND TUBERS
Cyclamen

FERNS
Asplenium
Polypodium

Hosta 'Golden Prayers'

PLANTS FOR MOIST SOIL IN SHADE

TREES
Acer

SHRUBS
Aucuba
Hamamelis
Hydrangea
Kalmia
Mahonia
Sarcococca

PERENNIALS
Aquilegia
Aruncus
Astilbe
Astrantia
Calla
Cimicifuga
Convallaria
Digitalis
Helleborus
Heuchera
Hosta
Lysimachia
Polygonatum

Primula
Pulmonaria
Rheum
Rodgersia
Thalictrum
Tiarella
Tricyrtis
Trillium
Trollius
Viola

PLANTS FOR EXPOSED SITES

TREES
Acer
Carpinus
Crataegus
Fagus
Fraxinus
Populus
Prunus
Salix
Sorbus

CONIFERS
Chamaecyparis
× Cupressocyparis

Cupressus
Juniperus
Pinus
Thuja

SHRUBS
Berberis
Buddleja
Calluna
Erica
Euonymus
(deciduous)
Ilex
Kalmia
Prunus

PERENNIALS
Achillea
Ajuga
Bergenia
Cimicifuga
Coreopsis
Iris
Persicaria
Primula
Pulmonaria

ANNUALS AND BIENNIALS
Hesperis

BULBS, CORMS AND TUBERS
Allium
Crocus

ALPINES
Campanula
Sempervivum

GRASSES
Miscanthus
Stipa

Stachys byzantina

Sarcococca hookeriana var. dignya

Sempervivum arachnoideum

Calluna vulgaris 'My Dream'

Ceanothus 'Delight'

Wisteria × *formosa* 'Yae-kokuryû'

PLANTS FOR ACID OR LIME-FREE SOIL

TREES
Acacia
Arbutus
Eucryphia
Magnolia

CONIFERS
Abies
Picea
Pinus

SHRUBS
Callistemon
Calluna
Camellia
Daboecia
Erica
Fothergilla
Hamamelis
Kalmia
Magnolia
Pieris
Rhododendron

PERENNIALS
Iris
Tricyrtis
Trillium

CLIMBERS
Lapageria

BULBS
Lilium

ALPINES
Corydalis
Gentiana (autumn-flowering)
Lewisia
Phlox
Primula

PLANTS FOR CHALKY SOIL

TREES
Aesculus
Betula
Carpinus
Cercis
Crataegus
Fagus
Fraxinus
Gleditsia
Laburnum
Laurus
Malus
Paulownia
Prunus
Pyrus
Robinia
Sophora
Sorbus

CONIFERS
Juniperus
Taxus

Iris reticulata

SHRUBS
Berberis
Buxus
Ceanothus
Cistus
Cotoneaster
Daphne
Deutzia
Euonymus
Forsythia
Fuchsia
Genista
Hebe
Helianthemum
Ilex
Kerria
Lonicera
Olearia
Osmanthus
Paeonia
Phillyrea
Phlomis
Rosmarinus
Sarcococca
Syringa
Viburnum
Vinca
Weigela
Yucca

PERENNIALS
Anemone
Anthemis
Campanula
Convallaria
Dianthus
Iris
Paeonia
Rudbeckia
Salvia
Verbascum
Viola

ANNUALS AND BIENNIALS
Bellis
Lobularia
Papaver
Salvia
Viola

CLIMBERS
Clematis
Hedera
Lonicera
Parthenocissus

BULBS, CORMS AND TUBERS
Anemone
Colchicum
Crocus
Gladiolus
Iris
Narcissus
Tulipa

ALPINES
Aubrieta
Campanula
Dianthus
Pulsatilla
Saxifraga

PLANTS FOR CLAY SOIL

TREES
Acer
Alnus
Arbutus
Carpinus
Fraxinus
Salix

CONIFERS
Abies
Chamaecyparis
Cryptomeria
Metasequoia

SHRUBS
Cornus
Magnolia
Weigela

PERENNIALS
Aconitum
Astrantia
Digitalis
Helenium
Hemerocallis
Lysimachia
Lythrum
Persicaria bistorta
Rudbeckia

CLIMBERS
Lonicera
Wisteria

BULBS, CORMS AND TUBERS
Anemone
Camassia
Leucojum
Narcissus

FERNS
Matteuccia
Osmunda

GRASSES
Cyperus

PLANTS FOR COASTAL SITES

TREES
Acer
Arbutus
Ilex
Trachycarpus

CONIFERS
Chamaecyparis
Cupressocyparis
Pinus

SHRUBS
Artemisia
Ceanothus
Cistus
Cotoneaster
Cytisus
Elaeagnus
Erica
Euonymus
Fuchsia
Genista
Halimium
Hebe
Hydrangea
Ilex
Lavandula
Olearia
Phlomis
Pittosporum
Potentilla
Rosmarinus

Hakonechloa macra 'Aureola'

Narcissus cyclamineus

Santolina	Penstemon
Spiraea	Phormium
Yucca	Sedum
	Stachys

PERENNIALS
Achillea
Agapanthus
Anthemis
Artemisia
Dianthus
Eryngium
Euphorbia
Geranium

ANNUALS AND
BIENNIALS
Antirrhinum
Matthiola

CLIMBERS
Fallopia
Wisteria

BULBS, CORMS
AND TUBERS
Canna
Chionodoxa
Crocosmia
Crocus
Narcissus
Zantedeschia

ALPINES
Aubrieta
Dianthus
Gypsophila
Sedum
Sempervivum

**PLANTS FOR
AUTUMN AND
WINTER
COLOUR**

TREES
Acer
Aesculus
Arbutus
Betula
Cercidiphyllum

Crataegus
Eucryphia
Malus
Populus
Prunus
Pyrus
Quercus
Robinia
Sorbus

CONIFERS
Cryptomeria
Ginkgo
Larix
Taxodium

SHRUBS
Berberis (deciduous)
Ceratostigma
Calluna
Cornus
Cotinus
Cotoneaster
(deciduous)
Daboecia
Erica
Euonymus

Fothergilla
Hamamelis
Paeonia
Photinia
Pyracantha
Spiraea
Viburnum
(deciduous)

PERENNIALS
Helleborus
Ophiopogon
Tiarella

CLIMBERS
Celastrus
Humulus
Parthenocissus
Vitis

FERNS
Osmunda

GRASSES
Festuca
Hakonechloa
Miscanthus

Plant Hardiness Zones

This map was developed by the Agricultural Research Service of the U.S. Department of Agriculture. Every plant in the directory is given a zone range. The zones 1-11 are based on the average annual minimum temperature. In the zone range, the smaller number indicates the northern-most zone in which a plant can survive the winter and the higher number gives the most southerly area in which it will perform consistently. Bear in mind that factors such as altitude, wind exposure, proximity to water, soil type, snow, night temperature, shade, and the level of water received by a plant may alter a plant's hardiness by as much as two zones.

	Zone 11	Above 4°C (40°F)
	Zone 10	-1 to 4°C (30 to 40°F)
	Zone 9	-7 to -1°C (20 to 30°F)
	Zone 8	-12 to -7°C (10 to 20°F)
	Zone 7	-18 to -12°C (0 to 10°F)
	Zone 6	-23 to -18°C (-10 to 0°F)
	Zone 5	-29 to -23°C (-20 to -10°F)
	Zone 4	-34 to -29°C (-30 to -20°F)
	Zone 3	-40 to -34°C (-40 to -30°F)
	Zone 2	-45 to -40°C (-50 to -40°F)
	Zone 1	Below -45°C (-50°F)

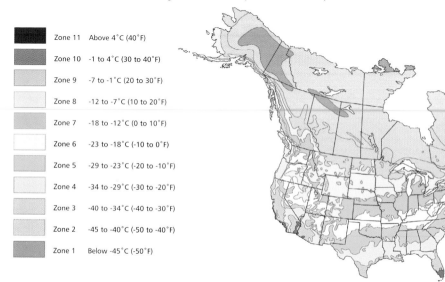

Glossary of terms

Annual A plant that grows from seed, flowers, sets seed again and dies in one year.

Aquatic A plant that lives in water: it can be completely submerged, floating or live with its roots in the water and shoots in the air.

Bare-root A plant that is sold with no soil or compost around the roots. They are dug up from the nursery field and are ready for planting during the dormant season.

Bedding plant A plant that is raised for use in a temporary garden display; spring, summer and winter types are available.

Biennial A plant that grows from seed to form a small plant in the first year and flowers and sets seed in the following year.

Biological control The use of a pest's natural enemies to control its numbers in the garden or greenhouse.

Bog garden An area of ground that remains permanently wet and is used to grow bog plants that thrive in such conditions.

Capillary matting An absorbent material that holds a lot of water on which containers are placed and from which they can draw all the moisture they need via capillary action.

Certified stock Plants that have been inspected and declared free of specific pests and diseases. They can be used as stock plants for propagation material.

Chit A technique used to encourage a potato tuber to begin to sprout before planting.

Cloche A small structure made from glass, clear plastic or polythene that can be moved around easily to warm small areas of soil or protect vulnerable plants.

Compost (soil mix) A mixture that is used for growing plants in containers. It can be loam-based or peat-based. Peat-free versions are now available based on coir, composted bark or other organic waste material.

Compost, garden A material that has been produced from the decomposition of organic waste material in a compost bin or heap. Useful as a soil improver or planting mixture.

Cordon A trained form of tree or bush with a main stem, vertical or at an angle, and with sideshoots shortened to form fruiting spurs.

Crop covers Various porous materials used to protect plants or crops. Horticultural fleece is a woven fabric that can be used to protect plants from frost and flying insect pests; insect-proof mesh is a well-ventilated fabric, ideal for keeping out insects throughout the summer, but offers no frost protection.

Damping down Wetting surfaces in a greenhouse to raise air humidity and to help keep temperatures under control.

Deadhead To remove spent flowers to tidy the display, prevent the formation of seeds and improve future flowering performance.

Earth up To draw up soil around a plant forming a mound. Potatoes are earthed up to protect new shoots from frost and to prevent tubers from being exposed to light, which turns them green.

Espalier A trained form of tree or bush where the main stem is vertical and pairs of sideshoots are at a set spacing and trained out horizontally.

Fan A trained form of tree or bush where the main stem is vertical and pairs of sideshoots are pruned at set spacing and trained out either side to form a fan shape.

Grafted plant An ornamental plant that has been attached on to the rootstock of another, more vigorous, variety.

Ground cover plants These are densely growing, mat-forming plants that can be used to cover the ground with foliage to prevent weeds germinating.

Hardening-off A method of gradually weaning off a plant from the conditions inside to those outside without causing a check to growth.

Hardiness The amount of cold a type of plant is able to withstand. Hardy plants can tolerate frost; half-hardy and tender plants cannot.

Herbaceous plants Plants that produce sappy, green, non-woody growth. Herbaceous perennials die down in winter, but re-grow from basal shoots the following spring.

Horticultural fleece *see* crop covers.

Humus The organic residue of decayed organic matter found in soil. It improves soil fertility.

Insect-proof mesh *see* crop covers.

Leafmould A material that has been produced from the decomposition of leaves in a leaf bin or heap. Useful as a soil improver or planting mixture.

Manure A bulky organic animal waste that is rotted down and used to improve soil structure and fertility.

Mulch A material that is laid on the surface of the soil to prevent moisture loss through evaporation and suppress weed growth. Can be loose and organic, such as composted bark or garden compost, loose and inorganic, such as gravel, or a fabric, such as mulch matting or landscape fabric.

Perennial A plant that lives for more than two years. Usually applied to a hardy non-woody plant (*see* herbaceous). A tender perennial is a non-woody plant that cannot tolerate frost.

Pricking out The spacing of seedlings while still small so that they have room to grow on.

Rootball A mass of roots and compost that holds together when a plant is removed from its container.

Runner A horizontal shoot that spreads out from the plant, roots and forms another plant.

Slow-release fertilizer A specially coated inorganic fertilizer that releases its nutrients slowly.

Sucker A shoot that arises from the roots underground. The term is usually applied to shoots from the rootstock of a grafted plant that has different characteristics to the ornamental variety.

Transplanting The transfer of seedlings or young plants from a nursery bed where they were sown to their final growing position.

Windbreak A hedge, fence, wall or fabric that is used to filter the wind and reduce the damage it may cause.

Rosa 'Frühlingsgold'

Index

Acknowledgements

Additional step-by-step text by Peter McHoy,
Richard Bird, Andrew Mikolajski, Ted Collins,
Blaise Cooke, Christopher Grey-Wilson, Lin
Hawthorne, Jessica Houdret, Hazel Key, Peter
Robinson and Susie White.

Photography by Peter Anderson, Jonathan
Buckley, Derek Cranch, Helen Fickling, Paul
Forrester, John Freeman, Michelle Garrett, Janine
Hosegood, Andrea Jones, Simon McBride and
Marie O'Hara.

Illustrations by Neil Bulpitt, Liz Pepperell and
Michael Shoebridge.

311tr, 311bl, 312t, 312bl, 313tl,313tr, 313br,
314tr, 315tc, 315br, 316tl, 316tc, 317tl, 324tc,
324bl, 325br, 330tc, 330br, 331tr, 332tl, 332tc,
333tl, 334bl, 335bl, 336br, 340tl, 341tl, 341tr,
341br, 350br, 351bcl, 352tcl, 352tcr, 352b,
353tl, 353bl, 353br, 354br, 360tl, 360bl, 360bc,
361tr, 361bl, 361bt, 362b, 363tr, 364bc, 365tc,
365tr, 365bl, 366tl, 366tr, 366bl, 366br, 367tr,
372tr, 372bl, 373tl, 373tc, 373bl, 374br, 375tc,
376tc, 377bc, 378b, 379t, 379bl, 379bc, 380br,
383bl, 383br, 388tl, 388tc, 388tr, 388b, 390tc,
392tc, 393tl, 393tc, 394tl, 394tc, 394b, 395tl,
416tl, 416tr, 416bc, 416br, 418tr, 421bl, 430tr,
430b, 438tl, 438tc, 438tr, 438bl, 439tl, 439bl,
439br, 440tr, 440bl, 440br, 441tl, 441tr, 442tr,
442bl, 442br, 443tr, 443bc, 443br, 444tl, 445tl,
445br.

The publisher would like to thank the following
picture libraries for permission to use their
photographs.
Peter Anderson 450br.
A-Z Botanical 263t, 265tr, 265br, 267tl, 267br,
272br, 274tr, 274br, 340tr, 367bl, 395bl, 450tl,
451tr.
Jonathan Buckley 260, 262, 263b, 278, 281t,
290, 292t, 326, 368, 370, 384, 387, 412, 414,
446, 448, 454, 456t, 457t, 474, 476, 477, 482,
484l, 485t.
Andrew Mikolajski 256, 270tr, 271tl, 318tl,
331tc, 383tl, 386l, 389tr, 417br.
Peter McHoy 18t, 22bl, 22bm, 22br, 23bl,
23bm, 23br, 49b, 140bl, 140bm, 140br, 141bl,
141bm, 141br, 295tl, 300tl, 300tc, 300tr,
301br, 302tl, 303br, 306b, 308bc, 309br, 311tc,